Medievalism and the Modernist Temper

Medievalism and the Modernist Temper

Edited by
R. Howard Bloch and
Stephen G. Nichols

The Johns Hopkins University Press
Baltimore and London

© 1996 The Johns Hopkins University Press
All rights reserved. Published 1996
Printed in the United States of America on acid-free paper
05 04 03 02 01 00 99 98 97 96   5 4 3 2 1

The Johns Hopkins University Press, 2715 North Charles Street
Baltimore, Maryland 21218-4319
The Johns Hopkins Press Ltd., London

A catalog record for this book is available from the British Library.

Library of Congress Cataloging-in-Publication Data
Medievalism and the modernist temper / edited by R. Howard Bloch & Stephen G. Nichols
    p.   cm.
Includes bibliographical references
ISBN 0-8018-5086-X (alk. paper).—ISBN 0-8018-5087-8 (pbk. : alk. paper)
    1. Literature, Medieval—History and criticism. 2. Civilization, Medieval.
I. Bloch, R. Howard. II. Nichols, Stephen G.
PN671.M42   1995
809′.02—dc20   95-21794

Contents

Introduction

R. Howard Bloch and Stephen G. Nichols

WORD'S OUT. There's something exciting going on in medieval studies, and maybe in the Renaissance too. The study of medieval literature and culture has never been more alive or at a more interesting, innovative stage. On the other hand, those who study classical French literature have seen the virtual disappearance not of a field but of the battlefield upon which the modern critical wars—known in the mid-1960s as "La Nouvelle Critique"—erupted, and modernists are so mired in the question of who did what to whom during World War II that they have lost a sense of intellectual urgency.

The institutional signs of a New Medievalism are everywhere: in the appointment of medievalists at major universities, many of which remained without specialists in Old French after the death or retirement of the dominating philological figures of the 1940s to 1960s; in renewed interest among graduate students, many of whom recognize that material artifacts, such as manuscripts, are the new frontier for a theoretically oriented philology; in a number of recent scholarly gatherings aimed at new understandings of the Middle Ages or attempting to plot the future of medieval studies; in the founding of scholarly journals such as *Assays, Exemplaria, Médiévales,* and *Envoi* devoted to the Middle Ages; in special issues of such established reviews as *Yale French Studies, Romantic Review, Esprit Créateur, Littérature;*

1

and—*mirabile dictu*—in the recent appearance of an issue of *Speculum* devoted to the so-called New Philology.

An important consequence of the recent renaissance of interest in the Middle Ages is that questions once taken for granted as being the immutable and natural defining issues of the field have begun to seem increasingly opaque. Indeed, those who write about the millennium between the fall of Rome and the discovery of the New World have come more and more to see that their assumptions regarding this period are as historically determined by the framing perceptions of the last century as they are by the artifacts of the medievalist's study. The historicization or relativization of the past entailed by such a perception might be nothing more than a liberating pretext for change, or simply for imagining possibilities other than those already in place.

In this the field of medieval studies is not alone but part of a larger movement: almost every discipline within the social sciences and the humanities is currently wallowing in the question of its origins. Historians since Haydn White's work in the 1970s have become more aware of the rhetorical underpinnings of the historical enterprise, just as anthropologists since the publication of *Tristes tropiques* by Claude Lévi-Strauss have discovered the literary and even biographical elements that comprise the anthropological voyage otherwise known as fieldwork. Medievalists, too, have begun to write the external history of the discipline from perspectives that would have been unthinkable twenty years ago. Here one can identify several stages, which are, in reality, more logical than chronological.

A first stage can be seen in the attempt to write the history of medieval studies from within the perspective of the discipline itself, that is, from a point of view implying a minimum of distance of the historian from his or her object of study. The Iordan-Orr history of Romance philology springs immediately to mind.[1] This work's highly narrative structure, based on intellectual genealogies that record filiations from *maître* to disciple, inevitably reflects the philologist's desire for origins while also mirroring medieval thinkers' own obsession with etymologies.

The lengthy study by Janine Dakyns of medievalism in nineteenth-century France, which assimilates medieval material in both primary literary works and in criticism, and seeks to define a multiplicity of Middle Ages according to the political motivations of particular classes and regimes, is an important step beyond the old history.[2] So, too, the first chapter of Lee Patterson's *Negotiating the Past: The Historical Understanding of Medieval Literature* is a more nuanced version of Dakyns's approach applied to the field of Middle English studies.[3]

A second stage implies, indeed is defined by, a recognition of and insistence upon a certain identity between the medieval period and our own. Here one thinks of a number of articles, books, and lectures by several scholars during the past fifteen years, for example, Eugene Vance, "The Modernity of the Middle Ages in the Future: Remarks on a Recent Book" (1973); Peter Haidu, "Towards a Problematics of Alterity: Making It (New) in the Middle Ages" (1974); Hans Robert Jauss, *Alterität und Modernität der mittelalterlichen Literatur* (1977); Paul Zumthor, "The Modernity of the Middle Ages," lectures given at the Pompidou Center (January 1979); Alexandre Leupin, "The Middle Ages, the Other" (1983); and the first chapter of R. Howard Bloch's *Etymologies and Genealogies: A Literary Anthropology of the French Middle Ages,* which appeared that same year.[4] This disparate group of writings is united by an enthusiastic sense of wonder at the discovery of how familiar the Middle Ages seem within the context of the contemporary discourses of cultural criticism, and thus a sense of relief that those who studied medieval texts are not as irrelevant to the present as many of our own teachers had hoped we would be.

A recent generation of medievalists was astonished by the healing of a wounded narcissism among those no longer content merely to hide behind the veil of philological expertise, which for decades had served not as a tool to make medieval literature accessible, but as a *cordon sanitaire* to prevent the reading of such works and thus inhibit dialogue between medievalists and specialists in other fields. Lee Patterson has noted the almost eager acceptance by many medievalists of the marginality of medieval studies decreed by the "master narrative [of modernity] first put in place by the Renaissance."[5] It has, then, come as somewhat of a relief to discover that the period we study not only had something to say to modernists but also might serve to unsettle or historicize what for better or worse has come to be known as "literary theory."

Finally, for some time now a number of medieval historians, art historians, philologists, and specialists of almost every national literature have felt the need for a more sustained external history of the various disciplines of medieval studies. Brian Stock wrote a brilliant article suggesting a rethinking of medievalist methodologies along lines sympathetic with the Vichean historicism of Erich Auerbach; Stock's article inspired a further meditation by Stephen G. Nichols.[6] In a slightly different vein, Hans Aarslef gave a retrospective assessment of Joseph Bédier; and Hans Ulrich Gumbrecht contributed a ground-breaking essay on Friedrich Diez, Gaston Paris, and the development of Romance philology in both Germany and France.[7] Several years ago, Bernard Cerquiglini published *Éloge de la variante: Histoire critique de la philologie,* a synthesis of the relation between medieval textual practice and medievalism. His work had as corollaries within the field of history monographs by François Hartog on Fustel de Coulanges and by Alain Boureau on Ernst Kantorowicz.[8] This phase of the New Medievalism thus placed in historical context the cultural appropriations of the study of the Middle Ages as it has been practiced since the middle of the eighteenth century.[9] This leads to what we, in planning this volume, perceived to be a subject worthy of further study.

From the outset we imagined a history of medievalisms aimed at exploring the ways in which medieval studies have been determined by the specific ideological or local, nationalistic or religious, political or personal interests of those who have shaped them. This kind of history considers questions normally excluded from the canon of traditional or high medieval studies, topics such as connoisseurship, professionalization, and popularization. It includes, for example, not only the effects of the medieval work upon Bédier's famous popular-ization of the *Roman de Tristan,* discussed below in the chapter by Alain Corbellari, but the effects—through Denis de Rougemont's *Amour en Occident*—of Bédier's successful rewriting of the *Romance of Tristan and Isolde* upon contemporary medieval studies as well as upon modern poets such as Péguy and Cocteau. This volume also considers the relation of philology to other medieval disciplines and to semiology and linguistics; as well as the role of collections, journals, bibliographies, textual series, and authoritative manuals including the *Grundriss der romanischen Literaturen des Mittelalters.*[10]

This collected work also discusses the effects of presuppositions about palaeography upon editions and hence upon the interpretation of medieval texts; important figures, schools, and movements; defin-ing questions and debates (not simply rehashing the terms but con-textualizing the stakes and motivations), and even the scholarly quarrel as a form of communication conceived to be productive of knowledge. In addition, it seeks to evaluate the current rationale for the study of the Middle Ages as well as to assess the potential effects of the study of medieval concepts, theories, and texts upon contempo-rary criticism, upon the canon, and upon such modern disciplines as psychoanalysis and semiotics—the work of Jacques Lacan and Umberto Eco, for example. In what ways can the study of the Middle Ages teach us to historicize the field of critical theory?

Which is another way of asking: to what extent do our own strategies and desires determine the questions we pose and the answers we give? We cannot escape the obligation to clarify our own agendas. We can do so only by recognizing the degree to which the inquiring subject stands in a compromising position: on the one hand, involved in an enterprise that, since the Renaissance, has assumed the disinterestedness of knowledge, the objectivity of philological science; on the other, participating as a socially contextualized being in a network of predetermined subjectivities such as sex, social position, or ethnic origin.

Here one can identify a landmark in Paul Zumthor's *Speaking of the Middle Ages*, which not only addresses the question of what it means to study the medieval past in the twentieth century, but does so in the first person singular, thus recognizing the place and effects of the subject in the scholarly enterprise:

> Along the way, I will not apologize for speaking in the first person. This is not a stylistic device, but an intellectual necessity. . . . It is not a question of speaking about oneself, still less of retreating into a den of memories. It is a matter of choosing . . . the most directly accessible reference point. Others are free to illustrate a half century of scholarly or social achievement by tracing the biography of a mentor or colleague. But why take that course when what counts in the end is neither he nor I? What counts is the possibility of identifying in an emblematic way the social function fulfilled by that individual (that is, by his work) as part of a given project, a given task, a given field of thought or research to which events (for want of a natural inclination) attached him for a fairly long time. In this way, the project, the task, or the field may be considered through the mediation of a person, that is, otherwise than in the library.[11]

Zumthor's personalized voice is justified by what he rightly points to as a crisis of method in the social sciences, and especially in the field of medieval studies, coupled nonetheless to "the weight of mental habits inherited from the nineteenth century: a sort of inability to tear ourselves away from an unexamined positivism" that forms the basis of the prejudice called "objectivity," shared by Zumthor's mentors and eliciting, ironically, something on the order of confession:

> Edmond Faral, with his dry, distinguished manner and his aseptic language, who was good enough to encourage my early efforts

although they were unfaithful to his teachings; Karl Voretzsch, proud of the imperial title of "Geheimrat" which made up for his small size, who was said to have boasted, in August 1914, that he would soon enter conquered Arles at the head of the Provençal regiment; Walter von Wartburg, who knew everything but who had only a few, rather narrow ideas, and who left to his memory alone the task of structuring knowledge; Robert Bossuat, who in 1935 gave me a 2 out of 20 on my Old French examination. That is not my motive for writing these lines! But none of these details are "objectively" insignificant.[12]

We do not mean to imply that Zumthor's essay caused the sudden irruption of a personalized subject in the otherwise dispassionate discourse of medievalism. Certainly, both American and Continental feminism are responsible more generally for such a trend, which also informs recent Lacanian readings of medieval texts such as the Grail literature and courtly lyric. Still, *Speaking of the Middle Ages* may well be the first attempt, certainly in recent years, to propose the memoir as a legitimate exemplum within the domain of the "objective" history of medieval studies.

Zumthor's acknowledgment of the inescapable role of individual memory points to an essential characteristic of this volume: the chapters that follow mine sources not generally recognized by the medievalist, in order to explore some of the possibilities of a history of medievalism. The authors examine letters and written records of private conversations, unpublished notes, works of fiction by academics known primarily for their scholarly writings, title pages and prefaces of printed editions, manuscript images often ignored by textual editors, famous forgeries and specious restorations.

Some of these writers do not hesitate to raise the question of biography, once an important adjunct to literary studies, but more recently seen as irrelevant. Indeed, those who discuss individual figures enter the arena of private and domestic life. They emphasize the influence of family origins, crises, and fantasies, as well as the influence of friendship, envy, ambition, and such imponderables as character, temperament, inclination, foible, and even prejudice upon the shape of the discipline.

A number of contributors recognize the crucial role of paternal and grand-paternal relations. Carl Landauer identifies the turn toward Latinity of Ernst Robert Curtius in his *European Literature and the Latin Middle Ages* with "an act of filial sacrilege" when viewed in the context of his grandfather, a renowned Greek scholar, having directed the excavations at Olympia. Per Nykrog sees the scholarly career of Joseph Bédier as essentially defined by a wrestling with the oblique paternal ghost of his friend and master, Gaston Paris. When combined with certain character traits—a natural skepticism and a keen sense of personal mission—Bédier's specific scholarly views, Nykrog argues, come to be seen as more personally motivated than one might assume. This view is tempered by Alain Corbellari's reminder that Bédier had a truly filial admiration for his intellectual master. Indeed, Corbellari's brief personal and intellectual biography of Bédier suggests that one explanation for the intensity of his relationship to Gaston Paris lies in Bédier's loss of his own natural father at the age of five.

Several authors focus specifically on the father/son relationship of Paulin and Gaston Paris in the formation of medieval studies in France under the Third Republic. Michael Camille attributes the divorce of philology from its manuscript matrix in this period to a rejection of the real father, whose essentially appreciative approach to medieval manuscripts was inevitably linked to their visual images, in favor of the "academic father" Friedrich Diez, the father of Romance philology in Germany, and what appeared at the time to be a more scientific conception of texts. The erasure of pictures from medieval studies by the uniform process of printed editions was, Camille maintains, part and parcel of a father's replacement by his son. So, too, David Hult ascribes Gaston Paris's formulation of the concept of courtly love (1883) to the psychological effects of Paulin's death (1881) in what amounts to an "Oedipal moment in the family romance of scholarly careers." Along the same lines, Alain Boureau makes a convincing case that Ernst Kantorowicz's unconventional early career in the army and in his father's wine business, coupled with the non-academic character of his first book on Frederick II, might explain his drive in later life toward erudition and his obsession with footnotes. (In a famous quarrel with the editors of *Speculum,* Kantorowicz maintained that not even endnotes would do.)

The chapters dealing with father/son relationships emphasize the extent to which the discipline, from the beginning, has been defined as essentially masculine. Camille and Hult hone in upon the famous passage of Gaston Paris's inaugural address in which he reproached the father he replaced at the Collège de France of "currying the favor of society (*les gens du monde*), of dilettantes (*les littérateurs purs*), and even of women (*chez les femmes elles-mêmes*)." Camille and Hult insist that the displacement of appreciation (gendered female) by science (gendered male) cannot be detached from the exclusion, from the beginning, of women from the field, an interpretation confirmed by more private sources as well. Writing about a very different context and a much later time, Hans Ulrich Gumbrecht details with considerable irony the sometimes comic self-celebration of the directors of the *Grundriß*, their scorn for what they perceived as the laziness of some of the editors working under them, and their initial rejection of even the suggestion that women participate in the project.

Precisely because of this exclusion, which some see as one of the founding principles of the discipline, the editors of this volume felt it essential to include discussion of the role of women in medieval studies. In "Feminism and the Discipline of Old French Studies: *Une Bele Disjointure*," E. Jane Burns, Sarah Kay, Roberta L. Krueger, and Helen Solterer, writing at the intersection of the personal and the professional, pose a series of questions concerning ways in which the female subject has been constituted by medieval texts as well as by medievalists.

Given the fact that the study of women in the Middle Ages "has borrowed much from feminist theory but given little of *theoretical* novelty," what, they ask, can medievalism give in return? Their answer is, simply put, a new practice of reading and understanding texts, "a historical and material feminism grounded in the differences of the past as well as the uncertainties of the present." Beginning from the premise, for example, that chanson de geste studies have historically been a male preserve, they discuss the many significant contributions by women who "provide women readers with a useful point of leverage against the purported univocality of epic representation" and, in Patricia Stablein's terms, against "a univocal, masculine ideology."

Moving then to the question of how to locate the woman's voice in the *chanson de femme*, Burns, Kay, Krueger, and Solterer maintain that this early lyric genre "provides an especially cogent reminder that if there can be no totalizing or coherent women's voice in medieval French literature (or elsewhere), neither can the dominant male voice—whether of literature or culture—dominate totally or unproblematically." Finally, in a conclusion dealing with the question of mastery—which, to invoke again the chapters by Camille and Hult, has been gendered as masculine since the 1870s—Burns et al. ask a significant question. "What would an authoritative stance entail that would neither impose a *magis* upon others nor use it to blur the register of difference?" In other words, how might one imagine a feminist mastery? The answer is to be found, again, in a practice, a reading of one of the great power-of-women works of the thirteenth century, the *Lai d'Aristote*, which leads the authors to conclude that "feminist mastery promises a sort of creative destruction of medieval studies as it has long been formulated—destruction because it does destabilize, if not demolish, the very grounds of the field." By destabilizing ways of reading and understanding medieval literature, feminism, the authors argue, will open the discipline to a non-hierarchical model of theory, practice, and professional relations.

The theme of professionalization runs deep throughout this volume. Indeed, almost all the authors note that at a certain moment—earlier in some places, later in others—the field of medieval studies consciously ordered itself as a discipline in contradistinction to the antiquarianism and even religious motivation that had earlier characterized it. Thus Jeffrey M. Peck, in his study "'In the Beginning Was the Word': Germany and the Origins of German Studies," explores the shift in Germany just after the Napoleonic Wars "from theology to philology, the word of God to the love of the word," and the rise of philology as a form of "secular redemption." Similarly, in "The Myth of Medieval Romance," John M. Ganim distinguishes an allied trend, under the intellectual aegis of F. J. Furnivall, to combine educational populism with German scientific philology, and Per Nykrog stresses the influence of the model of the German university upon the notion of the professional medievalist in both France and the United States.

Where France is concerned, Laura Kendrick identifies in her chapter, "The Science of Imposture and the Professionalization of Medieval Occitan Literary Studies," the Revolution of 1789 as a key founding movement, the first in a series of crises of legitimacy out of which medieval studies were born. Kendrick first demonstrates how counter-revolutionaries, after 1789, sought to invent a middle ages that would restore the glories of feudalism. They did so by what amounts to "fabricating" medieval texts, for Kendrick an inevitable consequence of the Romantic editing methods of the day. She shows how this first post-Revolutionary nostalgia to restore the past gradually evolved to the July Monarchy's efforts, after 1830, to work out a rational restoration of medieval monuments under the leadership of Louis-Philippe's conservative Minister of Public Instruction, François Guizot.

In his chapter on the editions of the troubadours, John Graham perceives a trend away from publishing translations of medieval works in favor of learning the language of the troubadours by way of fostering greater appreciation of the original. He sees this trend as marking a movement away from exclusively historical concerns toward greater grammatical and linguistic precision as befits a nascent professionalization of troubadour studies grounded in empiricism and an emergent sense of the "science" of philological disciplines (discussed in the chapter by Stephen G. Nichols). Graham shows how the trend led to a heightened esthetic sense of the "original" lyric, and a concern for the kinds of distortions introduced into it by imperfect historical transmission. Again, the movement grew from a recognition, articulated, Graham notes, with firmness and "exasperation" by Gaston Paris, of the greater emphasis placed on philology by German universities. "The French university, . . . oriented around the two-hour lecture courses given by a small body of titulary professors, was ill-adapted for labor-intensive philological instruction. Not only did the typical German university have more professors than even the Université de Paris, but those professors taught as much as five times as many hours per week as their French counterparts."

While German philology was undoubtedly one influence on the professionalization of medieval studies, Alain Boureau notes yet another. He traces the development of professionalism out of a knot of vague dilettantish resonances with the Ancien Régime, through the Revolution of 1848, to the earliest occurrences of the words "médiéval" (1874) and "médiéviste" (1867), to, eventually, the notion of "medievalist" as a vocation in the early twentieth century. Again, the father/son struggle between Paulin and Gaston Paris was also sensed, even at the time, as Camille and Hult make clear, as a struggle of the adherents of a scientific professionalism based upon philological method against what the first French philologists perceived to be the amateur connoisseurship of their fathers' generation. "In any case, we understand differently today the study of the Middle Ages," Paris *fils* writes. "We are less attached to appreciation and to inspiring appreciation than to understanding. What we seek above all is history."

In identifying the moment when the field became a discipline, one must recognize that, wherever and whenever such a crystallization occurred, medieval studies did not stand alone but were part and parcel of a larger movement toward organizing knowledge along the disciplinary lines that still define our university system—and that are, in the case of literary studies, still deeply allied with the philological enterprise. In "Modernism and the Politics of Medieval Studies,"

Stephen G. Nichols demonstrates the extent to which the emergence of French academic medievalism was bound to a concept of modernity in the second half of the nineteenth century. Comparing the substance and context of Rimbaud's "lettre du voyant," written during the Paris Commune, to Gaston Paris's "leçon d'ouverture" during the siege of Paris in 1870, Nichols makes a case for the early medievalists' ambiguous relation to what they saw as the insidious modernism of the times as opposed to an earlier modernism of Newton and Descartes. Where the former emphasized incompletion, refusal of clear meaning, autonomy of artistic consciousness, and fragmentation along with a penchant for detail, the latter stressed rationalism, a sense of "timeless principles that hold good at all times," and nationalism based upon the concept of sovereign statehood. Thus the great early figures, such as Émile Littré, Gaston Paris, Viollet-le-Duc, and Léon Gautier, sought the certainty of scientific method and at the same time emphasized the importance of the historical detail, the *dit,* as Nichols puts it, over the performative *dire* of medieval texts.

They proposed a concept of language as fact, and thus as historical artifact. This led, in turn, to a theory of identity, especially national identity, which served the contemporary agenda of the French. Nichols notes how quickly the historical linguistics of the last century, explanations for the origin, development, and relation of languages, give way to models of cultural primacy and, ultimately, claims to territorial legitimacy. His case in point is the lexicographer Littré's notion of France as a perfect combination of the Gallic, Roman, and Germanic races, a theory that Littré uses to argue that the language of France is both the most ancient, because of its early literature, and the most modern, because of its rebirth in the sixteenth century. Such contradictory notions of "nationalist modernism" were subtended, as Nichols maintains, by models from the natural sciences—first geological and then biological—as well as by an underlying theological premise, which accounts for the traditional trope in medieval studies of the epic as the master genre.

If Littré belies the concept of historical grammar as a value-neutral area of study—a science, in the concept of historical linguistics developed in the late nineteenth century—Suzanne Fleischman's chapter on the methods and ideologies of historical grammar suggests just how illusory such a goal must be even today. Taking the particle *si* (clause-initial) in Old French, Fleischman uncovers the conscious and unconscious ideologies inevitably permeating historical grammar.

One such assumption holds that language in a given period is sufficiently stable and homogeneous to permit identification of a period and a dialect one can call "Old French" and from which one may constitute a grammar of the language. Fleischman calls this the "taxonomic approach" to historical grammar because it seeks to construct a normative description based in part on the concept that word classification is universal. Testing this assumption with reference to the particle *si*, Fleischman finds that it "fails to exhibit certain properties common to temporal adverbs while at the same time exhibiting properties that define conjunctions." This simple illustration suggests that assumptions about the scientific nature of language analysis really become a creator of norms that impede observation of linguistic phenomena. In this case, for example, they miss the lability of grammatical categories and fail to account for changes over time; in short, they propose an image of Old French conforming to an inappropriate taxonomic model.

Fleischman identifies another "scientific fallacy" in historical grammar: the "autonomous approach to language." This approach has been used to describe "Old French" based on "rules" governing instances of verbal behavior found in texts. But since the "rules" so constructed are not "data available for observation," as would be the case with a pool of native-speaker informants for a living language, they are necessarily constructs, inductive generalizations arrived at through linguistic procedures. These rules imply "covert norms" imposed on Old French through the choice of one dialect, for example, the famous "Francien," identified in the late nineteenth century as the koine of the Ile-de-France. Grammars and dictionaries of Old French, Fleischman argues, like the normalized edited texts with which they have intellectual affinities, are modernist rather than medieval phenomena.

To see how modernism could produce such powerful tools for hammering out, like Jean de Meun's picture of Nature at her forge, compelling images of the Middle Ages, one may look to the career of the Abbé Migne detailed here by R. Howard Bloch. If ever there were a modernist avatar of Jean's *Dame Nature*, it must surely be the abbé. Migne pioneered, Bloch writes, "a bibliographical assembly line capable of producing a standardized product at minimal cost for mass consumption." Although undertaken for religious purposes, Migne's extraordinary entrepreneurial energy changed "the entire economy of book production and distribution in the nineteenth century. For the first time, subscriptions for a major publication venture were marketed like household merchandise, for example, over the counter in dry goods stores in his native Auvergne."

While Migne modeled his "Ateliers Catholiques"—the premises at Montrouge on the outskirts of Paris where he combined editorial activities, printing plant, and distribution—on the medieval cloister and scriptorium, he did not adopt scientific principles of text editing based on reconstructing texts from manuscripts. By working with already printed versions that his "editors" simply "refined," Migne pioneered a method of production that depersonalized the church fathers and "captures at bottom the very essence of the industrial revolution of the last century, that is to say, the impulse toward standardization."

Even though Migne believed that making the works of the church fathers—the *Patrologia Latina* and *Patrologia Graeca*—available to the masses would stem the flight from the church that had begun with the French Revolution, he produced one of the most prodigious scholarly tools for the study of late antiquity and the Middle Ages yet conceived. Thus, while Migne may not have contributed to the scientific development of medieval studies as it evolved in the nineteenth century, he unwittingly furthered the achievement of that goal by providing tools that embodied one of modernist medievalism's chief aims, the publication of comprehensive text series. Without the example of the complete Latin and Greek texts of the church fathers, would there have been such confident initiatives at publishing comprehensive series as the Société des Anciens Textes Français, the *Early English Text Society,* or the *Monumenta Germaniae Historica*?

As Bloch, Fleischman, Nichols, and others prove, the emergence of scientific medievalism cannot be detached from the emergence of the fields of history, art history, classical studies, and the social sciences. This implies, again, that our understanding the history of the field is not simply a matter of writing the narrative of its appearance and evolution, but of contextualizing—socially, politically, and sexually—those factors that have made and continue to shape the discipline as we know it. If the chapters that follow are unified by the attempt to identify and account for the specific historical determinants that have made the field of medieval studies, by far the most common contributing factor is that of nationalistic rivalry between Germany and France. Indeed, throughout the nineteenth century, a pattern emerges according to which military defeat and wounded nationalistic pride give rise to the urge to recover the medieval past as a means, first, of compensating for loss and then, eventually, of refashioning territorial claims that potentially result in renewed military clash.

Thus, as Jeffrey Peck argues, the development of medieval studies in Germany served to heal the wounds of the Napoleonic Wars. Beginning with Jacob and Wilhelm Grimm's *German Dictionary,* "the most literal example of a Romantic hermeneutic project," which replaced the Bible as the Hausbuch of the German family, medievalism contributed to the creation of a German national ethnic identity. The theories of *Bildung and Wissenschaft,* a belief in the power of the German language to shape intellectual and moral character, were translated into educational policy by Humboldt, Schleiermacher, and Fichte, as philology and the study of the Middle Ages continued to serve as a unifying force after 1830 and 1848. "This confluence of scholarship and politics," according to Peck, "contributed to the eventual successful institutionalization and professionalization of *Germanistik* at the most crucial juncture of power and authority of the discipline, just as Bismarck was unifying Germany and carving out a place for it as a competitive industrial and colonial power." The German unification of 1871 under the Prussians can be seen, Peck concludes, as another version of medievalism in the service of state building, an imperialistic rather than *volkisch* realization of the original Romantic project of the Grimms.

As is clear from the chapters by Graham and Hult, the nationalistic purpose of medieval studies in France emerged primarily after the Franco-Prussian War and in reaction to defeat. The four years between 1876 and 1879 saw the endowment of 250 new chairs of literature and history supported by university libraries. Journals dedicated to medieval culture were founded: the *Revue des langues romanes* (1870), *Romania* (1872), *La revue de philologie française et provençale* (1887), *Le Moyen Age* (1888), and *Annales du Midi* (1889). The Société des Anciens Textes Français, conceived by Paul Meyer and Gaston Paris and underwritten by James de Rothschild, came into being in 1875. "It seemed to us that the center of Romance studies ought to be in France rather than in Germany," Paris and Meyer declared in the prepublication Prospectus of the journal *Romania* (1872) discussed by Graham, who also notes the significance of the creation of the École des Hautes Études in 1868. "Defined at the outset as distinct from the university and the literary teaching it offered, the École went on to prepare generations of text editors and historical scholars and thus helped to promulgate both in France and abroad a notion of the discipline as practical and methodological rather than theoretical or ideological." Like the Écoles des Chartes, whose founding in 1821 Nichols discusses, the Écoles des Hautes Études became, as Graham claims, the "institutional base" from which the French rivaled the Germans in what amounted to, in the field of Provençal studies, a philological "arms race," the weapons being those of edition and publication.

In "Gaston Paris and the Invention of Courtly Love," David Hult offers a synthesis of many of the elements seen thus far: paternal struggle, a politics of gender embedded in the scientific impulse, a nascent nationalistic spirit.

> Gaston Paris's obsession with the scientific study of literature be-
> came translated not only as a kind of mind/body dualism, . . . but
> also as an unresolved conflict between control . . . and appreciation,
> understood in manifestly passive and "feminine" terms. Patriotism
> and national devotion here fall on the side of "appreciation" since,
> by virtue of their instinctual grounding, they were conceived by Paris
> as a form of love: "c'est l'amour que vous trouverez au fond de toute
> nationalité réelle." In the course of his career, we may say that
> Gaston Paris's scientific ideal led him increasingly to repudiate love
> in its many related forms: naive poetry, patriotic fervor, his father's
> medievalism. That Gaston lingered upon his father's qualities of love
> and sincerity, even as he deprecated his scholarly output, was thus
> rhetorically quite apposite. His father came increasingly to symbol-
> ize the qualities inherent in the Romantic substratum of nineteenth-
> century medievalism that Gaston's scientific ideal gradually induced
> him to dismiss or dismantle.
>
> What makes this a poignant realization is that it was equally
> clear that pure science was not self-sufficient. In his patriotism
> lecture [1870], Gaston spoke admiringly of the Germans' sense of a
> national identity, which he attributed, interestingly enough, to the
> efforts of a single man, a scholar, a philologist: Jacob Grimm. . . .
> [He] was able to accomplish this through a combination of qualities
> unavailable in the history of French civilization: a man combining
> "scientific genius with an intense, deep, and childlike love of one's
> fatherland (*patrie*)." It is hard not to see that the French equivalent
> would be an impossible fusion between Gaston Paris and his father:
> science and love, genial and childlike impulses.

It is precisely this combination, Hult maintains, that captures the essence of the concept of courtly love as a synthesis of desire and self-restraint.

In the generation immediately following that of Paul Meyer and Gaston Paris, Joseph Bédier maintained the most resolutely patriotic posture. As Per Nykrog contends in "A Warrior Scholar at the Collège de France," Bédier's entire career was in some profound sense motivated by a Germanophobia that extended even to French scholars whom he felt had adopted German ideas too readily. According to Nykrog, the anti-Orientalism of Bédier's thesis on the fabliaux was in reality anti-Germanism directed at Theodor Benfey, Reinhold Koehler, Felix Liebrecht, and their "folklorist" followers in France Emmanuel Cosquin and Gaston Paris. Nykrog also argues that Bédier's theses regarding the late, individualist, clerical, and learned origins of the epic were posited, in essence, against Romantic theories of a popular, collective, oral, early, and therefore Germanic origin of France's oldest chansons de geste.

Bédier's edition as well as his popular vulgarization of the Tristan legend worked similarly, according to Nykrog, to reclaim for France what had come, through Wagner and the German versions of Gottfried and Eilhard, to be perceived as a German work. Bédier's theory of text editing, elaborated in the prefaces of his two editions of the *Lai de l'Ombre* (1913 and 1928) are anti-Germanic to the extent to which they are anti-Lachmannian and directed against those who adopted Lachmann's methods in France. In proffering the principle of editing "one good manuscript, with a minimum of emendation," as opposed to multipronged stemmata with invasive editing, Bédier upheld at the most basic level of scholarship an individualistic thesis that was of a piece with his individualizing theories on the origin of the epic. Alain Corbellari completes the complex picture of the relationship between Bédier's patriotism, his explanation of the origin of the epic, and his text editing principles by noting the ways in which Bédier tried to counter what he considered a false positivist theory of origins with a notion of the ontological preeminence of every individual work. Bédier was simply against the idea of determinism in literary studies. In place of a strict adherence to the question of source, which would have made the earliest French literature in essence of Germanic stock, he substituted neoclassical models. Nor is Corbellari unaware of the paradox of a Bédier at once Romantic, because of the notion of "genius" to which he has recourse, and anti-Romantic because of his anti-Germanic spirit on the eve of World War I. Finally, Corbellari places Bédier at the forefront of the modernist notion of the integrity of the individual text and thus, along with Gustave Lanson, in whose history of French literature he will participate, at the origin not only of modern literary history but of literary theory as we know it. This is a different Bédier from the one we are used to—indeed, a Bédier who can be seen as the potential predecessor of Erich Auerbach, of the American New Critics, and even of the structuralists and deconstructionists of our own era.

Both Nykrog and Corbellari concentrate on a little-known aspect of Bédier's career: his wartime activities and employment in the French Ministère de la Guerre (war office). During World War I, Bédier produced several small volumes in which he tried to prove philologically, through the analysis of journals taken from the bodies of dead German soldiers and live prisoners, the barbarism of the German people. He also wrote an anti-German one-act play based on the medieval tale of the heroic deeds of Vivien. After the war Bédier wrote a little book on the subject of French artillery. In essence, Bédier, who had spent time in Germany (Halle) as a student, never quite recovered intellectually from his experiences in the war office.

Some of the chapters in this volume deal with the attempt of scholars between the two wars and in the postwar period to counter the effects of nationalistic rivalry and to bring to medieval studies a new sense of internationalism. Alain Boureau emphasizes that for Ernst Kantorowicz the Middle Ages represented a "projected space," "a place of refuge" and "internal exile" between the time of Kantorowicz's expulsion from the German university and his arrival in the United States. Seth Lerer and Carl Landauer identify similarly covert political agendas (or reactions to nationalist politics in which they found themselves enmeshed) on the part of Erich Auerbach and Ernst Robert Curtius.

Although Erich Auerbach has commonly been viewed as apolitical, Seth Lerer argues that Auerbach's concept and practice of *dargestellte Wirklichkeit,* misleadingly translated into English as "mimesis," actually encrypt his opinions on serious political issues. Taking Auerbach's essay in *Mimesis* on the twelfth-century *Jeu d'Adam* as a proof-text, Lerer suggests that the techniques of figural interpretation Auerbach "develops for the study of medieval literature are encoded in his own narrative of the processes of textual criticism." From this insight, one can read the specific "political subtext" of the chapter.

The pivot of this chapter, for Lerer, turns on a philological argument Auerbach makes regarding the difference between the way two editions, one German, one French, read a particular passage (the dispute itself continues a long-running conflict between German-style and French-style philology). Lerer reads this argument, and the resultant interpretation Auerbach gives to Eve in the play, as a recasting of his interpretation of the behavior of European nations during World War II, specifically the collaboration of the French with Hitler's regime. "Again and again the character of Adam is affirmed as good, as noble, and as French" by Auerbach; for Lerer, then, Adam represents the good, decent, and democratic Frenchman. The collaborationists were the "childish, impetuous French like Eve, who would succumb to the temptations of a satanic *Verführer.*" In a final twist, Lerer shows why the reception of Auerbach's work failed to perceive the real agenda of this piece; medieval studies not being associated with political matters, *Mimesis* was received as a non-political work of criticism which Auerbach's exile in Turkey could permit one to see as "either a problem in research or a badge of honor, yet nowhere relocated in the critic's narratives."

Carl Landauer finds a related reaction on the part of Ernst Robert Curtius, for whom literary criticism functioned as a topos of the landscape or garden and for whom Dante represented the figure of the internal exile. Curtius's *Toposforschung*, his pan-Europeanism and emphasis upon the unity of Europe, his turn toward France as universal culture with a strong humanist tradition, but, most of all, the pride of place bestowed in his *European Literature and the Latin Middle Ages* upon classical culture as opposed to both Christianity and Germanness, were, Landauer convincingly shows, a means of distancing himself from the Third Reich.

Hans Ulrich Gumbrecht, writing about German medievalism after World War II, underscores the degree to which the editors of the new *Grundriß* rejected both the *Toposforschung* of Curtius and the obsessive search for sources by scholars such as Jean Marx and Roger Sherman Loomis, in favor of a unified vision of the Romance languages and literatures and the cultural unity of the West. The original decision of Hans Robert Jauss and Erich Koehler to organize the *Grundriß* along lines of genre was, like Curtius's vision of continuity with the classical past, a form of resistance to the nationalistic rivalries of the past century. Such an effort was only partially successful, however, for the unified European vision met strong resistance from medievalists who were less ecumenically inclined. Noting that, despite the appearance of a number of volumes, the *Grundriß* still remains incomplete, Gumbrecht ascribes this failure of completion in part to problems inherent in the strict disciplinary conception of the project. Beyond that, his analysis of the correspondence that passed between editors turns up evidence of a self-defeating belief in the rhetoric of their own project. Material conditions had also changed since the inception of the *Grundriß,* for example, the economics and politics of book publishing beginning in the 1960s, and a waning by the late 1970s of the original energy that generated the enterprise in the 1950s.

Though influenced tangentially by the nationalistic struggles between Germany and France, England, as John Ganim demonstrates, is somewhat of a case apart. Ganim uses the romance genre as a literary and political litmus test in order to follow the ways in which the Middle Ages have been pressed into the service of ideology from the eighteenth century to the present. Romance is, he maintains, "a crucial focus for tracing the politics of English medievalism."

Thus we find, in the eighteenth-century revival of medievalism by Thomas Warton, Thomas Percy, and Bishop Hurd, that romance takes on the role of an escapist utopian literature thought to offer a means of recovering a lost coherence. The Middle Ages are imagined as romance, history "is read as a literary genre," and, concomitantly, the importance of romance is minimized. Such a static view implies, Ganim stresses, a concept of history in which change can be imagined only by "constructing an opposite and prior world, in its own way as timeless as the present." Thus "the scholars of medieval romance in the late eighteenth century insistently denied the political relevance of their scholarship, but this denial masked the conservatism of their enterprise."

By the early nineteenth century, however, romance had become a more popular genre, even a style, and medievalism came to stand for a specific antirevolutionary religious, political, and cultural agenda of return to Anglican ritual. The aristocratic antiquarianism of the previous century was transformed into a symbolic masquerade of the "Young England" movement. By midcentury, the study of romance had joined the academic institutionalization of literature; and in the Victorian period, it passed, under the aegis of F. J. Furnivall and the Early English Text Society, from the original conservative antiquarianism of a century earlier to a more pluralistic ideal of educational populism sustained by German scientific philology. This reversal comes full circle with the advent of W. P. Ker's *Epic and Romance* (1897), which set the agenda for several generations of English medievalists in its emphasis on the mechanistic, secondary, and corrupt nature of romance as against the primal, heroic power of epic. This dismissal of romance, this insistence upon the Nordic and the primitive as opposed to what was perceived as cosmopolitan and French, must, Ganim maintains, be seen, again, in terms of a nationalist, fundamentally antimodernist, anti-Continental, and pro-English thrust.

Inasmuch as the rejection of romance and the rise of nationalism recur here as a leitmotif explaining why certain aspects of the discipline developed as they did, we thought it useful to include a largely forgotten and previously untranslated document that testifies in a fascinating way to the *mentalité* underlying modernist medievalism. The document, translated for the first time into English, is the *Vorrede* (*Preface*) to the 1819 edition of Jacob and Wilhelm Grimm's *Kinder- und Hausmärchen*, otherwise known, somewhat inaccurately, as "Grimms' Fairy Tales."

"One of the indispensable documents from the early history of the Western literary disciplines," as its translators Hans Ulrich Gumbrecht and Jeffrey Schnapp point out, the *Vorrede* "reveals a double movement of differentiation . . . between, on the one hand, an overarching fascination on the part of European intellectuals with cultural otherness . . . and, on the other, a specific interest in the otherness of their own nation's past."

The *Vorrede* outlines three functions for the *Kinder- und Hausmärchen* that suggest a move by academic teaching and research to embrace the public interest in cultural artifacts from the national past. The first function "reflects the aesthetic credo of early Romanticism." The oral tales collected by the brothers Grimm from informants who still recount them in rural settings exude "freshness and spontaneity" in contrast to the "'stiffness' of contemporary manners and mores." It is this freshness and spontaneity that connote innocence and nature and thus childhood. Education is the second function of the tales, but education in the sense of *Bildung* ("development"), celebrating the emotionally and intellectually matured individual. In this sense, the *Kinder- und Hausmärchen* announce the novel of development or *Bildungsroman*.

The third function is surely the most innovative one proposed by the *Vorrede*. This is the claim—"unthinkable before the institutionalization of the Romantic fixation with the national past"—that historical and ethnographic values take precedence over normative aesthetic factors when considering the social utility of artifacts like the *märchen*. At some level, we find in the articulation of this third function a consciousness in the *Vorrede* of that current that came to be known later in the century as realism and naturalism.

The *Preface* by the brothers Grimm makes a fitting epilogue to this volume. It warns that, in a real sense, each document from the rich fund of nineteenth-century testaments to the foundations of the discipline of medieval studies has its own tale to tell about the period, its own slant to impart on those foundations. To attempt to encompass in one work this rich lode of witness would be to espouse the totalizing optimism of the period itself, and it would require the boundless energy of an Abbé Migne to complete. We are not he, nor do we and the volume's contributors share the philosophy of the founders of the discipline, as much as we admire and respect their legacy. That's what this volume is about.

NOTES

1. Iorgu Iordan and John Orr, *An Introduction to Romance Linguistics* (London: Methuen & co., Ltd., 1937).

2. Janine Rosalind Dakyns, *The Middle Ages in French Literature, 1851–1900* (Oxford: Oxford University Press, 1973).

3. Lee Patterson, *Negotiating the Past: The Historical Understanding of Medieval Literature* (Madison: University of Wisconsin Press, 1987).

4. R. Howard Bloch, *Etymologies and Genealogies. A Literary Anthropology of the French Middle Ages* (Chicago: University of Chicago Press, 1983); Peter Haidu, "Towards a Problematics of Alterity: Making It (New) in the Middle Ages," *Diacritics* (summer 1974): 1–10; Hans Robert Jauss, *Alterität und Modernität der mittelalterlichen Literatur* (Munich: Fink Verlag, 1977); Alexandre Leupin, "The Middle Ages, The Other," *Diacritics* (fall 1983): 22–31; Stephen G. Nichols, "Remodeling Models: Modernism and the Middle Ages," in *Modernité au Moyen Age: Le défi du passé*, ed. Brigitte Cazelles and Charles Méla (Geneva: Droz, 1990), 45–72; Eugene Vance, "The Modernity of the Middle Ages in the Future: Remarks on a Recent Book," *Romantic Review* 64 (1973): 140–51.

5. "If it is the case, as I believe it is, that the master narrative first put in place by the Renaissance is the cause of all our woe as medievalists, then surely we should struggle against it at every level. And yet medieval studies has been all too eager to accept this account, and the professional sequestration it entails." Lee Patterson, "On the Margin: Postmodernism, Ironic History, and Medieval Studies," *Speculum* (1990): 87–108, at 101.

6. Brian Stock, "The Middle Ages as Subject and Object: Romantic Attitudes and Academic Medievalism," *New Literary History* 5 (1974): 527–47; Stephen G. Nichols, "A Poetics of Historicism? Recent Trends in Medieval Literary Study," *Medievalia et humanistica* 8 (1977): 77–101.

7. Hans Aarslef, "Scholarship and Ideology: Joseph Bédier's Critique of Romantic Medievalism," in *Historical Studies and Literary Criticism*, ed.

Jerome J. McGann (Madison: University of Wisconsin Press, 1985), 93–113; Hans Ulrich Gumbrecht, "'Un souffle d'Allemagne ayant passé': Friedrich Diez, Gaston Paris and the Genesis of National Philologies," *Romance Philology* 40 (1986): 1–37.

8. Bernard Cerquiglini, *Éloge de la variante: Histoire critique de la philologie* (Paris: Éditions du Seuil, 1989); François Hartog, *Le XIXe siècle et l'histoire: Le cas de Fustel de Coulanges* (Paris: Presses Universitaires de France, 1988); Alain Boureau, *Histoire d'un historien: Kantorowicz* (Paris: Gallimard, 1990).

9. For reflections on what has come to be called the "New Medievalism," see Stephen G. Nichols, "The New Medievalism: Tradition and Discontinuity in Medieval Culture," in *The New Medievalism,* ed. Marina S. Brownlee, Kevin Brownlee, and Stephen G. Nichols (Baltimore: Johns Hopkins University Press, 1991), 1–26.

10. This useful, multivolume tool, published in Heidelberg by Carl Winter Verlag, surveys different aspects of the foundation of medieval Romance literatures.

11. Paul Zumthor, *Speaking of the Middle Ages* (Lincoln: University of Nebraska Press, 1986), 3–4.

12. Ibid., 17.

PART ONE

FOUNDING THE DISCIPLINE

O N E

Modernism and the Politics of Medieval Studies

Stephen G. Nichols

GASTON PARIS AND ARTHUR RIMBAUD would not seem to have a great deal in common beyond contemporaneity. The adolescent poet, scornful of Charleroi, rebelling against adult authority, teasing Verlaine, strikes one as the very antithesis of the eminently respectable professor of Old French language and literature at the Collège de France. Yet they were both engaged in similar enterprises in their respective domains, and, in his own way, Gaston Paris fervently espoused Rimbaud's dictum "Il faut être absolumment moderne"— albeit his was a more expansive and conservative formulation of the concept.

Modernism for Rimbaud meant faith in progress, the invention of the new; the poet must make himself a multiplier of progress (*multiplicateur de progrès*), as Antoine Compagnon reminds us.[1] Rimbaud wrote his modernist manifesto, the famous "lettre du voyant," in May 1871, in the midst of the Paris Commune, one of many examples of his recognition of modernism's insistent linking of art with the present, "la modernité est le parti du présent contre le passé" ("modernity is the party of the present against the past")[2] And yet, his "Illuminations" and "Une saison en enfer," reveal how much at home Rimbaud was with a poetic tradition he felt bound to move beyond. Such contradiction—establishing traditions only to break with them—is, as Compagnon points out, one of the recurring paradoxes of modernism, and one that leads it to affirm and deny art.[3] Rimbaud serves as something of an icon of modernism because his quixotic career and writings illustrate its tenets and paradoxes so clearly.

Gaston Paris, too, conveyed many of those same tenets (and paradoxes), which makes him a convenient starting point for showing how modernism was the hidden agenda for the discipline of medieval studies as it developed in the second half of the nineteenth century. If Rimbaud wrote his "lettre du voyant" inspired by revolutionary solidarity with the *Communards* in Paris in 1871, Gaston Paris also produced a rather astonishing manifesto every bit as emotionally charged as Rimbaud's which he gave as the opening lecture for his course at the Collège de France on December 8, 1870. The Germans were laying siege to Paris even while Gaston Paris spoke, and it was not by accident that the title of both his lecture and the course that year was "*La Chanson de Roland* et la nationalité française." We will look at this fascinating monument to the paradoxically modernist agenda of Old French studies later.

MODERNISM AND PHILOLOGY

First, I want to suggest that Gaston Paris's case is not an isolated one. The anxiety of modernity, as Compagnon shows, pervades certain tenets of nineteenth-century literary sensibility. It is not the concept of newness per se that marks this sensibility. Compagnon cites Hans Robert Jauss's study tracing *modernus* to a late fifth-century low Latin coinage from *modo*, meaning "recently, now."[4] *Modernus* designated not what was new, but what was present, immediate, contemporaneous with the speaker. The modern was a way of distinguishing between what was current and what was old, or ancient—between the classical and the contemporaneous: "les anciens contre les modernes."[5] Jauss argues that the phenomenon implicated in the semantic history of *modernus* is the sense of a foreshortening of time, a narrowing of the time separating past from present, in short, a sense of the acceleration of history.

It is thus not "modern" or "the moderns" that is at issue in the nineteenth century, but the noun, *modernité,* which announces a new perspective, an awareness of new methodological approaches with new ways of producing knowledge and representation. Compagnon situates Baudelaire as the commentator of artistic modernism who first recognized the characteristics of the movement that set it apart from prior manifestations of artistic contemporaneity. Baudelaire recognized modernity much more ambiguously than Rimbaud. In Compagnon's aphorism, "Il loue la peinture de la réalité moderne, mais non la réalité de la peinture moderne."[6]

As found in Baudelaire's *La peinture de la vie moderne* (1863), the painting of modern reality lay in the subjects of contemporary artists like Constantin Guys: "les femmes, les filles, le dandy, la société de l'Empire" ("women, prostitutes, the dandy, Third Empire society"). The reality of modern painting occasioned much less enthusiasm, departing as it did from romantic modernism's "great chain of history" that Baudelaire had praised so enthusiastically in the *Salon de 1846* when analyzing Delacroix's *Dante et Virgile*. Baudelaire discovered four traits of modernist painting through his analysis of Guys's work which also helped to explain the resistance to modernist painting in the work of Courbet and Manet. These characteristics were (1) incompletion, (2) fragmentation or a penchant for detail, (3) refusal of clear meaning or loss of sense attendant upon a refusal of organic unity, and (4) autonomy, reflexivity, or circularity stemming from an artistic critical consciousness.[7] One cannot underestimate the significance of these traits for, taken together, they contribute to one of modernism's most important innovations: the destruction of illusion based on geometric perspectivism and the flattening of painting which goes along with its refusal of meaning.[8]

Baudelaire begins here to formulate principles that suggest not only new ways of painting, but of looking at and thinking about art and its implicit connections to history and historical traditions. This defining movement of modernism in art may seem remote or removed from medieval studies. We may feel that the reality of modern painting in the second half of the nineteenth century has nothing to contribute to our discipline. And yet, what we find in Baudelaire's tenets of modernism are the early warning signs of a slow coming to consciousness of the "hidden agenda of modernity," to use Stephen Toulmin's recent coinage. If Baudelaire was not comfortable with the reality of modern painting he perceived, it may well be because he, like Gaston Paris or Émile Littré, found himself more at home with an earlier agenda of modernism, one dating back to the time of Newton and Descartes. The traits of this primal modernism, in Toulmin's formulation, were (1) rationalism leading to a preference for theory over practice; (2) "timeless principles that hold good at all times," summarized by the motto "the permanent was in, the transitory was out," and nationalism based on the concept of sovereign nationhood.[9]

The traits Baudelaire identifies in modern art—incompletion, fragmentation, refusal of clear meaning, reflexivity—manifest a clear opposition to modernism's prior agenda. Yet both are undeniably tenets of modernism readily identified as motivating forces for art and literature in the nineteenth century. Indeed, the nineteenth century marks the apogee of sovereign nationhood in the guise of imperialism, in politics, while the rise of the modern university seemed to empower "science," both physical and humane, with limitless theoretical horizons.

The rise of the modern university also witnessed the beginning of medieval studies as a formal academic discipline with a defined methodology and course of study. Paulin Paris, the father of Gaston Paris, was brought from his job as archivist at the Bibliothèque Impériale (where he had been working since 1828) by Napoléon III and appointed France's first professor of medieval language and literature in 1852. He delivered the first lecture for the newly created chair on March 1, 1853, at the age of fifty-three.

Paulin Paris first, then his son Gaston, beginning in 1867, at the Collège de France, and Léon Gautier who assumed the chair of palaeography at the École des Chartes in 1871, played major roles in defining the nature of the new discipline of Old French literary studies. Each in his own way manifested the first agenda of modernism, although not necessarily as a conscious predilection. Indeed, one of the paradoxes of the modernism elaborated during the eighteenth century lay in its ability to polarize temporal perspective into a future-oriented modernism with its invitation to and celebration of technological change versus an historically oriented modernism resistant to the technological innovations and sociopolitical changes that were the logical fruits of the "other" modernism. Historical method, or what we may call an "ideology of history," occupied a place of honor in the perspective of past-oriented modernism, where it functioned to safeguard the values of rationalism, temporal duration, and nationalism that were so integral a part of the modernist agenda.

The academic study of medieval literature may with some justification be viewed as having been "invented," in the medieval sense of the term, as a reaction to avant-garde modernism's aggressive turning away from traditional forms. Just as Baudelaire had reservations about traits in Manet and Courbet that seemed to him to deny the principles of historical continuity he had celebrated in an earlier generation of painters, so the founders of the discipline of French medieval studies sought to find in the origins of the French language and national consciousness what Charles De Gaulle, at a later moment, but with the same motivation, would call "la grandeur de la France."

Medieval studies, at their inception, consequently straddled a fault line dividing modernism into closely linked but essentially opposing masses imbricated one upon the other. Men like Émile Littré, Gaston Paris, Viollet-le-Duc, and Léon Gautier infused their authoritative versions of medieval studies with ideals which we may recognize as correlating with historically centered modernism. Nevertheless, as we take a close look at tenets of medieval studies developed by them, particularly definitions of the language and the hierarchy of literary works they espoused, we will find deep within their work the fault lines of the modernist paradox.

If this be so, we may well ask some basic questions about their views of the discipline. For instance: what was their notion of the Middle Ages? One of alterity? Disjunction from the modern age? Or did they view its literature as analogous to that of their own age? That is, just as their avant-garde contemporaries viewed art as linked to *actualité* ("current events"), did these scholars see medieval works as reflecting twelfth- or thirteenth-century *actualités* in ways analogous to, and according to, the same agendas as modern works? In other words, are they in fact perpetrating historical decontextualization even as they strive to define "scientifically" the concept of a *contextual* literary history? Only through such questions can we understand the politics of reading in nineteenth-century literary history, a politics that manifested itself through a newly defined and narrower definition of philology and a hierarchical view of literary texts.

Turning away from the conception of philology as what we might call an anthropology of language, the sense given by theorists of the subject like Roger Bacon in the thirteenth century, philology assumed a new conceptualization as a scientific study of language according to historical and phonological principles.[10] Rigorous implementation of these principles were to inform an archaeological reconstitution of medieval languages and the methodical editing of texts in which the language would be showcased. The study of language and the editing of texts were complementary skills that had to be practiced together, especially in light of the "interventionist" principles of nineteenth-century text editing which authorized reconstructing the language of a text. But philology also had a good deal to do with determining the ways in which particular kinds of texts would be viewed and the temporal importance accorded to them in the historical timeline of medieval literature that literary historians were developing. Let us look first at philology and then at the canon it helped to establish to get a better view of this politics of reading and modernism's contradictory compression of the process.

MODERN PHILOLOGY AND/AS DECONTEXTUALIZED MEDIEVALISM

The role of time was fundamental to both philology and literary history as it was in modernism. Time had taken on a new role when Newton had adopted the modern B.C./A.D. dating system introduced by the Jesuit Dominic Petavius in 1627. In conjunction with Newton's principle of absolute time, the new dating system—which only became standard in the West in the eighteenth century—allowed scholars to quantify the relationship between events in a precise and "scientific" manner.

As Donald Wilcox has shown in *The Measure of Times Past*, the new system provided a conceptual grid to give universal applicability to historical measurements.[11] It also laid the foundation for a "scientific" history by allowing scholars to measure first and evaluate afterwards; that is, to first locate an event in time by establishing its chronology in absolute time, and only then to evaluate and interpret it. In a decisive manner, the modernist concept of absolute time, backed by the B.C./AD.D. dating system, reinforced the idea of the modernist present as superior in scientific perception and methodology.

Armed with the tools for accurate chronological measurement superior to any prior age, modernists made a very subtle shift when passing from measurement of the past to judging it. Belief that the cognitive tools of the present were scientifically superior to those of the past gave rise to an unconscious sense of the hegemony of the present manifested in a decontextualization of historical periods.

The belief that "la modernité est le parti du présent contre le passé" granted license for methodology in diverse disciplines to juxtapose modern theory and historical practice without necessarily correlating the modern theoretical agenda with its historical counterpart.[12] This led inevitably to cultural decontextualization of historical artifacts, interpreted according to theoretical agendas determined by nineteenth-century "scientific" viewpoints. In our discipline, philology as practiced by German grammarians and their disciples was one of the most salient examples of this kind of decontextualization.

Gaston Paris and his contemporaries placed history at the center of what Paris was fond of calling their *science,* which no longer carries the connotation of knowledge, but now took on the weighting of scientific method. The science of their methodology, it seemed, should shelter them from accusations of decontextualizing. Indeed, much of their energy was spent in recovering historical contexts. Léon Gautier's notes to his oft-reprinted edition of the *Song of Roland* contain a wealth of historical details. One of the paradoxes of modernism—particularly the modernism that turned back toward the past (and that is the modernism with which medieval studies has usually been linked)—was its historical dualism.[13] A history in the service of the present, which believes in the superiority of the modern age for understanding the past, is a history that will inevitably place great weight upon the archaeology of historical details, the individual facts, as proofs of its superior ability to recover and interpret a past hidden from itself.

This fixation with historical detail translates in the realm of language into a strong emphasis on "the said" (*le dit*), as opposed to the performative acts and contexts of speaking: *le dire. Le dit* and *le dire* are very different. The first emphasizes communication as historically determinate, that is, as fact and artifact. It is unconcerned—or need not be concerned—with context, with the conditions of articulation. "The said," as quotation, historical fact, and so on, may be taken out of context and used to support a thesis far removed from the original context of the speech act. It has the seductiveness of apparent factuality, however, precisely because of its status as artifact. *Le dire,* on the other hand, involves an interlocutor, a context of speaking—exactly what Augustine describes (with himself as interlocutor) in book 11 of *Confessions* when he analyzes the difference between oral recitation of a psalm and the (silent) memory of it. In the Middle Ages, *le dire* involves the dual considerations of orality and audience, on the one hand—phenomena that Paul Zumthor has described in such recent works as *La lettre et la voix* and *La poésie et la voix dans la civilisation médiévale*—while, on the other, one must take into account the interactions of performance as a written and as an oral phenomenon.[14] As oral performance, *le dire* has been lost to us; it is recoverable only obliquely from written, visual, and sometimes musical notations about which we can only speculate. In the form that has come down to us, *le dire* involves multiple insertions of given works into an ever-varied manuscript matrix. By studying a given work in its manuscript setting, one may begin to see how *le dire* functions performatively, albeit in a different setting and at a different moment from the twelfth-century oral performative representations. Both the oral and the manuscript manifestations involved the speaking/performative body in complex and different ways, as I have tried to demonstrate in a series of recent papers.[15]

Nineteenth-century medievalism had a reason to focus on *le dit*, the historical word per se, as opposed to *le dire*, the process and context of communication as a multiphase phenomenon. The former treats what was said as pure historical fact and could thus serve as a keystone for a theory of identity. Identity, above all national identity, became a crucial issue for the medieval scholars working in the last half of the nineteenth century. National identity was of paramount importance at this time, and these men considered it their duty to demonstrate the origin of French national identity in terms of language and literature. In his 1901 book on François Villon, for example, Gaston Paris quotes approvingly Montaiglon's praise of Villon in 1874 as a national icon, "the first poet in the true sense of the word of modern France."[16]

If Villon represents the quintessential modern French poet, he is so in part because his poetry, we are told, reflects paradigmatic elements of the conservative modernism cited by Toulmin: rationalism, "timeless principles that hold good at all times," and nationalism. Montaiglon cites versions of just those qualities in assessing Villon:

> le sentiment du néant des choses et des êtres est mêlé d'un burlesque soudain qui en augmente l'effet. Et tout cela est si naturel, si net, si franc, si spirituel; le style suit la pensée avec une justesse si vive, que vous n'avez pas le temps d'admirer comment le corps qu'il revêt est habillé par le vêtement. Il a tout, la vigueur et le charme, la clarté et l'éclat, la variété et l'unité, la gravité et l'esprit, la brièveté incisive du trait et la plenitude du sens, la souplesse capricieuse et la fougue violente, la qualité contemporaine et l'éternelle humanité.[17]

> [the sense of the emptiness of things and of beings is mixed with a sudden burlesque that enhances the effect. And all that is so natural, so sharp, so frank, so witty; style follows thought with such a lively appropriateness that one scarcely has time to admire how the body he assumes clothes itself. He has everything: vigor, charm, brilliance and panache, unity and variety, wit and gravity, the incisive brevity of the sure stroke and the plenitude of logic, capricious suppleness and violent ardor, the quality of contemporaneity and enduring humanity.]

Gaston Paris supplements Montaiglon's transformation of the poet into a national model by claiming that it was only the nineteenth century that had been able to discover the historical Villon: "Notre siècle devait rendre à Villon plus pleine justice encore, et mieux démêler ce qui fait sa véritable originalité" ("Our century should render still greater justice to Villon, and better yet, resolve just what it is that constitutes his true originality").[18]

In nationalist modernism, origins became central not only to matters of identity as historical fact, but also to prove teleological and ethical systems linked to a kind of national racial identity. Gaston Paris makes the connection very clearly between the origins of French literature and the ethical, moral, and racial connotations of French identity in the opening lecture for his course at the Collège de France for 1869, entitled "Les origines de la littérature française." There can be no question of "origins" simply meaning "beginnings" in his lecture; to show that "origins" conveys its full sense as identity, he speaks of "les origines et les commencements de la littérature française." Paris does not hesitate to make explicit the link between historical and genetic origins of a people and the literature viewed as the expression of those racial *genera*.

> Une littérature n'étant en somme qu'un des aspects de la vie d'un peuple, avant d'aborder l'histoire même de cette littérature il faut se rendre compte de ce qu'est le peuple qui l'a produite, se demander quelles influences il a subies, quels milieux il a traversés, par quelles phases s'est opéré son développement, avant l'heure où commence en réalité son histoire littéraire.[19]

> [A literature being only one of the aspects of the life of a people, before undertaking the history itself of that literature, one must recognize the specific nature of the people who made it, ask oneself what influenced them, what milieus they frequented, the phases of their evolution, all before the moment when their literary history really began.]

From the general law of origins to the specific example of the French as a uniquely privileged race (as proved by the history of their origins) is but a step that Paris does not hesitate to take in a manner instructive to follow. He makes the unification of different races superposed one on another a mark of the racial distinction of French origins. Underlying the logic of Paris's exposition are: first, a historical teleology suggesting that French identity was a historical imperative, and second, a geographical identity, a map of France, intelligible only in terms of nineteenth-century boundaries and terminology (he speaks, for example, of "la plus grande partie de notre sol," "notre pays," and so forth). Everything points to the desired vindication of the present-centered ideology of origin:

> Cette étude [of the people who make the literature], entourée de bien des difficultés pour toutes les nations, est particulièrement épineuse pour la nôtre: le peuple qui depuis plus de mille ans porte le nom de "français" n'est pas une de ces races simples dont l'histoire, quelque obscure qu'elle puisse être à certaines périodes, offre cependant une suite logique de faits identiques et continus; ce n'est pas un groupe naturel, demeuré pur de tout mélange depuis les plus anciens temps: c'est au contraire, si je puis ainsi dire, un produit tout historique, où des éléments divers et parfois antipathiques ont été combinés et fondus soit par la force soit par les siècles. . . . C'est en France, en effet, et seulement en France que la fusion des trois éléments [Gaulois, Romains, Germains] . . . se fit d'une façon complète, et qu'il en sortit un produit véritablement nouveau.[20]

> [This study, beset by difficulties for all nations, is particularly thorny for ours: the people who for more than a thousand years have borne the name "French" are not one of those simple races whose history, however obscure during certain periods, offers nevertheless a logical succession of identical and continuous deeds. This is not a natural group, free from any kind of contamination since its earliest history; it is, on the contrary, if I may say so, entirely a product of history where diverse and sometimes antipathetic elements have been combined and melded, sometimes by force, sometimes by time. . . . It is in France, and only in France that the fusion of three elements [Celtic, Roman, Germanic] . . . occurred in so thorough a manner, and there resulted a product so truly new.]

ÉMILE LITTRÉ'S ONCE AND PRESENT FRENCH

This view of the French race as a uniquely successful union of three prior "master races" in Europe rested on firm philological grounds articulated by that most eminent historical linguist, Émile Littré. Eight years before Paris gave his first course on the origins of French poetry in 1866, and eleven years before the lines quoted above, Littré published a series of five articles in the *Journal des savants* from October

1858 to June 1859, under the deceptively specialized title "Étude du chant d'Eulalie et du fragment de Valenciennes."[21] While Littré did eventually deal with the title texts, he did so only after elaborating a theory of the Romance languages that is nothing short of spectacular for its positioning of French as simultaneously the most ancient and the most modern of the major Romance tongues: Spanish, Italian, Provençal, and French. French is thus doubly preeminent: its philological primacy as the most ancient, and closest to Latin, gave it primacy of production of the greatest and most numerous texts in the eleventh through thirteenth centuries, while its rebirth as a new language in the sixteenth century assured that French would be the language most suited for the new technologies and sciences of the modern age.

For philological *chutzpah*, Littré can have few peers, but his theory—a perfect example of the modernist tendency toward abstract axioms—illustrates wonderfully the dualism of positivist historicism. He begins with a political strategy based on modern nation-states (*trois pays*) that unites French and Provençal into one group, the Gallic languages, set off against Italian and Spanish. Is it reasonable, he asks, to suppose that four brother languages, having Latin as their common father, would break off from the common trunk at the same time, in the same way, and all having the same characteristics?[22] Historical and political factors militate against a uniform development of the four languages. Once diverse rates of development have been admitted, it is legitimate to look at the language groupings in light of genetic and geographical evolutionary differences. From this perspective, one finds philological grounds for (1) taking *langue d'oc* and *langue d'oïl* as a group, and (2) asserting their fundamental difference from Spanish and Italian.

Those differences mark the Gallic languages as *plus ancien* than Italian and Spanish, not in the strict chronological sense, Littré specifies, but in the sense of retaining characteristics that recall an older state of Latin than that preserved in Italian and Spanish. The philological primacy of *langue d'oc* and *langue d'oïl* becomes crucial for Littré's whole theory, so we need to understand it. Latin is said in some ways to be more ancient than Greek not because it antedates Greek in any way, but because if one compares Greek and Latin with Sanskrit, the most ancient form known of the Aryan language, Latin has certain characteristics closer to Sanskrit than does Greek. Similarly, the Gallic languages possess more characteristics in common with classical Latin than do Italian and Spanish.[23]

The philological primacy of the Gallic languages results from their greater proximity to Latin. They retain the vigor of a Latin closer to the great period of its productivity. Italian and Spanish broke away from the paternal trunk later, when Latin was closer to its death throes and thus much less vigorous. Latin was spoken longer in Spain and Italy and thus was in a more decadent form when these vernaculars struck out on their own; they naturally would not retain the characteristics we associate with Latin as did the Gallic vernaculars which split off earlier. Chronology is less important to Littré than philology, for it is the records, the language-as-artifact, *le dit,* on which he will rely for the next, important movement: "En vertu d'aperçus qui me sont propres, j'essaye de montrer qu'un certain droit d'aînesse, sinon chronologique, du moins philologique appartient à la langue d'oc et à la langue d'oïl.[24] ("By virtue of my own insights, I try to show that a certain law of primacy, if not chronological, at least philological, belongs to Old Occitan and Old French.")

Philological primacy suggests the strength and resources of the Gallic languages. Their proximity to Latin also allows them to bask in the aura of classical Latinity, permitting them to profit from the associations of high culture attached to Latin. Philology studies language as historical artifact, *le dit.* What the Gallic languages retain from Latin which the other Romance idioms did not have are the distinguishing markers of written Latin, particularly its case systems. The survival of nominative and accusative cases in Old French and Provençal, but not in Italian and Spanish, makes Old French and Provençal intermediary languages which record the process of decadence and degradation of Late Latin, but which, by the same token, preserve remnants of its vigor.[25]

Philological primacy, once established and scientifically demonstrated, particularly with the case system, serves as the basis for asserting the primacy of literary productivity of the Gallic languages in the twelfth and thirteenth centuries. From a high cultural perspective, it was natural for Littré to equate the brilliant linguistic development he identified in those centuries with an equally brilliant literary productivity.

> La langue d'oïl et la langue d'oc sont, sinon anciennes, du moins intermédiaires, tenant du latin des caractères qui ont tout à fait disparu dans l'italien ou dans le français moderne et qui établissent un anneau philologique entre l'antiquité et nos temps. *Aussi faut-il partager autrement qu'on ne fait l'histoire littéraire de ces trois*

grandes nations. A la langue des Gaules, sous la forme provençale ou sous la forme française, appartient, avec la priorité philologique, la priorité de production; c'est là que commencent les oeuvres nouvelles, celles qui ne relèvent plus du latin, le gai savoir, les chansons de geste, les poèmes d'aventure; on les lit, on les goûte, on les traduit, on les imite dans tout l'Occident.[26]

[Old French and Old Occitan are, if not ancient, at least intermediary, retaining from Latin traits that have entirely disappeared in Italian or modern French and which establish a philological ring between antiquity and our time. *Consequently, one must apportion differently than has been the custom the literary history of these three great nations.* To the language of the Gauls, be it in the Provençal or the French form, belongs, along with philological primacy, the primacy of production. For that is where new works begin, those no longer beholden to Latin, the love poetry, the epic, the poems of adventure; these were read, appreciated, imitated, translated all through the West.]

This completes the first movement of Littré's exposition, establishing the priority of Old French and Provençal in linguistic and cultural terms. He locates the alterity of the Middle Ages in its status as a mediating or linking period which is, of course, why modernism inevitably assigned to it the name "middle" ages. What is new in Littré is the proportional rewriting of the relations between the three dominant Romance languages and their relation to Latin and modernity. *Langue d'oïl* and *langue d'oc* are not only the "oldest" Romance idioms, they are the only truly medieval vernaculars. Italian and Spanish are modern languages which came into their own when the Gallic tongues fell into decadence—sharing the fate of their Latin forebear—in the fourteenth century. The myth of decadence allows Littré to explain the decline of Old French and Provençal just at the moment when he would have to explain how the heretofore weaker Italian and Spanish languages suddenly burst into vigorous productivity. That production, which includes Dante, Boccaccio, Romanceros, Cervantes, and so on, becomes the beginning of European modern culture, a fallow period for French while it gathered its strength for a rebirth in the sixteenth century. Once reborn, in an entirely new form, French quickly reasserted its primacy—linguistic, cultural, and political—over its two sister languages.

Le xive siècle est l'avènement de l'Italie, qui, pendant l'époque antécédente, avait préparé son essor et qui se signale par le chef-d'oeuvre de la grande poésie dans le Moyen Âge, *la Divine Comédie;* tous les arts se donnent la main, et rien de plus brillant que cette période. Peu après, l'Espagne vient à son tour sur la scène; et toutes deux servent de modèle à la France, qui jadis leur avait servi de modèle. Mais la langueur momentanée de la France se dissipe, le xvie siècle entre dans toutes les voies de la pensée; une nouvelle langue française et une nouvelle littérature reprennent les hauts rangs et gagnent, comme jadis, la faveur générale et l'universalité. Telle fut, dans l'Occident latin, la série des choses littéraires.[27]

[The fourteenth century marks the ascendency of Italy, which, during the preceding period, had signaled its rise by that masterpiece of great medieval poetry, the *Divine Comedy.* All the arts join together and nothing more brilliant than this period can be imagined. A little later, Spain in turn comes on the scene, and both serve as models for France, formerly their model. But France's momentary lassitude soon dissipates; the sixteenth century penetrates all realms of thought. A new French language and a new literature regain the high ground, winning, as before, general approbation and universality. Such was, in the West, the sequence of literary events.]

Littré's tableau of a once and present French uses one of modernist historiography's most enduring master tropes: the theory of evolutionary cycles first proposed by Giambattista Vico in his *Scienza nuova* at the beginning of the eighteenth century. Vico proposed different stages for cultures moving from a primitive state which he called poetic wisdom because thought moved by metaphor and analogy as it does in poetry. A vigorous stage of the culture followed in which rational, truly philosophical thought permitted the development of institutions leading to a national identity and consciousness. Inevitably this state yielded to decline and decadence which, in its turn, could lead to a gradual renewal as the cycle began again.

When Littré speaks of the Middle Ages as a "philological ring" (*anneau philologique*) linking the classical period "to our times," and of the fourteenth and fifteenth centuries in France as a period of exhaustion (*épuisement*), a "momentary languor," he uses Vichean concepts in a revealing manner. The Middle Ages had its own concept of transition and transmission which it called *translatio.* But *translatio* was a movement across space and time, a movement of spatial concepts through time which declared themselves in new ways and in new forms (*renovatio*), all the while proclaiming their adherence to the old. This was a linear movement through a single, prolonged *durée,* not a sequence of Vichean cycles, indeed, not a sequence at all, as Littré claims.

One may dispute the hold of *translatio* over the fourteenth and fifteenth centuries, just as one rejects out of hand today the notion of a falling off in either the quality or the quantity of literary production in fourteenth-century France. If anything—as a series of brilliant books beginning with Daniel Poirion's *Le poète et le prince* (1965) to Jacqueline Cerquiglini-Toulet's *La couleur de la mélancholie* (1993) have shown—the fourteenth century was a period of incredible innovation of new genres and themes frequently based on sophisticated appreciation of the French and European literary output of the twelfth and thirteenth centuries.[28] This constituted nothing less than a recognition and celebration of the vernacular: recognition that it *had* a tradition and one worthy of building upon. It also marks a massive shift in historical emphasis from the far past to the recent past and present, a turn marked by a strong practice of historiography in Middle French. The *Roman de Mélusine* by Jean d'Arras or Antoine de la Sale's *Le paradis de la reine Sibylle* construct themselves brilliantly as, in part, a sophisticated reading of prior literary, historical, and folkloric motifs from medieval vernacular culture. They, and other works by Deschamps, Machaut, Christine de Pizan, to name but the most obvious, circle back on the previous centuries to produce something as different from what had been seen previously as it was from later production. This phenomenon is less cycle or linear sequence than "recurrence" in the medical or mathematical sense of a recurrent nerve that curves back upon itself, or a recurrent series in which each term may be calculated according to a certain number of coefficients that precede it.

Littré, of course, saw none of this. His philological otherness of the Middle Ages turns out not to be one on which to locate a truly medieval identity or a methodology truly based on that identity. In fact, the Middle Ages fade out in Littré's configuration, as they always do in the modernist frame. Philological alterity creates an illusion of independence for *langue d'oc* and *langue d'oïl,* but finally they serve as an interesting philological coda to Latin, and a poetic preface, in Vico's sense, to the French of the present. They were, for all their philological primacy, incapable of producing a truly premodern masterpiece like Dante's *Commedia.* In short, the Middle Ages had no conception of high culture as Littré understood the term.

Recalling the title of this series of articles—"Étude du chant d'Eulalie et du fragment de Valenciennes"—we realize that language and culture are for him indices of a perspective in which the Middle Ages not only play an ancillary role of precursor and witness to a later age, but are themselves constituted through fragmentary and intermittent works. As we shall see in the next section, this perspective determines the kind of works selected as worthy of study, but even more important, it serves as a powerful means of projecting back upon the Middle Ages the inconvenient aspects of progressive modernism that Baudelaire identified. Fragmentation, incompletion, and lack of meaning could conveniently be exorcised from modernism and identified instead as marks of the otherness of the Middle Ages, causes of the decline and fall of the period to be avoided in "true" modernist works.

Medieval literature, then, needed to be recontextualized, that is, studied in its "historical" setting—as reconstructed by modernist methodology—to demonstrate at once its value as historical artifact, witness to the origins and first grandeur of France. At the same time, medieval literature would display the inherent defects that led to its own eclipse, an obscurity only beginning to dissipate, as Gaston Paris remarked, through the efforts of the new class of academic medievalists. As Léon Gautier remarked in the *Préface* to his second edition of *Les épopées françaises: Étude sur les origines et l'histoire de la littérature nationale* (1878), "L'histoire des littératures romanes est une science nouvelle, mais qui a fait en peu d'années un long chemin" ("The history of Romance literatures is a new discipline, but one that has accomplished much in a few short years").[29] Let us see briefly how this new methodology set about recontextualizing what became for over a century the Old French literary canon.

CONTEXTUALIZING A/THE CANON

Three primary principles underlay the concept of literary formation espoused with impressive consistency by the first generation of academic medievalists: (1) historical function; (2) rational and organic connections between historical moment, literary forms, and the social formation (*le peuple*); and (3) a historico-genetic conception of medieval language that made it a reflection of people, social formation, and moment.[30] I will trace only the first principle, historical function.

The early discipline of medieval studies viewed history as a highly theoretical and interpretive gift. It was not to be confused with the technical skills of palaeography and diplomatics necessary to gain material access to the documents and manuscripts on which the historical interpretations would ultimately rest. In February 1821, one of Louis XVIII's ministers, le comte Siméon, placed before the king a proposal for the formation of an École des Chartes. The purpose of the school was to preserve "une branche de la littérature française à laquelle votre majesté prend un intérêt particulier, celle relative à l'histoire de la patrie" ("a branch of French literature in which your majesty takes a particular interest, that relative to the history of the country").[31] The means of preservation would be the creation of a category of "paléographe-archivistes" indispensable for preserving and transcribing historical documents. At no time in this founding document are the prospective palaeographer-archivists perceived as anything more than "collaborators" with historians; in other words, they were viewed as a class of technicians:

> Je veux parler, Sire, de ces hommes qui, par de longs efforts d'application et de patience, ont acquis la connaissance de nos manuscrits, se sont rendus familières les écritures si diverses de nos chartes, des documents de tout genre que nous ont laissés nos ancêtres, et savent traduire tous les dialectes du Moyen Âge.[32]
> [I am speaking, Sire, of those men who, by applying themselves diligently and with patience, have acquired a knowledge of our manuscripts, have familiarized themselves with the widely diverse handwritings of our records, of documents of all kinds left to us by our ancestors, and who know how to translate all the medieval dialects.]

The count goes on to distinguish for the king the difference between the technician and the historian:

> L'homme instruit dans la science de nos chartes et de nos manuscrits est sans doute bien inférieur à l'historien; mais il marche à ses côtés, il lui sert d'intermédiaire avec les temps anciens, il met à sa disposition les matériaux échappés à la ruine des siècles.[33]
> [Anyone trained in the knowledge of our records and manuscripts is certainly inferior to the historian; but he walks beside him, he acts as an intermediary between him and times past, making available to him materials that have escaped the ruin of the ages.]

This strict division between palaeographer and historian—rather like the medieval distinction between *poète* and *jongleur*—does not long survive in quite so "class conscious" a formulation. I cite it here, however, because it shows, first, the modernist bias for theory over practice discussed earlier, and second, because its underlying premise that historical interpretation somehow transcends the material artifact remained basic to medieval studies and the formation of the canon. For purposes of rational, that is, theoretical, elaboration of the historical function of literary works, historians had an obligation to place them in a historical milieu that transcended the artifacts of the material culture itself.

Léon Gautier incorporates the split between history as artifact and history as teleology (function) in the structure of his monumental *Les épopées françaises* (1865 and 1878). In a tripartite structure that recasts in new methodological terms what we recognize as the medieval levels of reading—literal, metaphorical, and anagogic—Gautier divides his work into "I. *Origine et histoire;* II. *Légende et héros;* III. *Esprit des épopées françaises.*" The first part systematically suppresses any discussion of content or ideas, limiting itself strictly to a history of the successive material forms the epic assumed from its origins to the present day. He organizes this "objective" history of manuscripts and editions into yet another tripartite schema that we recognize from Littré: "Trois grandes périodes (de formation, de splendeur, de décadence," described as follows:

> Mais nous montrerons qu'avant d'être le héros d'une longue épopée, Roland avait été chanté en des cantilènes religieuses et militaires; qu'à ces cantilènes ont succédé des chansons de geste; qu'à ces chansons de geste, de plus en plus développées, ont succédé des romans en prose, et à ces romans en prose, les grossiers volumes de la *Bibliothèque bleue.*[34]

> [But we will show that before being the hero of a long epic, Roland had been the subject of short military and religious songs; these short songs gave way to the chansons de geste; the chansons de geste, more and more elaborate, gave way to prose romances, and these prose romances gave way to the vulgar editions of the *Bibliothèque bleue.*]

This is a typical example of how the historical perspective of these scholars recontextualized epic in an evolutionary schema that linked literary history to patterns of cyclical historicism. Gautier's positing of relentless literary activity in successive layers motivates his historicist method. The method is both structural and temporal in that each layer forms a period when a particular kind of genre dominated. The genre,

in this theory, structures the period and names it. Perhaps coincidentally—but then again perhaps not, given the pride this generation of
medievalists took in their "scientific" methodology—the postulates
for this literary historical approach strongly resemble the historicizing
principles of pre-Darwinian nineteenth-century geology, particularly
stratigraphical geology.

In his fascinating book *The Great Devonian Controversy: The
Shaping of Scientific Knowledge among Gentlemanly Specialists,*
Martin Rudwick describes the stratigraphical geology that dominated
early nineteenth-century geology in both England and France, the
Société Géologique in France and the Geological Society in England
having a significant overlapping membership.[35] Stratigraphical geology postulated a development of the earth based on the analysis of
distinct strata of materials each one different from the next strata but
consistent within itself. Like their medieval literary-historian counterparts, geologists researching the strata focused on structural elements,
research and analysis into the genres and their language. Like the
geologists, however, they never lost sight of the fact that "the structural sequence of strata also represented a temporal sequence of past
events."[36]

This theoretical approach aimed at nothing short of a total "scientific" explanation of the phenomena to be studied, an explanation
residing literally on bedrock. Just as deposits in geology signified a
historical period, so Gautier perceives literary genres functioning as
synecdoches for given periods. For what he describes as successive
"transformations" of *epic* are the same transformations Littré saw
in *languages.* During the great period of the "chanson de geste," the
epic establishes itself as the preeminent literary form for defining the
age. Later, under the impact of new literary forms, the epic yielded its
old form to take on a new one in conformity with the then reigning
genre.

The fact that the epic can still be recognized despite its transformations tells us something about the links between deterministic
literary history and canon formation. If the epic defined a first
period in medieval French literature, then it cannot simply disappear to be replaced by *historia* or chronicle; it retains its ide-
ational identity, albeit in a different material form. Indeed, it is the
alteration of the form that serves to confirm the change in the
period paradigm. Throughout the changes, however, even down to
the despised *Bibliothèque bleue,* the epic remains as a foundational
work for medieval culture. One cannot *not* read epic as a defining

criterion for its own period, in the first instance, and as a gauge for change in later times.

The issue of change as opposed to sedimentation suggests that geology gives way to biology as scientific paradigm when the question of *déchéance* of the master genres arises. Why is Gautier so harsh in speaking of the last stage of epic decadence in "les grossiers volumes de la Bibliothèque bleue"? These popular versions of medieval tales that Gautier described as debased avatars of epic signify the fate of the Middle Ages in the modern period. The volumes seem wretched or vulgar, shadows of the former grandeur of the age and genre, because they do not take the form of splendid manuscripts ornamenting royal libraries. They appear in modern garb as printed books, but books bearing the stigma, for Gautier, of serving a popular social function. The high cultural forms of modernism do not appear in the *Bibliothèque bleue*. Epics have lost their grandeur, their seriousness, and thus their status as the master genre, to become popular literature, mere entertainment serving not the rational but the emotional faculties. Like the Middle Ages themselves, the epic has become transient and meaningless, no longer worthy of representing national identity.

This material history of epic reinforces the inability of the *Middle Ages* to sustain on their own the primary modernist agenda of temporal duration, rationality, and sovereign nationhood. More to the point, the sketch at least unconsciously ascribes to medieval epic precisely the traits of modernist alterity that Gautier firmly opposed.

But how did epic come to play the role of master genre in the first place? Why should epic have been so prized by the founders of our discipline as to become the standard for canon construction? The answer lay in the historical function ascribed to epic in the theoretical revision of history undertaken by Gautier's generation. For these men, the epics were the cave paintings of the nascent French spirit and nation; viewed anthropologically, as Vico had taught, epics gave a prehistory of the French nation.

- "C'est la narration poétique qui précède les temps où l'on écrit l'histoire" (Paulin Paris, quoted in Gautier, 1:6). ["Poetic narratives precede the era when one begins to write history."]
- "[Les] épopées primitives [sont des] poèmes dans lesquels certains peuples, avant la culture littéraire, ont célébré leurs dieux et leurs héros" (Littré, *Dictionnaire de la langue française* under the word "Épopée"). ["The earliest epics are poems in

which certain peoples, before there was a literary culture, celebrated their gods and their heroes."]
- "La poésie épique se divise en poésie religieuse et héroique, en
chants consacrés aux dieux et aux héros" (Karl Bartsch, *Revue
critique* 52 [1866]. ["Epic poetry divides into religious poetry
and heroic poetry in songs devoted to gods and to heroes."]

These are interesting, but Gaston Paris provides still more insight
by defining epic as the genre that constructs the idea of the nation; his
formulation comes closest to showing how the theory of medieval epic
really serves as a covert description of the reactive modernist project
itself, as well as a description of how a temporal period takes on
structural unity (the stratigraphical model):

L'épopée n'est autre chose en effet que la poésie nationale
développée, aggrandie, centralisée. Elle prend à celle-ci son inspiration, ses héros, ses récits même, mais elle les groupe et les coordonne
dans un vaste ensemble où tous se rangent autour d'un point principal. Elle travaille sur des chants isolés et elle en fait une oeuvre une
et harmonieuse. Elle efface les disparates, fond les répétitions du
même motif dans un thème unique, rattache entre eux les épisodes,
relie les événements dans un plan commun, et construit enfin, avec
les matériaux de l'âge précédent, un véritable édifice.[37]

[The epic is nothing more in effect than national poetry developed,
enlarged, centralized. It takes from the latter its inspiration, its
heroes, even its narratives, but it groups and coordinates them in one
vast whole where everything places itself around a principal point.
Epic works on isolated songs, making of them a unified and harmonious work. It effaces disparities, melts repetitions of a similar motif
into a unique theme, attaches episodes between them, links events
according to a common scheme, and builds, finally, a veritable
edifice from the materials of the preceding age.]

The *point principal* around which the epic constructs an organic and
harmonious "one" is the religious principle that is never far from the
surface in nineteenth-century medievalism. Especially for Léon Gautier, literary anthropology is intertwined with philosophical anthropology in the doctrinal sense of the term. The *cantilène* at the heart of
epic is not simply a lyric inspiration; it is the earliest manifestation of
human word in the service of the Logos. As Gautier observes, the oral
etymology signified by the Greek word εἰπεῖν ("to speak or recite")

does not imply communication alone, but manifests the human need to celebrate its links with God in the first instance, then, at a more evolved moment, to tell the story of the nation under God.[38] Before man speaks, Gautier writes, he sings:

> Représentez-vous le premier homme au moment même où il sort des mains de Dieu et où son regard se promène pour la première fois sur son nouvel empire. . . . Hors de lui, enivré, presque fou d'admiration, de reconnaissance et d'amour, il lève au ciel ses beaux yeux que le spectacle de la terre ne satisfera jamais; puis, découvrant Dieu dans ce ciel et lui rapportant tout l'honneur de cette magnificence, de cette fraîcheur et de ces harmonies de la création, il ouvre la bouche; les premiers frémissements de la parole agitent ses lèvres, il va parler. Non, non, il va chanter, et le premier chant de ce roi de la création sera un hymne au Dieu créateur.[39]

> [Imagine the first man at the very moment when he steps from God's hands and when his gaze wanders for the first time over his new empire. . . . Beside himself, intoxicated, almost mad with admiration, with gratitude and love, he raises his beautiful eyes to heaven, for an earth-bound spectacle will never satisfy them. Then, discovering God in the heavens and attributing to Him all the honor of this magnificence, of this freshness, and the harmonies of creation, he opens his mouth. The first tremblings of language agitate his lips, he is going to speak. No! No, he's going to sing, and the first song of this king of creation will be a hymn to God the Creator.]

Besides illustrating romantic medievalism's tendency toward dramatic hyperbole, this passage suggests a delicate equilibrium between lyric and epic. No matter how inspirational the song was perceived to be, in this first period of literary development, it represents but the first step toward epic form. In a gesture that assigns different values to epic and lyric in the strata of the High Middle Ages, Gautier asserts: "La poésie lyrique, est *humaine:* la poésie épique (car il est temps de la nommer) est *nationale*" ("Lyric poetry is *human:* epic poetry, for it is time to name it, is *national*").[40]

In other words, lyric poetry unlocks the philosophical anthropology that shows the simultaneous origins of human symbolic consciousness and poetry, but it is epic that reveals the nation as cast in the image of God's order. Epic is a microcosmic recontextualization of divine providence. As the master genre, it gives humans the world and assigns them an appropriate role. More important, epic assigns meaning to the other genres, showing us how we are meant to read them in the schema of philosophical anthropology.

For example, one can cite Gautier's own study of the fragmentary tropes of religious poetry from the ninth to eleventh centuries, a poetry that belongs to the canon by virtue of showing the connection between the first song of praise and formal medieval liturgical song. Gautier discovers serious sociological insights conveyed by the tropes because of the prior link established between historical function of poetry and literary genres. After describing the tropes ascribed to the Virgin, he moves to those dedicated to saints:

> Les Saints s'étagent, pour ainsi parler, au-dessous de la Vierge, et c'est ici le cas de rappeler ce que nous avons jadis appelé "la théorie des types." Pour tous les âges, pour tous les sexes, pour toutes les conditions et toutes les conjonctures de notre vie, Dieu nous a préparé et forgé des modèles spéciaux. . . . Les types ne nous manquent point, et il ne nous manque que d'y ajuster nos âmes. Le Moyen Âge n'a pas ignoré ces choses, *mais il est certains traits qui lui ont échappé dans la physionomie des Saints.* Il a vu très clairement leur action surnaturelle, et même l'a plus d'une fois dénaturée par la légende; mais . . . il a moins nettement saisi leur rôle social.[41]

> [The saints mass themselves, so to speak, under the Virgin, and this is the place to recall what we have already termed "the theory of patterns" (*types*). For all ages, for all sexes, for all the conditions and circumstances of our life, God has prepared and forged special models for us. . . . We do not lack for patterns; all that's lacking is to fit our souls to them. The Middle Ages did not *not* know these things, *but certain characteristics of the physiognomy of the saints escaped it.* It saw very clearly the supernatural action of the saints, even deforming more than once that supernatural by legends; but . . . it grasped much less clearly their social role.]

No matter how inspirational, other genres belong to the human or social sphere; they do not exhibit the high-flying vision of epic that engages national purpose. Epic does not distract the reader from history, nor from the contemplation of the providential construction of the world. The conditions necessary to realize epic for Gautier, as for Gaston Paris, are historical: (1) "a primitive epoch," indicative of a liminal social organization and a minimum level of collective identity; (2) "a national and religious milieu," by which Gautier envisions an emergent collectivity whose religious and social unity may be further developed into a national collective identity through the action of epic; and (3) "heroes who may be the true personification of an entire country and a century."[42]

Religion and language cement Gautier's vision thanks to the philological conception prevalent in his day which held that the language of the heroes in surviving works faithfully reflects their "naïve" consciousness objectified in a simple religious faith:

> À quels éléments se réduisent les notions religieuses de nos chevaliers et de nos poètes du douzième siècle? Ils croient, du fond de leurs âmes très simples et très viriles, à l'unité d'un Dieu *espirital* et *qui fist le ciel et la rosée.* Ils croient, d'une foi plus précise et plus vive, à ce Dieu incarné qui est le *fils de sainte Marie.* Ils meurent volontiers pour la sainte église; mais il ne faudrait guère leur rien demander de plus. "Ô notre vrai père qui jamais ne mentit,—Qui ressuscita saint Lazare d'entre les morts—Et défendit Daniel contre les lions,—Sauve, sauve mon âme et défends-la contre tous périls, à cause des péchés que j'ai faits en ma vie."[43] Telle est la prière naïve de ces primitifs. . . . La foi de nos barons n'a rien de subtil, et ils ont inconsciemment horreur de la rhétorique et des rhéteurs. Un faiseur de tropes et un chevalier, quel contraste![44]

> [What are the main tenets of the religious ideas of our knights and poets in the twelfth century? They believe, from the bottom of their very simple and very virile hearts, in the unity of a God at once spiritual and [material] who made the heavens and the morning dew. They believe, with a more precise and lively faith, in this God incarnate who is the Son of Saint Mary. They die willingly for the holy church, but one can scarcely ask them for anything more. "Oh, our true Father who never lies, who resurrected Saint Lazarus from the dead, and protected Daniel against the lions, save, save my soul and protect it from all dangers caused by the sins I committed in my life." Such is the naïve prayer of these primitive men. . . . The faith of our barons has nothing subtle about it, and they have a visceral horror of rhetoric and rhetoricians. A maker of tropes and a knight, what a contrast!]

This grandiose schema notwithstanding, epics fail the test for temporal duration. They do not represent the final French destiny, but only an imperfect beginning. Lecturing on the *Song of Roland* in December 1870 as the Germans laid siege to Paris, Gaston Paris celebrated the work for its ability to demonstrate the first example of a national unity that could bring a truly French (i.e., non-Carolingian) monarchy into harmonious alliance with the barons and the people. At the same time, he notes the geopolitics of the *Song of Roland* and argues that the French Middle Ages, as illustrated by their master genre, failed to achieve a sufficiently viable fusion of the two elements out of which it constructed itself: "le germanisme" (by which he means the Frankish element) and Christianity (the Gallo-Roman, Merovingian substrate).[45]

Fragmentation and incompletion within the epic reflect the same fatal traits within the national fabric or rather the fabric of nationalism. If the epic was the great national expression of the people in the twelfth century, by the fourteenth and fifteenth centuries—precisely the period Littré cites as the *décadence* of the French Middle Ages— the epic had been replaced by the *mystère,* a sign for Paris, as for Gautier, of internal social fragmentation:

> Plus tard encore, malgré la séparation du peuple en deux, malgré l'introduction de la science des clercs dans la littérature vulgaire, il y eut une poésie qui s'adressa à toute la nation: ce fut le théâtre. Aux xive et xve siècles, les mystères furent ce qu'avaient été autrefois les chansons de geste. Leur sujet, exclusivement religieux, leur donnait les droits égaux à la sympathie et au respect de tous; l'unité chrétienne, suppléant l'unité nationale, faisait battre un seul coeur dans la poitrine des milliers de spectateurs.[46]

> [Still later, despite the separation of the people in two, despite the encroachment of clearly learning on popular literature, there was a poetry that spoke to the whole nation: the poetry of the theater. In the fourteenth and fifteenth centuries, mysteries became what the chansons de geste had formerly been. Their exclusively religious subject matter gave them equal rights to the empathy and respect of all. Christian unity, replacing national unity, inspired the beating of a single heart in the breast of thousands of spectators.]

As Villon knew and put it so well in the "Ballade pour prier nostre dame," religion is the refuge of the impoverished. Placing the beginning and ending of the Middle Ages between the *splendeur* of epic and the pious *décadence* of the *mystère* guaranteed that the hard-edged alterity we need to discover in our period would be effectively effaced. In its place, the modern originators of medieval studies substituted an alterity proper to modernism itself. Medieval modernism espoused the Middle Ages as a subject matter to recover works from oblivion that it sincerely admired and sought to hold up for all to scrutinize. But the canon it established, like the image of the period it projected, was made in the image of an other that it was seeking to exorcise from its own contemporary history. The greatest paradox of nineteenth-century medieval studies was that it created a modernist canon in a medieval setting.

NOTES

1. Antoine Compagnon, *Les cinq paradoxes de la modernité* (Paris: Éditions du Seuil, 1990), 17.

2. Ibid., 29.

3. Ibid., 8.

4. "Si le substantif de modernité, au sens de caractère de ce qui est moderne, apparaît chez Balzac en 1823, avant de s'identifier véritablement à Baudelaire, et si celui de *modernisme,* au sens de goût, le plus souvent jugé excessif, de ce qui est moderne, apparaît chez Huysmans, dans le *Salon de 1879,* l'adjectif *moderne,* lui, est beaucoup plus ancien." ("If the noun modernity, in the sense of the quality of that which is modern, appears in Balzac in 1823, before becoming primarily associated with Baudelaire, and if *modernism* in the sense of a taste (most often judged excessive) for that which is modern, appears in Huysmans, in the *Salon de 1879*, the adjective *modern* itself is far more ancient.") Ibid., 17–18.

5. Ibid., 18.

6. Ibid., 33.

7. Ibid., 33–36.

8. "Tous ces traits, une fois entendus formellement, contribuent à la destruction de l'illusion liée à la perspective géométrique, et à l'aplatissement de la peinture, qui va de pair avec sa perte de sens." ("Once understood formally, all these traits contribute to the destruction of illusionist perspective and to the flattening of the painting plane, which naturally accompanies its loss of meaning.") Ibid., 33.

9. Stephen Toulmin, *Cosmopolis: The Hidden Agenda of Modernity* (New York: Free Press, 1990), 34.

10. Bacon believed in establishing a credible text, for which he urged adopting a comparative method of textual study, but also in the need to study works in context. He was concerned with what we would call the cultural horizon surrounding a given work as well as with accurate texts: "Non oportet nos adhaerere omnibus quae audimus et legimus, sed examinere debemus districtissime sententias maiorum, ut addamus quae eis defuerunt, et corrigamus quae errata sunt cum omni tamen modestia et excusatione."

("It's not necessary for us to stick to everything we hear and read, but we ought to weigh in the most thorough fashion the opinions of the majority, so that we may add what is absent and correct what is false, with all due modesty and excuses.") *Opus Maius,* I. Also: "Notitia linguarum est prima porta sapientiae, et maxime apud Latinos qui non habent textum theologiae nec philosophiae nisi a linguis alienis et ideo omnis homo deberet scire linguas et indiget studio et doctrina harum." ("The knowledge of languages is the first door to wisdom, and especially among the Latin peoples [Romance language speakers] who don't have a theological or philosophical text that's not in a foreign tongue, and for the same reason, every man ought to know languages and needs their study and doctrine.") *Opus Tertium,* J. S. Brewer, ed., *Frater Rogeri Bacon Opera quaedam hactenus inedita* (London: Rerum Britannicarum medii aevi Scriptores, 1859), 102; 20, 21, 33, 34, 42; *Opus Maius* I. "Qu'on examine attentivement les oeuvres de Bacon et l'on constatera que toutes ses recherches et tous ses travaux furent subordonnés à ce but: procurer à la chrétienté un bon texte de la S. Bible et des oeuvres d'Aristote. En plus, ces deux textes qui doivent former la base de l'enseignement théologique et philosophique ne peuvent être interprétés correctement sans une culture très intense des diverses sciences." ("One has only to examine Bacon's works attentively, and one will clearly see that all his research and all his labors were in the service of this end: to obtain for Christendom a good edition of the Holy Bible and of the works of Aristotle. What's more, these two texts which must form the basis for theological and philosophical instruction cannot be interpreted correctly without a very intense culture of numerous branches of learning.") Ch. Borromé Vandewalle, "Roger Bacon dans l'histoire de la philologie," *France franciscaine* 11 (1929): 373–74.

11. Donald J. Wilcox, *The Measure of Times Past: Pre-Newtonian Chronologies and the Rhetoric of Relative Time* (Chicago: University of Chicago Press, 1987), 8–9.

12. Toulmin sees decontextualization, abstract axioms, privileging of theory over praxis, and rationalism as part of the historical forces constructing modernism from the seventeenth century on. See Toulmin, esp. chaps. 1–3.

13. For a discussion of this type of modernism, of which Baudelaire's was an example, see Compagnon, chap. 1.

14. Paul Zumthor, *La lettre et la voix* (Paris: Éditions du idem, Seuil, 1987); *La poésie et la voix dans la civilisation médiévale* (Paris: Presses Universitaires de France, 1984).

15. See Stephen G. Nichols, "Voice and Writing in Augustine and in the Troubadour Lyric," in *Vox Intexta: Orality and Textuality in the Middle*

Ages, ed. A. N. Doane and Carol B. Pasternak (Madison: University of Wisconsin Press, 1991), 137–61; "Marie de France's Common Places," in *Style and Value in Medieval Art and Literature,* ed. Daniel Poirion and Nancy Regalado, *Yale French Studies* (June 1991):134–48; "Deflections of the Body in the Old French Lay," *Stanford French Review* (spring-fall 1991):27–50; "The Image as Textual Unconscious: Medieval Manuscripts," *L'esprit créateur* 29 (spring 1989), 7–23; "1127: William IX and the Early Troubadours," in *A New History of French Literature,* ed. Denis Holier (Cambridge, Mass.: Harvard University Press, 1989), 30–36; "Picture, Image, and Subjectivity in Medieval Culture," *MLN* 108 (September 1993): 617–37; "Seeing Food: Ekphrasis and Still Life in Late Antiquity and the Middle Ages," *MLN* 106 (September 1991): 818–51.

16. Here is the context of the remark Paris quotes: "Tous sont, avec raison, unanimes à reconnaître l'originalité, la valeur aisée et puissante, la force et l'*humanité* de la poésie de Villon. Pour eux tous, et ce jugement est aujourd'hui sans appel, Villon n'est pas seulement le poète supérieur du xve siècle, *mais il est aussi le premier poète, dans le vrai sens du mot, qu'ait eu la France moderne. . . . L'appréciation est maintenant juste et complète."* [emphasis added] ("Everyone is rightly unanimous in recognizing the originality, the effortless and powerful value, the force and the *humanity* of Villon's poetry. For all these people—and this judgment is now definitive—Villon is not only the superior poet of the fourteenth century, *but he is also the first poet in the true sense of the word in modern France. . . .* Our appreciation is now fair and complete.") Gaston Paris, *François Villon* (Paris: Hachette, 1901), 180.

17. Ibid., 180.

18. Ibid., 176.

19. Gaston Paris, "Les origines de la littérature française," *La poésie du moyen âge,* 2d ed. (Paris: Hachette, 1887), 43.

20. *La poésie du moyen âge,* 43–44, 73.

21. Émile Littré, "Étude du chant d'Eulalie et du fragment de Valenciennes," *Journal des Savants* (Octobre 1858): 597–606; (December 1858): 725–37; (February 1859): 82–94; (May 1859): 289–300; (June 1859): 336–48.

22. Littré, I (Octobre 1858): 597–98.

23. Here is how Littré reasons:

Je prends *ancien* au sens qu'on lui a déjà attribué en des questions de ce genre, par exemple, quand on dit qu'à certains égards le latin est plus ancien que le grec; ce qui ne veut pas dire que le latin ait été écrit avant le grec, cela serait historiquement faux, ni qu'il ait été parlé avant le grec, de cela on ne sait rien; mais on entend que, rapporté au sanscrit, qui nous présente la langue des Ariens dans la forme la plus antique à nous connue, le latin a certains caractères qui avoisinent plus le sanscrit que ne fait le grec. De même, la langue des Gaules a certains caractères par lesquels elle avoisine le latin, tronc commun des idiomes romans, plus que ne font l'espagnol et l'italien.

[I understand *ancient* in the sense that one has already given it in questions of this kind, for example, when one says that in certain respects Latin is more ancient than Greek; which would not mean that Latin was written before Greek—that would be historically false—nor that it was spoken before Greek—of that we know nothing; but one understands that, in respect to Sanskrit, which gives us the language of the Aryans in the most ancient form known to us, Latin has certain traits which approach Sanskrit more closely than does Greek. Furthermore, the language of the Gauls has certain traits by which it appoaches Latin, the common root of the Romance vernaculars, more closely than do Spanish or Italian.]

Littré, I (October 1858): 599.

24. Littré, I (October 1858): 600.

25. Littré, IV (May 1859): 296–300.

26. Littré, I (October 1858): 603.

27. Littré, I (October 1958): 603–4.

28. Daniel Poirion, *Le poète et le prince: L'évolution du lyrisme courtois de Guillaume de Machaut à Charles d'Orléans* (Paris: Presses Universitaires de France, 1965); Jacqueline Cerquiglini-Toulet, *La couleur de la mélancholie: La fréquentation des livres au XIVe siècle, 1300–1415* (Paris: Hatier, 1993). As instructive as it might prove, this is not the place to list the many excellent books that have appeared in the last thirty years showing the richness of the French fourteenth century.

29. Léon Gautier, *Les épopées françaises: Étude sur les origines et l'histoire de la littérature nationale*, 2d ed., (Paris: Société Générale de Librairie Catholique, 1878), I:v.

30. Thus Paget Toynbee in his influential and widely circulated anthology, *Specimens of Old French: IX–XV Centuries* (Oxford: Clarendon Press, 1892), expressed a widely held conception that language reflected biological and social givens when he wrote in his introduction: "The marked difference between the races in the North and South of Gaul, which must at an early date have produced a corresponding difference in the forms of speech employed by them, gave rise in the course of time to two languages (both derived

from the popular Latin) as distinct from each other as French and Spanish are at this day" (xviii).

31. Martial Delpit, "Notice historique sur l'École royale des Chartes," *Bibliothèque de l'École des Chartes* 1 (1839–40): 3.

32. Ibid., 3.

33. Ibid., 3.

34. Gautier, *Les épopées françaises*, "Préface à la première édition," 2d ed., 1:viii. The *Bibliothèque bleue* were among the first mass-circulation vulgarizations of (originally) high culture literary texts. So-called because they may have been printed on blue stock or had blue paper covers, these slim and inexpensive volumes were first published in Troyes by Nicolas Oudot beginning around 1608 or 1610. "From the start, the 'Bibliothèque bleue' was above all a publishing formula appropriate to the distribution of strongly different texts. Nicolas Oudet used this formula to print three general types of texts. First there were the medieval romances, which elite culture in the sixteenth century had discarded and which had therefore been abandoned by the more 'ordinary' avenues of publication. Second, there were the texts that belonged within the traditional store of hagiographic literature. And third, there were certain titles from the learned literature that found their 'pocket book edition' in the Troyes booklets." Roger Chartier, "Publishing Strategies and What the People Read, 1530–1660," in *The Cultural Uses of Print in Early Modern France* (Princeton: Princeton University Press, 1988), 170–71.

35. Martin J. S. Rudwick, *The Great Devonian Controversy: The Shaping of Scientific Knowledge among Gentlemanly Specialists* (Chicago: University of Chicago Press, 1985). See chap. 2 for a discussion of the Société Géologique and the Geological Society, and p. 29 for a Venn diagram illustrating, among other things, overlapping membership in the two.

36. Here are the relevant passages from Rudwick (42): "The primary intellectual goal [of stratigraphical geology] was the delineation of a 'succession' or sequence of distinctive major groups of *strata* which could be recognized throughout the world. . . . In research on the sequence of the strata, temporal modes of analysis were usually subordinate to structural ones. Nonetheless, all geologists were well aware that the structural sequence of the strata also represented a temporal sequence of events."

37. Gaston Paris, *Histoire poétique de Charlemagne*, reproduction de l'édition de 1865 (Paris: Librairie Émile Bouillon, 1905), 3–4.

38. The context merits quoting in full since it illustrates the genetic logic underlying the idea of stratigraphical structure:

La poésie des hymnes ne suffira bientôt plus aux besoins de ces nations primitives. Ces hymnes, à l'origine des choses, n'étaient dus et adressés qu'à Dieu: on ne tardera point à en faire honneur aux chefs des nations, aux grands guerriers, aux héros. Mais c'est ici qu'il fallait élargir le cadre trop restreint de l'hymne ou de l'ode: car malgré tout, on n'y put faire entrer, comme on le désirait, toute l'histoire ou, plutôt, toute la légende des héros. Alors un nouveau genre de poésie naquit de la nécessité: dans une série de chants moins enthousiastes et plus narratifs, on raconta tout à son aise les grandes guerres, les grandes adversités, les grands triomphes des peuples. Le premier caractère de ces récits fut souvent le mythe: car le sens historique ne devait naître que plus tard. De plus, ces récits légendaires furent essentiellement nationaux. La poésie lyrique est *humaine:* la poésie épique (car il est temps de le nommer) est *nationale.* Επὼ [sic] est un mot grec qui signifie "dire, raconter": il convient bien à cette poésie qui, avant tout, est un récit.

[The poetry of hymns will soon no longer suffice for the needs of these primitive nations. Originally these hymns were due and addressed to God alone: one will not long delay paying homage to heads of state, great warriors, and heroes. But it is here that it was necessary to widen the overly restricted frame of the hymn or the ode: for after all, one could not include, as one wished, all of history or rather the entire legend of the hero. And so a new poetic genre arose from necessity: in a series of songs less enthusiastic but more strongly narrative, one easily recounted the peoples' great wars, great adversities, principal triumphs. The early character of these narratives was often mythic: for historical meaning would only come later. What's more, these legendary narratives were essentially national. Lyric poetry is *human:* epic poetry (for it's time to name it) is *national.* Επὼ [sic] is a Greek word that means "to say, to tell": it's well suited to this poetry which is, above all, a narrative.]

Les épopées françaises: Étude sur les origines et l'histoire de la littérature nationale, vol. 1 (Paris: Société générale de librairie catholique, 1878), 4.

39. Ibid., 3.

40. Ibid., 4.

41. Léon Gautier, *La poésie religieuse dans les cloîtres des ixe–xie siècles* (Paris: Victor Palmé, Alphonse Picard, 1887), 25 (emphasis added).

42. Gautier, *Les légendes épiques,* 13.

43. This is Gautier's own translation quoted from his edition, the official classroom text in lycées (Édition classique à l'usage des élèves de seconde). *La*

Chanson de Roland, ed. Léon Gautier, 8th ed. (Tours: Maison Alfred Mame et Fils, 1887), 2384–88.

44. Gautier, *La poésie religieuse,* 5–6.
45. Gaston Paris, *La poésie du moyen âge,* 112.
46. Ibid., 29.

T W O

National Identity and the Politics of
Publishing the Troubadours

John M. Graham

RECENT INTEREST in the history of philology has brought a renewed awareness of how editorial method determines the shape of the texts we read, but there has been no extended account of how theoretical concepts have historically influenced the decisions made by editors of lyric texts. My purpose is to examine when and how troubadour texts came to be published, and how the tension between literary theory and editorial practice has influenced the direction of research and the form of publication. I argue that the establishment of critical institutions organized around nationalist principles has in large part determined what has been and can be said about the vernacular lyric poetry of the south of France in the High Middle Ages. My observations concentrate, then, not on the content of scholarship on the troubadours, but rather probe the thoughts and actions of the men who built a discipline. I examine the role of personal conflicts and ambitions, specialized institutions of higher education, academic chairs, journals and publication series, the access to library sources, and even the quality of students. Because the history of troubadour scholarship is to a large extent that of Romance philology itself, my account is by necessity selective; while I have made use of previous histories of the discipline, I do not intend to replace them.[1] My examination begins with a look at the manuscript text as it functioned before the invention of philology. The notion of the printed critical edition has become so naturalized during the century or so it has been in existence that it is necessary to show what an exceptional, if not to say strange, form of publication it was when it first appeared.

Before the critical edition, to the degree that medieval vernacular literature was studied as a text, the questions asked were either linguistic or historical in nature. To the degree that medieval literature was studied as literature, the text was seen as superfluous and the work retold in contemporary language. Between the Albigensian Crusade and the French Revolution, a relatively large body of linguistic and historical scholarship on the troubadours was produced independently in France and Italy based on the manuscripts and the critical apparatuses they contained.[2] This scholarship was augmented by the activities of a loosely connected group of eighteenth-century aristocratic antiquarians centered around Jean-Baptiste de La Curne de Sainte-Palaye, whose thorough and scrupulous research on the troubadours produced twenty-five folio volumes of manuscript notes but only a single book, the *Histoire littéraire des troubadours,* which was brought to fruition by the Abbé Millot.[3] The reason why the texts themselves were not published lies both in their irrelevance to royal institutions and in the working conditions of aristocratic scholars. Troubadour poetry bore no direct significance to institutions of state or church. Because it could not contribute to the understanding of either theology or law, it was not the object of university teaching, and thus led to no career. Study of the troubadours was the pastime of noble antiquarians whose peer connections and personal loyalties could get them access to the libraries where the manuscripts were held.

Although Sainte-Palaye himself did not own any Provençal manuscripts, he had copies of twenty-one chansonniers held in French and Italian collections. With the notes, tables, and glossary he had established with the help of a small staff of copyists, he could not only offer his antiquarian friends information on the whereabouts of manuscripts, but even produce on demand collations of individual poems, with variants.[4] In spite of exceptions such as Lévesque de la Ravalière's *Les poésies du roi de Navarre* (1762) or Abbé Nicolas Lenglet du Fresnoy's *Le roman de la rose* (1735), the public market for medieval works was mostly limited to chivalric or humorous stories that could survive translation and abridgment. Even Sainte-Palaye's translation of *Aucassin et Nicolette,* published in 1756 as *Les amours du bon vieux temps,* offered the satisfaction not of documentary evidence but of "artful simplicity."[5]

Between eighteenth-century medievalists such as Sainte-Palaye and the first generation of Romance philologists, François-Juste-Marie Raynouard and August-Wilhelm von Schlegel, there is a world of difference. It was not just the French Revolution that put an end to this world by modifying the working conditions of scholars. In fact, the real changes occasioned by the events of the 1790s were probably slight. Like Sainte-Palaye, Raynouard was elected to both the Académie des Inscriptions and the Académie Française; he used Sainte-Palaye's copies of manuscripts and benefited, like later scholars, from extended loans from owners of chansonniers. But the difference between the 1774 *Histoire littéraire des troubadours* and Raynouard's 1816 *Choix des poésies originales des troubadours* is immediately apparent: Raynouard's title bears witness to a conception of poetry radically different from that of earlier medievalists. Raynouard's interests were not primarily literary-historical, as had been Sainte-Palaye's, but linguistic. His research on manuscripts had led him to the theory that the language of the troubadours, the "Provençal" of the twelfth and thirteenth centuries, had been spoken all across southern Europe before the year 1000 and that it was thus the "langue romane primitive" ("original Romance language"), the common ancestor of all the Romance idioms.[6] Hence the linguistic evidence brought forth in support of this thesis, which included the poetry of the troubadours, could only be useful if printed in the original.

The adjective *originale* signals, in an admirable instance of polysemy, both the fact that the poems were published in Old Provençal and that they are to be regarded not as reproductions, representations, or translations of an absent and anterior model, but as unique texts in themselves. For Raynouard this was undoubtedly the secondary and unimportant by-product of regarding troubadour poetry as the belated representative of the "langue romane primitive." But in his appreciation of the lyrics anthologized in the second volume of his *Choix,* he valorized this originality in a literary sense:

> The new literature thus borrowed nothing from the lessons and the examples of the Ancients. It had its distinct and independent ways, its native forms, its local and foreign colors, its own spirit . . . everything contributed to make the literature of the troubadours stand out by this character of originality which had not been suffi-

ciently remarked; it is in this respect that one should examine and appreciate the content and the form of their compositions.[7]

Raynouard reveals his debt to Enlightenment scholars by the interest (perhaps superficial) in historical mores, customs, and beliefs; but the rest could not be more different. The insistence on native, local, and national aspects of textuality to the exclusion of the universal; the notion that both the "content and the form" of troubadour poetry are worth study, rather than just the historical context and "a few sentimental phrases"; and the idea that the troubadour lyric was not born of imitation, and thus, by implication, itself cannot be imitated, are all new.

All of this is, of course, part of the wider epistemological mutation described in Michel Foucault's *Les mots et les choses*.[8] A much more specific idea of what was at stake in Raynouard's work can be gained through A. W. von Schlegel's 1818 *Observations sur la langue et la littérature provençales,* written in French and published in Paris. In this book-length review of the *Choix,* Schlegel's immediate goal was to dispute Raynouard's contention that the "langue romane primitive" was the common ancestor of all Romance idioms. More important, however, he cross-pollinated the nascent Romance philology of Raynouard with the grand theories of comparative linguistics developed by his brother Friedrich and by Franz Bopp, and with his own vast knowledge of literature. Schlegel's long and detailed exposition of the linguistic context of the *Choix,* situated at a crossroad of ideas, at once critiques, develops, and contextualizes Raynouard's often jumbled account of a vast area of linguistic and literary inquiry. Schlegel touches, in fact, on virtually every topic to be disputed in subsequent scholarship up to the present day, and a detailed analysis of his argument will make clearer the range of possibilities available to him as well as the choices made by later scholars. For the purposes of exposition, Schlegel's ideas will be presented in five main points, although his eighty-one-page text is not divided in any way.

First, Schlegel, in justifying the scope and dryness of Raynouard's work, asserts the impossibility of procuring an adequate translation of troubadour poetry. Translation succeeds when the work to be translated is based on imitation, and has its equivalent in "all cultivated literatures." Provençal poetry, however, has nothing to do with ancient ideals of the beautiful; its appeal is local, not universal. Schlegel subtly circumvents the dilemma of reconciling troubadour poetry with a universal notion of art by alluding at once to fundamental differences that separate it from both classical Latin verse (based on meter rather than rhyme) and folksong:

> The original imprint . . . of a nascent art is difficult to render in translations. I think it would be impossible to imitate Provençal poetry with a successful fidelity. . . . One cannot consider the songs of the troubadours to be the spontaneous effusions of a nature still in the savage state. The songs are artistic, often even very ingeniously so; they have above all a complicated system of versification, a variety and an abundance in the use of rhyme that have never been equaled in any modern language. . . . [The poetry] was not drawn from the wellspring of books, nor in models thought to be classical; it came to them uniquely from their poetic instinct.[9]

Schlegel's appeal to an undefined notion of "poetic instinct" serves to beg the question of imitation, by idealizing the Middle Ages as a time when poetry was closer to life itself. But the insistence on cultural difference also introduces, within the range of cultural possibilities offered by French and German Classicism, a troubling question. If troubadour lyric is neither imitable nor imitative, then what lessons can it hold for contemporary readers (or poets)? What cultural-theoretical justifications might be offered for the study of this poetry in replacement of prescriptions such as that of Winkelmann, that imitation of the Ancients is the only way to become inimitable?[10]

At this point, Schlegel abruptly shifts the discussion from aesthetics to linguistics. Language itself is now conceived not as an instrument but as the privileged source of culture. Schlegel's notion of "poetic instinct" reflects the conviction that the ultimate sense of poetry is determined by the structure of the language in which it is written. What a culture can accomplish is limited by its language, and thus "the history of languages is that of the human spirit."[11] Here Schlegel embarks on a description of the well-known "general theory of languages" propounded in his brother Friedrich's *Essai on the language and ancient philosophy of the Indians* (1808), which classified languages into one of three types—isolating, agglutinating, or inflecting—based on morphology. Inflecting languages are further subdivided into synthetic and analytic languages, according to whether relations between words are expressed by a system of declension and conjugation, or by word order and the use of articles, pronouns, and auxiliary verbs. In this theory, linguistic change conserved both the grammatical structure and the organization of sounds within the language; however, the evolution of the latter, through the activity of speaking subjects, tended to erode the former. Languages were thus always in a state of decline from an earlier state. Analytic languages, such as modern French or Old Provençal, were born from the disintegration of synthetic languages, such as Latin.

This evolution in turn is indissolubly linked to changes in the way people think and express themselves. Because language reflects the human spirit—one never quite knows which term drives the argument and which one follows by analogy—it must follow that grammatical structure represents mental functioning. Thus modern languages (including medieval languages) "are severely subjected to the regime of logic, because having lost most of the inflections, they must indicate the relation between ideas by the place that the words occupy in the sentence" (26). The obscurity that makes the translation of troubadour poetry difficult results not from the intention of individuals, but from a temporary grammatical insufficiency along the road from synthetic to analytic language, due to the wear imposed by speaking subjects. The medieval speaking subject, he asserts, "had not yet learned to observe all the precautions necessary to obtain the same clarity that Latin owed to the inflections, when these inflections were shortened or omitted. That is what forms the distinctive character of the Romance language. There results from this both advantages and disadvantages: this language is of a surprising brevity; but it sins occasionally by obscurity" (30–31). Poetic ambiguity is not a question of interpretation or of reading, but of the grammatical possibilities of the language. As a result, the meaning of a difficult verse is to be sought not in relation to the content of the poem, but in the history of the language. If only one fully understood the process of linguistic evolution, the grammar would become clear again, and with it the thoughts of its speakers. Obscurity is not a poetic tool but is imposed by the structure of the language itself.

Furthermore—and this is the third point—the notion of linguistic change implicit in such a formulation must also imply a causality of change, and thus an intentionality residing not in individual speech acts but in the collective linguistic community itself. Now, Raynouard had asserted that the "langue romane primitive" was identical in all the provinces of the Roman Empire; yet it was obvious that the languages of medieval Europe had undergone separate development at some point and that their literatures were in large measure independent. Schlegel's critique of Raynouard on this point is decisive. But while Schlegel is able to document the differences between the languages descended from Latin, he can say nothing of the causes, underlying this evolution, that would allow us to "know the history of peoples [and] their private life in past times" (53–54). Here his linguistic arguments begin to have clear implications for reading poetry. Since meaning is now a question of grammatical structure, and word form (determined by the alteration of sounds) a result of the activity of speaking subjects, this form in itself must somehow represent the preferences of the people who shaped it: "If all the letters written were pronounced, and they were without a doubt, Provençal must not have been exempt from harshness; but it was a flexible language, and which lent itself easily to imitative harmony: one detects an insinuating sweetness in the love poems, and, on the other hand, in the war songs of Bertran de Born, one seems to hear the clash of arms" (56–57).

At this point it is clear that Schlegel's argument that linguistic structure reflects mental functioning is based on assertion rather than proof. He is describing his own reading of texts rather than the conditions of their production, and thus he has returned to aesthetics by way of linguistic speculation. Schlegel's emphasis on regional diversity is here conjugated with somewhat older ideas of Mediterranean civilization, and the result recalls nothing so much as Rousseau's *Essai sur l'origine des langues*. His notion of "imitative harmony" links what properly belongs to the domain of rhetoric (the catalog of figures of speech, such as alliteration) to the older speculations on the origins of melody in the imitation of the accents of a language. In so doing, Schlegel surreptitiously reintroduces the notion of poetry as "spontaneous effusion" that he had earlier banished.

The fourth point follows upon the discussion of phonetics and brings us into the thick of the main argument of this chapter. Schlegel remarks on the abundance of homonyms in Provençal and on the variations of orthography. Some of these variations indicate real changes of pronunciation encountered as one moves from northern to southern dialects, such as *chantar* and *cantar*, and indicate Provençal's central geographic position. Other variations are due to the uneven adaptation of the Roman alphabet to indicate sounds foreign to classical Latin. Thus palatalized L is written –*ill*– in French, –*gli*– in Italian, –*ll*– in Spanish, –*lh*– in Portuguese, and these variations were introduced, according to Schlegel, at the moment when the orthographic system was fixed. The manuscripts of troubadour poetry show an even greater variation of notations for this sound, and indeed for many similar sounds. We know now that this variation is due to the complex process by which a poem composed in one dialect was filtered through several other dialects as it was fixed in writing and recopied. For Schlegel, however, this variation was a simple lack of method on the part of the scribes, whose ambiguous text should be clarified by methodical compensation on the part of the modern editor:

> As a result of this observation, I think that one could venture to correct the spelling of the troubadours, that is, to choose among the variations of the manuscripts one single way of writing the same words and the same sounds, preferring the one that best recalls the etymology. . . . An original text loses all its value with its authenticity. To advance the philology of the Middle Ages, one should apply to it the principles of classical philology. (61–62)

We will examine the principles of classical philology shortly; for now let us observe that authenticity is to be gained through the rigorous application of method. It is implicit in Schlegel's suggestion that the lack of method that characterized both eighteenth-century editors and medieval scribes renders their texts inauthentic, and that this inauthenticity arrives at the moment of translation into writing. It is the graphic system that introduces needless complications. But here Schlegel commits the same error he denounced in Raynouard: where Raynouard assumed that the geographical coherence of classical Latin must imply the coherence of the "langue romane primitive," Schlegel assumes that, because nation and language are assumed to be one and the same, medieval languages must have possessed a coherence comparable to modern national languages. The Provençal language, however, has never corresponded to any historical political unity. Furthermore, the troubadour manuscripts were themselves copied not just in the Midi, but also in Italy, northern France, and Catalonia. Thus Schlegel's suggestion assumes the existence of a linguistic identity—which is also a national identity—on the basis of grammar alone. The authenticity of the text is assumed to stem from its grammar, which is in turn the royal road to understanding the thought processes of a single, unified group of speakers.

The final—and for our purposes, most important—assertion of Schlegel's text is that literature is the source of national culture, and thus that Raynouard merits the government support given to his work. This idea links Schlegel's French-language "observations" with the movement of national history being developed in Prussian universities (Schlegel was called to the University of Berlin in 1818, the same year the *Observations* were published), whose initial form and ultimate consequences have been described by Jauss and Gumbrecht.

Schlegel comes to this assertion by way of an examination of versification and music, which leads him to compare the production of the troubadours with that of poets working in other languages, especially Arabic. Here he returns to the notion of "poetic instinct" to establish the connection between poetry and living voice. Many of the troubadours, he asserts, were illiterate, and their poetry was transmitted by memory, with the result that the earliest lyrics have been lost (65–66). Since "the taste for rhyme is in nature," one must distinguish between analogies between different poetries and the classical ideal of imitation (68). The validity of poetry, Schlegel insists, derives from the authentic speech acts of native speakers: "All gifted peoples have had the need and the taste for poetry; it has developed everywhere where the circumstances have been favorable. . . . Poetry partakes most of the intimate impressions produced by the maternal language; it is always null and artificial, when it is not national" (73).

Here the early Romantic Middle Ages as other blends imperceptibly into the teleological national history soon to be developed by Humboldt and Gervinus. Gumbrecht has asserted convincingly that the national history paradigm never dominated in France as it did in Germany; if he is right, then Schlegel's views would have been a dead letter in France, but decisive in Germany.[12] Schlegel's text would appear as the fleeting attempt to reconcile the incredible contradictions between Enlightenment views of the influence of climate and geography on cultural products, Romantic notions of the popular voice, and the emergent theories of language driven in equal parts by the discovery of manuscripts and comparative hypothesis. Here for the first and last time do we find an attempt to deal adequately with the entire sum of knowledge pertaining to the troubadours, from literary and linguistic theory to the minutiae of biography, graphic systems, and rhyme schemes. Schlegel's *Observations* are the first and only *Grundriß* that could pretend to totality; and what he did not or could not know, the enthusiastic flush of theoretical speculation could fill in.

In fact, neither Raynouard nor Schlegel were to have an immediate impact in France. While Raynouard's work was, so to speak, imported into Germany by way of Schlegel and others, in France the rising crest of Romantic enthusiasm favored the broad analogies between various national literatures that were being developed to "explain" the origin of epic poetry. In Germany, the increasingly nationalistic orientation of university life tended to marginalize studies in foreign literatures to the extent that those studies did not facilitate the study of modern foreign languages.[13] There was thus a significant parting of ways between French and German Provençalistes; or more accurately, the coincidence of their paths was only illusory in the works of Raynouard and Schlegel. This divergence was of great consequence for the future publication of troubadour poetry. As we shall see, in the period from 1816 to 1864, French scholars shunned troubadour manuscripts to edit and publish important works relating to the Provençal language and narrative poetry, while the Germans published lyric texts and established the scientific bases of textual criticism and Romance philology. The organization of French and German universities played a significant role in this evolution, and the manifesto launched by Gaston Paris against French philology in 1864 takes as its central exhibit precisely the German publication of troubadour manuscripts. The opening salvo of the civil war in French philology was fired, not by Gaston Paris, but by the man he would adopt as his academic father, Friedrich Diez. This requires some explanation.

In spite of the passion for German Romanticism sweeping French intellectual circles, Schlegel's ideas bore little fruit in France. In a defensive review of Schlegel's book, Raynouard defended his position on the universality of the "langue romane primitive" as preferable to Schlegel's recourse to a universal instinct insuring the same results.[14] Raynouard saw his role as the exposition of facts and plausible working hypotheses, not the solution of the broadest questions by speculative theory. Although his approach bears a more than superficial resemblance to later positivist scholarship, his branch of the scholarly family tree never developed. According to Jeanroy, Raynouard had no disciples and undertook his work uniquely out of his professional duty as member (from 1807) and *secrétaire perpétuel* (from 1816) of the Académie Française.[15]

In Germany, however, Schlegel was very successful as a teacher, drawing many students, among them Friedrich Diez. Diez's path from young student imbued with German Romanticism and "bellicose nationalism" to founding father—out of political disillusionment?— of Romance philology has been laid out in Gumbrecht's remarkable article, to which the reader is referred. Diez's interest in the troubadours seems motivated, on the one hand, by a love of poetry more typical of early Romanticism, and on the other by the scholarly need to make available to students of philology all of the manuscript texts.

Raynouard, as he himself had admitted to Diez, had published only what he could understand, with the result that, in Diez's estimation, his selection of troubadour lyric in volume 2 of the *Choix* did not reveal anything that had not already been said by Millot.[16]

In the preface to his 1826 *Die Poesie der Troubadours,* Diez challenged Raynouard on the question of publication: "The most suitable anthology is still not much more than an expedient. It will always refer to what is missing, but that is available in the present case in manuscripts, which only a few can ever inspect. The publication of the entire corpus of songs is thus the only means of fulfilling the legitimate demands of the friends of poetry, and until that has been accomplished the job is only half done."[17] Raynouad was quick to justify himself. A native of the Var as well as a member of the Académie Française, he had intended his *Choix* to revalorize the language of the Midi in the absence of any corresponding political unity.[18] Diez's attack revealed a misunderstanding of his original motives, and in reviewing Diez's book he explained himself: "I wanted to make known the language of the troubadours and establish its grammar; after this essential work, I hoped that one might apply the principles of this language to a selection or collection of original texts, and I limited myself to this."[19]

Referring to the editorial difficulties stemming from the imperfect state of the manuscripts, and then to Diez's assertion that "even the defective or corrupted texts have too great a worth for experts,"[20] he asks: "Was I to discourage those who wished to study this language, in offering them riddles that neither Mr. Diez nor I will ever explain! Certainly not: it was necessary first to accredit the language. . . . I persist in maintaining that the precipitate publication of defective and incorrect texts will be more harmful than helpful to knowledge."[21] However, the "defigured and amputated texts" to which Raynouard referred in his review often owe their mutilation to purely external contingencies such as the removal of illuminations,[22] which could be mitigated by recourse to other copies of the same song. Raynouard did in fact collate his texts with other manuscripts when necessary; but what Diez wanted was the source materials themselves in their entirety, not the limited anthology of "classical" texts offered by Raynouard.

Here we need to return a moment to the idea of philology present in germ in Schlegel's *Observations.* Schlegel's assessment of the nascent discipline implies that a period of linguistic exploration would need to precede any work on troubadour poetry proper. Since language expresses the will of the people, and grammar is what conserves language, poetry is interesting only insofar as it illustrates grammar: in other words, insofar as the philologist can establish a link between the attested forms of a corrupt and defective analytical language and corresponding forms of a synthetic (or grammatical) language. But the only way to guarantee that one possesses the grammatical structure in its entirety is to inspect all of the texts known to exist in the language; furthermore, one must distinguish between mere variations of spelling and grammatical error. Thus, during the first phase of research, the study of poetry is first of all a study of grammatical difficulties, and for this it is necessary to have convenient and regular access to as many texts as possible.

For the purpose of training new philologists, especially those far from major manuscript collections, this means publishing everything that can be found. Once the source materials are available, however, the difficulties intensify. The fact that there are multiple, divergent copies of each poem makes it impossible to accept any copy as authentic merely because it was written down in the Middle Ages. Authenticity becomes a matter of negotiation between notions of grammatical correctness, poetic diction (different for "art-poetry" and "folk-poetry") and historical veracity that depend on criteria that will seem objective and scientific only to those scholars who share the presuppositions on which they are based.[23] There can be no doubt that Schlegel and Diez had sufficient knowledge of troubadour manuscripts to see this problem on the horizon, even though it did not fall to them to address it in practice by editing texts.

The difficulty of establishing an authentic text is, of course, bound up with the view one takes of the production and transmission of poetry. Schlegel asserted that a period of oral transmission preceded the first written collections, and that the poetry was the product of a living voice and a poetic instinct. But these ideas were not the fruit of his reflection on the troubadours: he was simply applying to troubadour lyric the theory of the collective oral origin of epic poetry, which he had exposed in numerous lectures and publications since 1802.[24] In this theory, epics were the late and partially reworked combination of earlier, short songs; because of the collective nature of this work, the epic was seen as the product not of a single author but of entire generations. This idea was not particularly new, but it arose in conjunction with the development of increasingly sophisticated techniques of textual criticism, associated in particular with the works of Ferdinand Wolf and Karl Lachmann. In Germany, where classical studies and nascent Germanic philology occupied a privileged place in national culture, it provided a prime illustration of the role of poetry in mediating between national identity and popular voice, at the same time that it guaranteed interest in critical editions of epics such as the *Nibelungenlied.*

In France, where Raynouard had focused attention on the origins of the Romance languages rather than on that of troubadour poetry, the question of origins and authenticity presented itself not for troubadour lyric but for the chanson de geste. Schlegel's theory of the collective origins of the epic was taken up by Claude Fauriel, who held the chair of *littérature étrangère* created for him in 1830 at the Sorbonne. Fauriel lectured on the history of Provençal poetry, but his main interest was clearly in narrative and the epic. His thesis that the French chanson de geste originated in Provençal models provoked a debate with Paulin Paris; while his "literary imperialism" (the word is Jeanroy's) was discredited, Paulin Paris did later concede that Fauriel had been correct in postulating the origin of the epic in short songs.[25] What finally was published in France during the twenty years following the death of Raynouard in 1836 were texts that reflect both Raynouard's interest in language and Fauriel's interest in epic: the *Histoire de la croisade contre les hérétiques albigeois* (Fauriel, 1837); the compendium of rhetoric and poetics known as *Las leys d'amors* (Gatien-Arnoult, 1841–48); the grammars of Uc Faidit and Raimon Vidal (Guessard, 1843); and the epic *Girard de Roussillon* (Fr. Michel, 1856).

In Germany, however, the situation was quite different. While in France at this time only one professor taught the Old Provençal language (Guessard, at the École des Chartes),[26] and the teaching of Provençal literature at the Faculté de Paris came from a chair of *littérature étrangère* (Fauriel), the German academic machine had already begun turning out scholars. Besides Diez in Bonn, there was Adrian (Giessen), Emmanuel Becker (Berlin), Eduard Brinckmeier (Halle), Adalbert Keller (Tübingen), Karl August Friedrich Mahn (Berlin), and somewhat later Karl Bartsch (Rostock).[27] During the 1840s and 1850s, these and other professors, heeding the call first made by Diez, began publishing the manuals and text collections needed to train the next generations of students: transcriptions of unpublished texts,[28] anthologies and study manuals,[29] editions of individual poets,[30] grammars, and an etymological dictionary.[31]

It is also in Germany in the 1850s that the marriage of literary and linguistic scholarship celebrated by Schlegel began to fall apart.

Bartsch's 1857 edition of Peire Vidal was the first to apply to the works of a troubadour "the principles of scientific criticism, as Lachmann first established and practiced them for Middle High German texts."[32] Bartsch's appeal to Lachmann is not a simple pledge of methodological allegiance, however; it reveals a delicate three-way negotiation between Germanic, classical, and Romance philology, literary history and linguistics, and more broadly between the claims of nationalist cultural theories and an atheoretical "scientific" objectivity. The stakes of this negotiation were the legitimation, by association with more prestigious fields, of Provençal studies and Romance philology; but while the "scientific" method seems to have prevailed, in reality Schlegel's theory of popular origin continued to exercise considerable influence under the surface. To understand this process, it is necessary to present in some detail the circumstances in which it developed.

Lachmann's name is today associated with a method of editing classical Latin texts based on rigorous criteria for reconstructing the genealogical relation between a set of manuscripts, and for determining mechanically which readings go back to the archetype, or (lost) original text.[33] His method of editing medieval texts was different, however.[34] In a series of articles and reviews published between 1816 and 1820, Lachmann had adapted to the *Nibelungenlied* the hypothesis of Wolf, Schlegel, and others that the song had been gradually assembled rather than composed by a single author. This led him, in his widely accepted editions of the song published beginning in 1826, to base his text on the oldest, but also the most poorly written text, and to postulate that the other manuscripts had descended from it in a straight line, which meant that they could not be used to reconstruct the archetype. By the 1850s his views were coming under increasingly severe attack by Germanists such as Friedrich Zarncke, who "contended that Lachmann had based his *Liedertheorie* on the supposition of the superiority of one manuscript, and the superiority of that manuscript on the validity of the *Liedertheorie*."[35] It would ultimately fall to Karl Bartsch, in his 1865 *Untersuchungen über das Nibelungenlied,* to determine through an examination of the song's versification that it could only have been composed by a single author, demolishing Lachmann's *Liedertheorie*. It was also Bartsch who, according to Mary Thorp, was the first to establish the genealogical relationship between the manuscripts with "no reference to any theory of the epic's origin" (135).

Bartsch's 1857 edition of Peire Vidal was a milestone in troubadour edition because it was the first to attempt a systematic classification of manuscripts. Bartsch was aware that there were more manuscripts than he knew of (he did not dispose of mss. J, U, a, c, e, f), and began with the questionable assumption that the manuscripts he did not know would not form any new branches on the genealogical tree. In the assessment of D'Arco Silvio Avalle, who reedited Peire Vidal a century later, Bartsch's edition was not as persuasive as Lachmann's work in classical edition; Bartsch did not justify the critical text he offered or attempt to trace the relation between the texts of individual poems. But, on the other hand, he was, according to Avalle, the first to observe that the various manuscripts were composed of individual *Liederheften,* or "song-notebooks."[36] This is, of course, a significant departure from Schlegel's theory, borrowed from the epic, that the songs were preserved by memory. Bartsch in fact took care to make clear the differences between epic and lyric manuscripts, placing his discussion of editorial technique in his dedicatory foreword, rather than with the list of manuscripts at the end of his ninety-six-page introduction:

> The chansonniers often have their origin in troubadours' and jongleurs' individual song-notebooks, which recorded the songs either from a written copy or from oral delivery that they had learned (*apres*). This explains why manuscripts agree in the readings of the songs of one poet and differ from one another for another poet, since they are based on different song-notebooks. . . . For now let us remark only that this manner of formation of the manuscripts makes a substantial distinction between the treatment of epic and lyric texts.[37]

Bartsch's hypothesis of mixed oral and written transmission offered two advantages. On the one hand, because it assumed a written tradition, it allowed the use of editorial techniques developed for classical texts, and avoided the theoretical questions inherent in postulating an oral origin. On the other hand, by leaving open the possibility of at least some oral transmission of an unspecified nature, the hypothesis was no longer vulnerable to refutation by the isolated references to memorization or oral transmission that occur with some frequency in troubadour lyric.

In the closing pages of his foreword, Bartsch took pains to address the observations of a French critic that troubadour poetry merited only public indifference from an aesthetic point of view. His justification reveals the complexity of the negotiations he was engaged in. Bartsch felt that troubadour lyric, no less than Middle High German lyric, had a properly literary as well as a linguistic worth. However, the reader who sought to judge medieval Germanic or Romance poetry according to the aesthetic standards of ancient or modern poetry, who was "unable to regard the manifestations of the human spirit in all periods with unprejudiced eyes," would find no pleasure in such reading. Bartsch addressed his edition to the "unprejudiced reader" who might, through careful study, recognize the poetic vision (*poetische Anschauungen und Gedanken*) of a Peire Vidal and detect a genuine feeling (*wirkliches Gefühl*) through the conventions of his poetry.

"The Middle Ages," he claimed, "will not be judged by the standard of either ancient or modern aesthetics; it has its own aesthetics, which it developed in both theory and practice."[38] Bartsch offered, it would seem, no less than a declaration of independence for medieval studies, a clean break with Schlegel's theory of the Middle Ages as the mirror image of future national identity. Yet his reasoning is riddled with contradictions. Medieval poetry has no more claim to attention than any other "manifestation of the human spirit"; yet at the same time he plays on the cultural prestige of the Minnesänger in valorizing the troubadours. Medieval poetry is the equal to classical and modern poetry and cannot be judged by their standards; at the same time he proposes to his reader that the specifically modern values of poetic vision and genuine feeling are what make Peire Vidal worth reading. It is not implausible to advance that Bartsch chose to edit Peire Vidal precisely because the legend recounted by the Provençal *vida,* the medieval biography transmitted with his poetry, fit so well the profile of the wandering cleric, the medieval prototype of the Romantic poet-hero.

––––––––––

The tensions visible in Bartsch's edition between the pretension to scientific objectivity and the unobserved reliance on Romantic theory; between modern, medieval and classical literature; between Germanic and Romance philology; and between literary history and linguistics, are so many symptoms of the nineteenth-century crisis of literary history analyzed by Hans Robert Jauss in his 1968 manifesto "Literary History as a Challenge to Literary Theory." In Jauss's analysis, the development of positivist literary history in nineteenth-century Germany came from the increasing inability of scholars to believe that national individuality was the whole that explained every part, that connected all the facts. "To the extent that this conviction disappeared," Jauss states, "the thread connecting events had to disappear as well, past and present literature fall apart into separate spheres of judgment, and the selection, determination and evaluation of literary facts become problematic" (8).

Positivism not only lived but thrived in the perennially unaccomplished task of keeping all the facts sewn together, and its history is the story of the hardening of humanistic study into professional academic disciplines. But positivism also brings with it a self-perpetuating logic, which is that the knowledge produced by the purely external exploration of literary events generates a demand for still more knowledge to fill in the gaps this knowledge makes apparent. Specialization breeds more specialization, and the surplus of knowledge thus created is seen as a sort of national intellectual capital in spite of its lack of practical utility. This was, and still is, the reason for the international success of the German model of the research university.

The academic success of Romance philology in Germany was due in good part to the organization of university teaching. The French university, on the other hand, oriented around the two-hour lecture courses given by a small body of titulary professors, was ill-adapted for labor-intensive philological instruction. Not only did the typical German university have more professors than even the Université de Paris, but those professors taught as much as five times as many hours per week as their French counterparts.[39] The institution of the *Privat-Docenten* allowed the teaching of subjects not officially consecrated by a titulary chair.[40] This permitted instruction of a much more practical nature, essential to philological study, and also attracted more serious students.

It was precisely the specialized aspect of German pedagogy (with the devotion to detail and expense of time it implied) that was most resisted by French faculties, as Gaston Paris, graduate of the École des Chartes and onetime student of Diez, noted with exasperation in his 1864 manifesto, "La philologie romane en Allemagne":

> Are we too exacting in regretting that French philology is not taught more than it is? Alas, yes, much too much, for one can answer us that one does not teach in France any kind of philology, and that it would be bizarre and even revolting to see chairs of French linguistics in faculties where one studies even of antiquity only its *literature*; the word *philology* itself has something heavy and forbidding about it . . . all those things are pedantic, obscure and rather ridiculous; the humanities, *humaniores litterae,* as Cicero said, that's

what we need! And don't tell us that your philology is needed to understand these authors we admire, for we understand them in our own way, and a well-wrought misinterpretation is better, to be sure, than a tedious exactitude. (437)

For the young (and then unemployed) Gaston Paris, the creation of new positions for philological instruction was more than a matter of principle.[41] His manifesto had as its goal the creation of a second position parallel to Guessard's at the École des Chartes, and took as its point of departure a discourse pronounced by Karl Mahn at the 1863 philologist's convention at Meissen. Mahn, referring to Diez's 1826 call to publish all of the poetry of the troubadours, pointed with pride to the decision of the Berlin Society for the Study of Modern Languages to award its 500-Thaler travel stipend to a certain Mr. Grützmacher for the purposes of transcribing and publishing all of the manuscripts of troubadour poetry held in Italian libraries. Grützmacher's "Reports to the Society" appeared in the *Archiv für das Studium der neueren Sprachen und Literaturen* in 1863 and 1864. Paris exclaimed, "one doesn't like to see foreigners take charge of the ashes of your fathers and give them monuments befitting their worth."[42] Gaston's father, Paulin, however, was very much alive, and his son's reception of the intellectual heritage left to him was hardly respectful.

In 1866 Gaston, who had just read Bartsch's *Untersuchungen über das Nibelungenlied*, exclaimed in a letter to its author, "Your work . . . is a genuine event in literary history. . . . From now on we will have to apply *the Bartsch method* to all of medieval poetry."[43] When Gaston substituted for his father at the Collège de France in 1867, Paulin Paris's course of literary *explications de texte* became instead a history of French phonetics. "I have taken up," he wrote to Bartsch, "one by one the first words of Cassel's glossary . . . and I have given for them all the phonetic explications they call for, with the result that in ten lessons I've now explained eight words."[44] Gaston's response to this crisis of paternity took the form of founding journals in collaboration with another young and underemployed former student of the École des Chartes, Paul Meyer.[45] In 1865 came the *Revue critique d'histoire et de littérature,* founded "to evaluate works of contemporary scholarship from an exclusively scientific point of view," but also to practice in France the method "applied every day in the periodicals of Germany and England."[46] In 1872 appeared *Romania,* intended to compete with the Leipzig *Jahrbuch für romanische und englische Literatur,* because, as Paris and Meyer declared, "it seemed to us that the center of Romance studies ought to be in France rather than Germany."[47]

The twenty-five-year-old Paris was not the only one unhappy with the French system, however, and a movement to reform the universities along German lines led to the creation of the École des Hautes Études in 1868. Its mission, according to Gaston Paris, an instructor there from the beginning, was "the initiation into the rigorous methods of history and philology, as it was practiced in Germany."[48] Similar to the École des Chartes in that its teaching was to be practical, advanced, and scientific in character, Hautes Études differed from the other *grandes écoles* in that it did not prepare one for any career, and thus tended to draw more foreign students than French ones.[49] Defined at the outset as distinct from the university and the literary teaching it offered, the École went on to prepare generations of text editors and historical scholars and thus helped to promulgate both in France and abroad a notion of the discipline as practical and methodological rather than theoretical or ideological.

Once endowed with an institutional base, French philology set as its goal to rival—in the context of the dispassionate advancement of science—the German competitors. In the field of Provençal philology, Diez's 1826 challenge to Raynouard meant this was first and foremost a question of publication. Grützmacher's reports touched off a philological "arms race," which resulted in the publication, in the space of five years, of indexes to the most important chansonniers.[50] Indexes to most of what was left were published over the next decade in newly created philological journals.[51] Once the indexes were published, scholars began publishing transcriptions of the manuscripts themselves, an enormous undertaking that continued into the 1920s.[52]

The publication of such an overwhelming wealth of source material made necessary the weaving of an organizational fabric to hold it all together, and this raised the very theoretical problems that positivist scholarship wished to avoid. The symptom of this tension is the conflict, sustained by Paul Meyer, over the attribution of sigla to the chansonnier manuscripts. Behind Diez's call to publish the troubadours remained, of course, the question of whether the texts should be published according to the version of a single manuscript, as Raynouard preferred, or in a composite version produced according to the methods of classical philology, as Schlegel indicated. Bound up with this question was Schlegel's theory of the popular origin and oral transmission of song. Bartsch's edition of Peire Vidal had attempted to deny the applicability of his predecessor's theory of origins by attempting a rigorous classification of lyric manuscripts and showing how the lyric thereby differed from the epic. In 1872 Bartsch finetuned his classification in his *Grundriß zur Geschichte der provenzalischen Literatur,* a reference manual listing all of the known works of Provençal literature and their bibliography. Paul Meyer, however, had offered his own sigla three years earlier in *Les derniers troubadours de la Provence,* and his system was based not on a qualitative classification of the manuscripts, but on their place of residence. Meyer's review of the *Grundriß* in volume 1 of *Romania*[53] bristled with envy at having been beaten by Bartsch in publishing the urgently needed manual, and launched a frontal attack in the name of positivist science. After condemning Fauriel's work as derivative and conjectural, and praising Bartsch for having abstained "from entering the domain of hypothesis,"[54] Meyer turns to Bartsch's manuscript classification.

[It] cannot . . . claim any scientific value. As I have explained elsewhere, the chansonniers of the troubadours resist all classification by family. One can classify the various readings of such and such a text, but this classification can never extend to an entire manuscript. That is because the Provençal chansonniers that have come down to us are made up of the combination of earlier collections. Consequently the order adopted by Mr. B., and that I for my part have always rejected, is absolutely arbitrary. (380–81)

Meyer's own approach to the problem of classifying the manuscripts can hardly be called scientific in the elevated sense he gave to the word. Not only did he never give any extended treatment of the problem, but he never modified the opinion he first expressed in 1868: that the surviving manuscripts were copied from older manuscripts, and thus are not original; that their derivation is so confused that they cannot be grouped into families; and that any further work is a waste of time.[55] By this he meant the classification of the manuscripts themselves; for although he declared in 1881 that many of the stemmas established by editors for individual songs were "purely chimerical," he admitted the utility of attempting them and relied on such a grouping himself in reediting a song of Peire Vidal.[56]

Meyer's inclinations in any case would not have led him to undertake such a speculative project. Thomas and Langlois, in writing their necrology, noted his "apprehension of synthesis" and predilection for the role of "censor of the works of others."[57] His editorial projects were above all works held in single manuscripts, as witness his editions of the chansonnier Giraud (*Derniers troubadours*), *Flamenca*, *La chanson de la croisade albigeoise,* and *Girart de Roussillon.* For him, the immediate role of text editing was not a search for national identity, but the preservation of documents from revolution in the streets. The literary value of the works was unimportant. Thus he wrote of *Brun de la montagne,* "It's a mediocre poem . . . nevertheless, with the Communes [sic] that are going around, one would rather see printed than unpublished the manuscripts of our Parisian libraries."[58] Of *Guillaume de la Barre,* he was more indulgent: "The romance is rather bereft of poetry, but the language is interesting. And then there is only one manuscript: it could have been lost, like so many others of greater value. It had to be published."[59]

While Meyer virtually refused to discuss, at least in print, the relationship between the manuscripts, others were not so reticent. In 1877 Gustav Gröber published a monograph investigating the sources of troubadour manuscripts and their interrelationship.[60] Citing a long series of examples from the *vidas* and *razos,* Gröber concluded that the troubadours composed in writing and, disputing the claims of Diez and Schlegel, argued that inability to write was the exception rather than the rule among troubadours (339). The songs were written down on *Liederblätter,* or "song-sheets," by the troubadour or by someone in his or her entourage. These song-sheets were then collected into song-books at a later time. Gröber's work was based on the hypothesis that, to demonstrate his point, he had only to show that the manuscripts (as distinct from individual songs) fell into groups (342). Since there is indisputable evidence of written transmission (in the scribal preface of Bernart Amoros), and of written collections made by the poets or contemporary scribes (in the songs of Guiraut Riquier and in Miquel de la Tor's copy of the songs of Peire Cardenal), he had only to show a continuous written tradition back to the first written copies in order to demonstrate the possibility of producing an authentic text (344). Gröber was unable to establish an overall stemma of the manuscripts and thus spare editors the task of collating variants for each song; but he did conclude that the transmission of troubadour lyric was "almost exclusively written" (657).

In 1883, U. A. Canello published an edition of Arnaut Daniel in which he declared himself unable to construct a genealogical stemma "in the manner of the Berlin school."[61] The text of Arnaut was so contaminated that the classification of the texts was a "Sisyphean labor" which allowed the editor to obtain a text that was only "relatively authentic" (iv–v). In his review of the edition, Bartsch had high praise for Canello, and expressed an opinion utterly opposed to Gröber's, but yet consistent with his own earlier views. A clear division of the texts into families is not possible, he wrote, unless one understands, as none of "our philologists" have, the expedient of the manuscript collections: the manuscripts had been collected primarily from the memory of singers, and the variation between the copies of a given poem were due not to the comparison of manuscripts in a scriptorium, but to the nature of oral transmission.[62] For Gröber, such a hypothesis meant that it would be impossible to procure an authentic text.[63] Gröber and Canello had each reached, independently, the limits of philological science, and yet the solution they sought to the genealogical puzzle was beyond the horizon. Bartsch's hypothesis of an oral tradition was seductive, but it shared the one fatal flaw of Fauriel's lost Provençal epic: "it did not exist."[64]

Meyer seems to have shared Bartsch's views of mixed oral-written tradition in spite of his sharp critiques. He opened his 1872 review by noting that Provençal literature "not only ceased producing at the moment when the literary works had the greatest odds of being collected and preserved, but even the works that had already been collected in writing were neglected: one took scant care to make new copies and those that already existed were allowed to disappear."[65]

However, unlike Bartsch, Meyer does not seem to have taken pains to distinguish between the origins of lyric and those of epic poetry. This emerges from his early disagreement with Gaston Paris over the oral transmission of epic poetry. In his 1865 thesis, *Histoire poétique de Charlemagne,* Paris had submitted that the epic had been assembled out of short, disparate, lyrico-epic songs composed directly after the events they describe. Meyer reviewed Paris's thesis in 1867 and concluded, "This is the system of Wolf for the Homeric poems, and of Lachmann for the *Nibelungenlied,*" that had been disproved by Bartsch in his *Untersuchungen.*[66] Meyer believed instead that the songs were composed (i.e., written) by poets who relied on an oral tradition which transmitted a song containing the entire dramatic action in germ. But Meyer argued against Paris's hypothesis—echoing Fauriel—that there had existed a Provençal epic cycle subsequently lost (46). First of all, the loss of an entire cycle of texts could only be explained by negligence or suppression. Troubadour lyric had been suppressed when the poets' noble protectors, the counts of Toulouse and Provence (335), were ruined by the Albigensian crusade (49); but, he asked, if the works of the late troubadours survived, why would a popular genre such as the epic leave no trace? Second, there was no reason to assume such a loss in the Midi, but not in the north. His refutation, however, supposes another lost work: "In the South, as far as our knowledge of its literature extends, we see minds busy with highly thoughtful and artistic works: lyric songs, which obviously come from a popular poetry, about which we can form only conjectures, but whose inspiration was not the kind that produces an epic" (49–50).

Meyer's supposition of a lost popular lyric seems no more plausible than that of a lost popular epic. He was simply following the suppositions of Diez and Fauriel that troubadour lyric was preceded by an older popular lyric. It is possible that Meyer avoided discussion of the relationship of the lyric manuscripts because it brought forth these logical flaws in other areas of his research.[67] The final irony is that the same idea was later picked up by Gaston Paris who, in "Les origines de la poésie lyrique en France," argued that troubadour lyric had its origins in dance songs originating in an intermediary region between the north and south, perhaps Poitou. Käte Axhausen, in her 1937 survey of theories of the origin of Provençal lyric, concluded that Paris's *Volksliedertheorie* "stands entirely in the influence of a conceptual world whose principles were conceived in the spirit of Romanticism. From that, it was inevitable that he was assailed by a younger generation for whom this conceptual world had become problematic."[68] Meyer avoided a similar assessment by never developing the contradictory suppositions he advanced against Paris.

The contradictions in the thought of Paris as well as Meyer are in each case the result of the unexamined legacy of Romantic theory. This legacy had become problematic, following Jauss's analysis of positivism, because of the increasing impossibility, in the later nineteenth century, of reconciling the idealistic nationalism constitutive of the philological project—the restoration of the link between text and the voice of the people—with political reality. Gaston Paris's reaction was to avoid recognizing the paradoxes inherent in his own intellectual position by blaming the entire social organization of his country. Reminiscing in 1892 on the educational reforms so central to the philological project and so dear to him in the 1860s and 1870s, Paris wrote:

> I no longer have the hopes—I will gladly say the illusions—of former days: I hardly think that any kind of measures could change from one day to the next a state of things that is due to all the material,

political, administrative, intellectual and moral conditions of our society. . . . Let us take advantage of what we have; let us strive to fill the chairs of our Faculties in a worthy manner . . . and let us renounce the great hopes we had once been able to hold.[69]

Coming from the future *administrateur* of the Collège de France (he was named in 1895), such a statement represents not just a personal disillusionment but an institutional *immobilisme*.

———————

The generation of Provençalistes that came of professional age in the 1870s reached the limits of their discipline in the standoff over the classification of manuscripts. In the face of a problem that brought into question the entire edifice of unexamined presuppositions, the easiest solution was simply to ignore them and publish editions that were, if not always philologically rigorous, at least respectable entries on a curriculum vitae. The publications of the 1860s and 1870s made possible the establishment of a cottage industry of critical edition, which began slowly in the 1870s.[70] Paul Meyer described, with his customary malice, the mediocrity of the work procured:

> Since Mr. Bartsch published in the back of his *Grundriß der pro-*
> *venzalischen Literatur* a useful, if not always exact, index of the
> poetry of the troubadours, young German students of Romance
> languages looking for dissertation subjects are eager to undertake
> treating the life and works of some troubadour. They are seduced by
> the apparently advantageous circumstances in which the work pres-
> ents itself to them. The sources of their publication are given to them
> by the *Grundriß*, the principal historical information is generally
> furnished by Diez's *Leben und Werke der Troubadours;* course notes
> and their professor's assistance give them the means to fill in the
> framework sketched out in advance, and it is thus that little by little
> the former poets of the South of France are published in separate
> editions, as we await the collective edition on which Mr. Bartsch has
> long labored. The benefit that accrues to Provençal studies from this
> way of proceeding is more apparent than real. The poetry of the
> troubadours is difficult to understand; it raises a mass of questions,
> some linguistic, others historical, that a beginner is hardly able to
> resolve. Thus, among the numerous dissertations relating to the
> troubadours that have appeared in the last years, only a few rise
> above a fair mediocrity.[71]

Bartsch's general edition of all of the troubadours never appeared, and the pace of individual editions gained momentum, fed in part by the need to redo earlier efforts. In the 1890s, the creation of text series at a small number of publishing houses (Max Niemeyer[72] and N. G. Elwert[73] in Germany, Privat[74] in France, and Ermanno Loescher[75] in Italy) provided a reliable outlet for a narrowly defined product. The mechanical editorial practice described by Meyer continued well into the twentieth century, fostered by the development of a French school of Provençalistes in Alfred Jeanroy and Joseph Anglade. Neither one showed a particular interest in the problem of manuscript classification. Anglade's best work, like that of his master, Camille Chabaneau, centered on late troubadours, from Guiraut Riquier to the fourteenth-century "Consistori del gai saber." His 1913 edition of Peire Vidal reproduced Bartsch's text, "typographical errors included," according to Avalle.[76] Jeanroy's editions[77] are most often of poets whose works are found primarily in only one or two manuscripts; it was Salverda de Grave who classified the manuscripts of Uc de Saint Circ (and made the stemmas), and Jeanroy's edition of Jaufré Rudel relied heavily on Stimming's precedent.[78] Aside from a few remarkable efforts (such as Appel's 1915 *Bernart von Ventadorn*), troubadour edition from the 1880s on had reached a dead end that condemned it to repackage information already available in print from other sources. In this perspective, the two monumental works of 1933–34, Pillet and Carsten's *Bibliographie der Troubadours* and Jeanroy's *La poésie lyrique des troubadours*,[79] represented the twilight of an era rather than the possibility of a new beginning from fresh principles.

The reaction against positivist edition in France came with a change in editorial technique on the eve of World War I. In the preface to his revised edition of Jean Renart's *Lai de l'ombre*, Joseph Bédier renounced attempting to organize the different manuscripts of the *lai* into a single genealogical tree.[80] Bédier's rejection of the Lachmannian method imported into France by Gaston Paris confirmed the bad faith long implicit in the editorial endeavor. His critique was based less on philosophical or logical principles than on a psychoanalysis of the Lachmannian editor: "Obscure forces, confined to the depths of the subconscious, have exerted their influence. . . . Through the consequences of almost imperceptible psychological movements, that is what one or another of my readers will be able to observe, if he attempts to establish a text . . . and if he watches what happens inside him over the course of the operation" (175).

The "obscure forces" Bédier had discovered were a *force dichotomique* which, he claimed, compelled the editor to pursue his or her classification of common faults until the stemma had been reduced to just two branches. With three branches, the correct reading will be given mechanically by the agreement of two branches against one, and the editor is a robot, a slave; with two branches, the editor "frees himself from an overly harsh law" (173–74). In the case of the *Lai de l'ombre*, the problem was not in grouping the manuscripts into families, but of finding the point where the different families converge into a single trunk that would allow the recovery of the original text, O. It is at this crucial moment that the Lachmannian method leaves the editor vulnerable to his subconscious, and this shortcoming impeaches the method itself. The convergence of branches, Bédier concluded, is "out of our grasp for the moment," and perhaps forever (181). As a result, he decreed, the establishment of a text through the classification of manuscripts is legitimate only if it leads to the reproduction *tel quel* of one manuscript; a composite of several manuscripts cannot be legitimate. The conditions of transmission of medieval French literary texts were not the same as those of Antiquity, nor sacred or legal texts (354–55). As a result: "We must admit, with the humanists of old, that we dispose of only one tool: taste. . . . Thus the most advisable method of edition is perhaps, in the last analysis, the one governed by a spirit of lack of trust in oneself, of prudence, of extreme 'conservatism'" (356).

Bédier's psychoanalysis led not to the liberation of the editor from the neurosis of positivism, but to the imposition of a veritable psychosis through its denial of the reality of editorial judgment. Bédier's wager is that the lapses, parapraxes, and judgments committed by the scribe are more interesting than those of the editor because they are closer in time to the original work. In such a perspective, the original itself becomes a function of the unconscious of its scribes. But editors using this method still must correct faults of grammar and spelling; and whatever amount of faith one may put in the medieval scribes and the documents they created, the underlying question of intentionality and interpretation affect the scribe as much as they affect the modern author or editor.[81] By prohibiting the editor from giving in to the "obscure drives" that haunted his subconscious, Bédier preserved a façade of objectivity but left no real criteria for determining which manuscript was the "best" or under what circumstances it had to be emended.

The effect of the single-manuscript method, rigorously applied, was to save the scribal text by killing the authorial work it transcribed. In the case of troubadour lyric, however, none of the manuscripts offers an even minimally satisfactory text for each and all of the songs of a given poet, if the poet has more than a few songs and if those songs are transmitted by more than a few manuscripts. Thus Bédier's impeachment of composite texts deprived the lyric editor of the logic that drove the classification of variants, while still requiring the emendation of an obviously flawed text. The result was to leave the editor to choose a base manuscript and correct it only when the meter, sense, or grammar was faulty. But this was, in fact, what many editors, from Raynouard to Jeanroy, had always done. Of the lyric anthologies, two in particular—A and C—had stood out in the judgment of many editors as the "best" manuscripts because of their size and the tendency of their scribes to correct "mistakes" and homogenize the language of the poems.[82]

István Frank's 1855 article "De l'art d'éditer les textes lyriques," which acknowledged the importance of Bédier's critique, represented less a new departure than the recognition of an established state of affairs from this point of view. But the real importance of Frank's article—and in this Bédier was instrumental—was to draw attention to editorial technique as a special problem as regards lyric texts. It was special in the case of the lyric for the very reasons already put forth by Bartsch, Gröber, and Canello: the variation due to oral transmission, to multiple divergent sources, and to contamination. The Lachmannian method, he wrote, "should be used with moderation and with extreme caution"; but the scrupulous editor must still use its principles in classifying variants.[83] Most important, Frank pointed to the limits of the Lachmannian method; there would be cases where it would not yield secure results, and in such cases the editor would have to resort to publishing only one branch of the tradition (136–37).

In Italy, however, Lachmannian criticism had been raised to a new level of sophistication through the work of Giorgio Pasquali, especially as regards the previously fatal problem of contamination. Already in the 1950s, Aurelio Roncaglia demonstrated the value of a rigorous application of the Lachmannian technique to lyric poetry in his editions of individual songs of Marcabru,[84] which stood in stark contrast to the posthumous 1909 edition of Dejeanne.[85] The most spectacular defense and illustration of Lachmannian edition, however, came in D'Arco Silvio Avalle's 1960 edition of Peire Vidal, followed in 1961 by his manual *La letteratura medievale in lingua d'oc nella sua tradizione manoscritta*, which integrated the findings of the edition within the broader context of manuscript traditions and textual criticism.[86]

Occitan lyric, Avalle asserted against Frank, is clearly a case where Lachmannian methods should apply (*P*, vii). The base-manuscript technique facilitates the multiplication of editions, but "has contributed to diminish interest in more general studies of the type, for example, of Gröber . . . , with grave damage for the advancement of our knowledge in this particular field" (*L*, 110–11). Following Gröber's argument that troubadour lyric proceeded from a written tradition, Avalle launched a counterattack against both the Bédieristes and the partisans of oral transmission. These editors, he claimed, either expected the Lachmannian method to do more than it could or compromised it in some way. The study of the relations between texts in a given manuscript tradition is an arduous task; the temptation to hypothesize oral transmission, he charged, is inversely proportionate to the patience of the researcher (*L*, 110–11; 57). Other mistakes can occur. Thus, in the *Lai de l'ombre*, Bédier had indiscriminately mixed scribal innovations and significant errors. Scribal innovations are significant but unreliable; only those significant errors that can be clearly distinguished from a genuine reading are to be used in constructing a stemma. In spite of this, Bédier has been correct to conclude that the Lachmannian method could not tell him which stemma of the *Lai de l'ombre* was authentic; he had reached the limit of the method, but this was not reason to reject it (*L*, 167–70). His attack did not compromise the logic of the Lachmannian system (*P*, lxi, n. 1).

Avalle's strategy in the edition was to move beyond the song-by-song process imposed by relying uniquely on internal criteria (the classification of textual variants), through the additional recourse to external criteria (the order of songs in the different manuscripts), applied much as Gröber had done in 1877. The presupposition was similar to Gröber's: given multiple channels of transmission, it is possible that more than one text was conveyed at a time, and thus the individual stemmas and single problems may shed light if considered together. In an oracular introduction, he put forth the hypothesis that Peire Vidal's corpus had been transmitted in four stages, through three different "traditions," and drew up a series of composite stemmas that led from an incomplete original, arranged by the poet himself in

1201–2, to the extant manuscripts. These were stemmas unlike any-thing Provençalistes had ever seen before: manuscripts appeared in more than one place; contamination was rampant; there were tradi-tions, families, subgroups, collectors, and virtually an entire Greek alphabet of hypothetical intermediaries.

The demonstration was so magisterial that reviewers felt com-pelled to insist on the subjectivity of the entire edifice and to wonder if the results "justify the time spent on it."[87] But Avalle's "unbelievably complicated structure"[88] served to draw attention to the fact that contamination, the despair of Canello in his edition of Arnaut Daniel, was produced as a matter of course by the normal operation of scriptoria. The transmission of troubadour poetry occurred through the collation of exemplars; certain manuscripts bore variants in their margins, and were constantly compared and corrected against other manuscripts that passed through the same scriptoria (L, 57–64). None of these variant manuscripts have survived, but some manuscripts, such as D, lend support to this theory in their handling of variants (see the examples in P, xlvii–xlix, lxxxv–lxxxvi, xcv–xcvi).

The effect of Avalle's reaction against Bédier is, I believe, a positive one for Provençal studies in that it encouraged a new attention to the medieval texts themselves. As Stephen Nichols has observed, "Bédier's insistence on a single manuscript had the effect of putting that manu-script into a relationship with its printed edition analogous to that of a unique manuscript of a modern printed book."[89] Avalle's research into contamination, on the other hand, is an attempt to understand medieval textuality within the historical conditions of its production, beginning with an acceptance of the contingencies of manuscript transmission. Avalle's list of manuscripts was not just an inventory, but a sort of report card on their scribes showing their different competencies, agendas, and resources. Thus ms. C chose among the variants in its source those that "rendered the text immediately intelli-gible" and aimed for an "ideal semantic mean" (P, xcv); E revealed "a notable latitude of philological interests" (xcviii); Q was made by a scribe who showed uncertainty in reproducing the signs of his model (cxi); the scribe of R was "ever ready to intervene without rhyme or reason wherever he didn't understand and absolutely refractory to respect for the letter" (cxii). Such judgments reveal the absurdity of trying to choose which manuscript offers the "best" text of the works it transmits; the work can emerge only from the comparison of how each scribe made sense of the model he or she copied.

This is also, of course, where the edition comes to betray the medieval conditions of textuality: in choosing the one composite configuration shown to represent the original. In this Avalle's edition is a virtuosic display of method, a wager that a strict Lachmannianism can identify the authentic text within a tradition assumed at the outset to be entirely written. Avalle's judgment that the temptation to posit an oral tradition is inversely proportionate to the researcher's patience may well be true; but it also makes devotion to a strictly written tradition a tenet of Lachmannian faith. Avalle in fact dismisses the "problem of the oral tradition" with a reference to the "most convincing" thesis of Gröber (*L*, 47). Yet it is precisely here that the most productive exchange between text editors and literary critics might take place. In particular, the consideration of medieval textuality from the point of view of communication and reception, in the works of Paul Zumthor and Brian Stock among others, points the way to renewing the study of the social function of literature without recourse to the Romantic myth of the popular voice.[90] The medieval history of troubadour song is the road by which a poetry of "pure voice," unquestionably designed for oral performance, paradoxically came to constitute the prime example of a written canon of literary classics, as is evident already in Dante's *De vulgari eloquentia*.[91] In the study of such a phenomenon, the positivist divorce between questions of theory and the establishment of historical fact can lead only to a misunderstanding of the medieval text itself.

There are signs that the barriers between theoretical inquiry and editorial practice have begun to break down in recent years. Rupert Pickens's edition of Jaufré Rudel and Maurizio Perugi's edition of Arnaut Daniel both begin from Lachmannian principles and attempt to push beyond the limits of a strict Lachmannian faith, albeit in very different ways. Pickens found himself in precisely the same position as Bédier: his stemmas of Jaufré Rudel forced him to choose between two equally valid hypotheses with no means of determining which might be authentic. But instead of selecting one "best" manuscript, he chose to print all the extant versions because, given the impossibility of determining the author's intentions, "each manifestation of a song must be considered to be, in its own right, as valid a whole complete poem as any other versions."[92] Pickens's hypothesis that the different versions may be "second or third 'editions'" (28) prepared by the author are, of course, only conjectural; but his observation that "the evidence cannot deny Jaufré's having 'authorized' two or even three different versions" (24) opens room for maneuver at the limits of the Lachmannian method.

Perugi's approach is on the whole far more speculative and, at the same time, more removed from the manuscripts themselves. Where Pickens is fascinated with the production of variant poems in the gap between poet and manuscript, Perugi is fascinated with the diachronic evolution of language in the same gap. The diversity of regional dialects and their evolution over time meant that the scribe constantly engaged in an active process of translation to make the text readable for a wide public. In doing so, the scribe faced a relatively limited range of choices that ought to be susceptible to detection through the techniques of structural linguistics. Perugi attempts to determine the rules that govern this recodification through an investigation of hiatus and diffraction in a large sample of published editions of troubadour lyric. For Perugi, "the image of the manuscript tradition proves to be, with respect to Lachmannianism, completely overturned: since not error but structure ought to inform the concept of critical edition."[93] His use of printed editions rather than manuscripts is questionable, however, in such exacting linguistic research, as is his assumption that "the whole arc of troubadour production [is] inscribed inside a well-defined linguistic synchrony" (xxxii). But Perugi's approach is an imaginative attempt to couple original linguistic research with the practical demands of procuring a text.

If an edition represents "a theoretical structure, a complex hypothesis designed to account for a body of phenomena in the light of knowledge about the circumstances which generated them,"[94] then one can only hope that editions such as those of Avalle, Pickens, and Perugi become the rule rather than the exception. The preparation of editions of troubadour poetry has accelerated more since 1960 than at any previous time, especially in the United States, aided by the relative ease of travel and the availability of microfilms of the manuscripts. Yet the proliferation of new editions hides the fact that the teaching of editorial technologies and linguistic knowledge, on which they are predicated, is suffering a serious decline in major American universities. The availability of ancient and medieval texts in printed editions and translation may be enough to guarantee them a place in the curriculum, but cannot by themselves allow us to understand the cultures that produced them. If the history traced in this chapter shows anything, it is that the broad theoretical questions raised by medieval textuality cannot be solved by purely theoretical or purely positivistic research alone.

NOTES

1. J. Bauquier, "Les provençalistes au XVIIIe siècle," *Revue des langues romanes* 17 (1880): 65–83, 179–219; 18 (1880): 179–82; Santorre Debenedetti, *Gli studi provenzali in Italia nel Cinquecento* (Turin: Loescher, 1911); Émile Ripert, *La renaissance provençale (1800–1860)* (Paris: Champion, 1918); Alfred Jeanroy, "Les études provençales du XVIe siècle à nos jours," *La poésie lyrique des troubadours* (Toulouse: E. Privat, 1934), 1:1–44; Käte Axhausen, *Die Theorien über den Ursprung der provenzalischen Lyrik,* Inaugural-Dissertation, Philipps-Universität zu Marburg (Düsseldorf: Dissertations-Verlag G. H. Nolte, 1937); Nathan Edelman, *Attitudes of Seventeenth-Century France toward the Middle Ages* (New York: King's Crown Press, 1946); Lionel Gossman, *Medievalism and the Ideologies of the Enlightenment: The World and Work of La Curne de Sainte-Palaye* (Baltimore: Johns Hopkins University Press, 1968); Hans Robert Jauss, "Literary History as a Challenge to Literary Theory," in Toward an Aesthetic of Reception, trans. Timothy Bahti, Theory and History of Literature 2 (Minneapolis: University of Minnesota Press, 1982), 3–45; Hans Ulrich Gumbrecht, "'Un souffle d'Allemagne ayant passé': Friedrich Diez, Gaston Paris and the Genesis of National Philologies," *Romance Philology* 40 (1986): 1–37; Bernard Cerquiglini, *Éloge de la variante: Histoire critique de la philologie* (Paris: Éditions du Seuil, 1989). I am also indebted to Prof. Margaret Switten for her comments on an earlier version of this chapter.

2. See Edelman, 338–61, and Debendetti.

3. Jean Baptiste de La Curne de Sainte-Palaye, and Claude Millot, *Histoire littéraire des troubadours* (Paris: Chez Durand neveu, 1774), 3 vols.

4. Bauquier, 201.

5. Gossman, 261.

6. Because the sources I discuss mostly do not differentiate between the different southern dialects (Languedocian, Limousin, Rhodanian, and so on), I have kept the term "Provençal" in the wide sense throughout to avoid confusion.

7. François-Juste-Marie Raynouard, *Choix des poésies originales des troubadours* (Paris: F. Didot, 1816–21). vol. 2 (1817): ii.

8. Michel Foucault, *Les mots et les choses: Une archéologie des sciences humaines* (Paris: Gallimard, 1966), esp. 292–313. Raynouard is mentioned on pp. 298 and 303.

9. A. W. de Schlegel, *Observations sur la langue et la littérature provençales* (Paris: À la librairie Grecque-latine-allemande, 1818), 8–9.

10. See Hans Robert Jauss, "Fr. Schlegels und Fr. Schillers Replik auf die 'Querelle des Anciens et des Modernes,'" in *Europäische Aufklärung: Her-*

bert Dieckmann zum 60. Geburtstag, ed. Hugo Friedrich and Fritz Schalk (Munich: W. Fink, 1967), 117–40, esp. 122.

11. Schlegel, 18.

12. Gumbrecht, 20–28. Gumbrecht (14) sees Raynouard as the only exception in France to this hypothesis, and attributes it to Raynouard's desire to preserve Provençal identity within French society.

13. See Gumbrecht, 18–19.

14. François-Juste-Marie Raynouard, review of *Observations sur la langue et la littérature provençales,* by A. W. de Schlegel, in *Journal des savants* (October 1818): 590.

15. Jeanroy, 1:17, 24.

16. Letter of April, 18 1826, in A. Tobler, "Briefe von Friedrich Diez an Jakob Grimm," *Zeitschrift für romanische Philologie* 7 (1883): 486.

17. Friedrich Christian Diez, *Die Poesie der Troubadours. Nach gedruckten und handschriftlichen Werken derselben dargestellt,* 2. vermehrte Auflage von Karl Bartsch (Leipzig: 1883; rpt. Hildesheim: Georg Olms, 1966), preface to the first edition of 1826, x. Translated by Gumbrecht, 19.

18. See Ripert, 50–56.

19. François-Juste-Marie Raynouard, review of *Die Poesie der Troubadours,* by Friedrich Diez, in *Journal des savants* (June 1828): 349.

20. Diez, x.

21. Raynouard, review of *Die Poesie der Troubadours,* 350–51.

22. Raynouard refers to ms. C (BN Fr. 856), which he found to be "the purest and most classical" in style. The manuscript was made by a scribe who in fact seems to have reworked poems that did not make sense to him: see François Zufferey, *Recherches linguistiques sur les chansonniers provençaux,* Publications romanes et françaises 176 (Geneva: Droz, 1987), 152.

23. On this see Lee Patterson, "The Logic of Textual Criticism and the Way of Genius," in Jerome J. McGann, ed., *Textual Criticism and Literary Interpretation* (Chicago: University of Chicago Press, 1985), 55–91.

24. On Schlegel's theory of the epic, see Mary Thorp, *The Study of the Nibelungenlied. Being the History of the Study of the Epic and Legend from 1755 to 1937,* Oxford Studies in Modern Languages and Literatures (Oxford, Clarendon Press, 1940), esp. 13–20.

25. On this, see Jeanroy, 1:25–26; Henri Alexandre Wallon, "Notice sur la vie et les ouvrages de M. Paulin Paris," *Académie des Inscriptions et des Belles-Lettres. Mémoires de l'Institut National de France* 33.1 (1888): 285–86; Joseph Bédier, *Les légendes épiques: Recherches sur la formation des chansons de geste,* 3d ed. (Paris: Librairie Ancienne Édouard Champion, 1929), 3:200–230.

26. Jean Boutière, ed., *Correspondance de Frédéric Mistral avec Paul Meyer et Gaston Paris,* with an introduction by Hedwige Boutière, Publications de la Sorbonne, Documents 28 (Paris: Didier, 1978), introduction, 8.

27. See Ripert, 65.

28. The collections of Keller (*Romvart,* 1844), Mahn (*Werke der Troubadours,* 1846–53, and *Gedichte der Troubadours,* 1856–73), Delius (*Ungedruckte provenzalische Lieder,* 1853), and Heyse (*Romanische Inedita,* 1856).

29. The anthologies of Brinckmeier (*Blumenlese,* 1849) and Bartsch (*Provenzalisches Lesebuch,* 1855, and *Denkmäler der provenzalischen Literatur,* 1856).

30. Editions of William IX (Keller, 1848), Guilhem de Berguedan (Keller, 1849), and Peire Vidal (Bartsch, 1857).

31. The works of Adrian (*Grundzüge zu einer provenzalischen Grammatik,* 1825) and Diez (*Grammatik der romanischen Sprachen,* 1836–44, and *Etymologisches Wörterbuch der romanischen Sprachen,* 1853).

32. Karl Bartsch, *Peire Vidal's Lieder* (Berlin: F. Dümmler, 1857), foreword, first unnumbered page.

33. Sebastiano Timpanaro, *Die Entstehung der Lachmannschen Methode,* 2., erweiterte und überarbeitete Auflage, German translation by Dieter Irmer (Hamburg: Helmut Buske Verlag, 1971), esp. chap. 7.

34. My discussion of the *Nibelungenlied* relies heavily on Patterson, esp. 82–85, and Thorp.

35. Thorp, 49–50.

36. D'Arco Silvio Avalle, ed., *Peire Vidal Poesie. Edizione critica e commento,* Documenti di filologia 4 (Milan: Riccardo Ricciardi, 1960), cxx.

37. Bartsch, *Peire Vidal's Lieder,* foreword, second and third unnumbered pages.

38. Foreword, fifth unnumbered page.

39. See Gaston Paris, "La Philologie romane en allemagne," *Bibliothèque de l'École des Chartes* 25 (1864): 444, and *Le haut enseignement historique et philologique en France* (Paris: H. Welter, 1894), 20; Franz Pfeiffer and Karl Bartsch, *Briefwechsel,* ed. Hans Joachim Koppitz (Cologne: Green, 1969), 256–68.

40. Paris, "Philologie romane," 439.

41. Gaston Paris seems to have begun his teaching career giving independent *cours libres* in 1865: see H. A. Todd, "Gaston Paris: Romance Philologist and Member of the French Academy," *PMLA* 12 (1897): 352.

42. "Philologie romane," 442.

43. Letter of August, 31 1866, in Mario Roques, ed., "Correspondance de Karl Bartsch et Gaston Paris de 1865 à 1885. Première partie: 1865–

1867," *Mediaeval Studies in Memory of Gertrude Schoepperle Loomis* (New York: Columbia University Press, 1927; Geneva: Slatkine, 1974), 427–28.

44. Letter of February, 19 1867, Roques, 433.

45. It was Meyer who was allowed to offer a *cours libre* at the École des Chartes, and he who replaced Guessard in 1869, gaining full title to the chair in 1879. See Boutière, 8, and also Antoine Thomas and Charles-Victor Langlois, "Notice sur Paul Meyer," *Histoire littéraire de la France,* vol. 35 (Paris: Imprimerie nationale, 1921), xxii.

46. "À nos lecteurs," *Revue critique d'histoire et de littérature 5* (January 1867): 1–3.

47. Pre-publication prospectus for *Romania,* ed. Paul Meyer and Gaston Paris (Paris: A. Franck, 1871), 5.

48. Paris, *Haut enseignement,* 12.

49. Ibid., 35.

50. Grützmacher published tables of contents for mss. AF^aF^bGHLO-$PQUVabceg^1g^2$, and rho. In 1867 the Vienna kaiserlichen Akademie der Wissenschaften published an index to D in its *Sitzungsberichte.* In 1868 the long-delayed *Catalogue des manuscrits français* of the Paris Bibliothèque Nationale finally went into publication, furnishing the complete indexes to BCEIYZ. In 1869–70 the Bibliothèque de l'École des Chartes printed Paul Meyer's *Les derniers troubadours de Provence,* which gave indexes to Rf, and the contents of f.

51. The index to ms. F was published in vol. 11 (1870) of *Jahrbuch für romanische und englische Literatur,* founded 1858; J and N in vols. 1 (1872) and 2 (1875) of *Rivista di filologia romanza;* S^g and N^2 in vols. 10 (1876) and 19 (1881) of *Revue des langues romanes,* founded 1869; K^p in vol. 1 (1877) of *Zeitschrift für romanische Philologie.*

52. Grützmacher's indexes were supplemented with transcriptions of unpublished poems. Two complete manuscripts, UV, were published immediately after his "Reports" in vols. 35–36 (1864) of *Archiv für das Studium der neueren Sprachen und Literaturen,* which later published P, 49–50 (1872–73), and N^2, 101–2 (1898–99). Edmund Stengel published F as *Die provenzalische Blumenlese der Chigiana* (Marburg: N. G. Elwert, 1878); O appeared in *Atti della R. Accademia dei Lincei* (1886); the series *Studi di filologia romanza* published AB, in vol. 3 (1891); H, 5 (1891); c, 7 (1899); J, 9 (1903); and L, 16 (1921); W appeared in *Romania* 22 (1893); a in *Revue des langues romanes* 41–45 (1902); Q and G in *Gesellschaft für romanische Literatur* 8 (1905) and 28 (1912); b in *Annales de Midi* 21 (1909); a (again!) and a^1 in *Collectanea friburgensia,* 20–21 (1911); and S in *Elliott Monographs in the Romance Languages and Literatures* 21 (1927). One facsimile—ms. X—was published by the Société des Anciens Textes Français (1892).

53. Paul Meyer, review of *Grundriß zur Geschichte der provenzalischen Literatur*, by Karl Bartsch, in *Romania* 1 (1872): 379–87.

54. Clearly a barbed compliment, for Meyer went on to lambast Bartsch for assuming the existence of a lost Provençal epic poem, a "hypothesis [that] could have been left aside in a work whose goal is to compile and classify the facts definitively secured by scientific knowledge," 382. This after Meyer complained that Bartsch did not have "a complete knowledge of the printed literature on his subject," 381!

55. Paul Meyer, "Troisième rapport sur une mission littéraire en Angle-terre et en Écosse," *Archives des missions scientifiques et littéraires. Choix de rapports et instructions* publiés sous les auspices du Ministère de l'Instruction Publique, 2d ser., 5 (Paris: Imprimerie Nationale, 1868), 165–66. Meyer refers to these pages in taking up the question in his *Derniers troubadours*, 140, and quotes them in his notice on Gustav Gröber's *Die Liedersamm-lungen der Troubadours*, *Romania* 6 (1877): 476.

56. Paul Meyer, review of *Guilhem Figueira, ein provenzalischer Trou-badour*, by Emil Levy, and *Leben und Werke des trobadors Ponz de Capduoill*, by Max von Napolski, in *Romania* 10 (1881): 268; Paul Meyer, "Explication de la pièce de Peire Vidal *Drogoman seiner s'agues bon des-trier*," *Romania* 2 (1873): 423–36.

57. Thomas and Langlois, xxii, xxvii.

58. Boutière, 115.

59. Ibid., 172.

60. Gustav Gröber, *Die Liedersammlungen der Troubadours*, in *Ro-manische Studien* 2 (1875–77): 337–670.

61. U. A. Canello, *La vita e le opere del trovatore Arnaldo Daniello, edizione critica corredata delle varianti di tutti i manoscritti* (Halle: Max Niemeyer, 1883), 91.

62. Karl Bartsch, Review of *La vita e le opere del trovatore Arnaldo Daniello*, by U. A. Canello, in *Zeitschrift für romanische Philologie*, 7 (1883): 582.

63. Gröber, 343: "In this case [if the written text was transcribed from memory] the attempt to procure an authentic text of the songs of the troubadours would come up against insuperable difficulties."

64. Paulin Paris, quoted in Wallon, 286.

65. Meyer, review of *Grundriß*, 379.

66. Paul Meyer, "Recherches sur l'épopée française," *Bibliothèque de l'École des Chartes* 28 (1867): 28–63, 304–42; quotation, 333.

67. This is the conclusion drawn by J. Bédier in examining the case of the epic: Bédier, *Légendes épiques*, 3:274. Bédier does not refer to lyric manuscripts.

68. Axhausen, 30–31.

69. Paris, *Haut enseignement,* 17, 42.

70. Editions of Jaufré Rudel (Stimming, 1873), Bertran de Born (Stimming, 1879), Ponz de Capduoill (Napolski, 1879), Guilhem Figueira (Levy, 1880), Peire Rogier (Appel, 1882), Bertolome Zorzi (Levy, 1883), and Arnaut Daniel (Canello, 1883).

71. Paul Meyer, review of *Guilhem Figueira,* 261.

72. *Romanische Bibliothek* published editions of Bertran de Born (Stimming, 1892), Sordel (De Lollis, 1896), and Folquet de Romans (Zenker, 1896); *Gesellschaft für romanische Literatur* published an edition of Rambertino Buvalelli (Bertoni, 1908), as well as the transcriptions of mss. Q and G.

73. *Ausgaben und Abhandlungen aus dem Gebiete der romanischen Philologie* published an edition of Monge de Montaudon (Klein, 1885), and Selbach's study of the debate genres (1886).

74. *Bibliothèque méridionale* published editions of Guilhem de Montanhagol (Coulet, 1898), Bertran d'Alamanon (Salverda de Grave, 1902), Elias de Barjols (Stronski, 1906), Marcabru (Dejeanne, 1909), Uc de Saint Circ (Jeanroy and Salverda de Grave, 1913), to name a few.

75. *Studi di filologia romanza* published a collection of *inedita* (Bertoni, 1901), as well as ms. transcriptions.

76. Avalle, *Peire Vidal Poesie,* cxxvii.

77. Berenguier de Palazol, 1908; Uc de Saint Circ, with J.-J. Salverda da Grave, 1913; Bertran Carbonel, 1913; William IX, 1913; Jaufré Rudel, 1916; Pujol, 1921; Cercamon, 1922; *Jongleurs et troubadours gascons,* 1923; "'Coblas' provençales relatives à la croisade aragonaise de 1285," 1926.

78. Alfred Jeanroy and J.-J. Salverda de Grave, *Poésies de Uc de Saint-Circ,* Bibliothèque méridionale 15 (Toulouse: Privat, 1913), vii; Alfred Jeanroy, *Les chansons de Jaufré Rudel,* 2d ed., Classiques français du moyen âge 15 (Paris: Champion, 1924), xiii–xiv.

79. Alfred Pillet and Henry Carstens, *Bibliographie der Troubadours,* Schriften der Königsberger gelehrten Gesellschaft, Sonderreihe 3 (Halle: 1933); Jeanroy, *Poésie lyrique.*

80. Joseph Bédier, "La tradition manuscrite du *Lai de l'ombre,*" *Romania* 54 (1928): 161–96, 321–56. The article is a revised and extended version of the preface to the 1913 edition.

81. Bédier himself, arguing against the possibility of an oral tradition for the chanson de geste, argued that one should not think that "there lived in France men who were different from those we can observe with our own eyes," *Légendes poétiques,* 3:271. See also David F. Hult, "Reading It Right: The Ideology of Text Editing," *Romanic Review* 79 (1988): 74–88.

82. See Zufferey, 35, 152.

83. István Frank, "The Art of Editing Lyric Texts," trans. Arnold Miller, in *Medieval Manuscripts and Textual Criticism,* ed. Christopher Kleinhenz, University of North Carolina Studies in the Romance Languages and Literatures, Texts, Textual Studies and Translations 4 (Chapel Hill: University of North Carolina Department of Romance Languages, 1976), 135.

84. See, for instance, Aurelio Roncaglia, "Marcabruno *Lo vers comens quan vei del fau* [BdT 293, 33]," *Cultura neolatina* 11 (1951): 25–48; and "Il 'gap' di Marcabruno," *Studi medievali* 17 n.s. (1951): 46–70.

85. J.-M.-L. Dejeanne, *Poésies complètes du troubadour Marcabru,* Bibliothèque méridionale 12 (Toulouse: Privat, 1909).

86. Avalle, *Peire Vidal Poesie,* cited in text as *P;* D'Arco Silvio Avalle, *La letteratura medievale in lingua d'oc nella sua tradizione manoscritta. Problemi di critica testuale* (Turin: Giulio Einaudi, 1961), cited in text as *L.*

87. Frank M. Chambers, review of *Peire Vidal, Poesie,* by D'Arco Silvio Avalle, in *Romance Philology* 15 (1962): 474. Werner Ziltener observed that Avalle's stemma for the *vida* did not match that of Favati's Lachmannian edition of the biographies (Guido Favati, ed., *Le biografie trovadoriche, testi provenzali dei secc. XIII e XIV. Edizione critica,* Biblioteca degli *Studi mediolatini e volgari* 3 [Bologna: Libreria Antiquaria Palmaverde, 1961]), which appeared at the same time, and concluded that "a certain proportion inevitably stands on subjectivity." Review of *Peire Vidal, Poesie,* by D'Arco Silvio Avalle, in *Zeitschrift für romanische Philologie* 79 (1963): 272.

88. Chambers, 473.

89. Stephen G. Nichols, "Introduction: Philology in a Manuscript Culture," *Speculum* 65 (1990): 6.

90. See Paul Zumthor, *La lettre et la voix: De la "littérature" médiévale* (Paris: Éditions du Seuil, 1987), and Brian Stock, *The Implications of Literacy: Written Language and Models of Interpretation in the Eleventh and Twelfth Centuries* (Princeton: Princeton University Press, 1983).

91. Zumthor, 316, 176.

92. Rupert T. Pickens, ed., *The Songs of Jaufré Rudel,* Studies and Texts 41 (Toronto: Pontifical Institute of Medieval Studies, 1978), 39.

93. Maurizio Perugi, ed., *Le Canzoni di Arnaut Daniel: Edizione critica,* Documenti di filologia 22 (Milan: Riccardo Ricciardi, 1978), xvii.

94. George Kane and E. Talbot Donaldson, eds., William Langland, *Piers Plowman* (London: Athlone Press, 1975), cited in Patterson, 68.

THREE

The Science of Imposture and the Professionalization of Medieval Occitan Literary Studies

Laura Kendrick

IF A TWELFTH-CENTURY TROUBADOUR could be resuscitated and asked to criticize what had been written about him or attributed to him by subsequent scholars, he would be baffled by our distinctions between authentic and pseudo-medieval texts, between scholarly editions and amateur inventions, between history and fiction. "Marcabru," for example, supposing we were "he," could hardly help but be surprised to learn from Jean de Nostredame's late sixteenth-century *Vies des plus célèbres et anciens poètes provençaux* that he was a late fourteenth-century "nobleman from Poitou [who] went to live in Provence with his mother, who was the boldest courtesan there had been for a long while in Provence, . . . the most famous poetess in our Provençal language, [who] held an open Court of Love in Avignon, where all the poets . . . came to hear the answers to questions and love debates proposed there."[1] The "real Marcabru" would surely judge that Nostredame's was an impostor, but it hardly seems likely that he would find it any easier to recognize himself in the thirteenth-century biography or *vida* accounts (lives concocted mainly out of imaginative readings of certain lyrics)[2] that Nostredame imaginatively (or, fraudulently, to use the accusatory terms of late-nineteenth-century scholars) transformed.

That the "real Marcabru" would invalidate both Nostredame's *Vies* and the *vidas* comforts us in our opinion of our own rectitude, but how can we possibly believe that "he" would not be just as surprised to learn what we professional medievalists have attributed to him? Would he recognize anything as "his own" in the various poetic accretions and adaptations that have been ascribed to him as an individual, first by later medieval manuscript compilers, then, with some adjustment, by us? Would "he" even recognize himself in the sayings ascribed in some poems to Marcabru (internal allusions that usually prompted ascription of whole poems to him)? What could the "real Marcabru"—or the person at the beginning of the legend, assuming there was one—possibly think of the critical edition of his collected works in their modern printed form, except that it is a "supposed" work, Dejeanne posing as Marcabru?[3] From "Marcabru's" point of view, the history of Occitan (or Provençal or Romance)[4] literary studies can hardly be perceived as anything but a series of pseudo-medieval texts, each new imposture demasking a previous one, delegitimating previous claims in order to legitimate itself, a series of impositions passed off, with increasing seriousness and professionalism, as authentic and "original." (My own pretence of "our" perceiving the history of medieval Occitan studies from Marcabru's perspective is only the latest in the series of claims to originary insight serving to displace previous "impostors.")

Have I not stated the obvious? The products of medieval scholarship—even the most meticulous edition of a poem—are inevitably pseudo-medieval texts because they are, literally, *not* medieval texts. Yet what any novice can see is precisely what the thoroughly professional medievalist—or Occitan literary scholar—cannot see or admit seeing. The basic rule for becoming a professional medievalist has been that we must believe ourselves to be returning to, restoring and founding our criticism and literary history upon, authentic medieval texts that are as close as possible to authorial originals. Our erudition is fundamentally falsifying, our science a discipline of imposture—and this from the beginning, but increasingly so, and with less and less tolerance for such self-critical analysis, from the turn of the nineteenth century on. This chapter focuses on that turning, and the reasons for it, from "amateur" or "antiquarian" to "scientific" or "professional" medievalism in the realm of Occitan studies, although this restriction of the field is itself a late product of the process of professionalization, for the late eighteenth- and early nineteenth-century actors in this history did not so restrict themselves.

The crucial impetus for the turning serious of medieval studies in France was not so much, as in England, unwelcome changes brought on by industrialization (although these changes, occurring later in France, would eventually play a role in sustaining interest in the medieval there), but rather a dramatic political event: the Revolution of 1789, which provoked a long-running crisis of legitimacy and questioning of how legitimacy should be defined, and the Reign of Terror of the early 1790s, which destroyed so many legal instruments and symbolic reminders of the "feudal" past and dispossessed so many emigrant nobles.[5] Many of these aristocrats fled to England in the 1790s, where Macpherson, Percy, and Chatterton had aroused scholarly and public controversy with their pseudo-medieval verse, and to Germany, where classicists such as F. A. Wolf were insisting on a more careful, "genealogical" consideration of manuscript tradition in order to restore the truth of the original text. Emigrant French noblemen such as Charles Vanderbourg, "editor" of the supposedly fifteenth-century *Poésies de Clotilde de Surville* (1803), immediately applied this new science to authenticate pseudo-medieval texts of their own invention,[6] texts that attempted, at least figuratively, to supply the lack of family documents destroyed and to restore the legitimacy of their discoverer-inventors in various ways. During the Revolutionary period, there was a certain audience eager, not only for a literature with an implicitly counter-Revolutionary content, but also for a new science with an implicitly counter-Revolutionary intention, a science aimed at restoring (or reinventing) the past, even to the point of publishing an "original" text in antiquated language, which now had a positive political value and provoked nostalgia (instead of disgust or condescending amusement for its lack of refinement). In order to appreciate more fully the novelty of this sudden politicizing and turning "serious" of medieval literary scholarship, this new mingling of science and imposture, we need to examine the attitudes of scholars toward medieval texts prior to the nineteenth century.

Jean de Nostredame's *Vies des plus célèbres et anciens poètes provençaux* (1575) is the obvious place to begin, for it was through Nostredame that the troubadours entered modern literary history "odiously disfigured"—in the judgment of the professional medievalists of the second half of the nineteenth century who, by so vehemently prosecuting Nostredame and exposing his "dishonest" scholarship of three centuries back, prosecuted in effigy their own immediate scholarly predecessors, the generation that disappeared around 1850, the generation that Alfred Jeanroy characterized as largely made up of "amateurs or entrepreneurs of premature popularization" (as compared to the generation of "specialists" who followed them and "methodically organized the scientific work").[7] Indeed, Nostredame's attitude toward manuscript sources seems to be nearly the opposite of that of later, professional scholars. Although he had access to medieval manuscripts containing *vidas* and troubadour verse and translated bits of these into French, Nostredame also invented medieval authorities (whose names were anagrams of his friends' names), made up many colorful incidents in the lives of the troubadours, attributed invented titles of didactic treatises and other works to them, passed off his own verses as troubadour compositions, deliberately changed the names of troubadours to locate them in Provence, and flattered local Provençal families by depicting their current members as friends or patrons of troubadours.

Nostredame's French *Vies,* dedicated to the queen of France, was a witty way for a provincial lawyer to show his Provençal patriotism and boast the former glories of the language (after François I, in 1539, had limited the written language of the courts throughout the kingdom to French).[8] Nostredame's proclaimed purpose was to make the troubadours more widely known by publishing their lives from late medieval manuscript sources, which he meticulously listed at the very beginning of his narrative. The novelty here is not that he professed to be translating a text in a language rendered illegible by age and disuse (for that is a traditional claim in the medieval romance genre, where it sanctions inventive improvements of many sorts rather than guaranteeing against change). What is new is that Nostredame has imitated the forms of sixteenth-century Italian humanist scholarship to the extent of listing his source manuscripts (albeit largely invented).[9] Nostredame has gone beyond the conventional allusion to a prior source and dressed his fictions up as a composite based upon careful comparative analysis of late medieval manuscripts lost, as he claimed, in the "troubles of 1562." This contemporary scholarly dress was not intended to mean, however, that Nostredame would forgo "romancing" his "sources," with all the revision and invention and modernizing anachronism that conventionally entailed—right down to writing his contemporaries into the text. Nostredame's *Vies* is a patriotic *roman* intended to intrigue and amuse, but hardly to dupe for any length of time his Provençal friends and aristocratic contemporaries, who found themselves therein rubbing elbows with troubadours.

The *Vies* has some of the qualities of an insider's joke: only a foreigner to Provençal society or a dunce would take it for truthful history in 1575, but a few decades later Provençals themselves, most notably Jean's nephew Caesar, were willing to accept many of the anachronisms of the *Vies* as fact and incorporate them into an official history of Provence, which in turn served as a source for other histories, which were thus "contaminated" by Jean de Nostredame's fictions.[10] Yet why should Jean de Nostredame be held to blame for subsequent misinterpretation of his intentions? If there is any fault, is it not his naive nephew's? Would we blame Umberto Eco for his fraudulent intentions if succeeding generations of readers of *Il nome della rosa* (*The Name of the Rose*) were to take his prefatory claim— that his book is an Italian version of a lost "neo-Gothic French" translation of a lost seventeenth-century Latin edition (by Mabillon, no less) of a lost fourteenth-century Latin chronicle by the German monk Adso of Melk—as proof that Eco's book is intended to be a factual historical account?[11] Yet that is just what nineteenth-century medieval scholars did to Nostredame, beginning in 1874 with Karl Bartsch's investigation of Nostredame's professed literary sources,[12] and continuing with Camille Chabaneau's critical edition and analysis of the *Vies* published by Joseph Anglade, after Chabaneau's death, in 1913. The outraged vehemence of the professional medievalists' prosecution of the dishonest amateur—their insistence that Nostredame intended to dupe by presenting fiction as history and should be punished for it—deserves examination for what it suggests about how the profession disciplined and constructed itself.

For Chabaneau, himself Provençal, Nostredame's duplicity was also an act of treachery against Provençal scholars, for it contaminated their histories and made them look foolish to other, northern and foreign, scholars. Chabaneau's patriotic professionalism motivated him to carry his criminal investigation of Nostredame as far as it could go, ferreting out the lies not only in Nostredame's *Vies* but also in all those later literary and political histories that had incorporated them. Joseph Anglade, Chabaneau's former student, perhaps impatient that he had been burdened with bringing Chabaneau's work before the public, insinuated that Chabaneau's view of what was necessary to extirpate corruption was, albeit a model of scholarly discipline, somewhat obsessive. What Chabaneau intended was a whole series of studies on Nostredame, a "Corpus Nostradamicum" that would include a study of the family of Nostredame, his influence, his correspondence, his friends, and so forth; a critical edition of the text of the 1575 *Vies;* and also, to demonstrate Nostredame's fraudulent methods with incontrovertible material proofs (or, as Chabaneau

put it, "to penetrate into his lie factory" [1:87]), an edition of
Nostredame's first draft of the *Vies* (surviving in manuscript in the
library of Carpentras). On Chabaneau's working copy of Nostredame's first draft, Anglade remarked that Chabaneau had noted "with
extraordinary minuteness . . . the least details" of change, from
different inks to words erased or added. Anglade acknowledged the
exemplary "precision and conscientiousness" of Chabaneau's working methods, but he went on to question whether Nostredame really
merited this "excess of work and this excess of honor" (1:8).

In treating the manuscript draft of the *Vies* as the scene of the
crime of corrupting history and trying to discover every clue as to how
and why Nostredame went about committing this crime, Chabaneau
was pursuing error to its source, just as he wanted to pursue it to its
"last refuge" by exposing histories that had been "spoiled" by incor-
poration of Nostredame's fictions. Blinkered by his own positivistic
fictions of detection, Chabaneau diligently compiled the dossier
against Nostredame, but it was Anglade who argued the case and
called for severe judgment on the impostor, reminding us that, even
though Nostredame's attempt to restore the honor of the vernacular
might incline us to indulgence, we should "refuse this indulgence,
because, in awkwardly trying to pastiche the troubadours, he wanted
to trick his readers" (1:51). What Nostredame did was further fictionalize and modernize medieval *vidas* that were, in his view, already
fictions (both those "sources" he invented and those that earlier
interpreters had invented before him). Chabaneau, Anglade, and
Bartsch all insisted that Nostredame's *Vies* (and the medieval *vidas*)
ought to be history and would not countenance any other possibility,
even though Anglade admitted to being at times "disarmed by such
candid imposture" (as in Nostredame's changing of troubadours'
names in order to place them all in Provence). Such "naive and
infantile procedures" were, in these professional scholars' view, "sufficiently crude to make us aware of his bad faith and at the same time
his foolishness" (1:87). To these professional medievalists, it was
immoral not to respect manuscript sources, to fictionalize (what they
considered to be) fact, and so they tried to "purify" Nostredame's
historical romance into history.

The purified and rehabilitated Nostredame would amount to very
little, those fragments "accurately" translated from his "real" medieval manuscript sources, posited as truth incarnate. What Bartsch and
Chabaneau were working toward through their detection of fictions

was the creation of an expurgated Nostredame that was every bit as much their own invention, every bit as much an imposture as Nostredame's *Vies* was an imposture with respect to the *vidas*. Yet professional Occitan scholars of the late nineteenth century did not allow themselves to see this, that the truth they discovered and restored was really a fiction.[13]

Pre-Revolutionary scholars, on the other hand, even those most famous for advocating a return to manuscript sources, tended to be skeptical about the truth or historical value of those sources, and ignored or modified them blatantly (as did Nostredame) to serve present interests. A scholar as interested in textual criticism as Erasmus, for example, was not above the occasional total imposture; in his edition of Cyprian in 1530, he published as authentically as Cyprian's his own treatise responding to Reformation extremism, *De duplici martyrio*.[14] When Mabillon in 1681 tried to establish palaeographic and diplomatic rules for distinguishing true from false medieval charters, he provoked a skeptical rebuttal from the Jesuit Germon, who claimed that most of those pre-Capetian documents Mabillon published as authentic, and hence as models for determining the authenticity of other documents, were either forgeries ("supposed") or "corrupt copies substituted for originals as age consumed these." Mabillon himself outlined the major reasons for the fabrication of "false" documents (to steal what belonged to others, to replace worn or lost originals), and he argued, not very reassuringly, that if the documents he considered authentic were false, then there were no authentic ones left from early times.[15]

Eighteenth-century French scholars, even those of the Royal Academy of Inscriptions involved in the collection and "centralization" of relics of the "national" past under an absolutist monarchy, tended not to set as much stock by the historical or truth value of these artifacts as by their aesthetic value, which was lacking by eighteenth-century standards, and thus warranted improving change. Indeed, the conviction that medieval documents, literary texts included, were largely fictions, impostures upon impostures, confirmed eighteenth-century scholars in their aesthetic emphasis. For example, Le Grand d'Aussy, in the preface to his translated and extracted *Fabliaux ou Contes du XIIe et du XIIIe siècle*, published in 1781,[16] depicted himself in a long line of "improvers" of fabliaux and lyrics that went back to the medieval performers and scribes themselves. Le Grand's improvements are stylistic: he says he has "reformed" the style, cut out the boring and distasteful parts, and tightened the narrative (xciii), and he justifies these changes by the enormous variation he found in comparing different manuscript versions:

> All this would make me think that the minstrels, when given fabliaux to set to music, or the jongleurs, when they went to recite them in the provinces, or perhaps even the copyists, when they made the collections, took the liberty of altering them according to their desires.
>
> I experienced the same difficulty in the manuscripts containing lyrics. Often they differed by whole strophes, and this reminds me of an amusing story about the famous Jesuit Hardouin: He was chatting familiarly with a young friend to whom he laid out all the reasons he had to prove that the poems of the ancients were a recent invention and that they were composed by monks in the early Middle Ages. But, father, said the friend, laughing, if your system is true, think what a horrible blow you would level against the holy scriptures, the canons of the councils, the writings of the fathers? The Jesuit, surprised, looked at him hard, and after a moment's silence, shook his hand: my friend, he exclaimed, in a sort of transport, only God and I know the force of the objection you have just raised. (xcvii–xcix)

If the medieval transmitters of the fabliaux were constantly improving upon them, why should Le Grand not continue in that tradition and refine them to eighteenth-century taste? Only a full-fledged crisis of legitimacy, the French Revolution, could turn this attitude around (just as, in Le Grand's anecdote, the young man's suggestion that the holy scriptures must then be a human invention stopped the Jesuit in his tracks); only a crisis of their own legitimacy could so suddenly make scholarly aristocrats start treating medieval documents of all sorts, not as aesthetic objects to be embellished at will for present use, but as sacred repositories of truth—even, and especially, when they were inventing those "medieval" documents.

Eighteenth-century academicians did not publish medieval texts in the "original" vernacular of the manuscripts because they conceded little authority to originality and did not consider surviving medieval texts to be original anyway. The attitude of the man who initiated Le Grand d'Aussy into medieval literary studies, La Curne de Sainte-Palaye, the most learned medievalist of his day, is exemplary.[17] Sainte-Palaye, who was a member of the Academy of Inscriptions from 1724, spent his entire life working with medieval manuscripts, both doing and supervising the copying, collecting, describing, cataloging, and "centralizing" of all the vernacular medieval literary documents (in *langue d'oc* as well as d'oil) produced in the lands held by the French crown (the literary heritage of the "nation" in its kingly, absolutist incarnation). Prior to his death, Sainte-Palaye sold his huge collection of manuscript copies of medieval texts to the king in the view that it would become part of the royal collection available to scholars working in Paris. To amplify, complete, and organize the royal—and, in that sense, national—collection was, from Sainte-Palaye's point of view, an appropriate, and patriotic, goal. Publication was not required.

One of Sainte-Palaye's early projects, which he carried out with the help of other southern aristocratic (*robe*) scholars like himself, was the collection of at least one version (but often several) of every surviving troubadour poem from all known manuscripts in Italy as well as France (thus repatriating parts of the dispersed literary heritage).[18] A modern, professional medievalist, for whom scholarly labor is "justified" more by dissemination (publication and teaching) than by hoarding up a unique treasure, cannot help but be amazed by the enormous effort "gone to waste" of Sainte-Palaye's troubadour corpus and by the enormous difference between these compilations and what he thought fit to present the public in the form of the three slim volumes of his *Histoire littéraire des troubadours,* written by the Abbé Millot and published in 1774.[19] From the "fifteen folio volumes containing Provençal pieces with the variants from the different manuscripts, eight other volumes of extracts where some of the pieces are translated, where each is designated by alphabetical order of author, not to mention the glossary, the tables, and an infinite number of notes," from all this material Millot assured his readers he had at his disposal (vii), he produced a history of the troubadours containing no quotations of troubadour lyrics in medieval Occitan. This was probably what was expected of him. Sainte-Palaye knew that Millot could not read Occitan and would therefore be entirely dependent upon his translations and selections. As Millot acknowledged in his preface, he was "spared the boredom of research" by Saint-Palaye and his collaborators and could thus devote his whole attention to improving the style of Sainte-Palaye's translations, making them "freer and more varied," and everywhere possible trying to remedy the "boring uniformity" of the material (x).

In Millot's Enlightened judgment, troubadour verse was interesting, chiefly as a negative example, for "the history of customs and of the human spirit,"[20] but it was aesthetically deficient, very far from "real [eighteenth-century] perfection" (which is reached "only slowly as society enlightens and polishes itself"):

> Several [troubadours], to distinguish themselves from the multitude, affected painful faults that drew admiration: a combination of verses and rhymes capable of extinguishing the fire of genius, a stylistic obscurity whereby everything seemed enigmatic, and nothing merited guessing. Thus the progress of taste ... was stalled not only by the ignorance and crudeness that reigned then, but also by a sort of corruption produced by the cultivation of an *art without principles*. (xxviii, emphasis added)

As outrageous as they may seem to us, coming from a literary historian who could not read the literature about which he was writing, Millot's condescending judgments regarding troubadour verse are not out of line with those of Sainte-Palaye himself or of other Enlightenment scholars, most of whom placed a low value on "wretched gothic monuments" (the general term for medieval artifacts).

In a letter of 1739, written on his first Italian journey, Sainte-Palaye described his collection of copies of the texts of troubadour lyrics from French and Italian libraries as the "most ample, most laborious, and *worst* [aesthetically speaking] collection ever undertaken by a respectable man."[21] Sainte-Palaye acquiesced in the general Enlightenment view that eighteenth-century literature, language, and taste were greatly superior to their medieval counterparts, and that it would be "an abuse of the press to make it roll over the crude morsels of our ancestors."[22] To edit and print medieval vernacular literary texts without first "improving" (translating, extracting, expurgating, revising, fictionalizing) them would be too offensive to people of "good taste." Sainte-Palaye made his low opinion of the aesthetic value of medieval romance languages and literatures perfectly clear (in a way that no doubt also flattered the prejudices and ambitions of the other members as regulators and guardians of linguistic purity) in the speech he gave at his reception into the French Academy in 1758:

> This language, subjected without constraint today to the laws of a grammar, ... was a confused mixture of ill-assorted idioms, a mass of brutal and rustic words whose orthography, pronunciation, and even sense were never fixed, a shapeless jargon without rules or principles, bearing the imprint of that feudal anarchy which disregarded the laws or tended to destroy them; finally, [this medieval French] was a monstrous assemblage of lifeless allusions, of absurd

metaphors, of extravagant allegories, of figures of every sort packed together without order or intelligence.[23]

In one of his notebooks, where he would have less reason to exaggerate, Sainte-Palaye wrote: "Compare the writings of those barbarous times with those that printing has put into our hands for about two hundred years now. Let us be penetrated by gratitude especially for those respectable men who, towards the middle of the last century, succeeded in purifying our language."[24]

The most learned medieval Occitan and French specialist of the eighteenth century published no medieval texts in the original, and only four short poems in translation: three pieces as historical documents on medieval customs in his *Mémoires sur l'ancienne chevalerie,* and a literal translation of *Aucassin et Nicolette* in the February 1752 issue of *Mercure,* later republished as a slim little volume with a pretty engraving and subtitled "Les amours du bon vieux tems" (Loves of the Good Old Days). The Enlightened eighteenth-century Frenchman's self-congratuation for his superior refinement also had its flip side, a nostalgia for naiveté and natural sentiment (as opposed to civilized eighteenth-century decorum) that often dictated the kind of revisionary treatment medieval literary texts were given for publication (as, for example, the subtitle "loves of the good old days"). Ideally, medieval literary texts were supposed to "paint nature" exactly as it was—with heavy emphasis on "nature" as sentiment (if not passion).[25] To medievalists like myself, troubadour poetry is all art, and a naive troubadour would be a monster. But naive, plain-speaking troubadours were exactly what the eighteenth-century French public wanted, and anything that might make them seem otherwise was censored in one way or another. In the left-hand margins of Sainte-Palaye's corpus of extracts and translations, we find approving annotations such as, beside a poem by Arnaut de Maroill, "natural," "flowing," "This piece is agreeably written and also full of tenderness. It could be translated or at least given in a longer extract" (Paris, BN ms. Moreau 1584, fol. 114v, col. 1); however, anything that draws attention to the language itself is denigrated as, for example, "too rich, and the author sometimes affects therein to play on the same word" (fol. 115, col. 1).

In the opinion of Sainte-Palaye and other eighteenth-century scholars, medieval texts were improved by translation; if they were to be published at all, they had best be presented in free translations and extracts accommodated to eighteenth-century taste. Rather than making elaborate claims for the authenticity and originality of the medieval texts they published, eighteenth-century scholars and literary men emphasized their own perfecting skills; they made no pretence of restoration, but prided themselves on their ability to produce pseudo-medieval texts of greater aesthetic value than the "barbarous" or "corrupt" originals. Sainte-Palaye's and Millot's *Histoire littéraire des troubadours,* like Nostredame's *Vies des plus célèbres et anciens poètes provençaux* two centuries earlier, presents no troubadour lyrics in medieval Occitan, but rather in brief, translated extracts; this is as far as Sainte-Palaye and Millot go in the creation of pseudo-medieval texts (never inventing pieces of poems and ascribing them to troubadours, as Nostredame did). Yet the Enlightenment's naive troubadours are surely as fictive as some of Nostredame's inventions.

As Henri Jacoubet has noted in his study, *Le Comte de Tressan et les origines du genre troubadour,* when eighteenth-century medievalist-novelists such as Tressan referred to their medieval manuscript sources, it was never to give an idea of their palaeographic expertise, but rather of their "unlimited capacity for fantastic conjecture, if not, as in the case of *Ursino* [an entirely "supposed" medieval romance], of . . . talent for mystification."[26] In fact, although Tressan and his associates in the publication of medieval romances in the *Bibliothèque universelle des romans* had access to texts in medieval manuscript versions and to eighteenth-century copies of these (Le Grand d'Aussy had worked as a copyist for Sainte-Palaye, and the Marquis de Paulmy bought from the king the bulk of Sainte-Palaye's literary compilations),[27] they did not often use medieval versions, but usually culled extracts for adaptation and further fictionalization from the latest printed (and translated) edition of the romance in question, often a sixteenth-century gothic-letter one.[28] These romances, full of gallantry and naive sentiment, aimed at and read by a largely female audience, were nominally medieval, but not expected to have any historical value. Eighteenth-century French readers had no interest in authentic medieval literary texts (which were stigmatized as crude); they wanted their medieval literature sublimated into sentimental fiction fit for the entertainment of aristocratic and bourgeois females. Scholars such as Sainte-Palaye acquiesced in, even encouraged, this trivialization of the medieval history and the medieval literature they published. The two pretty little (duodecimo) volumes of the printed edition of his *Mémoires sur l'ancienne chevalerie,* which he had originally read at the Academy of Inscriptions, Sainte-Palaye dedicated, with a gallant flourish, to a female readership: "May the ladies welcome this last fruit of a pen that has always been used by preference on a kind of literature that they make their dearest entertainment."[29]

The Revolution of 1789 put a temporary halt to the publication of the pseudo-medieval texts of the *Bibliothèque universelle des romans* and to the appreciation in public of anything medieval. The Jacobin Republic (1791–94) was characterized by the wholesale public destruction of all sorts of reminders of the Ancien Régime—paintings, sculpture, manuscripts, and charters—all stigmatized as "feudal" or "gothic," as symbols of a barbarous past characterized by superstition (i.e., religion) and tyranny. During the Jacobin Reign of Terror, medieval artifacts were punished in effigy for the crimes of the Ancien Régime. In 1794, for example, a member of the Conservatory of the Museum (the group charged with purifying and forming the collection of the current Louvre) wrote:

> It is by our hatred for tyranny that we will measure our love for liberty. Animated by these sentiments, we ask you, legislators, to authorize us to rip from the walls of the aforementioned academy of painting the portraits of certain villains, as well as several paintings, productions of their corrupt genius. We will drag them to the foot of the statue of Liberty and, in the presence of our fellow citizens, we will deliver them to the flames, thus sending to infamy these traitors and all those who try to imitate them by refusing to use all their faculties and talents to affirm the rule of equality.[30]

The Revolution invested medieval artifacts with great political value as symbols of the past. Where one stood in the Revolutionary political spectrum determined whether the medieval had a positive or a negative value, whether one wanted to destroy it or restore it to its original, authentic state. This sudden change in the perception of the medieval artifact—from a largely fictitious and corrupt detritus of little aesthetic value to a supercharged symbol of the past—is perhaps most dramatically demonstrated with respect to the plastic arts, although, as we shall see, a similar revolution occurred in attitudes toward medieval literary texts.

Alexandre Lenoir's *Musée des monuments français,* where, as a child, "history was first revealed" to the great Romantic historian Jules Michelet,[31] had its beginnings in 1791 as a depot, in the former monastery of the Petits-Augustins, for "condemned" medieval and Renaissance sculpture and painting (from ransacked chateaux, churches, and abbeys, such as Saint-Denis) whose fate—to be burned, melted down for their metal, sold off—had yet to be decided. In charge of the depot, Lenoir worked relentlessly and often deviously (for example, plastering bronzes to make them appear to be worthless stone) to acquire and save medieval and Renaissance sculpture from destruction and to make the depot into a museum of the history of French monumental (chiefly funerary) art. To this novel purpose, Lenoir grouped and "classified" the art by centuries, beginning with the thirteenth, in a consecutive series of rooms that gave the visitor the impression of proceeding through French history. By 1800 Lenoir was already publicizing the *Musée des monuments français* through a descriptive catalogue.[32]

Although reputedly authentic, much of what the visitor saw in Lenoir's museum was, in the words of later scholars, "perfectly voluntary inexactitude" and "charlatanism."[33] Lenoir pieced together fragments of sculpture into wholes of his own invention and dubbed them monuments to rulers and medieval luminaries who lacked commemoration. One of the most successful of these "supposed" monuments was the tomb of Abelard and Héloïse among the trees of the *jardin elysée* of the museum.[34] This monument, within which he supposedly reunited the ashes of the medieval lovers, Lenoir constructed in 1779 from the debris of a chapel from Saint-Denis, within which he placed the supposedly original tomb of Abelard from the infirmary of Saint-Marcel-les-Châlons, and added to it reclining statues or *gisants* of Abelard and Héloïse (commissioned from a contemporary sculptor, who was ordered to fashion statues as authentic as possible from the supposedly authentic plaster casts of the skulls of Abelard and Héloïse).[35]

Later nineteenth-century historians of medieval art such as Lenoir's biographer, Louis Courajod, credited Lenoir with the first "scientific" treatment of medieval plastic art in that he regarded medieval artifacts as pieces of history to be classified for their truth value (rather than as aesthetic objects to be admired or rejected as examples of good or bad taste) (1:ii). Courajod had to overlook Lenoir's creation of "supposed" monuments in order to hold him up as an example of the scientific spirit in opposition to the "mystifications" of previous connoisseurs:

"What does it matter," said these audacious mystifiers, "what period, what country, what author such and such a work came from, what subject or person it represented?" Some, kneeling before the crudest fakes, even went so far as to pretend that it did not matter whether the admired piece was authentic or fake, modern or ancient, original or pastiche. It sufficed that it should appear beautiful in the abstract, regardless of the conditions of place or time. . . . To be a competent judge of sculpture, it sufficed to have taste. (1:iii)

Lenoir's desire to restore what never, in fact, existed (except in his own wishful imagination) led him to make historical claims for and to try to use archaeological "science" to validate his own inventions of an idealized past.

Soon after the restoration of the French monarchy, in 1816, Lenoir's museum was dissolved and the tombs of monarchs and aristocrats restored to their "original" ecclesiastical settings. The Restoration thus put a stop to Lenoir's fictionalizing restorations, but, as we shall see, gave impetus to restorations of similarly "supposed" medieval originals in other domains, such as troubadour verse. Medieval artifacts could never again be taken for granted in quite the same way as prior to the Revolution. No longer merely "wretched gothic things," they had become potent symbols of a contested past, a past that was idealized or debased, fictionalized without acknowledging the fictions, in order to sanction actions in the present and visions of the future. Under the July Monarchy, beginning in 1834, King Louis-Philippe's minister of public instruction, Guizot, would institutionalize the conservation and "intelligent" restoration of "monuments" of the medieval past in all domains, with history and literature looked after by one commission and all the other arts by another.[36] With the creation of these commissions, one might say that professional medieval studies as a science of restoration were officially instituted in France.

The medieval manuscripts in the royal collection in Paris did not undergo the same destructive physical treatment during the Revolutionary period as medieval plastic arts exposed more publicly. Yet later scholars evoke the Paris Commune's intention to destroy the royal library as proof of its fragility, and many manuscripts in private aristocratic collections were indeed burned and destroyed as symbols of the past during the Reign of Terror. The actual or threatened destruction of medieval literary manuscripts and other texts that eighteenth-century scholars and the Enlightened public considered to be of mediocre aesthetic and historical value had the effect of turning these, especially in the eyes of legitimist aristocrats, into valuable originals, witnesses to a stolen inheritance.

Some of the earliest evidence of this changed attitude toward medieval literary artifacts appears in the prefaces to "supposed" medieval texts in the *genre troubadour,* a novelistic genre that usually involves the pretence of translating a medieval manuscript that is "found" / "invented" (*trouvé*), and thus supposes a certain erudition on the part of the "translator." In 1803 the Parisian editor Heinrichs published two especially "scientific" specimens in this genre, both using the same idealized engravings (such as the frontispiece of a knight in plate armor shielding a young woman carrying a lamb). In the two volumes of his *Le Troubadour: Poésies occitaniques du XIIIe siècle,* Fabre d'Olivet used some of the trappings of a scholarly edition of a classical text, the "science" of textual criticism, for the purpose of authenticating Occitan texts almost entirely of his own invention.

He even published some shorter pieces such as "La Poudestad de Diû" and verses by Sapho to Phaon [*sic*] in what he claimed to be the "original" Occitan (really an eighteenth-century dialect antiqued and made strange). Modern French translations appear on facing pages, and the "editor" supplies scholarly notes of a historical or geographical nature, as well as, in an appendix to the second volume, a vocabulary of "occitanique" and a treatise on its orthography and pronunciation. Fabre d'Olivet's treatment of Occitan texts is philological in the sense that he considers them under the rubric of history of the language. The main value of these texts, from this point of view, lies in their priority. In his scholarly preface, the "editor" takes up the claim of Caseneuve and previous Provençal patriots (a claim that François Raynouard continued to support adamantly) that Occitan was "the true romance language used in France under the first and second races of our kings, . . . the common stock of French, Spanish, and Italian" (xxix–xxxi).

Fabre d'Olivet's proclaimed intention is to revive the renown of the troubadours as the "fathers of modern [French] poetry," just as the publication of Ossianic poetry (equally factitious) had revived the reputation of the "bards of the north" (iii–iv). In 1803 these claims of originality and authenticity made on behalf of texts in a provincial vernacular might have a counter-Revolutionary political import. Fabre d'Olivet suggested as much in his dedicatory poem to his mother:

> Usurpers of a heritage
> that our respectable ancestors
> have transmitted to us from age to age,
> they tread our fallow lands under their damaging feet;
> but in our houses, which they possess,

black phantoms obsess them;
from the bottom of their tombs our sleeping ancestors
awaken offended. . . . (vii)

By publishing these "supposed" thirteenth-century troubadour texts, Fabre d'Olivet figuratively revived ancestral claims, his own and those of other dispossessed southern aristocrats. To the counter-Revolutionary mind, an "original" medieval document, even a literary one, had an almost legal status, for it witnessed to the priority of its owner's claims and thus to his legitimacy (equated with past precedent). The restoration of troubadour verse symbolized the wished-for restoration of past privileges.

Whereas eighteenth-century scholars tended to take the vagaries of the transmission of medieval literary texts lightly, Fabre d'Olivet focused on the problems of transmission in his prefaces, for it was "original" texts that he professed to value most. Rather than presenting himself as improving upon his sources by judicious cutting, extracting, and refinement (as late eighteenth-century *troubadour* novelists such as Tressan had done), Fabre d'Olivet insisted (while inventing every bit as much or more than Tressan) that he was faithful to sources he was trying to piece together and restore to their original wholeness. By his own account, a sheaf of parchment gatherings containing troubadour lyrics was sent to him by an anonymous person from Montpellier who knew Fabre d'Olivet to be a restorer of medieval literary texts through reading his first novel, *Azalaïs et le Gentil Aimar* (iv). Fabre d'Olivet claimed this first novel to be a tissue of fragments translated from old Provençal chronicles that fell into his hands by chance, as a result of "the vengeances licensed against feudality, the ravaging of ancient castles by fire, and the pillaging and dispersing of archives" (iii).

Supposedly, the anonymous sender of the packet of troubadour manuscripts accompanied these with an explanatory letter assuring Fabre d'Olivet that these manuscripts had been passed down from father to son for generations "as a family inheritance" and that family tradition had it that "this poetry had been bequeathed to them by one of the most skilled troubadours of the time, a native of Esperou, a small village within the family's once-extensive feudal domain" (vi–viii). Though he found this poetry "marked with a native originality hard to imitate," Fabre d'Olivet, pretending to be a judicious textual critic, raised the possibility that the anonymous letter-writer who sent the manuscript might have, like Macpherson was believed to have

done, "discovered scattered fragments that he then arranged, connected, and perhaps extended, conserving the spirit, tone, and flavor
of his model" (ix–x). Yet, before giving his readers the complete
"facts" of transmission such as he knew them, Fabre d'Olivet also
pointedly left it to "the sagacity of the reader to judge what degree of
confidence these manuscripts merit" (ii).

According to François Raynouard, who put a substantial body of
medieval Occitan poetry before the public in the six volumes of his
Choix des poésies originales des troubadours (1816–21), some readers were indeed duped by the "science" of Fabre d'Olivet's presentation into thinking that his texts were genuinely medieval. Raynouard
set the record straight about how many of these texts were authentic
by citing the one *chansonnier* in the Royal Library that Fabre d'Olivet
had consulted and the handful of lyrics from it that he had translated
in bits and pieces into his antiqued eighteenth-century Occitan. Yet,
given the liberties he had himself taken with medieval history in order
to deliver a contemporary political message in a highly successful
tragedy of the Knights Templar (read "French nobility") with which
he began his literary career,[37] as well as his patriotic belief (like Fabre
d'Olivet's) in Occitan as the "original" Romance tongue,[38] Raynouard
did not go out of his way to denounce Fabre d'Olivet's fictions and,
indeed, gave the impression that readers who were duped by them
were the ones really to blame.

Raynouard set the record straight on the troubadours only in
passing, and not until 1824, in the context of a review of a new
historical anthology of French literature.[39] His main concern was that
this anthology, intended to present French literature to a broad public
including foreigners, featured in its medieval section the fictitious
fifteenth-century poetry of Clotilde de Surville, which had been published by Heinrichs in 1803, the same year as Fabre d'Olivet's *Le
Troubadour*. The "editor" of *Poésies de Marguerite-Eléonore Clotilde
de Vallon-Chalys, depuis, Madame de Surville, poëte françois du XVe
siècle* was one of Raynouard's colleagues at the French Academy,
Charles Vanderbourg (Charles de Boudens, Viscount of Vanderbourg), an emigrant aristocrat who had made his reputation as a
textual critic with the publication of Clotilde in 1803 (which went
through three printings that year) as well as a scholarly edition and
translation of Horace's *Odes* in 1812–13, and who was, with
Raynouard, on the editorial board of the *Journal des savants* at the
time Raynouard published his carefully worded review. Congratulat-

ing the true author of the supposed verse of Clotilde, a man "of wit and good taste," for having "attracted and pricked up the public's curiosity for a moment until serious examination had evaluated and characterized these compositions as pseudonymous," Raynouard went on to blame the editor of the anthology for dereliction of his responsibility as a literary historian in printing the pseudo-Clotilde as a medieval poet and merely noting that the various arguments for and against the authenticity of her verse were beyond the bounds of the edition. "Certainly," Raynouard wrote, "if there is someone called to pronounce upon the authenticity of works, it is undoubtedly the person who assigns them a place in the history of the literature" (410).

The affair of the pseudo-Clotilde is one of the most fascinating in the history of the professionalization of medieval literary study, fascinating for what it reveals, not only about the politics of the new science of restoring "original" medieval artifacts, but also about how this science of detection began as a detective fiction, how science served to disguise fiction as history.[40] The highly sentimental "fifteenth-century" poetry of Clotilde apparently began as the invention of the Marquis de Surville, who made no effort to "age" his verse and admitted among friends to being its author, while publicly pretending to have discovered his ancestress's verse in an old family manuscript. Surville's verse had a tasteful contemporary form and a nominally medieval, historical content in much the same way as did the Count de Tressan's "medieval" romances. Like Tressan's novels, "Clotilde's" verse seemed to be initially aimed at a female audience (and, perhaps, through his medieval female persona, enabled Surville to express emotions inexpressible otherwise). The pieces published as Clotilde's during Surville's lifetime, while he was in exile, in Madame de Polier's *Journal littéraire de Lausanne* (an entertaining mixture of literary criticism, poetry, charades, and word puzzles), were quite incredible, especially the genealogy of female poets—from Héloïse to Agnès de Bragelongne (head of the Old French school) and Beatrix d'Arragon (the Occitan) and their respective pupils, Sainte-des-Prez and Barbe de Verrue and on and on to Clotilde. This genealogy, supposedly recorded in Clotilde's memoirs, served to prove why her verse seemed so modern: the female line of poets managed to preserve good taste down through the centuries of barbarity and never stopped writing correct *alexandrins* and following other poetic, linguistic, and orthographic rules otherwise unknown in the Middle Ages.[41]

Following the execution by firing squad of the Marquis de Surville in 1798 at Le Puy (for trying to raise a counter-Revolutionary rebellion in favor of the Bourbons), Vanderbourg took it upon himself, in his 1803 edition of the *Poésies de . . . Clotilde,* to try to prove the historical authenticity of at least some of these fictions, that is, that they came from Clotilde, who was sincerely representing the past in her "memoirs" and the fifteenth century in her verse. What this authentication involved was extracting the most credible pieces from Surville's manuscripts, aging the vocabulary of the verse somewhat (with the help of La Combe's *Dictionnaire du vieux langage français* of 1766), and, above all, publishing it in a very scholarly format that included a lengthy preface investigating the written transmission of the verse, and accompanied the "original," untranslated verse with copious explanatory notes filling every facing page (two-thirds of which, critics claimed, were totally unnecessary). The striking thing about the Vanderbourg "edition" of Clotilde is that "real" medieval verse had yet to receive such respectful, valorizing editorial treatment.[42] The science of textual criticism was first applied in publishing medieval French verse in order to authenticate a fiction (that Vanderbourg tacitly recognized as such in his consideration of marketing strategies, such as his copious scholarly notes, in private letters to the widow Surville).[43] Just as Chabaneau, later in the century, decided that Nostredame's *Vies* ought to be history (and not historical romance), so Vanderbourg, for reasons to be discussed, decided to use the textual science he had recently discovered in Germany (along with a number of creative revisions of his own, such as "aging" the vocabulary, which may well have come from his acquaintance with the Macpherson, Percy, and Chatterton "impostures" in England and the scholarly defenses of authenticity these provoked)[44] to turn the Marquis de Surville's verse in the historical romance or *troubadour* genre into "authentic" medieval verse.

When they posed as editor-translators, Fabre d'Olivet and other historical romancers assured their readers that they were working from ancient manuscripts they had fortuitously found and which were presumably still in their possession (a claim they expected their readers to take for what it was worth and not ask for material proof). Vanderbourg, on the other hand, began the preface to his edition with a very different announcement:

> It is always a fairly hazardous enterprise to publish the posthumous
> works of an entirely unknown author. Critical suspicion, always

wakeful, does not stop at searching out the faults of the work; it raises doubts about the very existence of the author, or at least of the authenticity of the productions attributed to him; it demands the display of the original manuscripts. The editor's surest resource is, undoubtedly, to produce them; but how difficult his situation is when he does not have this means in his power! (v)

Vanderbourg admitted at the outset that he worked from Surville's translated copies, and not from the original manuscript of Clotilde, which was supposedly burned during the Terror, along with all the other Surville documents, agents and symbols of "feudalism." Vanderbourg thus called attention to a problem of legitimacy (of considerable interest, by analogy, to the expropriated French aristocrat) which, with the scientific fictions of his edition, he attempted to resolve: how to prove originality in the absence of original documents and how to authenticate proprietary claims with such proofs.[45]

According to Vanderbourg's own account, he first became acquainted with Clotilde's verse while in the Rhineland, where certain pieces were being passed around by Surville in emigrant circles that admired the patriotic, royalist sentiments and thinly veiled allusions to contemporary events expressed in poems such as the "Heroïde à son espoulx Bérenger," supposedly written by Clotilde to her husband off fighting in the cause of the dauphin. The great interest these poems reportedly elicited was due to their contemporaneity—their royalist allusions—and it was this interest that Vanderbourg decided to tap and exploit with his "edition." However, to publish these poems as (the executed traitor) Surville's was politically problematic in 1802–3, and Vanderbourg knew it.[46] Therefore he insisted in his scholarly introduction that they were authentically medieval, at least in content, if not entirely in form, and that his own enterprise of edition was a disinterested, scientific one.

To those who would argue that the language and form were too modern, he replied that one of Clotilde's late sixteenth-century female descendants, Jeanne de Vallon, had the project of publishing them and had done some modernizing editorial revision of the original manuscript. To those who would argue that the language was antiquated in very peculiar ways, he countered that Surville himself, once Clotilde's original manuscript had been burned, may have tried to reproduce them from memory by antiquating his own translations (lxxxii). To every imagined critical opposition, Vanderbourg provided a reply that affirmed the fundamental authenticity of the verse by blaming all faults on the corrupting interventions of its subsequent transmitters (himself excluded).

The true value of the poetry Vanderbourg erected as authentically medieval—through these fictive detections of transmission errors and deprecation of all modern revision as corruption—was that it was contemporary: it satisfied the needs (legitimized the royalist and religious sentiment) of a certain contemporary audience and did so in a language and form that was sufficiently legible and correct by their standards. Although the Revolution provoked an increased respect for the medieval artifact as a symbol of the past and for "originality" as a guarantee of precedent-based authority, it did not immediately produce a great admiration for "real" medieval language and style.

Charles Nodier, "editor" of the second volume of Clotilde's verse in 1827 (the year of Vanderbourg's death), described the appeal of Clotilde's antique (pseudo-medieval) language thus in his *Questions de littérature légale:* "The old language has this property of being so marvelously appropriate to simple sentiments and touching ideas that one cannot hear it without some sort of emotion, because it transports the mind back to bygone days which we always represent as those of innocence and happiness."[47] Fake medieval was still more to the public's taste than "real" after the Revolution, as before. By the turn of the century, however, there were many people who, for broadly political reasons, no longer wanted to acknowledge as fictions the inventions involved in projects of "restoration."

After the restoration of the monarchy put the Bourbons on the throne, one of the first things Louis XVIII's favorite minister, the Comte de Blacas, did was finance the restoration of some "original" medieval texts. That Blacas was also the name of a troubadour may have played a part in the enthusiastic ministerial approval of François Raynouard's project for restoring troubadour verse. His *Choix des poésies originales des troubadours,* published in six volumes by Didot from 1816 to 1821, was the first scholarly edition of "real," as opposed to "supposed," troubadour verse—in the sense that Raynouard did not make these texts up out of his own imagination, but edited them from medieval manuscripts and presented them, not in modern translation, but in medieval Occitan (or, as called it, *Roman*), the "original" (his thesis) romance language.

That troubadour lyrics are valuable historical artifacts that Raynouard has discovered and restored, historical objects as valuable as the Grecian and Roman ones the Revolutionaries brandished to symbolize their ideal past, is at least one of the implicit messages of the engravings that ornament the volumes of his *Choix:* antique objects (lamps, lyres, urns, and so forth) and scenes of excavation (presumably for such antique objects) in natural landscapes. Yet, in many respects, these scholarly restorations of "original" troubadour lyrics—heavily edited composites of Raynouard's preferred readings with no mention of variants or manuscript contexts, poems punctuated and spaced on the printed page as if they were nineteenth-century poems—are also "supposed" texts, albeit much more meticulous and careful impostures than Nostredame's or Fabre d'Olivet's.

The past as it really was cannot be recuperated, only invented in ways that satisfy present exigencies. Raynouard needed to idealize his "originals" to make them palatable to a nineteenth-century public. Like Sainte-Palaye's and Millot's before him, Raynouard's "choice" of lyrics featured the less complex (more naive-seeming) poems in terms of language and content (for Raynouard considered anything he could not understand not worth printing). This subjective principle of selection he reportedly admitted to the visiting German medievalist, Friedrich Diez, who spent three months in Paris preparing his own *Leben und Werke der Troubadours* (1826).[48]

Furthermore, Raynouard devoted the greater part of the first volume of his *Choix* (109–438) to a "Grammaire de la langue romane" that rationalized and tried to unify medieval Occitan by insisting that, underneath the superficial orthographic variety of word forms, there was regularity in the formation of words (out of Latin) via conjugation and declension. As Bernard Cerquiglini has shown with examples from later editions, such as Gaston Paris's critical edition of the Old French *Vie de saint Alexis* (1872), the "discovery or invention" of these grammatical rules (which required overlooking many "exceptions") provided a justification for the editorial correction or expurgation of "irregularities" to produce more pleasingly regular printed editions,[49] pseudo-medieval texts adapted to contemporary values much more subtly than by the eighteenth-century method of "perfection" by translation, extraction, censorship, and forthright invention.

Nineteenth-century Romance philology, the founding of which Friedrich Diez attributed to Raynouard,[50] performed its impostures at the more hidden level of the medieval language itself, through the invention of the instruments of the science, artificially regularizing grammars and dictionaries, such as Raynouard's *Lexique roman,* which worked to reduce the polysemy of medieval Occitan and continued the work of his "Grammaire" in reducing its polymorphism.[51] To be sure, nineteenth-century medievalists were not the first regulators of medieval Occitan; they were following in the path of self-proclaimed thirteenth-century regulators such as Raimon Vidal with his *Razos de trobar*, Jofre de Foixa with his *Regles de trobar*, Uc Faiditz, with his *Donatz Proensals* (*Provençal Donatus*), and the fourteenth-century *Flors del gay saber* and *Leys d'amors*.[52] However, whereas the medieval rule makers acknowledged their corrective (and thus improving) project, nineteenth-century philologists disguised theirs as a discovery and restoration of original, historical truths about the proper functioning of the language.

The professional discipline of medieval literary studies has depended, from the beginning, on our repressing the knowledge that we are inventing a fictive object that fills our own needs and our professing the belief that, through our editions, we are restoring historical artifacts (usually imagined as the products of individual proprietary authors) or that, through our interpretations of these, we are restoring "original" meanings (those of "original" authors or audiences). The turning "serious" of every domain of medieval studies in France was accomplished gradually after the Revolution through such erudite acts of self-disciplinary repression, beginning with the hiding of one's fictions only from others (exemplified in the attempt of the budding academician, Charles Vanderbourg, to make flagrantly fictive verse in the *genre troubadour* into authentic medieval texts through a scholarly edition) to the hiding of one's fictions even from oneself (exemplified by the attempts of Chabaneau and Anglade to expurgate Nostredame's fictions in order, through their own detective fictions, to restore the truth of history as these late nineteenth-century medievalists imagined it).

The charges Chabaneau and Anglade laid against Nostredame—and, by extension, any previous or future medievalists who would deliberately fictionalize and modernize medieval "sources"—were heavy: he was a fraud. Fear of such a sentence has disciplined us all, has guided our increasingly subtle impostures, our fictions disguised, even to ourselves, as disinterested historical restorations. Having admitted the impossibility of recuperating troubadour lyrics as they "really" were, have I not grasped at an equally chimerical project: trying to recuperate, at least, the truth about why, over the course of centuries, we fictionalized them as we did? And what if I were to admit now that this essay is, inevitably and deliberately, just another self-and-society-serving fiction posing as history? Would that really destroy its value?

NOTES

1. Jehan de Nostredame, *Les vies des plus célèbres et anciens poètes provençaux,* ed. Camille Chabaneau and Joseph Anglade (Paris, 1913; rpt. Geneva, 1970), 2:125. To avoid confusion in citing parts of this volume, which is really two in one (with page numbering beginning again at one with Nostredame's text), I will treat the prefacing critical material as volume one and the edition as volume two. Unless otherwise noted, all English translations in this chapter are my own.

2. J. Boutière and A. H. Schutz, *Biographies des troubadours* (Paris: Nizet, 1973).

3. J.M.L. Dejeanne, *Poésies complètes du troubadour Marcabru* (Toulouse: Privat, 1909).

4. All these terms are modern inventions that would surely surprise a twelfth-century troubadour. Nostredame called it Provençal (and relocated Limousin and Gascon troubadours to his native Provence to do so); his term stuck for more than three centuries and is still used by many scholars, including myself at times. The early nineteenth-century historical novelist and poet, Fabre d'Olivet, who was from the Cevennes region (not Provence proper), claimed credit for inventing the more appropriate term "occitanique" to describe the languages of southern France or *langue d'oc.* (Fabre d'Olivet's inventions will be discussed in more detail later.) François Raynouard, the nineteenth-century publisher of the first dictionary of the language, *Lexique roman,* promoted the general term *Roman* (Romance) in order to underline his support for the thesis of the language's priority with respect to the "newer" dialects of Old French, Italian, and Spanish. The terms of the popularizing "impostors" had more success than did Raynouard's. The tide seems to have turned nowadays toward using the term Occitan (as I have done throughout this essay) rather than Provençal.

5. For the history of the French Revolution, I have relied on François Furet's long view (1770–1880) in the two volumes of his *La Révolution* (Paris: Hachette, 1988). A historical analysis that treats the post-Revolutionary idealization of "the Middle Ages, the people, and the noble savage" is Eric Hobsbawm's, *The Age of Revolutions* (London: Weidenfeld and Nicolson, 1962), esp. chap. 16 on the arts.

6. Charles Vanderbourg, for example, was well aware of what was going on in Germany. In 1802 he published French translations of Lessing's *Laocoon* and of Friedrich Meyer's *Voyage in Italie.* In 1812–13 he published a three-volume edition and French translation, *Les Odes d'Horace, traduites en vers, avec des argumens et des notes, et revues pour le texte sur XVIII manuscrits de la Bibliothèque impériale* (Paris: Schoell), which was modeled

on "the new German editions that discuss the opinions of interpreters and the readings of early editors" (iii–iv). From the prefacing materials of the Mitscherlich edition of the *Odes,* he discovered that there were about forty manuscripts in the Imperial (former Royal, now National) Library in Paris that the editors of the best French editions had not consulted. Consequently, in order to "repair the negligence of my compatriots," Vanderbourg decided "to collate . . . all the manuscripts anterior to the invention of printing . . . and to make them the base of a new recension of this part of Horace" (iv). Vanderbourg, "editor" of pseudo-Clotilde, was abreast of the latest German textual science and helped introduce it into France. On the beginnings of this critical science, especially the preface to Wolf's *Prolegomena ad Homerum* (1795), see Sebastiano Timpanaro, *La genesi del metodo del Lachmann* (Florence: Le Monnier, 1963), 23–25.

7. Alfred Jeanroy, *La poésie lyrique des troubadours* (Toulouse: Privat, 1934; rpt. Geneva, 1973), 30.

8. Claude Hagège, *Le Français et les siècles* (Paris: Jacob, 1987), 232.

9. Chabaneau and Anglade point out in their edition of the *Vies* (1:135–49) that Nostredame cited by name Equicola, Velutello, Gesualdo, and Bembo, and thus knew of the printed editions of sixteenth-century Italians who had investigated the troubadours in their learned commentaries on Petrarch and Dante. On Italian humanist study of the troubadours during the sixteenth and seventeenth centuries, see Santorre Debenedetti, *Gli studi provenzali in Italia nel Cinquecento* (Turin: Loescher, 1911) and Eleonora Vincenti, *Biografia antica dei trovatori* (Milan: Riccardi, 1963).

10. Chabaneau and Anglade, *Vies,* 1:153–59.

11. Umberto Eco, *Il nome della rosa* (Milan: Fabbri-Bompiani, 1980).

12. Karl Bartsch, "Die Quellen von Jehan de Nostradamus," *Jahrbuch für romanische und englische Sprache und Literatur* 13 (1874): 1–65, 121–49.

13. An equally meticulous prosecution (and fictive detection) of a previous scholarly fraud had recently been published in England with the three volumes of John W. Hales and Frederick J. Furnivall's *Bishop Percy's Folio Manuscript* (London: Trübner, 1867–69). Percy's *Reliques of Ancient English Poetry* (1765) was a work in the *troubadour* vein, first seriously attacked a quarter of a century later by that "cantankerous attorney" Joseph Ritson. In his own *Ancient Songs* (1790), Ritson accused Percy of preferring "elegance" to "truth" and fraudulently corrupting and even forging (in the name of refinement) "original" medieval documents. In the second half of the nineteenth century, Hales and Furnivall did their "duty" (as Furnivall put it) by printing exactly as it was, with no corrections, the "foundation document of English balladry" (1:ix)—Percy's much-mutilated seventeenth-century manu-

script—and thus demonstrating (as well as by their notes), much more thoroughly than Ritson had done, how Percy had corrupted his sources. Furnivall assessed this patriotic contribution—none too clearly—in the foreword to the first volume, "It is something to have helped to secure the Ms. for the nation, something that ballads like *The Childe of Elle* . . . can be read without Percy's tawdry touches" (1:xi). "Something" indeed. (In this same foreword, Furnivall quotes from Ritson's attacks on Percy, xvii–xviii.)

14. For a discussion of Erasmus' textual criticism and his imposture, see John F. D'Amico, *Theory and Practice in Renaissance Textual Criticism* (Berkeley: University of California Press), 36–37.

15. The debate between Mabillon and Germon is summarized and mise-en-scène to interest the public in Father Lallemant's *Histoire des contestations sur la diplomatique* (Paris: Delaulne, 1708).

16. Le Grand d'Aussy, *Fabliaux ou Contes du XIIe et du XIIIe siècle, traduits ou extraits d'après plusieurs manuscrits du tems, avec des notes historiques et critiques et les imitations qui ont été faites de ces contes depuis leur origine jusqu'à nos jours* (Paris: Onfroy, 1781; rpt. Geneva, 1971). See also Geoffrey Wilson, *A Medievalist in the Eighteenth Century: Le Grand d'Aussy and the "Fabliaux ou Contes"* (The Hague: Nijhoff, 1975).

17. On La Curne de Sainte-Palaye and the medieval scholarship of his day, see Lionel Gossman, *Medievalism and the Ideologies of the Enlightenment: The World and Work of La Curne de Sainte-Palaye* (Baltimore: Johns Hopkins University Press, 1968).

18. Part of the correspondence among these Provençal antiquarians has been published by J. Bauquier, "Les Provençalistes du XVIIIe siècle: Lettres inédites de Sainte-Palaye, Mazaugues, Caumont, La Bastie, etc.," *Revue des langues romanes* 17 (1880): 65–83, 179–219.

19. La Curne de Sainte-Palaye and Claude Millot, *Histoire littéraire des troubadours contenant leurs vies, les extraits de leurs pièces, & plusieurs particularités sur les moeurs, les usages, & l'histoire du douzième & du treizième siècles,* 3 vols. (Paris: Durant, 1774; rpt. Geneva, 1967).

20. Millot, xxxi: "One sees there the ignorance and fanaticism of a sinful clergy, the petulance of a troubled and untamed nobility, the activity and boldness of a bourgeoisie just released from servitude, the vices rather than the virtues of men of all estates, still given over to barbarous habits, and beginning to refine themselves by false ideals."

21. Bauquier, 209.

22. Bauquier, 193, quoting from a letter of Joseph de Bimard, Baron de la Bastie-Monsaléon.

23. *Discours prononcés dans l'Académie françoise le lundi 26 juin 1758* à la reception de M. de la Curne de Sainte-Palaye (Paris: Brunet, 1758), 6–7.

24. Gossman, 255, quoting from Paris, BN ms. Bréquigny 154, fol. 6.

25. For further examples of this insistence on the naiveté of medieval French literature, from the Count de Caylus in the mid-eighteenth century on, see R. Howard Bloch, "Naturalism, Nationalism, Medievalism," *Romanic Review* 76 (1985): 347–49.

26. Henri Jacoubet, *Le Comte de Tressan et les origines du genre troubadour* (Paris: Presses Universitaires de France, 1923), 257. Also useful are Jacoubet's *Le genre troubadour et les origines françaises du romantisme* (Paris: Belles Lettres, 1929) and his *Comment le XVIIIe siècle lisait les romans de chevalerie* (Grenoble: Drevet, 1932).

27. On the Marquis de Paulmy's acquisition of Sainte-Palaye's copies, in part even before the latter's death in 1781, see Henri Martin, *Histoire de la Bibliothèque de l'Arsenal,* vol. 8 in his *Catalogue des manuscrits de la Bibliothèque de l'Arsenal* (Paris, 1899), 226–27. For Le Grand d'Aussy's contribution to the *Bibliothèque universelle des romans,* see Wilson, 297.

28. Jacoubet, *Comment le XVIIIe siècle,* 1.

29. La Curne de Sainte-Palaye, *Mémoires sur l'ancienne chevalerie considérée comme un établissement politique et militaire,* 2 vols. (Paris: Duchesne, 1759), 1:vii–viii.

30. Louis Courajod, *Alexandre Lenoir, son journal, et le Musée des monuments français,* 3 vols. (Paris: Champion, 1878–87), 1:xcvii.

31. Courajod, 2:7, citing Michelet's *Histoire de la Révolution:* "How many souls have taken the spark of history in this museum, the interest in great memories, the vague desire to go back through the ages! I still remember the emotion . . . that made my heart beat fast when, as a small child, I entered beneath those somber vaults and contemplated those pale faces" (6:117).

32. Alexandre Lenoir, *Musée des monuments français* (Paris: Guilleminet, 1800). This is the first in a rapid series of new editions of the catalogue.

33. Courajod, 1:clxvii, 2:207.

34. There is a reproduction of a romantic engraving of this tomb of Abelard and Héloïse, as well as of other parts of the museum, in Courajod (2:25).

35. Lenoir, 223–24.

36. Courajod, 2:14–15.

37. Raynouard's *Les Templiers* went through five editions and an Italian translation in his lifetime, beginning with the first in 1805 by Giguet and Michaud (and the first representation at the *Théâtre français* on May 14, 1805). His second play representing French history, *Les États de Blois,* was performed only once, before Napoleon at St. Cloud on June 22, 1810,

because Napoleon did not appreciate the play's obvious politics and squelched it. Raynouard, a lawyer from Brignoles in the south of France who participated in the legislative assemblies of the Revolutionary period, and was arrested during the Terror, restored the "medieval" past in his historical plays in order to influence events in the present. Charles Nodier's critical appreciation, written in 1824, of *Les États de Blois* makes this abundantly clear:

> It displeased him [Napoleon] very much. Indeed, how could he and his court enjoy the implication of the following verses: "How guilty these vile conspirators are! / They dare to reject and do battle against a Bourbon. / Judge the criminal audacity of the Duke de Guise; / he shoves Bourbon down to climb into his place." A host of other verses expressing the same sentiments . . . would necessarily indispose the man who, even more ambitious and more guilty than the Duke de Guise, had declared himself the head of a new dynasty and was intent on hindering the expression of opinions in favor of the old. . . . Comparison of the two great historical periods of the League and the Revolution was apt to tempt a poet who knew the power of allusions; thus those Mr. Raynouard's play offers are numerous and striking. (*Bibliothèque dramatique ou répertoire universel du théâtre français. Auteurs contemporains. M. Raynouard, M. Baour-Lormian* [Paris: Dabo, 1824], 306, 321).

38. In the first volume of his six-volume *Choix des poésies originales des troubadours* (Paris: Didot, 1816–21; rpt. Geneva, 1982), François Raynouard supported the outdated views of the sixteenth- and seventeenth-century literary historians Fauchet, Caseneuve, and Huet, whom he quoted to the effect that medieval Provençal was the same as *roman* (the language into which classical Latin supposedly devolved in Gaul), and that French, Italian, and Spanish derived, not directly from Latin along with Provençal, but directly from *roman* (i.e., Provençal) (xxxv–xxxvi).

39. François Raynouard, review of the first two volumes of *Les poëtes français depuis le XIIe siècle jusqu'à Malherbe, avec une notice historique et littéraire sur chaque poëte [by M. Auguis]* (Paris: Crapelet, 1824), *Journal des savants* (July 1824): 412.

40. There is a copious nineteenth-century scholarship aimed at exculpating or blaming Vanderbourg, Surville, another member of the Surville family, or upholding Clotilde's authenticity. Not to mention review essays and articles covered in M. H. Vaschalde's twenty-three-page *Bibliographie Survilienne* (Paris, 1876), the following books were devoted to the subject in roughly the last quarter of the century: A. Mazon, *Marguerite Chalis et la*

légende de Clotilde de Surville (Paris, 1873); Antonin Macé, *Un procès d'histoire littéraire: Les poésies de Clotilde* (Grenoble, 1873); Anotole Loquin, *Réponse à M. Antonin Macé (Bourdeaux, 1873)* [418 pp.]; Eugène Villedieu, Marguerite de Surville, sa vie, ses oeuvres, ses descendants devant la critique moderne (Paris, 1873); William Koenig, *Étude sur l'authenticité des poésies de Clotilde de Surville* (Halle, 1875); and, finally, Abbé Édouard Peyron's two volumes in 1901, *Le Marquis de Surville* and *Les poésies de Clotilde.*

41. Macé, 62, on Madame de Polier's journal; ibid., 64–66, on the fanciful history of medieval female poets published anonymously therein in 1797–98. For Vanderbourg's narrative of this incredible feminine poetic genealogy (which he says, in a letter to the widow Surville, he would gladly leave out of the edition had it not already been published in Switzerland), see his scholarly preface to *Poésies de . . . Clotilde,* xxi–lv.

42. The exception, although its scholarly notes are by no means so extensive, is Étienne Barbazan's poorly selling 1756 Old French edition with glossary of the *Fabliaux et contes des poètes françois des XI, XII, XIII, XIV et XVes siècles,* the first volume published in Paris by Vincent and the second and third in Amsterdam by Arkstée and Merkus in the same year. In 1808 Meon's expansion and reedition of Barbazan was published in four volumes by Crapelet in Paris with much greater success.

43. Macé, 142. Vanderbourg also planned to make the "edition" look "even more "Gaulish," as he put it, by printing the title of each poem in gothic lettering and by ornamenting the text with antique-looking woodcuts (143).

44. In a letter to the widow Surville dated 1805, Vanderbourg recounted Macpherson's imposture. In a letter of 1803 to the Marquis de Surville's younger brother, Vanderbourg defended his deprecation of the defunct Marquis's poetic skills as necessary in order to answer the objections of critics that Surville was just another "Chatterton who, toward the end of the last century, published supposed verse in ancient English that he attributed to a monk named Rowley . . . [and] pushed this deceit to the point of forging original manuscripts on parchment yellowed on purpose" (Macé, 113, 154). Heinrichs, the Parisian editor of both Fabre d'Olivet's and Vanderbourg's supposed medieval poetry, had spent ten years as an officer in the English army (Macé, 159) and must have been well aware of the polemic evoked in England by the "supposed" medieval verse of Macpherson and Chatterton. Heinrichs and Vanderbourg would probably also have seen the scholarly format (with explanatory footnotes) of authenticating editions of "Rowley's" verse, such as Jeremiah Miles's *Poems Supposed To Have Been Written at*

Bristol in the Fifteenth Century by Thomas Rowley, Priest, with a Commentary in which the Antiquity of Them Is Considered and Defended (London: Payne, 1782).

45. In light of the analogy between literary and legal documents and property rights, it is interesting that Vanderbourg, on the widow Surville's behalf, tried to get a decision from the Ministry of the Interior under the Consulate of Napoleon assuring the widow the property rights to her husband's manuscripts of Clotilde's verse (some of which were not then in her possession) and, more crucial, forbidding anyone to publish them without her permission. To give the widow exclusive publication rights to Clotilde's verse (of, supposedly, over three centuries back) would have been to authenticate officially Clotilde and a literary property right inherited down through a family over three centuries (rather than the ten years the heirs of an author legally possessed the rights to his work after his death at this period) (Macé, 140).

46. Vanderbourg's and Heinrichs's printer, Didot, balked at the royalist sentiments and allusions midway through the printing of the first page of the first poem and would not proceed without special ministerial authorization, but the minister refused to take responsibility and deferred the question to Napoleon, who was supposedly persuaded by Josephine (and perhaps also by the flattering allusions to his own battle victories that Vanderbourg seems to have written into Clotilde's "Chant royal à Charles VIII") (Auguste Le Sourd, *Autour de Clotilde de Surville: Lettres inédites de Vanderbourg et du Marquis de Surville* [Aubenas: Habauzit, 1928], 22.). Among the marketing strategies Vanderbourg explained in his letters to the widow Surville was the necessary distribution of some free copies of the edition "to close the mouths of Republican journalists so that they do not sound the alarm on the subject of the allusions you are familiar with" (Macé, 152).

47. Charles Nodier, *Questions de littérature légale: du plagiat, de la supposition d'auteurs, des supercheries qui ont rapport aux livres,* 2d ed. (Paris: Crapelet, 1811), 85. In this same volume Nodier judged, speaking of Chatterton's impostures, that to invent works and ascribe them to unknown older poets is "the most innocent thing one can do" for "the slight breach of truth is hardly of a nature to deserve reproach from a scrupulous probity" (76). Nodier and Roujoux published out of the Marquis de Surville's manuscripts a second volume (which announced itself "ornamented with engravings in the gothic genre"): *Poésies inédites de Marguerite-Eléonore Clotilde de Vallon et Chalys, depuis Madame de Surville, poëte français du 15e siècle* (Paris: Nepveu, 1827).

48. Adolf Tobler, "Briefe von Friedrich Diez an Jakob Grimm," *Zeitschrift für romanische Philologie* 7 (1883): 486.

49. Bernard Cerquiglini, *Éloge de la variante: Histoire critique de la philologie* (Paris: Editions du Seuil, 1989), 87–88, 91–94.

50. Joseph Körner, "François-Juste-Marie Raynouard," *Germanisch-romanische Monatsschrift* 5 (1913): 486, quoting from the third edition of Diez's *Grammatik der romanischen Sprachen.*

51. François Raynouard, *Lexique roman, ou dictionnaire de la langue des troubadours,* 6 vols. (Paris: Silvestre, 1838–44).

52. For further discussion of these medieval regularizing efforts, see my *The Game of Love: Troubadour Word Play* (Berkeley: University of California Press, 1988), 74–94.

FOUR

"In the Beginning Was the Word": Germany and the Origins of German Studies

Jeffrey M. Peck

THE FRONTISPIECE OF Jacob and Wilhelm Grimms' *German Dictionary* contains an angel sitting in an idyllic setting: her left hand holds a torch and her right the message "In the Beginning Was the Word." The popularized Enlightenment image of the light and Word of God was known to as many Germans from Goethe's *Faust* as from John's Gospel, as much from their reading of a literary text as of a theological one. That the most monumental and ambitious project of nineteenth-century German philology was also situated in a Christian religious tradition points to some of the circumstances in which *Germanistik* (German studies) originated. This study proceeds from the biblical account of its origins in the word to the study of the word later in the discipline which bears the traces of these beginnings. This shift highlights the transformative power of some significant manifestations of the word and philological reflections on it. Considering it as part of the all-encompassing notion of German *Bildung*,[1] I examine the pivotal moment when philological practice and discourse coincide

An earlier version of this chapter was presented at a meeting sponsored by the Group for Research on the Institutionalization and Professionalization of Literary Study (GRIP). It has benefited from the collaborative spirit in which it was discussed there. My thanks especially to James Sosnoski.

with the struggle for national identity: the Grimms' massive enterprise of writing a dictionary within the institutional context of German philology at the "new" University of Berlin. This confluence of scholarship and politics contributed to the successful institutionalization and professionalization of *Germanistik* at its most crucial juncture of power and authority, just as Bismarck was unifying Germany and carving out a place for it as a competitive industrial and colonial power.

Today, in writing histories of literature and language disciplines, we can learn a great deal from the beginnings of *Germanistik* because its history shows how critical practice is shaped by interests and ideologies closely associated with formal institutions such as church and state. Its development reflects how disciplines are like texts, insofar as they are constituted for very compelling reasons at particular historical moments, which set them on a course that continues to shift direction and assume different meanings as their function changes. Institutional interests, national and patriotic urges, academic and scholarly philosophies intermittently erupted and converged to shape the course of a discipline which, as part of philological practice, would significantly influence what constituted scholarship, research, and learning, especially in England and America.[2]

Yet ironically, German philology and its offspring *Germanistik* were marked by their problematic origins, especially after World War I and the ideological excesses of the Nazi period. These events compelled German academics to reflect critically on their own practices as they tried to reform the university and "interpretive" disciplines such as literature and history in the late 1960s and 1970s. For American critics, traditionally less sensitive to worldly concerns, the problematic German example draws attention to the important function of disciplinary histories, especially for national literatures. Suddenly we see how what has been done in the past to build a national literary and disciplinary tradition informs politically and culturally what we do today in our practice of literary study.

In an essay on the genesis of national philologies in France and Germany (i.e., Prussia), Hans Ulrich Gumbrecht begins by establishing "Romanticism as an age in cultural history" or "the Romantic concept of the nation" as "the most important preconditions for the origins of what we now call the 'modern philologies.'" He then elaborates: "It suggests an analogy (and even an identity) between Romantic enthusiasm for the Middle Ages and the exceptional position of medieval studies in the early days of modern philology."[3]

While his observations are important, they are not new. He concludes, however, with a more salient critique relevant to any work being done on national literatures that tries to tie together scholarship, its practice, and political struggles for national identity: "It also permits critical modern philologists to 'unmask' the political abuse of research as, so to speak, the eventual consequence of 'national birth trauma.'"[4] He connects in fact the rise of national philologies in Romanticism and their experience of alterity in the past according to "what function the evocation of knowledge about the culturally "other" had in each period."[5] Thus he implies that disciplinary history can have an anthropological and political function when it is carried on in the context of contemporary practice.

Any critical history of *Germanistik* that wants to unearth its origins, especially in struggles for national identity, seems always to begin with the Grimm Brothers.[6] The Grimms represent in their work what Gumbrecht typifies for Romanticism: "National identity—as a representation of collective identity—seems to depend—at least for the early 19th century—on the experience of socially distant folktales and historically distant medieval cultural forms, which can be identified as the objectivations of one's own 'people.'"[7] Merely the titles of the Grimms' publications reflect their preoccupation with "the German" and the German past: *German Legends* (2 vols., 1816–18) and their periodical *Old German Woods* (1813–16); Jacob's own projects, *Old German Song* (1811), *German Grammar* (1819–37), *German Monuments of Law* (1828), *German Mythology* (1835), *History of the German Language* (2 vols., 1848); and, of course, their well-known *Fairy Tales* and the *German Dictionary*.

The preface to the second volume of the tales clearly sketches the connections between a past in a particularly German form and the tales' contents. Just as in their other works, the instructive and the pleasurable are harmoniously joined in this aura of Germanness:

> Nothing is more reliable and at the same time more certain than that which comes together from two springs that, once separate, have flowed together into the same bed. In these folktales lies resonant German myth that had been considered lost, and we are entirely certain that, if one were now to search in all the blessed corners of our fatherland, unnoticed treasures would be found transforming themselves in unsuspected ways. They will help to establish a science of the ancestral source of our poetry. . . . We wish in the meantime, through our collection, not merely to show that the history of poetry

can perform a service; it was at the same time our intention that the living poetry itself should work its effect, should delight if it can, so that it can take on the function of a virtual book of instruction (trans. Gumbrecht, 11). It has been said against this last point that one thing or another in it is questionable. It is unsuitable or disturbing for children (there have been the same discussions about the devil because children are not to hear anything evil). Parents do not want to put the tales into their children's hands. . . . However, we know of no healthy or powerful book that has educated the people (*Volk*), even if we place the Bible at the top of this list, where such considerations have not arisen to various degrees (my trans.).[8]

For comparison, Wilhelm Grimm uses the holiest of texts, the Bible, which draws on the mythic and the real and brings the past into the present in forms that also can teach as well as delight. It is a standard against which he and his brother can measure the validity of projects like the fairy tales and even the dictionary, the latter an enterprise which for them will also be as influential for the German people as the Bible.

In the case of the dictionary, Jacob Grimm takes a philological project, invests it with nationalistic presumptions and expectations, and then projects what might be considered a mere practical or diligent exercise in lexicography, etymology, or onomastics onto a transcendental and religious level.[9] His rather rhetorical question only emphasizes the magnitude of the project: "What is the purpose of a dictionary? In accordance with its encompassing universality, there can be only one great goal. It should establish a holy place/sanctuary of language, preserve its entire treasure, and remain open for all. Our legacy grows like a honeycomb and becomes a sublime monument of our people, whose past and present are connected in it."[10] Although Grimm may have believed in 1838, when the project was first announced, that he could produce "six or seven large narrowly printed volumes,"[11] the completion of such a Romantic endeavor literally "growing out" of the German past, taken up in the Romantic present, and carried on into the German future seems to have been illusory. The paradox comes through in Grimm's anonymously published advertisement of 1838 which describes the dictionary as including "the infinite wealth of our fatherland's language, which no one as of yet has surveyed and judged."[12] As the project was dedicated to collecting a "living"[13] and metaphorically alive language, the dictionary, in common Romantic organic imagery, was planting the seeds for the continuing growth and future of the German language, not only for the people (*Volk*) but also ironically for the generations of German philologists to come. The first volume was completed in 1854 and the last, thirty-two volumes later, in 1961, 123 years after the project was first announced. No sooner was it finished, however, than work began again![14]

Marking the dictionary as a kind of Romantic fragment, this openness toward the future of the German language is represented in the unidentifiable and unidentified angel, a common nineteenth-century icon. With this image Grimm is trying, in the very first pages, to make the dictionary accessible to interpretation for "the common people, not the educated/clever people who come from a landed estate."[15] They should be able to enter freely into the holy realm of the German language. He parallels here the Protestant theologian Martin Luther, who three hundred years earlier had translated the Bible and brought a heavenly realm down to earth literally and spiritually. By making these two books accessible theologically and philologically through the word, both men tried to open up, so to speak, a "new land" of interpretation and understanding to the German people. Both men encouraged a Romantic speculation on language, which, while it enlarged the territory of hermeneutic participation for the *Volk*, also inscribed the beginnings of an exclusionary ideology based on ethnic superiority.

The sanctity of this new holy book leads Grimm, who naturally then becomes the priest of this new religion, to counsel his readers: "If people could have access to the simple fare of their native language, the dictionary could thus become a household necessity and could often be read with desire and devotion. Why shouldn't the father select a few words in the evening and go through them with the boys in order to test their language ability and freshen up his own."[16] Thus the German dictionary, as one critic has pointed out, becomes the "household book (*Hausbuch*) of the German family in place of the Bible . . . the learning of the German language becomes a sacred act."[17]

In the spirit of his now famous definition of "people (*Volk*) as the essence of mankind who speak the same language,"[18] Grimm's secularized theology provides linguistically and culturally the religious faith and the political ideology for the symbolic unification of a country without a political identity. Grimm confirms his faith in a heritage that has transfiguratory power: "Since the Wars of Liberation there has arisen in all noble classes of the nation continuous and unfading yearning for the heritage that unites and does not divide

Germany . . . if after the storm of 1848 long and arduous setbacks occur, language and history can best use their inexhaustible power to calm."[19] German philology, whose most ambitious project was the dictionary, could therefore even be for Grimm's successor, Rudolph Hildebrand, "a worker for the health/healing of the nation," "when a people is sick."[20]

How was it that the dictionary, a mere book of words, could have such seemingly magical power to heal the wounds of defeat in the wars with Napoleon, two unsuccessful revolutions in 1830 and 1848, and the fragmentation of the ideal of the German nation and people into dozens of political entities? The German nation seems miraculously, for Grimm at least, to start taking shape and appears to be unified, past and present, beginning and end, through just the careful collection of German words in a book. How was it that the shift from theology to philology, the word of God to the love of the word and its study, could take place so smoothly?

The answer lies in Romanticism's (largely Friedrich Schlegel's) theoretical program of *Transzendentalpoesie* ("transcendental poetry"), which would synthesize the ideal and the real on a higher level of transcendence through the poetic word and make every poet a priest. In this spirit, Grimm has invested the word with religious significance and validated what on one level was merely a linguistic or philological exercise. Any practitioner of literary study would confirm Frank Kermode's comparison of religious and philological/literary institutions: "Of institutions having a primary duty to interpret texts, and to nominate a certain body of texts as deserving or requiring repeated exegesis (interminable exegesis, indeed) the Church is the most exemplary. Self-perpetuating, hierarchical, authoritative, much concerned with questions of canon, and wont, as we are, to distinguish sharply between initiate and uninitiated readings, it is a model we would do well to consider as we attempt to understand our own practice."[21] While the dictionary was clearly not a text to be interpreted in the strict philological sense, it does function to bring understanding (the light in the angel's hand) to the German family. It succeeds not only in the literal philological fashion (giving meaning to a word), but in the broadly cultural and political sense (giving meaning to a people) without a state. Unfortunately Grimm could not foresee how such a concept of a Germanic *Kulturnation,* while it might be based on a Herderian cosmopolitanism and universalism, would be interpreted for more narrowly patriotic and nationalistic purposes.[22]

If for the Romantics the magic or key word (*Zauberwort, Schlüsselwort*) could, as it does for the exemplary German Romantic hero Heinrich von Ofterdingen, open the door to the interpretation of life, as well as literature, the dictionary, the book of words, becomes the book of life (*Lebensbuch*), that is, literature in the broadest poetic sense. Like the tenth-century Merseburger magical charms (which Grimm himself edited) or the word on the chalice which unlocks the secret of the Grail for the German medieval hero Parzival, the German words collected in the dictionary could, at least, perform the Romantic magical function of creating a new reality, a new unified Germany in the consciousness of the German people.

This shift from word to world, from the meaning of a book to the meaning of life, from theology to philology, was mediated through the form of critical practice common to all scholars in those fields that dealt with texts and the accompanying problems of interpretation. Hermeneutics developed originally for the exegesis of and commentary on the Bible. It was secularized during the Romantic period into a general theory of understanding (*Kunstlehre des Verstehens*[23]) by thinkers such as Friedrich Schleiermacher, an established theologian who also was, as could be expected, recognized for his philological expertise in translating Plato. He has come to be known therefore as "the father of Romantic hermeneutics." The Romantic texts of philologists/philosophers like Schleiermacher, but especially Friedrich Schlegel and Novalis, drew attention to their self-referentiality. These texts became blueprints for their own interpretation. Every experience of reading and interpretation is a metacritical act, when each text points to its own poetic categories and characteristics. Novalis sums up in a few words what would evolve into a central Romantic theoretical program: "A novel is a *life* as a book. Every life has a motto—a title—a publisher—a preface—introduction—text—*notes*—and so forth, or can have it."[24]

Therefore the dictionary becomes a *Lebensbuch* and as such represents the most literal example of a Romantic hermeneutic project, at least on the philosophical idealized level above the failures of real political practice. It was, however, in the words of one critic, "a Pyrrhic victory for *Germanistik*,"[25] an enterprise that outlived its own Romantic and nationalistic impulse. Grimm's fixation on alterity in the past did not prepare the Germans for coping with a world that no longer could be satisfied with Romantic ideals. This obsession with the past, as the spring from which a national identity could grow, moved him and others, as Gumbrecht pointed out, to find those texts where German language, myth, and legend all began. They therefore sought the beginnings of the word in medieval texts. Grimm asks rhetorically, "What do we have more in common than our language and literature?"[26] He could have answered himself when he pointedly states, "Our language is also our history."[27] This exaggerated concern with the German medieval past prompted philologists to conceive history regressively and therefore produced a mythology of a kind of Golden Age (*goldenes Zeitalter*) founded in German antiquity. It presumed that the older texts were more German and therefore better. Further, while it stimulated in the early part of the nineteenth century the founding of chairs in German philology, it concentrated literary study on medieval texts, and produced a dilettantish scholarship practiced by men who were more patriot than philologist.

One of the best examples was Friedrich Heinrich von der Hagen. Considered the first professor (extraordinary) "for German language and literature" at the newly established University of Berlin in 1810, von der Hagen was a lawyer by training, as was Grimm. He was, in fact, reported to have received the post since he had established "in Germany a name as an enthusiastic patriot."[28] Similarly, von der Hagen's replacement, after his call to Breslau, the second Prussian university, was August von Zeune, a geographer, who is described by a sentimental historian of the University of Berlin in 1925 as one "who replaced what he lacked in philology with heartfelt patriotic enthusiasm."[29] Zeune was therefore moved enough to edit one of the four editions of the medieval epic the *Nibelungenlied,* which was produced in the embattled political years between 1806 and 1815. This volume was a "field-tent edition for the Prussian soldiers" in the war against Napoleon that began in 1813.[30]

Von der Hagen also edited the *Nibelungenlied,*[31] which, as the focus of the most lively philological debate in Germany, was "the center of German literary history . . . the crystallization point of the national literary 'treasure.' It was the starting point and goal for all historically linguistic and mythological concern: it was plainly the object of identification for German philology."[32] It was natural, then, that von der Hagen should give his first and only course in the opening semester of the university the rather baroque title "An introduction will be given to the history of the older German literature in general and especially to the *Nibelungenlied* and the poem explained in its grammar and content." It is clear from von der Hagen's title that the study of the text was not even what we would call literary criticism but rather literary history, grammatical study of the Middle High

German language, and content analysis. Even in today's German departments, medievalists along with philologists/linguists are responsible for teaching Middle High German, since understanding the text is first of all a task of translation and understanding a foreign language. This alliance of the general field of German philology with medieval study hindered the development of more critical methods in *Germanistik* into the twentieth century. Until the advent of more theoretical approaches such as structuralism, semiotics, reception theory, and poststructuralism, medievalists, like classicists even today, approached the text philologically, that is to put it most generally, they began with the word.

This explains, then, at least in part, the placement of von der Hagen's single course under the category "Modern languages and literature" (*Neuere Sprachen und Literatur*), which not surprisingly completed the first semester with twelve courses by more illustrious colleagues in the "Philological disciplines" (*Philologische Wissenschaften*) such as Friedrich August Wolf and August Boeckh. In this semester Boeckh began his now famous series of lectures, "Encyclopedia and methodology of all the philological disciplines" (*Enzyklopädie und Methodologie der gesamten philologischen Wissenschaften*), which forms a significant part of the corpus on nineteenth-century hermeneutics. In the second semester von der Hagen's course on the *Nibelungenlied* makes its way into the category of philological disciplines along with his new course, "History of old German literature" (*Geschichte der alten deutschen Dichtung*). But here it competes with Homer and Pindar, Tacitus and Horace. The rivalry between the study of German philology, that is, medieval study, and classical philology is partly assuaged by the appointment in 1825 of Karl Lachmann, considered to be one of the best philologists of the nineteenth century, as professor "for German *and* classical philology" (emphasis added).

This short descriptive review of the curriculum reveals not only the evolution of medieval study in the new university, but also the status of classical philology against which German philology was competing, but, even more, from which it was drawing sustenance and legitimation. Studying the word, especially the Greek word of classical texts, drew the student into the entire cultural world of antiquity. As the central experience of *Bildung* at the newly reformed university and the *Gymnasium,* the younger partner in this new educational enterprise, classical study humanized and cultivated him as a whole human being without regard for practical and professional training. It also gave the budding scholar the methodological tools and scholarly framework for interpretation and understanding when he studied German literature. It is not surprising to note, then, that from a representative sampling of a hundred Germanists during the period from 1806 to 1848, only twenty-one had courses of study in German philology, whereas the largest number (fifty-one) had studied classical philology. Even more noteworthy in this context is that the next largest group (thirty-three) had chosen to study theology.[33]

As Werner Richter points out, "even into the 1880s, when *Germanistik* had become institutionalized at the University of Berlin and Wilhelm Scherer was establishing the seminar for modern German literary history, it was taken for granted that the learned Germanist was conscious of the original connections with classical philology."[34] It is, in fact, reported, that as Scherer approached his teacher Müllenhoff (von der Hagen's replacement) and inquired what he as a Germanist should do, the elder Germanist replied, "Read Propertius!"[35] Clearly what we have here is a set of performances that are validated and shape academic careers. Lodged in an "official" set of beliefs, these practices "*authorize* our professional discourse within our institutions." This is how James Sosnoski characterizes what he calls the *magister implicatus*.[36]

Classical philological study had already been institutionalized as early as the beginnings of the eighteenth century in Göttingen which attracted the likes of the Schlegels, F. A. Wolf, and Wilhelm von Humboldt himself.[37] The philological seminar was, in fact, established at Göttingen and Halle, modeled not surprisingly on its theological predecessor.[38] Humboldt, who considered Wolf his mentor, was particularly complimented by the fact that the latter had been influenced by his ideas on *Bildung* and classical antiquity presented in an essay that has been called "a manifesto proclaiming the relevance of classical scholarship to Germany's cultural needs in a time of national humiliation."[39]

Theories of *Bildung* were translated into educational policy that became institutionalized at the University of Berlin. Those responsible—Humboldt, Friedrich Schleiermacher, and J. G. Fichte—reveal in their writing their own kind of conviction in the power of the German language to shape intellectual and moral character through *Bildung* and *Wissenschaft*. They institutionalized the interconnection of language, scholarship, and politics in the context of what is called the "most incisive German university reform since the sixteenth century."[40]

Berlin became the model of reform and under Humboldt's leadership established the unity of *Bildung* and *Wissenschaft* in an environment of *Lernfreiheit* ("freedom of learning"). These notions are still, at least, a desired ideal at the heart of the modern university when we think of scholarship, research, and learning. In Humboldt's own plan for the university, outlined in his short but seminal essay "On the inner and outer organization of the higher scholarly institutions in Berlin (1810)," he begins by describing *Wissenschaft* in these higher institutions "as the peak in which everything that has to do with the moral culture of the nation comes together."[41] It is "something seen as not yet to be found and never completely to be found, to be searched for continuously as such." He also uses words like "uninterrupted," "to reenliven itself again and again," "uncompelled," and "purposeless working together."[42] He clearly attributes an unusually dynamic and spiritual character to *Wissenschaft* in Berlin. He can speak therefore about such high expectations of "a great part of our fatherland" for the new university and acknowledges it "would exert a significant influence on all Germany."[43] The university, in one of Humboldt's biographer's words, "would be capable of fulfilling a supreme cultural function for the German people."[44]

Although Humboldt does not develop a philosophy of language explicitly connected to German national identity, his concept of "language as world view" based on his ethnological and linguistic studies, is a theoretical premise for more concrete nationalistic language propositions. At the core of Humboldt's strikingly humanistic anthropology is the unity of language and thought as the constitutive basis for human existence. Language is the "shaping organism of thought" and is for him *energeia* rather than *ergon,* a dynamic and lively, organic and active process, akin to the power of *Wissenschaft* to regenerate itself and to carry thought and spiritual life forward.[45]

In Fichte's "Speeches to the German nation" (1807–8) and "Dedicated plan for established higher institutions of learning in Berlin" (1807) are rooted concepts of language which Grimm would develop in his preoccupation with the "language nation." In the latter essay, Fichte emphasized the creative aspect of *Wissenschaft* in the mother tongue: "Lively art (art = learning in the sense of the classical fields of study from antiquity and the Middle Ages) can be practiced and documented solely in a language that is not already limited through itself, but rather in which one may be *fresh* and *creative* and in which as our mother tongue our own life is interwoven."[46] His colleague Schleiermacher, in the title of his treatise "Occasional thoughts on universities in the German sense," implies that there is a special relationship between language, nation, and *Bildung*. He sets up in the educational treatise the methodological bases of all disciplines in language: "all activities of learning that form in the area of one language have a naturally exact relationship. . . . For what is produced and illustrated in *one* language with regard to scholarship/learning shares the special nature of this language."[47]

Although these three educational reformers' and philosophers' plans for the university diverged, they were all committed to a philosophy of language, to a notion of philology that invested the word with unusual power to generate thinking and reflection. The "linguisticality of understanding" (*Sprachlichkeit des Verstehens*), which we now identify with Hans Georg Gadamer's twentieth-century philosophical hermeneutics, had its origins in these men's attitudes toward language and understanding, toward the interpretation of the word.

By emphasizing philology's central place in the work of Boeckh, Schleiermacher's student, the linguist and historian of scholarship Hans Aarsleff establishes the strongest bond between philology and hermeneutics: "In Germany philology became the central academic discipline—'philology' in the German sense as the historical knowledge of human nature or in August Boeckh's comprehensive definition 'Die Erkenntniss des Erkannten,' i.e. no less than the study of the history and knowledge of all human thought and activity."[48] *Bildung* and *Wissenschaft* were no less than the means through which human beings could come to know themselves, and philology in this universal sense was not only the key to enter this world but also the realm in which understanding became conscious of itself.

For the Romantics and hermeneutic philosophers/philologists like Boeckh, philology was synonymous with philosophy, the queen of the disciplines as it was called, since it provided the comprehensive mechanisms for reflection and interpretation on all of life as well as work. In this rather overly speculative context, classics, as well as its methodological offspring German philology (and its grandest project, the dictionary), did indeed become a kind of "secular redemption."[49]

Thus, in an article on the beginnings of literary study, Lionel Gossman sees that for the Romantics and especially the Germans, "Literature . . . was nothing less . . . than a Revelation of the hidden and forgotten world of the origins. The early teachers of Literature were consequently transformed into priests of a new religion. They were the guardians and interpreters of its sacred texts,"[50] particularly those inspiring medieval texts, literally (and reverently) called "language monuments" (*Sprachdenkmäler*) by the philologists. They were verbal relics fastened firmly to pedestals of the past in a dusty museum of masterpieces. They were devoutly received and treated to exegesis by the devoted priests of *Germanistik* smitten by their quasi-religious mission. These men's sacred philological regard for the German word through which they entered these texts was instilled with political fervor and still bore the traces of its theological origins. As part of their holy charge, they thought they could fulfill the task of healing "the divisions and discontinuities,"[51] "creat[ing] a unified and total culture without ruptures or exclusions."[52]

Germany's unification in 1871 under Prussian leadership could be interpreted, then, as the realization of Grimm's Romantic project, albeit from the emperor above rather than from the people (*Volk*) below.[53] In the spirit of Grimm, *Germanistik* continued to be involved in national affairs. Thus in 1872 Wilhelm Scherer was called (*berufen*) from Vienna to the now German university of Strassburg. Scherer's academic move was based, according to one critic, on the university's role of "firm[ing] up the German spirit against France . . . as fortification of German imperialism."[54] Another critic elaborates that, for Scherer himself, going to the recently Germanized city was "less academic/scholarly than much for the founding and intensification of 'the German'."[55] Scherer reports in a letter that in Strassburg there was "a very pleasant association between the university [i.e., the German professors] and the military," especially as the Alsatian population was very reserved toward these (German) academics.[56] Scherer, in fact, describes his own work there as "colonizing."[57] These circumstances explain, at least in part, his decision to stay on in Strassburg after his first offer from Berlin. Bismarck himself intervenes: "I would like this even more since Herr Professor Scherer, even beyond the circles of the university, has enthusiastically encouraged, through his writing and speaking, the German language and the German manner, and I lay special value from a political standpoint on these influences of his work in the lands of the empire."[58]

While such a nationalism emerging from religious origins may have inspired and then validated philological political efforts like Grimm's, and even Scherer's, the projects remained idealized and otherworldly. They romanticized, on the one hand, the legendary past and the mythical world of the Middle Ages, and on the other, the glorious future of political, economic, or colonial successes, literally in exotic, other worlds like Africa or the South Seas. The "ideal of totality and presence, the goal of restored and unified national culture"[59] that Gossman claims for Romanticism could not be achieved in a Wilhelminian Germany that was being transformed by industrialization, technology, and *Machtpolitik*.

Even Scherer becomes increasingly dissatisfied with the German drive for political and imperialistic national power. He sees it producing "human isolation" which is intensified by the social alienation accompanying economic and technological advancement.[60] He himself seems to want to return to a liberal-humanistic age more reminiscent of Humboldt, Fichte, and Schleiermacher sixty years earlier. Disappointed, Scherer finally admits that the ideal of "unity of thought, sensibility, and desire" (*Einheit des Denkens, Empfindens und Wollens*) was not to be achieved in this new *Reich*.[61] Scherer was confronted with a kind of fragmentation and alienation that Grimm had not known or perhaps even could imagine in preindustrial Germany. These dramatic changes were undermining any hope of recovering a Romantic vision of unity or all-comprehensiveness, at least in this new Germany, or in the one that tried to realize the ultimate Romantic dream of a thousand-year Nazi *Reich*.

Such romantic hopes seemed to have faded, or were at least tempered by the realism of postwar boundaries that divided rather than united. Two Germanies and two Germanistics emerged from the failure of what for a long time seemed to be the last attempt to translate Romanticism into a national program. Both Germanies struggled to claim a common political and literary history that was decisively altered by the defeat of the Third Reich. Then, in the debate surrounding German unification, both within both Germanies and in the world, the issues of national identity and political power surfaced even more dramatically; the existence of a new Germany was based, to some observers, on a questionable reliance on traditions, symbols, and myths that were being used to enhance the continuities to a collective national history and to underplay the disruption of the terrible twelve years of Nazism.

It is not surprising that reflections on "Germany and the Origins of German Studies" should end by referring to the unifications and disunifications (1871, 1933, 1945, 1990) in German history that emerge as variations on a theme preoccupying German philologists as well as politicians. After Scherer, there indeed do emerge extreme nationalist German philologists such as August Sauer and Josef Nadler. However, interpreting Grimm and Scherer as intermediaries in a continuous tradition from German Romanticism to a German nationalism culminating in the Third Reich is extremely problematic.

The ambivalence and contradiction in the German tradition around "unification" and continuity are exemplified precisely by the history of Grimm's reception,[62] especially in recent years, and Scherer's own vacillation. This uncertainty was reflected in the Federal Republic's own confusion about thorny political and trying emotional issues such as patriotism and national identity in the decade before the unexpected unification. What will come in the wake of such a historic event is yet to be seen. However, a solution other than the traditional simplistic dichotomy of the "good" and the "bad" Germany needs to be found, whether this opposition refers to a German tradition leading to the Third Reich, then to the postwar West-East era, and now more recently to a united Germany.

Disciplinary history might mediate this interpretive dilemma by drawing on the theoretical foundations of critique and self-reflection constitutive of the very same German Romanticism that seems to have initiated the problem. If a discipline is understood as a set of practices that acquires meaning over time, the history of disciplines will reveal the classification systems and narrative models that have been used to constitute, represent, and empower the discipline for specific interests. The constant reinvention of the discipline through the histories written about it draws our attention to the conditions under which disciplinary practices acquire meaning. We see how important it is to ask who practiced the discipline, what kinds of knowledge did it produce, what function did it serve. Thus, rather than merely affirming or legitimizing an origin, disciplinary history questions the entire premise of beginnings by making the various instances of historicizing scholarly discourse (*wissenschaftlicher Diskurs*) the proper subject of its inquiry.

While the impact of politics and ideology on academic and critical practice is more obvious in situations as tragic and traumatic as the Third Reich, disciplinary history exposes the foundations of its subject in less dramatic historical instances as well. In both cases the history of *Germanistik* reveals how the constellation of language (the word), philology (the study of the word), and national identity (here the empowering of the word) can constitute dangerous alliances. The German experience, which includes the events and their histories, can remind us how important it is to disentangle this triadic nexus of power relations wherever and whenever it may appear. Such activity is necessary for our continued vigilance and critique of any fetishizing of the word which might lead to oppression and ultimately to silence.

NOTES

1. *Bildung,* as well as *Wissenschaft,* are two concepts associated with the newly reformed German university in the nineteenth century. These two words are particularly difficult to translate from German into English because they represent notions of scholarship, research, and learning specifically identified with the German tradition. *Bildung* means most broadly education and cultivation. I quote here the definition used by Fritz Ringer in his now classic study *The Decline of the German Mandarins: The German Academic Community 1890–1933,* which he has taken from the standard German *Brockhaus* encyclopedia.

> The fundamental concept of pedagogy since Pestalozzi, *Bildung* means forming the soul by means of the cultural environment. *Bildung* requires: (a.) an individuality which, as the unique starting point, is to be developed into a formed or value-saturated personality; (b.) a certain universality, meaning richness of mind and person, which is attained through the empathetic understanding and experiencing (*Verstehen und Erleben*) of the objective cultural values; (c.) totality, meaning inner unity and firmness of character. (86)

Wissenschaft is often misrepresented in English by being translated as merely "science," that is, natural science. It also means scholarship and discipline.

2. In the latter half of the nineteenth century, hundreds of young English and American students flocked to German universities, especially Berlin and Göttingen, to take advantage of German scholarly methods and research facilities. Many of them returned to later become presidents of prestigious American colleges and universities such as Noah Porter of Yale and George Bancroft of Berkeley. The Johns Hopkins University, founded in 1876, and regarded as the first American graduate school, was overwhelmingly influenced by the German university.

3. Hans Ulrich Gumbrecht, "Un souffle d'Allemagne ayant passé: Friedrich Diez, Gaston Paris, and the Genesis of National Philologies," *Romance Philology* 40, no. 1 (1986):1.

4. Gumbrecht, 2.

5. Gumbrecht, 5. Gumbrecht goes on to undercut this "explanatory pattern" to explain the emergence of Romance philology in the Prussian university instead of in France, Italy, or Spain.

6. Although both brothers worked on the dictionary and wrote the introduction, in my discussion I refer to Jacob because he has come to be the one most identified with the project. A number of significant political events

influenced the Grimm Brothers, the most noteworthy being their expulsion from the University of Göttingen with five other professors for refusing to break their oath to a rather liberal constitution that had been dissolved by Ernst August, the new monarch of Hannover. This group has come to be called the "Göttingen Seven." Wilhelm Scherer, the famous Berlin Germanist at the end of the century, went so far as to attribute the writing of the dictionary to their expulsion. The dictionary was "the form in which their lives that had been destroyed by a German government and not supported by any other, could be most honorably taken care of." In 1848 Jacob was also a representative to the Frankfurt National Assembly, which was the first such constitutional meeting in Germany. For further discussion see "Grimm-Wörterbuch. A bis Zypressenzweig," *Der Spiegel*, No. 20 (May 1961), 65–74.

7. Gumbrecht, 12.

8. Wilhelm Grimm, "Vorrede zum zweiten Band," *Kinder- und Hausmärchen*, in Johannes Janota, ed., *Eine Wissenschaft etabliert sich 1810–1870* (Tübingen: Max Niemeyer Verlag, 1980), 83. As indicated in the note, this and all following translations are my own.

9. For a more conventional discussion of the religious and political elements in Grimm's concept of *Vaterland*, see Roland Feldmann, *Jacob Grimm und die Politik* (Kassel: Bärenreiter Verlag, n.d.).

10. Jacob and Wilhelm Grimm, *Deutsches Wörterbuch* (Leipzig: Verlag von S. Hirzel, 1854), 1:xii.

11. Quoted from Grimm by Ulrich Wyss, *Die wilde Philologie: Jakob Grimm und der Historismus* (Munich; Verlag C. H. Beck, 1979), 176. By taking into account contemporary theoretical work on language, signification, and history, the author in this very sophisticated analysis has made Grimm a much more provocative figure for study today.

12. Wyss, 176.

13. Quoted from a Grimm letter of August 24–31, 1838 in Walter Boehlich, "Ein Pyrrhussieg der Germanistik: Die Vollendung des 'Deutschen Wörterbuchs' der Brüder Grimmm," *Der Monat* 13, No. 154 (1961): 40. Grimm's point is that the dictionary "will not only include the entire range of the living High German language . . . but rather, also old words of the 16th, 17th, and 18th centuries . . . which rightly or wrongly are out of date." He includes, in other words, the new High German language from Luther to Goethe.

14. Without going into the complicated details of the dictionary's history, it is worth mentioning that the project, which took longer than either of the Grimms could have imagined, continued to be supported by Bismarck, when he was still chancellor of the North German Confederation in 1868 (he called it "an important national undertaking"). It continued to be sustained after the country had been unified (1871) and later by both Germanies after

the country had been divided again. At the project's completion, scholars in East Berlin at the Academy of Sciences and at the University of Göttingen in West Germany had worked on it together since 1946. Ironically, the year in which the dictionary was completed with both Germanies' cooperation was the same year as the erection of the Berlin Wall.

15. Quoted from Grimm, *Altdeutsche Wälder,* ed. Brothers Grimm, 1:1813–16; rpt. with an introduction by Wilhelm Schoof (Darmstadt, 1966), in Janota, 32–33. I follow Janota's argument here.

16. Grimm, *Wörterbuch,* 1:xii–xiii.

17. Jutta Strippel, "Zum Verhältnis von Deutscher Rechtsgeschichte und Deutscher Philologie," *Literaturwissenschaft und Sozialwissenschaft 2. Germanistik und Deutsche Nation 1806–1848: Zur Konstitution bürgerlichen Bewußtseins,* ed. Jörg Jochen Müller (Stuttgart: Metzler, 1974), 165.

18. Jacob Grimm, *Kleinere Schriften* (Berlin: Dümmler, 1884), 7:557.

19. Grimm, *Wörterbuch,* 1:vii.

20. Quoted in Horst Albert Glaser, "Philologien-Allgemeine und Vergleichende Literaturwissenschaft-Literaturtheorie Literaturkritik," *Grundzüge der Literatur- und Sprachwissenschaft,* ed. Heinz Ludwig Arnold and Volker Sinumus (Frankfurt: Dtv, 1973), 1:17.

21. Frank Kermode, "The Institutional Control of Interpretation," *Salamagundi* 43 (winter 1979): 75.

22. In Walter Boehlich's article "Aus dem Zeughaus der Germanistik: Die Brüder Grimm und der Nationalismus," *Der Monat* 18, No. 217 (1966): 56–68, an extremely one-sided nationalistic interpretation of the dictionary is presented. He goes so far as to see the entire history of *Germanistik* as steeped in a "sickness of nationalism."

23. See the discussion in Friedrich Schleiermacher, *Hermeneutik,* ed. Heinz Kimmerle, from the newly edited and introduced manuscripts, Abhandlungen der Heidelberger Akademie der Wissenchaften, Philosophisch-historische Klasse (Heidelberg: Carl Winter Universitätsverlag), 1959), 9–24.

24. Friedrich von Hardenberg (Novalis), *Schriften,* ed. Richard Samuel in conjunction with Hans-Joachim Mähl and Gerhard Schulz (Stuttgart: W. Kohlhammer Verlag, 1960), 2:599.

25. Boehlich, "Ein Pyrrhussieg."

26. Grimm, *Wörterbuch,* iii.

27. Jacob Grimm, *Kleinere Schriften,* ed. Karl Müllenhoff and Eduard Ippel (Berlin, 1864), 1:290.

28. Janota, 17.

29. Quoted by Norman Balk, *Die Friedrich-Wilhelms-Universität zu Berlin, Mit einer Darstellung des Berliners Bildungswesens bis 1810* (Berlin: Speyer and Peters Verlag, 1926), 107.

30. Rainer Rosenberg, *Zehn Kapitel zur Geschichte der Germanistik: Literaturgeschichtsschreibung* (Berlin: Akademie Verlag, 1981), 53.

31. Janota notes that von der Hagen's edition was "torn apart" by Wilhelm Grimm.

32. Jörg Jochen Müller, "Germanistik—eine Form bürgerlicher Wissenschaft," *Literaturwissenschaft und Sozialwissenschaft,* 2:90.

33. Müller, 31–33.

34. Werner Richter, "Berliner Germansitik vor und nach dem Hundertjährigen Jubiläum der Friedrich-Wilhelms-Universität," *Studium Berolinese: Aufsätze und Beiträge zu Problemen der Wissenschaft und zur Geschichte der Friedrich-Wilhelms-Universität zu Berlin,* ed. H. Leussink et al. (Berlin: de Gruyter, 1960), 490.

35. Richter, 490.

36. See James Sosnoski, "The *Magister Implicatus* as an Institutionalized Authority Figure: Rereading the History of New Criticism," *GRIP Report* (N.p.: n.d.), 1 (second draft), 5.

37. For a provocative discussion of philology in the German university in the years preceding the University of Berlin, see Robert Leventhal, "The Emergence of Philological Discourse in the German States 1770–1810," *ISIS* 77, no. 287 (1986): 243–60.

38. Hans Aarsleff, *The Study of Language in England 1780–1860* (Princeton: Princeton University Press, 1967), 180.

39. Paul Sweet, *Wilhelm von Humboldt: A Biography* (Columbus: Ohio State UP, 1978), 25.

40. Müller, 51.

41. Wilhelm von Humboldt, "Über die innere und äussere Organisation der höheren wisseschaftlichen Anstalten in Berlin," *Studienausgabe,* ed. Kurt Mueller-Vollmer (Frankfurt: Fischer, 1971), 2:133.

42. Humboldt, 134.

43. Humboldt to Dohna, *Gesammelte Schriften,* 10:31–32; quoted in Sweet, 56.

44. Sweet, 57.

45. Humboldt, "Grundzüge der allgemeinen Sprachtypus," *Gesammelte Schriften,* ed. Albert Leitzmann (Berlin: B. Behr, 1907), 5:374.

46. Müller, 52; quoted from Ernst Anrich, ed., *Die Idee der deutschen Universität: Die fünf Grundschriften aus der Zeit ihrer Neubegründung durch klassischen Idealismus und romantischen Realismus* (Darmstadt: Wissenschaftliche Buchgesellschaft, 1956), 184.

47. Muller, 52; quoted from Anrich, 225. For another discussion see Heinrich Dieters, "Wilhelm von Humboldt als Gründer der Universität Berlin," *Forschen und Wirken: Festschrift zur 150* Jahre Feier der Humboldt-

Universität zu Berlin 1810–1960, Beiträge zur wissenschaftlichen und politischen Entwicklung der Universität (Berlin: VEB Deutscher Verlag der Wissenschaften, 1960), 1:15–40.

48. Aarsleff, 180.

49. Lionel Gossman, "Literature and Education," *New Literary History* 13, no. 2 (1982): 351.

50. Ibid., 355.

51. Ibid., 349.

52. Ibid., 347.

53. It is worth noting here that Austria was excluded in Bismarck's "small German" (*kleindeutsch*) political solution to German unification. It must also be mentioned that the connection of Grimm and Scherer is based not only on their nationalistic orientation. Scherer wrote extensively on Grimm's work, completed a volume on the famous Germanist himself, and gave the commemorative speech at the University of Berlin on the occasion of what would have been Jacob Grimm's one hundredth birthday, January 4, 1885.

54. Franz Gress, *Germanistik und Politik: Kritische Beiträge zur Geschichte der nationalen Wissenschaft* (Stuttgart-Bad Canstatt: Friedrich Frommann Verlag, 1971), 60.

55. Quoted in Jürgen Sternsdorff, *Wissenschaftskonstitution und Reichsgründung: Die Entwicklung der Germanistik bei Wilhelm Scherer, Eine Biographie nach unveröffentlichen Quellen* (Frankfurt: Peter Lang, 1979), 175.

56. Scherer cited by Sternsdorff, 175, who also reports that Scherer saw his move to Strassburg as his "mission" and a "true good deed." I follow here and in the following references Sternsdorff's interpretation of Scherer's statements.

57. Wilhelm Scherer, *Kleine Schriften,* vol. 2; quoted in Gress, 61.

58. Sternsdorff, 177–78.

59. Gossman, 354. Although Gossman refers here to Matthew Arnold's realization that this Romantic ideal could not be fulfilled in England, in the context of Gossman's argument this point is applicable to the German situation in the 1870s and 1880s.

60. Scherer, cited in Sternsdorff, p. 184.

61. Ibid., 185.

62. In an article from a respected weekly political newspaper, "Das Parlament," a political scientist turns his attention to the Grimm Brothers in the context of contemporary German polemics about national identity. He surveys the reception of the Grimms through the nineteenth century to National Socialism and recent responses in the Federal Republic and the German Democratic Republic. This historical review illustrates how the Grimms' attitudes about nationalism could be interpreted in a variety of ways

depending on political ideologies and interests. One particularly interesting example is the President of the Federal Republic, Richard von Weizsäcker's speech at the opening of the Seventh International Germanic Studies Congress in Göttingen in August 1985. As the first such conference to be held on German soil, it behooved von Weizsäcker to see the Grimms as conscientious and humanistic linguists/philologists. The author makes the point that, for the president, "language . . . is not a vehicle of national socialistic exclusion and arrogance, but rather the medium of communication (*Verständigung*) between human beings and peoples" (10–11). See Wilhelm Bleek, "Die Brüder Grimm und die deutsche Politik," *Das Parlament,* no. 1 (January 4, 1986): 3–16.

FIVE

The Myth of Medieval Romance

John M. Ganim

TO THE LATE-TWENTIETH-CENTURY lay reader, medievalism, in both its scholarly and popular varieties, is almost synonymous with escapism. Filtered through the lenses of Tolkien, Disney, various theme restaurants, commercially produced "fairs," and even Las Vegas (where one of the most recent casinos is called "Excalibur"), popular medievalism has acquired the function of licensing innocence. This situation was by no means always the case. In the nineteenth century, medievalism was constructed as a fierce reproach as well as a utopian escape from the present, and that reproach was framed in explicitly political terms. The most famous exemplars of nineteenth-century medievalism in its position as social critique are such authors as Sir Walter Scott, Thomas Carlyle, William Ruskin, and William Morris. That is, literary medievalism in the nineteenth century seems to chart a political trajectory from conservative paternalism to socialist utopianism, from right to left, in however halting a manner. Beneath this apparent pattern, however, medievalism is a more continually contested terrain, problematizing the political implications its proponents wish to draw.

This more problematic politics of medievalism is revealed, oddly enough, in what might seem to be the innocent pastime of medieval scholarship. Where many objects of modern literary study were institutionalized (in however contested a manner) in the modern university during the nineteenth and the early twentieth century, the study of medieval English literature had a prior history. It was fostered, even invented, by several generations of amateur scholars.[1] This was also the case with some other literary subjects, but the peculiar conditions of preacademic medievalism, and the prestige of its connoisseurs, meant that their attitudes toward medieval literature, and the cultural value they accorded it, had an extremely powerful influence on academic study. The study of medieval literature in general is born in a nostalgic love for the age and its imputed values, rather than in a veneration of authors (such as Shakespeare) or of particular texts. This sentimental romance of the period precedes any response to any particular work.

The studies of medieval romance provide a convenient and crucial focus for tracing the politics of medievalism. Implicit in these studies are conceptions of society, history, and the uses of literary language that still complicate our own responses to these works. This chapter seeks to trace some of these complications, particularly the peculiar circularity in which the study of medieval romance takes the form of its object of study. From its earliest formulations in the eighteenth century to the brief centrality of romance criticism in the mid-twentieth century, critical discourse surrounding the romances first imagines the Middle Ages as a romance, and then gradually becomes a species of romance itself.

"We have lost," wrote Richard Hurd, "a world of fine fabling."[2] Along with Thomas Warton and Thomas Percy, Bishop Hurd, especially in his *Letters on Chivalry and Romance,* was one of the leaders of the revival of medieval literature in the eighteenth century. His statement is heavily freighted with a set of characteristic assumptions. The world of the Middle Ages is a lost Golden Age, perhaps even a childhood, to which we can never return. Imagination holds the place in the Middle Ages that reason holds in the eighteenth-century present—a way of defining and creating culture. Romance itself is valued as a therapeutic and subjective means of recovering that imaginative coherence. If, rather than unpacking these assumptions, we rewrite them, the message is even clearer: the Middle Ages is imagined as a romance. "Romance," defined as escapist and utopian, is emplaced as the stereotypical genre of the Middle Ages. History is read as a literary genre. The Gothic revival of the late eighteenth century propounded a conception of the Middle Ages that apparently bore no political relevance to the present save nostalgia and inspiration. The utopian possibilities inherent in romance remain implicit in their construction of the genre, but both nostalgia and renewal are imagined by them in terms that require as little contingency with the present or the future as possible.

This aestheticized view of the Middle Ages and of romance was by no means inevitable or itself without a context. Interpretations of English medieval history had been deeply fought over in the seventeenth and the early eighteenth century. The parliamentary and legal debates that surrounded both the Puritan Revolution and the Restoration depended heavily on historical precedent. It mattered profoundly in political terms whether the Norman Conquest was a conquest or a legitimate assumption of power. Equally important was the question of whether anything like parliamentary representation existed among the "Saxons," a position favored by supporters of Parliament, and whether there was any political inheritance from the pre-"Gothic" world of the Celtic Britons, a position favored by supporters of the monarchy. Those making efforts to legitimize monarchical or parliamentary authority found themselves constructing highly elaborate arguments as to the nature of the conquest, the Magna Carta, or the "Gothic" freedoms of preconquest Saxon England.

By the early eighteenth century, the most sophisticated of these arguments had developed into an interpretation of the English medieval past as a series of historical stages. Partisan debates about this historiography had dwindled, and historians imagined medieval history as one of a series of phases through which history passed before arriving at a far preferable present. The various conflicts that the partisan ideologues of the previous century had seen in the Middle Ages were now envisioned as separate streams flowing into the institutions of the present.[3] The political utility of the Middle Ages was reduced and the Middle Ages represented as a step through which civilization moved to the present, enlightened, quite other, stage. This Whig interpretation of history—the vision of the best of the past informing the institutions of the present—replaced conflict and struggle with concord and stability. The odd result was a minimization of the importance, cultural or political, of the Middle Ages. By the time of the Gothic revival's rediscovery of romance in the late eighteenth century, the political and social dimensions of romance, and of its now metonymic period, the Middle Ages, were reduced.

The result of this minimalization of the historical and political centrality of the Middle Ages is a conception of medieval romance as mythic invention. In keeping with this, romance is imagined as both strange and faraway, its origins typically described as Oriental, and as indigenous, national, and local, as a form of history before historical consciousness takes shape. It is both familiar and strange. For part of the appeal of medieval romance for its earliest champions was that it represented a wilder, freer past, one that gave free reign to an imaginative freedom that contemporary aesthetics and mores had repressed. For the early romance scholars, however much we may dismiss their antiquarianism, romance is a model of aesthetic liberation.

We soon find these assumptions developed in the celebration of the Gothic, especially in Hurd's *Letters on Chivalry and Romance,* quoted earlier. Here the Gothic is to be valued because of its almost precivilized status, a status that seems peculiarly timeless and devoid of actual social or political contexts. The Gothic (and by extension the romance) are not just aesthetic forms but ancestral traditions that Warton's and Hurd's modern world can reinvoke through imagination. A steady-state conception of history conceives of change only by constructing an opposite and prior world, in its own way as timeless as the present. Romance is nostalgically celebrated for its preservation of our wilder past, which is constructed as both a lost world and an other world. But it also offers an avenue toward utopian renewal of our underdeveloped imaginative capacities.

This therapeutic and regenerative strain in eighteenth-century medievalism, however conservative its proponents might have been, led to one of the chief inspirations for high Romantic poetry. The alterity represented by the "gothic" was one of the ideological sources for the Romantic poetic program, however askew its understanding of the "gothic." Coleridge and Keats were directly inspired by medieval sources. The Romantic poets in general especially found in the quest romance a form congenial to the exploration of the poetic Self, even if, as in Shelley's case, the romantics knew little of medieval romance and found medievalism, as did Byron, acutely distasteful and reactionary. The conception of nature essential to Romanticism's self-definition grew out of a conception of nature linked to gothic wildness, even if no such conception of nature was held by the actual inhabitants of the Middle Ages. The challenge to the canons of poetic form and poetic language represented by medieval poetry inspired the revolution in poetic form and poetic language that was Romanticism. Through the misty haze of the "gothic," medieval literature seemed to embody the organic coherence Romanticism sought in its own aesthetic. Despite this connection with the revolutionary politics and aesthetics of Romanticism, the curation of medieval romances was to remain a largely conservative enterprise during the early nineteenth century.

The scholars of medieval romance in the late eighteenth century insistently denied the political relevance of their scholarship, but this denial masked the conservatism of their enterprise.[4] This politics becomes overt in the reception of the fruits of their labors in the early nineteenth century. The tremendous surge in enthusiasm for, and a considerable number of collections of romances, which appeared in England during the wars against France, almost certainly appealed to an antirepublican bias, and the main popularizers of the genre, including Sir Walter Scott, adopted strongly conservative and hierarchical political views. (In this light, Scott's multivolume biography of Napoleon is an ironic testament, reading Napoleon as a romantic antihero, and shifting blame to the Republic). The Middle Ages was presented as a critique of modernity, a critique of industrialization, urbanization, and democratization. The social world imagined in this scheme idealized both aristocracy and folk. The aristocracy was imagined almost entirely in terms of chivalry, to the exclusion of other traits, and "romance" was valued chiefly to the degree that it reflected chivalric models. The rest of society was honored with the capacity for cultural production, but imagined as fully itself when accepting, even demanding, hierarchical paternalism.

By the early nineteenth century, romance had become a "popular" genre and the medieval revival had become a widespread style. Not only were medieval romance and medievalism fashionable, they defined social ideals. Medievalism was propounded as an ideology, with a specific religious, political, and cultural agenda. Medievalism was associated with a return to high Anglican ritual. Antirevolutionary at base, conservative reform groups like the "Young England" movement sought to transform noblesse oblige into a political platform. The idiosyncratic antiquarianism of the eighteenth century was magnified into a symbolic cultural masquerade, the inspiration for which was the medieval romance. Nevertheless, medieval romance was a profoundly unstable center for such an enterprise. The study of popular culture has alerted us to the ways in which forms such as romance embody private desires as well as shared public values. These uneasy negotiations result in a ceaselessly contested form. Such contestation marks the unofficial history of medieval romance in the nineteenth century. In *Idylls of the King,* his retelling of Malory, Tennyson is unable to reconcile the subversive eroticism of romance with the public vision of medievalism, but the effort to do so accounted for the work's enormous and continuing popularity. Similarly, later in the century, William Morris and others appropriated medieval romance for revolutionary politics, precisely the position the romance revival of the early nineteenth century defined itself against. In works such as *News from Nowhere,* Morris's utopian tale of a future in medieval dress, romance becomes the formal vehicle of apocalypse and utopia, an association it briefly held in high Romantic poetry.

One particularly interesting case is that of the scholar Joseph Ritson, not because he reflects the early-nineteenth-century pattern of conservative medievalism, but because he defies it, and in defying it exemplifies some of the difficulties implicit in the entire enterprise for both left and right positions. Ritson was early on a radical republican (as well as a vegetarian, traits that Sidney Lee in the *Dictionary of National Biography* associates with his eventual madness) and fearsomely irascible. Yet despite Ritson's radicalism, which did not prevent a respectful association with Sir Walter Scott, his version of romance is consistent with the idealizing patterns of late-eighteenth-century antiquarianism, even as he rejects its most egregious misconceptions. The introduction to Ritson's edition of *Ancient Engleish Metrical Romanceës* gores many oxen necessary to drive the eighteenth-century conception of romance. He ridicules the notion of romance, expounded by Warton, emerging as a result of contact with the Arab invaders of Spain. More important, Ritson attacks the idea of an infinitely receding origin for romance: "That they may likewise, 'have a multitude of sagas or histories on romantick subjects, some of them written SINCE the times of the crusades' will be readily admited; but there is not the slightest proof or pretext for asserting that 'others' were so 'LONG BEFORE.'"[5] Ritson is here concerned with the possibility of Scandinavian origins of romance, but his rejoinder expresses his skepticism at the lack of manuscript evidence or reliable witnesses.

Ritson's skepticism about the racial origins of romance is not confined to Scandinavian or Arab. He is only partly persuaded by theories of primitive Celtic origins. "The Welsh," he writes, "have no 'tales' or 'chronicles' to produces of 'the elder Welsh bards,' nor any other writeër mor early than by Geoffrey of Monmouth" (xvi). Much firmer is his vitriolic dismissal of any Anglo-Saxon origins of romance. Speaking of the Saxons, he writes: "Though these treacherous strangers are not known to have brought over with them books or letters, or,

154 • Founding the Discipline

in short, any kind of literary stock, while they continue'd pagans, they were unquestionably a brave and warlike nation, but, upon their conversion to Christianity, their kings became monks, their people cowards and slaves, unable to defend themselves, and a prey to every invadeër" (lix–lx). The politics of Ritson's analysis here is interesting. Alfred, normally the hero of progressive political imagining in the seventeenth and eighteenth centuries, is dismissed by Ritson as a "wretched bigot." At the same time, Ritson echoes the trope of the "Norman Yoke": William "would make them draw the plough like oxen" (lxix). In an earlier formulation, the theory of the Norman Yoke celebrated Anglo-Saxon political institutions. Democratic change, such as that imagined by the radicals of the seventeenth century, meant a return to a birthright of free English yeomen. Ritson, while contemptuous of Blackstone's legalist view of the conquest as a form of contract, nevertheless does not romanticize the Anglo-Saxons. His radical republicanism explodes in anger at the already corrupting influence of the church over the Anglo-Saxons, even before the invasion, and in the earlier acceptance of royal dominion.

Where does this radical skepticism leave romance in Ritson's scheme? Eighteenth-century definitions of romance were concerned with both the romances' origins and their ambiguous national status. Ritson dismisses both of these as obsessions rather than realities. Moreover, the appeal of romance as history, the other side of otherness, is equally brushed aside by him: "Bevis and Guy were no more English heroes than Amadis de Gaule or Perceforest; they are mere creatures of the imagination, and only obtain an establishment in history because (like mister Wartons) it was usually written upon the authority of romance" (xciv). The claims to a particular national excellence in English romance is also rejected by Ritson. He accepts French romances not only as obviously earlier, but as obviously better.

Ritson's criticism of the idea of uniqueness of Middle English romance as compared to French romance is the first expression of a disenchantment with the former. His motivation may have been partially a reaction against a certain provincial nationalism that he critiques elsewhere, and partly an allegiance to the France of the Revolution, but it was almost certainly driven by Warton's elevation of minstrelsy and romance as part of the splendor of Norman aristocracy, against which Ritson can barely contain himself. Ritson finds himself lashing out at overgeneralizing schemes on the one hand, but at specific historical placement on the other. For all his quarrels with other scholars, Ritson ends up by ratifying the urge toward romance as a universal human trait, sometimes more successfully expressed than at other times. By so doing, Ritson enacts precisely the quandary that scholars of romance find themselves in to the present day. The scholarly study of romance ends up by disenchanting the very idea of romance that draws us to it.

His contemporaries, such as Sir Walter Scott, could admire Ritson's accuracy at the same time that they felt free to ignore some of his positions as the products of a deranged mind. Yet Ritson's skepticism and the chivalric fantasies of the early nineteenth century left a problematic dual legacy. For by midcentury, the study of Middle English romance had partly joined the academic institutionalization of literature.[6] In so doing, it was subject to a number of forces that threatened to minimize its place in the canon, and to retard its study except for the editions of texts. The Germanic model of scientific philology had no particular allegiance to romance as a privileged form. The Arnoldian stress on high culture threatened to marginalize all but major medieval authors, and, given Arnold's famous observation on Chaucer lacking high seriousness, even some of them. The institutionalization of literary study in the nineteenth century academy was led by medieval studies, but the ironic result was the relegation of the study of medieval romance in England, which had been at the center of the medieval revival of the eighteenth century, to the periphery.

The most important of the Victorian publishing series was the Early English Text Society, inextricably intertwined with its chief founder, F. J. Furnivall.[7] Earlier literary societies were gentlemanly, even exclusive affairs, in keeping with the social values of medievalism. A lawyer and amateur editor, committed to Christian Socialism, Furnivall's energy and enthusiasm are reflected in the original series, both in its indiscriminate attempts at comprehensiveness and in its varying quality of scholarship. Where earlier antiquarians defined the Middle Ages through the privileged genres of romance and ballad, Furnivall's projects suggest a broader sense of a medieval social world, one consistent with his own politics. Such a broader sense was not one necessarily limited to left politics, but was rooted in the social consciousness of high Victorianism. While impelled by a sense of mission, Furnivall's medievalism is nevertheless relatively secularized, and the literary past imagined in the Early English Text Society, taken as a single project, is pluralist and multifaceted. The odd collection that makes up the EETS series, while it may reflect the range of medieval discourse, hardly even fits the literary idea of the Middle Ages constructed by the antiquarians of the previous generation, let alone a contemporary public. Furnivall's agenda combined an educational populism with the scientific model of Germanic philology, and it is through the publishing societies, as much as through the universities, that this scientific model was institutionalized. It was an agenda that opposed itself to the amateur aristocratic antiquarianism of the previous generation as much as it was to be in opposition to the gentlemanly belletristic impressionism of the next. As a result, the romances that did not fit the romantic conception of romance inherited from the previous generation were rendered safe from commentary.

Although the value of romance is debated, even devalued, in certain strains of Victorian medievalism, the general hypostatization of romance survived through the nineteenth century to emerge in some of the most influential academic works on medieval romance. In W. P. Ker's *Epic and Romance,* which crystallized its positions for several generations of scholars, Middle English metrical romances are excluded from the outset: "whole tracts of literature," he writes, "have been barely touched on—the English metrical romances."[8] For Ker, the mythic Middle Ages is embodied in epic, and romance is a mechanistic, secondary simulation of the primal power of romance. "Epic" is the literature of an earlier epoch; it is heroic rather than chivalric. Even the Battle of Hastings is allegorized as the battle of epic against romance. For Ker, romance is medieval modernity; epic is medieval traditionalism. Romance is "hot and dusty and fatigued. It has come through the mills of a thousand literary men, who know their business, and have an eye to their profits. . . . [It] is almost as factitious and professional as modern Gothic architecture. . . . A 'romantic school' is a company for the profitable working of Broceliande, an organized attempt to 'open up' the Enchanted Ground" (371).

The language of Ker's description, moreover, introduces metaphors whose implications he would seem to be aware of. Romance is "brilliant and frequently vainglorious" (3). "Whatever epic may mean, it implies some weight and solidity; Romance means nothing, if it does not convey some notion of mystery and fantasy" (5). Ker is aware enough to retreat from too hard polarization, but he does so in caricature rather than description: "The Crusader may indeed be natural and brutal enough in most of his ways, but he has lost the sobriety and simplicity of the earlier type of rover" (5). Ker significantly, and apparently naturally enough, equates military strategy with literary form: "If nothing else, his way of fighting—the undisciplined cavalry charge—would convict him of extravagance as compared with men of business, like the settlers of Iceland for instance" (5). But there is a heavy and perhaps ironically late Victorian freight behind these images, for romance is described as crusading warfare, which is described as the military style typical of the romantic native. Romance is described again as Foreign, becoming so in its conquest of the Foreign, an associational move more akin to Conrad than to Kipling. Ker's opposition of epic and romance inverts the duality of eighteenth-century medievalism, which privileged romance over epic. Implicit in Ker's move is the difficult place of "civilization" in late-nineteenth-century imperialism. Ker's celebration of epic over romance, while on the surface dismissable as a militarizing and imperial fantasy, on a deeper level reveals an anxiety about the possibilities of, combined with a nostalgia for, the heroic virtues.

Ker redefines the relatively romantic medievalism of Morris into a historical continuum. Despite its aristocratic base, heroic society is represented as more egalitarian, without the "contempt of the lord for the villein" (7). The later chivalric age is complex, specialized, and striated. Moreover, for Ker, romance is the cultivation beyond proportion of one of the "fairy interludes" of epic. But in romance, this "mystery and the spell of everything remote and unattainable" is taken out of context. Romance is not only effete and foreign, it is also monstrous. Ker's Provence is Ruskin's Venice. One suspects that, for Ker, romance takes on the qualities of Wilde and Swinburne, to which the study of medieval epic seems almost an antidote. Another association, again metaphoric, also expressed in a revised Ruskinianism, is between romance and production, as if romance were manufactured, professional, reproducible (as opposed to the "natural" growth of epic). Romance, oddly enough, is projected by Ker as unfettered and amoral capitalism. Ker is obviously extending the politics of romantic medievalism to its contradictory conclusion, but the association of capitalism and romance is bizarre and striking at best. For Ker, the *frisson* of romantic poetry is what he means by romance, and he reads medieval romance as an unnatural attempt to manufacture it.

Ker published *Epic and Romance* in 1897, when he was forty-two. The Scotland that Ker had been born into was still indebted to Sir Walter Scott's cultural program, and Ker's division is an inverse homage to Scott's chivalric heroism, despite Ker's devaluation of romance. Ker also adhered to the political tradition of romantic medievalism; a lifelong conservative, his celebration of heroic poetry appropriates some of the virtues the socialist Morris also ascribed to it. As what we would call a comparatist, Ker could also explicitly pay homage to Gaston Paris. Yet in rejecting precisely the idea of romance that Paris was helping to construct and in celebrating an image of an earlier Middle Ages, Ker was in fact constructing a paradigm of medieval literature that was English, nordic, and primitive rather than French and cosmopolitan. Perhaps because it was a convenient cultural strategy, perhaps because this marginalization of romance carries forth into twentieth-century scholarship, the almost preacademic attitudes toward romance form the basis for romance scholarship in English literature in the twentieth century. The great exception to this marginalization, the study of Malory's Arthurian work, finds its most powerful expression in a content-obsessed, anthropological ahistoricization of Malory, in which myth becomes romance.

The understanding of romance as myth in the twentieth century is firmly rooted in some of the canonical texts of high modernism, the most notorious being T. S. Eliot's footnotes to *From Ritual to Romance* in *The Waste Land,* and, in fact, *The Waste Land* itself. This approach to romance was born in the "Cambridge School" interpretation of Greek drama, which flourished in the early twentieth century, as displaced ritual, and fostered by the enormous influence of Frazer's *The Golden Bough.*[9] Partly anthropological, partly ritualizing, the project is carried out in greatest detail by R. S. Loomis and his collaborators, working chiefly on Arthurian materials. Loomis's importance for our schema here is that he manages to express the romantic and neoromantic reverie about the genre with the scholarly apparatus of professional medievalism. "To think of Medieval Romance is to gaze through magic casements opening on the foam of perilous seas in faery lands forlorn," his first book (1927), a source study, opens.[10]

Loomis's importance partly derived from his energy and unprecedented thoroughness in tracing as many possible conceivable details of Arthurian romance back to Celtic myth.[11] Where the pursuit was carried out by previous scholars, most of them were much more heavily indebted to ritualistic and seasonal explanations. Loomis rendered the possible chain of associations a matter of precedent and source rather than forgotten associations. In so doing, he subsumed the sometimes free associations of previous scholars to the rigors of philology and literary history. Indeed, in Loomis's schemes, Celtic myth itself took on the trappings of a literary tradition. Interestingly, his rigor did not exclude a certain concern for the nonspecialist public's appreciation of medieval literature, and he edited translations of medieval texts, many non-Arthurian. Presumably, for Loomis the power of the literary work, romance or other, did not necessarily reside in the unique language of the text. Loomis's combination of anthropology and literary history rendered his enterprise still useful despite the withering barrages of the opponents of both his Celticism and his mythic priorities. Stressing the ultimately British roots of Arthuriana pitted Loomis and his followers against a French Arthurian establishment that still strives to minimize Anglo-American Arthurian studies. Loomis's obsession with sources and origins (one of the prime categories, as we have seen, of eighteenth-century romance scholarship) was itself minimized by the New Critical concern with individual texts and with the ways in which the language of literary forms such as romances is chiefly responsible for its effects.

For our purposes, in fact, the most interesting opposition develops not between Celtic and continental theories of Arthurian origins, but between one of the later formulations of myth criticism, a book by John Speirs entitled *Medieval English Poetry: The Non-Chaucerian Tradition* and C. S. Lewis (himself the author of fictional works frequently classified as "myths" or "romances").[12] Speirs resurrected a Frazerian anthropology and rationalized it through a Leavisite concern with identifying an Englishness and a tradition. Hence, while Chaucer was associated with continental and self-consciously literary creation, other Middle English works, argued Speirs, continued a folk tradition of pre-Christian myth. Works like *Sir Gawain and the Green Knight* are powerful because they embody such vegetative myths as the struggle of Winter and Spring. Speirs argued that such mythic images lay behind the language of the text, and the power we feel is the power of the myth. The work of Loomis and others was important, said Speirs, but it was not "literary criticism." C. S. Lewis could hardly have cared to defend Loomis; indeed, he begins his essay with a critique of Loomis. He was probably more concerned with Speirs's allegiance to F. R. Leavis and to his paganization of medieval literature. Lewis attacks Speirs's substitution of ritual origins for specific literary effects. Yet, interestingly, Lewis's attack was not based on the importance of literary language in the New Critical mode (for this was Speirs's rather ill-fitting armor), but on the generic nature of romance as a specific type of literary work created by authors and read by readers who responded directly, rather than indirectly, to the power of the narrative:

> The romancers create a world where everything may, and most things do, have a deeper meaning and a longer history than the errant knight would have expected; a world of endless forest, quest, hint, prophecy. Almost every male stranger wears armor; not only that there may be jousts but because visors hide faces. Any lady may prove a fay or devil; every castle may conceal a holy or unholy mystery. . . . Until our own age readers accepted this world as the romancers' "noble and joyous" invention. . . . It was invented by and for men who felt the real world, in its rather different way, to be also cryptic, significant, full of voices and "the mystery of all life." There has now arisen a type of reader who cannot thus accept it.[13]

Lewis's description is quite lovely, but it disguises a complex circularity. Ostensibly defending the literariness of romance, Lewis in fact implies that the modern reader (with Speirs as his exemplar) cannot respond to a lost belief system, and therefore must invent an extreme referent to explain what is already obvious and there. But what Lewis sees as there is precisely the highly mythologized world of romance. What Lewis objects to is that Speirs must remythologize the already magical. In the case of the study of medieval romance, the debate engages not history against myth, but myth against myth.

Such debates were nevertheless overshadowed by the politicization of mythic, ritual, and folkloric approaches in the 1920s and 1930s. Folklore studies always had close ties to both left and right populism, and sometimes Frazerian anthropology found itself allied with Social Darwinist and racialist impulses in the early part of the twentieth century. Nazi rhetoric and official scholarship then appropriated ritual and mythic discourse to the extent that its liberal adherents were forced into defensive moves. For the editorial circle around the French journal *Annales,* for instance, the question arose as to how or whether to continue the publication of its research into popular culture, which might then be seen to be an act of collaboration.[14] More generally, the resurgence of interest in myth and anthropological interpretation in the post-World War II period was tied to a sanitization of the entire enterprise, freeing myth and ritual criticism from its heavily politicized context.

The single most influential statement on the nature of romance in the twentieth century has undoubtedly been Northrop Frye's *Anat-*

omy of Criticism, which allowed romance to overcome its status as secondary to the novel and to realism:

> The romance is nearest of all literary forms to the wish-fulfillment dream, and for that reason it has socially a curiously paradoxical role. In every age the ruling social or intellectual class tends to projects its ideals in some form of romance, where the virtuous heroes and beautiful heroines represent the ideals and the villains the threats to their ascendancy. This is the general character of chivalric romance in the Middle Ages, aristocratic romance in the Renaissance, bourgeois romance since the eighteenth century, and revolutionary romance in contemporary Russia. Yet there is a genuinely "proletarian" element in romance too which is never satisfied with its various incarnations, and in fact the incarnations themselves indicate that no matter how great a change may take place in society, romance will turn up again, as hungry as ever, looking for new hopes and desires to feed on. The perennially childlike quality of romance is marked by its extraordinarily persistent nostalgia, its search for some kind of imaginative golden age in time or space. There has never to my knowledge been any period of Gothic English literature, but the list of Gothic revivalists stretches completely across its entire history, from the Beowulf to the writers of our own day.[15]

No one could accuse Frye of either lack of sophistication or of naiveté. Yet the picture of romance he paints here reinforces a certain sense of the Middle Ages as naive. Frye's brilliant essay, which might have promised a freedom to regard Middle English romance on its own terms, ends up by establishing as self-conscious method the celebration of mode over any particular exemplar of that mode. While it may be argued that genre criticism always assumes such prioritization, Frye seems as much concerned with defining an ur-romance, or super-romance, of which all expressions are copies. In his later, more biblically oriented work, this agenda is made explicit. While aware of and critical of the fallacy of Gothic revivalism, with its nostalgia for an ur-form that existed only in the work recalling it, Frye finally constructs a formal parallel to precisely such a fallacy. He recognizes at the outset the social component of romance (in terms almost certainly influenced by William Empson), but almost immediately, within a sentence or two, shifts to the perennial idealism of romance.[16] Frye's own work mimics the form of romance, moving from adventure to adventure without worrying about the precise relations of these adventures.

In one sense at least, Northrop Frye's celebration of myth in *Anatomy of Criticism* involves liberating ritual and mythic criticism from its political and historical associations. And he succeeds in doing so partly by relying on the traditional affiliation of myth and romance. Frye's defense of romance as a significant mode (a move reflected in the influential work on the novel during these years by such scholars as Richard Chase and Leslie Fiedler) makes myth criticism free for liberal humanism. Romance (along with myth) becomes one of the dominant critical categories of the 1950s and early 1960s, precisely at the moment when North American political and social thought, with awkward timing, announces the end of ideology.

The effort of the past few years has been to remedievalize medieval romances. In so doing, its agenda is also to replace a static and romanticized conception of the medieval past with one more complex and striated. Such an effort involves the demythologization, even the deromanticization of romance. This common agenda connects, for example, the extreme historicization of Susan Crane's *Insular Romance* and the high structuralism of Susan Wittig's *Stylistic and Narrative Structures in the Middle English Romances*.[17] Crane places the Middle English romances securely within a very specific English cultural and political setting. Wittig similarly treats the apparently conventional patterns of the Middle English romances as part of a particular cultural code. Neither seeks to defend the romances as transcendent literary forms. Rather than seeking to make a case for romances as high literature, or to claim a hegemonic role for romance (as C. S. Lewis and Northrop Frye respectively might be said to have attempted), the newly historicized versions of medieval romance are, perhaps more implicitly than explicitly, part of a larger deconstructive agenda.

It becomes increasingly difficult to speak of a unified "Middle Ages," or even a "later Middle Ages," with its Hegelian, and largely Burckhardian echoes. The historiographic innovations of the study of early modern Europe have suggested as many continuities as discontinuities between what we have thought of as medieval and Renaissance centuries. The influence of *Annales* historiography has emphasized gradual rather than abrupt change, and abrupt change itself is now understood as the result of long-standing cultural and social undercurrents. But these conceptual transformations are common to many forms of cultural and social history. In literary history, however, even in the history of literary criticism, medieval romance has a special place. The canonization of medieval romance, coincidental with the earliest stirrings of romanticism, is inseparable from the critical agenda of romanticism: the establishment of national literary histories, the self-representation of the romantic poet as the hero of the quest romance, the valorization of "primitive" epochs over classical and neoclassical periods. The late romantic aesthetic itself, with its celebration of the fragmentary, the supernatural, and the transcendental, declared its version of medieval romance as one of its chief sources. To the arguable degree that modernism itself is an extension of Romanticism, our very idea of literariness grows out of the appreciation of romance.[18] The conception of the literary work as possessing an irreducible aura, as being a fundamentally different kind of discourse than other writing, is one central to the Romantic-modernist tradition, and it evolves in no small part from the sense of medieval romance as enchanted other. There are, of course, other strains in modernism than its Romantic origins, and there are other traditions for the inspired nature of the poetic, but the vehicle for the formulation of these, into a coherent aesthetic was medieval romance.

The disenchantment of romance current in modern criticism of medieval romance, then, has wider repercussions than a more comprehensive understanding of its historical context and its relation to other medieval writings. It may be seen as part of a larger questioning of the idea of the literary, a skepticism as to whether literary discourse does differ in important fundamental ways from other sorts of discourse. The evidence of the preponderance of medieval writings, frequently found together with romances, would seem to suggest that in the Middle Ages, such a distinction was either not made or had not yet been fully formulated. In one sense, we find ourselves returning to the idea of the preliterary. In another sense, of course, recent cultural studies in fact valorize literary discourse, insisting on the textuality, hidden narrativity, and allusive connotation of all discourse, perhaps even of all events. Such an imperial claim for the literary, even if in the name of historicity, resembles the impulse, however inversely expressed, that initially defined medieval romance as myth.

NOTES

1. The best guide to the rediscovery of romance in the eighteenth century remains Arthur Johnston, *Enchanted Ground* (London: Athlone, 1964). For a larger framework behind these literary ideas, see René Wellek, *The Rise of*

English Literary History (Chapel Hill: University of North Carolina Press, 1941) and *A History of Modern Criticism: 1750–1950*, Volume I: The Later Eighteenth Century (New Haven: Yale University Press, 1955). My focus here is on the ideological assumptions behind the literary ideas that Johnston recounts. I am indebted throughout on Lee Patterson's important analysis of the ideology of Chaucer criticism, *Negotiating the Past: The Historical Understanding of Medieval Literature* (Madison: University of Wisconsin Press, 1987), 3–39.

2. Richard Hurd, *Hurd's Letters on Chivalry and Romance, with the Third Elizabethan Dialogue,* ed. Edith J. Morley (London: Frowde, 1911), 154.

3. See Christopher Hill, *Puritanism and Revolution: Studies in Interpretation of the English Revolution of the Seventeenth Century* (London: Secker and Warburg, 1958), 50–122; R. J. Smith, *The Gothic Bequest: Medieval Institutions in British Thought* (Cambridge: Cambridge University Press, 1987).

4. On the politics of medievalism, see Alice Chandler, *A Dream of Order: The Medieval Ideal in Nineteenth-Century English Literature* (Lincoln: University of Nebraska Press, 1970) and Mark Girouard, *The Return to Camelot* (New Haven: Yale University Press, 1981). The story of popular medievalism and chivalric nostalgia in the nineteenth century has been well told by Girouard. Girouard is especially helpful in detailing the influence of chivalric ideals upon the "Young Englanders" and the nostalgia, social as well as cultural, represented by the Middle Ages in their program. Chandler's *A Dream of Order* characterizes the high literary use of the medieval revival as a retreat from a critique of the present in its formulation of the Middle Ages as Golden Age. No matter how different the uses nineteenth-century writers and politicians put medieval romance to, the ideal of romance remained more important than the individual works that made up the genre.

5. Joseph Ritson, *Ancient Engleish Metrical Romanceës,* 3 vols. (London: W. Nicol, 1803), xxviii.

6. In any case, the relative lateness of British academic literary study meant that room was still left for men of letters and nonacademic scholars to play an important role in the establishment of the field. In the earlier part of the nineteenth century, this gap was filled by the book clubs, of which the Roxburghe club was the most productive, for which see Harrison Ross Steeves, *Learned Societies and English Literary Scholarship* (1913; rpt. New York: AMS, 1970). Composed largely of aristocratic and gentlemanly amateurs, the clubs originally concerned themselves with antiquarian matters of all kinds, increasingly centering, however, on editions and literary miscellany. By midcentury, few of the clubs still functioned actively, and their place was

taken by publishing societies. The tone of the clubs is best communicated by the rancor that met Sir Frederick Madden's edition of *Havelock the Dane,* largely because Madden was a nonmember. Madden represents one aspect of nonacademic professionalism, through his appointment at the British Museum. Irascible and difficult, he combined an early fascination with medievalist antiquarianism with a sure sense of judgment, both textual and aesthetic. His work on the Pearl manuscript is best known to modern scholars, but he also produced important editions of *Havelock the Dane, William of Palerne,* the *Brut, Sir Gawayne,* the Wycliffe Bible, and Mathew Paris's chronicle. In his dyspeptic dismissal of the efforts of other projects, he also predicts the judgments of modern editors upon nineteenth-century pioneering editorial efforts. Madden seemed attracted to the nexus of historiography and fictionalization that marks medieval literature for twentieth-century rather than eighteenth- and nineteenth-century scholars. Even in treating the most exotic Middle English romances, he refrains from the rapture of his predecessors. His critical observations are understandably lean, but the fact remains that the nature of his profession minimized the influence he would have other than in terms of the standards of his work. See Robert W. Ackerman and Gretchen P. Ackerman, *Sir Frederick Madden: A Biographical Sketch and a Bibliography* (New York: Garland, 1979).

7. A recent biography is William Benzie, *Dr. Frederick J. Furnivall: Victorian Scholar Adventurer* (Norman, Okla.: Pilgrim Books, 1983).

8. W. P. Ker, *Epic and Romance: Essays on Medieval Literature* (London: MacMillan, 1897), p. a.

9. Sir James Frazer, *The Golden Bough: A Study of Magic and Religion,* 3d ed. (New York: St. Martin's Press, 1966).

10. Roger Sherman Loomis, *Celtic Myth and Arthurian Romance* (New York: Haskell House, 1927), 1.

11. See Roger Sherman Loomis, ed., Arthurian Literature in the Middle Ages: A Collaborative History (Oxford: Clarendon, 1961).

12. John Speirs, *Medieval English Literature: The Non-Chaucerian Tradition* (London: Faber, 1957); C. S. Lewis, "The Anthropological Approach," in Norman Davis and C. L. Wrenn, eds. *English and Medieval Studies Presented to J.R.R. Tolkien* (London: Allen, 1962), 219–30.

13. Lewis, 129.

14. See Traian Stoianovich, *French Historical Method: The* Annales *Paradigm* (Ithaca: Cornell University Press, 1976); John M. Ganim, "The Literary Uses of the New History," in *The Idea of Medieval Literature: New Essays on Chaucer and Medieval Culture in Honor of Donald R. Howard,* ed. James M. Dean and Christian K. Zacher (Newark: University of Delaware Press, 1992), 209–26.

15. Northrop Frye, *Anatomy of Criticism: Four Essays* (Princeton: Princeton University Press, 1947), 191.

16. See William Empson, *Some Versions of Pastoral* (London: Chatto and Windus, 1935).

17. Susan Crane, *Insular Romance: Politics, Faith and Culture in Anglo-Norman and Middle English Literature* (Berkeley: University of California Press, 1986); Susan Wittig, *Stylistic and Narrative Structures in the Middle English Romances* (Austin: University of Texas Press, 1976).

18. In *The Critical Romance* (Madison: University of Wisconsin Press, 1990), Jean-Pierre Mileur discovers the quest romance not in modern literature but in modern criticism. The chief structuralist and poststructuralist critics, according to Mileur, carry on in their own writings the project of Romanticism.

PART TWO

FOUNDERS OF THE DISCIPLINE

"Du bon et du bon marché": The Abbé Migne's Fabulous Industrialization of the Church Fathers

R. Howard Bloch

THE ABBÉ JACQUES-PAUL MIGNE published a book every ten days for thirty years, and like some Balzacian self-made man who could have been his contemporary, he did it practically without money. Migne arrived in Paris in the early 1830s, almost penniless and with only a meager education. In a decade he had created what Firmin Didot would refer to as "the greatest publishing enterprise since the invention of printing—the Ateliers Catholiques of Montrouge, worth more than 3 million francs at the time of his death. Migne is best known, of course, for the *Patrologia latina,* in 217 tomes and 218 volumes, issued in two series between 1844 and 1855, and the *Patrologia graeca,* which appeared in a Graeco-Latin edition (161 tomes in 166 volumes) between 1857 and 1866 as well as an edition of the Greek fathers in Latin only, 81 tomes in 85 volumes. Yet they represent only about half of his total output, Migne having published four hundred books before the first page of the patrologies had even gone to press.

Unless we assume that Migne read between fifty and one hundred pages of Latin or Greek each day, in addition to the fifty to one hundred pages he published a day, we can conclude that he did not read, could not have read, as much as he published. Indeed, questioned by the authorities about an article that had appeared in one of the ten newspapers he also owned and managed in the same thirty-year period, Migne defends himself before the Ministre de l'Intérieur by claiming not to have read even a tenth of what appeared under his name. Even at that, his days were full. Migne is alleged to have worked sixteen hours a day, reserving, as the letterhead of his stationery asserts, the hour between 1 and 2 P.M. for visits, and never, by his own account, taking recreation, not even one hour a year. As abstemious where food was concerned as he was with time, Migne lived like a monk: "in order to preserve the freedom of our spirit, we do not eat more than a simple seminarian or a worker." "The more we work, the better off and the happier we are," Migne writes to Dom Pitra, the man most responsible for the general plan as well as the editorial execution of the patrologies.[1]

Migne sacrificed himself materially, even bodily, to a sense of mission. He pictured himself as a medieval monk staving off the barbarians in what were the new invasions and threat to the church of the century following the French Revolution, and his personal history represents an extraordinary conjunction of the moment and the man. Following a movement within France toward the capital, Migne found in the Paris of the 1830s a world of fervent industrial and technological progress, especially within the realm of printing. In this world, what must have seemed like the intense capacities of capital to feed fantasies of ambition encouraged not only a sense of the feasibility of epic undertakings, but of the infinite potential of the individual will in their realization.

It is, of course, unthinkable within the present context to attempt to retrace the history of the church in the period from Migne's installation as a curé in Puiseaux in 1825 to his death in Paris half a century later. Yet, in the most general terms, the destruction of the church in the decades immediately following the Revolution—the closing of abbeys and churches, the alienation of property and revenues, the dissolution of whole religious orders, the abdication of priests, the dispersal of ecclesiastical teaching institutions and libraries—began to reverse itself following the Napoleonic Concordat (1801). It is in the spirit of restoration that one can best situate Migne whose unique contribution was the reparation of what he saw as a lack of libraries and texts.[2] Toward that end Migne associated himself with the most powerful clerical figures of the "reconstruction catholique," Dom Guéranger and Dom Pitra. Guéranger, who in fact first suggested the project of the patrologies, was an early collaborator and signed a contract with Migne such that the monks of Solesmes would edit the *Cours* and would have sole responsibility for their doctrinal contents, typography, and tables.[3] The collaboration with Solesmes, which called for three volumes per month, was abandoned, however, when Guéranger failed to obtain the consent of his monks, suspicious of the very tenacity of Migne's character that would have made such a project possible in the first place.

The monks of Solesmes were no match for Migne, whose ambition and capacity for work place him among the epic entrepreneurial figures of the century. Indeed, this "Rastignac auvergnat en soutane" is often compared to that other printing giant in whose *Comédie humaine* he could so easily have figured. The Ateliers Catholiques represented, as contemporary witnesses confirm, an enormous undertaking. At any given time Migne employed hundreds of workers: typesetters, smelters, manuscript and copy editors, printers, proofreaders, binders, couriers, and accountants. The approximately three hundred employees of 1842 had almost doubled by 1854 (to 596); and Migne claimed that he had an equal number working on the outside.

Much more than a simple print shop, Migne created on the "Rue d'Amboise, au Petit-Montrouge, barrière d'Enfer de Paris," as his letterhead reads, an autonomous universe dedicated to the book. The Ateliers Catholiques contained a library, a bookstore, a chapel, a bindery, a warehouse, an artist's atelier, and Migne's own apartment in addition to the workshops and the factory in which the *Bibliothèque universel du clergé* was actually printed. Migne conceived the Ateliers Catholiques along the lines of ancient models—the cathedral building site, but also the medieval scriptorium. Most of all, Migne thought of the company he had founded in terms of the monastery and the cloister, whose communal perfection he had recreated in the banlieue of Paris. The Ateliers Catholiques were a miniature City of God. "The first time I visited the Abbé Migne at Montrouge," writes R. du Merzer in the popular magazine *L'Illustration,* "an employee said to me: come into the warehouse, take Bible Street on your right, then Bossuet Street on your left, and at the end you will find M. l'Abbé Migne on Fathers of the Church Square. I crossed long aisles formed of enormous piles of books, and at the far end I found the Abbé Migne pointing out, on Fathers of the Church Square, the place reserved for Tertullian's building."[4]

Migne's relation to the monastery, not to mention the City of God, was, however, at best ambiguous. The reality of the workplace was far from ideal. Migne was a formidable taskmaster, and the Ateliers Catholiques resembled more a feudal manor, of which he was the lord, than the ideal city. Within the walls of the Ateliers Catholiques, Migne appears to have exploited his editors and workers in the mold of any nineteenth-century capitalist entrepreneur. Migne paid his workers badly, which is not without its hidden blessing for the historian: because he paid them badly, they were often discontent; because they were discontent, they came to the attention of the authorities; and because they came to the attention of the authorities, we are able to recover to some extent their story. "Three hundred and fifty to four hundred workers on the average, women included, work in the ateliers of the Abbé Migne," we read in a letter from the Cabinet du Préfet de Police to the Ministre de l'Instruction Publique et des Cultes written on October 27, 1857. "As the salaries he offers are low, he accepts just about any worker who shows up without worrying too much about their past; usually they don't stay long in his workshops and leave as soon as they find something better elsewhere."[5] Not only were they badly paid, but the workers of the Ateliers Catholiques also submitted to conditions that even the police inspector found harsh. Migne imposed a regime of silence according to which the medieval monastic rule becomes indistinguishable from that of the factory worker of the industrial revolution. "He has, moreover, established in these workshops a severe discipline that he has rigorously observed; thus it is explicitly forbidden to sing or to indulge while working in even the most frivolous conversation" (AN F19, 5842).

The silence imposed upon Migne's workers did not prevent disputes with them. On the contrary, the Ministre de l'Intérieur (direction de la Presse) characterizes him in a *rapport* of December 23, 1853 as "a violent man who often gets into fights with his employees" (AN F18, 283 and 333a). The Ateliers Catholiques represented more than just a mobile work force, for Migne deliberately recruited his workers from among the most dispossessed element of the population, which was not only unstable but vulnerable by definition to his offer of low wages. "He welcomes at Montrouge all the suspect characters who cannot find work in Paris," the police inspector notes (AN F18, 333a). The demimonde of the Ateliers Catholiques attracted, again as in a Balzacian tale, political "refugees" of the Revolution as well as the revolutions of 1830 and 1848. "L'abbé Migne," writes the police inspectors, "is known as a schemer (*intrigant*) and surrounds himself with all the priests on the index throughout the dioceses of France" (AN F18, 333a).

If Migne was known as a "schemer," it was not because of the patrologies but because he also owned and edited at least ten newspapers in the course of his lifetime. He had, in fact, originally left his post as curé in the town of Puiseaux in order to enter the world of journalism. The *exeat* signed by the bishop of Orléans specifies that "M. Jacques-Paul Migne, . . . to our regret leaves the diocese to devote himself to the editing of a newspaper called *L'univers religieux,* by which he hopes to do good works."[6] The first volume of *L'univers religieux,* printed on the Presses de Bailly, 2 Place de la Sorbonne, appeared on November 3, 1833, and after that everyday but Monday, until Migne changed the name the following year to *L'Univers*—and until the entrepreneurial abbé encountered the first in a long series of legal battles involving almost every aspect of his journalistic activity. On October 23, 1834, less than a year after the first appearance of *L'univers religieux,* Picot, editor of the rival *Ami de la religion,* accused Migne of plagiarism. On December 24, 1835, Migne was convicted by the Tribunal de police correctionnelle de la Seine of attempting to bribe a postal employee and sentenced to pay a fine of 200 francs.[7] Migne left *L'Univers* in 1836.

By 1838 Migne had installed himself in Montrouge and founded the Ateliers Catholiques. He did not reenter the world of journalism until 1846 with the founding of the newspaper *La voix de la vérité,* which appeared in both a daily and a triweekly edition until it was divided (1854) into a daily called simply *La Vérité* and a biweekly that kept the original name. On May 31, 1850, Migne founded another paper aimed more toward a secular than a clerical readership, the *Journal des faits,* which was, however, closed down by the government on February 10, 1854 as a result of two condemnations, one for printing false news and the other for *contrefaçon* ("illegal reproduction") of articles from *Le Constitutionnel* (AN F18, 333a).

The *Journal des faits,* like *La voix de la vérité,* was a *journal reproducteur* ("newspaper digest"), of the type that abounded at mid-century, for example, *L'Estafette, Le Journal des journaux, L'Écho des feuilletons.* As such, it did not so much publish articles written expressly for it but reproduced what had already been printed elsewhere. Migne is absolutely without pretension where the question of originality is concerned. "The nature of this newspaper being to reflect other sheets means that it needs no editor in chief," Migne writes to the Ministre de l'Intérieur on December 13, 1853 (AN F18, 333a). "I am one of the busiest men in France, for my print house is without doubt the largest that has existed since the invention of print," he writes to the Ministre de l'Intérieur on June 28, 1854. "For this reason I am forced by circumstances to have confidence in several editors and proofreaders. Thus, too, my inability to read even a tenth of what I print" (AN F18, 333a). Migne thus rhetorically displaces editorial responsibility in such a way as to answer preemptively, indeed to render absurd, the very charges that eventually shut down the *Journal des faits*. There can be no such thing as *contrefaçon*, Migne seems to say in advance, when the very essence of the journal is to reproduce what has already been published elsewhere. Nor does the notion of false news make sense. For Migne manages through the *journal reproducteur* to detach his repetition of the news from his own voice, and therefore from anything resembling individual responsibility or intent.

In this poly-positioning of an unascribable veracity of others, Migne becomes simply the vessel through which the truth, unmediated, seems to pass. He is the voice of the truth, the passive, mere mechanical agency by which the impartial universal becomes manifest: "the editor is a pair of scissors," he assures the Direction de la Sûreté Générale on February 6, 1854, "given the fact that this newspaper is a simple reprint digest" (AN F18, 333a). In the pages that follow we shall see how the figure of the absent editor not only occupies pride of place in Migne's journalism, but comes as well to define the essence of his fabulous industrialization of the church fathers.

The publication of the patrologies was, first and foremost, the work of a publicist. The *cursus completus* was sold by subscription, the conditions of which were detailed in the numerous prospectuses Migne also published. Indeed, this "Napoléon du prospectus," as he was known by contemporaries, was practically as prolific in his sales promotion as he was in the actual editorship of the fathers; and the series of "abominable posters" (Dom Pitra) that flowed from his presses are not only monuments to his effectiveness as a publicist and to his shrewdness as a businessman, but they are, again, of a piece with his journalistic endeavors.

Migne's prospectuses openly sing the praises of the *Bibliothèque universelle*—the most complete, the most informed, the best annotated, the most readable, the most accurate, the most beautiful. . . . More important, they confirm the tendency, which we have seen in relation to his journalism, toward displacing his own voice, and thus creating the impression of a discursive neutrality assimilable rhetorically to a self-evident universal truth. Thus, in a broadsheet entitled

"*Curieux Détails* Sur la Bibliothèque Universelle du Clergé," Migne not only presents the "curious details" as if they had appeared out of nowhere, but he speaks of himself in the third person, as if he were simply reporting dispassionately the sanctioned public opinion of the patrologies held by the great prelates of France. Out of modesty, he will cite only seven. Thus "the most illustrious son of the father of nineteenth-century Christian philosophy, le cardinal de Bonald, Archbishop of Lyon," writes that "we cannot recommend enough the editions of l'abbé Migne." An "extract from a letter of the late Mgr Affre, Archbishop of Paris," applauds "a work destined to reproduce excellent books at a moderate price." Another "extract of a letter from the present Archbishop of Paris" claims to encourage "by my word and my subscription your theological publications." A "letter from Mgr the current Bishop of Saint-Flour" names Migne "honorary canon of my cathedral." An "extract from a letter from Mgr the Bishop of Luçon" offers prayers for "the prodigious works of your *Patrologies.*" Another "extract of a letter from Mgr the Bishop of Montauban" reminds the clergy of his diocese that they are eligible to receive bonus books by subscribing to the *Cours de théologie et d'Écriture sainte* in 28 volumes. And, finally, an "extract from a letter of Mgr de Gap to his clergy" lets it be understood that no priest should be without "at least one of the complete courses of writings on Theology, canon law, the Fathers, etc., published by M. l'abbé Migne at such a good price."

Here we behold the continuity between Migne's activities as a journalist and publicist. The "*Curieux Détails* Sur la Bibliothèque Universelle du Clergé" is the equivalent of a *journal reproducteur.* Indeed, the broadsheet pretends, like *the Journal des faits* or *La voix de la vérité,* merely to reproduce the voices, or the words, of others— gossip heard on the street, common knowledge and thus received truth, about l'abbé Migne. Which is, in the context of all we have seen thus far, a tip-off to the most curious detail of all.[8] That is, by writing about himself in the third person, and thus rhetorically appearing to absent himself from what is said about him, Migne's reproduction of the testimony of important Christian witnesses sounds awfully much like what Migne says elsewhere both about himself and about the publications of the Ateliers Catholiques.

Migne wrote a letter to the journalist Louis Veuillot, for example, which is significant in that it demonstrates with clarity the inner workings of his concealment of his own voice behind that of another. Migne had evidently requested that Veuillot, editor of *L'Univers,* of which, it will be remembered, Migne was the founder, make some positive mention of the publications of the Ateliers Catholiques. Veuillot has not responded, and in a second letter of February 13, 1858 Migne informs Veuillot: "I have 50,000 letters of this type in my files; I have in addition the praises of more than one hundred Catholic newspapers spread out throughout the whole world, and I cite among others the *Annales-Bonnetty,* the *Civiltà* of Rome, the *Revue* of Louvain. Whence it follows that you would not compromise yourself in the least in praising in my publications that which appears to you to be praisworthy." Should Veuillot, however, not be moved by the virtue of praise of that which is praiseworthy for its own sake, l'abbé Migne offers to increase the inducement that has apparently already been extended: "I am offering you again, not two hundred francs worth, but three hundred francs worth of your choice of my publications, if you will only include the name between the beginning and end of your sheet" ("la nomenclature entre une tête et une queue de votre main") (BN n.a. 24633, fol. 478).

The letter to Veuillot is stupendous in the glimpse it offers of Migne's placement of advertisements for himself in the mouth of others. For, one is tempted to ask: if Migne has offered an inducement of 200–300 francs to the journalist Veuillot to praise works that are, he maintains, praiseworthy because they have already been praised elsewhere, what prevents us from assuming that he has not made the same request of the editors of the *Annales-Bonnetty,* the *Civiltà,* and the *Revue* of Louvain? Indeed, one can assume, from the letter to Veuillot, that Migne will take Veuillot's praise, which has been traded for 200–300 francs in books, and trade it to other editors for more praise; or, as in the case of Bonnetty, for regular publicity for the publications of the Ateliers Catholiques. The possibilities of such speculation, the playing of one editor off against the next, seem almost infinite, and support the further supposition that it is entirely possible that Migne wrote to the high clergy quoted in "*Curieux Détails* Sur la Bibliothèque Universelle du Clergé" with similar claims to their admiration. Or, to hone the vicious cycle of self-glorification just a bit, it is possible that he wrote to Cardinal de Bonald with the praises of the archbishop of Paris and the bishops of Saint-Flour, Luçon, Montauban, and Gap, suggesting that he do the same; and that he wrote, in turn, to each of the bishops with the commendations of Cardinal de Bonald and the archbishop of Paris accompanied by a similar request.

The request to Veuillot seeks to publish under the name of another what in fact belongs to Migne's own voice, and what will in turn be quoted in another of his apparently objective descriptions of the unsolicited opinion of others—of either the high clergy of France or of the 50,000 letters supposedly tucked away in cartons. Indeed, Migne promises (or threatens), again in the "*Curieux Détails* Sur la Bibliothèque Universelle du Clergé*," that once the *Cours complets* are finished, the letters will be taken out of their cache and published in toto: "More than 50,000 [similar letters] coming from the [ecclesiastical] hierarchy at every level and from all countries could be produced! This unbelievable but true number of congratulations, and those that might still come in, will be gathered in ten or twelve volumes of the format of the *Cours*" (AN F18, 369). The ten- or twelve-volume collection of the letters of praise, which Migne has to a lesser or greater degree solicited either directly or simply by apprising other potential correspondents of their existence, constitutes a fitting culmination to the patrologies, a self-generated summa of the good that Migne has accomplished; for his goal, as stated to Veuillot in the letter of February 13, 1858, is to "render to the Church the greatest service that has ever been rendered."

In this communicative cycle, the director of the Ateliers Catholiques creates a chorus of voices speaking on his behalf. And though those voices, ultimately, are but one voice because they either are Migne's own or are motivated by his own, the fact remains that he fashions around him a web of support, a crowd of supporters each desiring to speak on his behalf because others have spoken, each convinced that his opinion is sanctioned by that of others, each desiring to speak because the others have spoken. Or, finally, and here resides the ultimate effect of Migne's ventriloquistic salesmanship, each desiring to buy because the others have bought. "Mgr Dupanloup, whose name itself is sufficient praise, just carried a step further his zeal for that which M. Migne produces," Migne writes about himself, as if he were simply an uninterested listener, in the "Curieux Détails"; "he wanted, without indicating any bias against the other *cours complets on every branch of religious science,* that on *theology* should serve as the cornerstone of the libraries established in the thirty deaneries of his diocese. Almost all the bishops of France intend to follow in this matter their illustrious colleague from Orleans." The crowd of voices singing their praises is thus transformed into a crowd of visitors, pilgrims to Migne's typographical shrine: "If you would like to see carried out *all at once and on a grand scale* all the arts relating to printing, you are invited to honor with you presence the *Ateliers catholiques* of Petit-Montrouge." "M. l'abbé Migne is available every day and at any hour of the day, except between eleven o'clock and noon, and except also on Sundays and holidays"—thus the invitation is printed at the top of his stationery opposite the address. Most of all, however, the chorus of Christian witnesses singing Migne's praises are transformed through his prospectuses into paying subscribers.

Thus far we have seen how similar the journalistic personality that emerges from Migne's secular and religious *journaux reproducteurs* is to that of the publicist attached to the marketing technique of the *Bibliothèque universelle.* Whether a simple sales strategy or a more efficient means of spreading the word, whether self-interested or interested, as per his claim, only in a higher good ("le plus de bien"), Migne develops consciously or not a voiceless, anonymous, universal persona which seems to come from nowhere and which thus becomes the mere vessel of a universal truth. What's more, and here we move closer to the heart of the matter, Migne's journalistic practices and publicity schemes are of a piece with his editorial policy in the production of the patrologies.

First of all, there can be no doubt that Migne did make some small bona fide effort to locate and publish original manuscripts of the fathers. A few volumes of the patrologies are, in fact, completely new. The edition of Tertullian, for example, was prepared by Dom Pitra especially for the first volume of the Latin *cursus;* the text of the *Vies de Métaphraste* in the second Greek series appeared in print for the first time. In the overwhelming majority of cases, however, it is clear that Migne simply reprinted wholesale the editions of others. He drew extensively from previously published great collections as well as selected collections of the writings of the fathers: *Maxima bibliotheca veterum patrum et antiquorum scriptorum ecclesiasticorum,* 27 volumes in-fol. published at Lyon (1677); the sixth edition of the *Bibliotheca SS. Patrum,* 8 volumes, edited by Marguarin de la Bigne in Paris (1575) and completed under the auspices of the *Bibliothèque des pères* (1616), the liturgical collection of Hittorp and the publications of P. Fronton du Duc (1618–24); the 14-volume *Bibliotheca veterum patrum antiquorumque scriptorum ecclesiasticorum* of A. Galland, which supplemented the Bibliothèque de Lyon by adding the Greek and eastern fathers (1765–81).[9] In this Migne invented nothing new; rather, he participated in a long tradition going back to at least the twelfth century of copying the fathers in collections. Given the extreme rarity of manuscripts predating the Carolingian period, it is hard to imagine things otherwise. Thus, in the vast majority of cases, Migne did nothing morally or legally wrong. Most of his reprints of already published material theoretically belonged to the public domain, that is, were derived from editions no longer protected by the law of July 19, 1793, governing copyright (*les droits d'auteur*), which prevented the reproduction of original works as well as editions for a period of ten years after the author's or editor's death.[10]

In many instances, however, Migne walked a fine line between legitimacy and piracy.[11] Nor is he duplicitous about the fact that the *Bibliothèque universelle* is, at bottom, taken from elsewhere. His prospectuses never promise originality, but "the best available editions"—"the chronological and complete reproduction of the first twelve centuries of Catholic tradition, according to the most respected editions" (AN F18, 369). And his voluntary acknowledgment of sources, published when the patrologies were almost complete, looks more like an advertising ploy than a confession: "As for *éditions*," he writes in the *Annales de philosophie chrétienne* of 1864, "we will recall only that we have given a completely new edition of Tertullian and reproduced for St. Cyprian, that of Fell and Baluze; for Arrobius, that of Orelli; for Lactantius that of Lenglet-Dufresnoy; for Juvencus, Dracontius, Sedulius, Prudentius and St. Isidore, those of d'Arevalo; we followed Dom Coustant for the papal letters; . . . the Benedictines of Saint-Maur for St. Hilary, St. Ambrose, St. Augustine, St. Gregory the Great, Cassiodorus, Gregory of Tours, and so and so forth right to the end."[12]

A good proportion of the *Patrologie latine* and the *Patrologie grecque* was pirated. The rest, with the exception of a couple of volumes, was either reproduced from other editions or reproduced along with an apparatus, which was in some instances also pirated and included only minor additions or changes. In some cases, Migne reprinted editions, mistakes and all, or he reprinted older or even recently published works without indicating his sources. Migne's dictionaries were sometimes simply lifted without acknowledgment from eighteenth-century works or from more contemporary publications. His friend and publicist Bonnetty notes with obvious annoyance, for example, that the *Évangiles* of the Arian Ulfilas were simply the reproduction of the recent edition of Gabelentz and Loebe: "We bring to the reader's attention that one finds neither the place nor the date where it was published," admonishes Bonnetty. "M. Migne should never have forgotten them."[13] At an extreme, Migne purposefully attempted to cover his tracks by giving a false origin. In 1861, for example, he published volume 117 of the *Patrologia graeca,* the *Novels* of Leo VI, which he reproduced from the edition of Zachariae von Lingenthal, without, in the phrase of Alphonse Dain, "missing a single typographical error" (*sans en manquer aucun, les lapsus typographiques*).[14] However, since Zachariae von Lingenthal's edition, which had appeared in 1857, was not yet in the public domain, Migne pretends to ignore that fact by referring specifically to older editions of the *Corpus juris civilis.*

Migne, the master of the *journal reproducteur,* realized in the patrologies a *bibliothèque reproductrice* produced by essentially the same methods as those employed in the newspaper world.[15] The patrologies are, in essence, an enormous theological version in another register and on another scale of the *journal reproducteur* which seems to come from nowhere, to belong to no one, and to have been edited by a ghost editor who has, because of an editorial strategy thoroughly assimilable to that of the newspaper digest, become invisible. Indeed, Migne deliberately suppressed the names of collaborators from the beginning. The contract signed with Guéranger and Pitra provides under Article 3 that "the names of the reverend fathers individually or collectively will appear nowhere (*ne sera mis nulle part*), neither in the prospectuses and the announcements, nor in the titles and the frontispieces of volumes." Migne's name, on the contrary, will, the contract stipulates, appear wherever he "judges it appropriate."[16] Thus the prodigious patrologies whose synechdochic title is simply "Migne"—"Le Migne"—is so radically fused with his name not because he did the work, which was not humanly possible, not because he owned the Ateliers Catholiques where they were produced, but because Migne the supreme publicist—in the nineteenth-century tradition of P. T. Barnum or Buffalo Bill—managed to subordinate all other names to his own, which thus became synonymous with his enterprise.

What the suppression of names suggests is a diffusion of the editorial voice of the patrologies that is, once more, thoroughly analogous to the displacement of the journalistic voice of *the Journal des faits* or *La voix de la vérité,* and to the diffusion of the chorus of laudatory voices of the publicity tracts. Migne transforms, in fact, the irreducible impossibility of situating the editorial voice of the patrologies into a virtue, one that is figured, first of all, in spatial terms. Migne insists over and over again that the publications of the *Bibliothèque universelle* are not specifically French but are truly universal; and they are universal because those involved in their production come from all over. "Also, there are at Montrouge proofreaders from all nations and in greater number than in twenty Parisian print shops combined."[17] Migne seems to suggest that the *Cours complets* cannot be situated geographically, and therefore belong nowhere, that is, to no one. He goes to elaborate lengths, in fact, to establish their diffuse universality in the attempt to show that the very idea of the patrologies occurs so naturally that no one can claim it as his own. Even if others might have had the idea first, that idea is such common knowledge that the question of literary property becomes null and void.[18] The publications of the Ateliers Catholiques, like the articles already published in newspapers from which Migne disseminated *La voix de la vérité* and *the Journal des faits,* are already in a public domain of sorts, not because the material conforms necessarily to the law, but because it is part of a common Catholic heritage.

So, too, the naturalness of the universal idea of the patrologies is allied with the universal desire to possess them in a fashion thoroughly analogous to that which we have encountered earlier in the form of Migne's self-created chorus of laudatory voices. That the conception of the patrologies would occur to everyone, joined to the knowledge that everyone is talking about them, translates rhetorically into the notion that no one should be without one: "May it please God that each reader of this *Prospectus* might also shout: 'Me too, I have often thought of these *Cours,* and often, by my prayers, I have speeded their execution!' Oh! then we would be overcome with joy, and we would say: 'This idea must be natural, since it is so universally shared; it must contain, in its breast, great seeds of fecundity, since everyone places his hope in it, and believes, when hearing it publicized, that someone has stolen his secret and his dreams of the good!'" (AN F18, 1803).

In place of individual editorial responsibility, which implies individual proprietorship of literary material, Migne substitutes quite literally the notion of a collective effort out of which the patrologies emerge. Even before launching his prospectuses, before selling a single subscription, he has, he claims, sent out five thousand questionnaires (*lettres de consultation*) to all "bishops, head vicars, theologians, superiors, and professors of all the seminaries of France, without exception" (AN F18, 1803). This questionnaire asked simply:

1. Which is the name of the author who has produced the best commentaries and treatises among the following lists, and even, if possible, the best part of each individual commentary or treatise . . . ? It does not matter whether the designated author is ancient or modern, French or foreign, dead or living, long or short, a member of the regular or secular clergy. The only thing that counts is that his commentary or his treatise is in your opinion the best of all those with which you are familiar.

2. What is the best edition of each of these commentaries or treatises?

3. What defects are contained in each of the following commentaries which we believe to be wise to faithfully reproduce? (AN F18, 1803)

Migne has, then, supposedly collated the responses in order to determine which editions of the fathers and which commentaries on them to publish.

Thus, if the editor of the *journaux reproducteurs* is a pair of scissors, the editor of the *Cours complets* is a pot of glue—more precisely, a community of respondents who collectively seem to make the editorial decisions, which, because of their very collective nature, appear to spring from nowhere and to belong to no one. In a certain sense, then, the voices of Migne's editorial committee of five thousand can be seen to produce that which the fifty thousand voices of the laudatory letters supposedly praise. Further, one can even safely assume, given the reduced numbers of the clergy in the period under scrutiny, that some of the forty thousand editors of the patrologies had to overlap to a great extent with its fifty thousand enthusiastic supporters. And if one also assumes that Migne, who has, after all, promised to publish the laudatory letters he has received, is telling the truth, then one must conclude that those who praise the project must also feel that they have had at least some small part in its creation.

Migne managed to produce, once again, through brilliant marketing technique, an identification between the producer and the buyer, who has, even before making the first payment on a subscription, a vested interest in the success to which he has already contributed and which, again, belongs to no one individual, but to a collective voice of the universal truth. Migne insists, in fact, that the very enormity of the number of questionnaires is aimed at transcending the particular and thus at forging the general, a composite that is a microcosmic reduc-

tion of the universal church. The comprehensiveness of the questionnaire is thus of a piece with the internationalism of the editorial team.
The patrologies were the result, Migne wants us to believe as part of
his fabulous industrialization of the fathers, of a poll; because they
express editorially the will of the universal Christian community, that
community is impelled to identify with them, that is to say, to purchase them.

The notion of the originless *Cours complets* is of a piece with what
we have seen elsewhere in that it offered several marketing advantages
for the patrologies, the first of which was a certain guarantee of the
truth value of its contents. An editorial committee of five thousand, in
which some voices will no doubt cancel out others, insures a neutrality
which, again, is synonymous with universal truth. For here too Migne,
in order to certify the authority of the patrologies, pretends to remain
absent from them; he is neutral, above any particular editorial stand,
claiming "to give no entrée, in our work, to any systematic spirit
(*esprit de système*), and never to espouse one opinion over any other"
(AN F18, 1803). Hence the official philosophy for the patrologies
reproduces almost word for word the phrase that appeared in the very
first edition of Migne's first *journal reproducteur,* the *Univers* of
November 23, 1833: "We will give the opinion of newspapers on
every major event because the truth almost always emanates from the
clash of opinions; but we will leave all systems aside, because systems
divide."

Herein lies a second advantage, which is not inconsequential for
Migne's mass-market sales strategy. The voiceless, absent editor of the
Cours complets can make the claim to plenitude, which coincides with
his encyclopedic spirit; but such neutrality also avoids the possibility
of offending anyone, and thus alienating any segment of the market.
This was particularly important in the conflictual climate of mid-
century that pitted Gallicans against Ultramontains, either side of
which would have been lost as a market had Migne been perceived to
have taken sides. What the prospectuses show, and the similarity can
hardly be a coincidence, is that Migne's editorial neutrality allowed
him to exploit maximally the potential of the mass market by appealing to the greatest number of potential buyers and, more important,
by offending none.

Finally, and the conclusion could hardly be more obvious, that
which is conceived to be natural, to have been fabricated collectively,
to represent a universal higher truth that is everywhere in general but

nowhere in particular, that belongs to no one, resolves once and for all the question of copyright. The neutral universalism of the patrologies justifies ideologically the enterprise of the reprint. Migne, in fact, quite explicitly transforms the act of reprinting that which already has been printed into a guarantee of perfection. The fact that one begins from an already corrected—that is, already edited—version of the original is less an act of piracy than an assurance that one begins the process of reconstructing the Catholic tradition out of the best possible building materials: "the Benedictines, like the Jesuits, almost always worked from manuscripts, which was a constant source of a myriad of errors, while the *Ateliers Catholiques,* whose goal is above all to revive Tradition, only work for the most part on printed sources."[19] Printing for Migne did not mean beginning from the beginning, working from a manuscript, as would be the case in the philological reconstruction of the later part of the century and especially after the Franco-Prussian War. It meant refining that which had already been set in print; thus the emphasis on the process of correction, and not, say, transcription or composition. "The essential part of a work like this is, one could say, *the correction of proofs*" (Bonnetty). Here lies the essence of publication for the Ateliers Catholiques, where book production is more a question of the refinishing of a preexisting product than beginning from scratch. "To begin with, the copy is most often a printed source, which reduces greatly errors made while typesetting."[20] The actual process of book printing is, again, of a piece with Migne's excision of the names of those who produce them, both undeniable elements of the attempt to depersonalize the industrial production of the church fathers. For the anonymity of those responsible for the *Cours complets* captures, at bottom, the very essence of the industrial revolution of the last century, that is to say, the impulse toward standardization.

Far from his former role as a simple *curé de campagne,* Migne gives the impression that the figure of the "PDG [CEO] de la Patrologie" lurks just below the surface of what is presented as a spiritual enterprise. The Ateliers Catholiques represented, above all, a book factory: "un palais à l'industrie catholique," according to Barbier, whose account of a visit to the site shows, even as early as 1841, Migne the industrialist filling orders and circulating among his workers: "The master visits his hundred and forty typesetters and printers; he perhaps revises the proofs of St. Augustine or St. Chrysostom, etc. He takes care of his vast correspondence with the bishops around the world." The visitor is most impressed, however, by the enormous effects of mechanical energy—the clouds of steam, the heat of the foundry furnace—emanating from Migne's book machine:

> go there, he will extend a hand; and you will see functioning through the power of steam the five great mechanical presses which he just set up in the back of the building; you will cross this immense workshop filled, like billowing black clouds, with sheets laid out for drying. Here the foundry men who mold typeface before a furnace; there tables set for folding; there again the men of his accounting services, and from the proofreaders' office.[21]

Migne was fascinated by the efficiency of the mechanical press and sings its praises in one of his printed advertising broadsheets: "Steam is harnessed to mechanical power, and their force of production is such that they can give birth to 2,000 volumes in quarto ever twenty-four hours. Then, too, the hand of a monk of yesteryear could not copy in three years what is done in the *Imprimerie Catholique* in a single minute" (AN F18, 369).

Though Migne's conversion of one mechanical minute into the equivalent of three years of manual labor may or may not be accurate, it reveals nonetheless the degree to which the Ateliers Catholiques served as a catalyst to a certain kind of industrial modernism based on the possibility of quantification, and, in particular, the quantification of labor.[22] Thus, for example, in excusing the delay in the appearance of the index of the *Patrologie latine,* Migne quantifies exactly what such labor involves: "In effect, we offer TWO HUNDRED AND THIRTY-ONE TABLES for our *Cours de patrologie latine,* which is 217 volumes strong. In order to compile EACH ONE of these tables, it was necessary to read and reread EACH ONE of these 217 volumes from beginning to end; and this operation was necessarily done 231 times; which yields an analysis of more than 50,000 volumes of our format." Unlike the case of the medieval monk, for whom time—the *tempus* of the secular world—could have little meaning, labor for Migne is almost automatically converted into time. And time is converted into money: "What can we say about the enormous expense we were put to? More than fifty men working on the tables for more than ten years, and with only the small salary of 1,000 francs a year per man, makes more than 500,000 francs, without even counting the cost of printing" (*PL* 218:col. 4).

Migne is a captain of industry responsible not only for the Renouveau Catholique, but for the economic reconstruction of mid-century based on the possibility of precise, easy conversion between time, labor, and money. Indeed, he not only revels in delirious calculation of the production costs—labor and time—of the patrologies, but concocts complicated formulas for determining their eventual price. In making available the *Bibliothèque universelle du clergé,* his first concern was, in fact, that of price. "Du bon, à bon marché" ("the good at a good price"); thus Migne's dictum comes to characterize the economic aura surrounding their distribution. The question of price is, in fact, inscribed at both the beginning and end of the very title of the *Cours complets: Patrologiae cursus completus, sive Bibliotheca universalis integra, uniformis, commoda, oeconomica, omnium SS. Patrum, doctorum, scriptorumque ecclesiasticorum qui abaevo apostolica ad Innocentii III tempora floruerunt.*

Migne is always quick to remind the potential subscriber that the 469 volumes of the patrologies, purchased separately, would amount to a cost of more than 100,000 francs. Bought as a series, the price is reduced to 1,000–1,200 francs for the Latin fathers and only slightly more for the Greek.[23] Migne was anxious, of course, to sell both *Cours* as a single package: "The two series go together" (*Les deux Cours marchent de front*). And the benefits for those who "go together" with them are considerable.

For those who take only the Latin or the Greek, the price is 6 francs a volume. Those who subscribe to both, however, gain six advantages: the first, of course, is that of price, "de ne payer le volume que 5 francs"; the second, less significant, is simply to avoid paying postage on the order; the third is credit—extended payment, a version of a layaway plan; the fourth involves shipping costs with the added advantage, not to be discounted in the primarily rural settings—the *curés de campagne* to which Migne's marketing strategy was pitched—is home delivery; the fifth, easy payment, or collection of the sums due COD; finally, the sixth advantage offered to the double subscriber is a chance to become part of Migne's shopper's world with all the rights and privileges of future purchases, "to have the benefit, according to what the administration of the *Cours* sends them, of the prices marked in the diverse *prospectuses* and catalogues to all bookstore items and ecclesiastical goods" (AN F18, 369).[24]

The discount is even deeper for those willing to pay for the entire *Bibliothèque universelle* in advance:

THE UNIVERSAL LIBRARY OF THE CLERGY AND
LEARNED LAYMEN OR *COURS COMPLETS*

on every branch of religious and human science. 2,000 volumes in-4o. Price: 10,000 fr. for subscribers to the whole *Library;* only 8,300 fr. for those who pay all at once, upon receipt of the completed volumes, those which have not yet appeared.[25]

The figure of 8,300 francs for two thousand volumes, or a bottom line price of 4.15 francs per volume, is adjusted to reflect the amount that this sum, paid in advance, would earn over the period during which the *Bibliothèque universelle* would be produced in order to bring the unit cost into consonance with the full retail price.

Migne's flexible purchase plan foresaw yet further possibilities of double purchase in what amounts to a nineteenth-century version of a pyramid scheme. Thus, if a priest wants only the Latin or the Greek *cursus,* he need only find a colleague in order to qualify for the reduced price of the combined series. The second purchaser must, however, find a third subscriber to benefit similarly, and so on, and so forth. In addition to the *primes* (bonuses) which Migne offered for mistakes found in the books he printed, he also envisaged an elaborate system of referral for the ecclesiastical bounty hunters who functioned, through procurement of other subscribers, as unofficial salesmen.

Thus "any person who, in addition to his subscription to the two *Cours,* and that which he has procured in order to be able to pay only 5 fr. per volume, will procure a subscriber to one of the two *Cours* will receive *gratis* or *franco,* a volume of Saint Theresa"; for two subscriptions "he will receive a complete Saint Theresa"; for three subscriptions, "three volumes of the *Pallavicini* or the *Démonstrations évangéliques,* and will pay only 5 fr. for the fourth"; for four, "a complete *Histoire du Concile de Trente,* by Pallavicini, or the *Démonstrations évangéliques* of Eusebius, Huet, Léland, Stattler, and Duvoisin"; for five, "the SUMMA of Saint Thomas"; for six, "he will receive the *Perpétuité de la Foi,* by Nicole, Arnaud, and Renaudot." And, finally, for the person who brings in ten subscriptions, the eleventh is free (AN F18, 1803). What this suggests, in conclusion, is that Migne's historical contribution consists only in part in the reconstitution of a theological library at the great moment of Catholic renewal. For alongside the actual publication of the fathers there lurks a fundamental rethinking of the means of production which assumes the possibility of a precise conversion between time, labor, and price, or between income and cost, calculable down to the minimal element—the typographical character—of the minimal unit, the book: "Each page contains 108 lines of 38 letters each, which makes 4,180 letters on each page, 66,880 on each sheet, and 2,508,000 in each volume" (AB F18, 1803). One can only assume that Migne was capable of calculating—indeed, the figures must at some point have entered his consciousness—not only the price of each unit (with and without discount), the profit generated by each unit (based on both advance payment and payment over time), but the cost, price, and profit emanating from each page, column, line, and letter of the *Cours complet de patrologie ou Bibliothèque universelle.*"

The fantasy of Migne's precision, or the precision of his fantasy, serve to consolidate the alliance, to create the criteria of conversion, between time, labor, and money necessary to the industrial revolution of the Second Empire. The Ateliers Catholiques are, in essence, a bibliographical assembly line capable of producing a standardized product at minimal cost for mass consumption: "We will have the satisfaction of making the *Patrologie* available and intelligible to all"—"accessible et intelligible à tous" (AN F18, 1803). Again, Migne's mission, in making a theological library available and readable, can be seen in the pastoral context of the recapture, part of the Renouveau Catholique of mid-century, of souls lost at the time of the Revolution. But it was also more. The very "accessibility and intelligibility" coupled with low prices contain the essence of production according to an economy of scale, a strategy based on extensive sale of low-cost individual standard units. In this, Migne, one of the great entrepreneurs of the nineteenth-century, changed not only the prices of books but the entire economy of book production and distribution. "In was a revolution for bookstores," writes Dom Cabrol, Pitra's biographer, referring to the question of price, "the complete works of the fathers have been made accessible to the purse of a simple country priest."[26] But the bookstore revolution was not merely a matter of price; the Ateliers Catholiques also altered the means of book distribution. When Bonnetty, for example, insists that never was such a thing as the *Bibliothèque universelle* seen in bookstores (*c'est ce qui jamais ne s'était vu en librairie*), he refers to both the books themselves and to Migne's sales technique.[27] All of Migne's sales schemes are, finally, the very essence of wholesale. Indeed, the booksellers of Paris, threatened by lower prices and a shift in marketing technique that eliminated the middleman, sought help from the archbishop of Paris, Mgr

Quélen, who not only tried to close the Ateliers Catholiques, but tried to do so, Barbier claims, by citing canons on a passage from St. Paul forbidding commerce.[28]

NOTES

1. Cited in A. G. Hamman, *Jacques-Paul Migne: Le retour aux pères de l'église* (Paris: Beauchesne, 1975), 73–74. The comparison did not escape contemporaries. The newspaper *Le Droit* (December 22, 1871) speaks of Migne's publishing enterprise as "the most colossal of this century, a work that recalls the patient works of the monks of the Middle Ages.

2. See Jean Leflon, "Crise et restauration des foyers de science religieuse dans l'église du XIXe siècle," in *Migne et le renouveau des études patristiques, Actes du colloque de Saint-Flour,* 7–8 juillet, 1975, ed. A. Mandouze and J. Fouilheron (Paris: Beauchesne, 1985), 53–59; Gérard Cholvy, "La restauration catholique en France au XIXe siècle (1801–1860)," ibid., 61–89.

3. See Louis Soltner, "Migne, Dom Guéranger et Dom Pitra: La collaboration solesmienne aux enterprises de Migne," in *Colloque de Saint-Flour,* 200.

4. *Illustration,* February 22, 1868, reproduced in André Vernet, "L'Abbé Jacques-Paul Migne (1800–1875) et les Ateliers du Petit-Montrouge," *Annuaire de la Société Historique du 14e* Arrondissement (1960): 46.

5. Archives Nationales (= AN F19, 5842). L. Marchal reports that, "en 1865, il engagea quarante correcteurs, pour dix ans, à des conditions très onéreuses, pour la révision minutieuse des planches stéréotypées" ("Migne," *Dictionnaire de théologie catholique,* 10.2:col. 1727).

6. Cited in Hippolyte Barbier, *Biographie du clergé contemporain par un solitaire* (Paris: A. Appert, 1841), 3:307–8. See also Hamman, 57. The standard work on Migne the journalist is the long article by Pierre Pierrard, "L'Abbé Migne journaliste," *Colloque de Saint-Flour,* 93–117.

7. Police report of February 1854, AN F18, 333a.

8. In another *journal reproducteur* that he owned, *La vérité canonique,* Migne literally reproduced "for the recreational part of the Truth" clerical hearsay and scabrous anecdotes. Thus we read, for example, in the issue of December 21, 1861, under the rubric "Anecdodal News," a story that "everyone knows": "*Everyone knows* that M. Boyer, a pious ecclesiastic, learned and zealous as few others among the French clergy, was the most distracted of men. One day, he had just said mass; and, as he was a bit hurried, he forgot. . . ."

9. For a fuller list, from which the above extremely partial group is taken, see Hamman, 107–11; Marchal, cols. 1732–34; Pierre Petitmengin, "Les patrologies avant Migne," in *Colloque Saint-Flour,* 15–38.

10. Claude Colombat, *Propriété littéraire et artistique* (Paris: Dalloz, 1980), 6–7.

11. He was on much less solid legal ground, for example, in the case of the dates of the following editions, which he also appropriated: the Bibliotheca sacra Patrum ecclesiae graecorum published by R. Klotz in Leipzig (1831–34); the *Bibliotheca Patrum eccl. latinorum selecta* of E. G. Gersdorf, which also appeared in Leipzig between 1839 and 1847; the revision of Th. Pelt's Homiliarum patristicum by Rheinwald and Voigt (Berlin, 1829–34); the *Scripta genuina graeca Patrum Apostolicorum* of C. F. Horneman (1829); the *Patrum apostolicorum opera* of C. J. Hefele (Tübingen, 1839); the *S. Clementis Rom. S. Ignatii, S. Polycarpi . . . quae supersunt* of W. Jacobson (Oxford, 1838; Basel, 1840); the *Bibliotheca Patrum ecclesiae catholicae . . . delectu presbyterorum quorumdam Oxoniensium,* 10 vols. (Oxford, 1835–55); A. Mai, (died 1854) *Spicilegium Romanum,* 10 vols., published in Rome between 1839 and 1844 and his *Classici Auctores,* also in 10 vols. (Rome, 1828–38); F. H. Rheinwald, *Anecdota ad historiam eccl. pertinentia* (Berlin, 1831–35); G. Heine (died 1848?), *Bibliotheca Anecdotorum* (Paris-Leipzig, 1848) (used in *PL* 99:1231); G. H. Pertz, *Monumenta Germaniae Historica* (Berlin, 1826); M. J. Routh, *Reliquiae sacrae,* whose second edition was published in Oxford, 1846–48; J. A. Cramer, *Catena Graecorum Patrum in Acta SS. Apostolorum* (Oxford, 1840); the *Scriptorum veterum novo collectio,* 10 vols. (Rome, 1825–38); M. J. Routh, *Reliquiae sacrae* 2d ed. (Oxford, 1846–48).

12. *Annales de philosophie chrétienne,* 5th ser., 10 vol. 69 (1864): 83.

13. Ibid., 3d ser., 20 (1849): 316.

14. Alphonse Dain, *Les manuscrits* (Paris: Belles Lettres, 1975), 181.

15. The Goncourts, who are hardly generous in their satire of the Ateliers Catholiques, focus particularly on this aspect of Migne's character: "He has established at Vaugirard a print shop full of priests on the index just like him, defrocked scoundrels, death defiers (*Trompe-la-Mort*) out of grace, who, spotting a police officer, scamper for the doors. He is then obliged to shout: 'Nobody move! This is not for you, but for a matter of plagiarism' (*une affaire de contrefaçon*)." *Journal des Goncourts,* vol. 6 (Monaco, 1956), August 21, 1864, p. 234.

16. Hamman, 119.

17. Prospectus reprinted in F. Mély, *"L'Abbé Migne," Revue archéologique* 5 (1915): 213.

18. "From the beginning of our relations with the honorable Société de Saint-Sulpice," Migne writes in the 1838 prospectus, "we knew that it, like us, had the idea for a *Cours complets,* and that only the preaching of high learning was able to make it give up a project already under way. Soon,

however, our vast correspondence led us to the conclusion that there are few members of the two clergies, regular or secular, who have not conceived the same idea" (AN F18, 1803).

19. Prospectus reprinted in Mély, 213.

20. *Annales de philosophie chrétienne,* 4th ser., 16, vol. 55 (1857): 247.

21. Barbier, 314–15.

22. Migne was a prophet of progress through tradition, an evangelist who proclaims the future by citing Tertullian: "Au monde avide de Progrès, nous donnons la Tradition du passé pour marcher en avant. *Traditio tibi praetendetur auctrix* (Tert., *de Coron. milit.,* cap. 4)." *Annales de philosophie chrétienne,* 5th ser., 10 vol. 69 (1864): 82.

23. See H. Leclercq, "Migne," col. 953; Mély, 214, 222–23.

24. Indeed, in addition to a private bank, Migne ran a business in religious art objects—paintings sold by the square centimeter, statues sold by the kilo, organs and church paraphernalia—which he refers to as his "museum."

25. Prospectus in Mély, 222–23; see also Marchal, col. 1727.

26. Fernand Cabrol. *Histoire du Cardinal Pitra* (Paris: Victor Retaux et Fils, 1893), 112.

27. *Annales de philosophie chrétienne,* 3d ser., 17 (1848): 164.

28. Cabrol, 112; *Annales de philosophie chrétienne,* 3d ser., 17, vol. 97 (1848): 164; Barbier, 315; see also Hamman, 61; E. Leterrier, *Les Contemporains* no. 21 (1913): 7.

SEVEN

Gaston Paris and the Invention of Courtly Love

David F. Hult

> Il est dans la destinée du Moyen Âge de
> suggérer aux modernes des idées fausses.
> —A. Pauphilet

WITH A BURST OF YOUTHFUL and belligerent scholarly enthusiasm, Gaston Paris published in one of his earliest articles the following programmatic remarks pointed at his medievalist forebears and the nature of the traditions they had established: "De toutes les études, celles qui touchent à la poésie du moyen âge sont celles où un contrôle sévère et incessant des autorités alléguées est le plus indispensable. On est surpris, en faisant ce travail, de l'étonnant développement que peut prendre une toute petite erreur lancée un beau jour au hasard; elle fait boule de neige autour d'elle, et au bout de quelque

The main lines of the argument developed in this article were presented in a much shorter version at the 1988 MLA Convention in New Orleans under the title "Gaston Paris's Lancelot." I thank Alice M. Colby-Hall for inviting me to participate in that forum. The current version, prepared especially for this volume, was completed in December 1990 and has benefited along the way from the judicious comments and suggestions of Robert F. Cook, George Hoffmann, and Martha Walker.

temps on la retrouve sous forme d'un système imposant, ayant ses partisans et ses adversaires, ses commentateurs, et obstruant par sa masse la seule voie qui mène à la vérité."[1]

One might initially be struck by the self-reflexive nature of Paris's critique of the academic establishment, his insinuation that textual interpretation can be more beholden to the terms set down by traditional debate than by the object of interpretation itself, for it is possible to recognize therein a glimmer of the modern hermeneutic insight that cultural and ideological constructs are themselves constitutive of the categories they purport to discover "independently" in the objects they study. Paris's last clause nonetheless strikes a familiar note: reference to "the only path leading to truth" reassures us that this is indeed 1865 and that critical positivism is in full swing. The superficially radical attack upon criticism's tendency to obscure or displace the essential issues through its own ponderous verbiage or devious agendas shades into a more orthodox version of the "querelle des anciens et des modernes." For Paris, it remained possible to seize the truth of the matter, and in that endeavor the *modernes* (perhaps because the last word is by definition theirs) always have the advantage.

Of course, yesterday's "truths" have an alarming propensity for becoming tomorrow's "errors," and modern hermeneutics makes use of this inevitability in order to comprehend the perspectivism inherent in any critical position and to use that comprehension for the purpose of foregrounding its own, equally inevitably, historicized formulations.[2] It thus turns from mild irony to instructive example when we note that Gaston Paris was himself, somewhat later in his career, responsible for launching an expression that had a snowball effect never since equaled in the field of medieval studies: "courtly love." This datum belonging to the history of literary history has been noted by many scholars over the past few decades, the most vociferous of whom have termed this nineteenth-century legacy one of the great critical anachronisms of all time.[3] But whatever the answer to the beleaguered question of whether "courtly love" ever in fact existed as a code of aristocratic behavior, the reception of the *expression* "courtly love" did follow a trajectory that is not without its resemblance to the sorts of cumulative philological errors described by Gaston Paris in 1865.

Advanced rather tentatively in an article devoted to Lancelot and Guenevere,[4] "courtly love" soon became the object of entire books and articles and entered our common vocabulary—indeed, our collective imagination—as the expression designating *the* ideal of love and desire in refined medieval society. Recent squabbles over the "meaning" of courtly love, inasmuch as they have primarily been concerned with the nature or correctness of the "imposing system" (as most authoritatively elaborated by Lewis in 1936),[5] have fallen into the very trap that Paris delineated above: is the concept a valid one, or has the mass of critical discussion obstructed the path to truth in the matter? The residual positivism of both approaches suggests that neither question is satisfactory for they both would deny a formative role to the traditions that have helped to frame the questions. To "abandon" the notion of courtly love is as simplistic as to accept it as a fully formed, historically viable term: both positions assume a disinterested stance that by not taking stock of its own historical situation actually risks, as Gadamer puts it, a "deformation of knowledge."[6]

What I am interested in developing is an approach to courtly love through the specific circumstances leading to Gaston Paris's formulation of the concept, an approach that will elicit less obvious factors of scholarly motivation than have been typically adduced. Indeed, much important work in the past decade has, quite cogently, situated Paris's achievements in the not unexpected context provided by intellectual movements or political events. Following largely upon Paul Zumthor's critically self-conscious remarks[7] concerning the profession of the medievalist as it had developed from the nineteenth century through to the critical revolution of the 1960s (within which movement Zumthor's own *Essai de poétique médiévale* [1972] betokened a decisive turning point), these studies have emphasized the unrelenting continuity of philological methods and goals since they were institutionalized some one hundred years ago. Making good on his early promise to clear out the dead wood of previous scholarship and pave his own path to "truth," Gaston Paris and his entourage proceeded in short order to "reprogram" the field of medieval philology.[8] Their success was nothing short of astonishing. The year 1865 saw the appearance of Paris's doctoral thesis, the *Histoire poétique de Charlemagne,* which provided a model for the sort of cultural/historical/literary discourse that would later in the century receive its institutional sanction as the domain of "literary history."[9]

Along with the equally industrious Provençal scholar Paul Meyer, Paris founded the *Revue critique d'histoire et de littérature française* in 1866 and *Romania* in 1872. The Société des Anciens Textes Français, a group venture aimed at consolidating French editorial projects through an ambitious publication program, was formed in 1875. Paris had already published the undisputed model for "scientific" textual criticism in 1872, his landmark edition of *La vie de Saint Alexis,* which can with no exaggeration be said to have completely revolutionized the ways in which French philologists would edit texts through its implementation of the so-called Lachmannian method.[10] Finally, intermittently until 1872 and permanently thereafter up to the year of his death, 1903, Paris occupied the most important outlet for the promulgation of instruction in French medieval literature, the chair at the Collège de France. Thus, in the space of seven years following the statement quoted above (and this period would certainly have been shorter had the Franco-Prussian War [1870–71] not intervened), Gaston Paris had indeed disabused his contemporaries of the errors of the preceding generations and set up the institutional mechanisms that would assure their transit on the path to truth.

Gaston Paris's early writings reveal with astonishing clarity, lurking behind this vigorous and influential scholarly program, the strong ideological current not only guiding his patterns of thought but also determining the very nature and content of his "scientific" discoveries. While positivistic certainty or scientificity per se was the impetus for a method of textual reconstruction that could determine the contours and the letter of the original text in spite of the corruptions of manuscript transmission, France's political uneasiness and craving for a strong national image following the events of 1870–71 explain the extraordinary prestige accorded to an individual work such as the *Chanson de Roland* at this time (cf. Bloch "842"). Indeed, the most blatant instance of the intrusion of social commentary upon Gaston Paris's scholarly work is undoubtedly his well-known inaugural lecture to the Collège de France in December 1870 entitled "La Chanson de Roland et la nationalité française," delivered as France was under siege by the Prussian forces.

In his opening lecture of the previous year (1869), Paris had implicitly called upon some of his arguments advanced in his earlier *Histoire poétique* (1865) in speaking of the French as a fusion of two races, Teutonic and Latin, just as the chansons de geste was a hybrid version of an essentially Germanic poetic mode.[11] In the 1870 address, however, Paris, without having totally abandoned his earlier scheme of literary history, accentuates questions of national unity, solidarity, love of one's native land, and cultural heritage. The discourse of "fusion" that he had professed earlier is here turned into one of conflict. Leaving aside the transcultural scientific ideal of a *human* solidarity, he speaks of international conflict as an unexpected source of cultural formation: "l'opposition des nations les unes aux autres est nécessaire pour qu'elles apprennent, non seulement à apprécier les autres, mais à se comprendre elles-mêmes . . . elles peuvent, si elles savent en profiter y perfectionner leurs qualités et y corriger leurs défauts" (*Poésie*, 99).

If we accept Gumbrecht's contention that the discourse of nationalism imported from Prussia never succeeded in effacing a deeply rooted French *episteme* inherited from the Enlightenment, predicated upon "the SYNCHRONIC framework of *science de l'homme*" (Gumbrecht, 13), then we are witnessing here the double irony of Paris using the precepts of German ideology in order to combat German ideology in a sociopolitical context that was itself inimical to that ideology. Cerquiglini has made a similar point about Paris's work in textual criticism: in order to resolve his own conflicted admiration of German academic accomplishments after the war, Paris doggedly pursued the imitation, and not the rejection, of their methods in order to "lachmanniser vigoureusement la littérature médiévale française, et de montrer aux Prussiens . . . que l'on fait bien mieux qu'eux" (*Éloge*, 81).

If, on the considerable strength of such studies, it has by now become a commonplace to contend that we can understand the "Middle Ages" as a historical moment only through an investigation of the nineteenth-century philosophical and aesthetic movements (e.g., Romanticism, positivism, naturalism) within which the dominant philological discourse was initially inscribed, it would be a mistake nonetheless to assume that Gaston Paris and his contemporaries were unaware of the awkward, ideologically charged situation in which they (and their "scientific discourse") found themselves. Paris's importation of German methodologies had been conscious and willful,[12] suggesting as it did the long-standing inadequacies and simple inertia of the philological movement in France. Léon Gautier, commenting upon Gaston Paris's thesis in his 1868 *Les épopées françaises*, provides an immediate witness to its German influence: "C'est la critique allemande pénétrant enfin dans les oreilles et dans les esprits des savants français" (654; quoted in Gumbrecht, 26). Indeed, before the war, undue patriotism could be considered an impediment to historical and scientific understanding.[13]

In the decades following the war, when enthusiasm and appreciation for the *Roland* became a rallying cry for French national unity in defiance of German aggression (largely under the double-edged intellectual aegis of Gaston Paris), the defense of medievalism became an overtly patriotic matter, especially for those critics of lesser wit or subtlety. Thus, in 1880, F. Brunetière ridiculed the association made between literary appreciation of the chansons de geste and a love of one's country that had been used to criticize his unfavorable assessment of the "new" medievalism and its dismal effect on literary studies: "on peut être bon patriote aussi, et ne faire pourtant grand cas ni de la *Chanson de Roland,* ni d'*Aliscans,* ni de la *Chanson d'Antioche.*"[14]

Gaston Paris himself acknowledged the patriotic fervor of his 1870 lecture when he decided, some fifteen years later, to publish it for the first time in an unedited version, along with a collection of other lectures, most of which had already appeared in print: "J'ai même laissé subsister quelques pages qui n'avaient qu'un intérêt momentané ou personnel. J'ai tenu à reproduire ces discours tels absolument qu'ils ont été prononcés; j'insiste sur ce point notamment pour le troisième (*la Chanson de Roland et la nationalité française*), qui a été composé et lu (décembre 1870) dans des circonstances douloureuses dont il conserve l'impression immédiate, déjà difficile à bien retrouver aujourd'hui pour ceux qui l'ont ressentie, et bien plus difficile à concevoir pour ceux que leur âge a empêchés de l'éprouver alors" (*Poésie,* vi–vii). With little sense of contradiction, Paris saw this document as both a subjective record of wartime experience and a scientific inquiry into the constitution of a nation and its literature. What he certainly would not have been willing to admit was that the "impressionistic" side of the essay occupied any other than a marginal position punctuating, but not essentially altering, its solid historical depiction. Or, as we can see it now, that the historical "data" might have served the political moment.

With the aid of texts such as these, written at a time when the newly formed academy had to fight for its subsistence and justification, it is perhaps not difficult to assess the interrelationships between scholarship per se and external influences of a political, social, or institutional stamp. Indeed, the candor of many of these writings imposes upon us the necessity to understand scholarship as itself a political act,[15] one that not only reacts to and manipulates power relations, but that contains within it the potential to redefine the very terms of those relations (as in recent debates over the canon).[16] But however true this observation might be, it is important to remember that power relations continue to function in the academy and that the stages upon which they play themselves out are manifold. To be more specific, the above-mentioned ideological critiques of Gaston Paris, in their nearly exclusive concentration on the power relations between men in a political or institutional arena, betray their own ideological commitment to a "masculine" history of ideas as a locus of origin and a generating source of metaphoric power.

This perhaps explains the absence of Paris's work on love literature from such discussions,[17] for eroticism has only recently been considered a compelling explanatory tool in the same league, for instance, as political ideology or philosophical ideas. What I am suggesting is a reversal whereby certain conflicted gender and generational issues might themselves serve as symbolic motors of Paris's "political formulation." Indeed, as with many writers of his time, one is struck by the metaphoric richness of a discourse that otherwise makes claims to scientific exactitude and impartiality. The political discourse of national unity, as we shall see, is also a discourse of family, generation, and love. Whereas the unidirectionality of metaphoric invention is typically assumed—the political being the generating one—I would like to "read" the critical discourses as a text in the Barthesian sense, a web of metaphors and associations that do not necessarily admit of a single origin. This represents in part an attempt to recapture the fluid boundary between critical and literary formations that is especially characteristic of critical writing of the period. The advantage of this approach is that it allows us to link discourses that are not usually associated, such as, in Paris's case, the political, the editorial, and the erotic. To acquire something approaching a full grasp of a writer whose corpus was so variegated as that of Gaston Paris, we need to extend the ideological investigation beyond the confines of political or purely aesthetic issues by way of probing personal and familial metaphors that can themselves be seen to coordinate otherwise disparate aspects of his work.

As I have already suggested, much of the recent work on the politics of nineteenth-century medievalism[18] could induce us to forget that the hotly debated issue of courtly love, quite possibly the contribution to medieval studies for which Gaston Paris is best remembered today, concerns neither the question of national origins and the early epic nor that of scientific textual reconstruction. Furthermore, there remains a huge gap between the sort of work that has attempted an archaeology of the discourse of medievalism and a more traditional research oriented toward intellectual or literary history. Emblematic of the widening chasm that separates the diverse approaches to nineteenth-century philology is the appearance of two articles on Gaston Paris in *Romance Philology* published within six months of each other. The first, to which I have already alluded, was Hans Ulrich Gumbrecht's seminal investigation of the political and cultural complexities surrounding Gaston Paris's importation of German philological method. The second, by Henry Ansgar Kelly,[19] appeared only two issues later and proposed an overview of Paris's various opinions concerning love literature, extending from his earliest published lectures on Old French literature (the 1866 lecture) to his last writings. Kelly, following in the footsteps of recent critics who have condemned an unreflective use of the term, prompts a sensible review of Paris's career by noting his own marginal implementation of the expression and his far from monolithic vision of medieval eroticism.

In addition to their obvious methodological differences, what is most striking about these two articles is their nearly total lack of intersection, even as they each pretend to characterize a broad aspect of Gaston Paris's scholarship. While Gumbrecht's analysis pivots around the epistemological question of how national and cultural formations can serve as the basis for divergent ways of framing intellectual issues, Kelly, in a traditional "history of ideas" approach, focuses upon the abstract, disinterested expression of ideas outside of institutional or social contact. We might be tempted simply to say that the two are interested in different issues, and yet the mutual implications (and silences) are not to be neglected. Can Kelly's "critical archeology," his insistence on the importance of Paris's "insights and judgments" (323), afford to neglect that scholar's place in a context that was so clearly marked by polemical and institutional struggles? On the other hand, should Gumbrecht's assessment of Gaston Paris as putative "founder of French literary history" (29) and his unsuccessful attempt to install a "Germanic" French national identity not take into account an important sector of that scholarly work—one not so obviously marked by questions of nationalism—and, in so doing, broaden its vision of the "succession of works from his last decade" (29)?[20]

The very appearance of Gaston Paris's seminal writings on "courtly love" raises certain questions that have never, to my knowledge, been answered or even raised. The two parts of Paris's now infamous study appeared, respectively, in 1881 and 1883 in *Romania* under the global title "Études sur les romans de la table ronde."[21] It has become a critical truism to recall that the term "courtly love" was coined in the 1883 installment and given there a full definition in accordance with the love between Lancelot and Guenevere as detailed in Chrétien de Troyes's *Chevalier de la charrette*. It is less often recognized that the plan for the two articles was set out as of 1881 and that in fact the term first appeared in that article, two years earlier: "il est possible que cette indication légère . . . ait précisément suggéré à un conteur postérieur, qui voulait donner à l'épouse d'Arthur un amant digne d'elle et montrer dans leur liaison le type de l'amour *courtois,* l'idée de choisir Lancelot du Lac pour ce rôle" (Paris, 1881: 478). While Paris did not in 1881 detail the signification of the expression, his reference earlier in the article to the depiction of the "amour le plus profane" and "chevalerie la plus mondaine" in the context of Lancelot and Guenevere makes it clear that he knew which direction he was headed in. An additional clue is offered by his qualification of the *courtly* element: "la courtoisie dans les romans de ce groupe est poussée jusqu'à un raffinement excessif et bizarre" (1881: 469).

There is nothing surprising about the fact that the two parts were conceived as a single unit and published two years apart, but some additional questions need to be raised: Why did Gaston Paris embark upon this area of study at this particular moment in his career? Why did he not pursue his initial program past the 1883 article? The answer to the second question is uncertain: as the ambitious global title would lead us to believe, and as Paris laid it out in 1881, Lancelot and Guenevere occupied only a small sector of his projected "exploration méthodique de ce grand domaine poétique qu'on appelle le cycle de la Table Ronde, le cycle d'Arthur, ou le cycle breton" (1881: 465). His vision of the work toward which he was leading was impressive in its scale: "Les premières de ces études concernent Lancelot du Lac, Erec, Ivain, Yder, Gauvain, Perceval et le graal; d'autres viendront sur l'histoire religieuse de l'Angleterre, sur les lais, sur Nennius et Gaufrei de Monmouth, sur Merlin, sur Tristran, etc.; la question des romans en prose, souvent touchée dans les divers articles, sera l'objet d'une investigation particulière" (ibid.).

As it turned out, the only article published after 1883 that can even remotely be considered a part of this project is the 1886 "Études sur les romans de la table ronde: Guinglain ou le Bel Inconnu,"[22] which, except for its title, bears no connection to the previous articles. The appearance of these two articles starting in 1881 is itself sudden and difficult to account for. Up to that time, Paris had dealt little with the Breton material and even less with Arthurian romance. Aside from his edition of several anonymous Breton *lais* in 1878–79 in *Romania,* and, according to the Roques/Bédier bibliography of his publications,[23] sporadic book reviews over the previous fifteen years, he appears to have shown little interest in this material.[24] To summarize the questions: why did Paris undertake a project of gargantuan proportions in an area for which he had shown little previous interest and then seemingly abandon it after publishing a lengthy two-part article that limited itself to a discussion of the origins and development of the Lancelot/Guenevere story?

Before approaching an answer to this perhaps unanswerable question (why indeed does any scholar pursue or discontinue work in a particular field?), a second misconception about Gaston Paris's "courtly love" article needs to be revised. In view of the attention it has received, it is commonly assumed that "courtly love" is the central focus of the 1883 article. In fact, this is the result of a highly selective reading, for out of a total of seventy-five pages devoted to discussion of Chrétien's *Charrette* and its relation to the prose *Lancelot,* only eighteen (slightly less than one-quarter) actually involve the question of love and its codification. Paris himself admits to a selective reading of Chrétien's romance, dismissing much of it by virtue of its being bizarre, lacunary, and frequently incoherent. This judgment induces him to eliminate much of Chrétien's work from consideration. But more important, the question of courtliness is itself subsumed under another one that is more directly related to the establishment of literary history: the chronological priority of Chrétien's romance vis-à-vis the prose cycle of Lancelot/Grail romances, a priority that is nowadays so much taken for granted that Paris's argument is largely ignored. And yet at the time it was the subject of considerable debate; judging from some of the literature, it was commonly believed that Chrétien had simply provided in his *Charrette* a verse translation of one episode drawn from the enormous prose cycle. Paris made use of the charge of incoherence he had leveled against Chrétien in order to "prove" the latter's priority over the more smoothly rational and ideologically acceptable prose version, while in turn seeing in "courtly love" the original mark of twelfth-century French society that Chrétien had imprinted upon his inherited Celtic source. The two articles, taken together, promote a revision of literary history and not primarily an interrogation of erotic ideals; it is thus not surprising that Paris concluded his article as follows:

> Il est démontré en effet que le récit de l'enlèvement et de la délivrance de Guenièvre dans le *Lancelot* en prose n'est pas la source du poème de Chrétien, n'est pas non plus dérivé indépendamment d'une source commune, mais qu'il provient directement de ce poème, et il est établi par là même que les romans arthuriens en prose ne sont pas antérieurs aux romans en vers, mais qu'au contraire ils en sont une imitation, un développement, une suite, et représentent, dans

l'histoire du cycle breton, une phase très distincte, secondaire et postérieure. (1883: 534)

Perhaps because attention has always been focused upon the 1883 article as a point of origin for "courtly love," critics have not noted the other event that occurred in 1881, the year of "courtly love"'s first brief appearance: the death of Gaston Paris's father, Paulin Paris.[25] What might, in the case of most other scholars, appear simply as a personal *fait divers* scarcely rippling the surface of an otherwise unrelated career assumes an added importance in this particular instance. Paulin Paris was not only a scholar in his own right; he was Gaston's predecessor at the Collège de France, having occupied the chair of Old French language and literature since its foundation in 1853. Paulin Paris, both father and mighty pioneering figure, died in February and the first "courtly love" article was published in the October fascicle of *Romania*. The connection is not pure coincidence, for the global title of Gaston's projected series, "Études sur les romans de la table ronde," alluded directly to his father's last important publication, a five-volume work entitled *Les romans de la table ronde*, published between 1868 and 1877. Strangely enough, his father's work is scarcely mentioned in the two articles, yet the covert polemic is striking: whereas Paulin had maintained from his earliest writings[26] the chronological priority of the prose cycle of Arthurian romances (of which the above-mentioned work was a modern French translation), Gaston, as we have seen, doggedly insisted upon their secondary and derivative status vis-à-vis Chrétien's romances.

It is difficult to think of a more certain way for Gaston to bury his father's memory than this critical gesture, deemed by Joseph Bédier "worse than irony," that silences his father in two ways, not even crediting him with sufficient esteem to enter into a direct polemic.[27] Moreover, to think of Paulin Paris's life's work lurking beneath the "courtly love" articles is to reconceive the symbolic thrust of the words quoted above: "[les romans arthuriens en prose] sont une imitation, un développement, une suite, et représentent . . . une phase très distincte, secondaire et postérieure." A discourse of secondariness and derivation, as Patricia Parker has recently suggested in the context of misogynistic rhetoric, carries strong implications of inferiority and powerlessness.[28]

Gaston Paris did find a more direct way of interring his father's career, and it took the form of his opening lecture to the Collège de

France in December of that same year, published in the January 1882 issue of *Romania* under the title "Paulin Paris et la littérature française du moyen âge." In this eulogy, Gaston provided his audience with a sentimental yet rigorous review of his father's career, accompanied by a brief sketch of the intellectual program of medieval studies as it was in the process of developing:

> Toute sa vie, [Paulin Paris] chercha à . . . répandre le goût [des productions du moyen âge], à leur conquérir des sympathies chez les gens du monde, chez les littérateurs purs, chez les femmes elles-mêmes. C'est dans cet esprit qu'il choisit souvent les textes dont il a donné l'édition, qu'il écrivit plusieurs de ses préfaces et de ses notices, qu'il mit en "nouveau langage" *Les aventures de maître Renart et d'Ysengrin son compère,* et *Garin le Loherain,* et enfin *Les Romans de la Table Ronde.* Il faut reconnaître que ses efforts n'ont pas été couronnés d'un plein succès, et peut-être y avait-il quelque illusion dans l'espoir qui les animait. En tout cas, nous comprenons aujourd'hui un peu différemment l'étude du moyen âge. Nous nous attachons moins à l'apprécier et à le faire apprécier qu'à le connaître et à le comprendre. Ce que nous y cherchons avant tout, c'est de l'histoire. (*Poésie,* 219)

This brief passage is packed with a number of significant clues regarding not only Gaston's attitude toward his father's scholarship but, more broadly, his profession in general. Paulin Paris's achievements—here as elsewhere in the article—are presented as emblematic of a certain approach to the Middle Ages that is outmoded, having been superseded by the methods of Gaston and his entourage. We are given the image of a pioneer in the uncharted regions of the library shelves (Paulin's medievalist career started when he assumed a minor position in the manuscript room of the Royal Library, now the Bibliothèque Nationale), a landscape that is also at one point referred to as a cemetery (*Poésie,* 227). Whereas Paulin exhumed the rotting bones of a past civilization, Gaston and his followers in the text editing trade offer a living, breathing specimen through the method of textual reconstruction. We can here note the significance of a radical shift in metaphors:

> Quant à la sympathie du public pour ces oeuvres, à leur diffusion comme sources de jouissances littéraires, à leur introduction dans l'éducation nationale, nous les souhaitons assurément, au moins dans de certaines limites; mais nous ne les attendons que d'un

progrès lent, qui ne peut s'accomplir et s'accélérer que si d'abord une critique sévère et rigoureusement historique *a préparé le terrain, creusé les sillons et trié les semences*: alors des mains plus hardies et plus heureuses pourront *confier à la terre nouvelle quelques-unes des graines de ces fleurs oubliées*, écloses jadis spontanément *sur le sol* de la douce France, et qui retrouveront peut-être, au milieu d'*une flore parfois bien différente et souvent exotique*, un peu de leur éclat éteint et de leur parfum évanoui. (*Poésie*, 220; emphasis added)

Not only is the "new medievalism" of Gaston's team to be seen as fostering a process of regeneration, as opposed to an archaeology, but it necessitates, prior to any access, a new type of horticulture that will alter the very contours or aspect of the terrain in question. As such, it places the "new medievalism" in an originary and even creative position insofar as it suggests a planned spatial organization of the medieval canon in the image of a landscaped garden.

Paulin's personal, passionate, and heroically tireless devotion to the frequently indecipherable manuscript pages turns to an image of isolated absorption and distraction: "[il laissait] passer les heures sans en avoir conscience, et [il se replongeait], après une interruption toujours importune, dans le monde enchanté qu'évoquaient ces pages antiques et où, pendant de nouvelles heures, il vivait tout entier" (233). The point is more poignantly expressed when Gaston quotes his father's own words comparing himself cautiously but proudly to Don Quixote: "'Combien de fois alors n'ai-je pas mis un frein à mon enthousiasme, en me rappelant avec une sorte d'effroi l'aventure du chevalier de la Manche! Honnête don Quichotte! les romans coupables de ta folie n'étaient que de longues paraphrases décolorées. . . . Que serais-tu devenu si tu avais lu les originaux?'" (217).

The solitary pursuit of the distracted loner is contrasted with the team effort of Gaston and his associates: "*We* understand the study of the Middle Ages somewhat differently; we are less interested in appreciating it or having it appreciated than in knowing and understanding it." Even more than marking the passing of a generation, Gaston's remarks provide an outline for the pedagogical, social, and cultural ramifications of two distinct medievalisms, each as conceptually different—indeed, as mutually incomprehensible—as the Old Law and the New Dispensation. Perhaps the most basic distinction is the contrast between the pleasure of unmediated experience, emblematized by his father's total immersion, and the objectified, distanced gaze of the scientific observer, whose task, as Gaston repeated throughout his career, was to "establish the facts and articulate the laws governing them." For Gaston, his father represented the unwelcome dilettantism of a previous generation, one that had gained access to the texts and their understanding without any formal instruction (cf. *Poésie*, 250–52). One that, in fact, had no need of Gaston's philology or his by now solidly entrenched pedagogical machine.

Gaston illustrates the difference between appreciation and comprehension, between pleasure and mastery, in two complementary ways: through the nature of the two men's scholarly production and through a characterization of the audience addressed by them. While summarizing the diverse achievements of his father, ranging from the publication of historical works, to a pioneering catalog of manuscripts in the Royal Library, to translations of fictional works such as the Renard and Arthurian cycles, Gaston singles out the latter as the target for his criticisms, referring to the project of translation somewhat disparagingly (or condescendingly) by using Paulin's own phrase, "mis en nouveau langage," in quotation marks, as though he were afraid, even obliquely, to allow it to penetrate his own discourse. Disregarding his father's obvious passion for the discipline of history, Gaston located his generation's innovation in its submission of poetry to history; specifically, it was not a matter of gleaning historical information from the poetic texts, but treating these texts as historical documents in their own right, as "les faits mêmes de l'histoire de la langue, des sentiments et de la pensée" (220).

Gaston's version of medievalism, as thus articulated, seemed to promote a devaluation of poetry's expressive qualities in favor of its status as an artifact in a larger historical framework—a "document" rather than a "monument," to borrow Paul Zumthor's well-known distinction. Thus we understand the role of Gaston's editorial project as exemplified by the *Alexis*: the reconstruction of a linguistic specimen that would have the virtue of representing a particular stage of language development, however much it might stray from the actual words emitted by an individual author, linguistic data separated from individual expressive intention.[29] In terms of the scholarly publication itself, what could be a more extravagant departure from Paulin Paris's popularizing translations than the presentation of the 600-odd lines of the eleventh-century *Alexis* text in 32 pages with variants at the bottom of the page, preceded by 85 pages of prefatory material? Paradoxically, to *understand*, to *comprehend*, here means not to read;

and Gaston certainly prided himself on the fact that his edition was as inaccessible as his father's translations were open to the appreciation of a lay reading public.

More revealing, perhaps, is Gaston's manifestly uncharitable characterization of the readership for which his father destined these translations: "les gens du monde, . . . les littérateurs purs, . . . les femmes elles-mêmes." Scarcely masked beneath the first two terms is a polemic aimed at the mission of public instruction and the role of medieval literature therein. As early as his first lecture at the Collège de France, standing in for his father, Gaston spoke of the Collège institutionally as a place where the study of material lacking any recognized practicality or utility was protected from the constraints of the university *facultés*, where young people were trained for particular careers. Many changes occurred in the ensuing fifteen years, not least of which was the solid establishment of a self-begetting professional group of teachers that was distinct from the aristocratic culture-seekers who would in the past have formed the bulk of the lettered class.[30] The legitimation of literary studies required the sort of scientificity insisted upon by Gaston Paris, but it also caused a decisive rift: the offhand reference to those deluded souls who continue to believe that universities should be "sanctuaires du goût" (*Poésie*, 212) certainly constitutes a rejoinder to Brunetière's recent (1879–80) fulminations against the literature of the Middle Ages.[31] The use of the expression "littérateurs purs" was not, moreover, an innocent one: Brunetière himself provided a gloss revealing its derisive implications for the nonprofessional lettered class to which it was applied.[32]

The nuance conveyed by the last pronoun, "elles-mêmes," merits especial articulation: if women "themselves" are third on the list, the suggestion is simply that the first two groups are by their very nature characterized as possessing womanly qualities. The chain of associations is transparent: feminine, frivolous, unscientific, amateurish. In sharp contrast, Gaston Paris's own speech is punctuated with some frequency by the simple address "Messieurs." The world of aristocratic culture-seekers—the "lettered" class in general—all characterized as feminine, clearly has a secondary, or even tertiary, status, well below the male-oriented and newly professionalized pursuit of academic disciplines. The lines thus drawn far exceed the superficial distinction between professionalism and dilettantism: they also encode and thus perpetuate sexual and social divisions within the discipline itself.

It would be simple to stop at the conclusion that Gaston's double-edged review of his father's career represents an Oedipal moment in the family romance of scholarly careers, "Gaston Paris's victory over Paulin Paris as an academic" (Gumbrecht, 24). And yet what I would like to suggest is that Gaston's intermingled admiration for, and rejection of, his father's medievalism represents an amplified expression of a conflict that he felt throughout his career and that received a most curious expression in the "doctrine" of courtly love.

At bottom, the difference between the two medievalisms is a difference between unmediated appreciation and distanced comprehension, between pure literary imagination and science, word-as-expression and word-as-artifact. Paulin is depicted as a man possessed, a man literally living outside of his century,[33] a man whose absorption in the periods he studied was so thorough that he actually participated in the fictional or historical events. The result for Paulin Paris as a scholar was that he could no longer "judge . . . from the outside" (*Poésie*, 248), a fact that entailed the loss of "la froide impartialité du jugement vraiment scientifique" (249). The central traits that Gaston uses to characterize—and ultimately to dismiss—his father's professional activity thus derive ultimately from the distinction between subject and object, between exterior and unmediated vision. This is, moreover, a gendered valence, the passivity of pure immersion being regarded as a "feminine" attitude, while the active stance of observation and mastery—Gaston's own—betokened a blatantly masculine one.

The two attitudes abundantly characterized and caricatured in the 1881 eulogy derive from a duality that can be detected as of the earliest stages of Gaston's career, a duality that contributed to his ultimately paradoxical vision of the professional study of the Middle Ages. For in his first address to the audience at the Collège de France (1866), Gaston, still imbued with an unrepressed Romanticism scarcely distinguishable from the discourse of a Chateaubriand or a Mme de Staël,[34] characterizes the origins of medieval literature as spontaneous, enthusiastic, unbridled, vital, and natural. The Middle Ages, he says with utmost concision, is "une époque essentiellement poétique."[35] The poeticity attributed to the early Middle Ages is, however, only one component of a larger historical vision that involves the suppression of the primitive culture by an increasingly influential learned tradition fostered within the aristocracy and the clerical ranks. As he puts it in a later lecture, "Il y a donc dans toute histoire littéraire du moyen âge deux parts bien distinctes à faire: l'une pour la littérature des clercs, l'autre pour celle du peuple" (*Poésie*, 82). Especially in these early lectures, Gaston was overtly critical of this clerical tradition, not only because it quelled the vital voice of the people as represented primarily in epic songs, but also because it was itself steeped in artifice and empty conventions. By imposing laws of composition and trivializing subject matter, courtly society was only masking an emptiness and a displaced center.

In a fascinating passage from his first lecture, Paris suggests a parallel between this scheme of literary history and his own critical position. The spontaneous vitality of popular poetry is due, in large measure, to the absence of reflection or observation: "ils ne s'observent pas, ils vivent naïvement, comme les enfants, chez lesquels la vie réfléchie que développe la civilisation n'a pas étouffé encore la libre expansion de la vitalité naturelle" (9). In short, ignorance is a necessary precondition for poetic originality. The birth of "la critique," in Paris's scheme, marked the end of true poetic inspiration. Reason, although it is *the* "faculté souveraine et maîtresse," constitutes the "negation of poetry." Elevated, cold, and lacking any distinguishable traits, reason contrasts with the multiplicity of events in the real world, replete with "ses formes et ses couleurs, ses chants et ses parfums, son puissant et joyeux désordre" (9). Poetry and Reason are not simply contrasting values; allegorized; they denote epochs in the developmental stages of individuals or of societies. "Plus nous vieillissons, hommes ou nations, plus la raison chasse en nous l'imagination" (10). The modern philologist's position can, in this developmental scheme, be doubly contrasted with the ignorance of naive primitivism, as maturity is to infancy: first, the rational scientific observer as he is confronted with the spontaneous primitive culture; and, second, on the level of the history of criticism itself, Gaston's method of research superseding the naive but sincere work of his father's generation, referred to tellingly in the eulogy as the "âge héroïque de nos études" (252).

It is not difficult to perceive in Paris's literary history the underlying mythical scheme of the Fall or the loss of the Golden Age. Especially poignant in this regard is his attempt to recapture the lost paradise through means that themselves negate the very existence of that paradise. In this same passage, he pretends with uncharacteristic naiveté that reason *can* provide a return to the primitive state of unreflexive ignorance: "La science peut suppléer et recréer, pour ainsi dire, dans les peuples, leur adolescence poétique. Pareille aux souvenirs où nous aimons à retrouver les illusions de notre jeune âge, elle nous apprend à nous refaire enfants pour goûter les joies naïves de l'enfance; elle nous rouvre les trésors de l'imagination de nos pères, et fait jaillir de nouveau, dans nos intelligences desséchées, les sources vives de la joyeuse et jeune poésie" (252).

This passage provides a revealing contrast with the eulogy for his father fifteen years later, for one can detect in the intervening period the dissipation of early illusions accompanied by a sense of the essential belatedness and frustration of the scientific ideal. When faced with an individual (Paulin Paris) who did manage to reach the living sources of these fruits picked in the earthly paradise of the library shelves (221), the scientific philologist can only reject this vision as a distracted and deluded one. Conceptually and institutionally, literary history must posit an unattainable mythologized paradise as justification for its activity, just as textual criticism must cling to the assurance of a "lost original."[36] But ultimately, as we have seen, the goals of the philologist subvert the features of the object under study. At first, Paris valorizes the fact that the primitive society has no inkling of the "idée de régularité prévue" that reason grants us; ultimately, however, what the science of literature will allow us to articulate is "la régularité des lois qui dirigent un mouvement tumultueux et fortuit en apparence" (37). In order for science to exercise its power, even primitive poetic expression must have underlying laws to be discovered. Its disorder and liberty can thus only be an illusion that scientific philology will unmask. Reason, in other words, will dismantle poetry by showing that it is not *really* poetry.

The contrast between the naive and the rational, between passive immersion and rigorous objectivity, likewise surfaces in Paris's thoughts about patriotism and national feeling in the crucial 1870 lecture, once again bringing up the vexing question of the role of the intellectual. As Howard Bloch has recently shown,[37] the motives governing the conception of a national spirit parallel those seeking to schematize literary history. It is thus not surprising that Gaston Paris's early notions of primitive poetry and its spontaneous vitality conform to an ideal of "natural" patriotism.[38] Complicating this scheme, at a time when contemporary patriotism and national solidarity were in jeopardy, was the place of the scientific observer. What must a scientific observer do when he is himself a member of the society being studied? Can one simultaneously be a patriot and a scholar? The answer, not unexpectedly, is a contradictory one. Initially, the answer appears simple: "Je ne crois pas, en général, que le patriotisme ait rien à démêler avec la science" (*Poésie,* 90). Science and its principal object, truth, have no truck with polemics of any kind, be they political, religious, or moral. It is in this context that Gaston speaks of the ranks of intellectuals as themselves forming a great fatherland (*patrie*) inimical to political upheaval and, ultimately, comparable to the City of God (91). Thus there exists a supernal nationalism, one that belongs to another "political" order. Paris further concretizes the metaphor when he refers to the lecture hall as a fortification (*enceinte*), impregnable site of the scientific mind contrasting with the predicament of the besieged French capital surrounding him and his listeners.

But such profound indifference, even in the name of scientific ideals, is potentially dangerous, and Gaston showed himself to be as incapable of relegating himself to an "ivory tower" as he was of choosing a topic that had no bearing upon France's current woes. Nonetheless, in a brilliant display of intellectual *mauvaise foi,* he protested his deep-seated resistance to such coincidentally relevant historical material: not only does the true scholar not seek out "useful and applicable" consequences of his work, but he has a "secret repugnance" toward any immediate application of that work. The purity of scientific research resides in its distance from practical consequences or concessions of any kind: "[Le savant] laisse cette tâche aux vulgarisateurs habiles qui ont le goût et le talent de répandre l'instruction plus que le besoin de la vérité rigoureuse" (92). The problem, at bottom, is that the distanced purity of the scientific gaze risks running afoul of the most basic attitudes required of citizens in a period of political necessity. Gaston's solution is to place the scientist outside and above the political context, in no uncertain way a gesture that parallels his putative ability to detect the laws governing a poetic discourse that manifestly obeys no laws, that can by definition *know* no laws. Thus he contrasts true national spirit with that of societies held together by force or simple habit, as a natural organism contrasts with a mechanical artifact. Interestingly enough, he finds a way to exempt the scientist from this scheme through an odd triangulation: "il faut qu'elle [l'habitude] se transforme, qu'elle passe de la simple habitude extérieure à l'instinct intime, qu'elle devienne, *pour tout autre oeil que celui de la critique scientifique,* quelque chose de profondément différent et d'un autre ordre" (97; emphasis added). Gaston does not in fact state whether the scientist, *as citizen,* is ultimately subject to the instinctual bonds of national feeling, but he does place in an absolutely exceptional position the scientific gaze, which remains abstracted and . . . unnatural.

We might appear to have gotten far afield from our discussion of Paulin Paris and "courtly love," and yet I would submit that the dilemma of scientific observation and mastery articulated in Gaston's early writings lies at the heart of the 1881 events. Gaston Paris's obsession with the scientific study of literature became translated not only as a kind of mind/body dualism, the scientist being unfettered by all associations with concrete or material circumstance, but also as an unresolved conflict between control, schematized as a function of one's knowledge (an accumulation of "cultural capital," in the economic terms of Bourdieu), and appreciation, understood in manifestly passive and "feminine" terms. Patriotism and national devotion here fall on the side of "appreciation" since, by virtue of their instinctual grounding, they were conceived by Paris as a form of love: "c'est l'amour que vous trouverez au fond de toute nationalité réelle" (97). In the course of his career, we may say that Gaston Paris's scientific ideal led him increasingly to repudiate love in its many related forms: naive poetry, patriotic fervor, his father's medievalism. That Gaston lingered upon his father's qualities of love and sincerity, even as he deprecated his scholarly output, was thus rhetorically quite apposite. His father came increasingly to symbolize the qualities inherent in the Romantic substratum of nineteenth-century medievalism that Gaston's scientific ideal gradually induced him to dismiss or dismantle.[39]

What makes this a poignant realization is that it was equally clear that pure science was not self-sufficient. In his patriotism lecture in 1870, Gaston spoke admiringly of the Germans' sense of a national identity, which he attributed interestingly enough to the efforts of a single man, a scholar, a philologist: Jacob Grimm, "one of the veritable founders of modern German nationality" (113). Grimm was able to accomplish this through a combination of qualities unavailable in the history of French civilization: a man combining "scientific genius with an intense, deep, and childlike love for one's fatherland (*patrie*)." It is hard not to see that the French equivalent would be an impossible fusion between Gaston Paris and his father: science and love; genial and childlike impulses.

Gaston's ideological aim in his eulogy is accomplished rhetorically through a precise set of reversals that transform old age, indeed senility, into a state of infancy accompanied by a strong hint of emasculation; correspondingly, youth is elevated to a position of mature, masculine control. With this strong scenario of professional revisionism as a backdrop, the concept of "courtly love" takes on a powerfully ironic role within a literary historical picture that itself asserts priority, and thus authority, through the chronological reversal of the prose *Lancelot* and Chrétien's *Charrette*. "Courtly love" is, at bottom, in Gaston Paris's scheme, a submission of sexual passion to the laws of science, characterized by the distanced gaze of the observer and the notion of progress through the acquisition of knowledge. We recall the principal characteristic of "courtly love," according to Gaston Paris: "Enfin, et c'est ce qui résume tout le reste, l'amour est un art, une science, une vertu, qui a ses règles tout comme la chevalerie ou la courtoisie, règles qu'on possède et qu'on applique mieux à mesure qu'on a fait plus de progrès, et auxquelles on ne doit pas manquer sous peine d'être jugé indigne" (1883: 519). The formulation of a vision of love that subjects it to a set of rules, making of it an art and a science, represents a triumphant rewriting of literary history that offers an apparent resolution of the scientific dilemma.[40]

One of the most obvious signs of a critical revision can be detected in Paris's judgment of clerical/aristocratic literature as a whole. We recall that in his early lectures Gaston criticized the refined but vapid literature of the courts that displaced heroic poetry after the mid-twelfth century: "Le XIIIe siècle, qu'on regarde d'ordinaire comme le plus beau moment littéraire du moyen âge, n'est à mes yeux, par bien des côtés, qu'une époque de faux brillant, d'éclat extérieur sous lequel se cache un grand vide" (*Poésie*, 26). In this early, Romantic phase, the story of Tristan and Iseut received praise for its "incomparable" expression of a love myth that encapsulated the Celtic national spirit (51). In the "courtly love" article, he instead valorizes the "bizarre and excessive" refinement of love in Chrétien's romance, while dismissing the Tristan material as depicting "une passion simple, ardente, naturelle, qui ne connaît pas les subtilités et les raffinements de celui de Lancelot et de Guenièvre" (1883: 519). It is not at all the case that *Tristan* was being demoted as a work of literature, for Paris still considers it "le plus merveilleux poème d'amour qu'ait peut-être produit l'humanité" (1883: 521), but Paris's focus had changed to suit his current polemical interest. However grandiose the fierce passion of Tristan and Iseut might be, it was lacking the conventions and refinements of the twelfth-century courts: it was, quite simply, not French enough.

There are a number of ways of accounting for Gaston Paris's reversal in his thinking about the opposition between primitive and refined poetry. One of these involves a movement away from the well-known Romantic concentration on sources and origins. Such a discourse dictates an aesthetic valuation of the oldest, the most primitive or archaic form of poetic discourse. This point of view was espoused by Gaston in his earliest work, especially the *Histoire poétique de Charlemagne,* but it is clearly no longer a preoccupation in the "courtly love" article. Indeed, he there takes a nearly opposite stance by passing quickly over potential sources of the doctrine (Provençal lyric; English chivalry) in order to describe its definitive and fully formed incarnation at a particular moment in French society. What this amounts to, among other things, is Gaston's recognition that the philologist's real affinities lay with aristocratic/clerical literature and not with a primitive, naive poetry whose very principles are distorted by the scientific gaze that would attempt to comprehend it.

As the preceding discussion has attempted to show, the expression of personal, professional, and ideological conflicts in Gaston's discourse(s) was subject to a profoundly dichotomous arrangement. One can, with little difficulty or, I believe, distortion, summarize these dichotomies as follows:

Reason/science	Love/imagination
clerical literature	primitive poetry
objectivity	subjectivity
masculine	feminine
reflective	naive
active	passive

It is only when a final pair was added to the list:

Gaston Paris	Paulin Paris

that is, when Gaston faced Paulin, that the irreconcilable nature of the two series became patent; only at that point, perhaps, did he realize that his idealization of primitive poetry, in addition to being a remnant from the Romantic image of the Middle Ages, could only serve to justify his father's immanent and sincere approach to the texts, with which he fundamentally disagreed. In complementary fashion, a critique of his father's medievalism entailed an implicit solidarity with the clerical literary production patronized by an aristocratic audience, born of the same ideals of self-conscious and rational reflection to which he subscribed.

As a consequence, a new biological analogy was required: the genetic metaphor, so crucial to his early work on the *cantilènes* and their development into the chansons de geste, had become one of dissection, an alteration in perspective that entailed the delineation of what was "properly French" as opposed to the cataloging of the various sources that preceded the French creation.[41] Whether or not this was dictated as well by inherent political anomalies ("the troubling suspicion that French literature may in fact be German"),[42] it did leave an opening, perhaps even an imperative, to find in medieval literature evidence of the unique French national image such as the nineteenth century conceived it, one characterized by moral, erotic, and linguistic refinement, however extreme or perverse.[43]

Another contributing factor is certainly the growing institutionalization of medieval studies that, perhaps inevitably, induced it to forge links with the study of more modern periods of literature. In writing his early apology for primitive poetry, Gaston Paris had alluded to the first appearance of individual authors whose originality made them closer to us but somehow "less" medieval (*Poésie*, 27)—an aesthetic reversal that offered a paradoxical proof of the difference (and authenticity) of the medieval text (cf. Aarsleff, 103). In his "courtly love" work, however, and especially through its linkage to the author Chrétien de Troyes, we can detect a movement forward to a modern aesthetic sense, one grounded in a sophisticated and self-conscious poetic art. This aesthetic problem had been precisely the target of Brunetière's 1879 critique of academic medievalism and the latter's seeming enslavement to the rough-hewn contours of the *Chanson de Roland*. It is difficult not to detect in Gaston Paris's socioliterary construct of "courtly love" a conformity to the notion of a classical canon by virtue of his references to the salon atmosphere of the medieval courts (*pace* Andreas Capellanus), and, even more so, to his designation of Marie de Champagne and Eleanor of Aquitaine as "précieuses du XIIe siècle."

Judged according to its personal ramifications, and to the extent that psychological and intellectual affinities are related, Gaston's sketch of his father, loving and severe, admiring and disdainful, emulating and condescending, touches at the heart of an intellectual conflict very much in evidence from his earliest writings. More than the national epics, more than the fabliaux, aristocratic love literature focuses upon the conflicting demands of pure passion and reasoning intellect. Gaston's qualification of courtliness as essentially rule-governed activity bespeaks a desire to suppress or tame the spontaneous, instinctual, and possibly dangerous impulses in favor of the intellectual, the progressive, the artificial, the pedagogical.[44]

Finally, there arises the important problem of gender valuations to which I have alluded at several points and that has become an increasing source of interest in the discussion of "courtly love."[45] Feminist critics following upon Hélène Cixous[46] have noted the tacit gender-oriented dichotomies that have from ancient times differentiated intuition and knowledge, submission and domination, passive and active, matter and spirit. It is thus crucial to note that Gaston Paris's "invention" of courtly love takes place within a similar set of dichotomies related to his demotion of an effeminate and worldly dilettantism in favor of a masculine professionalism, itself effected in the broader, though not necessarily defining, symbolic space of a latent Oedipal conflict. The situation suggests, among other conclusions, that the construct of courtly love at its inception is rooted in an essentially homosocial professional discourse articulated through the collective masculine omniscience provided by the first-person plural pronoun, and the deictic use of "Messieurs."

It is, further, a discourse that must occult its own agency[47]; in this way, it imitates the medieval text that serves as one of its own points of origin, Andreas Capellanus's ultimately misogynous treatise on the art of loving. On the one hand, the apparent elevation of the Lady to the status of master or pedagogue simply masks her absorption by the clerical/professional mechanisms of power and mastery. On the other hand, just as the Lady, in Andreas's dialogues, occupies the position of respondent (shall we say Echo?) to the male *demande d'amour*, so is the *domina* in Gaston Paris's scheme objectified, since her role as master is subordinated to a further goal—the perfectioning of the adoring male lover: "pour être digne . . . il accomplit toutes les prouesses imaginables, et elle de son côté songe toujours à le rendre meilleur, à le faire plus 'valoir'; ses caprices apparents, ses rigueurs passagères, *ont* même d'ordinaire *ce but, et ne sont que des moyens* ou de raffiner son amour ou d'exalter son courage" (1883: 518–19; emphasis added). The woman is but a means to a masculine end. In this regard, Paris encounters some difficulties when it comes to characterizing the Lady. At first, he insists that Guenevere, in Chrétien's text, is the "modèle de toutes les perfections de la femme" (517). He is forced to admit, however, that this view of Guenevere as perfect queen and lover is scarcely visible in the source text and must be sought elsewhere: "Ces traits du caractère de Guenièvre sont peu marqués ici, mais se retrouvent dans d'autres romans de Chrétien et dans le *Lancelot* en prose, qui suit la même inspiration" (518, n.). We believe that love exists, we believe that the woman is an ideal presence, but somehow the proof is always to be found elsewhere, in another text.

The ramifications of the issues I have raised extend somewhat further than a simple questioning of whether "courtly love" does now,

or ever did, exist. Indeed, the question becomes increasingly meaningless as we come to see the seductive analogies between the medieval
and modern critical spirit. The invention of courtly love, as I have
tried to suggest, occurs strategically at the intersection of a personal
and professional dilemma in Gaston Paris's career. The fact that
Gaston Paris abandoned the grandiose project of which this essay was
only to be a small part hints at its localized, ad hoc role as a polemical
tool. The disproportionately widespread acceptance and vernacu-
larization of the term thus masks a profound irony, one that will
subsist only so long as its ideological and academic implications go
unrecognized. The suggestion of a continuity between the contradictions of professional academic life, its founding disjunction between
pleasure and science, and the ideal scheme of an eroticism grounded in
rules and progressive mastery perhaps explains "courtly love"'s enduring hold on succeeding generations, as the consummate (yet illusory) mythic image of the resolution of difference through rational
empowerment. The contradiction is far from resolved one hundred
years later, however much we might think it so; and, particularly in a
period when "minority discourses" are becoming a new source of
cultural and intellectual capital, it remains to be seen how far the
dominant discourse of mastery will be able to go in its conquest of
these fundamentally incompatible areas of experience, as illustrated
most recently, for instance, in the theoretical debate over "men in
feminism."[48] In this regard, "courtly love," in Gaston Paris's formulation, surfaces as an emblematic appropriation of the feminine on
behalf, once again, of the advancement of the male.

NOTES

1. Gaston Paris, "Ulrich de Zazikhoven et Arnaud Daniel," *Bibliothèque de l'École des Chartes* 26 (1865): 250.

2. There would be little need even to mention these questions were it not
still a common practice among philologists and literary historians to believe
in a positive solution to questions of interpretation and textual meaning. For
a recent programmatic statement of the positivist approach to authorial
intentionality, see Karl D. Uitti and Alfred Foulet, "On Editing Chrétien de
Troyes: Lancelot's Two Steps and Their Context," *Speculum* 63 (1988):
271–92, itself a response to David F. Hult, "Lancelot's Two Steps: A Problem
in Textual Criticism," *Speculum* 61 (1986): 836–58. The embarrassing philological inaccuracies of the former, which in essence undermine the positivist

argument, are detailed in David F. Hult, "Steps Forward and Steps Backward: More on Chrétien's *Lancelot*," *Speculum* 64 (1989): 307–16.

3. Cf. D. W. Robertson, Jr., *A Preface to Chaucer: Studies in Medieval Perspectives* (Princeton: Princeton University Press, 1962); E. Talbot Donaldson, "The Myth of Courtly Love," *Ventures* 5, no. 2 (1965): 16–23; F. X. Newman, ed., *The Meaning of Courtly Love* (Albany, N.Y.: SUNY Press, 1968).

4. As has been previously noted in the literature, Gaston Paris writes "*courtly* love" ("Études sur les romans de la table ronde: Lancelot du Lac," *Romania* 12 [1883]: 519), which suggests not only that he was coining a phrase for which there was hitherto none in existence, but that his use of the term as a shorthand to designate a set of characteristics (of which he listed four) was self-consciously arbitrary.

5. Lewis, Clive Staples, *The Allegory of Love; A Study in Medieval Tradition* (Oxford: The Clarendon Press, 1936).

6. Hans Georg Gadamer, *Truth and Method* (New York: Crossroad, 1982), 268.

7. Paul Zumthor, "Médiéviste ou pas," *Poétique* 31 (1977): 306–21, and *Parler du moyen âge* (Paris: Minuit, 1980).

8. Hans Ulrich Gumbrecht, "'Un souffle d'Allemagne ayant passé': Friedrich Diez, Gaston Paris and the Genesis of National Philologies," *Romance Philology* 40, no. 1 (1986): 1–37; Bernard Cerquiglini, "Éloge de la variante," *Langages* 69 (March 1983): 25–35, and *Éloge de la variante: Histoire critique de la philologie* (Paris: Éditions du Seuil, 1989); R. Howard Bloch, "842: The First Document and the Birth of Medieval Studies," in Denis Hollier, ed., *A New History of French Literature* (Cambridge, Mass.: Harvard University Press, 1989), 6–13.

9. Antoine Compagnon, "1895: Literature in the Classroom," in Hollier, ed., *History of French Literature*, 819–24, and *La troisième république des lettres: De Flaubert à Proust* (Paris: Éditions du Seuil, 1983).

10. David F. Hult, "Reading It Right: The Ideology of Text Editing," *Romanic Review* 79, no. 1 (1988): 74–88; Cerquiglini (above, n. 8). Paris notes in the introduction to the *Alexis* (Gaston Paris and Léopold Pannier, eds., *La vie de Saint Alexis, poème du XIe siècle et renouvellements des XIIe, XIIIe et XIVe siècles,* Bibliothèque de l'École des Hautes Études, Sciences philologiques et historiques, fasc. 7 [Paris: A. Franck, 1872], v–viii) that the editing method had been the object of his course in practical philology at the École Pratique des Hautes Études in the first six months of 1869. Publication of the work had been expected for 1870 and was already under way when the war broke out, a factor that delayed its appearance for two years.

11. Gaston Paris, *La poésie du moyen âge: Leçons et lectures,* 1st ser., 3d ed. (Paris: Hachette, 1895 [1885]), 73ff. (hereafter cited as *Poésie*). Cf. Bloch ("842," 13): "the founding discourse of medieval studies allows no distinction between explanations of the genesis of France's earliest linguistic and literary monuments and the identity of the nation." Bloch quite rightly detects in the genetic or evolutionary model a powerful ideological tool both in the creation of medieval studies and in the rehabilitation of the medieval period as a contemporary concern. This discourse accounts for the nine-teenth-century debates over the origins of the *Roland,* and, as Bloch brilliantly demonstrates, it finds a strikingly emblematic cross-cultural artifact in the *Strasburg Oaths.* However, I would term it "*a*" rather than "*the*" founding discourse of medieval studies, inasmuch as it does not apply to the bulk of works studied by these early medievalists (or, for that matter, to most of what they wrote). At least one other "founding discourse," which I will for the sake of simplicity call the philological, received its first (in the French tradition) important methodological elaboration and implementation in Paris's edition of the *Saint Alexis.* Rooted in the quasi-archaeological model of the concrete artifact and its reconstitution, the philological discourse was in no way conceived in nationalistic terms. Paris did indeed state in 1870 that "La littérature est l'expression de la vie nationale" (*Poésie,* 99), but, as he makes clear in the following pages of that essay, not all linguistic monuments are nationalistic ones: he reserves that place for works, typically epics, that take the history of a given people as an explicit theme (e.g., the Bible for the Jews; Homer for the Greeks).

12. Gaston Paris, "La philologie romane en Allemagne," *Bibliothèque de l'École des Chartes* 25 (1864): 435–45.

13. In "La philologie romane en Allemagne," Paris spoke of the efforts to cultivate the study of early Romance language and literature undertaken by the German government through its patronage of the university system and made his final jab at the French indifference to such study: "il est heureux, en attendant, que l'Allemagne fasse notre besogne" (445). A year later (1865), Paris referred obliquely to the "déplorable patriotisme" of many scholars ("Ulrich," 250) that had on occasion caused a distortion of their critical judgment and even of their good faith. Criticism of backward French research efforts had a long history before Gaston Paris started taking part; compare Paulin Paris, ed., *Li romans de Garin le Loherain publié pour la première fois et précédé de l'examen du système de M. Fauriel sur les romans carlovingiens,* Romans des douze pairs de France, 2, vol. 1 (1833; Geneva: Slatkine, 1969): "N'oublions pas, nous autres Français, si peu soucieux de tous nos genres d'illustration, que notre ancienne poésie est en ce moment étudiée et admirée par tous les hommes distingués de l'Europe. Tandis qu'à

grand'peine nous parvenons à publier les plus courts fragments de notre belle langue romane, on imprime à Londres, à Berlin, et à Florence, des in-folio qui lui sont empruntés. Il faut au moins marcher sur les traces des étrangers; il faut montrer pour ce qui nous appartient une sorte de jalousie et ne pas attendre, pour adopter sérieusement de vieux titres de gloire, que les barbares se réunissent pour nous les disputer" (xv–xvi).

14. Ferdinand Brunetière, "L'érudition contemporaine et la littérature française du moyen âge, in "*Études critiques sur l'histoire de la littérature française,* 1st ser., 4th ed. (Paris: Hachette, 1896), 1–61, which originally appeared in 1879 in the *Revue des deux mondes* (285). This text was republished a year later in the *Revue des langues romanes* (May 15, 1880), in response to a hostile article by Auguste Boucherie, who was taking issue with Brunetière's "L'érudition contemporaine." Brunetière had already in his first article played the game of national allegiances in a clever aside that politically justified his distaste for the *Roland:* "Non loin de ce grand fleuve épique, dont je consens, non seulement sans peine, mais encore avec plaisir, qu'on mette la source en Allemagne" (*Étude,* 25).

15. See in particular Lee Patterson's recent suggestion that the category of the "literary" is itself a screen used by criticism in order to "prove" its fundamental disinterestedness: "The refusal of criticism to acknowledge [the self-justifying idea of literariness as an ahistorical essence], and its counter-claim that it is called into being by an object that exists wholly apart from itself, is simply an effect of its reluctance to reflect upon the political nature of its authority" (*Negotiating the Past: The Historical Understanding of Medieval Literature* [Madison: University of Wisconsin Press, 1987], 41–42). On the cultural belatedness of the category "literature," see Terry Eagleton, *Literary Theory: An Introduction* (Minneapolis: University of Minnesota Press, 1983), and Paul Zumthor, "Critical Paradoxes," *MLN* 102, no. 4 (1987), 799–810.

16. John Guillory, "Canonical and Non-canonical: A Critique of the Current Debate," *ELH* 54, no. 4 (1987): 483–527.

17. It has become all too easy to decontextualize certain critical statements and claim that they represent a monolithic and unwavering outlook, as, for instance, one could gather from recent critical work that philology in the nineteenth century was solely determined by nationalism and the importation of German methods. An example of a different type, also involving Gaston Paris, can be detected in Stephen G. Nichols's introduction to an issue of *Speculum* devoted to "The New Philology," where certain of Gaston Paris's early statements (in his first lecture to the Collège de France in 1866) regarding the naive simplicity of medieval literature and its oral heritage are taken to represent *the* attitude of his entire career (Nichols, "Philology in a

Manuscript Culture," *Speculum* 65 [1990]: 7). However, this pigeonholing of
Paris, which leads Nichols to conclude that Paris's "conception of philology
does not use a language model" and to infer that his idea of poetry did not
involve a conception of "written and codified" language (5), is belied not
only by Paris's "authorial" approach to text editing (cf. *La vie de Saint
Alexis;* Cerquiglini, *Éloge;* Hult, "Reading"), but by qualifying statements
made by Paris in the same lecture, where he specifies that his view of the
"collective" origins of medieval literature is restricted to the earliest period,
prior to the mid-twelfth century, and thus applicable only to a few specific
works: "Cela n'est complètement vrai toutefois que de la première période du
moyen âge, de celle qui a été presque entièrement consacrée à l'épopée"
(*Poésie,* 22). This difference is important for our understanding of the role
played by aristocratic literature in Paris's system, as I suggest below.

18. For example, Janine R. Dakyns, *The Middle Ages in French Literature,
1851–1900* (Oxford: Oxford University Press, 1973); Patterson, *Negotiating the
Past;* R. Howard Bloch, "Naturalism, Nationalism, Medievalism," *Romanic
Review* 76, no. 4 (1985): 341–60.

19. Henry Ansgar Kelly, "The Varieties of Love in Medieval Literature
according to Gaston Paris," *Romance Philology* 40, no. 3 (1987): 301–27.

20. There is, I think, a problem here with Gumbrecht's suggestion that
only in his later years did Paris gravitate toward a more "French" vision of
his culture as one whose national image included a receptiveness to foreign
cultures. Even at his most fervidly patriotic, in the midst of his 1870 address
at the Collège de France, Paris defended the seriousness of his intellectual
endeavors from potential attacks against its partisan politics: "les études
communes, poursuivies avec le même esprit dans tous les pays civilisés,
forment au-dessus des nationalités restreintes, diverses et trop souvent hos-
tiles, une grande patrie qu'aucune guerre ne souille" (*Poésie,* 90). The concept of a nation of intellectuals that would overlap a more traditional
national formation is further discussed below.

21. Gaston. Paris, "Études sur les romans de la table ronde," *Romania* 10
(1881): 465–96, and "Études sur les romans de la table ronde: Lancelot du Lac,"
Romania 12 (1883): 459–534 (hereafter cited as 1881 and 1883 respectively).

22. Gaston Paris, "Études sur les romans de la table ronde: Guinglain
ou le Bel Inconnu," *Romania* 15 (1886): 1–24.

23. Joseph Bédier and Mario Roques, *Bibliographie des travaux de
Gaston Paris* (Paris: Société Amicale Gaston Paris, 1904).

24. During this period, *Romania* published at the end of each fascicle a
"Chronique" providing news of interest to its readers, including announcements of future publications and editions, books received, reports of meetings
of learned societies, and also titles of courses in Romance philology offered

each year in France and elsewhere in Europe. We see therein that, until 1879, Gaston Paris's courses at the Collège de France and at the École des Hautes Études were limited to epic, theater, and Oriental stories (the *Roman des sept sages*), along with some general courses such as "les plus anciens monuments" and "histoire de la littérature française au XIVe siècle." Only in January 1880 is it announced that the course for that year (1879–80) was devoted to "Les Romans de la Table Ronde."

25. Gumbrecht (24) and Cerquiglini (*Éloge*, 79) have both suggested connections between Gaston Paris's career and that of his father.

26. Cf. Paulin Paris, ed., *Li romans de Berte aus grans piés, précédé d'une dissertation sur les romans des douze pairs,* Romans des douze pairs de France, 1 (1832; Geneva: Slatkine, 1969), xi, and "De l'origine et du développement des Romans de la Table Ronde," *Romania* 1 (1872): 457–82.

27. The nuances of Gaston's questionable attitude toward his father's career and oeuvre were not lost on his own intellectual progeny and successor, Joseph Bédier. In 1910, in an open letter to Pio Rajna who had suggested in a review of Bédier's *Légendes épiques* that the latter had been disrespectful to his master's memory in his revisionist thesis regarding the chansons de geste, Bédier responded in his defense that his own criticisms of Gaston Paris's theories were no less a sign of "healthy" generational conflict than Gaston's criticisms (or neglect) of his father: "Il serait aisé à un chacun de placer ainsi sur la sellette de l'accusé le plus filial des disciples,—oui, Gaston Paris lui-même. Il avait, lui aussi, un maître aimé entre tous, son père Paulin Paris. Qu'a-t-il fait pourtant toute sa vie, que le contredire? . . . Si, vers 1865 par exemple, quelqu'un, grand admirateur de certaines théories de Paulin Paris, avait estimé que son fils faisait trop peu de cas de ces théories dans l'*Histoire poétique de Charlemagne*? . . . Ce censeur aurait dit par exemple: "telle théorie de Paulin Paris, Gaston Paris l'écarte en trois lignes: pourquoi? Telle autre, il la traite par le silence, chose pire que l'ironie: pourquoi?" ("Réponse à M. Pio Rajna," *Annales du Midi* 22 [1910]: 540).

28. Patricia Parker, *Literary Fat Ladies: Rhetoric, Gender, Property* (London and New York: Methuen, 1987); see also R. Howard Bloch, "Medieval Misogyny: Woman as Riot," *Representations* 20 (fall 1987): 1–15.

29. Cf. Hult, "Reading."

30. At the beginning of his 1881 eulogy, Gaston refers to the fact that finally the *facultés* are opening their doors to the study of medieval literature, the major problem being that there were not yet a sufficient number of qualified professors to occupy those positions (*Poésie*, 212).

31. Dakyns (208) reads Paris's reference in the same article (*Poésie*, 221) to "les rares protestations qu'il arrive parfois d'entendre encore" as an explicit response to Brunetière's attack.

32. Brunetière, 284: "nous autres, purs littérateurs, comme on nous appelle avec une indulgence aiguisée d'un peu de dédain."

33. "De toutes les époques de notre histoire, celle où mon père vécut n'était pas, à vrai dire, celle où il était le plus familier. Le grand mouvement d'idées qui se déroule depuis le commencement du siècle avait passé sur sa tête sans beaucoup le pénétrer. . . . il était au fond resté, par la direction générale de sa culture et la tournure habituelle de sa pensée, un bon Français du XVIIIe siècle" (*Poésie*, 249).

34. Cf. Albert Pauphilet, *Le legs du moyen âge: Études de littérature médiévale* (Melun: Librairie d'Argences, 1950), 56–58. Even though Pauphilet does not include Gaston Paris in this group, his sketch of the "Romantic" Middle Ages corresponds fairly exactly to Paris's vision of the earliest literary production: "c'est toujours une époque sentimentale, où les passions sincères, la foi, le dévouement à une idée, l'emportent sur le sens du réel. [Le moyen âge] se caractérise par le culte de quelques valeurs idéales, fierté nationale, honneur, amour, religion." Very early on, Bédier pointed out Paris's adhesion to the profoundly Romantic image of the Middle Ages that characterized his era, while adding that Paris's "realism" led him to somewhat different conclusions from his contemporaries; see Bédier, *Les légendes épiques*, 3d ed., vol. 3 (Paris: Champion, 1929 [1911]), 240–49.

35. Cf. Chateaubriand, who referred to the Middle Ages as "les seuls temps poétiques de notre histoire" (*Le génie du christianisme*, quoted in Dakyns, 11).

36. Cerquiglini (*Éloge*, 82) sees as characteristic of Gaston's editorial bias a "peur du vide" which led him to posit a seamless continuity of intervening linguistic stages. I would suggest a more paradoxical foundation for academic philology: the need to establish lacunae in order to have something to fill.

37. In his article "842" (above, n. 8).

38. In his 1869 lecture, Gaston details the Germanic contribution to Gallo-Roman culture, which it conquered and with which it ultimately fused. One important element of its contribution was "l'orgueil et l'enthousiasme national" coupled with "une poésie riche et puissante, qui devait, en se transformant, féconder l'esprit des nations auxquelles ils s'unirent" (*Poésie*, 70).

39. Bernard Cerquiglini (*Éloge*) and Hans Aarsleff ("Scholarship and Ideology: Joseph Bédier's Critique of Romantic Medievalism," in Jerome J. McGann, ed., *Historical Studies and Literary Criticism* [Madison: University of Wisconsin Press, 1985], 93–113) both stress the reconciliation between Romantic idealism and scientific positivism in Paris's work. While it is true that Gaston Paris attempted to coalesce the two discourses, most successfully perhaps in his work on textual criticism, what I am suggesting is a radical

division between the two, most visible on the level of scholarly affinities. On this point, see also Bédier, *Légendes épiques*.

40. Paris felt obliged to insinuate the interrelated ideas of science and progress even where they did not arise in his texts. In translating a pair of lines from one of Chrétien's lyrics ("Nuls, s'il n'est cortois et sages, / Ne puet riens d'amors aprendre"), Paris provides the following translation for the second line: "On ne peut faire aucun progrès dans la science de l'amour" (1883: 522).

41. In a review of Pio Rajna's book *Le origini dell'epopea francese,* which argued for the exclusively Germanic origins of the chansons de geste (Gaston Paris, in *Romania* 13 [1884]: 598–627), and which Bédier considered an important turning point in his teacher's thoughts on the epic, Paris's approval of a point of view that he admits being essentially his own ("Si M. Rajna n'avait pas écrit son livre, j'en aurais probablement écrit un sur le même sujet" (601)) is tempered by an insistence upon the essentially French amalgam that resembles none of its ancestors: "Notre épopée est allemande d'origine, elle est latine de langue; mais . . . elle est profondément, intimement française" (627).

42. Bloch, "842," 11–12.

43. We note an early (1870) contrast Gaston Paris makes between the "voix mâle et héroïque" of the *Roland* and the "voix moqueuse et légère," which he considers all too typical of the French national character (*Poésie,* 118).

44. Insofar as Paris's scheme rationalizes the pursuit of love, thus resolving any potential conflict between the two faculties, it is not insignificant that his account of Chrétien's romance (summarized at length in Paris, 1883: 464–82) suppresses the episode that itself emblematizes that conflict: the struggle between Love and Reason immediately preceding Lancelot's mounting of the cart. Paris quotes the passage in the original (466), but skips the lines corresponding to Mario Roques's edition (*Les romans de Chrétien de Troyes, III: Le Chevalier de la Charrette* [Paris: Champion, 1981; 1958], 365–74), and thereby writes Chrétien's Reason (clearly incompatible with Love) out of the romance.

45. E. Jane Burns and Roberta L. Krueger, "Courtly Ideology and Woman's Place in Medieval French Literature," special issue of *Romance Notes* 25, no. 3 (1985); Toril Moi, "Desire in Language: Andreas Capellanus and the Controversy of Courtly Love," in *Medieval Literature: Criticism, Ideology, and History,* ed. David Aers (Brighton: Manchester University Press, 1986), 11–33.

46. Hélène Cixous, "Sorties," in Hélène Cixous and Catherine Clément, *La jeune née* (Paris: UGE (10/18), 1975).

47. The curious character of Galehaut in the prose *Lancelot*, friend and erotic mediator, is here noteworthy. Christiane Marchello-Nizia, "Amour courtois, société masculine et figures du pouvoir," *Annales ESC* 36 (1981): 969–82, reveals Galehaut to be a central participant in the homosocial triangulation of desire recounted in the prose *Lancelot* by virtue of his amibiguous friendship with Lancelot. He is also one of the major elements used by Gaston Paris in order to demonstrate the prose work's derivative status. The effacement of a character revealing the true nature of triangulated courtly desire would, it seems, be necessary for the articulation of it as an idealizing passion.

48. Cf. Alice Jardine and Paul Smith, eds., *Men in Feminism* (New York and London: Methuen, 1987).

EIGHT

Feminism and the Discipline of Old French Studies: *Une Bele Disjointure*

E. Jane Burns, Sarah Kay, Roberta L. Krueger,
and Helen Solterer

> In raising the question of the gender of the producers of knowledge,
> women's studies always involves a radical questioning of the
> conditions of the production and dissemination of knowledge, of the
> constitution of the disciplines, of the hierarchical ordering of the
> faculties within the institution.
> —Naomi Schor, "This Essentialism Which Is Not One"

FEMINIST CRITICISM as it is practiced in our current moment
entails more than the empirical study of "women" or even of *woman.*
It involves calling into question one's own critical practice, one's
sexual and gender identity, one's relationship to authority and to
mastery, as we shall discuss in the last section of this essay. Feminist
studies entail, today as much as ever, taking the risk of bringing
together both the personal and the professional.

For the medievalist, this involves a radical critical investigation of
both the object of study in the past and of the critic's textual and
professional enterprise. The gesture is a vertiginous one: the feminist
writes from a destabilized position in the present to confront a *different* form of instability and *mouvance* in the past. Not wanting to lose
sight of the women whose bodies, experiences, and actions were the
sites of a historical difference, yet wary of essentializing that experi-

225

ence, the feminist medievalist does not abandon history but problematizes it, as she does her own moment in the present.

This collaborative study was prompted by an invitation from the editors to one of us to contribute a piece on feminism and medieval literature to a volume that would fill the need for a "sustained external history of the various disciplines of medieval studies." It evolved into a project by four of us corresponding between the United States and Europe on questions raised by the intersection of feminism and Old French studies. In so responding to the project of this volume, we have confronted several paradoxes and problems whose contours have shaped our enterprise. The first is the paradox of collaborative writing, a process where personal voices overlap and sometimes conflict to form a collective statement. The four sections that follow reflect individual differences in specialization, background, academic culture, and generation, but they also reflect the communal nature of our task.[1] We have written this essay together and in different voices.

The second problem we encountered was in responding to a call for an "external" history of feminism and medieval studies. The fields of women's studies and of feminist criticism have evolved in such a variety of directions, and with such amplitude, that it would be impossible to offer a full account of them. Suffice it to say that there is not one feminist "theory," but a plurality of feminist theories, wherein the politics of subject and gender identity, race, class, sexuality, and the body are hotly contested.[2] Perhaps more important, our position as critics who are engaged in an ongoing dialogue between feminism and medieval studies has made it difficult for us to perceive their history from outside the field. No history can ever be "external" in the sense of being "objective," and we are wary of the seemingly disengaged stance that a synthetic "survey" of the field of medieval women's studies could imply. Nor do we wish to reify the boundaries of an interrogatory, interdisciplinary discipline. Rather than attempt a definitive "external history," we offer a provisional and engaged account of recent queries and of our ongoing investigation.

Finally, in writing this chapter we have confronted the contradictions of our own position as feminist medievalist scholars.[3] The medieval feminist critic finds herself in a position like that of the feminist reader described by Diana Fuss who reads from a multiplicity of unstable subject-positions.[4] We encounter not only the shifting positions of our contemporary subjectivities, but also the elusiveness of textuality and identity in the past. When we turn to feminist criticism, we find intense disagreement over the notion of female difference and the category of "woman."[5] When we investigate the medieval text, we find not the stable presence of fixed documents but a textual tradition characterized by variants and *mouvance*.[6] The search for "medieval women" turns out to be a tricky enterprise, plagued by the perils of essentializing "woman" and of idealizing our foremothers as powerful or of portraying them as victims.[7] We also face resistance within the institution of medieval studies, as traditionally constituted, where any avowedly contemporary theoretical or political position embraced by the critic is frequently rejected as "anachronistic."[8] From this last perspective, the feminist medievalist is something of an oxymoron, a scholar at odds with her discipline.

Viewed from the more open perspective of interdisciplinary women's studies, the feminist medievalist moves continually *between* instabilities in the past and present, working against traditional categories of knowledge even as she employs her disciplinary training.[9] Ideally, the enterprise involves a creative questioning of the ways in which gender structures not only medieval thought in the past but also the discipline of medieval studies in the present. As feminist medievalists, we begin by acknowledging the divided nature of our critical identities and our conflicted, yet willingly embraced relationships to critical enterprises such as the one taken up by this volume.

The issue of feminism and Old French studies has shaped itself in our discussions as questions rather than answers, and it is around those questions that we have chosen to construct our collaborative work. We begin by attempting to situate medieval women's studies in the current critical moment, showing how the history of women in Old French studies is a history of presence through absence, of standing between different literary modes and categories of academic discourse. Emphasizing the ambiguous position of the feminist medievalist, this section will raise the question, "What is the place of women in the discipline of Old French studies?"

Then, taking epic and lyric texts as examples, the next two sections will reconceptualize the problem of woman as a sign and as a textual voice within the chanson de geste and the chanson de femme. They will emphasize how traditional genre studies have either marginalized women's concerns, as in the epic, or misapprehended the textual feminine, as in the lyric. Stressing the complex interrelation between feminine representation and female identity, these sections will ask in a variety of ways, "where is the female subject in Old French studies?"

Finally, returning to a self-critical mode, we shall reflect on what is at stake in the mastery of medieval studies for the female critic and will raise the inevitable question of how essays like this one can avoid imposing authority even as they engage in scholarly debate.

WOMEN AND THE DISCIPLINE OF OLD FRENCH STUDIES

In choosing not to privilege the "objective history" of feminism and medieval studies, we by no means imply that women have no history in the discipline. Women have a history first of all as scholars who have made substantial contributions to the field from the beginning of the century. Not surprisingly, even before women's studies militated for researching women's history and literary roles, many early works on Old French literature were devoted to women's issues. Such studies fueled a dialogue about authors like Christine de Pisan, and provided precious documentation about women in literary history.[10]

More recently female scholars in the United States, Britain, and France whose work has been influential in their respective fields have served as important professional examples to younger scholars. While many of these women may not tag their critical approach as feminist (though some indeed do), they have extended to the upcoming generation an intellectual generosity as impressive as their scholarship, sharing linguistic skills, erudition, and tactical support.

It would be dangerous, however, to paint too rosy a picture of a "female medievalist network" and its status within medieval studies, for indeed each of us has a more or less extensive anecdotal history of isolation, marginalization, or trivialization of our concerns, and in extreme cases, even harassment within the academy.[11] The editorial boards of the major medieval journals in France, Britain, and the United States are still predominantly in male hands.[12] Although these journals now publish an increasing number of studies by and about women, their philological and historical bias often precludes theoretical feminist approaches.[13]

Journals most receptive to publishing medieval feminist research over the last ten years have remained, generally, outside the medieval pale.[14] Interestingly, American university presses, realizing the audience that exists for feminist scholarship in all fields of the humanities and social sciences, have been quicker than specialized journals to

promote the work of feminist medievalists.[15] Some of the most exciting recent work has emerged at conferences and in special sessions
devoted to the topic of women in the Middle Ages.[16] An informal
newsletter exchanged among medieval colleagues to share feminist
research interests has an extensive membership of women and men
who debate gender issues.[17]

As more female medievalists are hired, promoted, and tenured,
and as they assume increased responsibility for personnel and curricu-
lar policy, as well as for publishing, feminists will be challenged to
maintain the edge of marginality and nonauthoritarianism that has
sparked feminist research from the beginning. There is also the danger
that a field defined primarily by white, middle-class academic women
to reflect their interest will overlook the differences between women,
and neglect the issues of race and class (more on this later).[18] Medieval
feminism is not immune to the elitism of medieval studies. As this
thumbnail sketch suggests, the history of women in medieval studies
cannot be divorced from the problems of feminist identity, which are
the chief concerns of this chapter.

Women also have a history in medievalism in the sense that the
"woman question" has been at the center of the debate about courtly
literature and misogyny ever since Gaston Paris first defined the
notion of *amour courtois* in 1883. Reading courtly narrative as a
refined idealization of the lady, he saw her empowered with a moral
and sexual superiority over the knight.[19] Paris's notion of female
empowerment through love represents a late-nineteenth-century ideal
of femininity rather than the historical reality of women in either the
twelfth or the nineteenth century. In both periods, an ideal of female
superiority obscures a profound cultural controversy about woman's
social place. For example, Paris's formulations offer striking parallels
with Freud's fears about the decline of the feminine ideal in the wake
of social legislation for women, reservations expressed in the same
year (1883) in a letter to his fiancée, Martha Bernays. As Sarah
Kofman has shown, Freud accepts reform as inevitable, yet wants to
maintain, as she translates, "la chose la plus délicieuse que le monde
ait à nous offrir, notre idéal de la féminité."[20] Freud's justification for
the legal status quo for women reads like a portrait of the courtly
couple as envisaged by Paris: "Bien qu'elle ne puisse voter et n'ait pas
de capacité juridique, toute jeune fille dont un homme baise la main et
pour l'amour de qui il est prêt à tous les risques, aurait pu lui en
remontrer" (268). If "courtly love" as a concept was invented in the

late nineteenth century, it was, at least in part, because the notion of a disenfranchised woman empowered by male mystification corresponded so well to the desires of modern men.

This is not to say that women were not an important concern of early scholarship in romance, epic, lyric, and didactic literature, for they often were.[21] But studies in the first half of this century rarely criticized the courtly ideal as it applied to women by revealing the strategies of containment that were at play.[22] The unquestioned acceptance of a late-nineteenth-century masculine definition of "feminine nature" in scholarship by both men and women has been, until very recently, a powerful impediment to the understanding of the historical role of women in the Middle Ages.

With the advent of women's studies in the 1970s, there has been a gradual but significant reconceptualization of the "woman question." Beginning with the ideas that textual inscription in the Middle Ages have more to do with the masculine consciousness that produced them than with the female reality they purport to describe, scholars began to read "woman" in the text as a textual sign rather than a historical entity.[23] Consequently, there developed a marked, if largely unarticulated, division about what the relation of woman as sign might be to the "real" women who would have read, commissioned, and in some cases written those texts. Some scholars persisted in reading women's roles or feminine voices as reflections, however refracted or attenuated, of historical reality.[24] With the appearance of historical studies about women of different periods, classes, and geographic regions, however, our sense of *who* "medieval women" were has become infinitely more complex and nuanced.[25]

At the other extreme from historical work are studies of Lacanian or poststructuralist bent which would read the "textual feminine" as a space within language unrelated to the biological sex of the author.[26] Those adopting a more avowedly feminist methodology struggle to reconcile the constructed nature of gender identities in texts with the material realities of female experience, as evidenced by the female body[27] or the historical female audience.[28] Tracking a course between, on the one side, naive historicism and essentialism that would reify either "women" or "woman" and, on the other, a masculine psychocriticism that erases historical women from the picture altogether, these scholars pursue the elusive question of the female subject, to which we shall return below. For feminists, the "woman question" has become a crisis of identities in which both critic and text are implicated.

Finally, women have played a role in medieval literary history as authors whose contributions to canonical and noncanonical genres have at last been given their due, in some cases after centuries of benign or disdainful neglect. Editions, critical monographs, and anthologies of women writers continue to emerge.[29] Recent interest in Marie de France or the *trobairitz* rivals that of Chrétien de Troyes for the twelfth century;[30] Christine de Pisan has achieved a stature as poet moralist that far exceeds that of her male contemporaries.[31] But no less the object of scrutiny are noncanonical writers such as mystics and letter writers, and the more elusive voices of other "women's poems," which we will examine in a moment.[32] At the current stage of feminist investigation, however, the "recanonization" of women writers who have suffered neglect is not, in itself, enough. With each woman writer who is resurrected as an *object* of study, female subjectivity, femininity, and the subject's relationship to history and class must be problematized.[33]

As the once marginalized question of "la femme médiévale" becomes a surprisingly fashionable topic, feminist academics who once fought to gain acceptance for their approach in a more hostile climate, and for whom women's studies is a vocation reflecting personal and political struggle, find themselves in the company of male scholars who eagerly pursue what is for them a "new" subject, often without the self-questioning and sense of struggle that accompanies feminist research. There is inevitable tension over the question of men's place in the feminist arena, arising in part from the suspicion that male scholarship on the "woman question," despite its interest or validity, might represent male academic appropriation in another guise.[34] The act of reading for the textual feminine, for example, can be taken up more readily and less problematically by male critics who do not experience the world through a female body. The question that emerges from such a conflict is not whether men can or should study women in the Middle Ages—surely no one would lament valid contributions to a field so long overlooked—but "what constitutes feminist research?"

Up until now, the study of women in the Middle Ages has borrowed much from feminist theory but given little of *theoretical* novelty in return. What medievalists can contribute to feminist studies is perhaps not a theory but a *practice:* a historical and material feminism grounded in the differences of the past as well as the uncertainties of the present. Let us offer by way of example two strategies, among many possible ones, of reading "for the feminine" in Old French literature. We have chosen the highly male-centered chanson de geste and the reputedly female-centered chanson de femme as two potentially fruitful arenas for investigating the problems of representation and interpretation that confront the medieval feminist *lectrice.*[35] Both readings address, if in very different ways, the issue of female subjectivity in its broadest sense, asking how the female subject has been constructed both by the texts that medievalists read and the politics of the profession. How, historically, have female critics, whether feminist or not, tended to read epic narrative differently from their male counterparts, thereby creating a kind of subculture of epic studies, a discipline within the officially recognized "discipline?" For the Old French chanson de femme we ask where one can reasonably locate the thirteenth-century woman—whether historical or literary—in songs traditionally attributed to female singers/composers.

NOT MUCH OF A SUBJECT: WOMEN IN THE CHANSON DE GESTE

Car au bien et au mal doit on son pere amer
          —*Les Quatre Fils Aymon,* ed. F. Castets, v. 3540

Entendez que le moi idéal lui-même n'est pas exempt d'ambivalence, mais que celle-ci doit viser à "reproduire et conserver le caractère du père"; elle lui aurait d'ailleurs emprunté sa "force."

    Voila encore des modalités d'élaboration du surmoi peu adéquates à la formation de la "féminité."
          —Luce Irigaray, *Spéculum de l'autre femme*

Chansons de geste often tell of the success and longevity of fathers, and the suffering and sacrifices of sons; perhaps that is why they enjoyed the highest prestige among the founding fathers of medieval studies, who all contributed substantial volumes elucidating the origins, and thereby (in their terms) the significance, of these powerful and violent poems.[36] Today chanson de geste studies remain a largely male preserve. It is very striking to what extent many *Roland* specialists in particular identify with the figures in the texts they study.[37] A position of implicit *parti pris* in favor of epic values is perceptible even in the most sophisticated writing on the *Roland* by male critics.[38] When they write about society, these men mean Frankish, aristocratic, male society. A recent book on the William cycle treats women characters quite separately from the depiction of "society," under the heading of "romance influence."[39] With certain notable exceptions,[40] the ideas of "history," "ideology," and "representation" are generally unsophisticated in epic scholarship. The question of origins may have dropped from the agenda, but the sense of a transparent relation between textual representation and historical "original" is often perceptible. To this extent, epic studies, though less authoritative than in the days of the founding fathers, are still patriarchal in their inspiration.

Nevertheless, the contribution of women scholars has been distinguished. It is significant that women have often chosen to devote themselves not to the *Roland*, where masculine ideology tends to predominate, but to the texts where it is more obviously in trouble, notably the epics of revolt. Rita Lejeune has studied the legends of Ogier the Dane; Mary Hackett devoted her life to *Girart de Roussillon*, which also forms the object of the longest and best essay in Micheline de Combarieu's *thèse d'état;* Jessie Crosland translated the first part of *Raoul de Cambrai*, and Pauline Matarasso wrote a book about it; scholarship on the Loheren cycle is dominated by women, both as editors and critics.[41]

These women might not all call themselves feminists, yet their work has kept alive alternatives to a univocal heroic ideal, and has drawn critical attention to the violence and disruptiveness of these poems. In the introduction to her translation of *Raoul*, for example, Jessie Crosland comments on the "gentler character" of Bernier and the "ideal of restraint" with which, through him, the poet counters the "brutality and lawlessness of the times" (viii–ix). In *The Old French Epic*,[42] Crosland links Bernier's greater reasonableness with his outrage at the death of his mother, Marsent, and his defense of her against Raoul's vilification (119). Such outrage at the treatment of women characters expressed by epic "heroes" can provide women readers with a useful point of leverage against the purported univocality of epic representation.

Marsent is a case in point. The text is explicit about her subjection, as a woman, to the degradation of powerful men:

> "Sire R[aous], a celer nel vos qier,
> ma mere fu fille a un chevalier—
> toute Baviere avoit a justicier.
> Preé[e] en fu par son grant destorbier;
> en cele terre ot un noble guerier,
> qi l'espousa a honor de mostier.
> Devant le roi qi France a a baillier
> ocist deus princes a l'espee d'acier:

grant fu la guere, si ne pot apaissier.
En Espolice s'en ala a Gaifier,
vit le preudoume, cel retint volentier;
en ceste terre ne vost puis repair[i]e[r],
toi ne autrui ne daigna ainc proier.
LXXXII
"Dont fu ma mere soufraitouse d'amis.
Il n'ot si bele en quarante païs—
Y[bers] mes peres qi molt par est gentix
la prist par force, si con je ai apris;
n'en fist pas noces, itant vos en devis.
LXXXIII
"Sire R[aous]," l'enfes B[erniers] dist,
"Y[bers] mes peres par sa force la prist
Je ne dis pas qe noces en feïst.
Par sa richese dedens son lit la mist,
toz ses talans et ces voloirs en fist—
et qant il vost autre feme reprist.
Doner li vost Joifroi, mais ne li sist;
nonne devint, le millor en eslist.
LXXXIV
"Sir R[aous], a tort faites et pechié.
Ma mere as arce dont j'a[i] le quer irié—
Dex me laist vivre tant q'en soie vengiés!"

["My lord Raoul, these are the facts; my mother was the daughter of a knight who ruled the whole of Bavaria, [but] she was snatched away from there, to her own lasting harm. There was a well-born knight in the region who married her with full religious honours. In the presence of the king of France he killed two princes with his steel sword: terrible warfare resulted which could not be stilled. He went off to Gaifier in Spoleto who recognized him as a valiant man and was glad to retain him; after that, he had no desire to come back to our country, he never condescended to beg favors of you or anyone.

"Thereafter my mother was friendless. She was the loveliest woman for forty countries—Ybert my father, who is a man of position, took her by force, so I learned; he didn't marry her, this much I grant you.

"My lord Raoul," said young Bernier, "My father Ybert took her forcibly—I cannot say that he married her. Because of his powerful

position he got her into his bed and did all he wanted with her—
then, when he chose, he took another wife. He wanted to make
Geoffrey her husband, but that didn't suit her; she chose the better
part and became a nun.

"My lord Raoul, what you are doing is wrong and sinful. You have
burned my mother, at which my heart is sore—may God let me live
long enough to get my revenge!"][43]

Pauline Matarasso's views on women characters do not always coincide with modern feminist thought, as when she remarks that Aalais,
Raoul's mother, "est féminine encore par son manque de logique.
Chez elle la logique est subordonnée aux sentiments" (235). Yet she
responds at some length to the character of Marsent, commenting in
terms similar to Crosland's on the narrative alignment of Marsent and
Bernier (238–39). For both Crosland and Matarasso, the dominant
values of aggression and acquisitiveness to which the text, despite the
ambiguity attaching to Raoul's behavior, at least partially subscribes,[44]
are undermined by a counterforce of restraint and gentleness displayed by Marsent and the son who defends her.

These women scholars are the mothers of more recent feminist
work on the chanson de geste, although the scope of such work is
limited by the prevailing tendencies of the discipline over the last
decades. These have tended to fall into three main areas, of which the
first two offer at best an unpropitious environment to feminist inquiry.
Manuscript transmission and textual criticism is a domain largely
ruled by "facts" that have little bearing on gender. A second area,
interest in which was fueled by Rychner's epoch-making monograph,[45] is comprised of studies analyzing the formal properties of epic
literature, in particular its adaptation to oral performance and recom-
position. This field too has a strong commitment to the factual, often
equated with the computable. Emphasis on the formula as the basic
unit of epic composition has distracted attention from other features
of rhetoric and has generally discouraged close reading, always such a
powerful tool of feminist criticism.[46] A third group of critics has read
the chansons de geste as fictional or historical representations. This
third field is most amenable to feminist studies, as witness, for example, the pioneering monograph of Ellen Woods on *Aye d'Avignon*.[47]

In a striking revision of Crosland and Matarasso, Patricia Stäblein
sees the plot of *Raoul* as caught between two "behavioral/emotional
complexes: (1) violence and anger are consistently associated with

high energy activity, maleness, and violation of cultural rules . . . and are consistently opposed to (2) peace and love, linked in their turn with the acknowledgement of cultural rules, with passivity, and femaleness. . . . Women can and do act in the behavioral mode associated with maleness . . . but this occasional crossing over serves only to underline the division in the cultural system.[48] Her article goes on to chart the structure of the entire epic in terms of this opposition. Stäblein's formulation is more "feminist" than that of her predecessors, in that it explicitly genders the ideological tension exhibited by the poem, while simultaneously releasing gender from the anatomical sex of the characters.

It is possible to expand on Stäblein's analysis of dual narrativity in *Raoul* by seeing the text as a meeting place of many competing stories.[49] When a character (such as Marsent) is killed, she is eliminated from the story but not from the text because the shock of the violence done to her is remembered by other characters, or by the narrator/audience. Outrages committed are stored up as a source of potential narrative renewal. Because there is so much violence, and so many outrages, this store of latent counternarratives is enormously rich. The most obvious examples are provided by Raoul himself. The energy with which he abuses, injures, and slaughters creates a shadow world of potential textual material. His insults to his mother and Marsent, and his burning of the latter, exhibit a violent repression; and that which is repressed returns in a variety of forms. Alais's curse contributes to Raoul's death; the burning of Marsent leads to Bernier's reiterated calls for revenge, and eventual achievement of it; and Beatrice, Raoul's cousin whom Bernier marries, succeeds in evading successive attempts by men to coerce and oppress her, thus retrospectively vindicating her female predecessors whose attempts at self-determination exposed them to men's aggression.

Reading the chansons de geste as containing latent narratives that conduce to the undermining of a univocal, masculine ideology involves most obviously the third of the three areas of epic studies detailed above: that concerned with historical or fictional representation. But textual criticism and formal organization also have a part to play in this approach. In *Raoul de Cambrai*, the practice of self-commentary and self-ironization to which counternarrativity gives rise is inextricably bound up with the practice of continuation. This is particularly evident in the theme of the two companions: Raoul and Bernier are more strongly differentiated from each other as the poem progresses through its successive continuations, Bernier being used in part as a site from which to criticize Raoul, and the delimitation of these continuations involves painstaking recourse to textual analysis.

A fine example of this kind of work is provided by the late Alison Goddard Elliott's study of *Girart de Vienne*[50]—itself an epic which, although carefully maintaining a foot in each of the three *gestes* that it is famous for delineating, devotes much of its plot to the revolt of the eponymous hero against his sovereign (as in the cognate *Girart de Roussillon*). Her article, drawing on a computerized concordance, analyzes the formulae and lexicon of the three parts that can be discerned in it and that apparently result from the addition, by Bertrand de Bar-sur-Aube, of an introductory (Part I) and a concluding section (Part III) to an older narrative (Part II), which he also to some extent reworked. Noting the greater frequency of formulae about concealment in I than in II, Goddard demonstrates that "Part I is a narrative of subterfuge and symbolic actions," whereas "Part II depicts the world of action in which physical prowess and valor are effective and respected. Values are black and white" (154–155). The third and concluding part, like Part I ascribed to Bertrand, is "closer to the ethos of I" and closes with the foreboding that "in the end, treachery and deceit will triumph" (155–156). The "monologism" associated with epic writing from the time the word was coined emerges from this study as characterizing the older part of the work alone; the late-twelfth-century continuations at either side of it are marked by the duality to which deceit gives rise. The martial is subordinated to the verbal, and a tissue of language replaces direct action. Whereas Aude, the chief feminine protagonist of Part II, is able to act alongside Roland, Charlemagne's queen, instigator of much of the plot of Part I, behaves as though deeds had no reality until clothed in language and assumes the primacy of calculation and deception (155).

Women characters in the later epic, such as Bertrand de Bar-sur-Aube's continuations, or *Raoul de Cambrai*, tend, therefore, to be a source of narrative plurality for one of two reasons. Either they instigate deception, or more commonly they found a critique of violence and abuse through their role as victims. They may therefore be seen as analogous to authors in their ability to devise stratagems, and as analogous to readers in their capacity to be exposed to, and eventually criticize, the narrative.[51] Either way they rarely enjoy narrative dominance for long. Women's marginality to the masculine world of the chanson de geste means that they are not fully empowered as subjects. What of the status, by comparison, of the women's voices that hold sway in the chanson de femme?

SUBJECT TO DEBATE: WOMEN'S VOICES IN THE CHANSON DE FEMME

Dex, tant est douz li nons d'amors:
[ja n'en cuidai sentir dolors].

A ces paroles et a ceste raison,
li siens amis entra en la maison.
Cele lo vit, si bassa lo menton:
Ne pot parler, ne li dist o ne non.

Dex, tant est douz li nons d'amors
[ja n'en cuidai sentir dolors].
                —Bele Yolanz en ses chambres seoit, vv. 11–18

[God, how sweet the name of love is. / [I never thought I would feel pain from it].

With these words and this thought (When these words were uttered and this thought formulated), / her lover entered the room. She saw him and kissed his chin. / Unable to speak, she did not say yes or no to him:

God, how sweet the name of love is; / [I never thought I would feel pain from it].[52]

This stanza and the refrain appearing on either side of it form part of what has traditionally been called "woman's song"[53] in Old French lyric. Taken from the *chanson de toile* "Bele Yolanz en ses chambres seoit," this excerpt falls into the wide-ranging category of chanson de femme that comprises, in Pierre Bec's definition, anonymous songs ranging from the lament for a lost lover in the *chanson d'ami*, the complaint against an unjust husband in the *chanson de malmariée*, the denunciation of a dawning day that separates adulterous lovers in the *aube*, and the tale of a longed-for lover in the *chanson de toile*. Bec draws together this vast corpus of varied poetic genres under the sign of "woman's song" because each contains "un monologue lyrique, à connotation douloureuse, placé dans la bouche d'une femme." The unique defining feature of these women's songs in Bec's schema is that they are spoken by women, not men, in contradistinction to the standard *canso* of the Occitanian troubadour or *grand chant courtois* of the Northern French *trouvère* which rarely admit women as the "centre subjectif de la pièce chantée"

But in what sense can female characters be considered speaking subjects in the chanson de femme or any other Old French literary work? To what extent does the heroine of "Belle Yolanz" speak in the excerpt quoted above? If the poem's opening stanza attributes the refrain unequivocally to its heroine, stating that "she sang this song: 'God, how sweet the name of love is; I never thought I would feel pain from it,'"[54] stanza two problematizes such a clear-cut attribution by inserting the narrator's descriptive commentary within the woman's supposed speech:

> Bels douz amis, or vos voil envoier
> une robe par mout grant amistie.
> Por Diu vos [pri], de moi aiez pitie.
> Non pot ester, a la terre s'assiet.
>
> Dex, tant est douz li nons d'amors:
> [ja n'en cuidai sentir dolors]. (vv. 7–12)

[Sweet love, I want to send you / a cloak as a token of my love. / I pray God you will take pity on me. / Unable to stand, she sits down.]

When Bele Yolanz's words are interrupted by the narrator's description of her physical condition ("Non pot ester, a la terre assiet"), the refrain that follows hovers uncertainly between two speakers; does it issue from the mouth of the heroine or from that of the poem's narrator?[55] The highly equivocal "A ces paroles et a ceste raison" of the third stanza (quoted above) suggests alternately that this same refrain may have been uttered by the newly arrived lover. Certainly someone other than the heroine is responsible for articulating the purportedly feminine words at the end of stanza three where Bele Yolanz is said to be mute and incapable of speech: "ne li dist o ne non, ne pot parler."[56]

These lyric moments, among many others in the *chanson de toile,* remind us that the dolorous voices sounded in medieval "woman's song," though emitted from the "mouths of women" as Bec describes them, issue from the rhetorical bodies of fictive protagonists situated at a far remove from the mouths of real historical women. If the women's voices we hear in the chanson de femme have been *placed* in female mouths, as Bec assents obliquely, they have been placed there by someone else. By a male author who has constructed and created female voices as products of his own literary imagination?[57] In which case these women's songs would really be men's songs in disguise. Are they then examples of men singing in drag? Of men speaking for women, that is to say, "in their place," literally displacing women from the stage of creative inspiration and literary production?[58] Or are we to assume, conversely, that these diverse women's songs have been gathered together by a manuscript compiler who has taken them from another source, perhaps from the dictated accounts of oral performance, once intoned by living women and reshaped by years of manuscript copying until they became contextualized within a literary narrator's voice? In both scenarios the status granted to the female speaking subject—whether as a mask for a male poetic voice or as real women whose voices have been appropriated into a written tradition—is more problematic than the notion of "women's song" would suggest. Rather than operating unproblematically as speaking subjects, the women's voices in the chanson de femme remain clearly *subject to* different forms of male subjective hegemony. But does this mean we should abandon the search for a female speaking subject in Old French lyric? Are there other ways of reading that could better address the paradox of the constructed female subject in the chanson de femme?

Feminist criticism of the past decade has shown us how complex the question of female subjectivity can be; how we must struggle to make distinctions between female authorship and the voices of female protagonists; how female agency in speech does not exist unproblematically for either real women or fictive constructions of them; and how individualized expression is a cultural construction conditioned by factors of class, family, patriarchy, and language as well as gender. The ground-breaking dialogue launched by Nancy Miller and Peggy Kamuf over "who is speaking" in literary texts written by female authors has played itself out over nearly a decade with no clear resolution.[59] The original debate, structured around the proper place of feminist critical practice in the university, found Miller committed to rectifying women's exclusion from the literary canon by insisting on the importance of female authorship, while Kamuf warned against the epistemological dangers of recentering feminist inquiry within a patriarchal, humanist tradition that privileges authorship.[60] The pitfall to be carefully negotiated by practitioners of the first approach is that of a possible "essentialism": the tendency to suggest, however indirectly, that women might speak naturally, biologically as women, and the corollary belief that an unbroken continuity exists between the lives of real, historical women and the depiction of them in literary texts.[61]

The danger facing those who want feminist criticism to address all literary productions that put the "feminine" into play without regard for the biological sex of the author is the risk of effacing the historical woman and issues of gender altogether. Calling into question the very identity of the speaking subject, or displacing it onto an intersubjective dialogue as in Lacanian criticism, can lead, in the worst case scenario, to obscuring the *sexual* identity of that speaking subject as well. This is but one example of the process Alice Jardine has termed gynesis, a kind of reading that puts woman into discourse while reducing her to a sign for something else.[62]

How, then, can we acknowledge a specifically female contribution to literary creation without essentializing historical women into the mythic category of woman? And how, on the other hand, can we locate woman in the literary text while remaining sensitive to the subtleties of the poststructuralist critique of subjectivity?[63] Or in Nancy Miller's more recent formulation, how can we get beyond the original terms of the debate that pit empiricism against theory, authorial identity against indifference to gender?[64]

Old French studies have not made this crucial leap beyond the binary impasse. Whereas Pierre Bec, following Alfred Jeanroy and Gaston Paris before him, pursues an essentialist search for a concerted *lyrisme feminin,* a truly autonomous poetic register that presumes the originary presence of historical women composer/singers,[65] Michel Zink's work on the *chanson de toile* provides a striking example of Jardine's gynesis. Arguing against the representational fallacy that has led critics to claim that the *chanson de toile* evolved from women's work songs simply because they depict women singing and working,[66] Zink reads the *chanson de toile* as a rhetorical device used by the male poet to seduce a male reader: "les chansons de toile ont pu plaire aux uns par les artifices qui veulent cacher leur rugosité, aux autres par leur rugosité perçant sous les artifices, comme une très jeune fille séduit le collégien par l'habilité de son maquillage et l'homme mûr par sa gaucherie" (2). The poem, then, is a flirtatious young girl defined in relation to the male reader's desire and seducibility. As the femaleness of woman's song is displaced onto the function of the text, woman as a historical personage or inscribed voice disappears altogether.[67]

However different they may be in other respects, the readings of woman's song offered by Bec and Zink come together in the binarism that conditions the initial question each poses. In asking "who's speaking?" in woman's song they lead us inevitably to discover a feminine or a masculine poetics, establishing either how the woman's lyric voice is distinctly different from the well-established tradition of male poetic expression or how the apparently female voice speaking to us from these poems is actually male.

Taking our cue from the ambiguous voice of "Bele Yolanz," could we try instead to move beyond this kind of polarization and read the female subject as she exists in a partial and fragmentary way within the medieval textual tradition? This is indeed a most difficult and vexing task: to imagine a kind of female subjectivity that might exist outside the obvious binary opposition of masculine and feminine. Western culture and convention have trained us to think subjectivity within that binary opposition. From the Stoics to Descartes, the status of the speaking subject in western philosophical and literary discourse has been defined as *homo loquens,* he whose identity derives from his activity as a thinking speaker.[68] Woman in this scenario functions often as the object of the male speaker's discourse, the listener or receiver of his words, the object of the desire articulated in his speech. This objectified female other moves with great difficulty into the position of speaking subject traditionally reserved for the male, whether she is a real-live woman or fictional creation.[69]

Rereading the *chanson de toile* in light of feminist arguments about subjectivity suggests that the inscribed woman's voice typically found there exists in a complex relational dynamic to the voices of both the narrator and the male protagonists figured in the song. The ostensibly female voice of the refrain is a floating voice. Not always contextualized or directly attributed to a specific speaker, it can hover between various actors in the lyric scenario, passing from male to female with relative ease.[70] If at times the voice of the refrain in the "Bele Yolanz" reads as distinctly female because articulated unequivocally by a female protagonist, at others it seems dislocated by the narrator's descriptive voice. To speak of a woman's voice in this and other 'women's songs" is then to describe voices that occupy an unstable and shifting place, voices that defy absolute categorization as either masculine or feminine.

By thinking in terms of this *mouvance* of gender identity—something akin to the well-known *mouvance* of the manuscript tradition that structures medieval literary production[71]—we might begin to shift the emphasis in our approach from "who is speaking?" in Old French literature to a more complex and intriguing question: "How do women speak from the pages of Old French literary works?" In what varied, muted, and partial ways do their voices enter into the relational dynamic that structures subjectivity in medieval literary texts? We might ask who can occupy the different subject positions, under what circumstances and to what effect? Or consider how the female voices inscribed in the written text change in relation to different reader/performers (male and female). In these ways we could begin to conceive of "voice" neither as an embodied essence that communicates the personalized and individual identity of a historical female nor as the depersonalized voice of literature or poetic craft. Why not look instead for a range of voices emerging from fictive female bodies in varying degrees and different ways across literary genres? Remembering how Bele Yolanz can speak to us despite her ostensible silence, could we search out a female subjectivity that comes to us through a literary tradition that neither reifies nor ventriloquizes it? Old French chansons de femme provide an especially cogent reminder that if there can be no totalizing or coherent woman's voice in medieval French literature (or elsewhere), neither can the dominant male voice—whether of literature or culture—dominate totally or unproblematically.

It is at this point that our study of female subjectivity in Old French texts overlaps with our own subjectivity as speakers and writers in a patriarchal institution, specifically one that authorizes and delimits speaking and writing.[72] When the question of female subjectivity posed by traditional studies of the chanson de femme is reopened by feminist medievalists of the twentieth century, how does that investigation call into question the role, function, and status of our own voices in the academy in general and within the discipline of medieval studies in particular?

TOWARD A FEMINIST MASTERY: WHEN THE DISCIPLINE MEETS DIFFERENCE

The manner in which you have made me your "confrère" I value as much as the membership itself. Thank you very much. I only wish you might have as good reason to think well of your "Soeur Brun de la Montagne" as I am proud of my "confrèrie" I see I seem to have.

I am delighted to be able to teach you a French word, you may call me a *consoeur* or *confrère* even (but I think this last is ugly), I find these two names for the sistern of the old guild of Culveriniens et Arquebusiers de Gand—only I do not aspire to be military.

—Lucy Toulmin Smith to Paul Meyer, January 29, 1877;
February 12, 1877

For Lucy Toulmin Smith, a pioneer in medieval studies and one of the first women to collaborate with her male peers, the question of her own mastery was double-edged.[73] Considering herself on a par with Paul Meyer, a leading medievalist in late-nineteenth-century France, indeed naming herself his *confrère*, did not insure parity and mutual respect. Her claims to mastery bespeak a concern that Meyer did not necessarily view her expertise in the same manner. Even her delight in choosing the medieval title *consoeur* somehow betrays her query as to whether it would be reciprocated. In letters to the master himself, Toulmin Smith speculates circumspectly about her standing in the male bastion of academia.

Such musings give us a glimpse into the dynamic between male scholars and women entering the discipline in the "early days." It is a complex dynamic: whereas women were being trained and began pursuing research themselves, their skills did not qualify them for a commanding position. Mastery, as the measure of competence, did not automatically translate into mastery as a form of recognized authority.

For many of us today, this *double* aspect of mastery continues to mark our intellectual lives. Whereas the numbers of women medievalists have certainly diversified since Toulmin Smith's generation, the stature of the female master is still very much at issue. If we consider our formation, the habitual pattern of our public activities, all these experiences are influenced by the institution of mastery, itself of medieval origin.[74] We have been brought up to expect a connection between competence and authority. Yet as faculty, we find that with respect to women the academy does not always make the connection straightforwardly. As teachers as well, we engage with students whose expectations and responses are still affected by the cult of the master—long deemed incompatible with women. The authority that comes with masterful competence is rarely, for women, a given.

It is this discrepancy between the social and intellectual aspects of mastery that we want to consider here. How does mastery function as a set of social relations long inflected by gender? In our academic setting, we work with an ever-shifting body of knowledge, a *gnosos*, shared between two principal groups: those who relay it and those to whom it is imparted. This exchange depends as a rule upon a differential relation linking a higher expert group to a lower one of apprentices. Whether we situate this exchange in the classroom, or in the encounters between colleagues, the relation typically involves an imbalance. The mechanism of mastery operates so as to redress an epistemological imbalance, but in so doing it often creates and exacerbates a social one. The process of passing on even a protean body of knowledge can serve to establish a social hierarchy, one that elevates the master to a place of utter superiority, while it puts the other in an inferior, lesser position. By virtue of knowing more, the master has sovereignty; knowing less means occupying a lower station socially. "The *more* there is of mine, the *less* there is of yours," as two feminist critics put it.[75]

Although this model of relations endemic to mastery need not be enacted socially, the history of intellectual life in the West from the medieval founding of the university onwards, shows just how common a structure it had become. If we consider the etymology and normative definition of mastery, it becomes all the more apparent that this principle of unevenness is predicated upon gender difference. The usual dictionary entry reads: "Master," from medieval Latin *magister,* based on the root *magis*—meaning more. The official master at the thirteenth-century University of Paris, for instance, possessed a certain something that his underlings did not—something that he was licensed to pronounce.[76] The *magister* stands over the *discipulus,* who will follow and revere his superior knowledge through the joint practice of their teaching profession (*disciplina*).[77] Tracing further the etymology of "master," we find his intellectual edge reformulated in the following modern definition: a man having control or authority, a teacher, a specific title held by such a man. In other words, the issue of the master's extra erudition and preeminence is collapsed into one of gender.

Thus it proves very difficult to distinguish between the identity of authority, the teacherly role, and a masculine stance. The social conditioning implicit to mastery has evaluated women as insufficient, and thereby found her ineligible to graduate to the status of master herself. She thus appears forever needful of the additive of masterful knowledge, always in someone else's hands. In the words of a medievalist from an earlier generation: "how strongly I appreciate the studious young girl who has replaced the innocent young thing of yesteryear. Instead of living in the skirts of her mother, she shares the studious work of her brothers, far superior in industry and perseverance, no less so in intelligence and knowledge."[78] Gustave Cohen's praise, expressed in the ambiguous terms of a double negative (*nullement inférieure*), qualifies his women students' capacity to attain mastery. Yet even in a contemporary context, where women rank among the most original critics and pedagogues, the paradox of the female master remains. No matter how women's intellectual achievements are perceived, no matter what prominence they gain, they risk being trapped in a hierarchy that refuses them the most powerful role. Opening up the preserve of knowledge to women has not dismantled completely its restrictive social caste. The master/disciple relation does not easily admit otherness.[79] In the past, its relations bound the woman academic to the inferior role, ever dependent upon the *magis* of other authorities. Even more recently, "more" intellectually has not necessarily signified, for women, "more" in the realm of social interaction.

However forceful the more/less dynamic may appear, we do not mean to suggest that we are governed by it. Far from it. Rather it accentuates the *symbolic* configuration of mastery that may still impinge upon intellectual women and men, and shape their professional choices.[80] And it thus leads us to examine the functioning of mastery in our own circumstances. More important, it underscores the critical importance of envisaging another concept of mastery that is not defined by the imbalances typical of our institutions. The problem of intellectual *magis* for the feminist medievalist thus takes this form: what would an authoritative stance entail that would neither impose a *magis* upon others nor use it to blur the register of difference?

Traditionally our discipline has proceeded in a manner that does not distinguish rigorously enough between the authoritative and what verges on the authoritarian; between the intellectual who explores knowledge in a commanding and liberating way, and the one who uses it to control. The fine line separating the teacher/scholar whose power is enabling from the one who wields knowledge manipulatively needs to be plotted out again and again. Because, as Carolyn Heilbrun reminds us, "power is the ability to take one's place in whatever discourse is essential to action and the right to have one's part matter."[81] For the feminist medievalist, the terms of that ability are constantly to be negotiated if we are to answer fully the questions: how to reckon with the effects of mastery's symbolic structures, how to create a truly feminist mastery?

Two medieval texts will help us to clarify the double edge of mastery's symbolic structures. The first, suitably enough, represents these structures in terms of the exemplary master: the *Lai d'Aristote*.[82] Its incongruous title highlights the upending of the *doctor doctissimus* by the quintessential heroine of *lai,* a fantastical, foreign woman. The sage pedagogue Aristotle reprimands his student, the emperor Alexander, for abandoning his Latin books in favor of a woman. It is, of course, the woman who brings the master down in a version of the nature/culture confrontation. Luring him away from his studies, she seduces him and rides him back triumphantly before Alexander. The audience can laugh richly, not only at the successful ploy of the woman, but at the very expense of Aristotle. The master who does not abide by his own lessons is the butt of the most satisfying joke.

The *Lai* exposes playfully just how precarious the social structure of mastery really is; the philosopher who occupies so disdainfully the position of more is turned on his head, demoted to the base position his teaching reserves for women.[83] However persuasive Aristotelian learning may be, the edifice of its authority is shown here to be easily undermined. Even more shockingly, the woman is seen to rise to the top, astride the figurehead of mastery. A sheer reversal of terms results in a sort of female *magis,* which the heroine turns against the bamboozled master. Her *magis,* however, looks to be completely vacuous. The joke lies less in the fact that the woman might exercise the prerogative of mastery than in her preposterous overtaking of the master's place. What is most amusing in this scenario is the prospect that a woman pretends to position herself authoritatively.

Cast as a fabliau, this text transforms the unnerving incident into a comic plot. The stunt of a woman displacing the most revered master is contained within the harmless frame of burlesque. Yet even as this text channels anxiety into laughter, it reveals a primordial danger. It sets into relief the threat represented by the woman who mimics the practice of what we might call one-upmanship: for, in the end, far worse than the destruction of the more/less social hierarchy of mastery is the possibility that it be turned completely around, used against its intended beneficiaries.

Taking this threat still further, the fifteenth-century farce *Les femmes qui se font maistresses* stages the occasion when several women aspire to the insignia of mastery.[84] A papal envoy arrives to sanction their ambition, bestowing upon them the University of Paris bonnet. Disreputable husbands intervene; yet their resistance only facilitates the way women come to dominate in all arenas. Not only can the women throw the book at their men, outwitting them in every scholastic disputation, but they rule them domestically and sexually as well. The fact that women enter the world of higher learning paves the way for their dominion.

At stake here is an instance of female *magis*—in substance as well as in stance. The women are represented, however comically, on the verge of undertaking a public intellectual life. Given the date of this text (early fifteenth century), it is hardly surprising that an image of women masters would crystallize in reaction to the larger numbers of educated lay women during the early-modern period.[85] Yet what remains constant is the fear that women can turn the authoritative hierarchy upholding mastery inside out. Like the late-thirteenth-century *Lai,* this text places the order of social relations in jeopardy. Once women gain academe, everything changes: the balance of home life, municipal life, the structure of society as a whole. The terms of that change, however, are always determined by the more/less paradigm. No new conception of mastery is forged: women merely step into the shoes of the former masters, thereby relegating them to the tenuous position of less.

Juxtaposing the *Lai d'Aristote* and *Des femmes qui se font maistresses* sets into relief the implacable quality of mastery's dynamic. On the one hand, the contrast between the two texts reveals that, as far as the technical competence of mastery is concerned, women were not to remain unqualified indefinitely. Moving from the single female figure of a single woman targeting the master to several aiming to be masters themselves, we can chart the positive trajectory of women intellectuals, one that extends into our own day. On the other hand, as far as the social relations of mastery are concerned, there is little sense of movement: two steps forward may well mean one step back.

In the academic community where Theory, today's *Latinitas,* offers a powerful form of mastery, it is the tension between feminists and latter-day Aristotles that merits the closest scrutiny. For this encounter enables us to gauge whether the institution of mastery will entertain a different structure of relation in response to feminism, or whether the power play of one-upmanship will continue to predominate.

Looking back over the history of the liaison between post-structuralist theory and feminism, we can comment on several episodes that stand out particularly. In the late 1970s, as Anglo-American intellectuals witnessed the arrival of the foreign women of feminist theory, the tendency was to make light of them. Elaine Showalter has pointed out wittily Terry Eagleton's cavalier dismissal of them, branding their discourse "theoretically thin," a position he would later nuance.[86] However attractive French feminist arguments appeared, they were deemed a minimal, even frivolous threat to prevailing theoretical models. Aristotle remained more or less unperturbed.

Through the 1980s, we could detect a different approach; the aim being, among leading theorists, to profit from various paradigms of feminist thought. As a result of the increasing notoriety of psychoanalytic and materialist-based feminisms, it appeared shrewd and even titillating to extend some collaborative gesture to several feminist theorists. There was a decided rapprochement initiated by Derrida, among others, which could be described as a kind of romance.[87] As if enacting one of the oldest scenarios around, the deconstructionist camp inched its way closer, seeking points of contact, possible affinities. Aristotle admitted that he let himself be taken, attracted by this other voice.

In the cycle of things, where courtship is followed inevitably by a falling out, this mutual admiration has subsided considerably. The sparring for academic mastery and reputation continues. However much it bemused the gurus of theory to discover the feminist in the latest theoretical vanguard, the stakes in reaffirming preeminence are too high to defer to a group of feminist intellectuals completely.

In the last two years, there have been several incidents that indicate another reaction in the face of what is often deemed feminist mastery. While leaving aside for a moment the imperative of exploring what this mastery entails, it seems clear that the increasing acceptance of feminist theory has given rise to open and stiff opposition. Our own fin de siècle is witnessing a backlash.[88] For example, in the volume *Men in Feminism,* as well as in the virulent exchanges between Frank Lentricchia and Sandra Gilbert and Susan Gubar in *Critical Inquiry,* we find what some call the "mind police" syndrome.[89] Several male theorists seem to be claiming that there is something coercive about feminist theory. The charge is that critics such as Gilbert and Gubar push notions of phallogocentric authority with such dogmatic force that there is little room for argument. Feminist theorists set themselves up as judges—so the argument goes—who police the discourse of the critical establishment, obliging them to comply.

Well into the 1990s, in the current polemical climate of political correctness, these accusations are gaining a certain credibility before the American public. Feminism has become, in certain circles, a code word for the very social intolerance it had decried.[90] Over a century after Toulmin Smith's cautious advocacy of *consoeurie,* more than fifty years after important numbers of women entered the university as students, a good generation after women began joining the professorial ranks, is it two steps back for every two steps forward?

If we take care to examine these various portrayals of dictatorial feminist theory, however, we should recognize in them a backhanded admission of feminism having gained authority. In many ways, the greater the perceived influence of feminism on the general scene, the greater the desire to challenge it; more significantly, the greater the desire to label it in what are the reverse or negative terms of mastery. Where mastery betokens an emancipatory power for male thinkers of whatever stripe, when detected in feminism, it can be taken to signal near-authoritarianism.

What are the ways to respond to the impasse of the mind-police charge, which is itself symptomatic of a belief in a superior/inferior dynamic? Here we are circling back to the unanswered question of the nature of feminist mastery. The test is to conceive of the disposition of knowledge differently—to debate it without enforcing it upon others. The very antithesis of a set of authoritarian strokes, the various feminist versions of theorizing medieval literature elect critical subjects long trivialized, while developing working relations that themselves do not trivialize others.

To draw an analogy from the social sciences, feminist mastery promises a sort of creative destruction of medieval studies as it has long been formulated—destruction because it does destabilize, if not demolish, the very grounds of the field. The textual frames of reference, the pedagogical programs, the way in which our readings are communicated in the academy—changing the basis of all these elements explodes the very notion of the arch, near-authoritarian intellectual. At the same time, this constitutes a properly *creative* destruction in the sense that such a transformation opens up the discipline in unforeseeable ways. Feminist mastery can energize the discipline, animating it to the benefit of its many practitioners: philologists, translators, teachers, literary critics. Rather than imposing the flipside of any number of more/less quarrels, it can project a nonhierarchical model of theory and praxis. In this manner, feminist mastery spurs us not only to envision, but also to conduct our professional lives otherwise.

CODA

Theory cannot be useful to anyone interested in resistance and change unless there is a reason to believe that knowing what a theory means and believing it to be true have some connection to resistance and change.

—Marai C. Lugones and Elizabeth V. Spelman

Our endeavor to reconfigure mastery brings us to reflect on the privilege inherent in that gesture, one that subtends our very enterprise as medieval feminists. We may be marginalized as female scholars within the high circles of the academy, but our scholarly endeavors are nonetheless those of a cultured elite. Only those who have achieved a modicum of power have the luxury of scrutinizing their practice. Theorizing the female subject in medieval texts, consulting manuscripts that are inaccessible to those without credentials—our critical enterprise might seem as privileged as was reading for the minority of literate woman in the Middle Ages.

If this is so, are our scholarly and pedagogic activities subversive of the patriarchal structures that they seek to critique? Or do we merely reimpose cultural hierarchy by teaching archaic texts at a time when basic literacy is in crisis? Involving as it does years of study to acquire languages, considerable spadework before a text can be "read" in the modern sense of the term, Old French literary studies constitute a labor-intensive discipline that can easily isolate its followers within the confines of comfortable anachronism. The question for feminist medievalists who would seek to apply a "theory . . . useful for resistance and change" is, to put it bluntly, why study this elite and rarefied past? How can fruitful change emerge from the seeming misalliance of philology and feminism?

As this chapter has shown, there is no comfortable *conjointure* between Old French literary studies and the theories of feminism. But the *disjointure* of their intersection generates a tension that can be creative and mutually illuminating. Feminist theory challenges medievalists to move beyond the analytic categories of the discipline as it has been conceived for a century. The attempt to account fully for women's participation in literary medieval culture—as absences and presences, objects and agents, creators and receivers—not only restores a missing element to literary history; it also effects a major paradigm shift in literary historiography. Reading gender as a category of literary construction and reception goes against the grain of the dominant cultural codes embedded in texts, revealing new patterns, conflicts, and questions. The study of women as an excluded group can lead to consideration of others who have been marginalized or oppressed: children, servants, serfs, the urban poor, non-Christians, people of color. The tricky negotiations of reading "women" in medieval writing brings scholars to the investigation of how subjectivity and sexuality are constructed within language. Finally, the feminist critique of the transmission of knowledge can lead to a tonic reconsideration of our roles as critics, authors, and teachers.

Now what can medieval studies contribute to feminist theory and to productive social change? The answer is not as evident. Contemporary feminists beckon us urgently to look beyond the problems of white, middle-class women whose interests have been the most visibly represented in theory. As women of color have argued, theorizing by one group of women about female differences can blur other differences between them.[91] Precisely because courses and publications reflecting this pressing need for cultural diversity are beginning to flourish, medievalists need more than ever to rethink their interpretative practice of the past.

Whereas our discipline may look to the lead of contemporary theories, medievalists can contribute substantially to feminist and multicultural studies. Demystifying the cultural constructions of the western European past can enable us to break out of the molds inherited from it. Studying the social relations of the past can reveal patterns of change that empower us to conceptualize change in the future.

Finally, negotiating the complex process of reading medieval women holds lessons for anyone who would theorize how difference is embodied. By a material and historical exploration of the past in all its particularities, medieval studies can enact the *practice* of reading difference. When we theorize how "women" can be read, we confront the problem of where lived experience intersects with social constructions of gender. As medieval literary critics, we are versed in the art of reading differences, variants, palimpsests, *mouvance*. Our training as readers of unstable texts that embody historical shifts, lexical quirks, and diverse generic registers in the past can be brought to bear on a theory of difference as a body whose precise contours can never be *known* but whose material existence should not be forgotten.

NOTES

1. Our collaboration is also indebted to the generous contributions of many who have read this chapter at various stages of its development: Marlyse Bach, Danielle Regnier-Bohler, Jacqueline Cerquiglini-Toulet, Cynthia J. Brown, Merrimon Crawford, Thelma Fenster, Elaine Tuttle Hansen, Alice Yaeger Kaplan, Linda Lomperis, Heather McLean, Nancy K. Miller, Mary D. Sheriff, Lisa Splittgerber; and, from the North Carolina Research Group on Medieval and Early Modern Women: Sarah Beckwith, Elizabeth

Clark, Michele Farrell, Judith Ferster, Valeria Finucci, Monica Green, Charlotte Gross, Ann-Marie Rasmussen.

2. The terms of the feminist debate have been continually reformulated since the inception of feminist criticism in the 1960s, as evidenced by ongoing discussions of essentialism, subjectivity, theoretical imperialism, race and ethnicity, sexual identity, and class, among other questions, in the journals *Signs, differences, Feminist Studies, Women's Studies, m/f,* and *The Women's Review of Books.* For a recent overview of contested areas within the field, see *Conflicts in Feminism,* ed. Marianne Hirsch and Evelyn Fox (London: Routledge, 1990). Other anthologies that present a useful spectrum of views are *Feminist Studies/Critical Studies,* ed. Teresa de Lauretis (Bloomington: Indiana University Press, 1986), and *Between Feminism and Psychoanalysis,* ed. Teresa Brennan (London: Routledge, 1989).

3. For an astute assessment of the contradictions of the medieval feminist as they are experienced by a Chaucer scholar, see Elaine Tuttle Hansen, *Chaucer and the Fictions of Gender* (Berkeley: University of California Press, 1992).

4. We employ the category "feminist medievalist" as a strategic term that describes a particular position within disciplines, even as we acknowledge that it cannot define a unified, stable identity or represent the diversity of medieval scholars who are feminists. On the multiplicity of subject-positions that feminist critics perforce adopt, see Diana Fuss, *Essentially Speaking: Feminism, Nature and Difference* (London: Routledge, 1989).

5. The challenge of postmodern theory to a feminist politics of identity has involved a radical questioning of the categories of "woman" and of the notion of the subject. See, most recently, Denise Riley, *Am I That Name? Feminism and the Category of the Woman* (Minneapolis: University of Minnesota Press, 1988), and Judith Butler, *Gender Trouble: Feminism and the Subversion of Identity* (New York: Routledge, 1990).

6. See Bernard Cerquiglini, *L'Eloge de la variante: Histoire critique de la philologie* (Paris: Seine, 1989), and *Speculum* 65, no. 1 (1990), a special issue edited by Stephen G. Nichols devoted to "The New Philology."

7. For discussion of the elusive female subject in light of poststructuralist and feminist theory, see the editors' introduction in *Seeking the Woman in Late Medieval and Renaissance Writings,* ed. Sheila Fisher and Janet E. Halley (Knoxville: University of Tennessee Press, 1989). For a cautionary word on the problem faced by historians, see Penny Schine Gold, *The Lady and the Virgin: Image, Attitude, and Experience in Twelfth-Century France* (Chicago: University of Chicago Press, 1985), xv–xxi.

8." Even among women medieval scholars of women, there is a resistance to postmodern theory that challenges the notions of female identity. For

254 • Founders of the Discipline

254 • FOUNDERS OF THE DISCIPLINE

a medievalist's perspective on this problem, see Laurie Finke, "The Rhetoric of Marginality: Why I Do Feminist Theory," *Tulsa Studies in Women's Literature* 5, no. 2 (1986): 251–72. Within French studies, the medieval period has not yet been reconceptualized by feminist *theorists* in the way that the modern period has by Nancy K. Miller, Naomi Schor, and Alice Jardine, to name a few.

9. On the goal of interdisciplinary scholarship to be *antidisciplinary* and work against traditional structures of knowledge, see Ellen Rooney, "Discipline and Vanish: Feminism, the Resistance to Theory, and the Politics of Cultural Studies," *differences* 2, no. 3 (1990): 14–28.

10. For example, Myrrha Lot-Borodine's early work on romance emphasized women's roles: *La femme et l'amour au XII siècle d'après les poèmes de Chrétien de Troyes* (Paris: Picard, 1909); Marie Josephe Pinet championed Christine de Pisan against virulent antifeminist attacks: *Christine de Pisan, 1364–1430: Études biographique et littéraire* (Paris: Champion, 1927); Alice Hentsch's *recensement* of didactic literature is a precious resource: *La littérature didactique du moyen âge s'adressant spécialement aux femmes* (Cahors: Coueslant, 1903).

11. See Sarah Kay, "French without Spears," *The Cambridge Review: A Journal of University Life and Thought* 108, no. 2298 (1987): 99–101. Concerning the current place of medieval feminist graduate students, see Merrimon Crawford and Alison Smith.

12. *Romania,* for example, has a lone male editor. *Cahiers de civilisation médiévale* has two male directors and three men compose its *comité scientifique. Le Moyen Âge* has four men and two women on its editorial board, *Romance Philology* has five males and one female. Of the assistant editors of *Speculum,* six are men and one is a woman. After long male rule, *Medium Aevum* now has two women editors out of three.

13. For example, a special issue of *Cahiérs de civilisation médiévale* 20 (1977) was devoted to "La femme dans les civilisations des Xe–XIIIe siècles." But see the response of female participants in the colloquium at which these articles were first presented and their critique of the sexist and exclusionary biases at work in the choice of subjects surveyed, sources invoked, stereotypes perpetuated, and the generally authoritarian delivery of papers that discouraged debate (262–64). Even the latest linguistic and philological investigations of medieval textuality and manuscript culture, which steer a course away from positivism and toward a radical examination of medieval representation, poetics, and hermeneutics are not necessarily more hospitable to feminist inquiry than were their more traditional predecessors. See, for example, the recent issue of *Speculum* on the "New Philology" which raises, only in passing, the prospect of feminism as a new direction in medieval

studies, in Lee Patterson's article, "On the Margin: Postmoderism, Ironic History and Medieval Studies," *Speculum* 65, no. 1 (1990): 106—7. The discourse of feminism is markedly absent from the list of "discourses of man (*sic*) such as philosophy, anthropology, and the social sciences," which serve to contextualize literature for new philologists. See R. Howard Bloch, "New Philology and Old French," ibid., 39.

14. See, for example, the special issue of *Romance Notes* devoted to *Courtly Ideology and Women's Place in Medieval French Literature* 25, no. 3 (1985), the medieval issue of *Signs* 14, no. 2 (1989), and *Women's Studies* 11 (1984). *Paragraph* 13 (1990) includes feminism among recent theoretical perspectives. One medieval journal that has devoted an issue to "Medieval feminisms" is Exemplaria, 4, no. 2 (1992).

15. See, for example, Penny Schine Gold, *The Lady and the Virgin;* Janet Halley and Sheila Fisher, *Seeking the Woman: Women and Power in the Middle Ages,* ed. Mary Erler and Maryanne Kowaleski (Athens: University of Georgia Press, 1988); Kathryn Gravdal, *Ravishing Maidens: Writing Rape in Medieval French Literature and Law* (Philadelphia: University of Pennsylvania Press, 1990), and others to be mentioned in the course of this chapter.

16. For example, the conferences hosted by the Center for Medieval Studies at Fordham University on "Women and Power" (1985), "Gender and the Moral Order" (1989), and "Men in Feminism" (1990); the King's College, Cambridge symposium on "Gender and Medieval Studies" (December 1988) and a follow-up at Warwick University (September 1989); special sessions organized in recent years by the *Medieval Feminist Newsletter* and individual medievalists at the annual Conference on Medieval Studies, Kalamazoo, Michigan, along with TEAMS sessions at Kalamazoo devoted to "Teaching about Women in the Middle Ages.

17. *Medieval Feminist Newsletter,* ed. Roberta L. Krueger, Elizabeth Robertson, Thelma Fenster, and E. Jane Burns.

18. On the exclusionary strategies of feminist theory, see Elizabeth Spelman, *Inessential Woman: Problems of Exclusion in Feminist Thought* (Boston: Beacon Press, 1988).

19. Gaston Paris, "Lancelot du Lac: *Le Conte de la Charrette,*" *Romania* 12 (1883): 459–534.

19. Gaston Paris, "Lancelot du Lac: *Le Conte de la Charrette,*" *Romania* 12 (1883): 459–534.

20. Sarah Kofman, *L'énigme de la femme: La femme dans les textes de Freud* (Paris: Galilee, 1983), 267. Kofmans further quotations from Freud's letter of November 15, 1883 show his fixation on an ideal feminity despite social changes: "La loi et la coutume doivent donner à la femme beaucoup de droits dont elle a été privée. Mais sa situation demeurera ce qu'elle fut

toujours, celle d'une créature adorée dans sa jeunesse et d'une femme aimée dans sa maturité" (268).

21. For a bibliography of work on women in Old French literature current to 1982, see Roberta L. Krueger and E. Jane Burns, "A Selective Bibliography of Criticism: Women in Medieval French Literature," *Romance Notes* 25, no. 3 (1985): 375–90.

22. One of the earliest attempts to demystify the effects of courtly love on women was by John Benton, "Clio and Venus: An Historical View of Courtly Love," in *The Meaning of Courtly Love*, ed. F. X. Newman (Albany: SUNY Press, 1968), 19–42.

23. See Joan Ferrante, *Woman as Image in Medieval Literature* (New York: Columbia University Press, 1975), and E. Jane Burns, "The Man behind the Lady in Troubadour Lyric," *Romance Notes* 25, no. 3 (1985): 254–70.

24. See, for example, the historian Joan Kelly's notion of female power in the literature of courtly love in "Did Women Have a Renaissance?" in Renate Bridenthal and Claudia Koontz, eds., *Becoming Visible: Women in European History* (Boston: Houghton Mifflin, 1977), 137–64. For a more nuanced approach, see Penny Schine Gold, *The Lady and the Virgin*.

25. The historian's contributions are too vast and various to summarize, especially if one considers the geographical field beyond France. As examples of recent studies that offer new perspectives on the structure of gender relations, we note Caroline Bynum's examination of female spirituality in *Holy Feast and Holy Fast: The Religious Significance of Food to Medieval Women* (Berkeley: University of California Press, 1987); Judith Bennett's study of rural gender relations in *Women in the Medieval English Country- side: Gender and Household in Brigstock before the Plague* (New York: Oxford University Press, 1987); Martha Howell's analysis of gender and economic relations in Northern European Cities in *Women, Production and Patriarchy in Late Medieval Cities* (Chicago: University of Chicago Press, 1986); and the essays on female participation in the labor force edited by Barbara Hanawalt in *Women and Work in Preindustrial Europe* (Blooming- ton: Indiana University Press, 1986). A review of how women have been idealized and marginalized by French historians from the Middle Ages to the present is provided by Susan Mosher Stuard, "Fashion's Captives: Medieval Women in French Historiography" in *Women in Medieval History and Historiography* (Philadelphia: Univerisity of Pennsylvania Press, 1987), 81– 100. For a useful bibliography on women in medieval France, see pp. 160– 71. For theoretical considerations of the impact of feminist research on historical studies, see Joan Kelly, "The Social Relation of the Sexes: Method- ological Implications of Women's History," in *Women, History, and Theory:*

The Essay of Joan Kelly (Chicago: University of Chicago Press, 1984); Joan Scott, "Gender: A Useful Category of Analysis," *American Historical Review* 91, no. 5 (1986): 1053–75; Gerda Lerner, *The Creation of Patriarchy* (New York and London: Oxford University Press, 1986); Judith M. Bennett, "Feminism and History," *Gender and History* 1, no. 3 (1989): 251–72; and Denise Riley, "Does Sex Have a History?" in her *Am I That Name?*, 1–17.

26. A reading of Marie de France as a textual voice unrelated to a biologically female author takes such a tack. See Jean-Charles Huchet, "Nom de femme et écriture féminine au Moyen Âge: Les *lais* de Marie de France," *Poétique* 12 (1981): 407–30, and, for discussion of the implications of such an approach to feminist theory, see Roberta L. Krueger, "Double Jeopardy: The Appropriation of Woman in Four Old French Romances of the 'Cycle de la Gageure,'" in Fisher and Halley, eds., *Seeking the Woman*, 21–50. Alexandre Leupin's *Barbarolexis: Medieval Writing and Sexuality* (Cambridge: Harvard University Press, 1989) offers the most recent and extensive instance of reading masculinity and femininity as textual functions; in Leupin's words, "In the final analysis, sexual difference is a textual matter, and it is important to perceive it this way" (166).

27. See E. Jane Burns, "Knowing Women: Female Orifices in Old French Farce and Fabliaux," *Examplaria* 4, no. 2 (1992): 81–104, and her "This Prick Which Is Not One: How Women Talk Back in Old French Fabliaux," in *Feminist Approaches to the Body,* ed. Sarah Stanbury and Linda Lomperis (Philadelphia: University of Pennsylvania Press, 1992); Kathryn Gravdal, "Camouflaging Rape: The Rhetoric of Sexual Violence in the Medieval Pastourelle," *Romantic Review* 76, no. 4 (1985): 361–73.

28. See Roberta L. Krueger, "Love, Honor and the Exchange of Women," *Romance Notes* 25, no. 3 (1985): 302–17; "Desire, Meaning and the Female Reader: The Problem in Chrétien's *Charrette*," in Christopher Baswell and William Sharpe, eds., *The Passing of Arthur: New Essays in Arthurian Tradition* (New York: Garland, 1988), 31–51; Helen Solterer, "Dismembering, Remembering the Chastelain de Coucy," in *Romance Philology* 46, no. 2 (1992): 103–24.

29. Peter Dronke, *Medieval Women Writers: A Critical Study of Texts from Perpetua to Marguerite Porete* (Cambridge: Cambridge University Press, 1984); Charity Cannon Willard, *Christine de Pizan: Her Life and Works* (New York: Persea Books, 1984); Katharina Wilson, *Medieval Women Writers* (Athens: University of Georgia Press, 1984); Meg Bogin, *The Women Troubadours* (New York: Norton, 1980).

30. See, most recently for Marie de France, articles in *Stanford French and Italian Studies* 58 (1988) by Diana M. Faust, "Women Narrators in the *Lais* of Marie de France," 17–28, and Stephen G. Nichols, "Working Late:

Marie de France and the Value of Poetry," 7–16; and Bloch "New Philosophy and Old French." On the women troubadours, see William Paden, ed., *The Voice of the Trobairitz* (Philadelphia: University of Pennsylvania Press, 1989).

31. See annotated bibliographies by Angus J. Kennedy, Christine de Pizan: A bibliographical Guide (London: Grant and Cutler, 1984), and Edith Yenal, *Christine de Pisan: A Bibliography of Writings by Her and about Her* (Metuchen, N.J. and London: Scarecrow, 1982 and supplement 1989). Additional bibliography in *Poems of Cupid: God of Love: Christine de Pizan's Epistre au dieu d'Amours and Dit de la Rose: Thomas Hocleve's The Letter of Cupid; with George Sewells' Proclamation of Cupid,* ed. and trans. Thelma Fenster and Mary Erler (Leiden: Brill, 1990). See also the recent special issue of *Revue des langues romanes* 92, no. 2 (1988) devoted to Christine studies and the first modern edition of the *Livre des trois vertus,* ed. Charity C. Willard and Eric Hicks (Paris: Champion, 1989) along with Charity Willard's English translation of it, *A Medieval Woman's Mirror of Honor,* ed. M. Cosman (New York: Persea Books, 1989).

32. See, for example, Renate Blumenfeld Kosinski, ed., *The Writings of Margaret of Oingt, Medieval Prioress and Mystic* (Cambridge: The Focus Library of Medieval Women, (1990), and for the most recent work on the lady's *Response* to the *Bestiaire d'amour,* Jeanette Beer, "Richard de Fournival's Anonymous Lady: The Character of the *Response* to the *Bestiaire d'amour,*" *Romance Philology* 42, no. 3 (1989), 267–73; Helen Solterer, "Seeing, Hearing, Tasting Woman: The Senses of Medieval Reading," in *Medieval Texts and Contemporary Reading,* ed. Anna Berthold (Ithaca: Cornell University Press, 1987); and *The Master and Minerva: Disputing Women in French Medieval Culture* (Berkeley: University of California Press, 1995).

33. See, for example, the debate about Christine de Pisan's alleged "feminism" and her class status: Sheila Delany, "'Mothers to Think Back Through: Who Are They?' The Ambiguous Example of Christine de Pizan," in Laurie A. Finke and Martin B. Schichtman, eds., *Medieval Texts and Contemporary Readers* (Ithaca: Cornell University Press 1987), 177–200.

34. For the problem of male academics' relation to feminism within the literary profession as a whole, see Alice Jardine and Paul Smith, eds., *Men in Feminism* (New York: Methuen, 1987). For an example of how the tension has played itself out in medieval circles, see the debate surrounding R. Howard Bloch's "Medieval Misogyny" (*Representations* 20 [fall 1987]: 1–24) in the *Medieval Feminist Newsletter* 6 (1988) and Bloch's response in *MFN* 7 (1989).

35. For feminist readings of the romance genre, see especially the work of Roberta L. Krueger, "Love, Honor and the Exchange of Women," in

Yvain: Some Remarks on the Female Reader *Romance Notes* 25, no. 3 (1985); "Desire, Meaning and the Female Reader: The Problem in Chrétien's *Charrette;* "Double Jeopardy: The Appropriation of Woman in Four Old French Romances of the 'Cycle de la Gageure,'" in Fisher and Halley, eds., *Seeking the Woman.*

36. Léon Gautier, *Les épopées françaises,* 3 vols. (Paris: 1865–68); 2d ed., 4 vols (Paris: V. Palme, 1878–94); Gaston Paris, *Histoire poétique de Charlemagne* (Paris: 1865); 2d ed. (Paris: E. Bouillon, 1905); Paul Meyer, editions of (inter alia) *Daurel et Beton* (Paris: S.A.T.F., 1880); *Raoul de Cambrai* (Paris: S.A.T.F., 1882); Joseph Bédier, *Les légendes épiques, recherches sur la formation des chansons de geste,* 4 vols. (Paris: Champion, 1908–13; 2d ed. 1914–21; 3d ed. 1926–29); Ferdinand Lot, *Études sur les légendes épiques françaises* (Paris: Champion, 1958); Edmond Faral, *La Chanson de Roland, étude et analyse* (Paris: Mellottee, 1932).

37. See, for example, Robert Pensom on the *Roland:* "The true subject of the poem is the confrontation of a transcendent ethical value (without which there can be no order) with ego-centered relativism such as we see depicted in the person of Ganelon," *Literary Technique in the Song of Roland* (Geneva: Droz, 1982), 114.

38. Pensom, *Literary Technique;* Robert F. Cook, *The Sense of the Song of Roland* (Ithaca: Cornell University Press, 1987).

39. Bernard Guidot, *Recherches sur la chanson de geste au xiiie siècle d'après certaines oeuvres du cycle de Guillaume d'Orange,* 2 vols. (Aix and Marseilles: Publications de l'Université de Provence, 1986).

40. E.g., Stephen G. Nichols, "The Spirit of Truth: Epic Modes in Medieval Narrative," *New Literary History* 1 (1970): 365–86; R. Howard Bloch, *Etymologies and Genealogies: A Literary Anthropology of the Middle Ages* (Chicago: University of Chicago Press, 1983).

41. Rita Lejeune, *Recherches sur le thème: Les chansons de geste et l'histoire* (Liège: Faculté de Philosophie et Lettres, 1948); *Girart de Roussillon, chanson de geste,* ed. W. Mary Hackett, 3 vols. (Paris: Didot, 1953); Micheline de Combarieu du Grès, *L'idéal humain et l'expérience morale chez les héros de chansons de geste,* 2 vols. (Aix-en-Provence: Publications de l'Université de Provence, 1979), 2:665–756; *Raoul de Cambrai, An Old French Feudal Epic,* trans. Jessie Crosland (London: Chatto and Windus, 1926); Pauline Matarasso, *Recherches historiques et littéraires sur "Raoul de Cambrai"* (Paris: Nizet 1962); Joseph E. Vallerie, *Garin le Loheren, according to MS A* (Norwalk, Conn., 1947); Pauline Taylor, *Gerbert de Mez, chanson de geste du XIIe siècle* (Namur: Secretariat de publications, facultés universitaires, 1952); Anne Iker Gittleman, *Le style épique dans Garin le Loheren* (Geneva: Droz, 1967).

42. Oxford: Oxford University Press, 1951.

43. Cited from the edition and translation by Sarah Kay (Oxford: Oxford University Press, 1990).

44. See the passage in which the dead Raoul's heart is compared favorably with that of the gigantic Jehan de Ponthieu whom he killed at Origini, vv. 3055–72 (ed. Kay).

45. Jean Rychner, *La chanson de geste: Essai sur l'art épique des jongleurs* (Geneva: Droz, 1955).

46. See, for example, William Calin's battle royal with Joseph J. Duggan occupying the whole of the spring number of *Olifant* 8 (1980–81). Calin's contention that "C'est une question de stylistique qui est au coeur de la dispute entre littéraires et 'oralisants'. Les oralisants voudraient nier le caractère et la qualité littéraire des chansons de geste" (267–68) may be somewhat overstated, but his own method of reading chansons de geste as suggestive, psychological, and political narratives tends to be closer to feminist practice than Duggan's more statistical approach. See below, however, how Duggan's approach has been used effectively in the service of feminist analysis by Allison Elliott; and, regarding close reading as a strategy of feminist critique, see Caren Greenberg, "Reading Reading: Echo's Abduction of Language," *Women and Language in Literature and Society,* ed. Sally McConnell Ginet et al. (Ithaca, N.Y.: Praeger, 1980), 300–9.

47. Ellen Rose Woods, *"Aye d'Avignon": A Study of Genre and Society* (Geneva: Droz, 1978).

48. Patricia Harris Stäblein, "Catastrophe Theory in Reading Narratives: A Way to Figure Out *Raoul de Cambrai* and Its Rôle in the Lyrics of Bertrand de Born," *Olifant* 8 (1980): 3–28. See also her *Narrer/nourrir:* La signification, la violence et la contamination dans la structure de *Raoul de Cambrai,*" in *Manger et boire au moyen âge, Actes du Colloque de Nice* (Paris: Les Belles Lettres, 1984), 451–65. Other feminist-inspired crtics to write on *Raoul de Cambrai* include Penny Schine Gold, *The Lady and the Virgin,* 12–18; Thelma Fenster, "The Son's Mother: Alais and Marsent in *Raoul de Cambrai, Olifant* 12 (1987): 147–53.

49. Sarah Kay, "La composition de *Raoul de Cambrai,*" *Revue d'histoire et de philologie belge* 62 (1984): 474–92; *Raoul de Cambrai* introduction, paras. 3.4.4-3.4.6.

50. Alison Goddard Elliott, "The Double Genesis of *Girart de Vienne,*" *Olifant* 8 (1980–81): 130–60.

51. See Sarah Kay, "Investing the Wild: Women's Beliefs in Old French *Chansons de Geste," Paragraph,* "Displacement and Recognition: A Special Issue on Medieval Studies" (1990): 147–53.

52. "Bele Yolanz en sa chambres seoit," from Michel Zink, *Les chansons de toile* (Paris: Champion, 1977), 77 (translation ours).

53. Pierre Bec, *La lyrique française au Moyen Âge* (Paris: Picard, 1977), 1:57–62.

54. For other examples, see Zink, 86, 93, 102, 103, 166.

55. As the typical opening stanza of most *chanson de toile* attest, the woman's voice figured in these poems, although it may be the first lyric "I" to appear in the poem, remains nonetheless a voice constructed by the narrator who reports the woman's words to us. The narrator's creative activity resembles that of the male lyric persona in the *chanson de malmariée* who gives to us, as the fabric of his poem, a song he heard three women singing, thus having appropriated their voices to his (Bec, *La lyrique française*, 2: poem 8), or any number of *pastourelles* that recount how the narrator's poem results from a woman's song he overheard (Bec, 2:poems 41, 42, 43, 49, 50).

56. For another example, see "Bele Ydoine," stanza 14, Zink, 117. For instances where the female protagonist speaks the refrain from a dead faint, see Zink, 86, 117.

57. Scholarly discussions of the *kharjas,* romance refrains in a woman's voice that were incorporated into Mozarabic poems called *muwashshahs,* and of the Gallego-Portuguese *cantigas de amigo* provide particularly striking examples of a critical blindspot regarding gender (Pierre Le Gentil, "La strophe zadjalesque et les khardjas," *Romania* 84 (1963): 1–27, 209–50, 409–11). See especially Peter Dronke's statement, "The greatest flowering of woman's songs in medieval Europe occurred in thirteenth-century Portugal. There both the court poet and the *jogral* composed *cantigas de amigo*": *The Medieval Lyric* (rpt. 1977; Cambridge: Cambridge University Press, 1968), 102. For a feminist reading of the *cantigas de amigo* against the *grant chant courtois,* see Ria Lemaire, *Passions et positions: Contribution à une semiotique du sujet dans la poésie lyrique médiévale en langues romanes* (Amsterdam: Rodopoi, 1988).

58. See Faral's thesis that women's songs were actually composed by men employing a consciously archaic style and his reasoning: that the *chansons de toile* were far too lascivious to have been sung by young girls: "L'héroïne de la chanson de toile n'était pas tout à fait dans le rôle d'une innocente, mais bien, comme on peut en effet le voir par le texte, dans celui d'une jeune femme qu'aucune règle ne fera renoncer à l'amour qui la tient. Ces raisons, de caractère moral, suffiraient à persuader que la notion de chanson chantées par des femmes est ici purement conventionnelle," Edmond Faral, "Les chansons de toile ou chansons d'histoire," *Romania* 69 (1946–47): 459 and more generally 453–59.

59. In *Diacritics* (summer 1982) see Peggy Kamuf, "Replacing Feminist Criticism," 42–47, and Nancy K. Miller, "The Text's Heroine: A Feminist Critic and Her Fictions," 48–53, and the update to their dialogue, "Parisian Letters: Between Feminism and Deconstruction," in Hirsch and Fox, eds., *Conflicts in Feminism,* 121–33.

60. The debate parallels a more general split between American and French feminist thought. For an explanation of their basic differences, see Alice Jardine, "Gynesis," *Diacritics* (summer 1982): 54–65, and Toril Moi, *Sexual/Textual Politics* (London: Methuen, 1985). On the distinction between gynocritics and feminist critique, see Elaine Showalter, "Toward a Feminist Poetics," in *Women Writing and Writing about Women,"* ed. Mary Jacobus (London: Croom Helm, 1979), 22–41.

61. See Mary Jacobus, "Is There a Woman in This Text?" in *Reading Woman: Essays in Feminist Criticism* (New York: Columbia University Press, 1986), 83–109. For recent discussions on essentialism, see Teresa de Lauretis, "The Essence of the Triangle, of Taking the Risk of Essentialism Seriously: Feminist Theory in Italy, the U.S., and Britain," and Naomi Schor, "This Essentialism Which Is Not One: Coming to Grips with Irigaray," both in *differences* 1, no. 2 (1988): 3–37 and 38–58; Fuss, *Essentially Speaking;* and Teresa de Lauretis, "Upping the Anti (*sic*) in Feminist Theory," in Hirsch and Fox, eds., *Conflicts in Feminism,* 255–70.

62. For a feminist reading of modernity's struggle with the issue of subjectivity and an assessment of the problematic turn toward a fascination with otherness, see Jardine, *Gynesis,* 118–44.

63. On the debate between feminism and poststructuralism, see Mary Poovey, "Feminism and Deconstruction," Leslie Wahl Rabine, "Toward a Feminist Politics of Non-Identity," both in *Feminist Studies* 14, no. 1 (1988): 51–65 and 11–31.

64. *Subject to Change: Reading Feminist Writing* (New York: Columbia University Press, 1988), 67.

65. Alfred Jeanroy, *Les origines de la poésie lyrique en France au moyen âge* (Paris: Hachette, 1889); and Gaston Paris, "Les origines de la poésie lyrique en France," *Mélanges de littérature française du moyen âge,* ed. Mario Roques (Paris: Champion, 1912), 539–615. Bec does not reiterate Jeanroy's *ad feminam* attack on the rustic spontaneity of woman's song's as a sign of primitive and precourtly lyric composition (Bec, 58). Nor does he echo Jeanroy's now famous virulent denunciation of the *trobairitz:* "J'avoue tout en admirant la simplicité et le naturel du style, que j'ai bien de la peine à croire à cette sincerité, et que cette singulière attitude me parait devoir s'expliquer autrement. Je me figure que nos trobairitz, esclaves de la tradi-

tion, incapables d'un effort d'analyse, se sont bornées à exploiter, des thèmes connus, à user d'un formulaire courant, en invertissant simplement les rôles." Alfred Jeanroy, *La poésie lyrique des troubadours* (Paris: H. Didier, 1934), 316–17. But the status of Bec's hypothetical woman poets does parallel, in a rough way, that of the Provençal *trobairitz* whose collective oeuvre has been carefully combed for evidence of a distinctive feminine poetics. See most recently William Paden, ed., *The Voice of the Trobairitz*, which includes extensive bibliography. For a sampling of studies of feminine poetics in Old French literature, see Michelle Freeman, "Marie de France's Poetics of Silence: The Implications for a Feminine *Translatio*," *PMLA* 99 (1984): 860–83; Stephen G. Nichols, "Medieval Women Writers: Aiesthesis and the Powers of Marginality," *Yale French Studies* 75 (fall 1988): 77–94; Christine Reno, "Feminist Aspects of Christine de Pizan's *Epistre d'Othea à Hector*," *Studi francesi* 71 (1980): 271–76; Liliane Dulac, "Inspiration mythique et savoir politique: Les conseils aux veuves chez Francesco da Barberino et chez Christine de Pizan," *Mélanges à la mémoire de Franco Simone: France et Italie dans la culture européene, I: Moyen Âge et Renaissance* (Geneva: Slatkine, 1980), 113–41; Kevin Brownlee, "The *Ditie de Jeheanne d'Arc*," *Discourses of Authority in Medieval and Renaissance Literature* (Hanover, N.H.: University Press of New England, 1989).

66. The only named poet of the chanson de femme, Zink reminds us, was a man: Audefroi le Batard, and the only poetic "I" that of a male speaker. Although one *chansonnier* contains a small number of anonymous chansons de femme, most are interpolated into romance texts (Jean Renart's *Le roman de la rose ou Guillaume de Dôle, Le roman de la violette, Le lai d'Aristote*), where they stand as "false citations" of putative women's voices.

67. This line of reasoning parallels Jean Charles Huchet's problematic erasure of the *trobairitz*, Marie de France, and Heloise as literary constructions of femaleness without historical referent. See his "Les femmes troubadours ou la voix critique," *Littérature* 51 (1983): 59–90; "Nom de femme et écriture féminine," *Poétique* 12 (1981): 407–30; "La voix d'Heloise," *Romance Notes* 25, no. 3 (1985): 271–87; or R. Howard Bloch's controversial argument that "If woman is defined as verbal transgression, indiscretion, and contradiction, then Walter Map, indeed any writer can only be defined as a woman," "Medieval Misogyny," *Representations* (fall 1987): 19. Within these critical frameworks, questions of gender appear central to an argument that actually speaks of woman only metaphorically. The woman becomes the seductive song for Zink, the process of writing for Huchet (see especially his *Le roman médiéval* [Paris: Presses Universitaires de France, 1984], and "literature itself" for Bloch (20). For a more nuanced reading of the complex

dynamics of male and female textual voices in Old French texts, see Alexandre Leupin, "La compromission (sur Le voyage de Charlemagne à Jerusalem et à Constaninople)," *Romance Notes* 25, no. 3 (1985): 222–38.

68. Jardine, 105–18; Luce Irigaray, *Spéculum de l'autre femme* (Paris: Minuit, 1974), 165–82.

69. Catherine Belsey, *The Subject of Tragedy: Identity and Difference in Renaissance Drama* (London: Methuen, 1985), chap. 6.

70. No one has proven this better than Pierre Jonin, whose diligent efforts to classify the refrains of the *chansons de toile* into distinct categories ("heroine's refrain" versus "narrator's refrain") led him to talk about merging voices, overlap, "collaboration," confusion of categories: "Les refrains dans les chansons de toile," *Romania* 96 (1975): 209–44. See also his "Les types féminins dans les chansons de toile," *Romania* 91 (1970): 433ff.

71. Paul Zumthor, *Essai de poétique médiévale* (Paris: Éditions du Seuil, 1972), 73.

72. Nancy K. Miller, "Changing the Subject: Authorship, Writing and the Reader," 112.

73. Little known to French medievalists, Lucy Toulmin Smith (1838–1911) was a British independent scholar who worked primarily in the area of economic history, editing several key texts. These projects brought her into contact with Meyer, with whom she jointly edited *Contes moralisés* (Paris: Firmin Didot, 1889). Bonnie G. Smith comments briefly on Toulmin Smith in her essay, "The Contributions of Women to Modern Historiography in Great Britain, France and the United States, 1750–1940," *American Historical Review* 89, no. 3 (1984): 723. See also her article, "Gender and Objectivity in the Writing of History," in *Objectivity and Its Other,* ed. Wolfgang Nader (New York: Guilford Press, 1995). Toulmin Smith's case offers an important corollary to the experiences of Jessie Weston, Gertrude Schoepperle, Charlotte Cipriani, S. Lutoslawska, Myrrha Lot-Borodine, and Mildred Pope, among other women working in medieval literary studies at the turn of the century. The story of these women is only now coming to light.

74. Two incisive readings of the institution of the master, as evidenced in France, are Emile Durkheim, *L'évolution pédagogique en France* (Paris: Félix Alcan, 1938), 91–98, and Pierre Bourdieu, *Homo Academicus* (Paris: Minuit, 1984), 127–28.

75. Sandra Gilbert and Susan Gubar, "The Man on the Dump versus the United Dames of America: Or What Does Frank Lentricchia Want?" *Critical Inquiry* 14 (1988): 389.

76. For a brief commentary on the status of the master in the High Middle Ages, see John W. Benton, "Masters at Paris from 1179 to 1215: A Social Perspective," in *Renaissance and Renewal in the Twelfth Century,* ed.

Robert Benson and Giles Constable (Cambridge, Mass.: Harvard University Press, 1982), 143–53; and Richard Southern, "The Schools of Paris and the School of Chartres," ibid., 135.

77. Alfred A. Ernout and A. Antoine Meillet, *Dictionnaire étymologique de la langue latine.*

78. Gustave Cohen, "Expériences théophiliennes," *Mercure de France* (February 1, 1937): 476 (translation ours).

79. See Jane Gallop's suggestive remarks on this issue in *Thinking through the Body* (New York: Columbia University Press, 1988).

80. For a discussion of this dilemma, see Adrienne Rich, "Towards a Woman-Centered University," in *On Lies, Secrets and Silence: Selected Prose* (New York: Norton, 1988), 18.

81. *Writing a Woman's Life* (New York: Norton, 1988), 18.

82. Ed. Maurice Delbouille, *Bibliothèque de la Faculté de Philosophie et de Lettres de Liège, no. 123* (Liège: Presse Universitaire de Liège, 1951).

83. This text was composed during the very period when the Aristotelian corpus was recovered and consolidated by masters at the University of Paris. Aristotelian thought argues, among many other things, for the material composition of women. See Prudence Allen, *The Concept of Woman The Aristotelian Revolution 750 BC–AD 1250* (Montreal: Eden Press, 1985), 415.

84. Ed. Gustave Cohen, Recueil de farces françaises inédites dy XVe siècle, Publications of the Medieval Academy of America 47 (Cambridge, Mass.: Medieval Academy of America, 1949), 113–22.

85. Myriam Greilsammer notes evidence for the extent of women's learning in her study, *L'envers du tableau: Mariage et maternité en Flandre médiéval* (Paris: Armand Colin, 1990), 14.

86. See "Critical Crossdressing: Male Feminists and the Woman of the Year," in *Men in Feminism,* 116–36; and "Rape and Clarissa," in Janet Todd, *Feminist Literary History* (Oxford: Polity Press, 1988), 121–25.

87. See Jacques Derrida and Christie V. McDonald, "Choreographies," *Diacritics* 12 (1982): 66–76; and Jacques Derrida, *Feu la cendre* (Paris: Des femmes, 1987).

88. Nancy Miller outlines this phase in "Philoctetes Sister: Feminist Literary Criticism and the New Misogyny," part of her forthcoming book, *Getting Personal: Feminist Occasions and Other Autobiographical Acts* (New York: Routledge, 1994).

89. Meaghan Morris' comments on this syndrome are germane; see "In any event . . . ," in *Men in Feminism,* 175.

90. Dinesh D'Souza refers to feminism in this manner: *Illiberal Education: The Politics of Race and Sex on Campus* (New York: Free Press, 1991), 190, 229, 235–36.

91. Barbara Christian, "A Race for Theory," *Feminist Studies* 14, no. 1 (1988): 67–79 and Marai C. Lugones and Elizabeth V. Spelman, "Have We Got a Theory For You! Feminist Theory, Cultural Imperialism, and the Demand for 'the Woman's Voice'," *Women's Studies International Forum* 6, no. 6 (1983): 573–81.

PART THREE

CONTINUATORS OF THE DISCIPLINE

NINE

Joseph Bédier, Philologist and Writer

Alain Corbellari

EXACTLY ONE HUNDRED years ago Joseph Bédier's thesis on *The Fabliaux* appeared, an important watershed in the then relatively "courtoise" field of French medievalism. This initial effort, a masterpiece, would remain for nearly seventy years the alpha and omega of a once again very controversial subject. It also marked the beginning of one of the most prestigious and disconcerting careers in the history of medievalism. The reputation of Bédier's *Roman de Tristan et Iseut,* which can be read as either a faithful transcription or a romantic reverie, made him a veritable myth among his peers, but also created misunderstandings that still exist. The average student of Old French, or even a section of the educated public, recalls in connection with Joseph Bédier, who was for more than thirty years the incontestable master of his discipline, a new method for editing ancient texts, assertions about the bourgeois character of the fabliaux or the clerical origin of the chansons de geste, and a heterogenous roman d'amour.

This image is certainly flattering—and one that even Gaston Paris did not possess—but it is truncated and hints of dilettantism and too great a facility at work—the very opposite of the real man, as I seek to reveal in these pages. Those who knew Bédier recall a man of extreme courtesy, willingly self-effacing, of hesitant speech (Ferdinand Lot emphasizes, in the monograph dedicated to his friend, how he was the opposite of Gaston Paris in this respect),[1] whose ideas were suspected because of the way he presented them. Paul Meyer, who always denied Bédier any originality, succumbed to this error. Ferdinand Lot indignantly claimed that this was "a great mistake!" as he reminds us of the epic (in every sense of the word) controversies that he himself had with Bédier. The latter not only developed revolutionary theories but also knew how to support them. This he did with a polemical vigor equaled only by the infallible precision and scrupulous exhaustiveness that he brought to the service, as he loudly claimed, of the sole and unique scientific "truth," or rather, philologic "truth," to avoid a term that Bédier used only with repugnance when speaking of his own work.

Bédier used his talents in service of the truth, but never to the detriment of art, this form that he venerated like a true classical writer. He used the French language as few of his contemporaries did, for if he was barely able to improvise the slightest conversation, in his writing he rivaled the best. Bédier exemplifies the conflict between a timid façade and an unshakable inner composure, the intransigeance of the disinterested seeker combined with great human generosity. We can clearly see a note of ironic complicity in the threat of "extermination" with which he menaced Ferdinand Lot, who described him, moreover, as a man whose ardent humanity we should not doubt.

His correspondence reveals a Joseph Bédier who was passionately attached to his friends. If Paul Meyer always refused to respect him, it was because he saw Bédier as the assassin of Gaston Paris (Les fabliaux, and later Les légendes épiques, would continue to ruin the theories of the thesis director!), without being able to admit Bédier's true filial admiration for his master. Nor could Meyer admit Bédier's sincerity, which was doubtless too idealistic, when the latter declared that Gaston Paris was the first to recognize his errors if he saw an advantage there for scientific truth. How can we explain the almost frivolous parenthesis of the Roman de Tristan et Iseut in a life's work so full of philological scruples? How can we express the tension between empiricism and dogmatism in a work that profoundly shook the habits and certainties of medievalists throughout the world? Finally, how can we measure the literary and even political importance in France, during the first half of the century, of a man who seemed to be so narrowly limited to his university specialty? By way of prelude to answering these questions, I offer here a short biographical sketch.

Charles Marie Joseph Bédier was born in Paris, at 6 rue Notre-Dame des Champs, on January 28, 1864, during a visit to the metropolis by his parents Adolphe Louis Marie and Marie Céline, born Du Tertre Le Cocq, who ordinarily lived on the Ile de la Réunion. They barely paused before returning to the island with their youngest child, who spent the first eighteen years of his life there.

The Bédiers' life on the island in the Indian Ocean is a familiar story whose complete details we know by chance thanks to a family record written in 1867 by Adolphe Louis Marie for his three children.[2] Although of peripheral importance, this long narration of about a hundred pages offers several keys to family influences on young Joseph. Although his close relations described him as in general not wishing to reflect on his past, whether private or professional, in middle age he never missed an opportunity to express his pride in his ancestors. As he said to Gustave Cohen: "You do not know, my friend, what to be born on the Ile de la Réunion and to be, like me, a blond with blue eyes, mean in terms of unbroken tradition and racial purity without any misalliance."[3]

Indeed, among Bédier's ancestors we find, described at length, a king's musketeer and even, on his mother's side, the historical proto-types of the heroes of *Paul et Virginie*! Close relations of Bédier report that he kept all his life the bearing of a musketeer, and his chivalric spirit was undeniable, both toward his opponents, whom he meant "to combat," and within his daily life, which explains his contempt for money. Upon succeeding Edmond Rostand in 1921 at the Aca-démie Française, Bédier expressed his great sympathy for the idealistic knights who expected nothing in return for their exploits. We may smile at this desire for selflessness in a man who died showered with honors, but we may still believe those who assure us that he did not seek, but only accepted, those that came to him.

But we must not anticipate. When he was only five years old, Joseph Bédier, who had a brother three years older and a sister two years younger, lost his father. His mother, who was not yet twenty-five years old, shortly afterwards married her cousin, Godfroy Le Cocq Du Tertre, who gave her two more children and looked after those from her first marriage. The dedication of the *Roman de Tristan et Iseut* tells us of the affection Joseph felt for him. Without entering too much into psychoanalytic explanations, it seems allowable to see in this precocious absence of a father one of the keys to Bédier's attitude toward Gaston Paris, "of whom he spoke always like a father," according to his own son. As an example of a "murder of the father," the thesis written on *Les Fabliaux* should absolve its author from all suspicion of scientific jealousy.

Bédier's youth on the Ile Bourbon is still not very well known. Emulation of his brother Édouard, who became a brilliant scientist at the Pasteur Institute but died tragically in 1892 of an acute inflammation of the lymphatic vessels, inspired the young student who, at fourteen, received as first prize in literature at the lycée of St.-Denis de la Réunion the edition of *La Chanson de Roland* by Léon Gautier, a work that had just appeared in 1872.

Bédier studied up to the Baccalauréat at the Réunion. A bachelor of arts (first part) in August 1880, he obtained his "capacité ès lettres" on August 19, 1881 and earned without difficulties a scholarship to pursue his studies in Paris. He embarked for the capital in 1881, returning to the Ile Bourbon a single time, for several weeks, just after passing the *agrégation*. In spite of the cost of the voyage and the many subsequent occupations of Bédier, we cannot help but be surprised by his attitude toward a land that he never disowned as his country. Clearly, when he arrived in Paris, he knew that a page had been turned and that the future awaited. A scholarship holder at Louis-Le-Grand, he entered the École Normale Supérieure on October 1, 1883. Of all his professors, two influenced him profoundly, and he sought throughout his life to perpetuate their ideal. The first was Brunetière, a model of integrity, of speech, and also of rigor. Bédier recognized in him his innate love of polished speech, that "academism" in the best sense of the term, which always caused him to reject with horror convoluted turns of phrase and neologisms. In his will, Brunetière named Bédier as literary executor for the edition of his posthumous writings, an unequivocal expression of confidence of which Bédier showed himself worthy.

The other master was, of course, Gaston Paris, thanks to whom medieval studies appeared to the young seeker as a branch of knowledge laden with such great future possibilities. *Romania*, founded in 1872, the same year that Gaston Paris succeeded his father Paulin at the Collège de France, blossomed; and, thanks to Gaston Paris's political skill in the creation of chairs, the study of Old French literature spread throughout France. Bédier felt his path completely marked out, and the moving letters (today in the Bibliothèque Nationale) that he addressed to his two masters show the veritable metamorphosis of a timid and worried student who found, thanks to the friendly protection of these "sacred cows" of the university, a confidence in himself that made him the most ruthlessly rigorous of medievalists. Earning his degree on October 31, 1884, he passed the *agrégation* on August 31, 1886. The great friendships that lasted all his life dated from this epoch. An example of fidelity, in his work as in his life, Bédier never renounced his camaraderie with Paul Painlevé, Joseph Texte, Paul Boyer, Durand, who became professor of Latin at the Sorbonne, Émile Mâle, the future author of *L'art religieux du XIIIe siècle en France* (to which we shall return), and especially Bernard Bouvier, the future professor at the University of Geneva and the editor of the *Journal* of Amiel, who served as a pallbearer at Bédier's funeral.

Bédier was admitted to the École Pratique des Hautes Études on January 20, 1887, but left for Germany on the first of October as a scholarship student attached to the seminar of Hermann Suchier. He gained from this sojourn primarily an excellent knowledge of German, from which he benefited not only in his works on Tristan (the study of the texts of Eilhart von Oberg and of Gottfried de Strasbourg) but also, in a more unexpected manner, during the war of 1914–18. Aside from Hermann Suchier, of whom he always spoke with respect and to whom he dedicated, moreover, the *Legendes épiques,* he formed scarcely any permanent connections in Germany. At most, the edition of Marie de France that Karl Warnke prepared in these same years inspired him with the idea for the article that appeared in 1891 in the *Revue des deux-mondes.* His virulent nationalism did not keep him, however, from welcoming German students to his courses with open arms when he was professor at the Collège de France and even after World War I.

As soon as he had returned, on October 1, 1888, Bédier was appointed *maître surveillant* at the École Normale Supérieure, the work of a "supervisor" rather than a researcher. On October 8, 1889, he was sent by Gaston Paris to the University of Fribourg (in Switzerland), which, newly created, sought a professor of French literature. Appointed for two years, Bédier remained there in fact less than one year, and experienced with difficulty the ponderous Catholicism of that city.

On August 1, 1891, he became a senior lecturer at the Faculté des Lettres de Caen, actively preparing the thesis that gave him the rank of doctor on September 30, 1893. In November, he became substitute senior lecturer at the École Normale Supérieure and henceforth did not leave Paris. Receiving tenure as a senior lecturer on April 1, 1896, he dedicated himself to modern literature. The *Études critiques* were the result of these years spent at the École Normale Supérieure, and it is not insignificant to note—and Lanson will cite Bédier among his precursors but without speaking of the *Études critiques*[4]—that, in applying philological methods to modern literature, Bédier purely and simply invented literary history.

However, Bédier returned definitively to Old French thanks to his appointment to the chair of Gaston Paris at the Collège de France on December 7, 1903. For thirty-three years his teaching was confined exclusively to the Collège de France, the chair of Gaston Paris at the École Pratique des Hautes Études having fallen to Mario Roques, then a very young researcher, who had been the student of both Bédier and Gaston Paris. For Bédier, the Sorbonne, whose dome he saw from his apartment on the rue Soufflot, was only "the house across the street." Needless to say, the internecine struggles between the great schools (which were so profitable to a Lanson or a Durkheim, as Antoine Compagnon has shown in *La Troisième République des Lettres*)[5] remained completely foreign to Bédier.

Thus it took only fifteen years for Bédier to climb all the rungs of the academic ladder to the highest chair in his discipline, which he attained in his fortieth year, although not without difficulty (Paul Meyer took his revenge by closing access to the Académie des Inscriptions et Belles-Lettres to Bédier). Meanwhile, he married, in the church of Saint-Clotilde on October 22, 1891, Eugénie Bizarelli, the daughter of Louis Bizarelli, a doctor of Corsican origin, who was a senator for the Drôme, Bédier gained from this marriage introductions in political circles and not insignificant political support. Even if Bédier loudly proclaimed himself as atheistic and apolitical, he never scorned, as we will see, the solicitations of politicians.

His three children—Louis, Jean, and Marthe—were born in 1894, 1898, and 1899. The testimonies they have left depict a father without any severity, of great gentleness, but one who was entirely absorbed by his work, accompanied by his books even in his vacation homes of Grand-Serre and Bray-Dunes (in the north). Besides, Bédier felt alive only in Paris, as the vibrant hommage he paid to the City of Light in his speech for the fourth centenary of the Collège de France makes clear: "Paris is an air that one breathes, so invigorating that a man who finds himself suddenly immersed in it, no matter what his profession, feels the rhythm of his life quickened and joyous."[6]

However, the period that preceded his election to the Collège de France remained above all the time when the *Roman de Tristan et Iseut* was conceived. And it is not perhaps by chance that it was precisely during the years when his children were born that Bédier, given the responsibility by the Société des Anciens Textes Français to edit the fragmentary roman of the Anglo-Norman trouvère Thomas, began ("in order to relax from this work and for fun," he later said) to translate and adapt the ancient fragments of the Tristan legend. Though habitually laborious, capable of rewriting up to ten times a simple lecture page, often discouraged by the mere idea of having to write a letter, Bédier for once wrote quickly, doubtless because without constraint, dictating part of the text to his wife, and finished the manuscript in the final days of 1897, while the edition of Thomas scarcely began to emerge from the enormous mass of documents that he had accumulated.

The text appeared in 1900, with a preface by Gaston Paris. Its success was immediate. France, then affected by acute Wagner mania, suddenly rediscovered the national origins of the legend immortalized all too well by the magician of Bayreuth. However, even if everyone agreed to praise the sovereign prose of Bédier, who became for a time the darling of Parisian literary circles, people quickly wondered how much faith to place in this "reconstruction" which very quickly became a subject of debate. Although Bédier always defended himself in this matter, his roman was quickly assimilated to the famous "archetype" that he reconstructed in the monumental introduction to the two volumes of the edition of Thomas, which did not appear until 1903 and 1905. We cannot enter here into the details of Bédier's argument. We must content ourselves with making clear that all the work—literary and philological—that Bédier accomplished on the legend of Tristan should be understood in the dialogue of three reconstructions: that (philologically solid) of the fragmentary text of Thomas with the aid of versions derived from it, a principal proof of the edition of 1903–5; that (more doubtful and inscribed at the heart of the Bédierist obsession with origins) of the so-called archetypal text from which all known written versions followed; and that (in which philological strictness gave place to more strictly artistic considerations) which was the *Roman* of Bédier himself.

The confrontation of the reconstructed narrative schema of the "archetype" with the table of contents of the *Roman de Tristan et Iseut* shows at once that the two texts do not match up. A detailed examination of the text of Bédier and his sources only confirms, synoptically, the divergences. For example, even if Bédier excluded from the "vulgate" the second half of Béroul's text, he reproduces in his *Roman* all that it is possible to conserve of it without harming the coherence of his narrative. He admitted, moreover, in a late and somewhat popularized work, that his attraction to Béroul was more instinctive than reasoned.[7] I will save for a later essay an analysis of the particulars of a text that has been, with reason but without emphasizing its literary impact, compared to a "restoration" in the sense that Viollet-le-Duc understood this term.[8]

The book, in just twenty years after its appearance, was translated into German (twice), Dutch, Swedish, English, Greek, Czech, Norwegian, Italian, and Catalan. The 576th edition appeared in 1946, and the *Figaro littéraire,* choosing in 1957 the twelve best French love novels of the half century, mentioned favorably the *Roman de Tristan et Iseut.*

At the appearance of his novel, Bédier was for a long time invited to dine every other week in the literary and Dreyfusard salon of the Marquise Arconati-Visconti. Henri de Régnier, Anna de Noailles Jean Jaurès, and many others became the familiars of our philologist. To those who were astonished to see as a Dreyfusard a man otherwise known for his nationalist commitments (we will acknowledge this later), Ferdinand Lot responded that here philology won over the man of duty. Bédier could not believe in the culpability of a man accused by a single piece of evidence, a note (*bordereau*) so crudely forged.

It would be interesting to study more fully the influence of the *Roman de Tristan et Iseut* on people such as Péguy, who held it in very high esteem, or on Denis de Rougemont and, through him, on the entire conception of medieval love that the public has today. It is certain that in French-speaking countries the romance of Bédier remains—naturally next to the opera of Wagner—the obligatory reference for all who evoke the ancient legend. Paradoxically, if Bédier did not rediscover the "vulgate," he has indeed invented a version of the legend that is seen today as *a posteriori* archetypal. It would be easy to show that the literary reconstructions after Bédier (to cite only André Mary, Jean Cocteau, René Louis, Michel Cazenave, and Catherine Hermary-Vieille) owe him an essential, although sometimes unavowed, debt. Let us also not forget that the text of Bédier inspired the great composer Frank Martin to create one of his purest masterpieces, Le vin herbé: "Bédier's text, as I believe no prose could have, served and affected me by its extraordinary sense of rhythm, proportion, and exacting psychological movement."[9]

Bédier himself tried to renew the charm. Here is where a character with a fateful name appears, whom one scarcely knows whether to view suspiciously or fondly: Louis Artus. A cousin of Joseph Bédier by his wife, Artus was as *arriviste* and worldly as his cousin was candid and disinterested. He inspired in Bédier, according to the philologist's son, an attraction in which envy mixed with scorn. A charmer, at ease with everyone, a fine speaker, comfortable in all circles, Artus was, basically, all that Bédier was not. The author of successful plays and of a Catholic novel of questionable interest that Bédier—thanks to family solidarity—held in high esteem, Artus proposed to his cousin, the day after the triumph of the *Roman de Tristan et Iseut,* to turn it into a theater piece. Without great enthusiasm, Bédier agreed.

Although skillful in society, Artus seemed to have the gift of offending possible collaborators, such as Debussy who, without Artus, would have gladly adapted Bédier's romance as an opera. And though Bédier eventually grew weary of Artus's insistence, he never overcame the temptation of the theater. At the very height of World War I, in fact, Bédier adapted an episode of the *Chevalerie Vivien* as a one-act play. With the help of circumstances, *Chevalerie* was a triumph at the Comédie Française. The fact that Bédier's work had been performed on such a prestigious stage is not an absolute sign of the value of the piece. But, even if it was a work of propaganda, *Chevalerie* simultaneously shows a real interest in the theater and a certain sense of dramatic speech in our author.

As for the adaptation of the *Roman de Tristan,* Artus, by sheer patience, finally got it from Bédier in 1928, not without difficulty, as Bédier's letters to Artus show. To give only one example: "My dear Louis, You maintain that your scene of the harp is excellent, and I insist that it is very bad. However, to be agreeable to you, I resign myself to countersign it." Under these conditions, it is not surprising that the play, presented at Nice in the Mediterranean Palace on January 30, 1929, and then at Paris at the Theater Sarah Bernhardt on March 19 of the same year, with incidental music by Paul Ladmirault, the national bard of Brittany, achieved success only with the critics, in spite of the title roles being played by André Brulé and Madeleine Lély. Ferdinand Lot comments on the experience: "The success did not equal the hopes of his friends. The characters of the Middle Ages are too spindly for the modern scene. They would play better in marionette theaters or even in the movies, if one wished to highlight the picturesque element that abounds in *Tristan.*"[10]

But let us return to the years before the war. For his courses of the year 1904–5, Bédier decided to study the cycle of Guillaume d'Orange. Believing in good faith that "all had been said on the question,"[11] he perceived little by little that new hypotheses were possible, that the old certainties were essentially built on prejudices. Thus the course of that year was continued in subsequent years. Notes accumulated along with the need to say that the scholars of the epic had been on the wrong track since the very beginning. Bédier published four large volumes by 1913, and continued to revise them. His research on the *Chanson de Roland* continued even into the 1930s. On the whole, it is scarcely an exaggeration to say that the last thirty years of Bédier's philological work were almost exclusively dedicated to the chanson de geste. *Les légendes épiques* remains, from the scientific point of view, his incontestable masterpiece. Although much weakened today, Bédier's theses have still not entirely collapsed. For more than one text, without excluding other interpretations that often complement them, his theories remain remarkably illuminating.

In many ways *Les légendes épiques* repeats the same refrain as *Les fabliaux* and the *Commentaires* of the Thomas edition (I have not summarized these two works, presuming that they are already known to the reader): where the popular origin was not vouched for, it was just fantasy. Have we indeed remarked at what point Bédier's theories can be compared, at their modest level, to Kant's "Copernican revolution"? Like the philosopher of Königsberg, Bédier left the known, let us call it "immanent reality," to speculate only secondarily about the conditions of existence of this given. In all three cases we end with a radical relativization of old certainties and, in a certain sense, with Bédier's belief in a "primitive author," which could pass for a manifestation of transcendental idealism.

In *Les fabliaux,* the lion's share is assumed by the problem of origins: so assertive, so radical is the destruction of the Indian thesis in the first part, Bédier appeared much more moderate, almost embarrassed, in the essentially synchronic second part. In the *Commentaires* on Thomas, the Celtic origins of the Tristan legend are not denied but put between parentheses, rendered ineffectual to explain the emergence in the twelfth century of the texts we have. In the *Légendes épiques*, Bédier exemplarily demolished the links between precise historic events and epic poems: not the participation of the popular spirit in the elaboration of the chansons de geste but its incapacity to create them in the absence of other factors.

In 1913, finally, publishing again the *Lai de l'ombre* (the first text of which he had edited, in Fribourg in 1890), Bédier added the final stone to the extremely cohesive edifice of his theories. Setting aside the Lachmannian method for its arbitrariness, he expressed the principle of the edition based on the single manuscript.

Thus we can say that all Bédier's efforts in the study of literary origins were to draw the unknown into the known. For him, the historical method was not a vertiginous plunge into the abyss of time, toward an absolute origin where peoples, races, and traditions found their common melting pot—the fantasy of German romantics whom Bédier opposed on this. Nor did he concede anything to them where nationalism was concerned. His long digression, in the *Légendes épiques*, on the harmful influence of German philology on French researchers was part of a very concerted strategy. As he could not deny the historic invasion of Graeco-Latin culture by the ancestral German base, and as Celtic heritage was suspect (for, after all, to go back thus in time, doesn't one move very far from France?), Bédier did not cease to reduce to its strictest minimum the gap that separated the idea of a work from its completed aesthetic realization. His study of the origin is in fact the study of the first author.

The historic vagueness—historic precisely by its very imprecision, which draws in relief the image, at once solid and opaque, of a duration—must disappear in favor of the exact stratification of different texts, which exist as so many streams of continuity from the same source—a source that differs finally from successive versions only by its anteriority, and not by some principle of ontological priority. Bédier, in fact, refused all creative responsibility, essential for others, to historic duration. The writer of genius continually transcends it and anchors his work, not in a living tradition, but in a context he himself creates, or at least whose sense he inflects sufficiently to monopolize it.

Finally, by his atomization of history and by the rigor of his historic method (and the paradox is precisely that it remained historic), Bédier succeeded by strongly calling into question, if not denying, literary determinism. To assume that a model was already perfect is to abolish all literary evolution: progress can express itself negatively only by the degeneration of initial models, or by the punctual appearance of new "works of genius" whose very genius—native and essential by definition—denied in advance any too narrow relation with that which had preceded them.

All successful literary work thus became the more or less distant approach of a formal ideal that transcended history, an ideal that Bédier recognized, according to a very common ethnocentrist logic, in classical French literature. Vinaver's remark on the resemblance between the writing of the author of *Athalie* and Bédier's writing has symbolic value.[12] It was, I believe, this obsessive fear of unity and the ascendency of French thought that can best resolve the paradoxes of a Bédier at once romantic (the notion of "genius") and antiromantic (the savage attack on the supporters of the "Germanic forest"). Beyond the apparent reversal of genetic theories that it replaced, Bédier's system supported the modern myth of the unchanging text.

In addition, World War I gave Bédier the chance to prove his attachment to his country. At the beginning of the war, his wife's cousin, Marcel Prévost, a lieutenant colonel who had free access to the Ministry of War (he was one of Bédier's two sponsors for admission to the Académie Française), asked him if he would put his good knowledge of the enemy's language at the service of France. Bédier hesitated, but his patriotism prevailed: he enlisted among the voluntary stretcher-bearers at the very moment his two sons were to leave for the front. Moreover, his audience at the Collège de France had dispersed, and he could abandon his work there without difficulty.[13] Thus for four years he worked at the Ministry of War and gave us, in the two pamphlets published in 1915, two rather unexpected contributions to the series "Studies and documents on the war" for the Publications Committee, where, surprisingly, we find the entire "Troisième République des Lettres": Lavisse was director, Durkheim secretary, and Bergson, Boutroux, Seignobos, and Lanson were part of the team.

While reproducing the letters found on the German soldiers taken prisoner, Bédier published *Les crimes allemands d'après des témoignages allemands,* a small pamphlet whose success (it was translated throughout Europe) and the polemic that followed it incited him to a second publication: *Comment l'Allemagne essaie de justifier ses crimes.* Clearly the fierce desire for justice that he expressed here must not be confused with impartiality; his hatred of Germany exploded, but the rigorous scholar was able to maintain a balance between his intellect and emotions.

As for the palaeographer, he gave himself to the job wholeheartedly. Bédier used the same methods in this work that he used in his philological tasks: "I have taken care to criticize here with as much meticulousness and scrupulousness as formerly when, during my peacetime work, I discussed the authority of an old chronicle or the authenticity of a charter."[14]

The French high command, enchanted, asked Bédier who, on August 30, 1916, had been appointed deputy mayor of Paris's fifth arrondissment, to write newspaper articles. These articles, published in various newspapers throughout the war, were gathered into a collection under the title *L'effort français* (1921) and were one of the prime reasons for Bédier's election to the Académie Française. Another reason was, of course, the *Roman de Tristan et Iseut,* as seen in the abundant correspondence of Bédier with Maurice Barrès, who, in a letter of 1919, urged him to become the fortieth member. Bédier was elected during the first round on June 4, 1920, and acceded to Edmond Rostand's chair on November 3, 1921. A discreet but faithful and greatly valued member, Bédier was particularly interested in the dictionary and knew how to form solid friendships with, among others, Raymond Poincaré and Georges Duhamel, respectively his predecessor and successor at the head of the Alliance Française.

What is striking in the last twenty years of Joseph Bédier's life (he died in 1938) was his neglect of new areas of research. Until 1913 he had shown an astonishing fecundity and an extraordinary force of renewal. After the war, with the exception of his edition and translation of the *Chastelaine de Vergy* (1927), he merely continued to rework, via successive editions of the *Chanson de Roland*, his technique of textual editing. His great articles in *Romania* against Dom Henri Quentin (1928) and on the old editions of *Roland* (1934) poorly hide the fact that henceforth Bédier's life was linked to the official realm. The Collège de France, which he directed from 1929 until his retirement in 1936, monopolized his time; it was under his administration that the premises of the venerable institution were renovated. Also, thanks to Bédier, Valéry (whom he described in private as a failure, however) was able to teach at the Collège de France.

His travels increased. As early as 1909 and 1913 he had been the official representative of the French government in America "in order to pursue studies on the spread of knowledge of French language and literature," as his first diplomatic orders stated. He returned to the United States again in 1927 and 1937, acquiring among his French colleagues, at a time when great international colloquia were still uncommon, the reputation of a globe-trotter. In the obituary dedicated to him by the journal *Pi Delta Phi* of Stanford University,[15] Bédier, who also taught a semester at the University of California, Berkeley, is hailed as the French philologist who had done the most for the development of medieval studies in America.

The universities and academies of Harvard (Cambridge, Mass.), Gøteborg, Copenhagen, Groningen, Dublin, Bucharest, Marseilles, Christiania, Helsinki, Rome, Louvain (on the occasion of the fifth centenary when Bédier gave a speech that was a vibrant homage to the humanist tradition of Flanders and Wallonia), Chicago, Lund, Boston, Vilnius, Oxford, Coímbra, Warsaw, and Philadelphia honored him successively. Bédier also ascended all the echelons of the Order of the

Legion of Honor: appointed *grand officier* on April 14, 1932, he received the decoration from the hands of the President of the Republic Paul Doumer several hours before the latter was assassinated.

In 1924 Bédier supervised a great *Histoire de la littérature française illustrée* for the publishing house Larousse in collaboration with Paul Hazard. He wrote almost nothing for this work (leaving medieval literature to his disciple Edmond Faral, he significantly wrote the chapter dedicated to Boileau), but marked it by his personality: the section on the Middle Ages is astonishingly important here. Cleverly, Bédier made room for many minor authors whose presence reassured the reader with the idea that great classics keep their reference value forever. So, too, The innovative illustrations that were included in the work are rich and suggestive. To integrate with literature the contemporary plastic arts was to take a step toward cultural history, or what is known today as cultural studies. At first glance, this step does not seem a natural one for Bédier, who had for a long time preferred specialization to synthesis.

In order to argue for a possible evolution, we can invoke his old friendship with Émile Mâle. Recall, moreover, that Mâle's book *L'art religieux du XIII siècle en France* developed a thesis very close to that of the *Legendes épiques* (that French religious art is an original emanation of the twelfth century). Now, in the years that preceded his death, Bédier planned to write a great book entitled *Le premier siècle des lettres françaises*. This work would have spoken not only of the French literature of the twelfth century, but also of the complete social, artistic, and political atmosphere that had surrounded what Bédier would not have hesitated to qualify as the "French miracle" (following the example of the "Greek miracle"). Of such a potentially magnificent synthesis of Bédier's thought, which would have contributed much to a notion still only halfheartedly accepted today (the "renaissance of the twelfth century"), there unfortunately exists not even a fragment of a manuscript.

Were official duties alone responsible for the "recyling" that Bédier devoted himself to in later life? As soon as the war was over, before his election to the Académie Française, he abandoned vast research projects on the twelfth-century lyric, entrusting to his students subjects he apparently held dear, as if the war had broken a spring in him. Ferdinand Lot has indeed noted that Bédier seemed to harden more and more in his positions;[16] and Gustave Cohen saw his master grow almost desperate when he dared question the thesis of the *Légendes épiques* (after having, it is true, ardently supported it in his course at the École Pratique des Hautes Études in 1914). While the first attacks made on the *Légendes épiques* when the first volume appeared had drawn an immediate response from Bédier in the following volumes, the publication in 1913 of *Tristan and Isolt, a Study of the Sources of the Romance* by Gertrude Schoepperle, an attempt to rehabilitate the hypothesis of direct Celtic influence, did not even provoke a review from him. Doubtless the war prevented this; but it was already too late, and the silence that Bédier kept until the end of his life on Tristanian problems is not the least enigma attached to this life of a researcher.

Ferdinand Lot had sufficiently frequented Bédier during his final years that his account of a certain ossification appears plausible. We can, however, reverse the diagnosis by saying that it was perhaps his doubts concerning his method that drove Bédier to abandon his reserve less and less often. Too great a certainty and chronic uncertainty often appear together, and there is still much to say about Bédier's attitude in his final years.

Although a member of the permanent Section of the Conseil Supérieur de l'Instruction Publique since December 14, 1931, Bédier was not spared by the restructuring introduced in 1936 by the Popular Front and had to take his retirement that year, awarded of course all the honors due to his rank. He settled at 10 rue du docteur Lancereaux in Paris. Free of all official activity, he devoted himself again entirely to study. He only had time to finish his last articles on the *Chanson de Roland*; the edition he had planned of the *Lais* of Marie de France never saw the light of day. He died abruptly of a stroke on August 29, 1938. He had suddenly lost consciousness the day before while fishing on the banks of the Galaure, at Grand-Serre, where he was buried in the strictest privacy. The intellectual world paid him unanimous homage.

Not having a personal fortune, Bédier had not made a will. His children shared his books and papers and gave to the Collège de France all the works that were too specialized. Two years later, the Germans, invading Paris, conducted a search at the Collège de France. They were told that the author of the *Crimes allemands* and of the *Légendes épiques* (it is difficult to say which of these was most responsible for his appearance on the black lists) was dead. One last time, Bédier triumphed over his adversaries.

The Grand-Serre had already given his name to a lycée and a public square, and on June 14, 1956, the avenue Joseph-Bédier was inaugurated in Paris. It was not until the 1960s that Bédier's theses, around which controversies were never lacking, began to collapse under the repeated blows of neotraditionalists and the followers of wholesale relativism. We must nevertheless ask ourselves, now that passions have cooled, now that literary criticism clears other paths, and the great certainties of the history of customs give way to the philosophies of nuance and restricted analysis, what remains of Joseph Bédier? To this question we respond: both little and much at the same time.

Little, in that the system of knowledge in which Bédier worked has indeed passed, and those who construct one after him can only consider his work as a stage. All the writings of the war are outmoded also, and of his properly literary work only the *Roman de Tristan et Iseut* may escape oblivion.

Much, however, in that the stage he represented retains a potential that should not be completely rejected. As for the exemplary precision of his analyses and commentaries, they will doubtless remain for a long time models of scrupulousness, elegance, and thoroughness, not to mention style, as a reading of Bédier makes us doubt that his aura is as ephemeral as has been said. Certainly we no longer believe in the transcendent virtue of form, and this is all well and good. Nevertheless, the miracle of the balance of Bédier's oeuvre remains: it had, in its time, been the *ne plus ultra* of what could be expected from a specialist and yet it never sought to discourage the profane, to exaggerate its effects by displaying its related knowledge (Émile Mâle, recommending to Bédier the *Villon* of Italo Siciliano, deplored however the "excess of juvenile erudition" in it) or by using jargon. An exemplary witness who was resolutely faithful to his epoch, a rare example, in spite of his nationalism, of intellectual probity, Bédier declared loudly "One will never make me do for money anything I would not do for literary reasons." He thus remains one of the dominant figures in the history of the French university.

In spite of his pusillanimity and his suspicion of modernity, his very doubt and the temptations he felt in his final years to renounce certain of his theories illustrate the conflict between science and poetry that is the lot of the literary critic and of philology since these disciplines have existed. It is difficult to trace the border between reason and insanity, between objective rigor and interpretative delirium, and Bédier, who wished to situate himself resolutely on the side of clarity and reason, in the great diurnal light of certitude, still remains the symbolist and the secretly tormented author of the *Roman de Tristan et Iseut*. As George Steiner said, "Philology is the quintessential historical science, the key to the *scienza nuova,* because the study of the evolution of language is the study of the human mind itself."[17]

NOTES

1. Ferdinand Lot, *Joseph Bédier* (Geneva: Droz, 1939).

2. Family archives; all specific personal information given in this chapter comes from memories or papers kept by the descendants of Joseph Bédier.

3. Cited by Gustave Cohen, "Joseph Bédier (1864–1938)," *Education nationale* 11, no. 3 (1970): 3.

4. See Gustave Lanson, *Essais de méthode, de critique et d'histoire littéraire* (Paris: Hachette, 1965).

5. Paris: Seuil, 1983.

6. *Revue de France* (July 15, 1931): 13.

7. See "Quinze visages de l'amour: Iseut la blonde, quelques-unes de ses métamorphoses," *Conferencia* 29 (1934): 21–31.

8. See the two articles by E. J. Gallagher, "'Le Roman de Tristan et Iseut': Joseph Bédier rénovateur of Béroul and Thomas," *Tristania* 5, no. 2 (1980): 3–13; and "Une reconstitution à Viollet-le Duc: More on Bédier's 'Roman de Tristan et Iseut,'" *Tristania* 8, no. 1 (1982): 18–28.

9. Frank Martin, *Un compositeur médite sur son art* (Neuchâtel: La Bâconnière, 1977), 36.

10. Lot, 11.

11. "Everything had been said, at least I believed, about the formation of these legends, and their mystery seemed to me to be explained" (*Légendes épiques,* 1:i–ii).

12. "His writing was not made to impress the reader; it was simply beautiful, and it could be mistaken for that of Racine" (E. Vinaver, *À la recherche d'une poétique médiévale* [Paris: Nizet, 1970], 17).

13. See Lot, 27.

14. *Les crimes allemands d'après des témoignages allemands* (Paris: Armand Colin, 1915), 5.

15. W. L. Schwarz, "Hommage à J. Bédier," *Pi Delta Phi* (November 1938): 8.

16. "Thus, he hardened his ideas into a system, he who hated the very word" (Lot, 31).

17. George Steiner, *After Babel: Aspects of Language and Translation* (London: Oxford University Press, 1975), 75 (p. 72 in French edition).

T E N

A Warrior Scholar at the Collège de France: Joseph Bédier

Per Nykrog

TOWARD THE END OF HIS LIFE, Joseph Bédier reviewed the discussions around the chansons de geste that he had provoked some twenty-five years earlier with his own epoch-making work. He found no reason to change any of his theses and promised his old friend and colleague Ferdinand Lot, who was also his most eminent opponent in the matter, that he would "exterminate" him. Lot was undaunted, but also somewhat taken aback by the promise, if one can judge from the fact that he mentions it twice in the small volume he dedicated to the memory of his friend shortly after his death.[1] It did not affect their friendship, however, for Lot knew very well that there was nothing personal in it, that it was not himself, but merely some of his ideas, that Bédier intended to annihilate. Besides, he had known for almost a half century that this was his old friend's style: in all his major works, Bédier takes possession of the field, crushes earlier divergent views with a massive barrage of meticulously gathered facts, and brands them with scorching irony, leaving those who would challenge his ideas thereafter to fight a defensive battle in which they would have to almost excuse themselves for disagreeing with the forceful master. Academic polemics can often be acrimonious, but the peremptory sharpness of Bédier's tone is striking even to modern-day students who are initiating themselves into research history. Wondering about it, one such student asked me a pointed question: why was Bédier so harsh?

To say: well, he was probably like that, is no answer. Bédier was obviously a perfectly healthy and well-adjusted person. At the most, he may have had a certain single-mindedness that at times could be blinding. Lot gives several examples of this[2] and also mentions an anecdotic trait that might suggest another side to the same explanation: "Chaque leçon [at the Collège de France] fut pour lui comme un modèle de composition et de style. Il s'y appliquait comme à une oeuvre d'art. Je l'ai vu dans son cabinet de travail me tendant une rédaction que je trouvais parfaite. 'C'est la neuvième,' me dit-il. Et comme je me récriais, il ajouta en souriant: 'Ce n'est pas la dernière. Je la corrigerai encore deux ou trois fois!'" (12). Admirable as it is, this way of writing tends to radicalize the text and make the writer dig in ever deeper as he rewrites with his own earlier texts as the only input.

However, the following search for a possible answer to the student's question will not be psychological. It will be literary and historical, looking at the author's texts, scholarly and others, in an attempt to grasp the bias that made him see what he saw. Every mind perceives the world through a bias. Believing is seeing.

———————

Two hypotheses present immediately themselves. Considering that Bédier's four major contributions to medieval scholarship are so many efforts to "exterminate" mainly German scholars (or French scholars who had adopted their ideas too readily), it is tempting to see a nationalistic undercurrent in them. These works all date from the period of the passionate French *revanchisme* between 1871 and 1914.

In *Les fabliaux,* Bédier dedicates two-thirds of the text to an all-out blitz against "Orientalism," the doctrine that allegedly dominated all scholarship on the subject and on folktales in general. It is difficult to determine, today, how crushingly universal this doctrine was in 1890—the pages in which Bédier presents its absolute predominance are more rhetorical than concise (part 1, chap. 1, 7). But the full text makes it clear that the villains (the word is not too strong) are Theodor Benfey, Reinhold Koehler, and Felix Liebrecht, none of whom had dealt significantly with the fabliaux. On the French side, the folklorist Emmanuel Cosquin is taken to task for his works on the migration of folktales; Gaston Paris somewhat less so, though he was the one who had most explicitly brought "Orientalist" ideas to bear on the fabliaux.[3]

Bédier's second major achievement were his two monumental works on the Tristan story in French: the freely elaborated "roman" (1900) and the reconstruction of Thomas's text (2 vols., Paris: Société des Anciens Textes Français, 1902–5). Neither is polemical against German scholars in particular, and yet Germany and Germans loom large in the immediate background of these works. Scholars would know that the Tristan story is part of French literature, but the less erudite public at the turn of the century would know it mainly from Wagner's opera (1865, first performed in Paris in 1900, the very year Bédier published his "roman"). And as the twelfth-century French versions are only extant in fragments, even the medievalists who wanted to study the complete story had to read it in the German versions by Gottfried or by Eilhard, or else in the Norse "saga." By a twist of fate, the Tristan story had become a German heirloom; what Bédier did was to reclaim it for France, first with a beautiful piece of uniquely successful vulgarization ("exterminating" Wagner), then with a most singular and unusual—and therefore probably significant—piece of reconstructive scholarship.

In retrospect, Bédier's introduction to his reconstruction of Thomas's lost text appears as a preparatory exercise before the great centerpiece of his life work, the famous four volumes on *Les légendes épiques* (vols. 1–2, Paris: Champion, 1908; 3–4, 1914). They seem to share the same central idea, the rejection of a gradual process of collective creation over several centuries, emphasizing instead the importance of a single and relatively recent (eleventh- or twelfth-century) genius. In the two volumes of 1908, however, Bédier is predominantly preoccupied with his brilliant (and uncontroversial) demonstration of the pilgrim routes and their sanctuaries as the backbone of the epic's production. These volumes would only elicit admiration. His polemic against the romantic idea of the epic as a gradual and collective creation by the anonymous "people" is outlined in the conclusion to the first volume, but cautiously and almost timidly.

Not until 1914, with volume 3, mainly on the *Chanson de Roland,* does that polemic unfold in its full force with a sarcastic overview of the research history. And not until the last half of volume 4, also from 1914, does Bédier openly defy almost the entire medievalist community, past, present, and to come, with his daring and dashing thesis—the one and only idea, or rather fact, as he says, that "dominates" his four volumes (473): "Les chansons de geste sont nés au XIe siècle seulement." He had been explicit about it in a preceding chapter: the chansons de geste are not of Germanic origin. By insisting on the relatively late creation of the genre, the conclusion locates the prestigious French epic at a safe distance from contamination by alien elements, in a period when it could be purely and authentically French: "cette poésie est toute nôtre; elle n'a rien de germanique, elle n'a rien que de français" (475).

Today the four volumes appear as one unit, and rightly so. Yet there are two theses in them, one stating the importance of the pilgrim routes for the extant texts, the other denying any oral tradition before the eleventh century. The second thesis needs the first one, but the first does not need the second. All the polemics against Bédier's doctrine have been directed at his denial of any oral tradition before the eleventh century: the importance of the pilgrim routes for the extant texts has hardly been challenged. The dates for the four volumes are perhaps irrelevant; Bédier may very well, as he says, have arrived gradually and cautiously at his definitive and controversial stance. But they might also be relevant. Pursuing the hypothesis of Germanophobia as a possible driving force behind Bédier's scholarship, one may find it significant that his most radical challenge to the German idea of a Germanic origin of the medieval French epic should have been published in the heady climate immediately before the outbreak of World War I.

This suspicion would have sounded more improbable had it not been for Bédier's activities during the war. As soon as the fighting had started, he abandoned academia and devoted all his talents to the war effort.[4] One of the first results was a one-act play, performed in February 1915, transparently picturing Vivien and his cousins as forebears of the young heroes of the present.[5] I will return to that text later. Another result was a small volume, carried by its tone of justified indignation, about the war crimes (as we would say today) committed by the advancing German armies against the civilians of Belgium and northern France in 1914. His documentation was as meticulous as in his peacetime scholarship: a collection of letters and diary notes found on German soldiers or printed in German newspapers, reproduced in German and French, in eighteen cases substantiated by facsimiles of the originals.[6]

> Most of the documents tell similar stories: as reprisal for an incident that occurred near a village, civilians are routinely massacred *by the scores or by the hundreds,* women, children, and old men; the village is plundered and burned down. In one case, three hundred civilians were shot and the women forced to bury them (18f): "they were

quite a sight, the women!" (*Das war ein Anblick der Weiber!*) In the next village, the same story: "burning, women, and all" (*Feuer, Weiber, und Alles*). In some cases men were thrown into the burning houses (10f); elsewhere civilians were used as a human shield pushed before a German advance (19f). It was not a matter of isolated aberrations: General von Bülow and Marchal von der Goltz offically approved orders to massacre large numbers of civilians (14). On August 26, General Stenger issued this order to his troops: "From today on, no more prisoners will be taken. All prisoners will be cut down (*niedergemacht*). Wounded, with weapons or unarmed, will be cut down. Prisoners that are also in major closed formation will be cut down. Let no enemy be left alive behind us" (29f, 39f). A German newspaper describes "a day of honor for our regiment" where this is put into practice (by another unit): they had been fired upon by Frenchmen sitting in the trees; they shot them down "like squirrels" and killed the wounded, some mercifully with bullets, others with bayonets, others by bashing their heads with rifle butts, "wisely using the Frenchmen's rifles so as not to damage their own." (31ff)

The following year Bédier continued with another small volume refuting a German newspaper that had tried to discredit his reports.[7] One can only praise this scholarly contribution to the national war effort. Yet the fact remains that few, if any, other scholars acted as radically as Bédier did. His emotional involvement with militant nationalism appears to have been particularly intense and active.

Some four years later, in 1918, he finished a substantial book extolling the virtues and exploits of the French armies.[8] The armistice intervened, so the book was not ready for publication until after the war had ended. Again, as a project, it must be considered a praiseworthy enterprise, especially by a man with two sons facing death and destruction at the front. Nevertheless, it is disturbing reading. The modern reader will be conditioned by the image of the unspeakable horrors of reciprocal mass murder perpetrated in trench warfare, as it has often been recounted since then by survivors. So Bédier's submissive respect for everything he sees or learns from the French military command, and his unconditional enthusiasm for the "beauty" and "greatness" of this monstrosity, cause one to shudder. Recalling that the book was published when there was no longer any need to boost wartime morale, the rare readers who find their way into it today perhaps cannot help feeling a deep uneasiness, as I did, over the elation Bédier expressed in his praise for that "Great War."

Did Bédier feel that way, too? Did he feel estranged from the world that emerged once the war was over and the emotional *engagement* in it was gone? Ferdinand Lot wonders, sympathetically, about the fact that this energetic scholar, who in twenty years had changed the landscape of French medieval studies (the expression is mine), did not produce any major work after the end of the war, in fact, after 1914.[9] Bédier published his classic edition, with translation, of the Oxford manuscript (1921), which he later completed with a volume of commentaries (1927). But these works, especially the edition, would not have had the immense prestige they enjoyed had it not been for their author's earlier achievements, in particular the *Légendes épiques*.

True, the definitive work in the fourth field on which Bédier left his mark, his epoch-making considerations on editing medieval texts, was published in 1928.[10] But, like the edition of the Oxford manuscript, it is, so to speak, an afterthought, an expansion of an earlier work: an edition of Jean Renart's lay had been part of his doctoral thesis (1890), and a second edition, for the Société des Anciens Textes Français had been published in 1913. The "surprising law" that is at the center of the 1928 article had been discovered in 1912 and presented in 1913. The law states, in substance, that three-prong stemmata (which oblige the editor to follow the two families against the one) appear only in review articles criticizing the work of an editor; text editors will always arrive at a two-pronged stemma for the manuscript filiation (thereby safeguarding their free choice of reading). Considering that it is impossible to reconstruct a reliable medieval text, the sound principle is to edit one good manuscript, with a minimum of emendation.

In question here is the so-called Lachmannian method of text editing, and so there is some "extermination" of German scholarship in this article: the method was German in origin, and German scholars had pushed the use of invasive editing to extraordinary heights.[11] But the irony of the "surprising law" is that it is mainly directed against French scholars, and its discovery was obviously inspired by Gaston Paris's review of Bédier's 1890 edition (*Romania 19* [1890]).

This observation invites one to place that discussion in the dossier for my second preliminary hypothesis: that Bédier's scholarship might be aimed at "exterminating," not so much German-type scholarship per se, as its most eminent representative in France, Gaston Paris. Indeed, Ferdinand Lot explicitly rejects the idea that Bédier could have been driven by nationalistic chauvinism: "Après comme avant la

Guerre, il reçut avec bienveillance les étudiants de nations ennemies. Il avait conservé d'excellents souvenirs de ses maîtres allemands: il dédia un des volumes des *Légendes épiqùes* à Hermann Suchier. Bédier n'était pas, ne pouvait pas être 'nationaliste.' Le 'nationalisme' est outrancier, donc incorrect et inélégant." (43).

It is true that Suchier was of French ancestry and spoke French at home. It is also true that Lot would not have written what he did, had Bédier not been suspected of a nationalistic bias. But Lot's characterization is indeed borne out by the remarkable fact that even in his book about the French war effort, Bédier never writes about the Germans with anything like hatred. The expressions he uses show that he conceived of them as equal, noble, and respected adversaries, not as odious demons and goblins.

If my first hypothesis, Germanophobia, does injustice to Bédier's noble character, my second one is even worse. But let us consider it for a moment, even if it is only to turn it on its head a moment later. All of his four great contributions to medieval scholarship "exterminate" ideas and teachings that had been dear to Gaston Paris; his *Légendes épiques* in particular relegated Gaston Paris's most cherished ideas on what he called *l'épopée nationale* to the ashcans of research history.[12] Could it be that one may detect, as a hidden driving force behind them, a filial desire to exorcise a father figure that dominated him? The hypothesis of nationalism could be supported by reference to the political climate of the times; a psychologizing one could be supported by the fact that those same times have provided many examples, explicit or implicit, of strong and ambivalent feelings in the younger generation toward their parents, biological or spiritual.[13]

Insulting as it is to Bédier's memory, the idea could be argued: a patricidal son can very well experience an intense love for the father figure he wants to "exterminate." Of course Lot does not even mention such a thought, and indeed there is absolutely no reason to doubt the sincerity of Bédier's often expressed feelings of gratitude and filial affection toward his great master, who admitted him into his intimacy when he was a student, whom he succeeded in the chair at the Collège de France, and whose memory he ensured by compiling a complete bibliography of his works.[14]

However, the first part of Bédier's inaugural lecture emphasizes, with three successive quotations, an idea that Gaston Paris had cherished as a fundamental principle. But it is an idea that seems to characterize Bédier's own style as a scholar (in particular the "harshness" discussed here) more than that of his gentle and generously all-embracing teacher:

> Je professe absolument et sans réserve cette doctrine que la science n'a d'autre objet que la vérité, et la vérité pour elle-même, sans aucun souci des conséquences bonnes ou mauvaises, regrettables ou heureuses, que cette vérité pourrait avoir dans la pratique.

And:

> Il faut, avant tout, disait-il, aimer la vérité, vouloir la connaître, croire en elle, travailler, si on peut, à la découvrir. Il faut savoir la regarder en face, et se jurer de ne jamais la fausser, l'atténuer ou l'exagérer, même en vue d'un intérêt qui semblerait plus haut qu'elle, car il ne saurait y en avoir de plus haut, et du moment où on la trahit, fût-ce dans le secret de son coeur, on subit une diminution intime qui, si légère qu'elle soit, se fait bientôt sentir dans toute l'activité morale. Il n'est donné qu'à un petit nombre d'hommes d'accroître son empire; il est donné à tous de se soumettre à ses lois. Soyez sûrs que la discipline qu'elle imposera à vos esprits se fera bientôt sentir à vos consciences et à vos esprits. L'homme qui a, jusque dans les plus petites choses, l'horreur de la tromperie et même de la dissimulation est par là éloigné de la plupart des vices et préparé à toutes les vertus.[15]

Taking a cue from these declarations (and others like it), I suggest a third and final hypothesis that turns the second one completely around: far from desiring, "unconsciously," to destroy Gaston Paris, Bédier desired, and most consciously, to *emulate* him and to be a worthy successor to him in the prestigious chair at the Collège de France. Gaston Paris had been epoch-making in the history of French medieval studies, giving them vast perspectives and a place they had never had before in the awareness of educated Frenchmen. He had modernized these studies and at the same time contributed to the modernization of humanistic research and higher education in France in general. In order to be worthy of him, his successor would have to do, in and for his time, what the old master had done in and for his.

———————

Gaston Paris (1839–1903) was what the French call an *enfant de la balle*: he had grown up surrounded by what was to become his métier. His father, Paulin Paris (1800–1881), belonged to the generation of pioneers in medieval French studies, together with men like Francisque Michel (1809–87), who published the Oxford manuscript of the *Roland* (1837), and Achille Jubinal (1810–75). But though Paulin Paris eventually became a professor at the Collège de France, he had little confidence in the French educational system and so sent his son to study in Germany, more precisely in Bonn (1856). On his return to France the following year, Gaston Paris brought with him considerable professional inspiration—though he had not, as has been often said, gone there to study with Friedrich Diez, the founder of modern Romance philology.[16] What he had mainly learned was what higher education could and should be.

In 1894, discussing a recent book by a young and fiery Ferdinand Lot,[17] Gaston Paris disapproved strongly of Lot's vehemence of expression (so Lot had been somewhat of a hotspur himself in his youth!), but he countersigned, in fact, most of the opinions that Lot had expressed. The book reminded him of his own homecoming thirty-five years before; at that time he had become an "angry young man" himself:

> Nous nous trouvâmes bientôt quelques-uns à avoir fait la même douloureuse expérience, et nous commençâmes à mener contre le haut enseignement universitaire une vive campagne, dans laquelle nous eûmes pour illustre auxiliaire le grand penseur et le grand savant que la France a perdu l'an dernier [i.e., Renan]. Pendant plusieurs années, nous sonnâmes avec confiance de la trompette autour des murailles de Jéricho.[18]

The situation they found in France was that higher education and research in the humanities were only conducted very modestly at the École Normale Supérieure and at the Collège de France. There were no "universities," only *des facultés*, which served mainly to give out diplomas for examinations passed after "studies" that added little to what the students had learned at the secondary level. All the criticism leveled against the system in the second half of the nineteenth century—and it was abundant—targets "la détestable organisation de tous nos examens de lettres" (21), which seems to have been something comparable to our day's "theory" preparation for the driver's license: memorizing answers to more or less predictable questions. Readers of nineteenth-century novels will be familiar with these "studies" (e.g., from Balzac or from Flaubert's *Education sentimentale*), but that insight is blurred by the fact that these young characters more often than not are very bad students, who fail. The point is that the good students probably studied the same way.

> La philosophie terminée et le baccalauréat passé, on quitte le lycée, à dix-huit ans en moyenne, et on s'imagine qu'on a une instruction générale suffisante et qu'on n'a plus qu'à se donner que la préparation spéciale à une "carrière". En fait, on ne sait rien et on est capable de parler sur tout; on n'a pas appris à travailler et on ne sent pas le besoin de s'instruire. (24)

An early result of the youthful revolt was the founding of the École Pratique des Hautes Études (1868), but as late as 1894, when Lot and Gaston Paris wrote, they both knew that "foreigners are struck by the ignorance of those who in France are supposed to have received a higher education" (G. Paris, 22):

> La faiblesse de notre enseignement supérieur [in the humanities] est incontestable si nous le comparons à celui de presque tous les pays de l'Europe, non seulement l'Allemagne, mais [. . .] des pays scandinaves, de la Hollande, de la Suisse, et même, au moins dans une certaine mesure, de la Belgique, de l'Italie et de la Russie. Cette faiblesse se marque essentiellement par les traits suivants: petit nombre des professeurs, petit nombre des leçons faites, petit nombre des étudiants, sujets peu scientifiques des cours, manière peu originale et peu instructive de les traiter. M. Lot s'occupe avec plus ou moins de détails de chacun de ces points.[19]

It is true that there was the Sorbonne, the old Faculty of Theology that had been abolished under the Revolution and reopened as a Faculty of Letters and Sciences under Napoleon. It had had a number of major names among its professors (A. F. Villemain under the Restoration, Victor Cousin under the July monarchy), but in medieval studies, the typical situation of the few scholars engaged in active research had been that they worked from an archive or a library, or as "gentlemen of independent means." This gave them a particular style that was inherited by Gaston Paris: he was an almost obsessively hard worker, but testimony about him as well as pictures show a princely, elegant man of the world who seemed to feel as close to poets as to scholars.[20]

In sharp contrast to this, the numerous nineteenth-century German scholars lived and worked in a highly developed and well-funded milieu, favored by the political powers and enjoying prestige among the population at large. The glorious story of the German universities during the nineteenth century has been told in many books.[21] Their rise to glory had sprung from the seminal reforms spearheaded by Wilhelm von Humboldt around 1810, as a key element in the national German revival against the predominance of Napoleon's France: they were created and maintained as the intellectual backbone of the nation. To be *Akademiker* (and so be able to put "Dr." before one's name) was to be part of a new and modern aristocracy, that of science, *Wissenschaft,* and the *Professoren* were the princes of that aristocracy. Hence the remarkable and sustained production of front-line research inspired by ambitious and far-reaching visions that poured out of the nineteenth-century German seats of learning.

When Paulin Paris sent his son to spend a year in Bonn in the mid-1850s, French Germanophilia was at its height: it was the romantic Germany as Madame de Staël had pictured it, a people of philosophers, musicians, and poets—but also of scientists and philologists.[22] So it was only to be expected that Gaston Paris, when he started his career in France, looked to Germany for ideas and inspiration for his studies in a wide variety of humanistic disciplines. It was simply there that ideas were to be found, for both his studies and his initiatives to modernize and strengthen higher education in France.[23]

All that changed, perhaps not in substance, but certainly in tone and attitude, after the defeat in 1870–71. Flaubert notes the transition in two sharp entries in his *Dictionnaire des idées reçues,* obviously completed after 1871:[24]

> *Allemagne:* Toujours précédé de blonde, rêveuse.—Mais quelle organisation militaire!
> *Allemands:* Peuple de rêveurs (*vieux*). Ce n'est pas étonnant qu'ils nous aient battus, nous n'étions pas prêts!

In the last decades of the century, the current toward reform of the French educational system became a tidal wave, and all the reformers, from the petulant young Ferdinand Lot to Gaston Paris to Ernest Lavisse, proclaimed the need to imitate the German example—now as the cornerstone of a national effort at rebuilding France into a strong, modern, and effective nation, and to win back the position of leadership in Europe it had lost to Kaiser Wilhelm's newly established Reich by decades of insouciance.[25]

This rush to imitate the German universities (which, incidentally, went into a certain decline under the invasive imperial administration)[26] was not limited to France: the entire western world (with the possible exception of Britain) imported German principles for use in educational reform. In the United States, these reforms were essentially the introduction of the Ph.D. degree (Yale, 1861) and of graduate schools (Johns Hopkins, 1876),[27] Harvard opened its Graduate School of Arts and Sciences in 1889, but as late as 1970, I heard both of these basics of modern academia denounced by conservative-minded Harvard professors as newfangled German ideas.

The figure of Gaston Paris in the best years of his full maturity should be seen in this historical context. He had tried to bring about a total reform of higher education in France, but had basically given up on that front. Instead he transformed the chair at the Collège de France that he had taken over from his father into a tribune from which he single-handedly spread the word about how modern scholarship sees and works with problems from linguistics, philology, literature, medieval history, and folklore.

He must have had an overwhelming capacity for work. His knowledge was almost encyclopedic, which, in medieval literature is even more impressive than it looks because many of the texts he discussed were unpublished and he had to read them in manuscript. He did not publish major monographs; his favorite medium was articles in learned journals (of which he founded several, most prominently *Romania*), often review articles, which demonstrate his untiring curiosity for and openness to new ideas: that he had gone public with different views himself did not keep him from entering sympathetically into those he came to discuss as a reviewer.

Gaston Paris was an innovator; if not exactly a modernist, he was at least a modernizer in his teachings (if seen against the background of his times) and mainly as a public figure. In the second half of the century, the Middle Ages à la Victor Hugo had become obsolete; instead a new far richer Middle Ages, had come out of the research of scholars, on the basis of primary texts and detailed knowledge. Gaston Paris brought the medieval past to the attention of a larger public and gave it national status and importance.[28]

But he was also a man whose sensibility had been formed by the Romantics: Herder, Grimm, Fauriel, Michelet. Personal taste—aesthetics—is a key factor in all research, determining the choice of field, the choice of method, the choice of subjects, and thereby the type of results the research obtaines. The subjects that appealed to Gaston Paris, emotionally or aesthetically, were those that could nourish a certain mystique, that allowed him to contemplate unknown and unattainable depths of the past, to dream of the endeavors of a bygone anonymous humanity, especially those that would demonstrate to him the creativity of *le Peuple*. That word was taken in its most exalted, positive sense: the creation of the Romance languages from Latin; folktales, myths, legends, and their surprising migrations; and, above all, the great works of art such as the chansons de geste that together constitute the People's "poetic history of Charlemagne." He did not value Chrétien de Troyes very highly; he could respect his art of writing, but in the pages he has devoted to him in his survey works, one clearly senses his regret for the authentically popular and presumably beautiful tales in oral tradition that have been thrown into oblivion by the prestige of the civilized, all too civilized, courtly romancer.[29]

Joseph Bédier was seven years old when the unified Germany under Kaiser Wilhelm was proclaimed from the Galerie des Glaces in Versailles. Nevertheless, his early career seems to have followed the pattern of the previous generation, including studies in Germany. The major difference, of course, was that he could study in a partly modernized system of French higher education, in particular that he could study with Gaston Paris, and thereby start his scholarly career from the point the master had reached at the end of his.

But behind all the facts that a biographer will gather when going over Bédier's life and scholarly works, there lies hidden a trait that may be more significant: his conception and understanding of what it meant to become a professor at the Collège de France in 1904. Gaston Paris had clearly understood that function as a national mission, but that was before the crucial date of 1871. The proclamation of the German Empire from the very building that symbolized France's glorious past was a traumatic event for French national feelings, adding insult to the injury of the defeat. In particular it had a decisive impact on the situation of French education. The effect is comparable to the jolt that Sputnik gave to American educational policies some ninety years later, only it was many times stronger: it triggered a broad and powerful movement for a national "rearmament" *of the schools*. The patriotic debates that followed the *débâcle* of 1870–71 called for a military rearmament, of course, but they also paid ample attention to the urgent need for accelerated educational reform at all levels:

> Aux Universités, les jeunes Français prendront les connaissances nécessaires à chacun d'eux pour exercer avec compétence et dignité la profession qu'il aura choisie; mais ils apprendront aussi que ces connaissances ne sont que le fragment d'un tout, et qu'au-dessus d'elles il y a des idées générales auxquelles il faut s'élever pour penser par soi-même et librement. . . .

Ils apprendront qu'ils ont des devoirs envers la patrie, le devoir militaire d'abord, puis le devoir civique. Ils apprendront que leur patrie est un être vivant, qui ne peut vivre que par eux comme elle a vécu par leurs pères, qu'elle sera ce qu'ils voudront qu'elle soit, ce qu'ils seront eux-mêmes, faible s'ils sont faibles, forte s'ils sont forts; qu'elle cesserait d'être s'ils venaient à l'abandonner; et qu'au contraire elle continuera dans le monde sa mission de justice, de liberté et d'humanité, s'ils ont eux-mêmes la claire conscience de cette destinée et les énergies nécessaires pour en assurer le développement.[30]

Did Bédier subscribe to these ideas and make them part of his self-understanding as a scholar and professor? Ferdinand Lot's comments seem to indicate that he had a very exalted idea of the Collège de France and its mission in the world.[31] But it is in other texts, more removed from his actual scholarship, that I find the most striking indication of how Bédier saw himself and his academic function, when these texts are read in the light of his scholarly practice as it can be seen in all his major works. In 1928 he spoke in Louvain on the occasion of that university's fifth centenary, and four years later he spoke to the scholars assembled to celebrate the fourth centenary of the Collège de France (see above, n. 2). In both texts he used the same sentence, with only slight modifications: in the Louvain discourse (20) as the final effect, in the later Parisian allocution (6), as an opening theme. In Louvain, he said:

> *En tout pays de noble culture, les forces contrastées, mais solidaires, des Universités sont les composantes de cette force une et indivisible que l'on appelle la patrie, et il y paraît chaque fois que la mère commune a besoin de tous ses fils.* Vous l'avez bien éprouvé quand on vit, aux jours récents, les diverses familles spirituelles de votre nation se ranger et s'ordonner toutes comme une belle chevalerie autour du Roi-Chevalier, fières de lui et dignes de lui.[32] (emphasis added)

Gaston Paris loved and respected his profession as a scholar and teacher, and he loved no less dearly the *épopée nationale*. But I very much doubt that he would ever, even in a flight of poeticizing rhetoric, have likened himself and his fellow professors to the twelve peers around Charlemagne, or to the knights of the Round Table, as Bédier seems to do in these two speeches. Is the almost verbatim repetition at four years' distance to be seen as economy of invention? I don't think so: Bédier was hardly short on words. It seems much more likely that these two similar sentences express an idea that was essential and precious to him.

When the war broke out in 1914, the first thing he did was, as mentioned, write a one-act play, *Chevalerie*.[33] It was performed at the Théâtre Français on February 18, 1915, and it must have been written under the immediate impression of the battle of the Marne (early September). It stages *le Covenant Vivien:* Vivien and his young cousins are preparing themselves to receive knighthood, and for that solemn occasion Guillaume d'Orange is returning, battle weary, from the "front" against the Saracens together with his two brothers. But old Aymeri de Narbonne refuses to let the boys join the fighting out there—he orders them to go to Gaifier in Spoleto, where they can live for some years in peaceful luxury: so many of their lineage have died in the war that he wants these three to enjoy life a little longer. The youngsters revolt in anger: they want to join the battle right away, and swear the fatal oath that they will never retreat before the enemy. Their fathers and uncles are horrified, but old Aymeri is pleased with their proud "covenant": he had merely wanted to test their mettle. And the three boys are knighted under a fanfare of "the trumpets of war." Curtain.

It must be legitimate to see this as a metaphor not only for the suicidal fervor of the young cadets from St-Cyr[34] but also for the idea behind Bédier's own resolution to leave the peaceful realm of scholarship and join the war effort as an "expert" in the Ministry of War.[35] I make note of this, not as a judgment of character, but as a source of insight into a "mentality" that springs not from psychology but from ideas (to the extent these two can ever be separated). Bédier's sentence, repeated in the two discourses, and his radical act in 1914 point in the same direction; they seem to reveal a Bédier who most seriously saw himself as a modern-day crusader knight.

And that is what I finally have to suggest as the key to the peculiar style of Bédier as a scholar: he understood himself as a Roland, a "chevalier sans peur et sans reproche," and he saw his major endeavors in scholarship as feats of arms.

The case is curious, for he does not seem to have been a right-winger, nor a militarist except in wartime. He had been close to Jaurès and a Dreyfusard: "the Affair" had been for him a noble battle that needed to be fought—Ferdinand Lot states that quite explicitly (42). What was, then, his cause? Again I will return to Lot, who knew him well: he characterizes him as essentially *français*—not a nationalist, but "French" in his entire being. The few snippets he gives as illustrations of what he means by that (39ff) tally neatly with the broader, but insightful and concise, picture Theodore Zeldin has given of "the national identity" of the Frenchman as it was seen under the Third Republic.[36]

Two characteristics stand out strongly in Lot's character portrait of Bédier: his "Cartesianism" and his strict conformity to established values in style and conduct—especially his strict fidelity to the traditional norms for the French language: "Lui, qui déclare ne rien comprendre à la philosophie, a la tête la plus 'cartésienne' que j'aie connue. Il n'accepte rien, absolument rien, même de Gaston Paris, dont il n'ait personnellement scruté l'argumentation" (18).

This will not surprise those who are familiar with Bédier's research and writings. The other trait may seem more surprising:

> Le Cartésien qui, dans le domaine de la critique littéraire ne veut rien admettre qu'il n'ait repensé lui-même, dans le courant de la vie est le "conformisme" incarné. Rien de la vie, de la vie française ne peut, ne doit être soumis au doute méthodique. Les choses sont ce qu'elles sont. Il est mal d'aller à l'encontre. . . .
>
> C'est à se demander si certaines lacunes de ses connaissances ne sont pas une manifestation de conformisme. Il sait mal la géographie, lui grand voyageur, et il semble en être fier. N'est-ce pas parce qu'il imagine—en quoi il se trompe—que le vrai Français l'ignore?
>
> De là aussi son aversion pour les lettres étrangères, en dehors des grandes oeuvres qu'il possédait naturellement à merveille. Il les juge funestes à l'esprit français, surtout les romans russes.[37] (39)

In the true French tradition of the nineteenth century, France, to be France, has to be the center and guiding light of civilization in the world, by the strength of French energy (*furia francese*) and the intellectual clarity that is the distinctive hallmark of its culture. For a while, French minds had let themselves be charmed by alien influences from the *brumes du Nord,* from the German "people of dreamers." Now France has fallen from the leader's position that is naturally hers; in order to regenerate the nation and give it back that position and its true identity, its sons would have to reinstate the traditionally French values in their purity: the traditional French forcefulness, and the critical spirit of French Cartesianism, sharp, clean, and unadulterated, the intellectual clarity that had distinguished its greatness in the past.

It would be the historical mission of Bédier's generation to clean out the house of ideas and free it from the *funestes* mistakes caused by imported alien obscurantism. The first *idolon libri* Bédier took on and "exterminated" was romantic, but not medieval: Chateaubriand's claim to fabulous traveling in America; he meticulously proved it to be plain humbug.[38] The second was the hazy idea of an influence from the Orient on French narrative tradition, coupled with the claim that grossly indecent stories from the thirteenth century could have anything to do with the noble traditions of French literature. "Orientalism" was ridiculed, and the fabliaux themselves branded with the withering epithet "bourgeois," which effectively expurgated them from the canon of French literature—culturally inferior, *uncivilized*. The third and fourth of his victims were noble ideas about great French tales and legends grown out of primitive and messy oral traditions, postulated but undocumentable and not even really French. As Bédier saw them, *Tristan* and the epics were the creation of sharp and orderly *French* geniuses who had constructed their plots as lucidly as Racine constructed his. The fifth scholarly mirage "exterminated" was that of artificially reconstructed texts presented as more authentic than any authentically medieval text.

"Ce qui n'est plus ne fut jamais," said Bédier one day to Ferdinand Lot (30 note). Lot was too much of a historian to accept that: he knew how large a part of reality has not left any tangible documents. One must assume that Bédier knew that, too, and that his statement was a paradox, meant to be shocking. It will be legitimate to understand it as a declaration of methodological principle, of strict "Cartesian" aesthetics in matters of research: the reconstructions of the past that I, Joseph Bédier, elaborate in my research allow no murkiness, no hazy dreams of what might have been, they admit only what is beyond dispute; therefore I will treat as nonexistent anything that I do not find clearly documented, and I will refuse to give it any place in my mental constructs. Gaston Paris would probably have agreed with the principle: he, too, rejected fakes and counterfeits that had been the delight of earlier generations, such as *Ossian* and the *Chant de l'Altobiscar;* yet in practice his aesthetics admitted as values large blocs of ideas that Bédier, according to his, had to reject as illusions.

The great Spanish medievalist Ramon Menendez Pidal was of the same generation as Bédier, five years younger than he, three years younger than Lot, but he survived them both by far. In 1959, at ninety-three years of age, but with youthful vigor, he rehabilitated Gaston Paris's "traditionalism" (with modifications) against Bédier's "Cartesian" skepticism, with a barrage of no less "Cartesian," though indirect, proofs of the existence of an oral tradition about

Roland and Roncevaux, from 800 to 1100: "El silencio de los siglos consiste, por una gran parte, en las forzadas negaciones de la hipercrítica tendenciosa y, por otra gran parte, en la deficiencia de la indagación."[39]

Even the most exacting "Cartesian" cannot escape the human condition. "Vous êtes embarqué," as Pascal says: not to bet is also to bet; to reject is also to pronounce and one who does not believe runs the risk of not seeing.

NOTES

1. Ferdinand Lot, *Joseph Bédier 1864–1938* (Paris: Droz, 1939), 14 and 32.

2. Lot mentions that Bédier never understood that his view of the Collège de France was without foundation in reality (13); regrets that Bédier polemicized against the *Volksgeist* at a time when no one took that concept seriously anymore (23); and notes that Bédier was unable to perceive any weaknesses in his own doctrines (31).

Add to this dossier a disquieting blunder that this exacting scholar has made twice, under solemn circumstances. As representative of the Académie Française at the celebration of the fifth centenary of the University of Louvain (1928), and again as administrator of the Collège de France addressing the delegated scholars celebrating the fourth centenary of that venerable institution (1932), Bédier spoke in praise of intellectual exchange: "Croyer, a dit Rabelais, que divine chose est prester; debvoir, vertu héroïque." One must hope that the learned audiences on the two occasions did not check the quotation against *Le Tiers Livre*, chapters 3–6. *Pour le 5e Centenaire de l'Université de Louvain* (Abbeville: Les Amis d'Édouard, 1928), and *Pour la science—Discours prononcés à l'occasion de 4e Centenaire du Collège de France,* Études françaises 28 (Paris: Belles Lettres, 1932).

3. Especially in *Les contes orientaux dans la littérature française du Moyen Âge,* a lecture published in *Revue politique et littéraire* 43 (1875). He deals mainly with the *Disciplina clericalis* as a source for French storytelling, seeing this, at first, as an amusing paradox. In later books he mentions an Indian origin for a type of fabliaux as an established fact, see, for example, his *Esquisse historique de la littérature française du Moyen Âge* (Paris: Armand Colin, 1907), §105f.

4. "Pendant plus de quatre années, il s'enferma au Ministère de la Guerre, mettant à la disposition de l'État-Major sa connaissance de l'allemand" (Lot, 27).

5. See below, n. 28.

6. *Les crimes allemands d'après des témoignages allemands* (Paris: A. Colin, 1915), 40 pp. Translations into several languages were all published simultaneously by the same Parisian publisher.

7. *Comment l'Allemagne essaye de justifier ses crimes* (Paris: A. Colin, 1915).

8. *L'effort français: Quelques aspects de la guerre* (Paris: Renaissance du Livre, 1919).

9. Lot, 27–30. Lot was of the same generation as Bédier (1866–1952), but he had by no means ceased producing in 1938. His main works, mostly on French history ca. 500–ca. 1000, were published between 1920 and 1950, culminating in the summa of his life work, the two volumes of *La Gaule* (1947) and *Naissance de la France* (1948, rev. ed. 1970).

10. *La tradition manuscrite du "Lai de l'ombre": Réflexions sur l'art d'éditer les anciens textes, Romania* 54 (1928).

11. For example, *Die Lais de Marie de France,* ed. Karl Warnke (Halle: M. Niemeyer, 1885, 3d ed. 1924), which rewrites the lays in the "correct" Anglo-Norman dialect of Marie's times. Note that Bédier's own reconstruction of Thomas's *Tristan* text on the basis of two foreign adaptations was at least as optimistic, his outline of the totally lost, hypothetical "archetype" (*Le Roman de Tristan* 2:194–306) even more so.

12. His only book, *Histoire poétique de Charlemagne* (1865) had been the bible for the study of the chansons de geste until Bédier. After *Les légendes épiques* it became obsolete.

13. The outstanding example is of course Freud's formulations of the "Oedipus complex," which may contain a general truth, but which more specifically reflects, I suspect, a particular social and cultural state, limited in time and space.

14. *Hommage à Gaston Paris: Leçon d'ouverture . . . prononcée au Collège de France le 3 février 1904* (Paris: Champion, 1904), and Joseph Bédier and Mario Roques, *Bibiographie des travaux de Gaston Paris* (Paris: E. Bouillon, 1904).

15. *Hommage,* 13f, quoting declarations from 1871 and 1897.

My colleague R. Howard Bloch has studied the correspondence between the two men and quotes to me, as *advocatus hominis,* examples of their mutual declarations of affection. Thus: "At one time when Paris seemed offended, Bédier writes back that he would rather have committed an error of science than of tact, and wishes at all costs to avoid offense." In my temporary role as *advocatus diaboli,* I find this interesting: knowing Gaston Paris, Bédier could expect that his master would refuse such sentimental protection at the expense of "truth."

16. The misunderstanding stems partly from the dedication to Diez of Gaston Paris's first major publication, *Étude sur le rôle de l'accent latin dans la langue française* (Paris-Leipzig, A. Franck, A. L. Herold, 1862). See Kristoffer Nyrop, *Gaston Paris,* Studier fra Sprog og Oldtidsforskning 68 (Copenhagen: Tillge, 1906) (in Danish). On the basis of Gaston Paris's letters from Bonn, the initiator of Romance studies in Denmark, himself a student of Gaston Paris, analyzes the year in Bonn: the young Gaston Paris studied mainly German; from Diez he took only a (boring) course in *Gerusalemme liberata* (83, note). But the master did help him out personally in a moment of practical difficulties.

17. *L'enseignement supérieur en France, ce qu'il est, ce qu'il devrait être* (Paris: Welter, 1892).

18. Gaston Paris, *Le haut enseignment historique et philologique en France* (Paris: Welter, 1894), 10.

19. Ibid., 20. Lot had shocked Gaston Paris by stating the point more brutally: "C'est un fait bien connu qu'un Français comparé à un Suisse ou un Allemand du même âge, de même condition sociale, d'intelligence égale, est véritablement un âne bâté" (Lot, 93).

20. "Princely" is Nyrop's expression (64): erect, carrying his head high, with a monocle in his left eye. It was functional: his right eye was blind, damaged by a boy's arrow in his early years, and he lived in constant fear of losing his eyesight in the other eye, too (58). A tragic detail: a few years later Nyrop lost his eyesight himself, and he lived the last twenty-five years of his life blind.

21. See, e.g., Thomas Ellwein, *Die deutsche Universitäte vom Mittelalter bis zur Gegenwart* (Königstein: Athenuaum, 1985); Laetitia Boehm and Reiner A. Müller, eds., *Universitäten und Hochschulen in Deutschland, Österreich und der Schweiz: Eine Universitätsgeschichte in Einzeldarstellung* (Düsseldorf: Econ., 1983); Charles E. McClelland, *State, Society, and University in Germany, 1700–1914* (Cambridge: Cambridge University Press, 1980); and David Fallon: *The German University: A Heroic Ideal in Conflict with the Modern World* (Boulder: Colorado Associated University Press, 1980).

22. On the French ideas about Germany, see Claude Digeon, *La crise allemande de la pensée française 1870–1914* (Paris: Presses Universitaires de France, 1959); J. M. Carré, *Les écrivains français et le mirage allemand 1880–1940* (Paris: Boivin, 1947); and the excellent condensed survey in Theodore Zeldin, *France 1848–1945,* vol. 2 (Oxford: Clarendon, 1977), 113–26. See in particular *Ernest Renan et l'Allemagne,* texts selected by Emile Buré (New York: Brentano's, 1945). See also Martin Thom, *Tribes*

within Nations: The Ancient Germans and the History of Modern France, in Homi K. Bhabha, ed., *Nation and Narration* (London: Routledge, 1990), 23–43, especially the section on Fustel de Coulanges, Durkheim, and Renan. The article is preceded by a translation of Renan's *What Is a Nation?*

23. Note that this has a bearing on the two hypotheses suggested and rejected at the beginning of this essay: if Bédier polemicized against German ideas and thereby implicitly against his own master, it may simply have been that there were hardly any ideas around in medieval studies that were not of German origin.

24. Quoted after Flaubert, *Bouvard et Pécuchet,* ed. Jacques Suffel (Paris: Garnier-Flammarion, 1966). Older editions do not give the final sentences from which I quote these entries here.

25. See, e.g., George Weisz, *The Emergence of Modern Universities in France 1863–1914* (Princeton: Princeton University Press, 1983); Jacques Verger, ed., *Histoire des universités en France* (Toulouse: Privat, 1986); Antoine Prost, *Histoire de l'enseignement en France 1800–1967* (Paris: A. Colin, 1968, 1970); and the detailed summary in Zeldin, 316–45.

26. See, e.g., Edward Shils, ed. and trans., *Max Weber on Universities: The Power of the State and the Dignity of the Academic Calling in Imperial Germany,* in *Minerva* 11, no. 4 (1973), Midway Reprint (Chicago: University of Chicago Press, 1976); Kurt Aland, ed., *Glanz und Niedergang der deutschen Universität: 50 Jahre deutscher Wissenschaftsgeschichte in Briefen an und von Hans Lietzman (1892–1942)* (Berlin-New York: De Gruyter, 1979).

27. See Richard Hofstadter and Wilson Smith, eds., *American Higher Education: A Documentary History,* vol. 2 (Chicago: University of Chicago Press, 1961); brief mention of D. Fallon on 51f.

28. It should be said that even in this respect, he followed the lead of the German Romanticists, who had done the same to their medieval past more than half a century earlier.

Nor should the importance of his lectures be exaggerated; witness the sigh he heaves in a long note in his *Le haut enseignement en France,* 35. He tells how, recently, he opened a lecture before some twenty students, but realized that they were all foreigners: *there was not a single Frenchman!* He left the auditorium deeply upset, but controlled himself and returned to complete his lectures. Since then, he says, he has decided to feel satisfied if there are just a few Frenchman who listen to him. Several of my colleagues, he adds, have had the same experience. The situation had not changed decisively in the times of Bédier; see n. 27 above.

29. See, e.g., *Esquisse historique de la littérature française du Moyen Âge . . .* (Paris: A. Colin, 1907), § 97.

30. Louis Liard, *Universités et facultés* (Paris: A. Colin, 1890), 158. Cf. also Ernest Renan, *La réforme intellectuelle et morale,* 3d ed. 1872 (Cambridge: Cambridge University Press, 1950).

31. "Cet établissement est l'honneur de l'Europe," m'a-t-il répété. Je n'ai eu garde de le contredire, pour ne pas le contrister. En réalité, cet établissement suranné souffre d'une plaie mortelle, l'absence d'étudiants français réguliers. D'ailleurs, la transformation perpetuelle des chaires rend impossible la continuité scientifique" (*Joseph Bédier,* 13).

32. The Paris version reads: "La diversité de tous ces corps savants, leur enchevêtrement, leur émulation, sont autant de richesses nécessaires à l'honneur du nom français. *En tous pays de noble culture, les forces contrastées, mais solidaires, des maisons de science sont les composantes de cette force une et indivisible qui s'appelle la Patrie, et il y paraît chaque fois que la mère commune a besoin de tous ses fils.* Il y paraît en ces jours où elle vous charge, Messieurs, de saluer nos anciens."

33. *Chevalerie* par Joseph Bédier, de l'Académie française; illustrations de Job (Tours: A. Mame et fils, 1931). It seems to be an edition for children. Note the late publication date.

34. The legend has it that they attacked the German line "with cold steel" in full-dress uniform and were mowed down in droves with machine gun fire. In *L'effort français,* Bédier commemorates the valor of the officers in the early days of the fighting; in many regiments they were almost all killed. But their example galvanized their soldiers: "grâce à eux, ils retrouvaient, intact, fidèlement gardé, leur propre patrimoine, le dépôt des vertus guerrières de leur race, et c'est pourquoi . . . tous d'un même coeur y allèrent, aussi purs que leurs anciens, les hommes d'armes de la Pucelle" (24f).

35. See above, n. 4. Lot adds, in a note: "Il m'a dit récemment que son rôle fut surtout de remonter le moral des gens employés au Ministère de la Guerre!"

36. *France 1848–1945;* see above, n. 22, vol. 2, chap. 1. But also in most of the following chapters: 4, on education; 5, on logic and verbalism; 8, on good and bad taste, and 9, on conformity.

37. Eugene Vinaver also writes at length about this respect for conformity and decorum, in his *Hommage à Bédier* (Manchester: Editions du Calame, 1942), 6–8.

38. *Chateaubriand en Amérique: Vérité et fiction,* in *Études critiques* (Paris: A. Colin, 1903), 125–294.

39. *La Chanson de Roland y el neotradicionalismo: Origenes de la épica románica* (Madrid: Espasa-Calpe, 1959), 253. French trans., *La Chanson de Roland et la tradition épique des Francs* (Paris: Picard, 1960). Earlier in the text, he had talked about Bédier's "sorprendente arrogancia en el tono entre profetico y conminatorio" in the conclusion of *Les légendes épiques* (14).

ELEVEN

Making Mimesis: Erich Auerbach and the Institutions of Medieval Studies

Seth Lerer

Nun ist der Unterschied zwischen Sage und Geschichte für einen etwas
erfahrenen Leser in den meisten Fällen leicht zu entdecken. So schwer es
ist, und so sorgfältiger historisch-philologischer Ausbildung es bedarf, um
innerhalb eines geschichtlichen Berichts das Wahre vom Gefälschten oder
einseitig Beleuchteten zu unterscheiden, so leicht ist es im allgemeinen,
Sage und Geschichte überhaubt auseinanderzuhalten. . . . Geschichte zu
schreiben ist so schwierig, daß die meisten Geschichtsschreiber genötigt sind,
Konzessionen an die Sagentechnik zu machen.   —Auerbach, *Mimesis*

La philologie est l'ensemble des activités qui s'occupent méthodiquement
du langage de l'homme, et des oeuvres d'art composées dans ce
langage. . . . Le besoin de constituer des textes authentiques se fait sentir
quand un peuple d'une haute civilisation prend conscience de cette
civilisation, et qu'il veut préserver des ravages du temps les oeuvres qui
constituent son patrimoine spirituel.

READERS OF ERICH AUERBACH'S *Mimesis* will remember
the first of these epigraphs as a moment in which history and legend
fuse to mark the making of his book.[1] The famous story of Odysseus's

---

This chapter was originally written in the spring of 1992. Portions of it appear, with
some modifications, as the introduction and the chapter "Philology and Collaboration:
The Case of Adam and Eve," in Seth Lerer, ed., *Literary History and the Challenge of
Philogy: The Legacy of Erich Auerbach* (Stanford: Stanford University Press, 1996).

scar has just been recollected, with its close attention to the detail of its characters and setting; and the story of the sacrifice of Isaac has been retold as a foil for the Homeric style, where the narratives of the Old Testament give us but little of the setting and motivations of its actors. Auerbach, in his opening chapter, has been distinguishing between the legendary flavor of Homer and the historical feel of the Elohist, when he announces that such a distinction "can be easily perceived by a reasonably experienced reader" (19). But what may not be so apparent, and what stands in the ellipses of my epigraph, is the history behind the making of *Mimesis* itself, and the ways in which that history has been transformed—by Auerbach, by later readers, and by the institutions of professional literary study—into a legend of the writer in exile, remembering the texts and contexts of a past.

What interrupts the reading of Odysseus's scar, and what interrupts Auerbach's own career, is "the history which we our- selves are witnessing." "Anyone who, for example evaluates the behavior of individual men and groups of men at the time of the rise of National Socialism in Germany, or the behavior of individual people and states before and during the last war, will feel how difficult it is to represent historical themes in general, and how unfit they are for legend" (19–20).[2] With the complexity of mo- tives, the bluntness of propaganda, and the ambiguities of political discourse, a simple understanding of these public events becomes nearly unimaginable. No "careful historical and philological train- ing" can distinguish true from false, *das Wahre vom Gefälschten,* in these matters. "To write history," he concludes, "is so difficult that most historians are forced to make concessions to the technique of legend" (20).

It is such moments in *Mimesis* that contribute to our understand- ing of the legacy of Erich Auerbach and that help construct his place in histories of criticism.[3] They separate him poignantly from his contemporaries, Leo Spitzer and Ernst Robert Curtius. All three are often grouped together as the great exponents of a German philologi- cal tradition; yet Spitzer is today largely remembered for his im- passioned, if idiosyncratic, teaching at Johns Hopkins and his acute application of techniques of *explication de texte* to medieval and Renaissance works, while Curtius remains, except to specialists in *Romanistik,* the distant compiler of the topoi that fill *European Literature and the Latin Middle Ages.*[4] It is the personal, the self- reflective, in Auerbach that late-twentieth-century readers treasure, as if what marked the *magisterium* of his work was the very suffering that brought him from Marburg, to Istanbul, to Pennsylvania State, and finally to Yale where he died as Sterling Professor of Romance Languages in 1957.[5]

The second epigraph is probably less well known to us. As the opening sentences to an introductory handbook of Romance philology, a handbook written originally for the Turkish students of Auerbach's exile, they seem, at first glance, to articulate the verities of a tradition rather than the idioms of an individual. Their definition of philology, the importance they place on textual criticism, and their loose associations between method and cultural understanding would have been familiar to most any European student at midcentury. With over a hundred years of institutional history behind them, Auerbach's opening lines affirm the centrality of philological investigation to recovering the character of "high civilization" and its origins.[6] They call to mind such affirmations of the "social value" of philology as those of Friedrich Dietz in 1821 (that the serious study of literature "reveals utterly characteristic directions and tendencies in the mind of man");[7] of Charles Aubertin in 1874 ("L'histoire des origines de la langue est l'histoire même des origines de la nation");[8] and of the many late-nineteenth- and early-twentieth-century French and German attempts to locate the search for national identity in the curricula of language study.[9]

These opening texts, most likely written in the same year, stand as the two poles of Auerbach's career and may introduce a reassessment of his project as a whole and of his reputation in the academic study of medieval literature. Both center on the techniques of recovery; both juxtapose a potentially destructive time against the endurances of culture; and both valorize the power of the philological-historical to distinguish true from false, the originary from the secondary, the authentic from the ersatz. They stimulate our efforts to separate the historical from the legendary in the scholar's work and may become, for such a purpose, subjects of textual inquiry themselves.

Much recent work has focused on the national origins and ideological consequences of the development of philology: on the tensions between French and German Romanists from the 1820s to World War I, on the agendas of post–World War II American New Criticism and the German revival of the *Grundriß* project, and on the changing status of medieval studies in the canons of professional training.[10] Some gestures have been made toward situating Auerbach in these various constellations, largely drawing on the more explicitly theoretical of his writings (the opening chapter of the early *Dante als Dichter des irdischen Welt* [1929] and the late essays "Philologie der Weltliteratur" [1952] and "Epilegomena zu Mimesis" [1953]).[11] Relatively little has been made, however, of Auerbach's critical practice in these contexts, that is, how it responds to, enacts, and influences the institutions of medieval studies.

By reading closely in one exemplary chapter from *Mimesis*—its seventh, "Adam and Eve"—this study seeks to turn Auerbach on himself. Its argument will be that the techniques of figural interpretation he develops for the study of medieval literature are encoded in his own narrative of the processes of textual criticism, historical recovery, and the writing of literary history. By reading Auerbach's own writing allegorically or figurally, I hope to make visible the powerful, political subtext behind his quarrel with a French editor and his reinterpretation of the quarrel between a French Eve and Adam. "Adam and Eve" has many purposes: an education in the arts of scholarly edition, an allegory of collaboration, a plea for the constructive ends of national philology. By chronicling the early reception of *Mimesis* in Germany and America, and in particular by illustrating the embracing of his reading of the medieval French drama together with the apparent rejection of his editorial arguments, I hope to show how the political subtext of this book has been carefully effaced by critics wishing to place Auerbach in a newly depoliticized medieval studies. The unique history that made *Mimesis* needs to be seen again, not only in the explicit self-references that charge the volume with its poignancy, but in the figurations of its philological interpretations and its allegories of power.

---

so daß ich auf fast alle Zeitschriften, auf die meisten neueren Untersuchungen, ja zuweilen selbst auf eine zuverlässige kritische Ausgabe meiner Texte verzichten mußte.

[I had to dispense with almost all periodicals, with almost all the more recent investigations, and in some cases with reliable critical editions of my texts.]

—Mimesis, 497

"Adam and Eve" begins by trying to establish a text. The opening quotation for this chapter—the dialogue in which Adam and Eve first quarrel, then debate, then fall—comes from a play "extant in a single manuscript" (145–46). Of the little that survives of the vernacular, liturgically oriented drama, the *Mystère d'Adam* is "one of the oldest specimens" (146). Unique and originary, marking both the starting point of a distinctive genre and of a vernacular literary history, the play's text stands here at the opening of "Adam and Eve" in ways far different from the quotations that begin *Mimesis*'s other chapters. It appears not as some randomly selected, exemplary section of a larger work; nor is it one of those "few passages" that, in the phrasing of the book's close, "can be made to yield more, and more decisive, information about [authors] and their times than would a systematic and chronological treatment of their lives and works" (548).

This is a passage carefully selected for its individualities and not its commonplaces. It tells a story of a set of firsts: the first human communication, first sin, first desire, and first text of a tradition that articulates the sublime in colloquial form. It is a story of a loss; yet, in the larger context of *Mimesis*, it provides the occasion for recovery. This passage from the *Mystère d'Adam* enables Auerbach to deploy those few resources of *Zeitschriften* and *Untersuchungen* in his Turkish exile. It enables him to use the techniques of philology to recreate "reliable critical editions" of his texts, and in the process, to restore methodological control over the study of the European Middle Ages.

Because the *Mystère d'Adam* and its manuscript encompass the discussion of first things, Auerbach seems anxious from the start to find its correct and originary form. Textual and literary criticism intertwine themselves here as in no other chapter of Mimesis, for the crux of Auerbach's interpretation turns on the correct edition of the manuscript. Adam and Eve speak in what Auerbach defines as the familiar idioms of French life. The first man "calls his wife to account as a French farmer or burgher might have done when, upon returning home, he saw something he did not like," while the first woman responds with "the sort of question which has been asked a thousand times in similar situations by naive, impetuous people who are governed by their instincts: 'How do you know?'" (147). The correct assignment of the dialogue is central to Auerbach's reading, not so much because it governs the play's action but because it helps articulate its characters. The opening paragraphs of the chapter have, in fact, already sketched out the broad contours of those characters: Adam, good, noble, a representative of the French citizenry; Eve, intuitive, childish, even clumsy in her wiles. The text of the *Mystère*—garbled by medieval scribe and confused by modern editor—must be brought into line with the essentials of these characters, their idiom, their motivations, and their sensibilities.

In his *Introduction aux études de philologie romane,* Auerbach sets out the methods of the editor, delineating the procedures for establishing a text beset by problems in transmission.

> Quant aux lacunes et aux passages irrémédiablement corrompus, il peut essayer d'en reconstituer le texte par des conjectures, c'est-à-dire par sa propre hypothèse sur la forme originale du passage en question; bien entendu, il faut indiquer, dans ce cas, qu'il s'agit de sa propre reconstitution du texte, et il faut y ajouter encore les conjectures que d'autres ont faites pour le même passage, s'il y en a. On voit que l'édition critique est, en général, plus facile à faire s'il y a peu de manuscrits ou seulement un manuscrit unique; dans ce dernier cas, on n'a qu'à le faire imprimer, avec une exactitude scrupuleuse, et à y ajouter, le cas échéant, des conjectures. (12)

This moment in the *Mystère d'Adam* offers a test case for this advice. The manuscript is, as Auerbach states, "somewhat confused" (148; ein wenig in Unordnung, 145). His goal will be to restore "la forme originale du passage en question," a task seemingly "facile" when faced with this "manuscrit unique." But there is little "facile" about the editing of this text. The distributions of these lines has been confused by S. Étienne who, in a note published in *Romania* in 1922, proposed a new reading of the lines.[12]

Adam:	Ne creire ja le traitor!
	Il est traitre, bien le sai.
Eva:	Et tu comment?
Adam:	Car l'esaiai!
Eva:	De ço que chalt me del veer?
	Il te fera changer saver.
Adam:	Nel fera pas, car nel crerai
	De nule rien tant que l'asai.
	Nel laisser mais . . . (280–87; Auerbach's edition)

Adam:	Ne creire ja le traitor!
	Il est traitre.
Eva:	Bien le sai.
Adam:	E tu comment?
Eva:	Car le'asaiai.
	De ço que chalt me del veer?
Adam:	Il te ferra changer saver.
Eva:	Nel fera pas, car nel crerai

              De nule rien tant que l'asai.
Adam: Nel laisser mais . . . (280–87; Étienne's edition)

This is, to Auerbach, clearly no "propre reconstitution du texte" but a complete misunderstanding; from a manuscript only "somewhat confused," Étienne constructs a reading now "completely confused" ("völlig durcheinandergemischt"). The problem with the manuscript lay in the assignation of the parts, signaled by the scribe with a capital *A* and *E* for the respective speakers. Now, in Étienne's note, this particular passage "ont embarrassé la critique." It is "très curieux," presenting a problem in what Étienne calls the psychological continuity of the speakers.[13] What seems clear to him is that the scribe has mangled the assignment of the lines, shifting radically the tone of Adam and Eve. Étienne's goal, therefore, is to rescue the text from its copyist's mistakes; in Auerbach's terms, defined in the first page of the *Introduction aux études de philologie romane,* "les sauver non seulement de l'oubli, mais aussi de changements, mutilations et additions que l'usage populaire ou l'insouciance des copistes y apportent nécessairement" (9).

For Auerbach, however, there is no "insouciance des copistes" in the text of the *Mystère d'Adam.* Rather, it is Étienne who misconstrues both the characters and the themes of the drama. Eve, in Étienne's edition, is far too knowing for Auerbach, far too skillful and self-assured. The emendation presents a dynamic of seduction and control, where the Serpent's intercession simply augments Eve's advance. To Auerbach, though, it is the Serpent who masterminds the Fall. Eve is clumsy (*ungeschikt*), "for without the Devil's special help she is but a weak—though curious and hence sinful—creature, far inferior to her husband and clearly guided by him" (149). Adam, the good French citizen ("ein braver Mann, ein französischer Burger oder Bauer" 147), must be approached "where he is weak," must be confused into compliance. After the Devil's intercession, Eve can take control; only after taking counsel from the Serpent can she master the situation. "The Devil has taught her how to get the better of her man; he has showed her where her strength is greater than his: in unconsidered action, in her lack of any innate moral sense, so that she transgresses the restriction with the foolhardiness of a child as soon as the man loses his hold (*sa discipline*) upon her" (150–51).

Eve's character, for Auerbach, remains stable, even though her actions shift in form and direction. Before and after her encounter with the Serpent she is childish, impetuous. Her earlier question was akin to that of "kindlichen, sprunghaften, instinktgebundenen Menschen"; here she has the "Tollkuhnheit des Unmundigen," the rashness of the underaged. By contrast, Adam is always adult, always the head of the household. His fall, in these terms, is the fall of the grown-up trapped by games of the child. The pathos of his situation lies in this vision of a "poor confused, uprooted Adam" with whom Eve plays (*spielt*). She eats, as if to goad him into playing—"und dann ist es geschehen," and then all is over and the game is won (English, 151; German, 148).

Auerbach offers this analysis as a case study of the way in which the Christian drama of redemption gives voice to sublime ideas in simple form. The juxtaposings of the learned and the popular, the Latin and the Old French, illustrate how vernacular literary experience becomes the vehicle for moral truth. The profundity of the Fall resounds in a scene of "everyday reality," a dialogue "in simple, low style." Its pathos and its power look back to those moments in the sermo humilis of Augustine while they anticipate the Tuscan idioms of Dante. The possibilities for figural interpretation—here as in nearly all the medieval texts Auerbach handles—lie precisely in this nexus of the high and low. God, the *figura* of the *Mystère d'Adam,* is both judge and savior, legal officer and spiritual father. He embodies the capacity of medieval literature to use historical or biblical personae to prefigure spiritual forms while holding both distinct as historical "realities." The simple surfaces of medieval Christian drama simultaneously shadow and reveal the underlying patterns of Creation, Incarnation, Passion, and Last Judgment that define what Auerbach identifies as "the very truth of the figural structure of universal history" (158).

> The everyday and real is thus an essential element of medieval Christian art and especially of the Christian drama. In contrast to the feudal literature of the courtly romance, which leads away from the reality of the life of its class into a world of heroic fable and adventure (*Sage und . . . Abenteuer*), here there is a movement in the opposite direction, from distant legend and its figural interpretation into everyday contemporary reality (*aus der fernen Legende und ihrer figurlichen Ausdeutung in die alltäglich-zeitgenossische*). (English, 159; German, 155)

But what precisely is this everyday contemporary reality for Auerbach? As he reminds us at the close of *Mimesis,* it is a scholar's life without the tools of scholarship: the journals, studies, and editions of the philological profession. As he announces at the opening, it is an exile's life without a nation, a moment when political and military action so challenges relations between truth and falsehood that "most historians are forced to make concessions to the techniques of legend" (*Konzessionen an die Sagentechnik zu machen*).

These similarities of phrasing blur the line between the philological and the political. Read in tandem, they point toward the construction of a scholarly *figura* of their own, a recognition that debates on the establishment of texts may adumbrate the arguments of nations. The high and low are not just styles of literature but styles of scholarship as well. The place of the sublime in the colloquial becomes an issue not just for the story of the Fall but for the narrative of its edition. To paraphrase the reading of the drama, we might say that "Adam and Eve" moves from distant readings and their scholarly interpretations into the language of everyday contemporary reality.

Throughout the chapter, technical analyses are couched in the colloquial expressions of feeling. Arrestingly informal, the conversational gambit that opens the discussion of the play disarms the reader: "Now let us examine" (147). But we are really asked, in Auerbach's *Betrachten wir nun* (144), to reflect and meditate, to move in that realm of impression and response that early German reviewers of *Mimesis* found characteristic of its *Feingefühl*, its almost belletristic sensitivity.[14] Auerbach asks us to share his imagination of the everyday. The ordinariness of his French Adam is translated into language full of idiom and commonplace. Eve's question, we are told, is asked a thousand times.

We are, in his translations and his paraphrases, on familiar turf here, much as we are in Auerbach's own analysis. "I find this impossible" (148; *Mir scheint es unmöglich*, 145), he rejoinds to Étienne's emendation. Exclamations, rhetorical questions, appeals to common sense—these are the argumentative devices of this scholar. "I know from experience": this might as well be Auerbach's as well as Adam's line. Indeed, it might as well be that of the reader of *Mimesis*, for what the scholar is relying on here is not so much a refined ability with ancient languages but simple clearheaded observation. Experience is what is at the heart of "Adam and Eve," an experience of how people react, of how men speak to women, and of how the stories from the past can resonate with present lives. Eve is, after the serpent's tuition, "Herrin der Lage" (147), idiomatically master of the situation. She is "to use the language of sport . . . in great form" (150; *wie man in der Sportsprache sagt, in großer Form*, 148), and as she plays (*spielt*) with her confused husband, we can see the transformation not only of the Fall into a game but of the discipline of textual edition into sportsmanship.

For it is Auerbach himself who is *in großer Form* here, Auerbach who deploys all the clichés of *his* everyday reality to offer up a *sermo humilis* of philological control whose simple, low style may conceal the subtleties of criticism. The quarrel with Étienne replays the quarrel of his Eve and Adam: a quarrel about what we know, about the control of *sa discipline,* about what might be thought of as the spiritual patrimony of high civilization. There is an allegory to the philological. Textual recovery becomes a kind of restitution, and these pages in *Mimesis* work out, in practical form, the directives of the *Introduction aux études de philologie romane.* Philology saves texts not only from oblivion but from the changes, mutilations, and additions that popular usage or the carelessness of copyists necessarily brings to them.

The emendation of Étienne, and its acceptance and reprinting in the published text of Chamard, presents a fallen text to Auerbach. Its misassignments of the dialogue place Eve over her husband, rewrite in effect the challenge of serpentine guile in the subversions of the first couple. Eve may play here, may be in the fine form of the competitor, may be the master of the situation; yet it must remain for Auerbach to show *his* form, to reaffirm the competitive edge of textual criticism to become the master of the interpretive situation. Auerbach, in short, replays a competition between French and German critics and philologists charged with the politics of the academy.

The story of Romance philology is a distinctively German story, as the discipline arose "in a period in which German intellectuals were accustomed to taking the French to task as effete (*Welsche*)."[15] The origins of *Romanistik* worked in tandem with the origins of European nation-states, and a good deal of the institutional support for literary studies hinged on the recovery of a cultural patrimony for the emerging political entities. The character of literature and the character of a people came to stand as elements in an equation whose solution was a national identity conceived through educational structures. Philology, to paraphrase von Clausewitz, became a form of politics by other means; indeed, it could become a form of war by other means.

The French responses to the "German science" often couched themselves in military terms. Léon Gautier could write of his defeated countrymen in 1870: "We find before us a nation which makes war scientifically. . . . For the Prussian fights in the same way he criticizes a text, with the same precision and method."[16] And in 1913 Henry Massis could complain that "there is a clear, logical link between our system of classical studies and the capitulation of Metz, as, of course, between the methodology of German universities and the invasion of Paris."[17] The rise of chairs of literature in France, the establishment of journals dedicated to medieval culture (*Romania* being among the first), all contributed to what Gaston Paris could think of as a medieval literature emanating from French soil: *plantes indigènes.*[18]

What was Auerbach to make of all this? He had been compelled, as a Jew, to leave his appointment at Marburg, the very university town where, Gautier had complained nearly seventy years before, "there were more Germans working on the chanson de geste than were French scholars in all of France."[19] For Auerbach, the anxieties of exile go beyond the mere lament for journals, up-to-date investigations, and reliable editions. They embrace something of the taint of having been a part of the ongoing war with France and French philology. The quarrel with Étienne, thus on the surface, seems to recapitulate these national philology wars, seems to revile the scholar in *Romania* for constructing an interpretation of the *Mystère d'Adam* that is *Welsche,* even feminized in its imaginations of a controlled and controlling Eve. But only on the surface. Rather than reinvest in the rhetoric of military conquest, Auerbach recasts his quarrel with philology and, in turn, his reading of the play as a story of collaboration. In reading his analysis of Eve, we find not the "invasion of Paris" but the infiltration of the French countryside. We find her assault on her husband—called, almost pathetically now, "ein braver Mann, ein französischer Burger oder Bauer"—worked not by the machinery of all-out war but in the machinations of betrayal.

Eve's claims, in her discussion with her husband, always rely on appeals to the here and now. She wishes for their betterment, speaks of experience in its most commonplace terms, and queries Adam on his understanding of the hard facts of life. Hers is the language of betrayal, and much of Auerbach's discussion hinges on Eve's failure to appreciate the line between her realistic questioning and her real betrayal. *Verrat, Verräter,* and *verraten:* these are the words that predominate in Auerbach's German. For Adam himself, the idiom is always that of being led astray: *verführen* is the operational verb, as Satan becomes the *Verführer* of the cause. The heart of Auerbach's objection to Étienne's reading is that Eve cannot be the "extremely skillful and diplomatic person" generated by his emendation. Diplomacy is far from Auerbach's concerns here. Eve's discussions with the serpent, and her temptation of Adam, do not go on in the realm of skill or political savvy. They transpire in the worlds of instinct, impression, and a blithe unawareness of the historical (if not the spiritual) consequences of her acts.

The picture of the Fall drawn here fits neatly in the terms of another, exiled essayist of collaboration. In his "Qu'est-ce qu'un collaborateur?" published first in New York in August 1945, Jean-Paul Sartre defines the logic of collaboration as the logic of realism.[20] Satre's paradigmatic collaborator succumbs to the "tentations de la défaite," the temptations not just of defeat but of defeatism. What he identifies as the "réalisme" of collaborationist thought devolves into a sense of the fait accompli, a sense that what is about to happen has already happened. "Réalisme," he writes, is the "refus de l'universel et de la loi" (60). It signals a confusion between judgment and experience. Instead of judging facts in the light of the law, the realist collaborator judges the law in the light of facts. He evidences an odd sort of passivity; indeed, he is not necessarily a *he* at all. There is a certain "féminité" about collaboration, not simply a docility in the face of facts but a participation in the subversion of natural laws and hierarchies.

Femininity might be thought of here as a figure for the fait accompli itself, and this is precisely how Auerbach defines the serpent's swaying of Eve in her Edenic collaboration. His counsel to the woman "upsets the order of things established by God, . . . makes the woman the man's master, and so leads both to ruin" (149): "The serpent accomplishes this by advising Eve to break off the theoretical discussion [of sin and treason] and to confront Adam with a wholly unexpected *fait accompli*." Adam's knowledge of the law, his sense of right now inextricably a part of his condition as a good Frenchman, finds its subversions in the claims of Eve. "Manjue, Adam," eat Adam, she implores, until she eats the fruit herself "and it is all over."

Auerbach tells the story of the Fall as the figural narrative of collaboration for specific pedagogical as well as political goals. It is not so much that he wishes to condemn Eve as much as he wants to save Adam. Again and again, the "character" of Adam is affirmed as good, noble, and French. This sense of character is what bridges the political and the philological, Étienne's misunderstanding of the characters of the *Mystère* now may be seen as standing for that larger misinterpretation of the French themselves and of the national characters of all the European peoples. What is "vollig durcheinandergemischt" ("completely confused") is the notion of responsibility in the face of political challenge. How do we evaluate, as Auerbach had put it in "Odysseus's Scar," "the behavior of individual men and groups of men at the time of the rise of National Socialism in Germany" (19)? To whom do we assign blame? What is the relationship between the national character and the individuals who live and act within, and sometimes for, those nations?

Such questions find their answers in the course of Auerbach's whole chapter, a sequence of brief assessments and long quotations designed to illustrate the humble and sublime in the religious literatures of the thirteenth century. From the *Mystère d'Adam*, we traverse the works of Bernard of Clairvaux, St. Francis of Assisi, and a range of early French and Italian dramas. Unlike the other chapters of Mimesis, in which ancillary texts appear as foils for the declared subject—the Old Testament to Homer, Proust to Virginia Woolf— here we seem to lose sight of the focus. The reader moves through a variety of European Latin and vernacular texts, from anonymous plays in unique manuscripts to named, canonical authors writing at their most authoritative. What remains a constant in this panoply is the editor. Each text, no matter how exemplary or marginal, receives its full citation. Editors are acknowledged: Förster-Koschwitz, Ferdinand Brunot, H. Boehmer, P. Eduardus Alenconiensis, E. Monaci. The volumes build, each with their comprehensive titles of the past half century of learning: *Übungsbuch, Histoire, Analekten, Crestomazia*. German, French, Latin, and Italian stand side by side, as Auerbach recreates on these pages the European resources he had abandoned. Now, in this chapter and only in this chapter, do we get the range of *Zeitschriften, Untersuchungen,* and *zuverlässige-kritische Ausgabe* whose loss he had lamented at *Mimesis*'s end.

"Adam and Eve" recites a literary history not in the narratives of the textbook but in the selections of the anthology. It compiles a chrestomathy in miniature, a selection whose illustrative texts may complement the story told in the *Introduction aux études de philologie romane*. As in that work, the *telos* of "Adam and Eve" is the restoration of a "patrimoine spirituel" for high civilization, or, as he puts it in the final paragraph of the chapter, "the character of the people" (173; *das Charakter des Volkes* 168). "Adam and Eve" thus answers questions about national character and individual motivation not by meditating on politics but by doing philology. By offering a miniature anthology of European texts, it recovers and sets out in clear order a moral conscience for a medieval and a modern Europe. By locating the *Charakter des Volkes* in the idioms of the vernacular, it illustrates the power of philology to find the ethic that inheres in nations.

Finally, by couching this discussion in the old debates between the national philologies, it realigns relations between literary origins and political types. Auerbach does more than seek to reclaim Romance philology from the French; he seeks to reclaim it from the Germans. He seeks a politically pacifist philology, one that restores the possibilities of language study and literary criticism to a humanist agenda. He is not depoliticizing scholarship, as later critics hoped to do. Rather, he repoliticizes it. The allegory of collaboration behind the *Mystère d'Adam* and its interpretation, by the chapter's end, takes as its moral the belief in the inherent goodness of the European peoples. We need not blame the good French like Adam, only the childish, instinct-governed, impetuous French like Eve, who would succumb to the temptations of a satanic *Verführer.*

"Sed inimici hominis domestici eius" ("but a man's enemies are the men of his own house"). These are Bernard of Clairvaux's words, quoted in this chapter, as a guide against "the prickings of temptation" (163). And when St. Francis of Assisi speaks, he gives voice to the very theme and method of the whole of Auerbach's enterprise. Developing the observation that the bulk of the saint's sentences, in one of his letters to Brother Leo, all begin with *et,* Auerbach notes (speaking as much, perhaps, for himself as for Francis): "But the person who writes these hurried lines is obviously so inspired by his theme, it fills him so completely, and the desire to communicate himself and to be understood is so overwhelming, that parataxis becomes a weapon of eloquence (*zu einer Waffe der Beredsamkeit wird*)" (English, 166; German, 162).

"Adam and Eve" may well be seen as something of an armory of those weapons of eloquence, an education in the powers of philology both to read and write figurally. It teaches us that the political occasions of linguistic study can, in themselves, come to be the subject of scholarly erudition. It teaches, too, that allegory may become a mode of writing far more "historical" than history itself, for to find the historical resonance of "Adam and Eve"—to discern its political subtext—we need to read the chapter allegorically, as if it were itself a text in need of figural interpretation.

This allegoricopolitical *Mimesis* outlined here may seem far from the received version of the book in current academic circles. Certainly, the

322 • Continuators of the Discipline

vision painted of Auerbach in the legends of the European and American academy is of a scholar almost willfully detached from social activism. The various interpretations advocated for the origins of Auerbach's projects—their Hegelianism, Viconianism, commitments to a humanist philology—are in their own way curiously removed from the history of German university life between the world wars.[21] And, to a certain extent, the criticisms of *Mimesis*'s reception in America after the war, and of its embrace by the formalist New Critics, hinge on the criticism of the work itself: its lack of a self-conscious methodology, its apparent garbling of the theoretical and the historical.[22] This apprehension of the book is due largely to its first reviews by German and American readers. As Paul Bové has argued, the original reviews in American journals were by German émigrés who, apparently unfamiliar with Auerbach's work on Dante and figuralism, considered *Mimesis* an idiosyncratic collection of essays without guiding principles of method or of style.[23] The historical moment of its making, and its thematic and ideological consequences for the book, were lost on early readers, who saw Auerbach's exile more as impediment than challenge to his project.[24] To Helmut Hatzfeld, who wrote the first American review in 1949, "The book was doomed to remain eclectic because of the working conditions of the author in Istanbul."[25] And to the audiences who heard him in the first Princeton Seminar in Literary Criticism (later to be called the Gauss Seminars) in the fall of 1949, Auerbach's personal experience was almost crassly heroic. "A Jew, an *émigré* from Germany, for years homeless, putting his big book together in Istanbul without benefit of the great libraries he longed for, Auerbach had faced with his flesh and blood the reality of evil force; the extremity of Pascal's thought [the subject of the first seminar] answered, for him, an extremity of experience."[26]

These two sides to the book's early reception—the one flat, the other romantic—share nonetheless a predilection for effacing the political subtext of Auerbach's reflections. The Turkish exile is externalized, made either a problem in research or a badge of honor, yet nowhere relocated in the critic's narratives.[27] This depoliticizing of *Mimesis* is in the interest of the institutions of postwar academic criticism. To find its origins, we need to turn not to the critic's early reception in America, but to the responses of his German contemporaries in the first years after the war.

The second number of the 1948 volume of *Romanische Forschungen*—perhaps the premier organ of German *Romanistik*—

opens with a long review essay by Gerhard Hess of Heidelberg, "Mimesis: Zu Erich Auerbachs Geschichte des abendländischen Realismus" (173–211); the volume's third number closes with a brief notice of the *Introduction aux études de philologie romance* by Peter M. Schon of Mainz. Sandwiched between them is a full review by Auerbach himself of Leo Spitzer's *Essays in Historical Semantics* and his *Linguistics and Literary History*. This volume of the journal represents Auerbach's postwar debut in the media of German scholarship: *Mimesis* had appeared, in Bern, in 1946, and with the exception of a piece in *Speculum* of that year, all of Auerbach's other publications from the end of the war until the Spitzer review appeared in Turkish volumes.[28] To call it a debut, though, or even a reemergence would be a misnomer, for the overall impression of these contributions to *Romanische Forschungen* is that, quite simply, there was nothing from which to emerge.

Hess's is certainly the most positive of the early reviews (it is certainly the longest), and it appears from Auerbach's "Epilegomena zu *Mimesis*" of 1953 that he did not consider it one of the negative assessments full of "Mißverständnisse" in need of defense.[29] What makes this review distinctive, however, is less its outright praise for the book—it is a little muted—than its desire to ground it in a tradition of a certain kind of scholarship. Hess begins by placing *Mimesis* not in the locus of the author's exile but in the genealogies of academic scholarship. There are, he begins, few "Außergewöhnliche Bücher . . . in den geisteswissenschaftlichen Disciplinen" (173), few truly unusual examples of scholarly work, such as Eduard Norden's *Antike Kunstprosa*, and, before that, Erwin Rohde's *Griechischer Roman*. Norden and Rohde stand as exemplars of a nineteenth-century scholarly control, a blend of an "unermüdichen philologischen Fleißes und literarischen Feingefühls" ("an untiring philological industry and a literary sensitivity"). They also appear as teachers, and Norden himself, as Auerbach's old teacher, stands as a fitting opening to this forthcoming account of the student's book. The legacies of scholarship present themselves as legacies of student and master, as the paternity of learning.

Now, Auerbach's *Mimesis* is, to Hess's mind, not quite up to the model of these masters: it seems a little spotty in its coverage, familiar in its choice of major texts, and relatively unimaginative in its focus on the old question of the representation of reality and its choice of a primarily "soziologische" mode of inquiry. Yet Hess's impression (*Eindruck*) is of a singular mind at work in *Mimesis*, an impression of "einer überlegenen, kunstverständigen, geschmackssicheren, im guten Sinne gebildeten Personlichkeit" ("a personality judicious, connoisseurial, sure of its tastes, and brought up with good sense," 173). Auerbach has a literary talent, one discernable from the book's opening pages, but not one that imposes itself through polemic or dogmatic judgments. "Der Leser lebt in einer wohltuend humanen Atmosphäre" ("The reader lives in a comforting, humane atmosphere," 174).

This attention to the humane atmosphere, to the more belletristic than primarily scholarly features of *Mimesis,* leads off Hess's chapter-by-chapter summary of the book. Though he begins with an allusive reference to "die Geschichte des Buchs" and to the writings of Auerbach's "Istanbuler Zeit" (174) there is no mention of the difficulties of his exile, no attention to the details of that *Geschichte* or to the contours of that *Zeit.* Hess's review preoccupies itself with placing *Mimesis* in its traditions—scholarly, institutional, and literary—rather than in its time. Its goal is to bring Auerbach back into the official organs of Gesistesgeschichte by emphasizing the continuities, genealogies, and detachments that enable *der Leser* to read *Mimesis* in the study. Instead of the fissures of exile, the limitations of a Turkish library, or the personal reflection on political conditions, Hess proffers the unbroken flow of learning.

The emphases on sensitivity and belletrism here—and, I would argue, in many of the early reviews—is not simply a misunderstanding on the part of Auerbach's contemporaries. It represents a conscious strategy to efface the disturbing political and personal themes of *Mimesis:* to make it safe for the reader in the study, the student in the library, the connoisseur in that literary gallery where we may all breathe that "humane atmosphere" of intellectual comfort. More informed than the American reviewers of the late 1940s and early 1950s, Hess relates *Mimesis* to Auerbach's other work on Dante and on *figura* (189). He recognizes that certain chapters, especially the Flaubert section, bring together work that Auerbach had written earlier. And he compares the work on Old French texts to scholarship by Curtius and Voretzsch (181–86, 187).

These citations do not necessarily imply that Hess's is a more objective account of the book than those by Hatzfeld, Ludwig Edelstein, or others. It is a more *informed* account, but one whose display of information presents an ideal of the worker in the institutions of the academy, where each book, each essay, has a place in the trajectory of apprenticeship, journeyman work, and mastery. The review, as a whole, papers over the hiatus of exile and the political subtexts of *Mimesis*'s readings. It brings the book back into the ambience of scholarship as if nothing had arrived to interrupt it, or as if even such an interruption (*die Istanbuler Zeit*) could be safely tucked away in the vagaries of euphemism. Discontinuities exist: discontinuities of style, of method, and of technical approach. But in spite of this apparent eclecticism of *Mimesis,* Hess writes: "hat der Leser nie das Gefühl der Uneinheitlichkeit. Ein klarer Geist durchdringt und verbindet scheinbar Disparates" (175–76). A clear and guiding spirit binds together all that seems disparate. For this, too, is Hess's purpose, to unite the disparate periods and products of Auerbach's career as part of a genealogy of *Geisteswissenschaft* at whose heart may lie that *Geist* that has no history or politics.

The pages of *Romanische Forschungen* that follow Hess's opening review article similarly leave us with a sense of academic business as usual. Studies of etymology, dialects, phonology, and literary topoi fill the volume in a manner hardly different from anything that had appeared before or during the World War II. The tone of scholarly detachment similarly permeates Auerbach's review of Spitzer's books, the first entry in the *Besprechungen* section of the volume. For the most part, Auerbach concerns himself with narrating the contents of Spitzer's volumes and with defining his particular method and its strengths and limitations. Only occasionally is there a reference to the personal in this review: to what, for example, Auerbach identifies as the "teilweise autobiographischen" introduction to *Linguistics and Literary History* (398), or to the letter from an American student, quoted in the book, criticizing Spitzer's approach as personal and intuitive.

The differences between the German review of this book and the one in English Auerbach published in the first volume of *Comparative Literature* (1949)[30] are subtly instructive in this regard. Though the American review is somewhat shorter than the one in *Romanische Forschungen,* it closes with a substantial reflection on the personal in academic study and teaching. Commenting on the idiosyncratic possibilities of Spitzer's method in his hands, Auerbach notes that we should not condemn the approach because of the excesses of the user.

> But it would be a great mistake not to study the method because of the imperfections of those who use it; or because, on the contrary, it requires so high a level of knowledge and so large an horizon that it is not adaptable to practical teaching or even to average research

work. I have had excellent results in using it on a very modest level, in Germany as well as Turkey. Our students learn too much biographical and other textbook material; they are like people who listen to lectures on fruits, but almost never get hold of an apple or a grape. . . . For such teaching [i.e., in national literature courses] Spitzer's book can serve as an excellent introduction, although practice would have to be simpler and less personal. (83–84)

For Auerbach writing in the pages of *Romanische Forschungen,* however, the practice has to be simpler and less personal. There are no comparable reflections in the German review, nothing of the "teilweise autobiographischen" that he attributes to Spitzer himself. Only in America, and only in English, could he give voice to the personal and the political concerns behind the practice of scholarship. For the readers of *Romanische Forschungen,* such concerns can only be slipped in, allusively, in other forms and other languages. Witness the curious, unique English quotation in the discussion of Spitzer on Racine: "Racine's main purpose was to show us the collapse of the world order as revealed to Thesée" (*RF,* 400). Or witness the moment, in the otherwise purely descriptive, brief review by Peter Schon of Auerbach's *Introduction aux études de philologie romane,* where the circumstances of the book's production can only be quoted in the French ("Ce petit livre fut écrit à Istanbul . . . . pendant la guerre . . . loin des bibliothèques européens et américaines" (*RF,* 490).

The Auerbachiana of these volumes of *Romanische Forschungen* take us far from the political allusions or the personal reflections of *Mimesis*—so far that when Auerbach eventually came to publish his "Epilegomena zu *Mimesis*" in the 1953 volume of the journal, he set out to rehistoricize the book. This essay, which opens the volume, offers an occasion to respond to queries about individual interpretations by catching up on current scholarship. Yet, in the course of his responses to reviewers and the extended rejoinder to Curtius's essay on the three styles, published in *Romanische Forschungen* in 1952, Auerbach grows more personal. He reminds the readers of the period in Istanbul (5), recalls his youthful training in Germany (15), and at the close explicitly addresses the historical and biographical moment in which the book took shape: "*Mimesis* ist ganz bewußt ein Buch, das ein bestimmter Mensch, in einer bestimmten Lage, zu Anfang der 1940er Jahre geschrieben hat" (18). A certain man, at a certain time, in a certain "situation" (*Lage*)—this is the closing key to understanding *Mimesis,* to reading its *figurae* of the person and the present. Auerbach's phrasing takes us back to the chapter on Adam and Eve, where Eve herself, "Herrin der Lage," overthrows the order of her God and man, and it reminds us, too, of Auerbach's quarrel with Étienne over who will be the master of the editorial situation.

It would be rewarding to close by naming Auerbach the winner in that quarrel and by showing that, in spite of all the manglings of *Mimesis* in the early reviews, and the later appropriation of Auerbach himself into the canons of literary studies, his editorial decisions on the *Mystère d'Adam* stood up to professional approval. But apparently, they do not. The critical edition of the play by Paul Aebischer, published in the *Textes Littéraires Français* series, accepts without question Étienne's distribution of the lines between Adam and Eve.[31] And while the diplomatic edition of Leif Sletsjöe, published with a facing-page facsimile of the manuscript, does not print the text of the speeches as Étienne edits them, it does state in a note to line 283 that Adam probably should speak this line and that the A used by the scribe to signal the speaker has probably been lost from the margin of the manuscript.[32] Sletsjöe and Aebischer both cite Étienne approvingly, and while their spellings of the individual words of the text may differ from the earlier scholar's, they both confirm an ordering of speeches first suggested on the pages of *Romania* in 1922. So powerful has been this editorial tradition that, in a recent American anthology of medieval drama edited by David Bevington, Étienne's version appears without question. And yet, so powerful is Auerbach's example for the institutions of American medieval studies, that Bevington can quote his interpretation of the play as received wisdom.[33]

This fissure in a classroom anthology, perhaps more precisely than the record of the histories of scholarship, shows the paradox of the place of Auerbach's *Mimesis* in the institutions of medieval studies. On the one hand, it accepts the critical interpretation, treasures its appreciation of the humble and the everyday in the articulations of the sublime in order to breathe fully in that atmosphere of humanistic scholarship. On the other hand, it rejects—or, better yet, ignores—the textual interpretation, bypasses the very heart of Auerbach's display of philological erudition that enables him to recover the character of European peoples and to write their literary history. One can only speculate on why Étienne's interpretation succeeds while Auerbach's fails, though such speculation might well say something about the

French control of a national textual legacy and its authoritative impact on later, American students.

Such speculation, too, might take us back to the very style of Auerbach's chapter and to the paradoxes of *Mimesis* itself. The colloquialism of the presentation in "Adam and Eve" shifts scholarly attention away from the details of his editorial technique and toward the sensitivities of belletrism. Ironically, it may be Auerbach himself who seems to lack the precision of method he demanded in the *Introduction aux études de philologie romane.* The paradoxes of *Mimesis* lie in the tensions between the scholarly and the colloquial, between the learned techniques of *Geisteswissenschaft* and the felt experience of *Feingefühl,* between what Auerbach defined as the historical and the legendary. "Again and again, I have the purpose of writing history."[34] This widely quoted passage has been used throughout much recent scholarship on Auerbach to emphasize the theory of historical understanding that grounds even his most affective of readings. But, as I have suggested here, we might do well to find his purpose not in writing *Geschichte* but *Sage,* and to recall, as he asks us, that in times such as those in which he wrote *Mimesis,* "most historians are forced to make concessions to the technique of legend."

NOTES

1. Erich Auerbach, *Mimesis: Dargestellte Wirklichkeit in der abendländischen Literatur* (Bern: A. Francke, 1946), 24–25. All subsequent quotations from *Mimesis* in German will be from this edition. English translation: "Now the difference between legend and history is in most cases easily perceived by a reasonably experienced reader. It is a difficult matter, requiring careful historical and philological training, to distinguish the true from the synthetic or the biased in a historical presentation; but it is easy to separate the historical from the legendary in general. . . . To write history is so difficult that most historians are forced to make concessions to the technique of legend." Willard R. Trask, trans., *Mimesis: The Representation of Reality in Western Literature* (Princeton: Princeton University Press, 1953), 19–20.

Throughout this chapter, I quote primarily from the English translation of *Mimesis,* save on those occasions when a close attention to Auerbach's German necessitates a full quotation in the text. Page numbers after quotations in each language refer to the respective publications. Erich Auerbach, *Introduction aux études de philologie romane* (Frankfurt am Main: Vittorio Klostermann, 1949), 9.

2. "Wer etwa das Verhalten der einzelnen Menschen und Menschen-gruppen beim Aufkommen des Nationalsozialismus in Deutschland, oder das Verhalten der einzelnen Völker und Staaten vor und während des gegen-wärtigen (1942) Krieges erwägt, der wird fühlen, wie schwer darstellbar geschichtliche Gegenstände überhaupt, und wie unbrauchbar sie für die Sage sind" (25).

3. There is a large and growing bibliography on Auerbach, most re-cently surveyed by Jan Ziolkowski in his foreword to the paperback reprint-ing of *Literary Language and Its Public in Late Antiquity and the Middle Ages,* trans. Ralph Manheim (Princeton: Princeton University Press, 1993), ix–xxxii, with a comprehensive listing of works cited (xxxiii–xxxix). Among those studies most relevant to his place in the traditions of literary criticism, and which have influenced my understanding directly, are: Paul Bové, *Intel-lectuals in Power: A Genealogy of Critical Humanism* (New York: Columbia University Press, 1986), 79–208; Luiz Costa-Lima, "Erich Auerbach: History and Metahistory," *New Literary History* 19 (1988): 467–99; Thomas M. DePietro, "Literary Criticism as History: The Example of Auerbach's Mime-sis," *Clio* 8 (1979): 377–87; W. Wolfgang Holdheim, "Auerbach's *Mimesis*: Aesthetics as Historical Understanding," *Clio* 10 (1981): 143–54. See also, now, Seth Lerer, ed., *Literary History and the Challenge of Philogy: The Legacy of Erich Auerbach* (Stanford: Stanford University Press, 1996).

4. On Spitzer, see Alban Forcione, Herbert Lindenberger, and Madeline Sutherland, eds., *Leo Spitzer: Representative Essays* (Stanford: Stanford Uni-versity Press, 1988), especially John Freccero's sensitive foreword on Spitzer as teacher (xi–xx). Spitzer and Auerbach are often paired in the impressions of midcentury German émigré medievalists. See, for example, the reflections of Paul Zumthor: "The work of the gentle Auerbach, with his large eyes and his expression of timid goodness, marked a generation, otherwise but no less than the work of the brilliant Spitzer, that great conversationalist, self-confi-dent and beloved by women" (Sarah White, trans., *Speaking of the Middle Ages* [Lincoln: University of Nebraska Press, 1985], 21). See, too, Harry Levin, "Two Romanisten in America," in Donald Fleming and Bernard Bailyn, eds., *The Intellectual Migration: Europe and America, 1930–1960* (Cambridge, Mass.: Harvard University Press, 1969), 467–83. On Curtius and Auerbach, see Geoffrey Green, *Literary Criticism and the Structures of History: Erich Auerbach and Leo Spitzer* (Lincoln: University of Nebraska Press, 1982). For a discussion of Auerbach's response to Curtius's *European Literature and the Latin Middle Ages* in his "Philologie der Weltliteratur" of 1952, see Bové, 205–6. For an amusing anecdote about Auerbach's encounter with Curtius in Princeton in 1949, related as an icon of their respective scholarly and emotional personalities, see Robert Fitzgerald, *Enlarging the*

Change: The Princeton Seminars in Literary Criticism 1949–1951 (Boston: Northeastern University Press, 1985), 21–22.

5. While there is, to my knowledge, no full-length biography of Auerbach, a brief sketch of his life and a bibliography of his works may be found in Ziolkowski's foreword to *Literary Language and Its Public,* and in the chronology appended to the book (393–407). An impressionistic account of Auerbach's institutional wanderings begins Costa-Lima's "Erich Auerbach" (467–68). Hans Ulrich Gumbrecht has recently completed a study, "'Pathos of the Earthly Progress': Erich Auerbach's Everydays," drawing on new access to the state archives in Marburg and on Auerbach's personal correspondence—an important and revisionary approach to the relationship between Auerbach's life and work. Gumbrecht's work was presented at a conference on Auerbach at Stanford University in October 1992, and should appear in the volume of papers drawn from that conference, *Literary History and the Challenge of Philology: The Legacy of Erich Auerbach,* ed. Seth Lerer.

6. Among the many recent reassessments of the history of Romance philology in Europe, see in particular Hans Ulrich Gumbrecht, "'Un souffle d'Allemagne ayant passé': Friedrich Diez, Gaston Paris, and the Genesis of National Philologies," *Romance Philology* 40 (1986): 1–37 (with a full bibliography of primary and secondary sources). The January 1990 issue of *Speculum* (vol. 65) is devoted to "The New Philology," and contains several essays relevant to my analysis: Stephen G. Nichols, "Introduction: Philology in a Manuscript Culture," 1–10; R. Howard Bloch, "New Philology and Old French," 38–58; Lee Patterson, "On the Margin: Postmodernism, Ironic History, and Medieval Studies," 87–108.

7. From Diez's remarks on his candidacy for a lectureship at the University of Bonn, quoted in Gumbrecht, "'Un souffle,'" 18.

8. From the opening of Aubertin's *Histoire de la langue et de la littérature française au moyen âge d'après les travaux le plus récents,* quoted in Gumbrecht, "'Un souffle,'" 26–27.

9. For a chronicle of these attempts, see Gumbrecht, "'Un souffle,'" and Bloch, "New Philology and Old French."

10. On the agendas of Franco-German philology in the nineteenth and twentieth centuries, see the studies cited above. For the responses of postwar American New Criticism, see Bové, esp. 106–7. For a history of the *Grundriß der romanischen Literaturen des Mittelalters,* and the larger context of postwar German philology, see Hans Ulrich Gumbrecht, "A Sad and Weary History: The *Grundriß der romanischen Literaturen des Mittelalters*" in this volume. On the changing canons of professional training in medieval studies, see Lee Patterson, *Negotiating the Past: The Historical Study of Medieval Literature* (Madison: University of Wisconsin Press, 1987), 3–74, and Allen

J. Frantzen, *Desire for Origins: New Language, Old English, and Teaching the Tradition* (New Brunswick: Rutgers University Press, 1990).

11. See the discussions in the articles by Costa-Lima, DePietro, and Holdheim cited in n. 3 and the treatment of Bové, 131–208. See, too, Edward Said, *Beginnings: Intention and Method* (Baltimore: Johns Hopkins University Press, 1975), 68–70. "Philologie der Weltliteratur" appeared originally in *Weltliteratur: Festgabe für Fritz Strich* (Bern: A. Francke, 1952), and has been translated as "Philology and *Weltliteratur*," by Marie and Edward Said in *The Centennial Review* 13 (1969): 1–17. "Epilegomena zu *Mimesis*" appeared in *Romanische Forschungen* 65 (1953): 1–18. *Dante als Dichter des irdischen Welt* (Berlin and Leipzig: Walter de Gruyter, 1929), has been translated by Ralph Manheim as *Dante, Poet of the Secular World* (Chicago: University of Chicago Press, 1961).

12. S. Étienne, "Note sur les vers 279–287 du *Jeu d'Adam*," *Romania* 48 (1922): 592–95. On this particular editorial problem, see Stephen G. Nichols, "Philogy in Aurbach's Drama of (Literary) History," in Lerer, ed., *Literary History and the Challenge of Philology*.

13. Étienne, 592, 593.

14. See the discussion of the early reviews of *Mimesis* at the close of this essay and the comprehensive survey of Herbert Lindenberger, "On the Reception of *Mimesis*," in Lerer, ed., *Literary History*.

15. Gumbrecht, "'Un souffle,'" 2.

16. Léon Gautier, "Chronique," *Revue des questions historiques* 9 (1870): 496, translated and quoted in Bloch, 40.

17. Henri Massis, *Les jeunes gens d'aujourd'hui* (Paris, 1913), 107, translated and quoted in Bloch, 40.

18. On the rise of chairs of literature in France and Germany in the nineteenth century, see Gumbrecht, "'Un Souffle,'" 31–32. For the rise "of a new paradigm in the history of French scholarship, which will create its own publication outlets in *Romania* (from 1872 on) and the *Société des Anciens Textes Français* (from 1875)," see Gumbrecht, 27. For the phrasings of Gaston Paris, see his *Les contes orientaux dans la littérature français du moyen âge* (Paris, 1875), 3, quoted in Bloch, 41–42.

19. Bloch, 40. Auerbach had left Marburg in 1936.

20. Jean-Paul Sartre, "Qu'est-ce qu'un collaborateur?" in *Situations III* (Paris: Gallimard, 1949), 43–61, with page numbers cited in my text. For a treatment of this essay in the context of another episode of academic politics and collaboration, see Werner Hammacher, "Journals, Politics: Notes on Paul de Man's Wartime Journalism," in Werner Hammacher, Neil Hertz, and Tom Keenan, eds., *Responses* (Lincoln: University of Nebraska Press, 1990), 438–67, esp. 447–48.

21. See, for example, Timothy Bahti, "Vico, Auerbach, and Literary History," in Giorgio Tagliacozzo, ed., *Vico Past and Present* (Atlantic Highlands, N.J.: Humanities Press, 1981), 249–66; Said, 363 (who calls Auerbach "Vico's principal and most profound literary student"); and Costa-Lima, 469–85.

22. For such a chronicle, see Bové, 79–208.

23. Ibid., 96–113.

24. One exception to this dehistoricized *Mimesis* among the early reviews is René Wellek, "Auerbach's Special Realism," *Kenyon Review* 16 (1954): 299–306. For a detailed reconsideration of the early reviews of *Mimesis*, see Herbert Lindenberger, "On the Reception of *Mimesis*," forthcoming in Lerer, ed., *Literary History and the Challenge of Philology*.

25. *Romance Philology* 2 (1949): 338.

26. Fitzgerald, 15. Fitzgerald's account, while published in 1985, is based on a report he prepared at the time of the original seminars, and its tone reproduces the clubroom atmosphere of Princeton in the 1940s.

27. For an impressionistic account of the German émigré intelligensia in Istanbul during the war, see Liselotte Dieckmann, "Akademische Emigranten in der Türkei," in Egon Schwarz and Matthias Wegner, eds., *Verbannung: Aufzeichnungen deutscher Schriftsteller im Exil* (Hamburg: Christian Wegner, 1964), 122–26. She reflects on the kind of bibliographical problems Auerbach experienced: "Für die Humanisten gab es zwar die schönsten alten Manuskripte, aber freilich keine Bibliothek. Nur wer eine private Sammlung besaß und sie hatte mitbringen können, konnte über Bücher verfügen. Und so ließe sich immer weiter erzählen" (125). I am grateful to Herbert Lindenberger for calling my attention to this essay.

28. For the details of Auerbach's publications from 1946–48, see the bibliography of his writings in *Literary Language and Its Public*, 399–400.

29. "Ausgewählt habe ich solche Motive, di mire besonders am herzen liegen—sei es, weil ich etwas einzuräumen habe, sei es, weil ich glaube meine Anschauungen gegen Mißverständnisse verteidigen zu müssen" (1).

30. From this review, Bové generates the following analysis, which I cannot find supported in Auerbach's text: "One particular dimension of Auerbach's project and of his own understanding of humanism's contradictory development seems particularly problematic, namely, the assumption that the scholar should or can legitimately be a universal intellectual whose leading role might be modified—from politician to mythographer—but can never be suspended without cataclysmic cultural consequences. The result of this belief is, as Auerbach notes, that humanists would be foolish to attempt to alter the modern tendencies that force them into the conservative role of mythographers. In other words, there is a tendency towards political quietism" (183–84).

31. Paul Aebischer, ed., *Le mystère d'Adam,* Textes littéraires français (Geneva: Droz, 1963), 51–52.

32. Leif Sletsjöe, ed., *Le mystère d'Adam,* Bibliothèque française et romane (Paris: Klincksieck, 1968), 21, 85.

33. David Bevington, *Medieval Drama* (Boston: Houghton Mifflin, 1975), text on 94, discussion on 79, quoting Auerbach's discussion of the everyday element of the play's realism (from *Mimesis,* 151) in support of an argument that the play was "intended for an audience of ordinary men and women." For a supple counterargument to this tradition of interpretation, reading the play as primarily a liturgical, Latin occasion rather than a popular, vernacular one, see Steven Justice, "The Authority of Ritual in the *Jeu d'Adam,*" *Speculum* 62 (1987): 851–64.

34. From *Literary Language and Its Public,* trans. Manheim, 20. This passage, and the historicist sentiment imagined behind it, generates the discussion of Auerbach's method in DePietro, "Literary Criticism as History," and forms the point of argument for the critique of Auerbach's "understanding of humanism's contradictory development" in Bové, *Intellectuals in Power,* 206–7; see, too, 183–84, from which the above phrase in quotations is taken. Auerbach's claim to write history has also recently formed the basis of a strikingly conservative foreword to the reprinting of *Literary Language* by Jan Ziolkowski (ix–xxxii of the Princeton University Press paperback reprint, 1993), who, among other things, avers that "readers should not exaggerate the topicality—or the ideological elements" of Auerbach's work (xxii), and who offers a vision of "the constancy of Auerbach in his self-understanding and in his lifelong engagement with European literature" as an "indeed attractive" alternative to the situation of "our days" in which "the self-definitions of the professors—the professionals—who are hired to teach and write about literature change with dizzying rapidity" (xxvii).

TWELVE

Ernst Robert Curtius and the
Topos of the Literary Critic

Carl Landauer

WHEN ERICH AUERBACH wrote his *Mimesis* in exile in Istanbul during World War II, he created a literary landscape in which he was very much at home, and one that was primarily European rather than German.[1] In the end, Auerbach styled himself a citizen of a European culture he had carefully constructed. In a similar effort—although carried out within Germany—another eminent Romance philologist of the same generation, Ernst Robert Curtius, created a European cultural realm that could stand in symbolic opposition to the Germanic mythology of the Nazis. If Auerbach's great work of the 1940s established his European identity, Curtius's *Europäische Literatur und lateinisches Mittelalter* represented a more urgent bid for European citizenship. Curtius was, in fact, quite explicit about his quest for citizenship. In the opening pages of his book, he asserted that it was possible to understand European literature as a whole only after acquiring citizenship in all of its periods from Homer to Goethe: "wenn mann sich ein Bügerrecht in allen ihren Epochen von Homer bis Goethe erworben hat."[2]

Such a narrative stretching from Homer to Goethe was an eminently German pursuit. And Curtius ended his opening chapter in a conventional German voice: "Homer is the founding hero of European literature. Its last universal author is Goethe."[3] But rather than

334

the Greece-to-Weimar commonplace of popular culture, this particular construction echoed the George-Kreis sentiments of his friend Friedrich Gundolf. Nevertheless, both Greece and Weimar were overshadowed in Curtius's story by Latinity, for ultimately the central theme of Curtius's work was the Latin core of European literature.

If Curtius, like Auerbach, inhabited the world of his great text, there was for Curtius also a sense of discomfort. He began the body of his text with the fourth canto of the *Inferno,* the canto in which Virgil introduces Dante to the circle of the great classical poets in Limbo, and where Dante feels that he has become a sixth in their circle. Curtius pointed out that the circle was composed of Homer, Horace, Ovid, Lucan, and his guide Virgil, which is to say that it was dominated by Latin rather than Greek poets. In a sense, Homer rather than Dante was the invited guest in a Latin world. Using this famous moment in the *Commedia,* Curtius not only introduced the major theme of his work—the Latinity of medieval culture—but provided at the same time a metaphor that would undercut it. Dante, as much as he was heir to the Latin tradition, was still a guest among the poets of antiquity. In this respect he provided a figure for Curtius himself. Just as the exile from Florence would never truly find his home among his classical models, so too would the inner exile from the Third Reich never be able to assume the European citizenship he so fervently sought. But finally, the classical poets were really guests in Dante's text, inhabiting a medieval world. Similarly, Curtius's Latinity was constructed with a German imaginative vocabulary; the world he created to reidentify himself against the German present was thoroughly German.

When *Europäische Literatur und lateinisches Mittelalter* was finally published in 1948, its pan-European message was immediately welcomed in reviews in Europe and America. Auerbach praised Curtius's radical rejection of all national or chronological isolation within European civilization, and the establishment of "European Literature as the intelligible field of study for historians of literature."[4] Curtius's political agenda was clear, but it was inextricably bound up with a scholarly agenda. His main complaint with literary study in Germany was the exaggerated influence of *Geistesgeschichte* with its focus on epochs and its narrative of the progression of styles. Curtius felt the enterprise entirely misguided: "Is Shakespeare Renaissance or Baroque? Is Baudelaire Impressionist, George Expressionist? . . . Is Goethe's *Faust* ultimately 'open' and Valéry's 'closed'?"[5] For him, the conventional strategy of German literary criticism was as harmful as it was foolish, impeding a true understanding of the cultural unity of Europe. For that reason, Curtius felt an intellectual affiliation with the art historian Aby Warburg, who was known for his bold attacks on the "border guards" (*Grenzpolizei*) of academic specialization, although for Curtius, Warburg's clever phrase took on a more literal meaning.

Curtius felt that modern scholars who lost sight of the essence of western literature would do best to return to the study of medieval literature, for medieval culture could provide a contrast with the ugly nationalism of the twentieth century. At the core of Curtius's medieval literature, however, was not the epochal unity of *geistesgeschichtlich* accounts. Rather, the bread and butter of medieval literature was its use of specific classical rhetorical elements he called "topoi." For Curtius, they served through the history of the West as the fixed points of literary creation. Avoiding the cultural-historical methodology of his contemporaries, Curtius focused on highly technical forms.

Curtius was trying to portray himself as a scholar of a different sort from the other denizens of the "political universities" of the Third Reich. Throughout his book, he framed himself as the knowing scholar who needed no Baedecker guide to the literature of the West. He was as fluent with the works of Denis Diderot, Heinrich von Kleist, and Gerard Manley Hopkins as he was with those of Jerome, Boethius, and Bernard Silvestris. But of more importance than a facility with the whole of western literature was his posture as an expert, perhaps unparalleled, on technical matters of classical rhetoric. Curtius maintained this chosen persona well after the publication of *Europäische Literatur und lateinisches Mittelalter*. In a review of Auerbach's *Mimesis*, Curtius upbraided his fellow Romance philologist for defining the classical doctrine of the separation of styles—so central to Auerbach's book—as a distinction between the higher and lower literary styles. Auerbach, Curtius was quick to point out, should have known that the doctrine of the separation of styles distinguished three rather than two levels.[6] Thus, far more important than the simple conceit of Curtius's 1929 essay on Joyce, in which he suggested that the task of fully decoding *Ulysses* was a rather simple matter, was his self-image as a philologist for whom the intricacies of Latin rhetoric held no mystery.[7]

Although there was a good deal of truth in Curtius's self-depiction, one should place it next to his other chosen identities, such as that of the critic of modern literature. It was as critic rather than philologist that he wrote appreciative essays on Hermann Hesse,

James Joyce, and T. S. Eliot, and his first major book on the new literary generation of France in 1919.[8] If some of his early essays referred to Cicero and Dante, they were basically critical in character.[9] They suggest the feuilletonist rather than the student of classical rhetoric.

In addition to Curtius's identity as critic, he had an early identity as a cultural commentator. Despite later attacks on the narrowness of *Geistesgeschichte* with its focus on national cultures, his own first works were themselves studies of French national culture: *Die literarischen Wegbereiter des neuen Frankreich, Französischer Geist im neuen Europa,* and *Die französische Kultur: Eine Einführung.*[10] Curtius, whose books were reviewed by Mario Praz, Benedetto Croce, and George Orwell, was immediately recognized as a courageous German who attempted to bridge the gulf between wartime antagonists. In an important sense, his early works were of a piece with his great work of the forties, for both were directed against the blind *völkisch* nationalism of the German right.[11] Indeed, internationalism was an important presence in almost all of his work. The scholar born in Alsace in proximity to both French and German culture spent much of his scholarly life trying to mediate between the two.[12] He saw himself as European in sensibility. And an important expression of this sensibility was his participation in the summer "Decades" at Pontigny organized by Paul Desjardins, meetings that were intended to encourage interaction among European intellectuals of different nationalities, attended by André Gide, W. B. Yeats, Walther Rathenau, Jacques Rivière, and Max Scheler.[13] At the Decades, Curtius made important foreign contacts, but most significantly the meetings symbolized the European reconciliation that was the aim of his scholarship.

Despite the agenda of his books on French culture and his highly polemical *Deutscher Geist in Gefahr,* his early books participated in some of the commonplaces of German *Geistesgeschichte.* At the end of the first chapter of *Die französische Kultur,* he expressed a hope that a new self-examination by French and German alike would "end the conflict between Culture and Civilization."[14] Here Curtius gave life to one of the stereotyped oppositions of French and German culture. In fact, the book continually defines French cultural characteristics against the cultural norms of Germany: "in the spiritual inheritance the French received from their Gallic forebears—we can find no memory of that primitive period, nothing comparable to the sagas that tell of the German tribal migration. The French soul does not know the drive to wander or the longing for distant places" (*Die*

Seele Frankreich weiß nichts von Wandertrieb und Fernsehnsucht).[15] Rather than avoid the prevalent clichés, Curtius's book takes its imaginative power from one of the basic tropes of *Geistesgeschichte*—the polar opposition between cultures.

Curtius's book of 1932, *Deutscher Geist in Gefahr,* reveals a similar *geistesgeschichtlich* tendency despite its attempt to diagnose the ailing German spirit and to provide a program of recovery through a renewed humanism. In it, Curtius announced the need to return to a study of medieval culture, providing a prelude to his studies of the 1940s. Still, despite his strong indictment of the *völkisch* right, Curtius shared some of its thought patterns. And in the midst of his cultural cliché mongering stands a several-page passage devoted to the part that Germany's Jews played in his nation's illness. This disturbing passage has recently come to attention in an apology for Paul de Man written by Geoffrey Hartman after the discovery of de Man's youthful anti-Semitic articles.[16] In an effort to place de Man's awful scribblings in a context that might diminish their brutality, Hartman cited the example of Curtius, whom he identified as "neither a nazi nor an anti-Semite." Curtius was far from a Nazi sympathizer.[17] But the second charge, that of anti-Semite, seems fully justified even by a generous reading of *Deutscher Geist in Gefahr.* His passage on the Jews appears in a discussion of the dangers posed to the German university by the advent of sociology, which Curtius thought helped to blur the boundaries between state and society. And right in the middle of the corrupting discipline he located the German Jew.[18] If, later in the book, Curtius identified the Jewish religion as a "venerable educational and formative source for Christianity," he was less generous to the Jews themselves, especially the assimilated Jews of Germany (111). Casually adopting one of the mainstays of turn-of-the-century anti-Semitism, he identified assimilated German Jews as "lapsed Jews who had abandoned the principles of Judaism, the beliefs of the chosen people" (85). In their skepticism, they posed a threat to German culture in its hour of need. Using the assimilated Jew to symbolize his nation's ills, he declared: "we are not fighting Judaism, but destruction; not a race, but a negation" (85). This is Curtius at his ugliest, and it makes apparent that his nationalism was overlaid with racial doctrine. Thus, if his book was designed to confront *völkisch* nationalism on the eve of its victory, the implications of Curtius's personal brand of nationalism, with its adoption of the worst right-wing hatreds, should be clear. We should not lose sight of it when we turn to the internationalist agenda of *Europäische Literatur und lateinisches Mittelalter.*

In writing *Deutscher Geist in Gefahr,* Curtius attempted to identify the threats to German culture that he perceived from the right and the left. Although he attacked the left and the ideals of socialism, his principal target remained the nationalist right, especially the circle around the right-wing magazine *Die Tat.* Despite the fact that the Nazis were only months away from taking over Germany, they appear in Curtius's book as no more than a segment of a general right-wing threat, only one of the groups preaching *Kulturhass,* while the circle around *Die Tat* were his real opponents. Essentially, the battle was over the soul of German humanism.

In the tumultuous last days of the Weimar Republic, Curtius's book made an impassioned call for German humanism as the only salvation from the *Barbarisierung* of the day. But when he invoked the spirit of humanism, Curtius was aware of the panoply of shallow humanisms unworthy of the name, including the pabulum humanism of the German Gymnasium education, "die offizielle Schultradition" (106). Against these, Curtius advanced a humanism that carefully balanced antiquity, Christianity, and Germanness: "All European lands sharing the common cultural tradition of the West have formed their cultural ideal from a balance of antiquity, Christianity and their own folk traditions" (22). "However," he continued, "an imbalance could produce altogether different results" (22). And *völkisch* nationalism represented just such an imbalance: Christianity and antiquity were sacrificed to *Deutschtum.*

Curtius felt that the nationalists of his day were responsible for bringing nationalism and humanism into conflict, foregoing the very combination that originally forged German culture. When they attacked Germans who answered "the siren call of the South" as somehow un-German, they came up against the "great stumbling block of their historical vision"—Goethe (30). Curtius felt they also fabricated a false image of the German medieval past. Citing the historian Konrad Burdach as his authority, Curtius asserted that even German mysticism, so often mythologized by the Romantic right, was not a homegrown product. Similarly, the great Middle High German epics, the pride of facile German nationalism, were based on French sources (31). Misguided nationalists, with their elaborate mythologies, overestimated the contribution of *Volkstum* to German culture while denying the importance of Christianity and antiquity. Making his own nationalist appeal, Curtius asserted: "If Germany neglected humanism and Christianity, it would soon arise that Eckhart and Luther, Goethe and Mozart and George would no longer be understood" (47). In short, the nationalists of the right were poor nationalists.

Basically, Curtius's book of 1932 invokes the nightmare of the German Mandarin. In contrast to the horrors that began on January 31, 1933, his worries focused on the inability of Germans to understand Goethe and George. In its unreality, one is reminded of Friedrich Meinecke's postwar plan for reviving the best of Germany through the creation of local Goethe societies, for Meinecke and Curtius drew breath from the same Mandarin atmosphere. Raised in that tradition, Curtius feared not so much the violence that accompanied the Nazis into power, but that the wall built between culture and the state, already crumbling, would fall into complete disrepair.

Curtius championed a particular humanist vision in the running struggle among German humanisms, and he located the best example of his ideal in the courtly culture of thirteenth-century Germany, a culture described by Hans Naumann as blending antiquity, Christianity, and Germanness (32). He felt consequently that a revival of humanism would come only through a renewed exposure to the Middle Ages" (31). His studies of the 1940s should thus be seen as an attempt to follow the program given voice in 1932; his massive volume would be a return to and an idealization of the medieval world.

One might easily read *Europäische Literatur und lateinisches Mittelalter* as driven by the same instincts as *Deutscher Geist in Gefahr,* linking an idealized humanism to internationalism. But despite its commitment to humanism and internationalism, as well as its engagement with an idealized medieval world, the program of Curtius's classic ultimately represented a sharp departure from the humanism of *Deutscher Geist in Gefahr.* From Curtius's equation of 1932—the triad of antiquity, Christianity, and Germanness—two of the elements were conspicuously absent. As many of his German colleagues complained, the medieval culture of *Europäische Literatur und lateinisches Mittelalter* was largely independent of German contribution.[19] And his medieval world was more Latin than Christian. Of the three forces he carefully balanced in 1932, only antiquity assumed a position of honor.

But if the idealized culture of the book abandoned the programmatic humanism of *Deutscher Geist in Gefahr,* it approximated the culture of *Die französische Kultur.* In part, Curtius made the link between French culture and his medieval literary sphere explicit by giving "Romania"—the "totality of the lands in which Romance languages are spoken"—a privileged place in his narrative.[20] But the unspoken and possibly unwitting comparisons of modern French culture outlined by Curtius in 1930 and the medieval literary culture he described in 1948 are remarkable. In *Die französische Kultur,* he distinguished French and German culture by describing the indissoluble tie of French culture to universalism. One of the characteristics of French nationalism was that it incorporated universalism. And for Curtius, that universalism was itself tied to France's identity as "the land of the humanist tradition."[21]

He sensed that France retained closer ties to antiquity, and that antiquity remained a vital part of French literature. Furthermore, literature itself assumed a more important position in French culture than in other cultures.[22] In Germany, literature shared the stage with music, philosophy, and science, but in France literature alone was the mainstay of the national culture. All of these traits were shared by the European culture idealized in *Europäische Literatur und lateinisches Mittelalter.* As explicit as Curtius's reference to "Romania" may have been, the unvoiced kinship between the portrait of France in *Die französische Kultur* and his portrait of the Latin Middle Ages suggests that his model of French culture was of immense significance for his idealizations of *Europäische Literatur und lateinisches Mittelalter.*

By comparison, the important absence of *Europäische Literatur und lateinisches Mittelalter* was German culture. The book's narrative retained enough traces of the absent culture to make that absence unmistakable. In his first chapter, he was quite explicit, asserting that "German literature is the most unsuitable of all the so-called national literatures to use as our starting point and as a field of observation."[23] Possibly more interesting than the absence of Germany in Curtius's medieval world was the relative unimportance of Christianity. Although Christianity did not disappear entirely from his narrative, it assumed a subservient position to the classical past. And, for the most part, it adopted antique formulae. Even the relation of theology to poetry, in Curtius's view, was borrowed from the classical understanding of poetry's relationship to philosophy. For that reason, the chapter on "Poetry and Theology" followed directly upon a chapter on "Poetry and Philosophy."[24] Clearly, the medieval literary world was Latin and not Christian.

With the decline in importance of Germany and Christianity, Curtius had in effect distanced himself from two important aspects of his own person. It is clear that he was a strong nationalist, if vehemently opposed to the *völkisch* strain of nationalism. But Christianity was equally important to him. Not only did he have a religious upbringing, but his mature writings were filled with expressions of Christian faith.[25] In a passage written in 1950 explaining why he remained at the periphery of Stefan George's Circle, Curtius wrote: "I loved the Greek world passionately, but I belonged to the Christian world" (*Ich liebte das Greichentum schwämerisch, aber ich gehrte der christlichen Welt zu*).[26] In his great study of medieval literature, however, Christianity was of only secondary importance.

Even his emphasis on the Latin rather than the Greek classical world involved a sort of self-denial. His neglect of the Greek tradition magnified his denial of German culture, for classical Greece had long assumed a special place of reverence in German culture; even Winckelmann's trips to the Italian peninsula were essentially in search of the Greek tradition. Not only was the Greek past sacred to German culture; it also had a special family significance for Curtius, since his grandfather, Ernst Curtius, was the renown classical scholar who had led the excavations at Olympia. Curtius's slighting of the Greek world was essentially an act of filial sacrilege. In its repudiation of important elements of his background, Curtius's great book of the 1940s can thus be understood as an effort at self-abnegation. Within the context of the Nazi regime, during which most of it was written, it should be read as an attempt at self-exile, an imaginary removal from his native land. The massive study thus offered him not only chronological escape, but an escape from his own Germanness. Always fond of French culture, the Romance philologist insinuated himself indirectly into its traditions.

In his studies, Curtius entered a world that was fully self-sufficient, a world characterized by self-absorption. The literary tradition of the West survived as a form of self-reflexivity, its strength deriving from adherence to certain formal norms adopted from Latin rhetoric—the topoi Curtius viewed as the "foundations of European literature."[27] Curtius's conception of the European literary tradition was extremely formal, for his study almost entirely neglected other aspects of literary production. He showed little interest, for example, in the sociological background of literary texts. Indeed, his framework was so formal that discussion of any type of content—even an interest in plot—seemed peripheral. He even went so far as to complain that the Shakespeare criticism of his day was too absorbed with the importance of character development and dramatic composition: "one is supposed to identify him as a playwright rather than a poet" (336). This objection indicates one of the weaknesses of his scholarship, his tendency to identify literary efforts by their working and reworking of rhetorical forms and their relationship to the Latin poetic tradition. Not only was he uninterested in the political symbology of *Richard III*, but he had no interest in the tragic development of *King Lear.*

Essentially, Curtius's authors were confined to a rhetorical literacy. But a problem emerged with the diminished place of Christianity: he could not ignore the importance of theology, particularly due to the impact of Dante on his imagination. Theology and philosophy entered his narrative but only with respect to poetry. Thus we are offered chapters entitled "Poesie und Philosophie" and "Poesie und Theologie." Ultimately, allegory allowed him to suggest that poetic forms could be made to articulate philosophical ideas; the ancient antagonism between philosophy and poetry was resolved by allegory (212).

Discussing poetry, philosophy, and theology, Curtius was especially interested in the self-consciousness with which European authors identified their relative roles—the deliberateness with which definitional questions were addressed. Consequently, Curtius announced that a large part of his effort was "terminological study" (215). This led him to a sort of metapoetics in which the definitions of rhetorical and poetic forms became a subject of study. Along with his catalog of topoi, Curtius dwelt on how the past understood poetic structure. The topoi already suggested the self-reflexivity of medieval literature. But in their terminological articulations, poets wrestled with the very structure of the poetic tradition. Their poetry was thus largely about poetry.

If Curtius's Latin world was essentially self-reflexive, it was emphatically so in his chapter on the book as symbol. After cataloging topoi and discussing the status of philosophy and theology, Curtius offered the reader one last trope—writing itself as a symbol. In a chronologically organized discussion, Curtius traced the fate of reading and writing as symbols within the literary tradition. And the chapter, much like the book itself, turns finally to Dante. Dante, we are told, used writing paper and the movements of his pen as metaphors. In Canto xxiv of the *Inferno*, he marked time by the duration used to write an "O" (330). Clearly, Dante was preoccupied with the scene of writing, just as all of Curtius's literary figures engaged in the highly self-conscious process of writing.

Since the authors of western literature were so deeply involved in the structure and history of their poetic tradition, and literature was largely about literature, literary production turned out to proximate Curtius's own philological project. Essentially, he brought the poet closer to the philologist. In all his talk about "precision methods" and the "technique of philological microscopy," Curtius cultivated the image of the profoundly professional philologist exercising highly technical expertise, the scientific metaphors suggesting distance from its subject (235). Curtius also made clear that what was so readily accessible to him was not always accessible to the medieval poet, so that he wrote excursuses on the "Misunderstandings of antiquity in the Middle Ages." But if Curtius gained a mastery of the Latin rhetorical tradition, that tradition remained the preserve of the poet. The implication was that the sphere of the poet had become his own.

I have described the literary tradition as a realm largely because Curtius himself does so. In fact, he uses almost exclusively topographical metaphors. Curtius, who devoted a chapter to the ideal landscape in literature, envisioned the literary tradition of the West itself as a landscape. The garden established itself as the principal symbol of the literary tradition. In his introductory chapter, Curtius speaks of "the garden of literary forms" (25). And late in his book, signaling his transition to a discussion of the poles of East and West, he mused: "Let us enjoy all the flowers and fruits of the gardens of Hesperides— and of the 'hanging gardens' of the East" (346). If the East was symbolized by the exotic luxury of the "hanging gardens"—an image of importance to George—the literary wealth of the West found its figuration in the gardens of Hesperides, the golden-appled garden set on a remote island. Curtius, who recognized the "ideal landscape" as one of the major topoi of western literature, described the literary tradition itself as a landscape abundantly populated with fruits and flowers, and remote from the agonies of the political world.

If the literary tradition is understood as a vast terrain, then Curtius's massive study signifies an expedition to map its contours and catalog its species. Indeed, several times Curtius described his book as a journey. Just after his reference to the gardens of Hesperides, he intoned "we end our wandering" (352). And his epilogue begins by using the journey as a figure for the reading of his book: "We have completed a difficult journey and now we can rest" (384). The book as odyssey is, of course, a major trope in the history of western thought, and there is little question that Curtius was conscious about its invocation. But within the tradition Curtius's invocation was precise, for he had in mind the ideal landscape of Dante's *Commedia*. In the chapter on the book as symbol he shows a deliberateness in his reference: "Our way has led us in spiral turns to a height that gives us a retrospect and a new prospect" (306). Who could read that sentence without recognizing Dante's path up the mountain of Purgatory?

The suggestion is that the book as a whole was modeled after the *Commedia*. With its twenty-five excursuses and loose structure, Curtius's study hardly followed the strict formal design of Dante's great poem. Indeed, there was some artifice even in publishing *Europäische Literatur und lateinisches Mittelalter* as a book; at one point Curtius referred to the "studies out of which the work grew" (385). His book lacks clear order. Although some of the transitions between chapters are smooth—as when he ends the chapter on poetry and rhetoric with a discussion of the "praise of contemporaries" directly before launching into a discussion of "heroism" in his chapter on heroes and rulers—even that transition is finally artificial, and the structure of Curtius's book is never clearly revealed (176). Erich Auerbach, whose own *Mimesis* suffered from a similar lack of structure, complained that "the organization of the book, in spite of the author's own explanations, is not always easy to understand."[28]

But despite the confused organization and the relatively unstructured catalog of topoi, Curtius would have his reader see his book as a journey over an ideal landscape. If, like Dante, Curtius was an exile from his own world, he constructed a realm in which he was very much at home. His study suggested an easy mastery of that world and its luxury of forms. At the same time, its replication of Dante's ascent in the *Purgatorio* represents the purgation of his own biography. Unlike the Florentine poet, Curtius was not forcibly exiled. Rather, his exile was self-chosen and the place of exile imaginary.

The world of literary artifice (*Wortkünstelei*) is itself an artifice, a construction set over by Curtius against the concrete world of the Third Reich. But the very notion that culture and politics occupy two separate realms was hardly a novelty in German scholarship. Curtius contributed to the German mythology of a cultural world sealed off from the mundane social realm. This mythology was one of the principal elements of German humanism clearly threatened by the "political university" of the Nazis. Well before Hitler's assumption of power, it was used by liberal professors like Max Weber and Ernst Cassirer to defend their vulnerable scholarly position. And it was adopted by other liberal professors, like Curtius in 1932, to protect their profession from the interferences of the modern world. If the apolitical ideal of culture had political uses, it represented one of the confessional doctrines of German professors attempting to create a protective Mandarin realm as their professional identity became increasingly threatened.[29]

One of Curtius's reactions to that threat was to raise the technical demands of his profession, to produce a book calling for immense technical mastery and command of a vast literature, seemingly the entirety of western literature. Curtius's book is in part a Jeremiad on the state of his profession, if sometimes expressed in sarcasm: "but to do that one must learn Greek and Latin—an unreasonable demand that no sensible person would even dare to utter."[30] If Curtius was the self-elected priest guarding the golden bough of literary culture, he emphasized that the literary culture of Europe had little to do with its political culture. He was fully aware that his project had an important political side—"The Europeanization of historical understanding has today become a political goal, and not only for Germany"—but his vision of culture itself was of a realm undisturbed by the exigencies of political life.[31]

I have mentioned the political uses of the ideal separation of culture and politics, but significantly the ideal was located in the works of the nation's greatest poets, Goethe and Schiller, and that the distinction between *Kultur* and *Politik* was considered part of the nation's inheritance from Weimar classicism. Consequently, any attempt to establish a border between the two has automatic suggestions of Weimar classicism and thereby automatic suggestions of legitimacy.

If Curtius's attempt to envision literary culture in isolation was thoroughly German, the overall force of *Europäische Literatur und lateinisches Mittelalter* remains its internationalism. And yet, even Curtius's internationalism, despite references to medieval notions of *Imperium* and *Studium,* developed from internationalist ideals distinctly German in provenance. In *Deutscher Geist in Gefahr* and in his works on French culture, Curtius advocated a strong internationalism, but one that maintained throughout the individuality of national cultures. If in *Deutscher Geist in Gefahr* he argued for a greater universality on the part of his German contemporaries, a universality that would issue from antique sources, he continued to recognize the place of *Volkstum* in German culture. In essence, Curtius's early understanding of European culture as a dialogue of separate cultures within a common western heritage adopted the historicist organic linking of separate cultures. His view reflected Friedrich Schlegel's dialectical understanding of the relationship between French and German culture, about which Curtius wrote an essay in 1932.[32] But more precisely, the internationalism of Curtius's early work approximated Goethe's *Weltliteratur*, in which various national literatures all played a part.

When Curtius referred to Goethe's concept of *Weltliteratur* in an essay written the year *Europäische Literatur und lateinisches Mittelalter* was published, he concentrated entirely on Goethe's attempt to transcend national literature.[33] Similarly, Curtius wrote in an essay in 1949: "If, however, Goethe represents the last concentration of the western spirit in a single great individual, he is at once more and other than a German poet."[34] This declaration followed directly on an enumeration of Dante, Shakespeare, and Goethe as the three great literary figures who had incorporated the whole of the western tradition. Here Curtius repeated the formulation of Friedrich Gundolf's *Dichter und Helden*, in which Dante, Shakespeare, and Goethe figured as the three "universal poets" and represented three steps in the historical development of European literature.[35] Gundolf's essay was highly historicist in character, and the universal poets he revered approximated the world-historical figures of Hegel. In fact, Gundolf compared them to Caesar, Alexander, and Napoleon, and believed that the universal poets represented a concentration of the history of European literature. They gave that literature new life in their own literary production. In addition, the history of world literature progressed through successive developments in individual national literatures. Gundolf was clearer on the place of national literatures in his *Shakespeare und der deutsche Geist*, but even in *Dichter und Helden* he was conscious that the three universal poets represented three separate national cultures.[36] Thus, if Curtius's translation of Goethe's *Weltliteratur* seems bereft of its national aspect, in its obvious reference to Gundolf it bears the traces of an earlier, more nationally oriented concept.

Curtius's very need to divest the European literary tradition of German contribution—which is related to his effort to eliminate the importance of national literatures—resulted in a dichotomy of the Mediterranean and the northern. When he began a chapter by stating that his "examination presupposed the historical unity of the Mediterranean-Nordic West," he undercut his argument merely by using the formulation *mittelmerrisch-nordisch*.[37] And this was compounded by all his talk of "Romania." By giving priority to Romania, he separated it from the experience of the North. There were certain cultural advantages Curtius conceded to the North mostly due to its less Latin background, such as the ability for some medieval northerners to speak purer Latin since there was less chance that they would confuse its forms with their vulgar tongue. Mostly, however, he favored the Mediterranean over the northern, and just such a juxtaposition echoed the old German mythology of North and South. Indeed, the tension present in the *mittelmeerisch-nordisch* formulation pervades the entire work.

Throughout Curtius's book, the uniformity of European culture threatens to turn into the blending of compass points, the integration of North and South, and East and West. If there is an ever-present North-South dichotomy, the final section of Curtius's chapter on the book as symbol focuses on the interaction of East and West. He even gives it an appropriately Goethean title, "West-Ostliches," suggesting that the ideas of Goethe's *West-östlicher Divan* have informed his imaginative vocabulary. In a tribute written to Hugo von Hofmannsthal in 1929, Curtius praised Hofmannsthal's cosmopolitan roots in Hapsburg Vienna: "Here the East and the West met, here blended ingredients of the great European nations. What a wonderful, rare mixture! Byzantium survives in Hofmannsthal, as it does in his beloved Venice."[38] The spirit of the passage did not disappear with Curtius's attempt to establish the unity of European literary culture. In subtle forms, it structured his work of the forties.

The figure who most symbolized the interaction of compass points was not Hofmannsthal but Goethe, and by making such prominent use of Goethe's *West-östlicher Divan,* Curtius established his debt to Goethe's form of internationalism. Thus, along with his separation of culture and politics, Curtius's appropriation of Goethe's internationalism summoned up eighteenth-century Weimar. If some of the leading ideas of Curtius's immense study led back directly or indirectly to Goethe, its guiding aesthetic was grounded in Goethe as well. Although the book was not meant to aid the formation of aesthetic judgments, it nevertheless reveals Curtius's aesthetic values. His sense of the critic's task is evident in an essay on "Goethe as Critic" published in 1948, where he spoke of "a task that is placed before all criticism of a higher type, but which usually remains unfulfilled: the ranking of authors. But that means as well the discrimination of minds."[39] In the midst of his vast philological project, Curtius did not evade the duty of the critic. He tells us, for example, that although the French and German epics of the Middle Ages represented significant works, none of them is a living part of our culture. "Why not? Not a single one could even at a distance reach the perfection and beauty of the *Aeneid*."[40] And he goes on to tell his reader that Dante's *Commedia* was the first work to reach the level set by Virgil. These are aesthetic pronouncements, and there are numerous other judgments and rankings.

Curtius, however, offers more than a canon. His book provides a rough set of aesthetic principles, if not a developed aesthetic philosophy. Initially, his reader is led to believe that knowledge of the literary tradition and facility with the topoi were the main criteria of Curtius's aesthetic judgment. Certainly, the greatest poets were well ensconced in the literary tradition, and the greatest works were broadly allusive. But knowledge is not poetry, even for Curtius. Thus one has to look elsewhere for the bases of aesthetic judgment, and although hinted at throughout the book, the answer comes mainly in the discussion of "mannerism," a term borrowed from the history of art.

Curtius insisted that the conventional literary opposition of Classicism and Romanticism was meaningless. Rather than referring to Romanticism with all of its nineteenth-century connotations, Curtius suggested a dialogue between classicism, defined as strict adherence to literary rules, and mannerism, which was defined by its gestures away from classical norms: "The mannerist attempts to say things not normally, but abnormally."[41] Curtius's tone and rhetoric reveal a personal fondness for mannerism, which he portrayed less as an escape from tradition as an attempt at free play with it. He believed, however, that mannerism could go too far, and showed a preference for a balanced mannerism, which in its play with tradition revealed its debt. Here Curtius's judgments approximate those of the art historian Aby Warburg—one of the two individuals to whom the book was dedicated—who also showed a fondness for a mannered mannerism. Curtius's taste for such balance, or rather such tension, related to his insistence that classical antiquity was not strictly "classical" in the common sense of the word. Instead of *die Klassik*, he preferred to talk about the Greek and Latin world as *die Antike*.[42] And this he shared as well with Warburg, whose formulation *Nachleben der Antike* has too often been translated as the "Survival of the Classics." For Curtius, as for Warburg, the antique world was a complicated tapestry, one that had little relation to the standard image.

The notion of a Latin and Greek past combining strict adherence to rhetorical rules with inventive gestures away from it brings Curtius close not only to Warburg. In his desire to see an interchange between classicism and mannerism rather than an opposition between *Klassik* and *Romantik*, Curtius approximated Goethe—or at least the common image of Goethe. Rejecting the conventional opposition of Classicism and Romanticism, Curtius offered the example of Goethe: How would you classify him, classic or Romantic? Here Goethe was not merely a useful example—ultimately he provided the symbol of Curtius's own aesthetic. But Goethe was not simply a passive vessel for Curtius's personal aesthetic. Rather the normative aesthetic that pervades Curtius's book came largely from his engagement with Goethe.

Goethe is the hidden presence in *Europäische Literatur und lateinisches Mittelalter*. He is, of course, hardly obscured from view, for his name frequently appears as a referent in Curtius's mapping of the European literary tradition. Even the genesis of the study of topoi—the core of Curtius's science—was located in Goethe's criticism.[43] In the context of Curtius's effort to limit the significance of German literary culture, Goethe could hardly assume the importance and visibility of Dante. Nevertheless, Goethe clearly made an immense impact on the structure of Curtius's imagination—and one that is most important where it is unvoiced.

The years of the Third Reich, during which most of *Europäische Literatur und lateinisches Mittelalter* was written, were framed by two Goethe Centennials, 1932 and 1947. Curtius produced several tributes to Goethe in the wake of the second *Goethejahr*, and he represented Goethe—in a way not unlike Friedrich Meinecke—as a refuge for German culture.[44] Similarly in 1932, *Deutscher Geist in Gefahr* could be read in its Goethean program as a tribute to the poet of Weimar. In both cases, Curtius turned to Goethe in an effort to save Germany. But in writing his great study of medieval literature, Curtius expressed little interest in the salvation of German culture. His project was the construction of a European literary space where he could live in self-imposed exile. That construction, however, was made largely of German materials. Relying on elements taken from the cultural imagination of the German professoriate, for which Goethe was so important, Curtius designed a rather German place for his exile. In the end, this imaginative exile, extremely bold in conception and courageous in its moral stance, did not take him far from home.

NOTES

This article was written with the support of the National Endowment for the Humanities.

1. Erich Auerbach, *Mimesis: Dargestellte Wirklichkeit in der abendländischen Literatur* (Berne: A. Francke Verlag, 1946); on this point, see Carl

Landauer, "*Mimesis* and Erich Auerbach's Self-Mythologizing," *German Studies Review* 11 (1988): 83–96.

2. Ernst Robert Curtius, *Europäische Literatur und lateinisches Mittelalter* (1948; Berlin: Francke Verlag, 1954), 22. All translations in this article are the author's; however, the author has consulted Willard Trask's translation, Ernst Robert Curtius, *European Literature and the Latin Middle Ages* (1963; Princeton: Princeton University Press, 1973).

3. Curtius, *Europäische Literatur*, 25.

4. Auerbach, review of *Europäische Literatur*, in *Modern Language Notes* (May 1950): 349.

5. Curtius, *Europäische Literatur*, 21.

6. Curtius, "Die Lehre von den drei Stilen im Altertum und Mittelalter," *Romanische Forschung* 64 (1952): 57–74.

7. Curtius, "James Joyce und sein Ulysses," *Kritische Essays zur europäischen Literatur* (1950; Berne: A. Francke Verlag, 1954), 290–314.

8. Curtius, *Die literarischen Wegbereiter des neuen Frankreich* (Potsdam: Gustav Kiepenheuer Verlag, 1919). It is interesting in this context to mention that in 1912 Gundolf praised Curtius for possessing "kein Gelehrtenton." Evidently, the tone was acquired later; Gundolf to Leonine Gräfin Keyserling (February 1912), in Gundolf *Briefe, Neue Folge,* ed. Claus Victor Bock (Amsterdam: Castrvm Peregrini Presse, 1965), 133.

9. See the essays in Curtius, *Kritische Essays.*

10. *Die französische Kultur: Eine Einführung* was the joint effort of Curtius and the younger scholar Arnold Bergsträsser, but the division of labor was clear enough that Curtius's name is on the title page of the first volume dealing with cultural questions, and Bergsträsser's name appears on the title page of the second volume dealing with politics and economics (Stuttgart: Deutsche Verlags-Anstalt, 1930); Curtius, *Französischer Geist im neuen Europa* (Stuttgart: Deutsche Verlags-Anstalt, 1925).

11. In his book on Maurice Barrès, Curtius confronted a similar form of nationalism in France; *Maurice Barrès und die geistigen Grundlagen des französischen Nationalismus* (1921; Hildesheim: G. Olms, 1962).

12. He also had a strong attachment to England. See Wolf-Dieter Lange, "Sinn für die geistige Lebensgemeinschaft Europas: Politik und Literatur im bisher unveröffentlichen Briefwechsel Ernst Robert Curtius-Romain Rolland," *EG Magazin,* Sonderteil (April 1986): 1.

13. A discussion of Curtius's involvement in the Decades de Pontigny can be found in Arthur R. Evans's chapter on Curtius in Arthur R. Evans, ed., *On Four Modern Humanists: Hofmannsthal, Gundolf, Curtius, Kantorowicz* (Princeton: Princeton University Press, 1970), 101–4.

14. Curtius (and Bergsträsser), *Die französische Kultur,* 1:27.

15. Ibid., 1:28. The major argument of Stefan Gross's *Ernst Robert Curtius und die deutsche Romanistik der zwanziger Jahre: Zum Problem nationaler Images in der Literaturwissenschaft* (Bonn: Bouvier Verlag, 1980) is that Curtius, despite an effort to reject "national stereotypes," still adopted an *Imagologie* in his description of France, thereby never really escaping the discourse on national essences (see esp. 85). I would add, however, that the images Curtius adopts were ultimately little removed from the conventions of French-German comparison.

16. Geoffrey Hartman, "Blindness and Insight," *New Republic* (March 7, 1988): 26–31.

17. Earl Jeffrey Richards has ably defended Curtius against attacks on his position during the Third Reich. In the context of criticisms by Peter Jehn ("Ernst Robert Curtius: Toposforschung als Restauration," in Jehn, ed., *Toposforschung: Eine Dokumentation* [Frankfurt, Athenaum Verlag, 1972]) and Michael Nerlich ("Romanistik und anti-Kommunismus," in *Das Argument* 72 (1972): 276–313), Richards has called attacks on Curtius for his anti-Semitism "patently false," arguing, among other things, that Curtius had all the right friends and enemies. Curtius was even praised by reviews in the journal of the Centralverein, the major self-defense organization of Germany's Jews, and attacked by the right-wing press; Earl Jeffrey Richards, *Modernism, Medievalism and Humanism: A Research Bibliography on the Reception of the Works of Ernst Robert Curtius* (Tübingen: Max Niemeyer Verlag, 1983), 12. See also Christoph Droege, "Das Exil und das Reich: Ernst Robert Curtius, Aline Mayrisch-de-Saint-Hubert und die Emigration in den dreißiger Jahren," in J.-C. Muller and F. Wilhelm, *Le Luxembourg et l'étranger: Présences et contacts* (Luxembourg: Association SESAM, 1987), 172–86. Droege describes Curtius's departmental struggles with the avid Nazi Moldenhauer and Curtius's failure to receive permission to visit Lisbon because the university deemed him distanced from the Reich. Droege tells an intriguing story of Curtius's surreptitiously aiding a Jewish student and sending correspondence to her from Switzerland. Establishing Curtius's dislike for National Socialism does not, however, negate the anti-Semanitism he expressed in 1932. The passage in *Deutscher Geist in Gefahr,* no matter how much he is working in the realm of symbols, is unambiguously anti-Semitic.

18. Curtius, *Deutscher Geist in Gefahr,* 84 ff.

19. See, for example, Hugo Kuhn's review, "Zum neuen Bild von Mittelalter," *Deutsche Vierteljahrsschrift* 24 (1950): 530–44.

20. Curtius, *Europäische Literatur,* 40–44.

21. Curtius, *Die französische Kultur,* 1:85.

22. Ibid., 1:74.

23. Curtius, *Europäische Literatur,* 21.

24. In his review of *Europäische Literatur und lateinisches Mittelalter,* Auerbach (150) took Curtius to task over this point: "The Bible interests [Curtius] insofar as it is supposed, by St. Jerome and Cassiodorus, to be the model of pagan rhetorics, and the fathers of the church insofar as they are philologists."

25. As Earl Jeffrey Richards writes in the introduction to *Modernism, Medievalism and Humanism,* Curtius was born in a strict Protestant family in Alsace. His father held the position of president of the Augsburg Confessional Church of Alsace-Lorraine. If Curtius had some interest in Catholicism, Richards (2) tells us that he adopted an "Anglican" (Curtius's own construction) posture—remaining outside the Catholic Church. Whatever the subtleties of his religiosity, Christianity remained important to him.

26. Curtius, "Stefan George im Gespräch," *Kritische Essays,* 112.

27. Curtius, *Europäische Literatur,* 89.

28. Auerbach, review of *Europäische Literatur,* 349.

29. The standard analysis of German Mandarinism is Fritz Ringer's *The Decline of the German Mandarins: The German Academic Community, 1890–1933* (Cambridge, Mass.: Harvard University Press, 1968).

30. Curtius, *Europäische Literatur,* 386.

31. Ibid., 17.

32. In his essay on Schlegel in France (1932) in *Kritische Essays,* Curtius describes Schlegel's dialectic of French and German culture, a dialectic that defined his concept of Europe. There is a good deal of Schlegel's French-German dialectic in Curtius, and Curtius's assertion that all Germans concerned with France must learn from Schlegel has autobiographical overtones.

33. Curtius, *Kritische Essays,* 47.

34. Ibid., 84. The translations are the author's. However, the author consulted Michael Kowal's translation, *E. R. Curtius* (Princeton: Princeton University Press, 1973).

35. Friedrich Gundolf, *Dichter und Helden* (1921; Heidelberg: Weiss'sche Universitätsbuchhandlung, 1923), especially Gundolf's essay, "Dichter und Helden" (1912). Although Earl Jeffrey Richards, in his article, "Curtius' Vermächtnis an die Literaturwissenschaft: Die Verbindung von Philologie, Literaturgeschichte und Literaturkritik," 1, does not make a direct connection between Curtius's image of great poets like Dante and Goethe and Gundolf's image of poet-heroes, he does describe Curtius's debt to Gundolf and George. He depicts Curtius's critical method as resulting from a "fruitful and constant tension between the Georgianer and the Gröber student," thereby suggesting a productive combination of philology and George-Kreis thematics.

36. Friedrich Gundolf, *Shakespeare und der deutsche Geist* (1911; Munich and Dusseldorf: Helmut Küpper, 1959).

37. Curtius, *Europäische Literatur*, 235.

38. Curtius, *Kritische Essays*, 124.

39. Ibid., 42.

40. Curtius, *Europäische Literatur*, 248.

41. Ibid., 286.

42. Curtius's move away from classical Greece and Rome was more than a Nietzschean undermining of the standard myths of the classical. It was tied into a growing scholarly appreciation of the breadth and variety represented by Greek and Roman culture, and—in part due to the work of Droysen on Hellenistic culture—an appreciation of the multitude of cultural forms in late antiquity. In this, Curtius was very much in the company of Aby Warburg and the scholars attached to the Bibliothek Warburg in Hamburg, who worked, as Fritz Saxl did, on Mithras cults, or, as Hellmut Ritter did, on the crab magic. Curtius tried to establish the term *Antike* instead of classical not only in *Europäische Literatur,* but more forcefully—if more briefly—in "Antike Rhetorik und vergleichende Literaturwissenschaft," *Comparative Literature* 1 (1949), esp. 43.

43. Curtius, *Europäische Literatur*, 30.

44. In 1948 Curtius published "Goethe als Kritiker." In 1948 he not only published "Goethe—Grundzüge seiner Welt," but in an attack on Karl Jaspers, summoned Goethe as the redemptive figure for Germany, "Goethe oder Jaspers?" *Die Tat* (the Zurich publication, not the nationalistic *Die Tat* that Curtius attacked in *Deutscher Geist in Gefahr*), April 2, 1949. In his essay "Ernst Robert Curtius," Arthur Evans writes that "Curtius's preoccupation with Goethe at the end of his life meant a return homeward after all the years spent with Romance and Latin literatures" (133–34); but I have been arguing that Goethean elements were formative even for *Europäische Literatur und lateinisches Mittelalter.*

THIRTEEN

Kantorowicz, or the Middle Ages as Refuge

Alain Boureau

THE HISTORY OF DISCIPLINES may be described generally in agronomical terms: "fields," "furrows," "harvests," "landmarks." Nevertheless, an urban metaphor would no doubt be more suitable because, since the places where it could be established should be peopled by dwellings, statues, and monuments. Great men and great institutions are necessary here, to name and to orient a space cultivated not out of the weeds, but on top of other habitats. Medieval history cleared its own space during the second half of the nineteenth century, when, in France for example, the Middle Ages were no longer seen as the ambivalent origin of the *ancien régime,* and as a distant time in which Christianity and the communal liberties were being formed. After the post-Revolutionary consensus, shared by the constitutional monarchy and the liberals, the aftermath of the Revolution of 1848 saw the development of a polemical inventory that gave the Middle Ages their own substance. The first occurrences of the words *médiéval* (1874) and *médiéviste* (1867) in French date from the 1860s and 1870s. At that time, the great philologists and erudites succeeded the *polymathes* of history, such as Michelet or Fustel de Coulanges. These specialists provided a strong and specific image of the medievalist vocation, which was durably installed.

Translated by David LaGuardia.

Medieval history called for vocations: it *elected* those who studied it. In the recent and brief autobiography that Robert-Henri Bautier provided in his preface to the collection of his articles, which the École des Chartes offered to him in 1990, the medievalist clearly manifests the substantial reality of the medievalist vocation. After writing an archaeological treatise at the age of twelve, he moves on forever to medieval history:

> A little later, when I was a sophomore [about fourteen] on a visit to the château of Vendôme, I was struck by what they told us about the history of its county and of its union with the Dunois, which seemed to me in error. I was eager to conduct some research at the Library of l'Arsenal, where I had been in the habit of consulting works of literary criticism for my scholarly dissertations; then, like sending a message in a bottle, I wrote to the conservator in order to give him my version of the Dunois. At that time this was Maurice Jusselin, the archivist of Eure-et-Loir, who took time to reply to me; he confirmed my suspicions, and also advised me to prepare myself later on for the École des Chartes. From that moment on, my resolution was firmly taken.[1]

The landscape of medievalism has thus been able to impose its essential nature after a century of professionalization. Still, in the actual development of medieval studies as a discipline, a vague state of being preceded its perfected essence. Thus I would like to demonstrate how one of the great figures of medieval history, Ernst H. Kantorowicz (1894–1963), built his reputation not on the basis of his innate nature, but rather at the end of conflicts and crises, which may enable one to grasp better the process of the medievalist's professionalization at the beginning of the twentieth century.[2]

When he died in Princeton in 1963, Ernst Kantorowicz was celebrated as the glorious image of the medievalist. The necrologies and obituary notices detailed the impressive list of honors and dignities that attested to his eminent presence in the academy: he was a member of the Medieval Academy of America, the American Numismatic Society, the German Archaeological Institute, the American Academy of Arts and Sciences, and the American Philosophical Society, a correspondent of the Royal Historical Society of Madrid, a recipient of the Haskins Medal awarded by the Medieval Academy of America, and so on. In its notice, the journal *Speculum* united three complementary and prestigious signatures, as if to represent the amplitude of Kantorowicz's medieval interests: Erwin Panofsky (for ico-nology), Gaines Post (for legal history), and Joseph Strayer (for the history of political institutions).[3] Each member of the academy could automatically associate the name of this lofty figure with the masterpiece whose very title conjoined its audacious thesis with the idea of "an instant classic": *The King's Two Bodies* (1957). Certainly, this book has been little read, and poorly at that; but is it not appropriate that a classic give this impression of false familiarity that dispenses one from having intimate knowledge of it? Are the medievalists who own a copy of Marc Bloch's *La société féodale* really that numerous?

Nevertheless, the very notice written by the three great scholars in *Speculum* ingenuously designated the faults that were cracking this statue of the perfect medievalist: they rewrote his life in accordance with academic unity, leaving aside the political adventures of the young Kantorowicz, and situating the beginning of his advanced studies before the war of 1914, which they reduced to a circumstantial interruption of a precociously thought-out plan. In fact, for this young man born of the industrial bourgeoisie of Poznan, the war had been the moment and prelude of a nationalist struggle, following his vague attempt to complete a commercial education.

Kantorowicz was an autodidact of medieval history: after the demobilization, and in conjunction with his political and military engagements, he registered, in a completely theoretical manner, for a semester of philosophy in Berlin. Then, in Munich (semesters 1919–20) and in Heidelberg (1920–22), he attended seminars on political economy for the most part, while also being interested in ancient history and the history of modern and contemporary Germany.[4] The thesis that he defended at Heidelberg, the subject of which is prudently left out of the notice in *Speculum,* was concerned with Muslim corporations and was written in the context of comparative historical sociology.

The biography of Emperor Frederick II (1927), which made its author famous, is not at all within the framework of academic medievalism, as we shall see. More profoundly, the work of Kantorowicz, before his last book, seems to have been rarely concerned with the substance of the Middle Ages. His closest disciple and friend, Ralph Giesey, reports that Kantorowicz was intrigued by the mystery of the king's two bodies because, for the first time, this figure of western political imagination did not seem to him to have any ancient roots.[5] The great essays collected in the *Selected Studies* (1964), almost all of which were written after his arrival in the United States, treat the Middle Ages as the medium of transmission and refraction for long schemas that link antiquity with the modern era. From this point of view, the thinkers and artists of the Middle Ages would have succeeded in continuing antiquity beyond its own existence, "in foreign soil," as a contemporary agronomist might say.

Yet, from 1930 onward, Kantorowicz presented himself as a medievalist and academic. How are we to understand this "conversion," which is so foreign to his education and propensities? It begins with the celebrated biography of Frederick II. Upon his arrival in Heidelberg in 1920, the young Kantorowicz entered the circle of the great poet Stefan George, who provided a lofty figure of the magus and the master thinker, at the boundaries of aestheticism and nationalism. George's circle was full of biographical frenzy. The renewal of the German soul came through the exaltation of the exceptional individual, but the biographers of the circle treated the historical science highhandedly, reducing it to the rank of a mediocre occupation of the "literati" or dry erudites. Within the circle, it was a question of using history as "a science of the soul and a revelation through the soul," in the words of Ernst Bertram,[6] who in 1920 composed his *Nietzsche,* which was presented as an "essay in mythology."

The choice of Frederick II was guided by George himself, who saw in the figure of the German emperor raised in Sicily the symbol of a secret Germany, always available for the regeneration of the German spirit. At the same time, the task seemed to be a challenge, as the master declared it impossible because of the incompatibility separating the time of the Gothic from that of "Individuality." The Middle Ages thus constituted some sort of handicap in the race toward aesthetic and nationalistic merit.

This biography, carefully documented, was presented as an historicopolitical essay, rather than as an academic work; it appeared without any commentary in the collection that issued from the review founded in 1891 by George and Hoffmanstahl, *Die Blätter für die Kunst.* This choice of publication was important to the perception of its author's seriousness. Marc Bloch devoted a few disdainful lines to the work in a "historical bulletin" of the *Revue historique* in 1928. He characterized Kantorowicz as an amateur and literatus, close to Hoffmanstahl(!), while four years later another note from Marc Bloch, in the same review, praised the same work, once it was flanked by its volumes of commentaries.[7]

The character of the emperor himself was based on his extratemporal aspect, as an untimely artist of political history, pushed by an ardent rationality to found an eminent state without any Christian attachments. Far from incarnating the Middle Ages, Frederick belonged to the small tribe of creative Heroes, whose emergence shone throughout history with discontinuous brilliance.

The book's success was rather considerable: ten thousand copies were sold in a few years. We know that it was highly valued by the future dignitaries of the Nazi regime—Hitler said that he had read and reread it; Göring gave it as a gift to Mussolini. It still remains to be seen how this work made Kantorowicz into an institutional medievalist. It has been said that, in spite of its thickness and the considerable documentation it carried, *Frederick II* was not intended for an academic public and did not imply any professional ambition. It appropriately belonged to the circle of Stefan George. In an astounding paradox, it was without a doubt its rejection by university critics that decided the career of its author. The scholarly reaction was late in coming, but violent. On May 16, 1929, Albert Brackmann, a respected and influential professor at the University of Berlin, who was the director of the well-known journal *Historische Zeitschrift,* read a paper entitled "Emperor Frederick II from a Mythic Perspective" before the Prussian Academy of Sciences. This speech was immediately echoed in the press, followed by its publication in 1930 in *Historische Zeitschrift.*[8]

First, Brackmann attacked Kantorowicz for his ideological presuppositions, which, according to him, tainted the latter's purpose and explained the historical errors of the work: "One cannot write history as a disciple of George, or as a Catholic, or as a Protestant, or as a Marxist; one may do so only as an individual devoted to the search for the truth." Kantorowicz had done the work of a mythographer by developing a superficial and brilliant image that linked together the rhetoric of the emperor's chancellors and the poetic and nationalistic ambitions of George's disciples. Brackmann then worked to demonstrate how an exact knowledge of the historical realities considerably reduced the interpretations of the figure of the emperor and of his grandiose metaphysics of the state. Thus, far from posing him as the master of the world, the crowning of Frederick in Jerusalem gave him the rather derisory job of governing a small Oriental territory that was recently and precariously conquered. The ceremony contained nothing of the titanesque defiance of the papacy, or of the imitation of Christ, that Kantorowicz had postulated. Frederick's governing practices in Sicily should have been measured point by point, according to a precise comparison with their neighboring systems. Observed in this way in their real context, that of the Christian West, the vertiginous

Roman and Oriental filiations lost their pertinence. For example, the famous "Constitutions of Melfi" (1231), which were the theoretical bases of the emperor's power in Sicily, did not accord the place to Nature that was given to it by Kantorowicz, but rather made manifest a desire to defend the church, which was proclaimed in all of the juridic texts of the period.

It is indeed difficult for a current historian to arbitrate the debate between Kantorowicz and Brackmann, which contains nothing caricatural. Recent research, such as it has been conducted in England, for example, by David Abulafia, tends to observe strong continuities with the Norman monarchic model of Sicily in Frederick's political system, which had not been noted by either of the adversaries in 1929. But rather than reactivating the terms of the dispute by mentioning new work in the field, it is important to recognize its general sense in relation to the profession of the historian. The vocation of the historian is measured, perhaps, by the desire to be both Brackmann and Kantorowicz at once, that is, to alternate incessantly between reduction and astonishment, the ordinary and the exceptional, the untimely and the historical, distance and projection. It is good to be able to thrust Frederick's megalomania into the distant and compact context of the Sicilian monarchy, and at the same time to dream of the breach of verisimilitude offered, for example, by the following passage on the medieval judicial ordeals from the Constitutions of Melfi, cited neither by Kantorowicz nor by Brackmann, and that breaks with our accepted notions of the medieval mentality:

> We, who study the true science of law, and who reject error, abolish from our hearts that evidence that the simple-minded call apparent, which neither takes physical nature into account, nor corresponds to the truth. We have decided that these opinions should be branded as null, and not simply corrected, since they lead one to believe that the natural heat of hot iron may be cooled, or, which is even more foolish, that it may become cold without a valid reason, or that cold water cannot receive a guilty man because of his bad conscience, while in fact, only the retention of a sufficient volume of air keeps him from sinking.[9]

A medievalist may find other texts from the 13th century to relativize such propositions without much trouble; indeed, it is well known that the church condemned judicial ordeals in 1215. Yet it remains true that this kind of vigor pierces the thickness of centuries, and incites the historian to pursue his game of oscillation between the present and the past.

The type of critique announced by Brackmann was found once again in several academic reviews of the work, the most noteworthy of which were those by Friedrich Baethgen (an esteemed scholar who later became Kantorowicz's friend), and by Karl Hampe, a medievalist of Heidelberg and sympathizer of the George circle, whose observations were more moderate. The Frederick II affair took a national turn when Kantorowicz was invited to the seventeenth German Historical Conference in Halle, (April, 1930), the subject of which was "the limits, the possibilities, and the tasks of historical interpretation." The discussion turned into a trial of Kantorowicz's work, along the lines sketched out in Albert Brackmann's article.

The stakes of the debate in 1929–30 largely superseded the context of George's circle. In his exposition, Brackmann had opposed the brilliant historical fresco of Kantorowicz with the humble and necessary task of erudition, and of the establishment of fact, which he called the "close work" (Kleinarbeit). This strong opposition of synthesis and analysis, of interpretation and erudition, had been current in western historiography for a century. A few years after the conference in Halle, in 1934, an analogous debate unfolded in France around the subject of the "Jassemin affair." Henri Jassemin was an archivist, educated at the École des Chartes, that bastion of French analytical erudition, and who had defended a doctoral thesis on the Accounting Office of Paris in the fifteenth century.[10] This work had been heralded by French and foreign historians. In 1934, however, Lucien Febvre, who had just founded the Annales d'histoire économique et sociale (Annals of Economic and Social History) with Marc Bloch in 1934, which became the crucible in which the French study of history was reforged, published a review of Jassemin's thesis. His review was rather ferocious, for the sake of rejecting the myopic erudition that considers all institutions indiscriminately, without comparisons or the elaboration of problems.

Jassemin replied briskly in an article published in the Annales, opposing the erudite scholar to the vulgarizer. The former performs the painstaking, obscure, and necessary work, while the latter employs the results of this work to produce brilliant syntheses intended to amaze the student body. A lasting conflict was installed in the historical academy that is still being waged today. It is not certain whether this type of debate has a salutary effect on historical reflection, insofar as it mixes methodological problems with political conflicts. The Jassemin affair probably swayed the career of Lucien Febvre in a perverse way, by inciting him in a concomitant and contradictory manner to accentuate the erudite allure of his research, and to amplify beyond measure his difference with respect to the tendencies of the Écoles des Chartes: tracing everywhere the "anarchronism" that he linked to myopia, Febvre fell into an excessive historicism that led him to construct the contestable notion of "mental equipage." On the other hand, the dispute at Halle had positive effects on the historical thinking of Kantorowicz.

In effect, this period of debate, from 1929 to 1930, seems to have been of capital importance in the life of Kantorowicz, because he left the cushioned atmosphere, the haughty and amiable complicity, of George's circle. He responded to his attackers in several ways: first, he composed a response to Brackmann, "A glance at myth," whose title (*Mythenschau*) was a reply to that of his critic (*Mythische Schau*).[11] While defending his book by citing its sources and the passages of the text that he considered misrepresented, Kantorowicz developed a theoretical point of view that would orient his work; he showed that, far from constituting a banal, rhetorical envelope of reality that had to be removed in order to attain the substance of the real, myths constituted entirely separate historical objects, which inferred their own causality. This crucial idea, to the effect that language, beside the structures of reality, constructs history, has not yet run its course in current historiography, which is divided unequally between the study of the real (which must push aside the film of language) and the analysis of images of the real, left to specialists in distortion and in mirror images. It is striking to note that this idea, which structures the thought of Kantorowicz, appears only sparingly in the work on Frederick II, which in many respects is drawn from the mythographic genre defined by Albert Brackmann.

A second type of reply oriented the professional life of Kantorowicz, who decided to proclaim his knowledge by exposing his erudition. He busied himself with the composition of a volume of notes and appendices, published in 1931 as the second volume of the work. A detailed examination of this second volume shows that most of Kantorowicz's research was completed after the fact, at the expense of an enraged labor, conducted mainly in locations that were admirably equipped with working instruments, the *Monumenta Germaniae Historica* of Berlin. History is an approximative science—could one imagine an experimental science that would construct its results before its experiments? And yet, sixty-five years later, Kantorowicz's work retains its powerful value, in spite of the detailed corrections that one could make of it. From that time, Kantorowicz swore never to publish anything without infra-paginal notes. In the United States, he protested violently when the Medieval Academy of America decided, for the sake of economy, to publish *Speculum* with endnotes.

The coexistence of minute erudition and complete freedom in the choice of subjects for study gives spice to the work of Kantorowicz, who was never a specialist or a guardian of a historical field. Rather, he was a nomad of specialization: arrested by the strangeness he noted in some object, he made himself an instant and provisional specialist in it. At the beginning, there was nothing but astonishment before the singularity of a graphic representation of a verbal formula; then came the moment of intense specialization: Kantorowicz went on a bewildered quest for all of the figures that multiplied or varied his object, and established the schema of its evolution and transmission. He then developed powerful correlations in the heart of symbolic and political history. For the historian, then, it was a question of attacking the obtuse massiveness of the past at its Achilles heel, advancing obliquely. This obstinate conservative was an anarchist of historical knowledge. The constraints of *Kleinarbeit*, which were dictated to him by the debate of 1929–30, pushed him toward a type of hermeneutics: the energy not invested in the extensive mythic reconstruction of the past he employed in deciphering minuscule sources. The freedom he lost by forcing himself to prove and verify everything was invested in his unruly vagabond trips through documents. Such is the enchantment of the oeuvre of Kantorowicz: while reading the particularly restrained enunciation of a study, one knows beforehand that some kind of spark will be thrown off from the tiny point of his flint.

Kantorowicz's third response was institutional: it seems likely that he took up the academic challenge by soliciting a professional post at the University of Frankfurt, notwithstanding the reception he received from the academy, and despite the fact that he had not obtained the required qualifications for this position in Germany. In the spring of 1930, a few weeks after the Halle conference, he sent a petition to the Prussian minister in charge of religious affairs, who, after consulting the university, granted him the status of honorary professor on August 11, 1930, without his having to traverse the ranks of *Privatdozent* and of distinguished professor. The status of honorary professor, however, did not include any salary, like that of the *Privatdozent* at a lower level. Furthermore, the young Goethe University of Frankfurt, founded in 1914, did not yet enjoy the reputation of its venerable older brothers, even though it was supposed to be open to new possibilities that were not recognized elsewhere. Curiously, aside from the reactionary Kantorowicz, the university received the first strongly progressive members of the famous Institut für Sozialforschung, which would give birth to the Frankfurt School. The strong presence of the favorites of George's circle must have accomplished the rest.

Kantorowicz took to his university service without haste, since he did not give his opening lecture until June 20, 1931, after having sent the second volume on Frederick II to his publisher Bondi. During the four semesters that he taught, he proposed classical and general class subjects and seminars that situated him in his new existence as a university medievalist: the problem of the nobility in the later Middle Ages, the era of humanism, Giles of Rome, the historiography of the thirteenth century, the history of the empire from the Interregnum to the abdication of Charles V. A peaceful and safe career was taking shape. On February 27, 1932, the titular professor of medieval history at Frankfurt, Fedor Schneider, died, and Kantorowicz maneuvered to secure his succession, which he obtained on August 18, 1932.

Hitler's ascent to power quickly interrupted the development of this career. The law of April 7, 1933, excluded the Jews from public functions, with the exception of active combatants from the war. In a letter sent to the Prussian minister of sciences on April 20, 1933, Kantorowicz protested against the law, and informed the minister of his decision not to guarantee his courses during the summer semester. Until his definitive departure, Kantorowicz was careful not to break off relations entirely with the university, perhaps in the hope that there would be a change of regime. His protest did not go so far as a resignation, and he attempted to resume his courses for the winter semester of 1933–34.

Kantorowicz did not intend to resign or go into exile (which he finally did, at the latest possible date, in autumn 1938); but, in fact, he would never again teach in Germany. With the return to classes in 1934, his classes were violently boycotted by the Nazi students, and, after returning from a year at Oxford, he refused to swear allegiance to Hitler, demanding an emeritus status that would exempt him from activity and from taking the oath. It should be noted that his mentor, Stefan George, had died in exile in December 1933 without truly condemning nazism.

It would be impossible, of course, to imagine what would have happened to a career that was interrupted in this way, during the same year in which Kantorowicz took possession of his chair. Approaching the age of forty, he had been placed in the most classic of academic molds: he had even made up for the "delay" caused by his years of military, political, and aesthetic service by means of the rapidity of his advance. Contemporary events destroyed the effect of this normalization, but, paradoxically, they pegged the Middle Ages more securely to the body of Kantorowicz, with this period becoming a place of projection, and not only a terrain that he inhabited merely by chance, having been forced to defend himself against the suspicion of an illegitimate occupation.

It was during the years 1934 to 1938, in interior exile and solitude, that Kantorowicz constructed his Middle Ages on a foundation of despair marked in this great laborer by the composition and translation of an anthology of English poems entitled *Poems of Death, Affliction, and Transfiguration*. The manuscript of this work was found by Eckhart Grünewald in the papers preserved by Beate Salz, the historian's niece. Kantorowicz spent long hours during 1934 to 1938 in the great library of the *Monumenta Germaniae Historica* in Berlin, but he produced little. Nevertheless, his articles, few in number, demonstrate clearly the way in which the Middle Ages captivated and sublimated his distress. Two significant and complementary articles date from 1937: the first was to have appeared in Stuttgart in the *mélanges* offered to professor Ludwig Curtius; its publication was suspended because the volume included too many studies signed by Jewish academics. The article, which appeared only later in the *Selected Studies,* concerned "the return of the scholarly anchoritic life in the Middle Ages."[12] The text opens with the following declaration: "This wise man's lot is solitude," and continues in this vein, in the midst of a scholarly examination of textual filiations: "Such is the wholesome life, which neither enervates the body with urban intemperance nor weakens it in monastic asceticism: the *solitarius* enjoys his 'savory lunch' and pays a light and simple price for it, in order to increase his well-being and bring forth the atmosphere necessary to scholarly work. Such is the fruitful intellectual and artistic life that allows one to pursue without troubles a correspondence with the great men of the past and to forget the distress of the present."

This encomium of the secular, agnostic asceticism of the scholar is sheltered rather precisely in the Middle Ages if one takes into account the other article of 1937, devoted to "Petrus de Vinea in England."[13] This rather technical study of chancellery formulas demonstrates that the royal administration of the thirteenth century used the style of classification and management perfected by Petrus de Vinea, the principal counselor (*logothete*) of Frederick II. It is with this article that Kantorowicz's consistent interest in the rhetors, jurists, and artists of the Middle Ages begins, which will blossom in the extraordinary hymn to the creative jurist that constitutes *The King's Two Bodies*. The ascetic retreat of 1934 had produced this reversal: it is no longer Frederick who makes history, but rather Petrus de Vinea. Yet, according to Kantorowicz's demonstration, which was corroborated from very different points of view by Jacques Le Goff and recently by Alan de Libéra, the central Middle Ages constitute the golden age of intellectual prestige.[14]

This prestige did not go without a powerful dream of taking action in the world, to the extent that the intellectual monopoly of the church up to the twelfth century and the emergence of new monarchies made it necessary to invent a secular vocabulary of legitimacy and a secular mode of argumentation. In Italy in the twelfth and thirteenth centuries, the wordplay between *rhetor* and *rector* took on an aura of reality when the cites choose intellectuals and not powerful people as their *podestà*.[15] The real pertinence of this self-consciousness of medieval intellectuals matters little: their image allowed Kantorowicz to find the traces and vestiges of his formidable construction of the *Two Bodies,* and it linked him profoundly to the Middle Ages, that great refuge of the annihilated intellectual of 1933. In Weberian terms, the Middle Ages of Kantorowicz became the place to exercise by procuration a kind of protestantism without God, and an intraworldly asceticism.

NOTES

1. R. H. Bautier, "Présentation," in *Chartes, sceaux et chancelleries: Études de diplomatique et de sigillographie médiévales* (Paris: Ecole des Chartes, 1990), 1:vi.

2. I will be referring to, and completing, the analyses contained in my brief essay, *Histoires d'un historien: Kantorowicz* (Paris: Gallimard, 1990). The German translation of this work (Stuttgart: Klett-Cotta, 1991) eliminates a few errors and adds, in appendix, a few reflections.

3. Their notice appeared under the rubric of "Memoirs of Fellows," *Speculum* 39, no. 3 (1964): 596–97.

4. On Kantorowicz's professional formation, see the indispensable biography of Eckhart Grünewald, *Ernst Kantorowicz und Stefan George: Beitrage zur Biographie des Historikers bis zum Jahre 1938 un zu seinem Jugenwerk "Kaiser Friedrich der Zweite"* (Wiesbaden: F. Steiner, 1982.

5. See the interview that Ralph Giesey gave to the journal *Préfaces:* "Deux modèles du pouvoir selon Ernst Kantorowicz," *Préfaces* 10 (1988): 114.

6. Cited in W. Lepenies, *Les trois cultures: Entre science et littérature, l'avènement de la sociologie,* trans. H. Plard (Paris: Editions de la Maison des Sciences de l'Homme, 1990), 272.

7. M. Bloch, "Bulletin historique. Histoire d'Allemagne. Moyen Âge," *Revue historique* 158 (1928): 108–58; "Bulletin historique. Histoire d'Allemagne. Moyen Âge," *Revue historique* 169 (1932): 616–55; and 170 (1932): 62–101.

8. A. Brackmann, "Kaiser Friedrich II. in 'Mythischer Schau,'" *Historische Zeitschrift* 140 (1929): 534–59.

9. Cited by R. Bartlett, *Trial by Fire and Water: The Medieval Judicial Ordeal* (Oxford: Clarendon Press, 1986), 76.

10. On the Jassemin affair, see C. Fink, *Marc Bloch: A Life in History* (Cambridge: Cambridge University Press, 1989), 158–59.

11. E. Kantorowicz, "Mythenschau: Eine Erwiderung von Ernst Kantorowicz," *Historische Zeitschrift* 141 (1930): 457–71.

12. E. Kantorowicz, "Die Wiederkehr gelehrter Anachorese im Mittelalter."

13. E. Kantorowicz, "Petrus de Vinea in England," *Mitteilungen des Österreichischen Instituts für Geschichtsforschung* 51 (1937): 43–48.

14. Cf. Jacques Le Goff, *Les intellectuels au Moyen Âge,* 2d ed. (Paris: Seuil, 1985), and Alain de Libéra, *Penser au Moyen Âge* (Paris: Seuil, 1991).

15. Cf. E. Artifoni, "Podestà professionali e la fondazione retorica della politica communale," *Quaderni storici* 63 (1986): 687–719.

PART FOUR

THE DISCIPLINE AND ITS OTHERS

FOURTEEN

Philological Iconoclasm: Edition and Image in the *Vie de Saint Alexis*

Michael Camille

THE BOOK IS FAR MORE REAL than the picture. It provides a truly ontological relationship and real participation with an intellectual entity. But a book, apart from anything else, is a "text." One understands it or one does not understand it. Perhaps it contains "difficult" passages. One needs a technique to unravel them: its name is philology. Since *Literaturwissenschaft* must deal with texts, it is helpless without philology. So-called *Kunstwissenschaft* (art history) has an easier time: it works with pictures and photographic slides. Here there is nothing intelligible. To understand Pindar's poems requires severe mental effort; to understand the Parthenon frieze does not. Knowing pictures is easy compared to knowing books.[1]

Making this distinction between the "superficial" image and the "real" word in the opening chapter of *European Literature and the Latin Middle Ages,* E. R. Curtius failed to realize he was himself using a venerable topos. St. Augustine had argued along similar lines that "a picture is looked at in one way and letters in another. When you see a picture, the matter is ended: you have seen and you praise. When you see letters, this is not yet the end, because you also have to read."[2] From ancient sources through the Middle Ages, in Renaissance writings on art and on to Lessing and the Romantics, this topos works to define a split between "discourse" and "figure," between seeing and

371

reading. It is a rupture that has literally divided the object/text that I want to look at/read in this chapter, a parchment manuscript of 209 folios measuring 276 × 194 mm, which belongs to the Basilika of St. Godehard in Hildesheim, Germany. It exists today as two quite discrete things with entirely different names, histories, contents, and contexts. Romance philologists and scholars of French medieval literature have designated it manuscript "L" of the Old French *Vie de Saint Alexis* as it appeared in Gaston Paris's 1872 edition of the work.[3] The same object is well known to art historians by a fuller name, the *St. Albans Psalter,* as it was called in Adolph Goldschmidt's 1895 study that first reproduced its full-page narrative miniatures.[4]

For the student of language and literature, nomenclature is a mere cipher. The "L" stands for the monastery of Lamspringen, near Hildesheim, which owned the manuscript after the Reformation and has nothing to do either with its present site, its originary place of production, or its functions. For the art historian the name is more important, signifying both its status as a common type of book, a Psalter, and locating its site of origin, which on internal palaeographic and liturgical evidence is thought to be the monastery of St. Albans in southeast England. "L" is in fact a sign not for a book, but for a text, the oldest extant version of the French *Vie de Saint Alexis* which this manuscript contains. In literary history the object is a mere repository for this text, like an obfuscatory *chasse* encasing a precious relic that has to be carefully extracted, cleansed, and retranscribed by the pseudo-scientific gaze of philological scrutiny.

The *St. Albans Psalter* was also the title of the definitive monograph on the Hildesheim manuscript published in 1960 by three scholars, Otto Pächt, C. R. Dodwell, and Francis Wormald, under the auspices of the "word and image" oriented Warburg Institute in London.[5] In a similar way to Gaston Paris's edition of "L," this large gray-covered volume has become something of a paradigm in the presentation of an illuminated medieval manuscript. However, the very multiplicity of its expert authors defined a less unified object: a collection of heterogeneous signs, both visual and verbal, yet all brought together, they argued, for one patron. This was the anchoress Christina of Markyate who, after finding a safe hiding place from her family at St. Albans in 1131, spent the rest of her life in a cell attached to the monastery where she was spiritual adviser to Abbot Geoffrey and an eremetic example for the whole community.

Christina's book opens with a calendar, rich in obitual evidence of her life, monastic friends, and the family she rejected in order to

FIGURE 1. *Basilika of St. Godehard, Hildesheim, Psalter of Christina of Markyate. Alexis Master, full-page image of the Deposition.*

become a hermit. Then come the thirty-nine full-page narrative pictures of the Life of Christ that carry no explanatory rubrics (fig. 1). A full-page picture of King David as musician precedes the vernacular Alexis poem, which begins with a half-page drawing and a long introductory rubric (fig. 2). The poem itself (fig. 4) is directly followed by an extract from a letter of Pope Gregory the Great, in Latin and French, defending the use of images (fig. 6). Three more pictures of Christ's appearance to the disciples at Emmaus precede the Psalter with its richly historiated text filling three-quarters of the manuscript (figs. 7 and 8). More pictures of local saints and another David scene close the volume. The few times the manuscript has been exhibited, as in the exhibition of English Romanesque art at the Hayward Gallery

FIGURE 2. *Basilika of St. Godehard, Hildesheim, Psalter of Christina of Markyate, pp. 56 and 57. King David enthroned as musician and inspired by the Holy Spirit on the left page, facing the Alexis Master's narrative picture*

in London some years ago, its tomblike status as a precious and unopenable object in the modern world, a mere repository of texts and magnificent art, was apparent in its display, open at one place (and not to be turned) in a climate-controlled, spotlit glass case as in a shop window.[6]

Most of the articles and books on the language, subject matter, and context of "L" never refer to its appearing in this peculiarly problematic artifact or picture-infested place. Goldschmidt's monograph went unnoticed by Romance philologists until the late 1950s.[7]

of St. Alexis leaving his bride before the prologue to the Alexis Song on the right page.

Even today the poem continues to be cited unsited, described deracinated from its place in space and history. This is between the imposing full-page image of King David as musician (fig. 2) and the text of St. Gregory's famous defense of pictures (fig. 6). Here it is called not a *vie* but a *cancun*. In this sense it appears carefully positioned between the singing King David as oral source for the Psalms and the arguments of *la peinture,* as sharing in both orality and spectacle, sound and sight. In the rest of this chapter, I want to explore how modern philology has erased all aspects of enactment—sound, sight, and sense—from this medieval text.

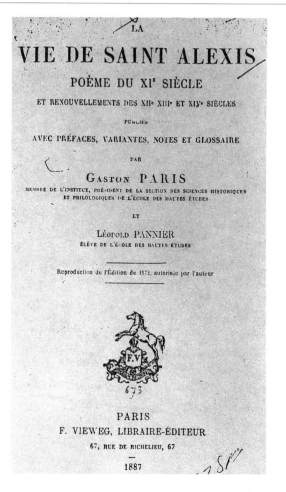

FIGURE 3. *Opening title page of Gaston Paris's 1872 edition of the* Vie de Saint Alexis.

It is worth remembering, however, that the discipline of art history is just as "guilty" as philology in creating this split between the discursive and visual aspects of the manuscript. In surveys of medieval art, the *St. Albans Psalter* is discussed as a "monument" of pure visibility—a collection of textless pictures (fig. 1) and not as a poetic locus, as it was displayed in the Hayward Gallery exhibition.[8] Even Pächt separates his analysis of the poem and its authorship by a scribe-artist he calls (after the poem the Alexis Master from his visual description of the miniature. Within his own discussion there is a split between the text and image, the latter being always *elsewhere:* "for a

FIGURE 4. *Basilika of St. Godehard, Hildesheim, Psalter of Christina of Markyate, p. 58. The beginning of the* Cancun de St. Alexis.

stylistic analysis see p. 120," states Pächt in a footnote in the middle of his treatment of the poem.[9] Just as Gaston Paris sought to find the text's anterior foundations, Pächt also undertakes a search for origins. He looks everywhere, in Italo-Byzantine and even ancient Roman art, for iconographic parallels and prototypes for the powerful narrative images like the Deposition, which replaces the Crucifixion as the climax of the cycle (fig. 1)—everywhere, that is, but the locus of the manuscript itself.

This method of tracing the stemmata of a miniature cycle as if it were a text was a German tradition of iconographic study greatly

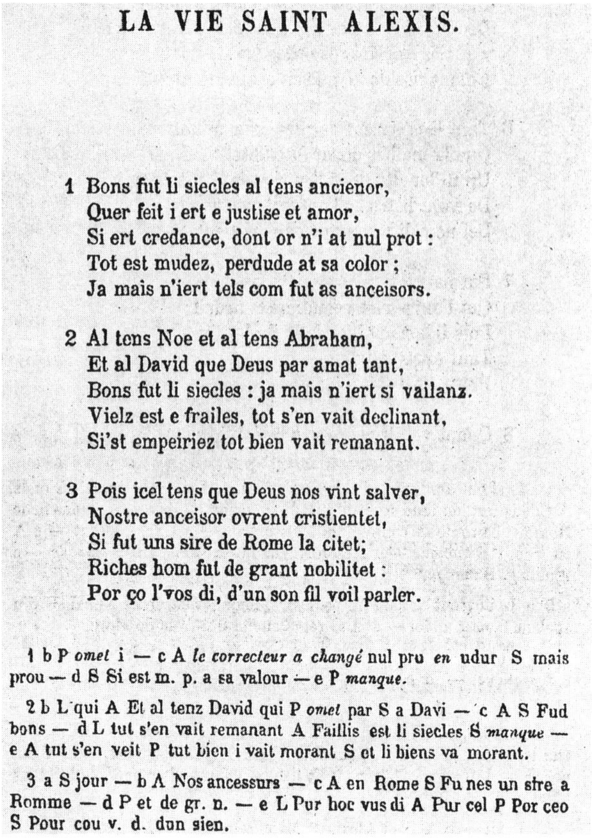

LA VIE SAINT ALEXIS.

1 Bons fut li siecles al tens ancienor,
  Quer feit i ert e justise et amor,
  Si ert credance, dont or n'i at nul prot :
  Tot est mudez, perdude at sa color ;
  Ja mais n'iert tels com fut as anceisors.

2 Al tens Noe et al tens Abraham,
  Et al David que Deus par amat tant,
  Bons fut li siecles : ja mais n'iert si vailanz.
  Vielz est e frailes, tot s'en vait declinant,
  Si'st empeiriez tot bien vait remanant.

3 Pois icel tens que Deus nos vint salver,
  Nostre anceisor ovrent cristientet,
  Si fut uns sire de Rome la citet;
  Riches hom fut de grant nobilitet :
  Por ço l'vos di, d'un son fil voil parler.

1 b P omet i — c A le correcteur a changé nul pru en udur S mais prou — d S Si est m. p. a sa valour — e P manque.

2 b L qui A Et al tenz David qui P omet par S a Davi — c A S Fud bons — d L tut s'en vait remanant A Faillis est li siecles S manque — e A tut s'en veit P tut bien i vait morant S et li biens va morant.

3 a S jour — b A Nos ancessurs — c A en Rome S Fu nes un stre a Romme — d P et de gr. n. — e L Pur hoc vus di A Pur cel P Por ceo S Pour cou v. d. dun sien.

FIGURE 5. *Gaston Paris's 1872 edition. The beginning of the* Vie de Saint Alexis.

influenced by the pseudo-scientific prestige of Lachmannian text edit-ing.[10] The 1960 Warburg Institute monograph is also a "visual" edition in that it presents only the frontispiece page, the opening lines of the poem (because of the initial), and the final page of the poem (because of Pope Gregory's statement), ignoring the body of the text in between. The written word is not judged to be visual "art" in modern scholarship. By contrast, the thirteenth-century canon, poet, and expert on word-image relationships Richard de Fournivall wrote, in his *Bestiare d'Amours,* that "writing contains depiction [*peinture*] for no letter exists unless painted."[11]

The corollary of this eradication of the text by art historians—the excision of the image by philologists—has to be seen in terms of the development of French literary studies in the nineteenth and early

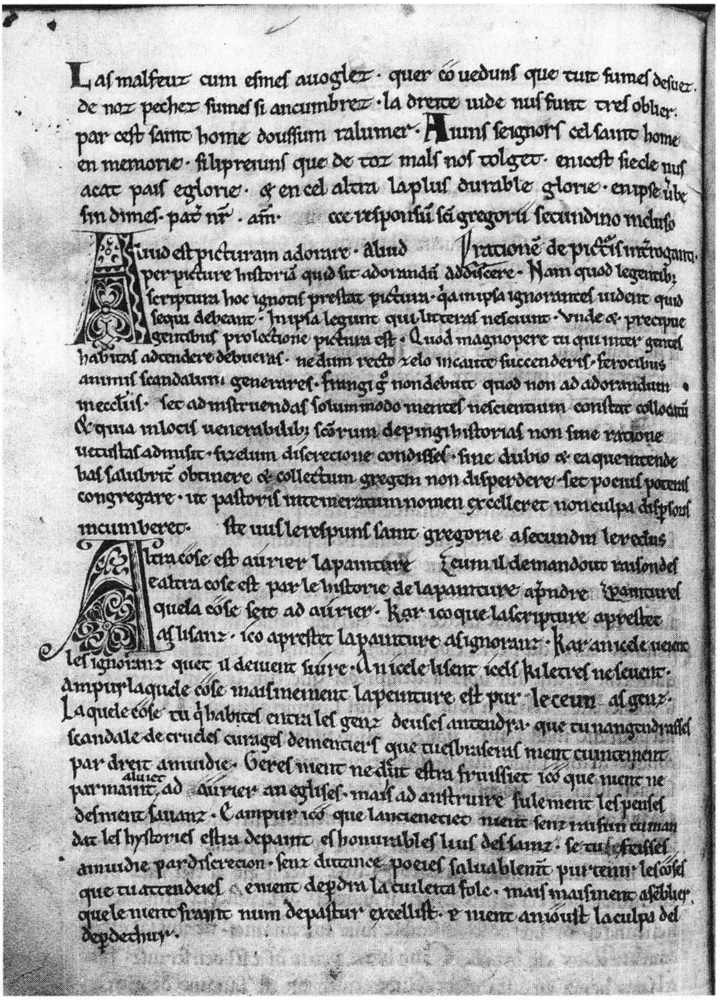

FIGURE 6. *Basilika of St. Godehard, Hildesheim, Psalter of Christina of Markyate, p. 68. The last lines of the Alexis Song and Gregory the Great's defense of images in Latin and French.*

twentieth centuries. The Alexis poem is a key construct in this history. Its importance as a founding text of the French language, like the *Chanson de Roland,* aids in its transcendence of any specific place, its disappearance apart from being designated by a point or "L" on a stemmatic tree. Crucial in its ascendence to the realm of pure invisibility as a "work" of French literature was its canonization in what has been called "a landmark edition in the ideology of Text Editing"

FIGURE 7. *Basilika of St. Godehard, Hildesheim, Psalter of Christina of Markyate, p. 72. The beginning of the Psalms with David the inspired author and the battle of knights drawn and discussed by the Alexis Master in the margins.*

Figure 8. *Basilika of St. Godehard, Hildesheim, Psalter of Christina of Markyate, p. 193. Initial to Psalm 65 (64).*

where, according to its editor Gaston Paris, the poem "s'ouvre véritablement la littérature française du moyen âge."[12]

Edition as Epitaph

Gaston Paris's critical edition of 1872 in fact closed off the poem for more than a century. Having "fait époque dans l'histoire de la philologie romane," it was reprinted first in 1885 for use in university classes and then again in 1903 with some changes caused by "innovations concernant la reproduction typographique."[13] But in this and the many subsequent editions such as that in the series Les Classiques Français du Moyen Âge (1974), "L" remains in its nineteenth-century typographic form. Externally it is a sliver of a volume in gray soft covers that might slip into one's pocket like an edition of Rimbaud or Baudelaire. Its sparse, almost ascetic regimentation on the page in five-line strophes is also, as we shall see, a monochromatic equalization of signs that in the Hildesheim manuscript are richly colored and variable graphic movements. This reduction to the purely optical on the part of the modern printed book is part of a regimen of uniformity and machine-speed legibility that marks the modern printed book as alien to the medieval mode of rapturous reading, rooted as it was in a somatic and sensuous experience. It is also a reduction of sensations to the purely optical distance that is a hallmark of late-nineteenth-century science. Editions of the poem in the last century have thus literally embalmed it. Their title pages have all the finality of epitaphs (fig. 3). Committed to the grave of an edition, Alexis' song as it appears in the Hildesheim manuscript has been erased from literary history.

Gaston Paris was not the first to bury the *Vie de Saint Alexis* in a text. He noted in his 1872 preface that the poem had been published four times before, first by a German philologist, Wilhelm Müuller, who "discovered" the "precious Hildesheim manuscript."[14] Paris stresses that his, the fifth publication of "L," has the "double innovation" of phonetic as well as grammatical critical apparatus and that the text has been *etabli* by comparison with other, later copies. This process of establishing a text achieved by methods of visual comparison between various copies, is also based on an erased ocular model.[15]

In terms of the history of editorial practices, this is indeed a new direction and part of that assimilation of German philological expertise by the nascent French nationalist educators as described by Hans Ulrich Gumbrecht.[16] But it is also part of a still little-appreciated appropriation of methods from other major and more visual discourses of the period such as comparative anatomy and the novel. Carefully classified blocks of print and their footnoted apparatus, together with clearly demarcated beginnings and endings, remade texts written in the twelfth and thirteenth centuries into nineteenth-century intellectual commodities. Presenting the Alexis poem as what he calls a "specimen of proper French Language such as it must have been spoken and written at the end of the eleventh century," Paris was not only ignoring its twelfth-century locus—the book or *chasse* in which his relic of language had been crystallized—but was also isolating its paradigmatic "voice."

Paul Zumthor has described literary communication as a process of stages, beginning with the "original communication" that is "generally beyond the limits of our gaze," which is first mediated by manuscripts but then mediated once again through the scholarly apparatus.[17] In literary production a crucial term is lost—the originary site. In Zumthor's words, "we listen to the discourse of an invisible other who speaks to us from some death bed (or some couch) of which the exact location is unknown to us."[18] The study of art history, by contrast, takes as its object that very place, the site of the originary gaze where the artist makes his stroke on vellum or in stone. Communication is not a lost voice mediated through a secondary visual process of writing but is through the image directly available at the point of origin.

This distinction can be seen in the differing strategies of the text editor and the art historian in dealing with the Alexis poem. Gaston Paris not only denied the pictures in the manuscript but the script as well since his philology was not language-based but was, as Stephen G. Nichols and R. Howard Bloch have suggested, rooted in the reflective notion of "literature as the image of life."[19] As a specular phenomenon, a poem could be deflected and displaced from the place of writing. Because the poem was itself an image, any actual images only interfered with the scholarly process of recouping the lost language reflected in the text. In his search for origins, Gaston Paris argued that "L" was not the first vernacular poem in the language (how could it be since it was written down in England!) but was rather a later version of a work composed a century earlier, toward 1040. He even tried to pin an author on the original text, Tebalt de Vernon, canon of Rouen. The scribe transcribing it in the Hildesheim manuscript was simply copying an already finished and imported French poem.[20]

Otto Pächt's art-historical study of the manuscript took issue with this and argued that, especially in the light of local interest in Alexis, there was nothing to prevent "L" from being the first vernacular version of the work. Moreover, he attributed its creation, its script, and also significantly its prefatory picture to an individual he named "the Alexis Master."[21] Although this reveals a similar nostalgia for origins and authorship, his argument rests on the materiality of the manuscript and a continuity between scribal and painterly practice totally ignored by the philologist. For Gaston Paris such a continuity between image and word has to be broken despite the search for paternal textual origins. What we know of Paris's life suggests that finding a text was not finding the "name of the father" but rather forgetting it.

Fathers and Sons: Images and Words

Why did philology become so completely divorced from the manuscript matrix in this way? Part of the answer lies in the institutional development of literary as opposed to art history in the course of the nineteenth century. Gaston Paris's inauguration of modern philology in France and his acceptance of the German Diez as his "academic father" have been described psychologically as a rejection of his real father, the medievalist Paulin Paris, who nominated his son to succeed him at the Collège de France in 1866.[22] What has not been fully realized is how much this denial of the "name of the father" was simultaneously a denial of the visual image. In a lecture at the Collège de France in 1881 in honor of his recently deceased father, Gaston described the trajectory from father to son as one of a transition from *apprécier* to *connaître,* from picture, to text.[23] The father emerges in his son's discussion as a Romantic connoisseur in an earlier tradition of medievalism now superseded by Gaston's own rigorous philological penetration which goes deeper than the surface. Another difference between image and text, father and son, was that Paulin Paris was one of the first great experts on manuscript illumination, having completed his great descriptive catalog of French manuscripts in the Royal Library—the very manuscript matrix that Gaston Paris was to so ardently ignore.[24]

Paulin Paris must also be seen in the context of medieval studies in the first half of the nineteenth century, which were far more "interdisciplinary" in today's sense than they were to become later. Gaston's lecture mentions his father's early work, *Apologie de l'école romantique,* which recounts his sources of early inspiration as Byron, "l'art du moyen âge," and the cathedral of Reims in whose shadow he had been raised.[25] During the first half of the nineteenth century, as Stephen Bann has shown, "the visual image became part of the general movement towards rediscovering and recreating the past."[26] The early enlightenment attitude that made images and texts equal evidence for a *science de l'homme* was continued in French museums of the early part of the century. The first and most influential of these was Lenoir's Musée des Monuments Français (1795–1818), which created a chronology of medieval monuments from the fragmented object of Revolutionary iconoclasm.[27] It was precisely the Romantic disorder of the Lenoir's museum that was later countered by Du Sommerard's Cluny Museum, which opened in 1832. This sought to organize materials in more thematic crystallizations of "the Gothic" and "the Romanesque" in a series of period rooms.[28] There is another father-son relationship here, too, in that Alexandre Lenoir's son, the beaux-arts architect Albert Lenoir, was involved in designing the newer museum. An increasingly didactic and evolutionary view of medieval art was further propagated by the new Musée des monuments Français opened with the help of Viollet-le-Duc at the Trocadéro in 1882.[29] This was an "ideal" museum in that it was composed totally of plaster casts of medieval and Renaissance sculptures and copies of paintings, each fragment restored, placed in its proper chronological sequence, and, significantly, ripped out of its spatial context.

This transformation of the vandalized medieval statue, from evocative Romantic fragment to classified "specimen" of style in a codified history of French art, was similar to that undergone by the medieval text. It too was "discovered" and presented to the public by a new generation of classifiers. As opposed to the dilettante fathers' delight in objects and fragments, the scholar sons' rigorous catalogs and editions were products of an anti-Romantic as well as an anti-aristocratic reaction. Like the plaster casts of the Trocadéro, where medieval images were totally removed from their places on portals and churches, medieval texts were likewise wrenched from their manuscript matrices as idealized fabrications in the evolving history of "literary" language.

The father/son, image/text split occurs in other leading nineteenth-century mediévistes. Emmanuel Viollet-le-Duc (b. 1781) was the father of the more famous restorer and architect. A polymathic man of letters in the Enlightenment tradition, he wrote to Didron, the director of the new organ of midcentury medievalism, the Annales archéologiques, in 1845 with articles entitled "De la poésie au Moyen Âge." The editor was pleased to see explorations of the "curious parallelisms" which he saw existing in the Middle Ages "entre la parole et l'image, entre la poésie et le dessin." The theme of what Didron acutely termed "les objets chantés et dessinés" continued to appear in this journal, with articles in the same year on "Iconographie des fabliaux" by M. le Baron Guilhermy.[30]

This is just one example of the innovatory approaches to medieval culture in its multiple media that was very much a part of the historicizing mid-nineteenth-century impulse. *Le Moyen Âge et la Renaissance: Histoire et description des moeurs et usages, du commerce, et de l'industrie, des sciences, des arts, des littéraires et des beaux arts en Europe,* published in 1848, had both a literary and an "artistic" editor, suggesting the beginnings of a split in expertise. Nevertheless, these lavishly illustrated texts continue the encyclopedic tradition of the Enlightenment where "All the arts must be seen as composing the one single family—Art," this volume announced.[31] This interest in the interplay of text and image in the mid-nineteenth century has to be seen in the context of new reproductive techniques in lithography and printing which allowed for reproductions of medieval illuminations and images on a mass scale such as those that filled Didron's *Annales archéologiques.*

But by the third quarter of the nineteenth century, the ubiquitous professionalization of evolving scholarly disciplines and the prestige of "scientific" discourse meant that the interests of art historians and text historians began to diverge. This was partly the result of the growth of specialist organizations and academies.[32] In France, the *Gazette des beaux arts* had a much less "academic" aspect than the equivalent German art periodicals, and one can say that, whereas Diez became the German godfather of French literary studies, French art history remained orphaned and untrained until well into the twentieth century. Lacroix's preface to his second 1870 edition of *Les arts du Moyen Âge* reveals an increasingly separatist attitude: "The numerous illustrations that adorn the work will engage the eye, while the text will speak to the intelligence."[33] This is the Augustinian topos repeated by Curtius and many others, which resurfaced as the tyranny of the text took over late-nineteenth-century culture.

Textual Restoration

"To restore a building is not to preserve it, to repair, or rebuild it; it is to reinstate it in a condition of completeness that could never have existed at any given time."[34] Viollet-le-Duc's 1840 restoration of the Romanesque abbey of la Madeleine at Vézelay created a new west façade with tympanum and doorway with sculptural ideas and details culled from other extant buildings. He literally restaged the threshold and altered how the viewer entered the building.[35] This redefinition of openings was also the method adopted by textual editors in their textual rather than architectural restorations of "ideal" texts that "never existed." Just as Viollet-le-Duc's rationalist restorations have been seen as heralding the rise of Modernism in architecture, Gaston Paris's, and later Joseph Bédier's, concern with authorship and establishing an edition from a single exemplar are protomodernist strategies for closing-off the text, purifying it of extraneous and supplementary forms whether they be images or readers. Paris described his edition of Alexis as "un essai de restauration intégrale" (vii).

Bedier's was not a radical restoration like Paris's but more akin to a single "reading" like the early iconographer's "reading" of a building. In his edition of the *Lai de l'ombre* published in 1913, Bédier actually cites "the archaeologist Didron" to the effect that "Il faut conserver le plus possible, réparer le moins possible, ne restaurer à aucun prix" and underlines its aptness for textual editing: "Ce qu'il disait des vieilles pierres doit s'entendre aussi, croyons nous, de nos beaux vieux textes." If the modernist Bédier sought to retain the purity of an authentic "original," Paris sought to construct it anew. Paris's first 1872 edition opens with the title of the autonomous poem "La Vie de Saint Alexis" in a bold and distinct typeface (fig. 3). By contrast, the opening of pp. 56–57 of the manuscript is a predominantly visual rather than verbal experience, beginning with the full-page picture of King David as musician on the left-hand page (fig. 2).

This image of inspiration and biblical song production provides the framing functional inauguration of the saint's song that follows as one's eye moves across to the right-hand page. A medieval manuscript is built out of openings and continuities between "before" and "after" rather than the isolated framed images, frontispieces, and title pages of the bound modern codex. The first thing that catches one's eye on p. 57 of the manuscript is the picture of Alexis leaving his wife on their wedding night. There are Latin *tituli* above the scene, but these are small, identifying names. The large "I" initial below inaugurates the textual beginning, "Ici cumencet" ("here begins"), the "ici," like the "hic" in the Bayeux Tapestry, defining a place of narrative opening that is both verbal and visual.

The next line of the 1872 title page tells us what we are reading: "*Poemè du XIe siècle*". There is no poem of the eleventh century, of course, the Hildesheim version being the oldest extant one; but this subtitle, like that of a contemporary novel, helps create the "fiction" that there was one. In the manuscript it is called a "song," not a poem: "Ici cumencet amiable cancun. . . ." The scholarly authority of the text is a crucial aspect of the presentation of the printed edition, which lists "Préfaces, variantes, notes et glossaire" by the editor/author Gaston Paris, whose honors and titles are enumerated. The printer's mark below is not an image internal to the poem but a sign of its commercial property value, followed by the place and date of publication. In contrast to this codified institutional list of the title page, the discursive opening of the work in the Hildesheim manuscript seems meandering, even free-floating, open to multiple subject-positions, rather than the perspectival gaze of a single objective viewpoint.

Recently the multiple meandering beginnings in the Hildesheim manuscript have been explored by Alexandre Leupin.[36] His approach is a good example of a welcome return to the manuscript matrix. However, that matrix is still seen in predominantly textual terms. The prose prologue is not, as he puts it, "the first threshold of the work"—surely the image is! (fig. 2). This image is what the French of the prologue below it on p. 57 refers to in its "opening" words.

> Ici cumencet amiable cancun e spiritel raisun d iceol noble barun Eufemien par num, e de la vie de sum filz boneuret del quel nus auum oit lire et canter.

> [Here begins the pleasurable song and spiritual account of a noble baron named Eufemien, and of the life of his blessed son, about whom we have heard reading and singing.][37]

The prologue is written in alternating black and red lines of script, which again serve to shift attention onto the surface, making text "play" image. It is by the same scribe that wrote out the poem, and as Pächt demonstrates by careful attention to the parchment object and its various markings, this writer is the maker of the drawing above. These words are those that might introduce the song as it was performed, and indeed have been linked to the liturgy and the inauguration of a chapel dedicated to St. Alexis in the church at St. Albans.[38]

The picture likewise inaugurates a mental performance by the viewer that focuses on the early part of the Alexis narrative rather than the revelation of the hermit saint to his parents, which is usually seen as the climax of the story (fig. 2). It depicts the renunciation of the saint in four segments. First he splits from his bride, giving back the ring over the bed that signals their unconsummated marriage and his rejection of the flesh. Next we see the isolated psychological effect of all this on the abandoned spouse who stands alone in the doorway. A *titulus* above her states that "the ultimate gifts are given to the chaste bride."

This draws out an identification with the single female figure and suggests how there are multiple subject-positions for Christina to inhabit within the image, not just that of the wanderer Alexis, but also that of the woman left alone in the constructed, cell-like space. Alexis leaves the bonds of family and the safety of civilization, represented by the rich textiles and architecture on the right, moving out through the open door into a marginal sea where his paying the boatman oddly echoes his return of the ring in the first image in the sequence. But this also serves to "close" the visual narrative, reminding us that images, too, have a logic and grammar that is just as temporal as texts and not instantaneous. The strong left-to-right thrust sets up the expectation of the reading eye/I that follows the prologue below and then turns the page to the realm of never pure textuality beyond.

Turning the page in the manuscript, we come to a brilliant decorated initial "B" (fig. 4). This letter preempts the later "B" in which King David plays his harp on p. 72 (fig. 7), and where the Alexis Master writes a long gloss on his marginal image of two warriors fighting as a spiritual image to be understood "spiritually" from the physical image. This is also the opening of the psalm *Beatus Vir.* But the big letter "B" earlier in the book begins "Bons fut li siecles al tens ancienor quer feit . . . " in the vernacular, not Latin. Such a play of decorative letters is a subversive strategy interposing the vernacular *as an image of* the Logos. Once again the appearance of the text is crucial to its interpretation. The saint's life is thus linked to the Psalter by a visual as well as a thematic christological bond.

The layout of the Alexis poem in Paris's and subsequent modern editions in numbered five-line strophes (fig. 5) is a radical reshaping of its long lines in the earlier manuscript where verses are indicated by a point and new strophes by a majuscule. One's pace of reading is also different. The first page of the edited poem, comprising the first three strophes, fill only one-third of the dense, almost cramped manuscript page (fig. 5). Gaston Paris, or at least his publishers, literally stretched out the spaces in and around the poem, pushed the words apart in order to purify and contain it as a specimen of medieval French. Now pinned to the page, it can be microscopically examined in relation to variants at the bottom of the page.

The whole enterprise works to the construction of something that never existed in the Middle Ages but is a creation for the *salle de classe.* The editor's prologue in the 1872 edition reads in many ways like the presentation of a scientific experiment or a preliminary to a dissection report: "Even assuming that here and there I have gone too far in attributing to the author of the *Alexis* one or other linguistic form to the exclusion of some other one, I think that it will indeed be recognized that the text of this poem, such as I am offering it to the public, offers an acceptable specimen of proper French language such as it might have been spoken and written in the middle of the eleventh century."[39]

In his scrupulous scholarly process, Gaston Paris does not, however, totally ignore the picture. He describes how "notre poème" is preceded by a "miniature qui représente Alexis prenant congé de sa fiancée". This separates the language—"our poem"—from the image, which is somehow other—theirs, not "ours." The image belongs to the past and cannot, unlike the enunciated poem, be recouped for modern tastes. Notice, too, how Paris's "naturalist" perception views the four-part narrative showing Alexis and his bride in the bedroom, her remaining behind, his leaving, and Alexis on the boat as one single framed picture of the saint "taking leave." There is other evidence that he was, unlike his manuscript-cataloging father, not very accurate in describing pictures. In the same edition he misunderstands a miniature in another manuscript of the Alexis poem.[40] The problem is that Paris reads medieval images, like medieval texts, through the codes and expectations of nineteenth-century naturalism in which pictures were "views" of an objective reality, outside language.

NATURALISM AND ART

The split between the discourses of art and literature that occurred in the last century did not prevent scholars on both sides from appropriating aspects of the other discipline, and the valorization of "lifelike" naturalistic art was one area where the Romance philologist and the art historian met. From Gaston Paris's statement that "littérature fut l'image de cette vie" to Winkler's 1927 article on the Alexis poem stressing its vivid naturalism, this poem in particular became a naive masterpiece, a "primitif français" like the paintings by early French artists exhibited in Paris in 1904 which saw the beginnings of a serious interest in medieval art among French intellectuals.[41] Winkler described the poem as being composed of "cleverly framed pictures of sadness and solemnity." His only criticism was of its cruelty in the scene of the saint leaving his bride on their wedding night, which revealed his twentieth-century sentimental bias. In fact he reads the poem as if it were an emotional *Bildungsroman*. Curtius, who saw this ascetical renunciation more historically as a topos, preferred to look at the poem from fourteen points of view. However, none of these is visual or even remotely concerned with actually *looking* at the manuscript itself, never mind the viewpoints of its first reader, Christina of Markyate.[42]

In another important article, in the very first issue of *Romance Philology,* Hatzfeld used the poem to encourage modern critics to have an aesthetic response to medieval literature, and, preferring Winkler's psychological to Curtius's topological reading of the poem, set the future of American philology on the "naturalistic" path for the next three decades.[43] Hatzfeld noted that an obsession with the history of ideas rather than the history of art "has impeded the Romance scholars in general, from comparing, for instance, the confused uses of the tenses in the authors with the false perspective of the painters."[44] The problem with this prescription is once again not being historical enough to see the tenses and perspectives as not "wrong" for medievals but right in their own cultural terms.

The impulse to continue Gaston Paris's view of literature as an image of medieval life continued as late as 1952 when Anna Hatcher reread the bride's silence as if one were appreciating a naive work of art: "similarly we are foiled if we attempt to visualize this lonely, mute figure. She has no substance in this scene." The girl's silence, according to another critic, which evokes "the restrained expressiveness of Romanesque sculpture," is not a very realistic depiction.[45] But she *does* exist! She is visualized by the scribe of "L," isolated in the center of the picture, her hand on her cheek in the "pathos formula" of dejection and sorrow, and as we have seen, signaled as a focus for contemplation by the rubric above her. She exists in both text and image in the picture, if not in the poem itself (fig. 2). She does not speak, but she is importantly represented in image if not in text. Under erasure in the works of Romance philologists, the bride's status as an image in the manuscript has led to her being imagined "naturalistically" from the text.

An extreme case for the visualization of the poem occurs in a series of densely argued articles by Heinrich Lausberg who holds that the numerical division of the poem (five groups of twenty-five strophes each) "may mirror a series of pictures on church walls in rows of five for the benefit of those who cannot read."[46] Here the poem is literally divided into twenty-five *Bilder* or pictures, the appended inscriptions to long-lost simulacra. More recently there has been a revival of interest in medieval iconography, and students of literature have begun to look to the methods of art history to help historicize their practice. However, too often this has been merely to raid images from various contexts in order to bolster, as does Lausberg, specific moralizations or readings of texts.[47] In these cases, too, the image is torn from its locus elsewhere in order to stand for or represent a "world view." What is needed is a literary history that incorporates not iconography (which many art historians now realize is as abstracting and idealizing a critical practice as philology) but a psychological materialism with regard to texts and images in medieval culture. Returning to the Alexis poem in one of its loci, we can begin, in the words of the "Alexis Master" (the scribe of "L"), to "learn from the picture."

"TO LEARN FROM THE PICTURE"

Just as the double pictorial threshold of the poem—its opening images of King David and the wedding night narrative—are erased in the 1872 edition, so too is its end curtailed. The last strophe calls on the "seignors" listening to hold the song in their "memorie" with a prayer to the Word "en ipse u(er)be: sin dimes pat(er) n(oster)" (fig. 6). Without a break, this is followed by a long quotation of a famous passage of Pope Gregory the Great, first in Latin and then in French, on the *raison des paintures*. Each is introduced by a rubric, which as Pächt noted, gives the "wrong" source for the text as the letter to *Secundinus inclusus* (another of Gregory's correspondents) rather than Serenus, bishop of Marseilles.[48] That audience was more important than origin in the twelfth century is shown by this intentional reattribution of the statement to someone who was *inclusus,* like Christina.

> Altra cose est aurier la painture eatra cose est par le historie de la painture aprendre quela cose fest ad aurier. Kar ico que la scripture appestee ad lizans. ico aprester la painture ad ignoranz. Kar an icele uerent les ignoranz quet il deivent liure.
>
> [For it is one thing to venerate a picture, and another to learn the story it depicts, which is to be venerated. The picture is for simple men what writing is for those who can read, because those who cannot read see and learn from the picture the model which they should follow.][49]

This passage has always been seen as an apology for the long picture cycle on pp. 17–56 of the manuscript, but it is much more intricately interwoven into the end of the Alexis poem. The word *historie* can refer to both poem and picture. Does this also relate it to the vernacular poem as much as the Psalter prefatory pictures, especially the opening image of the saint renouncing the secular married life, which was exactly the "model" that Christina herself followed in leaving her own husband? Because early text editors were obsessed with origins and establishing the personality of an author, they tend to be unconcerned with audience, with the reception and reading of texts. The particular circumstances of the reception of the *St. Albans Psalter*, so well researched by art historians and hagiographers, were still not considered as a context as late as 1973 when Maddox wrote that "further investigation of the relationship between L, the *St Albans Psalter* (of which it forms a major part) and the general intellectual and cultural life of St. Albans during the term of its illustrious abbot Geoffrey of Gorham (1119–46) might furnish additional background for the preceptive import of L."[50]

But how can the poem's "background" be contained in its structural site? Where something is located is surely not a background but a field that actually constitutes it. Christina of Markyate is not at the back of the text but right in front of it, turning the pages, seeing the images and intoning Alexis's song. Christina's life has clear parallels with that of the saint *peregrinus*. Both abandoned their intended partners and went against their worldly parent's wishes in order to live as hermits. The death-in-life of the recluse in her cell is also comparable to the long years of privation of Alexis under his father's stairs, until he reveals his body, origin, and name by writing his story down on parchment. Christina's *Vita* would also be written down after her death, but her living *vita* was the *St. Albans Psalter* itself.

It has only been with our current radical rethinking of the question of origins, authorship, and intention in the so-called "New Philology" that scholars of French medieval literature have begun to examine "the staging of writing" in the Alexis poem. Alexandre Leupin sees in the modern editions of the poem "a sort of erasure that destroys the materiality of its writing and obliterates the effect of the prologue's colors and punctuation . . . the text's calligraphy echoes its own divided language [between verse and prose], resonating with both voice and writing: the 'origin' divides itself internally and plays its entire problematic off language's mirrors."[51] While agreeing with this, I would want to add another mirror, that of the image itself, which is yet another means of division. Leupin, like many contemporary critics, enunciates the difference between competing linguistic modes, here poetry and prose as they are articulated in the manuscript, forgetting a crucial third term—the image. In the same way Stephen G. Nichols's invaluable discussion of the manuscript matrix in which the image is a supplementary gloss ultimately describes the image as "the textual unconscious."[52] For me, this comes too close to erasing it once again, relegating it to a subsumed and merely symptomatic place *elsewhere* when the image is eminently *there*. Why does the picture have to be the text's unconscious and not vice-versa, especially since the repetition and conventionality of most miniatures in manuscript culture can be subtly altered and even subverted by the "variance" of the moving, growing text that surrounds them? If we follow Lausberg's argument, the Alexis poem might itself have arisen from images, playing upon and reading out of their silent gestures. If words give voice to the mute image, the visual is like the unconscious in that it is always already there. Writing, although often preceding the image, is, as Derrida saw it, the real "supplement."[53]

The locus—the visual field that, after all, defines the place of writing—is itself a picture or representation of speech. Both word and image ultimately refer back to the primacy of the voice. This is true of the Psalms that comprise the main text in this manuscript, each of which opens with a vivid image of speech and declamation such as Psalm 65 (64), "A Hymn O God, becometh thee in Sion," which asks "O hear my prayer" in the second verse and shows figures pointing with the silent gesture that, in the twelfth century, signifies speech (fig. 8). According to the Latin grammarian Varro, "To talk (*loqui*) is said to come from place (*locus*); and he who speaks (*loquitur*) with understanding puts each word in its proper place."[54] The *Psalter of Christina of Markyate* (as I prefer to call the manuscript known as the *St. Albans Psalter*) is a place where image, voice, and text were enunciated for a particular gaze and where both the Psalms and Alexis were seen and sung. In the *Life of Christina of Markyate* is a passage describing how she read the Psalms, which also provides an insight into how this reader might have projected herself into her alter-ego's life before them: "She chose to read a very suitable passage and one that describes the situation of the reader. This she repeated often, lamenting at one moment her own weakness and blindness and at another the blindness and guile of her parents who were seeking her life: Psalm 37:12 'They that seek after my life lay snares for me.'"[55]

The voice of the ascetic female Christina, cramped in her tiny cell, brushing off the toads and demons that she saw in nightmarish visions clambering over the margins of her Psalter, performed this poem, and as a reflection, not in the sense of a naturalistic "picture" but rather as a set of prescriptive acts, renunciations, and staged self-explorations of her own life. These words and images gave her *consulaciun*, as the prologue states. Rather than closing off meaning as occurs in the very structure of nineteenth-century/modern editions, such an analysis of the place of performance erupts with tensions and paradoxes of intervisuality as well as intertextuality. Lee Patterson has bemoaned how research in literature has become trapped in "the labyrinth of textuality from which there is no exit."[56] One way out is to follow the directions, places, and positions in the manuscript, in what the early-nineteenth-century inventor of iconography Alphonse Didron, during a less logocentric period of medievalism, called "les objets chantés et dessinés."[57]

NOTES

1. Ernst Robert Curtius, *European Literature and the Latin Middle Ages,* trans. W. R. Trask (Princeton: Princeton University Press. 1973), 15.

2. Augustine, *In Joannis Evangelium,* tract. XXIV, cap. 2, *Patrologia latina* 35:1593. For a modern French Augustinian attack on images as deceptive, see Jacques Ellul, *The Humiliation of the Word,* trans. Joyce Main Hanks (Grand Rapids: Eardmans, 1985). For a study of the low esteem of the visual for French philosophers, which had enormous impact on the development of philology in the same period, see Martin Jay, "In the Empire of the Gaze: Foucault and the Denigration of Vision in Twentieth-century French Thought," in David Couzens Hoy, ed., *Foucault: A Critical Reader* (New York: B. Blackwell, 1986), and now his *With Downcast Eyes: The Denigration of Vision in Twentieth-Century French Thought* (Berkeley: University of California Press, 1993). The image in French letters has been redeemed recently for a libidinal postmodern desire, as against the conformity of the "dead" letter, in Jean-François Lyotard's seminal study *Discours Figure* (Paris: Klincksieck, 1971).

3. Gaston Paris and Léopold Pannier, *La Vie de Saint Alexis, poème du XIe siècle et renouvellements des XIIe, XIIIe et XIVe siècles publiés avec préfaces, variantes, notes et glossaire* (Paris: A. Franck, 1872), hereafter cited as Paris.

4. Adolph Goldschmidt, *Der Albanipsalter in Hildesheim und seine Beziehung zur symbolischen Kirchenskulptur des XII. Jahrhunderts, mit 8 Tafeln und 44 Text-llustrationen* (Berlin: G. Siemens, 1895).

5. Otto Pächt, C. R. Dodwell, and Francis Wormald, *The St. Albans Psalter* (London: Warburg Institute, 1960), hereafter cited as *Psalter.*

6. *Psalter,* 4–22. See also the fundamental historical exploration by Christopher J. Holdsworth, "Christina of Markyate," in *Medieval Women,* ed. Derek Baker (Oxford: Basil Blackwell, 1978), 189.

7. As Christopher Storey points out in his useful *An Annotated Bibliography and Guide to Alexis Studies (La Vie de saint Alexis)* (Geneva: Droz, 1987), 25: "Because this very important study was largely neglected by

scholars, the early editors of the VSA remained unaware of the significance of the presence of the story of the saint in the great St. Albans Psalter." Otto Pächt, in *Psalter,* 126, notes that "not until last year did philological circles take note of the sixty-year-old publication of the Hildesheim manuscript by Adolph Goldschmidt in which St. Albans was established as the place of origin of the book and where the date has been narrowed down to the years 1119–1146."

8. For example, Margaret Rickert, *Painting in Britain: The Middle Ages,* Pelican History of Art, 2d ed. (London: Pelican, 1965), 64–66. For a full bibliography on the ms., see C. M. Kauffmann, *Romanesque Manuscripts 1066–1190* (London: A. Miller, 1975), no. 29, and Rodney M. Thompson, *Manuscripts from St. Albans Abbey, 1066–1235* (Totowa, N.J.: D. S. Brewer, 1982), 119–21. The manuscript was brought from Hildesheim and was exhibited in *English Romanesque Art 1066–1200* (London: Hayward Gallery, 1983), no. 17, p. 93.

Except for this glimpse at one opening, I have never had a chance to see the manuscript, but a friend who has writes one of the most cogent art-historical analyses of the book I know: T. A. Heslop, "The Visual Arts and Crafts," in *The Cambridge Guide to Arts: II, The Middle Ages* (Cambridge: Cambridge University Press, 1988), 166–69. Part of the problem of incorporating manuscripts into literary study is, of course, that of accessibility.

9. Pächt, *Psalter,* 139 n. 4.

10. The most influential statement of this philological position in art history is Kurt Weitzmann, *Illustrations in Roll and Codex: A Study of the Origin and Method of Text Illustration* (Princeton: Princeton University Press, 1947), esp. 182, "The Relation between Text Criticism and Picture Criticism."

11. See Helen Solterer, "Letter Writing and Picture Reading: Medieval Textuality and the *Bestiare d'Amour,*" *Word and Image* 5 (1989): 131–147, and Jacqueline Cerquiglini, "Histoire, image: Accord et discord des sens à la fin du Moyen Âge," *Littérature,* 74 (1989): 110–26.

12. David F. Hult, "Reading It Right: The Ideology of Text Editing," *Romanic Review* 79 (1988): 84. Arigo Castellani, *Bédier avait-il raison? La méthode de Lachmann dans les éditions de textes du Moyen Âge,* (Discours universitaires , nouvelle sèrie, 20 Fribourg: Editions universitaires, 1957).

13. Mario Roques, "Avertissement" to the Champion edition of 1903, republished in many subsequent editions, which was based on an edition of Gaston Paris for the use of university students in 1885. For the publishing history of this edition, see Storey, 19.

14. Paris stresses that this great work of French literature was first published in a "Journal pour l'antiquité allemande" (1).

15. Paris, 1–138. See Bernard Cerquiglini, *Éloge de la variante: Histoire critique de la philologie* (Paris: Éditions du Seuil, 1989), 74, for what he calls the "second period" (1860–1913) of text editing. The larger context of Brian Stock's essay "Romantic Attitudes and Academic Medievalism," reprinted in his *Listening for the Text: On the Uses of the Past* (Baltimore: Johns Hopkins University Press, 1990), 52–85, is also useful in understanding this move towards textuality.

16. Hans Ulrich Gumbrecht, "'Un souffle d'Allemagne ayant passé': Friedrich Diez, Gaston Paris and the Genesis of National Philologies," *Romance Philology* 40 (1986): 1–37.

17. Paul Zumthor, *Speaking of the Middle Ages* (Lincoln: University of Nebraska Press, 1986), 26.

18. Ibid., 37.

19. Stephen G. Nichols, "Philology in a Manuscript Culture," *Speculum* 65 (1990): 45, discusses how Paris made "the collectivity the generative locus" of literature. See also the important essay by R. Howard Bloch, "New Philology and Old French" (ibid., 38–59), which explores Gaston Paris's methodology in the light of "French reaction to the losses of 1870." Paris alludes to the Franco-Prussian War having "interrupted" his work on the Alexis in the "Avant Propos" to his 1872 edition. For more on his biography, see R. Howard Bloch "'Mieux vaut jamais que tard': Romance Philology and Old French Letters," *Representations* 36 (1991): 64–87.

20. Paris, 208.

21. Pächt, *Psalter,* 126–46.

22. See Gumbrecht and Bloch (above, n. 19) for details.

23. Gaston Paris, "Paulin Paris et la littérature française du Moyen Âge," in *La poésie du Moyen Âge: Leçons et lectures* (Paris: Hachette, 1895), 214–15.

24. Paulin Paris, *Les manuscrits français de la Bibliothèque du Roi,* 7 vols. (Paris: Techener, 1836), who writes in a preface (1:xxiii) that the "passion des monuments du moyen-âge a saisi toute notre jeune France."

25. Gaston Paris, "Paulin Paris," 215.

26. Stephen Bann, *The Clothing of Clio: A Study of the Representation of History in Nineteenth-Century Britain and France* (Cambridge: Cambridge University Press, 1984), 54.

27. See Bann, 77–79, and Alexandre Lenoir, *Description du Musée des monuments français,* 3 vols. (Paris: Chez l'Auteur, 1812). A useful set of essays on museums and attitudes to the Middle Ages in nineteenth-century France are contained in *Les lieux de mémoire sous la direction de Pierre Nora: II, La Nation* (Paris: Gallimard, 1984).

28. For the Cluny Museum, see Bann, 80–85 and the lavishly illustrated tomes by its founder, Alexandre de Sommerard, *Les Arts au Moyen Âge,*

(Paris: Hotel de Cluny, published in 5 vols., 1838–46). For Albert Lenoir's association with the Cluny, see G. Duplessis, *Notice sur M. Albert Lenoir, Membre de l'Académie des Beaux-Arts* (Paris: Firmin-Didot, 1891).

29. For the new monuments museum, see *La Nation,* 424, and Camille Enlart, *Le Musée de sculpture comparée du Trocadéro* (Paris: A. Picard, 1911).

30. Viollet-Le-Duc père, "De la poésie au moyen âge," *Annales archéologiques* 3 (July–Dec. 1845): 7–10. Guilhermy's article follows directly (10–21). Viollet-le-Duc père has another article, "La littérature et l'architecture" (ibid., 201), which argues for the superiority of classical over medieval culture, with which the editor Didron disagrees in a footnote. In this sense the elder Viollet-le-Duc is part of the generation that argued about the classics vs. the moderns in the opening years of the century. For the importance of Didron and his journal, see Catherine Brissac and Jean-Michel Leniaud, "Adolphe-Napoléon Didron ou les media au service de l'art chrétien," *Revue de l'art* 77 (1987): 33–42.

31. Paul Lacroix and Ferdinand Sere, *Le Moyen Âge et la Renaissance,* 5 vols. (Paris: Administration, 1848–51). On the title page, the priority of "Le Moyen Âge" is indicated by its being double the print size of "la Renaissance." Lacroix went on to publish many illustrated books on medieval life and art. The preface (6–7) makes much of the execution and accuracy of the "gravures."

Many subsequent illustrated histories of French literature were published. In G. Larson, *Histoire illustrée de la littérature française* (Paris: Libraire Hachette 1903), one of the eight hundred gravures reproduces the Alexis prologue and illustration page from the Hildesheim manuscript as "Légende de Saint Alexis," with no information as to its location. The source is wrongly given as "Bibl. Nat. Imp." (54). For the latest maltreatment of the image, which at least cites the manuscript source, although it cuts out the picture from the page as a whole, see Michèle. Gally and Christiane Marchello-Nizia, *Littératures de l'Europe médiévale* (Paris: Magnard, 1985), 185.

32. See Anthony Burton, "Nineteenth Century Periodicals" and Trevor Fawcett, "Scholarly Journals," in *The Art Press: Two Centuries of Art Magazines,* ed. Trevor Fawcett and C. Phillpot (London: Art Book, 1976). For philological periodicals of the same decades, see Bloch "New Philology and Old French," 40. It is worth noting that the Benedictine-begun *Histoire littéraire de France* included articles on art, for example, Leopold Delisle's innovative study "Livres d'images destinés à l'instruction religieuse et aux exercises de piété des laics," vol. 21 (1893), 213–85.

33. Paul Lacroix, *The Arts in the Middle Ages and at the Period of the Renaissance* (New York: Appleton, 1870), trans. James Dafforne, x. This is a

condensed version of the five-volume French work by Lacroix and Sere which, together with its hundreds of engravings, was reprinted as recently as 1964: Paul Lacriox, *The Arts in the Middle Ages and the Renaissance* (New York: F. Ungar, 1964).

34. Emmanuel Viollet-le-Duc, *Dictionaire raisonné de l'architecture française du XIe au XIVe siècle,* vol. 8 (Paris: B. Bance, 1866), "Restauration."

35. See Bruno Foucart et al., *Viollet-le-Duc* (Paris: Réunion des Musées Nationaux, 1980), and F. Foucart and F. Berce, *Viollet-le-Duc: Architect, Artist, Master of Historic Preservation* (Washington, D.C.: Trust for Museum Exhibitions, 1987). For Joseph Bédier's remarks on Didron and restoration, see *Le Lai de L'ombre par Jean Renart,* publié par Joseph Bédier (Paris: Firmin-Didot, 1913), xlv.

36. Alexandre Leupin, *Barbarolexis: Medieval Writing and Sexuality* (Chicago: University of Chicago Press, 1989), 40–43. Another important study that came to my attention only after this study was finished, and which makes some of the same points as this essay is Laura Kendrick, "1123? A Richly Illustrated Latin Psalter Prefaced by a Vernacular *Chanson de Saint Alexis* is produced at the Monastery of St. Albans, for Christina of Markyate," in *A New History of French Literature,* ed. Denis Hollier et al. (Cambridge, Mass.: Harvard University Press, 1989, 23–30.

37. J. M. Meunier, *La Vie de Saint Alexis, poème français du XIe siècle, texte du manuscrit de Hildesheim, traduction littérale, étude grammaticale, glossaire* (Paris: Droz, 1933), 19, is one of the few editions to transcribe the prologue. See also M. Tyssens, "Le prologue de *la vie de saint Alexis,*" in *Studi in onore di Italo Siciliano* (Florence: L.S.Olschki, 1966), 1165–77, who argues that the scribe only reframes the earlier poem through the prologue.

38. This was first suggested by Goldschmidt in 1895, but see also Dominica Legge, "Archaism and the Conquest", *Modern Language Review* 51 (1956): 227–29.

39. Paris, 135.

40. Paris describes the miniature of the wedding in manuscript "S" as "Alexis mort, entouré du pape et des empereurs suppliants" (6), but then later in the edition correctly describes it as "le mariage de saint Alexis" (213).

41. Emil Winkler, "Von der Kunst des Alexiusdichters," *Zeitschrift für romanische Philologie* 47 (1927): 588–97. For the taste for "naive naturalism" in medieval art stimulated by the 1904 exhibition of the *Primitifs français,* see Michael Camille, "The *Très Riches Heures:* An Illuminated Manuscript in the Age of Mechanical Reproduction," *Critical Inquiry* 17 (autumn 1990): 86.

42. Ernst Robert Curtius, "Zur Interpretation des Alexiusliedes," *Zeitschrift für romanische Philologie* 56 (1936): 113–37.

43. Helmut A. Hatzfeld, "Esthetic Criticism Applied to Romance Literature," *Romance Philology* 1 (1947–48): 309–10. For the naturalism in the nineteenth century and its impact on literary studies, see R. Howard Bloch, "Naturalism, Nationalism, Medievalism," *Romanic Review* 76 (1985): 342–47. The literary implications of art critics like Champfleury, who wrote about the Middle Ages in his *Histoire de la caricature* (Paris: Dentu, 1877) as well as contemporary artists like Courbet, needs studying.

44. Hatzfeld notes that "more work has been done along these lines in Germanic philology" (322), which I would link to the prestige of art history as a humanistic discipline in prewar German universities.

45. Anna G. Hatcher, "The Old French Alexis Poem: A Mathematical Demonstration," *Traditio* 8 (1952): 120, which initiated the comment about "unrealistic" Romanesque sculpture from Alison Goddard Elliot, *The Vie de Saint Alexis in the Twelfth and Thirteenth Centuries* (Chapel Hill: University of North Carolina Press, 1983), 32.

46. Heinrich Lausberg, "Zum altfranzösischen Alexiuslied," *Archiv für das Studium der Neueren Sprachen* 191 (1955): 202–13, 285–320, and "Kann dem altfranzosischen Alexiuslied ein Bilderzyklus zugrunde liegen?" ibid., 195 (1959): 141–44.

47. Most notoriously D. W. Robertson Jr., *A Preface to Chaucer* (Princeton: Princeton University Press, 1962), and John Fleming, *The Roman de la Rose: A Study in Allegory and Iconography* (Princeton: Princeton University Press, 1969). In the past decade, the influence of semiotics and the various structuralisms has totally energized the field of verbal/visual inquiry in the Middle Ages that has modified the rather naive "naturalism" of the latter two publications. Two particularly important literary studies in this vein, both in medieval French studies, are Stephen G. Nichols, *Romanesque Signs: Early Medieval Narrative and Iconography* (New Haven: Yale University Press, 1983), and Sylvia Huot, *From Song to Book: The Poetics of Old French Lyrical Poetry* (Ithaca: Cornell University Press, 1989).

48. Pächt, *Psalter,* 138.

49. On Gregory's dictum in the twelfth century, starting from its place here in the *St. Albans Psalter,* see Michael Camille, "Seeing and Reading: Some Visual Implications of Medieval Literacy and Illiteracy," *Art History* 8, no. 1 (1985): 26–49.

50. Donald L. Maddox, "Pilgrimage, Narrative and Meaning in the 'Vie de St. Alexis,'" *Romance Philology* 27 (1973): 156.

51. Leupin, 44. On p. 52 he writes that "to the best of my knowledge," there exists "an illumination in manuscript A" showing Alexis as a scribe. While this is important to the scholar's argument, he makes this assertion without giving a folio or manuscript source or reference to a reproduction.

This "mystery" of the half-hidden visual is typical of the way even the postphilologists are careful to cite their textual sources but rarely treat visual sources with the same care.

52. See Nichols, "Philology in Manuscript Culture," 6. Some of his other terms, such as "manuscript matrix" and "interventions in the text," have been, however, crucial to the present study. For the *mater/materia* association that underlies the term *matrix* in the performance of gender, see Judith Butler, *Bodies That Matter: On the Discursive Limits of Sex* (New York: Routledge, 1993), 28–55.

53. For a Derridian reading of the manuscript matrix, see Michael Camille, "The Book of Signs: Writing and Visual Difference in Gothic Manuscript Illumination," *Word and Image* 1–2 (1985): 133–48.

54. Quoted from R. Howard Bloch, "The Medievalist's Desire," *Exemplaria* 2, no. 1 (1990): 215.

55. C. H. Talbot, *The Life of Christina of Markyate* (Oxford: Clarendon Press, 1987), 93.

56. Lee Patterson, "On the Margin: Postmodernism, Ironic History and Medieval Studies," *Speculum* 65, no. (1): (87–)108.

57. Didron, *Annales archéologiques* 3 (1845): 271.

FIFTEEN

Methodologies and Ideologies in Historical Grammar: A Case Study from Old French

Suzanne Fleischman

> The word as the ideological phenomenon par excellence exists in continuous generation and change; it sensitively reflects all social shifts and alterations. In the vicissitudes of the word are the vicissitudes of the society of word users. . . . One can study *the generation of language itself,* as *ideological material,* as the *medium for ideological reflection of existence,* since the reflection of the refraction of existence in human consciousness comes about only in and through the word.
> —Vološinov, *Marxism and the Philosophy of Language*

THIS VOLUME PROPOSES "a history of medievalisms." What distinguishes this undertaking from a more conventional history of medieval studies is an emphasis on exploring how the development of the constituent disciplines has been shaped by the prevailing ideologies (intellectual, nationalistic, religious, political, socioeconomic, or gender-related) of those disciplines and their practitioners. Consonant with this objective, I propose here to trace a history of methodologies, and of the (conscious or unconscious) ideologies that inform them, in one of the core domains of medieval studies: historical grammar.

The "historical grammar" rubric conflates two distinct approaches to language study: one has as its goal a synchronic linguistic description of an earlier *état de langue,* the other a diachronic analysis of the changes a language has undergone over the course of its history.[1] Of concern here is the first of these approaches, whose methodologies and ideologies I propose to examine with reference to grammatical descriptions (henceforth "grammars") of Old French and the role grammars play in the enterprise of textual criticism.

To focus the discussion, a case study will be included, highlighting a specific problem—and longstanding conundrum—of Old French syntax: the clause-initial particle *si* (vars. *se, s'*) that crops up in virtually every French text from the 9th-century "Strasbourg Oaths" through the fourteenth century. The examples below are from different genres and periods within this time span.

> Pro Deu amur et pro christian poblo et nostro commun salvament, . . . in quant deus savir et podir me dunat, *si* salvarai eo cist meon fradre Karlo, . . .
> [For the love of God and the Christian community and our common safety/salvation, . . . insofar as God grants me the knowledge and the power, # will I support this my brother Charles, . . .] ("Strasbourg Oaths," A.D. 843)[2]

> Ço est l'arcevesque, que Deus mist en sun num; / Cleimet sa culpe, *si* reguardet amunt, / Cuntre le ciel amsdous ses mains ad juinz, / *Si* priet Deu que pareïs li duinst.
> [This is the archbishop, whom God sent in his name; / [He] confesses his sins, # lifts up his gaze, / Pointing toward Heaven both his hands [he] has joined, / # [he] prays God to grant him [a place in] Paradise.] (*Song of Roland*, 2238–41; twelfth-century chanson de geste)

> Or t'ai dite la verité de ta devinaille, *si* me suis vers toi aquitez, ce m'est avis. *Si* te dirai ores la moie devinaille, *si* verrai qu'il en avendra.
> [Now [I] have told you the truth of your riddle, [and] # have [thus] taken care of my obligation to you, it seems to me. # [I] will tell you now my riddle, [and] # [I] will see what comes of it.] (*Prose Tristan*, 132:19–21, thirteenth-century romance)[3]

By the fifteenth century *si* is virtually extinct,[4] though it crops up in the 17th century as a quaint archaism in Molière's theater in attempts to reproduce uneducated/dialect speech.

In two publications dealing specifically with *si*, I offer a more detailed analysis of the related syntactic, semantic, and pragmatic issues than will be presented here.[5] I also situate my approach to *si* within the context of a broader methodological agenda concerning the practice of historical grammar, though this is not the primary focus of the articles. In this chapter, in line with the orientation of this volume, the methodological question moves to center stage, and with it an attempt to characterize the theoretical and ideological positions that have grounded the approaches used by grammarians and linguists of the last half-century to describe "text languages" of the Middle Ages.[6] My objective in this essay corresponds to what Roy Harris has called "demythologizing linguistics":[7] making explicit the (often covert) assumptions that underlie grammatical models, showing that they are historical constructs (rather than immutable truths given by the nature of the language itself), and subjecting them to critical scrutiny.

MODELS AND METAQUESTIONS

For expository convenience, the linguistic "paradigms" surveyed here will be grouped under three headings: taxonomic, autonomous, and pragmatic.

Under "taxonomic" approaches I subsume *traditional grammar*, with its emphasis on parts of speech, as well as varieties of *structural linguistics* (cf. n. 8). For traditional grammar, an exhaustive taxonomy of *la langue* is an end in itself. *Idem* for structural descriptions of a language, which typically take the form of inventories of the phonemes, morphemes, and syntactic categories of the language, *along with* a statement of the positions in which these elements occur (an "item-and-arrangement" model). "Grammar" may be seen as the rules governing substitution classes. Classifying a word as a noun, for example, indicates that it can substitute for a large number of other words, also nouns, without producing incomprehensible or outlandish combinations. Each class of words is divided into subclasses on the same basis. The principle of substitution possibilities underlies the structuralist theory of language that, with Leonard Bloomfield, came to be known as *distributionalism*.

"Autonomous" linguistics will be represented here, quasi in absentia, by *generative grammar*,[8] which moves beyond structuralism in being an "item-and-process" model. Work in autonomous linguistics ranges from simple accounts of changes in pronunciation and descriptive statements ("grammars") of the structural regularities in particular languages to ambitious attempts to characterize universal limits within which languages may differ structurally. Autonomous linguists, Newmeyer writes (5), approach a language "as a natural scientist would study a physical phenomenon, that is, by focusing on those of its properties that exist apart from the beliefs and values of the individual speakers of a language or the nature of the society in which the language is spoken" (whence the label "autonomous"). He adds (12) that autonomous linguists have traditionally viewed theirs as the only *scientific* approach to language.

The view of linguistics as a science, *a fortiori* a natural science, goes back to August Schleicher in the mid-nineteenth century,[9] and has provided a crucial piece of the methodological and mythological underlayment of virtually every linguistic movement since that time. It is this (largely unquestioned) belief in the "scientificity" of linguistics that has enabled its practitioners, notably partisans of "mainstream" paradigms,[10] to see their theories and practices as being objective and value-neutral, and to envision their discipline as being somehow isolated from ideology and from the ideological upheavals that, especially in recent times, have wrought major changes in the humanities and social sciences.[11] But as we shall see—and as any deconstructionist worth their salt would hasten to point out—this much-vaunted claim to scientific neutrality, so central to linguistic orthodoxy, is itself a cornerstone of its ideological foundation (cf. below, "Scientificity").

The remaining methodologies of Old French grammar to be surveyed here fall under the heading of "pragmatic." Linguistic pragmatics focuses on *contextualized uses of language,* that is, on language viewed not as an abstract system, the grammar of an ideal speaker-hearer, but as a communicative instrument of actual speakers that responds to and is shaped by the pressures of real situations of verbal interaction. It deals with "communicative competence," the knowledge that enables language users to produce and comprehend utterances in relation to specific communicative goals and contexts.

Two pragmatic methodologies have been brought to bear on Old French and on the particle *si.* The *théories de l'énonciation,* of French provenience, focus on issues of "context," in particular on how traces of a speaker and of speaker subjectivity are encoded in the utterances of language. *Discourse pragmatics,* a largely American brand of functional linguistics, targets relationships among elements in the "co-text,"[12] looking in particular at how larger utterances ("discourses" or "texts") and verbal exchanges cohere internally and with their extra-linguistic contexts.

While there is some overlap among these approaches to linguistic description, the thrust of each is sufficiently distinct to prompt different questions on the part of the investigator and, accordingly, yield different results.

This discussion will be informed by a set of metaquestions that it is appropriate at this point to articulate:

—Are "descriptive statements" about a language—whether in the form of rules or otherwise—really *descriptive,* or are they ultimately norms masquerading as value-neutral statements?

—Is it reasonable for descriptive linguistics to claim ideological neutrality, that is, that grammars are value-neutral, as practitioners of autonomous linguistics would have it?

—Can linguistics rightfully claim for itself the status of a science, given that its object of study—language analyzed as if it were a stable, unitary, homogeneous entity—has no existence in reality, having been constructed, through linguistic practices, out of the incessantly variable data of real language activity?

These questions often have different ramifications for text languages like Old French than for living languages, in regard to which they were originally raised. This discussion will focus accordingly on their implications for *historical* grammar, which poses two additional questions of its own:

—Given the methodology of mainstream descriptive linguistics (summarized below in "Autonomous Linguistics"), how can we write "grammars" of languages that have no native speakers?

—What is the relationship of linguistics to philology, and how have these two disciplines conspired to base grammar as much on the fantasies and desires of their practitioners as on the testimony of the texts—our medieval "native speakers"?

I wish to make clear that what follows is not an exercise in deconstructive linguistic historiography; it is an attempt to shed light on the ideological foundations of the methodologies we bring to bear on the language of medieval texts—methodologies that, insofar as they condition the kinds of questions we ask and the directions our inquiries take, will in turn influence the shape of our findings. Ideology, as understood here, is not limited to the imposition of external social and political values; as we shall see, it also inheres in intellectual values.

GRAMMAR AS TAXONOMY

Manuals of early vernaculars have traditionally been written by grammarians or older language "specialists," not by linguists. Accordingly, they are for the most part atheoretical and unreflective of new developments in linguistic theory and methodology.[13] The manuals still virtually all adhere to a "parts-of-speech" approach to grammar that seeks to impose order on the (often unruly) data of the texts by fitting them into the categories of a grammatical taxonomy. But whose categories? Whose taxonomy?

The practice of taxonomizing language dates back to antiquity, when Dionysius Thrax (100 B.C.) sought to apply Aristotelian principles of descriptive classification to the Greek language.[14] Thus began grammar's obsession with taxonomizing its object, as classical "linguists" established the categories into which their successors would subsequently download the data of many postclassical languages, with varying degrees of success.[15] A major objective of descriptive grammar in its various avatars has been to arrive at an "elegant" classification of language data, a task that often begins with assigning words to one or another of the recognized parts of speech (or, as they are now called, "word classes").

Not surprisingly, traditional grammars of Old French—which is to say, all grammars of Old French[16]—as well as many specialized studies have focused their analyses of *si* on determining its grammatical category status as a prerequisite to assigning it a meaning. The majority position takes *si* to be an adverb, notably an adverb of temporal sequence, albeit on the basis of differing syntactic criteria: Rychner stresses its ability to trigger subject inversion (cf. the example above from the "Strasbourg Oaths"), a property it shares with clause-initial adverbs but not conjunctions. Grad, on the other hand, emphasizes its distributional parallelism with a set of temporal adverbs (italicized in the examples below) that can likewise occur at the beginning of a main clause following a subordinate "when"-clause:[17]

Quant il veneit devant li rei, *si* li soleit li reis demander . . . [When he would come before the king, # the king would ask him . . .] (*Four Books of Kings*, 107)

Quant veit li pedre que mais n'avrat d'enfant . . . *Dunc* se purpenset del secle en avant. [When his father sees that he will have no more children, *then* he begins to contemplate the afterlife] (*St. Alexis*, 36–38)

Quant la douce Vierge Marie vit mort le trez dous fruit de vie, *Lors* se trait ele ver la crois. [When the sweet Virgin Mary saw the tender fruit of life [lying] dead, *then* she betakes herself toward the cross] (*Passion*, 1855–57)

> Quant derriers els le secors veient, *Idonc* se sont ravigoré. [When
> they see help on the way behind them, *then* their spirits are lifted]
> (*Eneas*, 3707–8)

This comparison leads Grad to label *si* a "conjunctive temporal adverb."
Via a different route, Kibler (§87.1) arrives at a similar classification.

Another distributional fact about *si*—that it always directly preceded the finite verb and its satellites, in most instances where there is
no overt expression of the subject—leads Blumenthal to classify it as
an "anaphoric personal pronoun"[18] and Cerquiglini[19] to assign it to a
class of "predicate markers" that includes *car, et, or,* and *mar,*
illustrated in the examples below, whose function, he claims, is to
signal "the presence of a speaking subject" (127).

Felun paien,	*si*	vindrent as porz.
Felun paien,	*car*	venez as porz.
Felun paien,	*mar*	i vindrent as porz.

[Dastardly pagans, [PARTICLE] (did they) come to the mountain
pass][20]

Cerquiglini sees this commutation procedure as a heuristic device
crucial to arriving at an understanding of the specificity of certain
grammatical morphemes. Thus he writes, apropos of *mar:*

> L'intérêt de l'analyse distributionnelle est qu'elle le [= *mar*] dépouille
> des considérations sémantiques . . . qui le rendaient proprement
> inclassable et intraduisible, et qu'elle permet de le rapprocher
> d'autres morphèmes, ouvrant la voie à une description plus correcte
> du fonctionnement sémantique et syntaxique de cet adverbe. . . .
> C'est sur de telles bases qu'il conviendrait de reprendre l'analyse
> d'un certain nombre de conjonctions et d'adverbes. (*Parole*, 151)

Distributionalism stands apart from European structuralist paradigms notably in its efforts to banish from the study of syntax all
considerations of meaning. How such a procedure can shed light on
the "semantic functioning" of an item is thus not at all clear. Distributionalism, in short, tells us nothing more about an item than its
syntactic distribution within a sentence; not even how it differs from
the other members of its distributional set, which, as Marchello-Nizia
(*Dire*, 143) points out, may turn out to be a spurious one, a "faux
paradigme."

Let us consider at this point some of the assumptions underlying taxonomic approaches in general, certain of which are shared with generative linguistics.

An implicit assumption of traditional grammar (and of generative orthodoxy) is that word classes, such as "noun," "verb," and "adjective," are discrete; a word either is or is not a "noun," "verb," "adjective," and so on.[21] But this assumption forces an arbitrarily rigid classification of the data. In many instances a word exhibits some but not all of the shared properties held to be criterial for a given class and/or exhibits defining properties of more than one class. To wit, *si* fails to exhibit certain properties common to temporal adverbs, while at the same time exhibiting properties that define conjunctions (for particulars, see Fleischman, 1991), whence the hybrid category labels adopted, uncomfortably, by several analysts.

Another metagrammatical problem for parts-of-speech or distributionally-based taxonomies, *a fortiori* in the case of text languages, is summed up by the questions posed earlier, to which we now return: Whose categories? Whose taxonomy? While linguists today readily acknowledge the nonuniversality of grammatical categories, grammars of Old French have with few exceptions adhered closely to the consecrated categories of Latin and/or Modern French, thereby falling into the methodological "traps" that Cerquiglini et al. refer to as "the historicist reflex" and "conceptual inertia."

THE HISTORICIST REFLEX AND CONCEPTUAL INERTIA

The "historicist reflex" entails deriving the grammar of a relatively elusive stage of a language, for example, Old French, from that of an earlier (Latin) or later (Modern French) stage whose grammar has been established with greater confidence.

An instance of this methodological fallacy cited frequently by Cerquiglini[22] involves the claim, found in every grammatical description of Old French, that the language had a case system—*cas sujet* vs. *cas régime,* the reduced legacy of Latin's more abundant case-marking apparatus. A careful scrutiny of the data, however, leads Cerquiglini and his colleagues to conclude that by the twelfth century the case system was an anachronistic "grammatical fiction" with no foundation in the reality of Old French texts, the so-called case morphology—or what remained of it (*–s* vs. "zero" and only in the masculine gender)—having been put to other uses. Yet Old French grammar has staunchly resisted acknowledging the "loss" of case from among the categories of the inherited taxonomy (this consecrated term of the metalanguage of linguistic diachrony is hardly innocent, participating as it does in a deep-rooted ideology of language change as a process of decline or decay). Seeking to maintain the illusion that this portion of the grammatical inheritance still exists, Old French specialists explain away the discrepancies between the grammar they have constructed and the testimony of the texts as "declension errors." Again, "change as decay" revealing the covert *normativity* of what bills itself as linguistic *description* (these issues will be discussed below). Telling, too, is that this "revisionist" view of declension, like most challenges to received ideas about Old French grammar and textuality (cf. the "actual/virtual" opposition discussed below), has had little if any impact on subsequent research.

The question of case-marking also provides a prime illustration of how grammatical fictions come to be *perpetuated* through curious— and unwitting—collaborations between linguistics and philology. Gaston Paris, it has been variously noted,[23] systematically regularized case-marking on all noun phrases in his edition of the *Life of St. Alexis* (1872) to conform to his belief (desire?) about how the case system ought to have functioned.[24] Paris's edition, and others of the same philological bias,[25] have constituted the data base for grammars of Old French, which subsequent editors have appealed to as the authority in matters of language (cf. Kukenheim's statement in n. 13). The circularity is striking. Through such unconscious conspiracies, grammars of text languages come to be constructed on a foundation part fact, part nostalgic desire . . . for earlier, more perfect taxonomies.[26]

The philological thinking about *emendatio* has, of course, evolved since Gaston Paris's time, now favoring less rather than more editorial intervention. Apropos of "declensional solecisms," Foulet and Speer urge that "unless the meaning of the sentence is thereby altered or obscured, it seems reasonable not to correct the scribe's 'error.'"[27] Their admonition is doubly revealing for our purpose. First, "evidential" quotes notwithstanding,[28] it assumes a grammatical rule for case-marking that, as Cerquiglini and others before him have pointed out, was no longer operative at the time the texts were copied down.[29] Second, it attributes the violation of this putative rule to the scribe rather than to the author of the text. The assumed inferiority of the language of scribes, central to the ideology of nineteenth- and twentieth-century philology and built-in to its core terminology, raises a number of questions relevant to the present inquiry that will be taken up below.

"Conceptual inertia," the second of the methodological fallacies discussed by Cerquiglini et al., involves applying the linguistic concepts and grammatical categories of a modern language straightforwardly to the data of an older language, on the assumption that basic concepts and categories remain stable over the course of a language's diachrony. A classic statement of this position appears in Lerond's tentative proposal for applying methodology of generative grammar to text languages: "Une solution existe: les jugements de grammaticalité n'étant possibles qu'en synchronie, on devrait donc admettre comme un postulat que les changements survenus au cours de l'histoire d'une langue donnée se réduisent à des modifications des règles de surface et que *la structure profonde n'a pas varié*. Mais c'est un postulat."[30] Examples of conceptual inertia discussed by Cerquiglini and his colleagues involve the concepts "word" and "sentence"[31] and the classification of clausal connectors ("conjunctions" in traditional terminology) as either coordinating or subordinating.

Another form conceptual inertia may take involves failure to recognize a category or distinction of an older language because it is no longer operative in the modern language. My interpretation of *si* as a "same subject" marker (outlined below) is a case in point; likewise the "actual/virtual" distinction brought to light by Pierre Guiraud. As Guiraud puts it, "c'est faute d'une opposition actuel/virtuel grammaticalisée en français moderne que cette notion étrangère à la terminologie grammaticale actuelle est passée inaperçue des grammariens, alors qu'elle est la base de toute la grammaire médiévale (articles, modes, temps, négations, etc.)."[32] First introduced by Guiraud in 1962, then elaborated in his sketch of Old French for the "Que sais-je?" series (1963; 5 eds. to 1975) and in an article on *Aucassin et Nicolette* (1964),[33] the actual/virtual opposition, not surprisingly, encountered initial resistance,[34] and ultimately failed to establish a place for itself in grammars of Old French.

The taxonomic approaches to *si* described above nearly all fall prey to one or the other of these methodological fallacies. They typically conclude by assigning the particle to one of the consecrated categories of Modern French and/or Latin: adverb, conjunction, personal pronoun. Yet, as it turns out, each of these interpretations of *si* arrived at via distributional analysis is ultimately an entailment of the "verb second" (V/2) constraint of Old French syntax, according to which the verb is assigned to second position in the clause and some stressable element must precede it. This rhythmico-syntactic "rule" of Old French grammar satisfactorily accounts for the distribution of *si*—and of all the morphemes with which it has been paradigmatically bracketed (as in the examples above).

Among the studies cited, only Cerquiglini's *La parole médiévale* alone breaks away from the traditional categories, precisely because the investigative framework of *énonciation* prompts one to look for other things, notably marks of speaker subjectivity. Cerquiglini's assignment of *si* to a class of "speech-marking" particles is entirely consonant with—even predictable from—the objectives of this approach to language.[35]

LANGUAGE AS "PLENITUDE": THE STRUCTURALIST LEGACY

As stated above, *si* has been generally construed as a piece of inter-clausal or intersentential connective tissue—an adverb, conjunction, or hybrid of the two—variously glossed as "and," "thus," "and so," "and then," "therefore," "however," or left untranslated, with meaning assigned contextually.[36] The grammarians' attempts to capture the meaning of *si* are all consonant with a structuralist view of language as *un système où tout se tient*—a verbal plenitude containing no gaps, no lacunae—and with a view of grammar that emphasizes relationships. Even more than the parts-of-speech grammarians, grammarians of structuralist inspiration[37] have sought to identify in the early language, and establish in its grammar, explicit connectives to bridge the interclausal gaps that Old French, like any language that has not yet developed "dedicated" discursive protocols for written language, typically leaves unfilled.

As modern text consumers in a culture of the written word, we have come to expect the connective tissue of discourse to be formal and grammaticalized; where it is lacking we supply it ourselves, as suggested by the grammarians' glosses of *si* and by their attempts to construe the particle as one of the "transitioning" parts of speech. Yet Old French texts were composed in a language that was not yet rigidly codified as a written idiom. From the standpoint of grammar and discourse structure, the language of Old French texts is still very much a paratactic spoken idiom.[38] It is our literate expectation of formal linkages in the environments where *si* occurs that has led investigators to analyze this particle as a sentence adverb, conjunction, or conjunctive adverb, or—skirting the parts-of-speech question altogether—simply a clause-level connector.[39] While I concur that the function of *si* relates to the connectivity of discourse, I am not persuaded that any of the proposals mentioned so far tells a convincing story.

Autonomous Linguistics: Generativism and Old French

Generative linguistics has not been widely cultivated as an analytical framework for studying Old French, nor for text languages in general.[40] Several reasons suggest themselves, the most pragmatic being that formal linguists speak a metalanguage quite foreign to Old French specialists. Nor is their work addressed to medievalists but to methodologically kindred linguists, for whom they make points about syntactic theory generally using Old French data, heavily "processed."[41] But in addition to the divorce between constituencies, there are reasons having to do with the premises and ideology of generative linguistics that render this orientation less hospitable to text languages.

The modus operandi of generative linguistics relies on a two-step procedure whereby the analyst (1) derives from the data a set of "rules" that ostensibly account for what native speakers know about their language (i.e., its "grammar"), then (2) submits the utterances "generated" by these rules—typically in the form of *sentences*—to the judgment of native speakers to determine their acceptability. The analyst repeats these procedures again and again, continually refining the rules, with a view toward formalizing the totality of (conscious and unconscious) knowledge native speakers[42] have about their language—a perfect grammar of this type has, of course, never been achieved—that enables them to produce and understand sentences that have never occurred in their experience.[43] The ability of a grammar to formalize this knowledge, in as economical and comprehensive (i.e., "elegant") a way as possible, and to relate such an account to a general theory of language and of grammatical structure, is the goal of generative theory as its exponents see it.

Marchello-Nizia, though not a hard-line generativist, assumes we can construct grammars of text languages like Old French using protocols analogous to those generativists use to construct grammars of living languages:

Les traces que l'on a conservées de l'ancien français sont assez riches et nombreuses pour rendre tout à fait possible l'élaboration de règles qui rendent compte des énoncés qui nous sont parvenus, qui puissent les générer, eux, et du même coup d'innombrables énoncés de même structure dont on n'a pas gardé trace, mais qui ont peut-être été prononcés un jour, ou écrits. . . , ou qui ne l'ont peut-être jamais été.[44]

Marchello-Nizia's statement, squarely in line with orthodox generative theory, reveals one of the major difficulties of autonomous linguistics. In line with its name, autonomous linguistics insists on a distinction between "linguistic" knowledge on the one hand, and contextual knowledge, pragmatic knowledge, knowledge of the world, of history, and so on, which ostensibly fall outside the purview of descriptive linguistics. Creativity is also denied to be a part of "language" except insofar as it is, in Chomsky's celebrated phrase, "rule-governed," that is, except as the theoretically predictable outcome of a determinate set of rules, taking the form of sentences which, although waiting to be used, have never actually been used. This view of language is explicit in Marchello-Nizia's statement.

Yet there are many combinations of words in a language that native speakers never spontaneously use even though their use would not infringe any general patterns or regularities ("rules") of the language (for examples from English, see Harris, 76ff). Speakers' rejections of such combinations have no explanation in terms of syntactic, semantic, or even pragmatic rules. They are simply "facts of usage" in that language.[45]

This issue is problematic *a fortiori* for text languages, where native speakers are unavailable to pass judgment on unattested utterances, for example, of the type Cerquiglini constructs in his distributional set for *mar,* discussed above. Marchello-Nizia, in "Question de méthode," tries to address this problem, proposing "controlled use of paraphrase" to determine the acceptability of utterances that have been generated by a rule one has formulated but are unattested in the corpus. That is, if we find an *attested* utterance that consistently paraphrases (i.e., is the semantic/functional equivalent of) the one under scrutiny, then we can hypothesize the latter to be ungrammatical (487f). But in the absence of a convenient paraphrase, this procedure leaves us with no way of determining an utterance's acceptability. In short, we have no reliable guide to *usage,* a state of affairs that poses a serious obstacle to the application of generative methodology to text languages. Moreover, for a language whose data corpus is finite—only the discovery of previously unknown texts will enlarge it—a grammar designed to generate "any and all possible sentences" is, in a word, overkill.

The methodologies discussed to this point—traditional grammar, structural linguistics, and generative linguistics—have certain common ground and subscribe to certain common ideologies which it is appropriate at this juncture to set forth along with their implications for historical grammar.

SCIENTIFICITY, MONOGLOSSIA, AND THE PROBLEM OF VARIANTS

It was in conjunction with its claim to the status of a science in the later decades of the nineteenth century that linguistics succeeded in emancipating itself from both pedagogical grammar and subservience to the ends of philology. Philology, as a branch of humanistic linguistics (cf. n. 69), is interested in linguistic facts as a key to understanding the literary monuments of earlier ages. But the new "science" of linguistics insisted that language be studied for its own sake, for intellectual interests of its own, and for no ulterior purpose.

In order to establish itself as a science, linguistics first of all had to constitute an object of study that was stable and homogeneous. The heterogeneous raw material of language activity had to be disciplined in order to make it stable enough for investigation; variation poses difficulties for any attempts to systematize language. Harris states the problem thus: "the variability which confronts the inquirer appears to be such as to make it questionable to what extent any elements of linguistic behavior are consistent enough or delimitable enough to be describable. . . . On what basis is it possible to disengage from the incessant variability of language any clearly defined object of analysis at all? This is the basic problem for a science of language" (31).

As suggested in Harris's statement, the scientificity of linguistics, taken comfortably for granted in most quarters,[46] is founded on an illusory object: a stable, unitary, monolithic entity that has no existence in reality—Harris speaks of the "myth of monoglossia" or the "'fixed-code' fallacy"—but is a construct of linguistic practices, an objectofourownfabrication.[47] In this regard linguistics distinguishes itself methodologically from truly scientific disciplines, Milner observes (64), by taking on an obligation no empirical science would ever assume: to reject any material for description that it has not itself constructed, either axiomatically (formalist version) or via observation (empiricist version). The object of linguistics, as Crowley sees it, is "twice removed from the reality of language," having been "unified by the repression of *heteroglossia,* and then . . . reified as a stable 'thing' of the world" (50). Sociolinguistics, notably the "variationist" or "quantatitive" paradigm associated with the work of William Labov,[48] represents a major attempt to challenge this doctrine of "the ideal speaker-hearer in a homogeneous speech community" (this is the familiar Chomskyan formulation,[49] though the crucial point that *linguistics must idealize its object in order to describe it* goes back through the structuralist paradigms to Saussure; see Crowley).

The philological analogue to variationist sociolinguistics is represented by Cerquiglini's proposal in *Éloge de la variante* to reconstitute textual criticism in French on a new foundation of *variation.* This proposal arises out of a discomfort, echoing that voiced by the linguists cited above, with philology's attempts to repress or ignore the essential heteroglossia of the language of Old French texts. This proposal has important consequences for historical grammar as well.

As stated above, nineteenth-century linguistics, in order to achieve a respectable academic status as a science, had to constitute for itself an object of study that was stable and simple, regular and homogeneous. From this perspective, Old French, in the eyes of the positivistic scholars who undertook to describe it, appeared to be characterized by a fundamental heterogeneity. To the ever-present textual variation among manuscripts was added a haphazard orthography, "pretty much an affair of the scribe's own choosing" (Foulet and Speer, 76), and variability of the linguistic forms themselves: a proliferation of seemingly equivalent suffixes, widespread apophony in verb roots, multiple paradigms for tenses, apparent freedom of word order, an overwhelming diversity of syntactic constructions, and so on. Nineteenth-century philology's response to this disconcerting heteroglossia, Sonia Branca opines, was not to seek out "a method to the madness" but to dissolve it, regularize it.[50] As Bill Bennett has observed (393), we value highly the social cohesion that results from the stability of the signifier; which makes it easy to write off as primitive those who varied it.

Cerquiglini, in *Éloge de la variante,* distinguishes three periods in the history of French philology. In the earliest, manuscript variation was simply accepted, the primary concern being simply to publish the data and make the texts available. The second period, dominated by Gaston Paris, favored collating the multiple manuscripts of a text into a "perfect" critical edition whose language was, in a word, a phantom, a homogenized composite idiom with little basis in textual reality—the philological analogue of the ideal speaker-hearer.[51] The prevailing methodology of the third period, associated with Joseph Bédier, involved selecting the best manuscript and editing it, ignoring the data provided by other manuscripts. While Cerquiglini prefers Bédier's method to that of Gaston Paris, he points out (101) that neither makes adequate provision for variation, at once the essence of medieval textuality ("la variance de l'oeuvre médiévale romane est son caractère premier," 62) and the nemesis of medieval philology ("[qui] rompt . . . l'unicité de l'oeuvre, l'unicité de sa composition, la perfection du chef d'oeuvre, et . . . traumatise notre pensée du texte," 63).

The "native speakers" of a text language are the texts. Yet the heteroglossia of Old French texts transcends that of living language users in ways that bear on how we conceive—and write grammars—of text languages. The language of each text is already a hybrid, reflecting not the idiolect of an individual speaker, but the language of an author/composer filtered through one or more textual copies and subject to greater or lesser modification in the process. Accordingly, it is likely to be dialectally heterogeneous, and will presumably contain genre-specific features as well.

Confronted with variation on so many levels, how have descriptivists proceeded? The prefaces to the grammars are instructive in this regard. All acknowledge the diversity: orthographic, morphological, and notably dialectal,[52] then proceed to seek out the "système de référence qui transcendait la variété des dialects" (Wagner, 22). The following statement from Kibler's *An Introduction to Old French* is particularly revealing: "Out of the diversity of Old French we can identify a period (c. 1100–1285) and a dialect (Francien) that, more than any others, *typify 'Old French' and constitute the basis of a grammar of the language*" (xxv; emphasis added). The "fixed-code fallacy" that underlies so many modern approaches to grammar and reveals itself in the very title of van Reenen's recent methodological essay "La linguistique des langues anciennes et la systématisation de ses données,"[53] could hardly be more entrenched than it is here, notwithstanding data that resist standardization at every level. The language of Old French texts, Cerquiglini writes (*Éloge*, 110), "ne produit pas des variantes, elle est variance." If heteroglossia can provide the cornerstone for a new philology, might it not also, *a fortiori*, provide a more solid foundation for linguistic descriptions of Old French?[54] *A fortiori*, as Wagner observes, "[car] les besoins des descripteurs débordent largement ceux des éditeurs. De leur point de vue, concordantes ou divergentes, toutes les sources se valent puisqu'authentiques" (68).

Bashing the Scribe: Language Change as Decay

The ideal speaker-hearer of autonomous linguistics is said to be a member of a "completely homogeneous speech community, who knows its language perfectly, and is unaffected by such grammatically irrelevant considerations as memory limitations, distractions, shifts of attention and interest, and errors (random or characteristic) in applying his knowledge of the language in actual performance" (Chomsky, 5). Philologists have long held similar views about authors of Old French texts to those autonomous linguists hold about the ideal speaker-hearer, ascribing the disconcerting variation and "errors" of the manuscipts—precisely those described by Chomsky above—to the negligence, defective linguistic knowledge, or mechanical copying methods of scribes.[55] Elaborating on his dictum "toute copie est un déclin," Cerquiglini writes:

> La thèse de la copie comme dégénerescence, qui fonde la philologie, présuppose un original sans faute: l'auteur n'a pas droit au lapsus. De même, l'idée de la dégradation langagière implique un original impeccable: l'auteur n'as pas droit non plus à l'incorrection, à l'à-peu-près, voire à la diversité de sa parlure. Tout manuscrit médiéval étant une copie, il est par définition la reproduction fautive (de par l'inadvertance des scribes) et disparate (de par la diversité de leurs interventions) d'un original par définition sans tâche et qu'homogénise l'unicité d'un scripteur de talent. *Myope, la grammaire historique est de plus fort soupçonneuse, et recherche, sous les graphies dégradées, le système [linguistique] homogène que l'original avait entrepris de transcrire.*[56]

Underlying this belief in the inferiority of the scribe's language is a long-standing and pervasive ideology of language that equates change with decay and seeks a return to an erstwhile state of imagined linguistic plenitude, of consummate regularity now lost.[57] The linguistic analogue of the topos of the *exordium*, this ideology underwrites all *normative* approaches to language (see below). Its force is apparent in the text-critical preference for the *lectio difficilior* (cf. Foulet and Speer, 82) and in the very language textual critics use to talk about their praxis: "declensional solecisms," "orthographic anomalies," "corrupt readings," "*loci desperati.*" The term "textual criticism" itself, as Vinaver observed,[58] implies a mistrust of texts; it presupposes that in any copied text errors are inevitable and that the critic's main function is to correct them, to restore order in language.

Along this line, text-critical methodology routinely sanctions some regularization of spelling. Noting, for example, that scribes tend not to write two *e*'s in a row—a seemingly innocent descriptive statement (but see below), Foulet and Speer advise "it is the editor's duty to insert the missing third *e* in feminine past participles of verbs like *creer*" (81)—a subtle slippage through which the philologist's desire for regularity, for felicitous (monoglossic) textuality, converts from a linguistic desideratum to a *moral* imperative.[59] Under the heading of "homonyms," Foulet and Speer observe (77): "In order to make their texts intelligible to the reader, editors usually regularize certain orthographical anomalies. Thus, they distinguish between *ce* 'this' and *se* 'if,' between *ces* 'these' and *ses* 'his, her,' and between *ci* 'here' and *si* 'so, and' [*sic*]. When the scribe blurs these distinctions he is set right."

This statement advocates "rapping the scribe on the knuckles" for neutralizing certain lexical distinctions. But whose distinctions? For the editor/grammarian conversant with Modern French and exposed to Old French exclusively in *written* form, the respective pairs are clearly homonyms. But for the medieval copyist and his audience, more familiar with the language in *spoken* form than in written, these forms might well have been construed as polysemous, as alternative meanings of the unitary morphemes /sə/, /se/, and /si/ respectively (cf. n. 3). (By this same principle, certain speakers of English have been observed to write *would of* for *would have*, assigning the contracted element of *would've* to the morpheme it most closely resembles in speech rather than to *have*.) Underlying editors' emendations of "corrupt readings" of this type is an unarticulated (and no doubt unconscious) desire for the stability and regularity that institutionalized written language offers. And what is "regularity" if not a value-neutral synonym for the more overtly ideological "normativity."

THE COVERT NORMATIVITY OF LINGUISTIC DESCRIPTION

As a "scientific" discipline, linguistics sees its methodology as being value-neutral. Autonomous linguists, in particular, inisist on the freedom of their praxis from ideology. Not that they have made a conscious decision to keep their discipline value-neutral; it is necessarily so, Newmeyer argues, particularly in its generative avatars, because its object of study, (universal) grammar, excludes all those elements to which political values might be attached.

Where we find ideology lurking in linguistics is precisely in its claim that description is value-neutral. Normativity and value inhere, first of all, in the very metalanguage linguists use to describe their object of study: terms such as "rules," "judgments," "acceptability," sentences that are either "good" or "bad." Secondly, as Talbot Taylor argues, the so-called descriptive statements of grammar are, ultimately, thinly disguised *norms*.[60]

To buttress this claim, Taylor (22ff) invokes the examples of lexicographic definitions (e.g., statements such as: *reticent* means "disinclined to speak readily")[61] and syntactic rules (discussed below). These, he argues, are normative, in contrast to truly descriptive statements like "grizzly bears hibernate in winter." Asserting the truth of a normative statement is to assert that the statement is normatively enforced (within some context, by some individual or group); asserting the truth of a descriptive statement is to assert that it corresponds to the facts. But the "facts" with which descriptive linguists deal are not of the same order as those of other sciences, in that they are not amenable to empirical observation. Take the purported "facts" that English has a syntactic rule: "verbs agree in number with their subjects," or Old French a rule: "the finite verb appears in second position in the clause." What is observable, in the case of a living language, is the behavior of individual agents, or in the case of a dead language, the data presented by individual texts. But these instances of verbal behavior are not the "facts" described by grammarians: the rules are. Yet the rules are not data available for observation; they are constructs, inductive generalizations arrived at through linguistic procedures (recall Milner's statement cited above).

Taylor argues his case with regard to living languages, where covert normativity has obvious practical ramifications. As he observes (25), what better way to get people to follow the norms you propose than to say: "I am not saying how you should or should not use this word; I am simply saying what it really means in English. You may use it any way you wish (although not to use it according to this definition amounts to making a mistake)." My example of *reticent* is a case in point. The definition given above, from Webster's dictionary, does not in fact correlate with the way this word is used by many speakers of English today, for whom it is synonymous with *hesitant, reluctant* (e.g., *I was reticent to discuss it with her*).

Similarly, the syntactic rule of Subject-Verb agreement is often "violated" in actual usage: commonly in speech, but also in writing, as any composition instructor can attest, at times even by careful writers in sentences with complex nominal embeddings. A genuinely descriptive grammar of English would simply state the conditions under which S-V agreement does not occur for some language users, that is, restate the rule as a "variable" to accord with the (changing) facts of usage. Descriptive grammars of French are notorious for their lack of recognition—or if recognition is given, stigmatized labeling —of utterances or constructions in widespread use that do not accord with the institutionally sanctioned grammar known as *bon usage* (e.g., "dislocated" topic constructions such as *Il est fou, ce type-là*). Taylor concludes his discussion by insisting that linguists start calling a spade a spade: "If purportedly descriptive discourse on language is best reconceived as a (covertly authoritarian mode of) normative discourse, then the assertion of the political irrelevance and ideological neutrality of linguistic science can no longer be maintained. Descriptive linguistics is just another way of doing normative linguistics and an ideologically deceptive one at that" (25).

Covert normativity is an issue for text languages too, though the stakes are obviously different, since it is no longer a question of influencing the verbal behavior of actual language users. Where the pressures of normativity are felt is in the practices of philologists and historical grammarians, independently and interdependently. Given the intimate connection between the two disciplines, the normative ideology of textual criticism (in all its historical avatars) has inevitably impacted Old French grammar. A telling instance, noted above, was the use of heavily rewritten, linguistically homogenized critical editions to constitute the data base for grammars. Text-critical praxis is still informed by the view, albeit no longer acknowledged, that the published text should reflect the verbal activity of "the most skilled users" of the language. Nor have historical grammarians always resisted the impulse to describe "comment un clerc du Moyen Âge *devait* s'exprimer" (Wagner, 67). This covert normativity is implicit in grammarians' unanimous choice of the Francien dialect as "typifying

'Old French,'" thereby legitimating this linguistic construct as "the basis for a grammar of the language" (excerpted from Kibler's statement cited in full above).[62] Confronted, then, with the question "whose language is delivered by grammars claiming to 'describe the facts' of Old French texts?" we can only respond: "no one's."

In making this acknowledgment, I am not proposing that we scrap all Old French dictionaries or abstain from making statements about its grammar—which would be tantamount to throwing out the baby with the bathwater. I am simply calling for an acknowledgment of the normative and provisional status of our generalizations (I prefer this term to "rules") about the language. These generalizations can have a heuristic value (see below); moreover, they are often restatable as variable rules. Take, for example, a generalization of my own that "if *si* co-occurs with an expressed (postverbal) subject, that subject will be the same as the (explicit or understood) subject of the preceding clause" (Fleischman, 1991, 1992). To accommodate "the facts" of Old French texts, which include some apparent counterexamples (see van Reenen and Schøsler, "Ancien français"), this statement might profitably be reformulated with variable conditioning factors.

As suggested above, grammatical generalizations can have a heuristic value. Just as grammarians depend on, and benefit from, the text-editorial work of philologists, philologists in their turn can profit from the statements of grammarians. For example, the statement that "*si* never occurs at the beginning of a text or of a thematic paragraph" might have dissuaded Alexandre Micha, had he encountered this statement, from inserting a paragraph boundary before the sentence beginning with *si* in the passage below from his edition of the *Prose Lancelot:*

> Et li rois s'en part, dolens et corociés de Lancelot que il ne peut retenir. (ix.1)
> > *Si* s'en va Galehout . . . (ix.2)

> [And the king departs, sorrowful and irate at Lancelot, whom he cannot hold back. (ix.1)
> > Galahad goes off . . .] (ix.2)

By the same token, should an editor encounter *si* at a point in the discourse that appears, on other grounds, to be a legitimate *incipit* (of a text or thematic paragraph), the above generalization should prompt consideration of whether the particle in question might not be a variant form of locative *ci* (see van Reenen and Schøsler, 115–16). In short, there is no reason to eschew syntactic generalizations altogether; we should simply be aware that they carry normative force.

As Bakhtin observed (288), the unitary language engendered by science is unitary "only as an abstract grammatical system of normative forms, taken in isolation from the concrete, ideological conceptualizations that fill it, and in isolation from the uninterrupted process of historical becoming that is characteristic of all living language." Moreover, if it is the case, as Bakhtin's statement suggests, that an understanding of the beliefs and values of its speakers and the nature of the society in which it is spoken is necessary for understanding the structure of a language, then an analytical model that makes no reference to beliefs, values, or social context is, per Taylor's simile, "as politically/scientifically neutral as the political model that purports to offer a 'scientifically neutral' model of social justice."[63] If the object of study (the grammar of a language) is itself the object of ideological determination or controversy in a community, then the scientific explanation of that object cannot but be itself an ideological statement. This argument obviously applies more directly to living languages, a case in point being the linguistic controversies raging in France today. It relates to text languages primarily in the suppression of heteroglossia, of variation, an ideological practice that skews in a not inconsequential way our understanding of the nature of medieval vernaculars and of medieval textuality.

Let us turn our attention now to linguistic methodologies that look at the forms of grammar in connection with the extralinguistic world they refer to, the speakers that produce them, and the contexts and cotexts in which they are used. The sterility of modern linguistic orthodoxy, Harris insists (166), is precisely that it relegates these essential features and conditions of language to the realm of the nonlinguistic.

IS THERE A SPEAKER IN THIS GRAMMAR?: THE PROBLEMATICS OF *ÉNONCIATION*

Among the basic presuppositions of language as a code for communication is the notion, which may at first seem trivial, that every utterance, every discourse, has a speaker and an addressee, and is produced in a specific extradiscursive context. This context includes the time and place of the speech-event, the identity of the participants and their relations to one another, plus a variety of cultural or real-world knowledge the participants presumably share. The utterances of language are not decontextualized pieces of information; even the act of writing, which may sever them physically from their origin, does not thereby obliterate connections to a speaker, a context, and the locutionary act that produced them—what the French subsume under the label of *Énonciation*.

Some of the most illuminating linguistic work on Old French is methodologically grounded in theories of *énonciation*. This particular brand of linguistic pragmatics is founded on the proposition that the utterances of a text inevitably contain traces of the locutionary activity that produced them, the context in which they were produced, and the subjectivity of the producer. A major research agenda has accordingly involved identifying and interpreting these traces through which the act of speaking and the beliefs and attitudes of speakers leave their imprint on the surface structure of discourse.

In the most exhaustive syntactico-semantic analysis of *si* to date, Marchello-Nizia interprets this particle, which she classifies as a sentence adverb, as an "evidential" of veridiction signaling the speech-act of *assertion*.[64] By means of *si*, she argues, speakers legitimate their authority to make an assertion and simultaneously vouch for the *truth* of the proposition contained therein. Suggestive as this hypothesis is, it presents a number of difficulties, which I elaborate elsewhere (Fleischman, 1991). The essential issue here is that an evidential interpretation of *si* as signaling "the speaker's assumption of responsibility for the veracity of an utterance" is a predictable *point d'arrivée* for an analysis grounded in the framework of *énonciation*.

KEEPING IT TOGETHER: SWITCH REFERENCE AND TOPIC CONTINUITY IN DISCOURSE

The last of the methodologies surveyed here that have been applied to Old French is a brand of functional linguistics that explicitly moves the locus of grammatical analysis beyond the sentence to the higher-level units of language referred to as "discourses" or "texts." Sentences never occur in isolation in the real world. In recognition of this fact, many linguists have come to acknowledge that certain phenomena, syntactic phenomena in particular, can only be understood properly from the viewpoint of their *functional* motivation in multipropositional *discourse*. Discourse pragmatics endeavors to explicate grammatical phenomena with reference to contexts larger than a single sentence, by showing either that sentence-level phenomena have some kind of grounding in discourse or that the sentence itself is suspect as a core unit.

In my two publications on *si,* I put forth the hypothesis that this particle has a pragmatic function paralleling that of subject pronouns (optional in Old French); working together, and for the most part in complementary distribution, *si* and the pronouns enable an addressee to keep track of participants (nominal referents) across the clauses of a discourse. More specifically (and simplifying considerably), I argue that *si* signals the *continuity* of a grammatical subject (which is generally also the primary "topic"),[65] that is, that the subject/topic of a (main) clause is the same as that of the preceding clause, while subject pronouns signal "switch-reference," that is, they alert the addressee to a change of subject and/or topic.

This interpretation of *si,* like the others that have been proposed, proceeds from and is constrained by the theory of language that grounds it, in this instance a theory that insists upon the fundamental interdependency of grammar and the pragmatics of discourse. Since the advent of structuralism we have become accustomed to thinking of grammar as a relatively stable system which all adult users of the language possess in reasonably similar form, and one in which *forms*—the recognized categories of the grammar—have *meanings* that hold constant independently of context (the "fixed-code" fallacy). Of late, however, there have been various proposals to abandon this a priori notion of grammar that founds standard theories of linguistics in favor of a view of grammar as a set of linguistic transactions that are continually being negotiated in individual contexts of communication. As Paul Hopper states it, "structure, or regularity, comes out of discourse and is shaped by discourse as much as it shapes discourse in an ongoing process."[66] It is precisely this view of grammar that yields an analysis of *si* and the subject pronouns as *grammaticalized* markers of (respectively) "subject/topic continuity" and "switch-reference" *in discourse.*

For philologists and Old French specialists, "switch-reference" and "topic continuity" are undoubtedly not household words. Switch-reference has been talked about in regard to a variety of exotic, nonliterary languages but not in regard to more familiar European languages, including Romance. This is not to say that devices for "participant tracking" are absent from Romance—all languages have them—but simply that Romance languages, tied as they are to the Graeco-Latin grammatical tradition, have for the most part not been looked at from this functional, pragmatic perspective.

One of the rallying points of structuralism, at least of the American variety, has been referred to as its egalitarianism, that is, its insistence on the position that all languages are equal irrespective of where their cultures figure along hierarchies of (notably western) civilization. Franz Boas, in particular, exposed the ideological thrust of earlier views (which have not been universally abandoned!), demonstrating that the grammatical sophistication of nonwestern languages is every bit as advanced as that of western languages of culture. *Mutatis mutandis* this has been demonstrated once again in recent times with regard to Black English. Yet philologists and scholars of western literature have generally shown little regard for the attention paid by linguists to nonliterary languages or, in so-called languages of culture, to the *sermo plebeius* or even the unmonitored speech of educated elites. French, eternally haunted by the specter of *bon usage*, is a case in point.

I raise this issue of linguistic elitism, in particular the view that vernacular usage and nonliterary languages have nothing to teach those who study the literary monuments of Europe, in an attempt to understand the reaction of medieval colleagues to certain of my own research that draws on linguistic protocols documented in everyday speech, or in nonwestern and nonliterary languages, to shed light on the workings of text languages of medieval Europe. What comes particularly to mind, in addition to my work on *si* (Fleischman, 1991, 1992) and on tense-switching,[67] is a study documenting the striking similarity of the "similar-*laisses*" phenomenon of Old French epic to a narrative protocol of formalized repetition observed in the story-telling practices of several unrelated and nonliterate languages.[68] Linguists' analyses of this "overlay" pattern can, in my view, only enhance our understanding of the functions of formalized repetition in the orally composed song poetry of medieval France. Yet, curiously, my work along these lines has aroused substantially more interest among general linguists than among the medievalists and Old French scholars to whom it is primarily addressed and whose object of study—the text language of medieval France—it is primarily intended to illuminate. In seeking to comprehend this disparity of response, I can only speculate on the part played by ideologies: the egalitarianism of modern descriptive linguistics vs. the elitism of the traditions of *belles lettres* and *bon usage* so deeply engrained in French culture.

CONCLUSION

This chapter has offered a retrospective reflection on the praxis of historical grammar, a discipline devoted to unraveling the linguistic mysteries of medieval texts. It has surveyed a range of grammatical methodologies from this century and looked at the theoretical and ideological presuppositions that underlie them in an attempt to see how these presuppositions have influenced the questions our research asks and the findings we come up with.

It seems not inappropriate to conclude by asking whether social and political agendas prominent in our culture today, in particular the problematics of gender and "diversity," have had any reverberations in a field so seemingly removed from political center stage as the grammar of medieval vernaculars.

Our current preoccupation (in America) with cultural pluralism—or "diversity," as it has come to be called—finds linguistic reverberations, not surprisingly, in the field of sociolinguistics, notably in variation studies, and in a heightened interest in dialect phenomena. It is too soon to say whether or how this emphasis on pluralism will impact Old French studies; a promising step in this direction is Cerquiglini's *Éloge de la variante,* a monograph on *variation* as "the name of the game" for a renascent philology. One thing Cerquiglini points out (112ff) is the increasingly important role to be played by the computer as an investigative tool for studying variation in medieval texts. In their recent study "Ancien français," which would have been unwieldy if not impossible without computer assistance, van Reenen and Schøsler analyze an extensive data base of Old and Middle French texts, seeking to identify statistically meaningful variation (dialectal, chronological, stylistic) in the use of *si.*

Our current preoccupation with gender issues in language has to date had only minimal resonance in the field of Old French. Two studies worthy of mention along this line are Doris Earnshaw's study of the female voice in lyric poetry and Cerquiglini's 1986 essay on *mar* as a distinctive feature of feminine discourse.[69] The syntactic formulas in which *mar* occurs, Cerquiglini contends, sum up "the misfortunes and anguished solitude of the feminine condition" in the twelfth and thirteenth centuries. Taking this argument further, he links the disappearance of *mar* in the course of the fourteenth century to an "ideological change" in the position of women which necessarily left its mark on women's language. His essay concludes with a germane reminder, very much in the spirit of Bakhtin, that "the arid diachrony

428 • THE DISCIPLINE AND ITS OTHERS

of linguistic change is not unrelated to the history of human societies"
(198).

Though gender has not emerged as a relevant factor in the debates
over *si*, it is perhaps not gratuitous to point out that the only women
participants in the discussion (Christiane Marchello-Nizia, Lene
Schøsler, and myself) have all, independently, eschewed formal, "autonomous" methodologies, which isolate the utterances of language
from actual speakers and contexts of communication, in favor of
"sociological" methodologies,[70] a fortiori paradigms that emphasize
the *interpersonal* aspect of language use. Speculating on these methodological affinities in the light of what we know about masculine vs.
feminine modes of communication,[71] we might consider the following
remarks by Robin Lakoff on women and autonomous (formal)
linguistics:

> Many of those who have in the past been turned off by undue
> obeisance to formalism have been women. . . . I feel that it is the
> emphasis on formal description of the superficial aspects of lan-
> guage that many of us find discouraging: hence many women, in an
> attempt to escape into relevance, go into psycholinguistics or socio-
> linguistics . . . but are lost to the mainstream and often end up
> dissatisfied anyhow. I don't know, nor does anyone, whether there is
> an inherent indisposition toward formalism among women, or
> whether it is a learned trait that may eventually be overcome; I know
> merely that it is the case now and is apt to remain so for some time
> to come.[72]

In 1928, in an appendix to the third edition of his *Petite syntaxe
de l'ancien français*, Lucien Foulet offered a series of cogent observations on the methodology of historical grammar that turned around
the implicit question: what kind of linguistic description is best suited
to a language like Old French, and what constraints does a text
language impose on the enterprise of grammar? Commenting on
Foulet's methodological vademecum nearly a half-century later,
Wagner writes, "La question demeure actuelle et le moment n'est pas
mal venu pour les médiévistes d'en reprendre l'examen, en s'en inspir-
ant d'abord d'une conversion que certains d'entre eux ont déjà opérée
dans un autre secteur de leur discipline" (67). A decade and a half
later—a generation in the evolution of linguistic theory, if only a
moment in the history of human thought—I acknowledge, in turn, the
timeliness of Wagner's own remark.

NOTES

My thanks to Jonathan Beck and to the volume editors for reading earlier drafts of this chapter and suggesting improvements; responsibility for the views expressed here is entirely my own.

1. On this distinction, see Christiane Marchello-Nizia, "Question de méthode," *Romania* 106 (1985): 483–92.

2. Glosses have been kept as literal as possible. Words not contained in the Old French but required for a smooth translation (e.g., subject pronouns, connectives of various types) appear in square brackets. Since in my view *si* is untranslatable, its place is indicated in the glosses by the number sign (#).

3. It is essential not to confuse this *si*, which I will refer to as "pragmatic *si*," with several look-alikes: (1) the subordinating conjunction *si* meaning "if" (vars. *se, s'*); (2) the adverbial intensifier *si* meaning "so, so much" (= MFr. *si, tant, tellement*); (3) the manner adverb *si* meaning "thus, so" (= MFr. *ainsi*); (4) the affirmation particle *si* used to counter a negative utterance (as in MFr.); (5) the 3d-person reflexive pronoun *se* (var. *s'*). Save for the reflexive pronoun (< Latin *se*), these morphemes are all traceable to Latin *sic*, though by the twelfth century it is unclear whether French speakers regarded them still as polysemes or as homonyms. To complicate matters further, the unstable orthography of medieval French texts occasionally yields *si/se* for the locative adverb *ci* (= *ici*) or the neuter demonstrative *ce* (= *ça/cela*). Given the opportunities for confusion, simply constituting a reliable data base for pragmatic *si* is a formidable task; even text editors and grammarians have mistaken one morpheme for another.

4. Cf. Christiane Marchello-Nizia, *Dire le vrai: L'adverbe "si" en français médiéval* (Geneva: Droz, 1985), and Pieter van Reenen and Lene Schøsler, "Ancien et moyen français: Si 'thématique': Analyse exhaustive d'une série de textes," *Vox Romanica* 51 (1992): 101–27.

5. Suzanne Fleischman, "Discourse-Pragmatics and the Grammar of Old French: A Functional Reinterpretation of *si* and the Personal Pronouns," *Romance Philology* 44 (1991): 251–83, and "Discourse and Diachrony: The Rise and Fall of Old French *si*," in M. Gerritsen and D. Stein, eds., *Internal and External Factors in Syntactic Change* (Berlin: de Gruyter, 1992) (hereafter cited as Fleischman, 1991 and 1992). The literature on this particle fills the pages of more than sixty studies. For bibliography and a comprehensive summary of viewpoints, see Marchello-Nizia, *Dire le vrai*, esp. 15–18, 162–64.

6. This terminus post quem is imposed by the lack of attention to French syntax (Old or Modern) prior to this time, save for German dissertations from the end of the last century and, in this century, the "psychomechanical" work of the Guillaumians. Cf. Louis Kukenheim, *Esquisse historique de la*

linguistique française et de ses rapports avec la linguistique générale (Leiden: Universitaire Pers, 1962), 143—44, and Bernard Cerquiglini, Jacqueline Cerquiglini, Christiane Marchello-Nizia, and Michèle Perret-Minard, "L'objet 'ancien français' et les conditions propres à sa description linguistique," in J.-C. Chevalier and M. Gross, eds., *Méthodes en grammaire française* (Paris: Klincksieck, 1976), 185–200, esp. 185.

7. See Roy Harris, *The Language Myth* (London: Duckworth, 1981).

8. Under the "autonomous" umbrella, Newmeyer includes, in addition to generative linguistics in its various avatars, the structuralist varieties that preceded it; see Frederick J. Newmeyer, *The Politics of Linguistics* (Chicago: University of Chicago Press, 1986).

9. See E. F. Konrad Koerner, "Towards a Historiography of Linguistics: 19th and 20th Century Paradigms," in Herman Parret, ed., *History of Linguistic Thought and Contemporary Linguistics* (Berlin and New York: de Gruyter, 1976), 685–718, esp. 699.

10. Mainstream syntactic theory is understood to refer to formal, primarily generative models (with and now without transformations) and their offshoots.

11. An exception to this generalization is provided by sociolinguistics, whose focus on language *in relation to society* obliges it to confront such determinants of linguistic usage as power, prestige, social class, gender, and ethnicity. Yet with respect to methodology, sociolinguistics is as committed as any field of linguistics to the use of "scientific" protocols.

12. The term "cotext" will be used to refer to the text surrounding an utterance (i.e., to linguistic or discourse context), "context" to its extra-linguistic or situational setting.

13. This statement is true of even the most recent manuals of Old French: the later printings of William W. Kibler's *An Introduction to Old French* (New York: Modern Language Association, 1984); the revised 3d ed. of Philippe Ménard's *Syntaxe de l'ancien français* (Bordeaux: Bière, 1988); Frede Jensen's *Old French and Comparative Gallo-Romance Syntax*, Beiheft zur *Zeitschrift für romanische Philologie* 232 (Tübingen: Niemeyer, 1990); and Geneviève Hasenohr's new ed. of Raynaud de Lage, *Introduction à l'ancien français* (Paris: SEDES, 1990). The following observation by Kukenheim, written in 1962, still holds today: "*à défaut de système méthodique*, les bonnes introductions sont très rares et les éditeurs d'anciens textes sont toujours à la recherche d'une description adéquate de la langue des textes qu'ils publient" (134, emphasis added). The "codependency" of text editors and grammarians will be explored below.

14. Cf. R. H. Robins, "Some Continuities and Discontinuities in the History of Linguistics," in Parret, ed., *History of Linguistic Thought*, 13–31, esp. 17–18.

15. Historians of French will recall with a smile the determined efforts of sixteenth-century grammarians to find a *locus amoenus* among the consecrated categories of Latin and Greek for such "recalcitrant" data as the French articles; cf. Peter Rickard, *La langue française au seizième siècle* (Cambridge: Cambridge University Press, 1968), 30ff.

16. I use the term "traditional" to refer to grammatical treatments (descriptive or historical) not overtly informed by a particular theoretical orientation.

17. Jean Rychner, *L'articulation des phrases narratives dans la "Mort Artu": Formes et structures de la prose française médiévale* (Neuchâtel: Faculté des Lettres; Geneva: Droz, 1970), and Antoine Grad, "Remarques sur l'adverbe de reprise *si* en ancien français," *Linguistica* 4 (1961): 5–19.

18. Peter Blumenthal, "Über gemütliches *si* in mittelalterlichen Erzählungen," in H. D. Bork, A. Greive, and D. Woll, eds., *Romanica Europea et Americana: Festschrift für Harri Meier* (Bonn: Bovier Verlag Herbert Grandmann, 1980), 55–67.

19. Bernard Cerquiglini, *La parole médiévale* (Paris: Minuit, 1981).

20. I leave the italicized particles untranslated, since elaborate commentary would be required to explain the glosses. At issue is their distributional parallelism, clear even without glosses. Of the three examples, only the last is attested (*Roland*, 1057); the other two have been constructed by Cerquiglini who insists that "even if they are not attested, they appear to be absolutely grammatical" (*Parole*, 156). I will return later to the matter of constructing data, a methodologically risky practice, *a fortiori* in the case of a text language.

21. I leave aside here altogether the problem of definition, that is, that there is no universally agreed upon criterion for identifying parts of speech. Differing results obtain if the criterion is semantic/referential (e.g., nouns designate substances or entities, verbs actions or states, adjectives qualities, and so on), formal (e.g., nouns are declined, verbs conjugated, particles invariable), or distributional, as in the attempts discussed in this section to find grammatical housing for *si*.

22. See, e.g., Cerquiglini et al., "L'objet"; Bernard Cerquiglini, "Für ein neues Paradigma der historischen Linguistik: Am Beispiel des Altfranzösischen," in Bernard Cerquiglini and Hans Ulrich Gumbrecht, eds., *Der Diskurs der Literatur-Sprachhistorie* (Frankfurt-am-Main: Suhrkamp, 1983), 449–63, and Cerquiglini, *Éloge de la variante: Histoire critique de la philologie* (Paris: Éditions du Seuil, 1989).

23. Pieter van Reenen and Lene Schøsler, "Le problème de la prolifération des explications," *Vrije Universiteit Working Papers in Linguistics* 27 (Amsterdam, 1987): 12–13; Cerquiglini, *Éloge*, 93–94.

24. Comforted, no doubt, by the stability, regularity, and coherence of the text produced by his rigorous editorial toilette, Paris writes: "Je pense qu'on voudra bien reconnaître que le texte de ce poème, tel que je le livre au public, offre un spécimen admissible de la bonne langue française telle qu'elle devait se parler et s'écrire au milieu du XIe siècle" (cited by Cerquiglini, Éloge, 94).

25. Comparing the several editions of the The Charroi de Nîmes with the nine manuscripts, Lene Schøsler documents similarly "fictitious" case-marking in editors' expansions of abbreviated proper names.

26. The situation is actually more complicated than what is suggested here. The "normative impulse" that emerges out of a nostalgic desire for grammatical correctness is not confined to modern editors. Old French authors, scribes, and copyists are also known to have Latinized (whence the existence of texts that *do* mark case rigorously); what this implies is that they themselves were already nostalgic—or browbeaten—about grammatical correctness. Cf. also n. 29 below.

27. Alfred Foulet and Mary Blakely Speer, *On Editing Old French Texts* (Lawrence: Regents Press of Kansas, 1979), 81.

28. "Evidential" as a term of the grammatical metalanguage is explained below in n. 64.

29. It is perhaps more accurate to say that the rule was no longer operative *as usage,* which is always at some distance from the *grammar* of written language. Reflecting on the broader implications of this observation, we might consider the idea that norms of correctness for written language exist precisely for the purpose of preserving linguistic practices that are "no longer operative" in the spoken language. Once again nostalgia.

30. Alain Lerond, ed., *Histoire de la langue* (= *Langue française* 10) (Paris: Larousse, 1971), 4–5 (emphasis added).

31. William Bennett, "*Scripta* and *signe:* A Defence of Scribes," *French Review* 39, no. 4 (1991): 385–94, esp. 391.

32. Pierre Guiraud, "L'expression du virtuel dans le 'Roland' d'Oxford," *Romania* 83 (1962): 289–302, at 300.

33. Pierre Guiraud, *L'ancien français,* "Que sais-je?" 1056 (Paris: Presses Universitaires de France, 1963; 5th ed., 1975), and "L'opposition actuel/virtuel: Remarques sur l'adverbe de négation dans *Aucassin et Nicolette,*" in *Mélanges . . . offerts à M. Delbouille* (Gembloux: Duculot, 1964), 1:295–306.

34. Nicol Spence, "Existe-t-il en ancien français une opposition actuel/virtuel?" *Revue de linguistique romane* 30 (1966): 183–97.

35. I should point out that Cerquiglini is interested in *si* only incidentally, the focus of his inquiry being *mar.* Thus his analysis of *si* goes no further

than to situate it within a class of "predicate markers" that he sees as signaling the presence of a speaking subject.

36. Thus Lucien Foulet, *Petite syntaxe de l'ancien français* (Paris: Champion, 1919; 3d ed., 1928; rev. 1974): "*Si* . . . signifie *ainsi*, mais adapte facilement son sens aux besoins de la phrase, au point qu'il est parfois malaisé d'en indiquer la nuance exacte" (§439). Similarly, Ménard: "Lorsqu'il marque la succession temporelle, lorsqu'il situe ou récapitule, on peut parfois le traduire par 'alors,' 'dans ces conditions,' 'ainsi,' 'et voilà,' parfois par 'aussi' ou 'donc' quand le contexte suggère une nuance consécutive. Parfois, il prend nettement la valeur adversative de 'mais' ou 'cependant.' Mais souvent il reste intraduisible" (§197). Robert Martin and Marc Wilmet, *Syntaxe du moyen français: Manuel du français du moyen âge*, vol. 2 (Bordeaux: SOBODI, 1980), deem it a "ligature passe-partout" (§460).

37. These two species of grammarian are not entirely distinct; by now, most traditional grammars of Old French are, if not consciously structuralist, at least structuralist by osmosis, though Ménard, writing in 1973, is skeptical about the possibility of a truly structural syntax "dans l'état présent de la recherche."

38. Cf. Cerquiglini et al., "L'objet"; Bennett, *"Scripta"*; and Suzanne Fleischman, "Philology, Linguistics, and the Discourse of the Medieval Text," *Speculum* 64 (1990): 19–37.

40. There have been no generative treatments of *si;* what little "formal" syntactic work has been done on Old French has concentrated on topics of interest to syntactic theory generally, notably the "V/2" phenomenon and "null-subjects."

41. By "processed data" I mean data extracted from grammars or edited texts, that is, at one or more removes from the manuscript sources. Claims based on these data are, of course, only as reliable as the philological foundation on which they rest (we recall here the problem of phantom case morphology). A notable exception to my generalization is represented by the "Paris philologists," whose (loosely) generative linguistic methodology is combined with a thorough familiarity with manuscripts and the philological dilemmas they pose. See in particular Cerquiglini et al., "L'objet"; Marchello-Nizia, "Question de méthode."

42. In the spirit of "affirmative action grammar," I reluctantly pluralize this referent to avoid stylistically cumbersome reiterations of "s/he," "his/her." Reluctantly, because pluralization camouflages the fact that that hero of mainstream linguistics, the "ideal speaker-hearer," is ineluctably singular. The implications of this singularity will be discussed below.

43. This mode of linguistic description has been labeled "epistemic," inasmuch as it endeavors to provide a formal description of *what the ideal*

speaker-hearer knows (the "grammar" of a language) rather than of the *actual verbal behaviors of real speakers*. Among the difficulties this approach runs up against, Roy Harris (35–36) points to the lack of any assumption on the part of linguistic theorists that in practice people always act linguistically in accord with what they know (implicit in the notion of "performance errors").

44. Christiane Marchello-Nizia, "Ponctuation et 'unités de lecture' dans les manuscrits médiévaux," *Langue française* 40 (1978): 32–44, at 32. In her later essay "Question de méthode," she suggests how generative methodology can be adapted to text languages, where the crucial element of native speaker judgments is lacking. This in contrast to Robert Léon Wagner, *L'ancien français* (Paris: Larousse, 1974), for whom the lack of native speakers "exclut d'emblée" the application of generative grammar to Old French. Cf. also Jean Batany, "Ancien français, méthodes nouvelles," in Lerond, ed., *Histoire de la langue,* 45–50.

45. Harris argues further (80) that the attempt to subsume such uncooperative facts of usage under "grammar," and thus place them on a par with, for example, rules of gender and number agreement, merely illustrates the confusion produced by autonomous linguistics' attempts to reinterpret the traditional notion of grammaticality in terms of some internalized principle of combinatorial structuring that organizes the totality of the formal content of native speakers' knowledge of their language.

46. Cf. Ranko Bugarski's assertion that "the scientific features of linguistics . . . have been adequately demonstrated through a precise analytical apparatus, systematic research techniques, the verifiability of hypotheses and the like, so that overt references to the scientific character of linguistics are no longer particularly called for" ("The Object of Linguistics in Historical Perspective," in Parret, ed., *History of Linguistic Thought,* 1–12, at 5). Among those who question the scientific ideology that founds the modern linguistic enterprise, compelling critiques are offered by Harris, *Language Myth;* Jean-Claude Milner, *Introduction à une science du langage* (Paris: Éditions du Seuil, 1989); and Tony Crowley, "That Obscure Object of Desire: A Science of Language," in John E. Joseph and Talbot J. Taylor, eds., *Ideologies of Language* (London: Routledge, 1990), 27–50.

47. Mikhail Bakhtin, "Discourse in the Novel," in *The Dialogic Imagination,* ed. M. Holquist, trans. C. Emerson and M. Holquist (Austin: University of Texas Press, 1981), offers a compelling *historical* critique of the type of linguistic research that posits a kind of monoglossia as the normal state of a language.

48. A "linguistic variable" is defined as "a linguistic unit [phoneme, morpheme, construction] with two or more variants involved in covariation

with other social and/or linguistic variables"; J. K. Chambers and Peter Trudgill, *Dialectology* (Cambridge: Cambridge University Press, 1980), 60. The variationist viewpoint on language is determined "first by a scientific interest in accounting for grammatical structure *in discourse*—be it spontaneous conversation, formal narrative or argumentation, or various written genres—and second with a preoccupation with the polyvalence and apparent instability *in discourse* of linguistic form-function relationships"; David Sankoff, "Sociolinguistics and Syntactic Variation," in F. J. Newmeyer, gen. ed., *The Cambridge Linguistics Survey*, vol. 4: *Language: The Socio-cultural Context* (Cambridge: Cambridge University Press), 140–61, at 141. A classic text of variationist linguistics is William Labov's *Sociolinguistic Patterns* (Philadelphia: University of Pennsylvania Press, 1972).

49. Noam Chomsky, *Aspects of the Theory of Syntax* (Cambridge, Mass.: MIT Press, 1965).

50. Sonia Branca, "Les débats sur la variation au milieu du XIXe siècle," GARS Université de Provence, *Recherches sur le français parlé 5* (1983): 263–90.

51. For a piquant critique of the Lachmannian method, with its ideological underwear in full view, see chapter 5 of Cerquiglini's *Éloge de la variante*, "Gaston Paris et les dinosaures."

52. Bennett (388) insists that for the manuscript culture of the French Middle Ages it is anachronistic to speak of dialects in the modern sense. The social dialects and local literary registers that were emerging, he argues, were no more than an aggregate of idiolects until the notion of a language provided a psychological focus for an increasing number of speakers.

53. Systematization, Pieter van Reenen observes, "est realisée par un processus de sélection, de raffinement, de classement": "La linguistique des langues anciennes et la systématisation de ses données," in A. Dees, ed., *Actes du IV Colloque sur le Moyen Français* (Amsterdam: Rodopi, 1985), 433–70, at 433.

54. A desiderative gesture in this direction is Wagner's suggestion (62–63) that a comprehensive grammar of Old French, still "premature" at the time of his writing (early 1970s), would have to take account of "la *varia lectio* des textes édités et des témoignages fournis par les manuscrits negligés." Cf. also van Reenen and Schøsler, "Problème."

55. Cf. Cerquiglini: "La philologie lachmannienne commence par automiser le scribe, a qui est déniée toute intervention positive et consciente: . . . Le scribe est une machine, et cette machine doit fonctionner mal, afin que la pluralité et l'excès des variantes s'ordonnent" (*Éloge*, 76).

56. Bernard Cerquiglini, *La naissance du français*, "Que sais-je?" 2576 (Paris: Presses Universitaires de France, 1991) (emphasis added); cf. also Cerquiglini, *Éloge*, 76ff.

57. As Cerquiglini (*Éloge,* 75) notes, this powerful ideology of language united the goals of philology and linguistics (historico-comparativism) during the later decades of the nineteenth century: while linguists busied themselves with classifying the Indo-European languages and trying to reconstruct the primordial, perfect *Ursprache,* philologists were classifying manuscripts and reconstructing the archetypal *Urtext.*

58. Eugène Vinaver, "Principles of Textual Emendation" [1939], repr. in Christopher Kleinhenz, ed., *Medieval Manuscripts and Textual Criticism* (Chapel Hill: University of North Carolina, Dept. of Romance Languages, 1976), 139–66, at 144.

59. Similarly "injunctive" among authorities on textual criticism are Vinaver: "'Impossible' readings are those which can be shown to result from scribal errors; such readings *it is our duty* to correct" (158–59); and Kleinhenz: "If there exists an obvious corruption or lacuna in the text (*divinatio*), then *the editor is duty bound* to correct it through *emendatio*" (23) (emphasis added in both instances).

60. Talbot J. Taylor, "Which Is To Be Master?: The Institutionalization of Authority in the Science of Language," in Joseph and Taylor, eds., *Ideologies of Language,* 9–26.

61. The role of dictionaries as an ideological instrument in language politics is widely recognized. Extralinguistic (and value-assigning) agendas invariably inform lexicographers' decisions about words to be included or omitted from dictionaries (again, the question "whose language?") as well as their choices of usage labels ("archaic," "rare," "popular," "vulgar").

62. The term "francien" was unknown before the nineteenth century when it was invented by Gaston Paris. Interestingly, not a single Old French text offers a *pure* specimen of this "construlect"; moreover, the paucity of texts localisable to the Paris region (see van Reenen, "Linguistique") would seem to pose a serious challenge to its privileged status. On the invention of francien as a projection back to the Middle Ages of the "ideology of the standard" (the term is from J. Milroy and L. Milroy, *Authority in Language* [London and New York: Routledge, 1985], see Gabriel Bergounioux, "Le francien (1815–1914): La linguistique au service de la patrie," *Mots/Les langages du politique* 19 (1989): 23–40; Suzanne Fleischman, "Medieval Vernaculars and the Myth of Monoglossia: A Conspiracy of Linguistics and Philology," in *Literary History and the Challenge of Philology: The Legacy of Erich Auerbach,* ed. Seth Lerer (Stanford: Stanford University Press, 1995), and "On Working with Older Languages: Methodologies and Ideologies," in *Textual Parameters in Older Language,* ed. Susan Herring, Lene Schøsler, and Pieter van Reenen (Amsterdam and New York: John Benjamins, 1996).

63. Talbot J. Taylor, review of F. J. Newmeyer, *The Politics of Language*, in *Language* 66 (1990): 159–62.

64. Marchello-Nizia, *Dire le vrai.* "Evidential" is a term introduced by Roman Jakobson as a tentative label for a verbal category that indicates the source of information on which a speaker's statement is based. Languages deploy a variety of evidential devices (lexical, grammatical, diacritical) for indicating whether or not a speaker vouches personally, or takes responsibility, for the information contained in an utterance—the function Marchello-Nizia attributes to *si,* albeit without invoking the term "evidential."

65. "Subject" is a *syntactic* category referring to the nominal in a sentence that governs agreement-marking on the verb; "topic" (grossly simplifying) is a category of *information structure* used to refer to the nominal under discussion at a particular point in the discourse (the noun phrase being talked about). Though topics often appear as sentence subjects, the two categories must be kept distinct at the theoretical level.

66. Paul J. Hopper, "Emergent Grammar," *Berkeley Linguistics Society* 13 (1987): 139–57, at 142.

67. Suzanne Fleischman, *Tense and Narrativity: From Medieval Performance to Modern Fiction* (Austin: University of Texas Press; London: Routledge, 1990).

68. Suzanne Fleischman, "A Linguistic Perspective on the *Laisses Similaires:* Orality and the Pragmatics of Narrative Discourse," *Romance Philology* 43 (1989): 70–89.

69. Doris Earnshaw, *The Female Voice in Medieval Romance Lyric* (New York: Peter Lang, 1988); Bernard Cerquiglini, "The Syntax of Discursive Authority: The Example of Feminine Discourse," *Yale French Studies* 70 (1986): 183–98.

70. These labels reflect Newmeyer's division of the field of linguistics into three broad orientations: humanistic, sociological, and autonomous. Under the humanistic rubric Newmeyer (8) places such fields as poetics, stylistics, and philology, which all study language primarily in the service of literature; sociological approaches include, in addition to the various branches of sociolinguistics, also pragmatics and discourse analysis, which "describe language use in its interpersonal context"; work in autonomous linguistics is largely concerned with "grammatical theory," attempting to formulate the principles governing structural regularity in language. (I invoke Newmeyer's typology for convenience, though I am not entirely comfortable with it; cf. Taylor's review of Newmeyer in *Language*.)

71. As set forth, for example, in Deborah Tannen's sociolinguistic bestseller *You Just Don't Understand: Women and Men in Communication* (New York: William Morrow, 1990).

72. Robin Lakoff, "Pluralism in Linguistics," in C. J. Fillmore, G. Lakoff, and R. Lakoff, eds., *Berkeley Studies in Syntax and Semantics* 1 (1974): xiv. Though more women are now engaged in formal linguistics than at the time of Lakoff's essay, her observation is still valid, and is borne out by the case study of *si*.

SIXTEEN

A Sad and Weary History: The *Grundriß der romanischen Literaturen des Mittelalters*

Hans Ulrich Gumbrecht

THERE IS A SET OF black binders on a shelf in my garage, about seven miles from the Stanford University campus, with hundreds of letters written since 1959 by the editors, authors, and publishers of the *Grundriß der romanischen Literaturen des Mittelalters*. They had been sent by Hans Robert Jauss (from Constance) and Erich Köhler (from Freiburg) to my address at the Ruhr-Universität Bochum in late 1976, some months after Ulrich Mölk and I had agreed to succeed our academic teachers in the role of "chief editors" for the GRLMA (this project had always been characterized by a quasi-military bent toward hierarchies and abbreviations). The binders had arrived at my California address by the time I moved from the Universität-Gesamthochschule Siegen to accept a permanent position at Stanford in the summer of 1989. These documents pertaining to one of the most ambitious projects launched by European medievalists after World War II somehow look strangely normal in their new

This article was written in September 1990. I presented an earlier version to the research seminar of Emmanuelle Baumgartner and Christine Marchello-Nizia in Paris on March 3, 1989. My thanks to Max Grosse for cautioning me against possible reactions to the following pages, and to Stephen Brown for his support in editing the manuscript for publication.

Pacific environment. Such an impression may have to do with the experience that nobody seems to care about their *translatio* across two continents. Indeed, no scholar or bureaucrat has ever asked me whether I found it problematic to continue in my role as a GRLMA editor from the American West Coast, and, for a long time, I was not even sure whether my colleague Ulrich Mölk knew that I had left Germany for good. Nevertheless, the *Grundriß* is still tenaciously alive.

Two volumes on medieval Italian literature, edited by Ulrich Mölk at Göttingen and August Buck at Marburg, have appeared during the last two months; a former student of mine has just finished the manuscript of the GRLMA documentation on French and Spanish historiographical texts; and as soon as this chapter is ready, I will read the galleys of a *Grundriß* volume dedicated to fourteenth- and fifteenth-century French texts. The situation I try to evoke has turned into reality two ironic predictions with which, almost since the beginning of the *Grundriß* project, some scholars used to play innocent academic language games. When Daniel Poirion was first speaking of the "horizon 2000," he wanted to express, with an undertone of mild irony, his skepticism about the possibility of finishing, before the end of the 1970s, all twenty-three planned volumes of the GRLMA; and when Raymond Joly, then a research assistant at the University of Heidelberg, in a letter to Hans Robert Jauss dated June 19, 1964, mentioned "l'Histoire du *Grundriß* que je compte écrire vers l'an 2000, si je suis encore de ce monde," he probably just wanted to flatter Jauss by cheerfully anticipating how important—not to say "classic"—the GRLMA might become during the thirty-six years then remaining until the end of the millennium.

In the late summer of 1990, however, it is, realistically speaking, no longer likely that the deadline of the year 2000 will be met (if the *Grundriß* will ever be finished at all). And, much earlier than Joly had imagined, I am trying to write a version of its history at a moment when the publisher's statistics show that most of the potential GRLMA readers have forgotten this handbook. But, if my own involvement with this project was intense enough to make such an effort understandable (even if it is only self-therapy),[1] why should anybody bother to read a narrative that does not even promise to yield a good story or any kind of exemplary learning because the *Grundriß,* as its main protagonist, has neither reached a successful closure nor been definitively shipwrecked?

My answer is that, in the context of reconstructing a broad variety of aspects from the history of academic medievalism, the GRLMA may

serve as a case study regarding the complex changes that have transformed this intellectual and institutional world since the mid-1960s.
Specifically so, because there were not only changes in the methods
and theoretical assumptions orienting the ongoing research, but
also—and, perhaps more important, although this has often been
overlooked—transformations in the dominating professional self-
image of medievalists, in the economic conditions of their work, and
in the conventions of academic sociability. Which were the specific
motivations that, before those changes, made young scholars opt for
an academic career as medievalists, how did they constitute their
disciplinary field and define its predominant tasks, in which forms and
discourses would medievalists from different European countries and
on different levels of the academic hierarchy work together, what
would they assume to be the extra-academic value of their work—
these are some of the interests that I wanted to pursue in analyzing the
history of the GRLMA.

My projects produced at least two surprising results. On a more
general level, whose relevance is probably not restricted to this particular case (and perhaps not even to the narrower disciplinary context
of academic medievalism), I found it impossible to separate the epistemological reorientations of which we have become increasingly—and
proudly—aware during the last two decades from those changes in the
values, styles, and norms of professional behavior and professional (or
perhaps simply male) sociability we normally downplay as "purely
anecdotal." Their tonality is certainly difficult to imagine for anybody
who entered the profession, say, after 1975. In other words, I argue
for taking such anecdotes (and what lies behind them) seriously in
their relation to our intellectual achievements and failures. Referring,
secondly, to the structures and, so to speak, to the rhythm that have
marked the history of academic medievalism, I take the *Grundriß* to
be indicative of an almost dramatic discontinuity. Whereas it would be
difficult to point to any profound differences between the institutionally dominant forms of medievalism around 1900 and around 1960
(the GRLMA, for example, was first conceived as a "new edition" of
Gustav Gröber's *Grundriß der romanischen Philologie* published in
1902), a question to be asked in 1996—and certainly the question that
will decide the GRLMA's fate—is whether we can seriously assume any
continuity with the auspices under which this handbook was first
founded in the late 1950s and on which, in the positive case, an at
least minimal intellectual coherence between its early and its late
volumes would have to rely.

I assume that it is the *Grundriß*'s undecided status that makes the binders in my garage look melancholic in their new West Coast normality. So much paper, so many working hours, and so much research money—and not even a negative end in sight, not to speak of a definitive assessment of the GRLMA's value, or a happy ending for the whole enterprise. In my account of its weary life and its tenacious survival, I will keep to the letters and documents in these binders, instead of relying on my own memories or on interviews with my academic elders. For, different from the written words in the GRLMA archive, memories would smooth out the double gap of intellectual and institutional discontinuity that I found so astonishing. A more personal story could hardly avoid becoming too apologetic.

BEGINNINGS, LATE AND EARLY

The earliest document in my *Grundriß* archive is dated April 30, 1959, and was typed by the then thirty-seven-year-old Hans Robert Jauss, who had obtained the *Habilitation* at Heidelberg in 1958 and was to be appointed "ausserordentlicher Professor" at the University of Münster within a few months. He invited Aurelio Roncaglia, professor of Romance philology at the University of Rome and invested with a seemingly awesome influence in the small world of academic medievalism, to participate in the task "den seit langem vergriffenen 'Grundriß der romanischen Philologie' von Gustav Gröber zu erneuern, genauer gesagt: einen neuen Grundriß der Romanischen Literaturen des Mittelalters zu beginnen." Jauss's rhetoric was strictly observing the academic hierarchy which still separated him from his addressee: he modestly presented himself as proxy of professors Jean Frappier from the Sorbonne and Erich Köhler from Heidelberg and recalled the "honor of having been introduced" to Roncaglia on the occasion of a Provençalistes' conference at Avignon. Roncaglia's positive answer is dated May 16, 1959, and emphasizes the importance of the now already common enterprise: "Ho trovato questo progetto del più vivo interesse, come quello che risponde a un'esigenza effettiva e largamente sentita nel campo dei nostri studi." Ten days earlier, Jean Rychner from the University of Neuchâtel, whose book on the oral character of the Chanson de geste was hailed as a breakthrough among his younger colleagues in the late 1950s,[2] had declined an analogous offer to participate in the new *Grundriß*. But he very strongly recommended that the editors try to establish "une sorte de catalogue raisonnée des oeuvres, classées par genres" instead of just presenting a bibliography at the end of each volume.

Many of these early letters bear witness to an astonishing traveling fever among specialists in medieval Romance literatures from different European countries around 1959 (long before professors became an economy class jet set). Jean Frappier lectured at Heidelberg in February 1959; a colloquy on "Medieval Humanism" was held at Strasbourg in April; the Société Roncesvals had its biannual congress at Poitiers in June; and it was followed by the gathering of the Société Arthurienne at Vannes in August 1960. At each of these meetings Erich Köhler and Hans Robert Jauss seem to have presented their project of a new handbook, trying to win the support of colleagues who were then the most renowned among their elder peers. Although they largely neglected the tensions between the particular working perspectives for which each of these "authorities" stood, Jauss and Köhler ended up not only exchanging letters with Jean Frappier, Aurelio Roncaglia, and Jean Rychner, but also establishing contacts with such venerable figures as Ramon Menendez Pidal, Damaso Alonso, and Martin de Riquer from Spain, Angelo Monteverdi from Italy, and Pierre le Gentil from France. Yet it is hard, if not impossible, to understand what motivated Köhler and Jauss to unfold their breathtaking activity. What kind of profit could they expect from launching the *Grundriß*?

The issue becomes even more complicated if one takes into account that both had already climbed the decisive steps on the ladder of professional promotion with considerable speed: three years after his *Habilitation* and only thirty-four years old, Koöler received a prestigious appointment as Ordentlicher Professor at Heidelberg in 1958. In spring 1959, the date of the first GRLMA letters, Jauss, who was three years older than Köhler, must have known about his forthcoming *Ruf* to Münster. Precisely because they were so successful, their encounter at Heidelberg lasted for just slightly more than a year, and it is probably not too benign to assume that it was indeed a striking convergence in their research interests that generated the first spark toward their shared GRLMA project.[3] After 1950, Köhler's academic teacher Werner Krauss had gone from Marburg to Leipzig where he formed, together with such figures as the philosopher Ernst Bloch and the historian Walter Markov, a center of innovative Marxist thought.[4]

This helps to understand why Köhler's *Habilitationsschrift* "Ideal und Wirklichkeit in der höfischen Epik" (1956) was a sociohistorical reading of Chrétien de Troyes's novels that stood out as a daring

challenge to the then dominating *Toposforschung* à la Ernst Robert
Curtius and to the obsessive search for (mostly Celtic) "sources" as
inspired by Jean Marx and Roger Sherman Loomis. Although, in the
intellectual atmosphere of "Reeducation" and the Cold War, it was
often misunderstood as a "political" statement, the main motivation
for Köhler's book was a sort of Hegelian historicism, which made him
see traces of early "individualism" in Chrétien's work. If he was soon
attributed the then exotic label of a Marxist, the simple reason was
that there were not very many non-Marxist models available for
someone who wanted to write a seriously historical monograph
around 1955. Köhler's first quotation, however, came from Gustav
Gröber's quite positivistic—and sometimes strangely romantic—
Grundriß der romanischen Philologie (1902), which had defined the
courtly Romance as "eine Reaktion des Individuums gegen die Masse,
des persönlichen gegen den Allgemeingeist."[5]

Hans Robert Jauss's *Habilitationsschrift* "Untersuchungen zur
mittelalterlichen Tierdichtung" not only appeared in the same *Bei-
hefte zur Zeitschrift für Romanische Philologie* three years after
Köhler's book, but shared both its Hegelian perspective and its osten-
sive disinterest in topoi and "sources." The reason why Jauss's discourse somehow seems to come closer to our present-day concerns—and
was perceived as less provocative by its contemporary academic community—has probably to do with the author's beginning effort to
develop a new concept of "literary genres." It was designed to become
a mediation between history and texts in order to overcome the
Marxist paradigm of "reflection," which, despite certain reservations,
Köhler would never abandon. But shouldn't their convergence on
some of the issues and options that were modestly innovative for
medieval studies in the late 1950s have prevented Jauss and Köhler
from the project of organizing a new version of the most traditional
handbook in their discipline? There is really no single "event" nor any
specific "inspiration" that we might identify as their starting point.

In these circumstances, the only way to understand the emergence
of the GRLMA project is to see it as the concretization of a historically
specific style of experiencing changes and transitions in the culture of
the 1950s (which perhaps had its strongest impact in postwar West
Germany). Innovative forms of acting and thinking were then often
initiated by great figures from the past, whose faces were familiar to
the general public, and many of the ideas and persons, whom our
retrospective tends to interpret as revolutionary, made their first appearance under extremely traditional circumstances. In 1958, for

example, when the *Grundriß* idea was born, General de Gaulle, who had become famous during World War II, inaugurated a radically new chapter in French politics; Werner Heisenberg, a nobel laureate in 1932, postulated the necessity of a paradigm change in nuclear research (which was symbolized as the strongest scientific potential for the future by the *Atomium* at the 1958 Brussels World Fair); Heinrich Lübke, a former architect of Nazi concentration camps, was minister of agriculture and became president of the Federal Republic of Germany in 1959; and, highlighting his dubious reputation as "father of the V-2 missiles," Wernher von Braun assumed the paternity of "Explorer 1," the first successfully launched American space satellite.[6] On the other hand, John XXIII, the new pope, who oversaw the theological transformation of the Second Vatican Council, looked as old and perhaps even more traditional than his deceased predecessor, Pius XII; the first political actions of Nikita Khrushchev, the new secretary general of the Soviet Communist Party, whose advances toward liberalization are now generally acknowledged, were interpreted as the dawn of a Stalinist Renaissance; and in Friedberg, a small, German town not too far from Heidelberg, Elvis Presley ended the first and often scandalous stage of his career in the classical uniform of a GI.

With this historical background in mind, one can begin to understand why Erich Köhler's and Hans Robert Jauss's convergent (and still rather vague) intellectual restlessness found its articulation in the most traditional academic form and institutional framework. Driven by a similarly opaque desire for change, their friend Wilhelm Fink, who had worked as an editor for the highly conservative Heidelberg publishing house Carl Winter Universitätsverlag, where the GRLMA would ultimately appear, tried to find a new, more independent position with Erich Schmidt Verlag, Berlin, and Ernst Hüber Verlag, Munich. He was supported by the *Grundriß* editors, who sent letters expressing their wish to work with Fink toward the publication of their manual in a new context: "Es handelt sich um einen auf 12 Bände . . . veranschlagten Grundriß der Romanischen Literaturen des Mittelalters, der den alten, seit langem vergriffenen 'Grundriß . . .' G. Gröbers ersetzen soll und für den wir im In- und Ausland bereits eine ganze Reihe namhafter Mitarbeiter gewinnen konnten" (December 5, 1959).[7] But, if at all, Schmidt and Hüber were only a little less conservative than Winter, so that the young professors' emphasis on academic continuity and international collaboration would neither compensate for their lack of reputation nor smooth the impression that Wilhelm Fink's admirably and sometimes fiercely daring mind must have made on his colleagues in the academic publishing business. Therefore, different from the situation of his academic companions, Fink's only possible choice was the foundation of his own Eidos-Verlag (which later became Wilhelm Fink Verlag and which, under new ownership, is today one of the most excellent academic publishing houses in Germany). In contrast, Jauss and Köhler found sufficient support to unfold their handbook project in the dusty world of a medievalism that had indeed not undergone any major changes since the times of Gröber—and which nobody has more eloquently described than Paul Zumthor: Un aspect doctrinaire et faussement systématique durcissait ce corps assez informé d'habitudes et de doctrines. . . . Ces habitudes de pensée, très inégalement distribuées selon le tempérament et la formation des chercheurs, les écoles, les lieux, maintenaient un ensemble de critères idéologiques plus ou moins implicites, liés à ce qu'on nomma le "discours humaniste." Discours de théâtre savant, dans les coulisses duquel les acteurs s'invectivaient à propos de "faits assurés" ou "d'hypothèses risquées," de "versions corrompues" et de "textes authentiques," en un conflit d'autant plus opiniâtre qu'il n'était jamais désigné par son nom: nul n'abattait ses cartes. Chacun revendiquait l'absence de point de vue, fondatrice de l'illusoire neutralité des valeurs, puis, retiré dans la paix livresque de son cabinet, reprenait force dans un lent, minutieux labeur d'établissement et de classification de ses fiches—dont l'effet dédramatisait la vie, la mort, le destin des hommes.[8]

The only traces of a potentially provocative aspect in the *Grundriß* project can be found in the reactions of some of Jauss's and Köhler's German colleagues, who, as Hermann Tiemann stated in a letter of June 8, 1959, were offended by the editors' selection principle of academic internationalism: "Das einzige, was ich nicht verstehe, ist, daß Sie vor diesen Besprechungen nicht einmal bei den wenigen deutschen Kollegen umgefragt haben, die für diese Aufgabe überhaupt in Frage kommen." Tiemann could not know (and was innocent enough not to suspect) that Jauss and Köhler had indeed approached Hugo Friedrich and Fritz Schalk, who by that time were the most influential representatives of West German *Romanistik*. Even in relation to these nationally dominating figures, however, it must be said in honor of the young editors that their negotiation strategy was somehow hesitant: "Es ließ sich nicht vermeiden, daß ich ihn da höflicherweise eben auch um seinen Rat . . . anging," writes Jauss in a letter to Köhler from May 19, 1960, referring to a recent conversation with Schalk.

But, besides such minor problems on the level of amateur diplomacy, the editors never incurred any criticism for the *Grundriß* as an intellectual provocation. For it was grounded on some of the most generally accepted assumptions of traditional medievalism, on which its founders insisted so frequently that they concealed any potentially innovative implications. Being presented as a new version of Gröber's *Grundriß,* the GRLMA shared its premise of a unity of Romance languages and literatures[9] and even extended it with its vision of the Middle Ages as a cultural totality.[10] From this perspective and by assuming, through the title of their project, an unproblematic continuity of the concept of "literature" across the centuries, Jauss and Köhler came very close to Curtius's interpretation of the Middle Ages, although they tended to make his "unhistorical notion of history" function as an antagonistic principle to their own enterprise.

They also adopted Jean Rychner's proposal to double the historical description of medieval literature through a "catalogue raisonnée des oeuvres," which later materialized in the decision to publish eleven of the twelve GRLMA volumes in two parts, that is, in a *Partie historique* and a *Partie documentaire.* There is no reason to think that they did *not* believe such a text catalog could become exhaustive. Though Jauss and Köhler may have personally found this goal all too positivistic, they probably accepted it as an opportunity to highlight the seriousness of their research in the eyes of the scholarly community. Both editors also largely profited from the *partie documentaire* in their regular reports to the Deutsche Forschungsgemeinschaft (which has been almost constantly funding the GRLMA from its beginnings to the present day): whenever they had to explain one of the countless delays that affected their working schedules, they could refer to the complexities coming from the task of establishing an exhaustive textual documentation. Finally, a concept of literary genres (in which the "literary" component was yet unproblematic) became *the dominant structuring principle* of what the editors wished to perceive as the "unity" of medieval Romance literatures.

Whereas Gustav Gröber had dedicated separate sections of his *Grundriß* to the different national traditions, Jauss and Köhler, during the first stage of their project and in a contract with the publisher, emphasized their preference for the genre perspective through a distribution of texts over the twelve GRLMA volumes which did not allow for any national specifications:

I: Allgemeine Probleme
II: Die geistliche Dichtung in den romanischen Volkssprachen
III: Das nationale Epos der Romanen
IV: Der romanische Vers- und Prosaroman
V: Die Gattungsgeschichte der erzählenden Kurzformen
VI: Die didaktische und satirische Literatur
VII: Die historiographische Literatur
VIII: Die allegorische Dichtung
IX: Die szenische Dichtung
X: Die Geschichte der provenzalischen Lyrik
XI: Die Geschichte der lyrischen Gattungen in den romanischen Literaturen
XII: Chronologie und Gesamtregister

Nevertheless, Köhler's and especially Jauss's interest in the theoretical issue of "literary genres"[12] was not the only driving force behind this original structure of the GRLMA. *Parallel to the Stilepochenforschung* of the 1920s, the emphasis on the genre principle allowed them to disregard differences between national cultural traditional, which, especially in Germany and for good historical reasons, was then seen as an expression of political goodwill. Yet it seems that Köhler and Jauss never understood that this was a specifically German concern— with a specifically German blindness. They therefore dedicated hundreds of letters to the creation of a kind of "balance of nations" on the organizational level of their enterprise. Not only did they persuade Ramon Menendez Pidal, Angelo Monteverdi, and Leo Spitzer to let themselves be named as *Éditeurs Honoris Causa* on the title page of the first GRLMA volume, but they also ceremoniously appointed Jean Frappier, Martin de Riquer, and Aurelio Roncaglia *nationale Konredaktoren* (thus establishing an organizational level immediately below the *Hauptherausgeber*). The *Konredaktoren* received individualized GRLMA stationery and a then considerable one-time honorarium of DM 1,000 from Carl Winter Verlag. But, perhaps with the exception of Frappier, they never quite understood how the GRLMA hierarchy was supposed to introduce a principle of division of labor between them and the *Hauptherausgeber,* nor did they fulfill their task of appointing (on a third hierarchical level!) some volume editors among their respective French, Spanish, and Italian colleagues.

EPISTEMOLOGICAL GOODWILL, TURNING INTO ANGER

As the scholars from France, Italy, and Spain certainly did not share (and probably did not even understand) Köhler's and Jauss's interest in playing down the differences between national literatures, tragicocomical interferences between the epistemological decision for the concept of "genre" as dominant orientation of the GRLMA and the diplomatic ideal of a "balance of nations" were soon to arise. Only seven weeks after he had agreed to accept the role of a national *Konredaktor* and expressed his appreciation for the general outlines of the GRLMA project, Aurelio Roncaglia sent a five-page single-spaced letter to Heidelberg on July 6, 1959, in which he prolixly problematized the handbook's exclusively genre-based structure. His arguments against the disregarding of national differences were hardly refutable, despite the editors' best "moral" intentions:

> Una divisione come quella tra "epopea nazionale" e "romanzo," perfettamente chiara e giustificata per la letteratura francese, non sembra poter essere mantenuta in maniera altrettanto rigida per la nostra letteratura, dove i due "generi" (entrambi importanti) tendono a sovrapporsi. . . . Penso ai "cantari" toscani. Dal punto di vista formale-stilistico . . . , come dal punto di vista storico-sociale . . . , la loro individuazione come "genere" non e meno legittima, ne meno netta, di quanto sia, in epoche anteriori ed ambienti diversi, per le "canzioni di gesta" e per i "romanzi cortesi." Non parebbe logico smembrarne la trattazione in due, o magari tre libri diversi.

Roncaglia's more general—and justified—objections against the genre concept, however, ended in a misunderstanding: "Non posso tacere infine qualche perplessità relativa al rischio di sproporzioni, dove l'impostazione per 'generi' portasse ad accentuare eccessivamente il punto di vista descrittivo a scapito non solo della valutazione estetica, ma propriamente della prospettiva storica. È un rischio che, secondo lo schema predisposto, mi sembra sussistere non soltanto per la prepotente personalità di Dante, ma anche per il Petrarca, il cui magisterio stilistico ha segnato per secoli le sorti della lirica europea." It had certainly never been in Jauss's or Köhler's mind to play out descriptive pregnancy against aesthetic and historical perspectives. Yet, by idealizing the community of specialists in the field of medieval literature to a sort of République des Lettres (or "Transcendental Scholarly Subject"), their excessive goodwill—which also was "a goodwill to power"—had not only underestimated the differences between different national literatures but also the distance between different, nationally specific approaches to literary history. Beyond the multiciplicity of scholarly traditions and perspectives, they were persuaded that it was possible to find, for each topic and object of their handbook, a single "adequate" approach.[13]

Since they did not understand that for their Italian colleagues a certain perspective was inseparable from "Italian literature" as its object, Köhler and Jauss were never ready to accept that the heritage of Croce's anathema against any categorizing concepts could not be overcome by a shared interest in historical differentiation (which had been their—very German—motivation to use the notion of "genre" as a historiographical tool). But while in the correspondence with their Italian colleagues they were at least eager to argue against what they saw as a Crocian prejudice, similar experience with Spanish scholars would only confirm the most trivial national clichés which, astonishingly enough, the *Hauptherausgeber* would never even modify. Against the (certainly well-founded) opinion of Martin de Riquer and José Manuel Blecua that, for example, it would be technically impossible to dedicate a GRLMA documentation to every single text found in the late medieval *cancioneros,* Erich Köhler wrote in a note of March 15, 1963: "Im übrigen gilt es, auf die Angst vor der Arbeit nicht allzu viel Rücksicht zu nehmen. Schließlich sind auch die Cancioneros kein Faß ohne Boden." Supposing, as Köhler did, "a typically Spanish laziness" behind every single reaction from his Iberian colleagues, Jauss adopted a blatantly angry and almost imperialistic attitude, when he found them reluctant to work what Menendez Pidal had described as "the *life* of the *romancero* "[14] into the *Grundriß* structure: "Ich finde es rührend, die Kriterien für 'alte Romanzen' nach wie vor bei Jacob Grimm (1815) zu suchen, zugleich aber äusserst besorgniserregend; das Beste wäre doch wohl, einige deutsche Doktoranden zu finden, die sich dieser ganzen Geschichte einmal annehmen."

Despite the obvious analogy between the reasons that caused such resistance in both the Italian and Spanish collaborators, it was also their confidence that they at least intellectually understood the "Crocian prejudice" that made Köhler and Jauss take Roncaglia's objections much more seriously. On the basis of such generosity, they even overreacted when, in the fear of losing the Italians' collaboration, they asked Hugo Friedrich in December 1959 *not* to write a contribution on Italian lyrical poetry which they had originally entrusted to him (Friedrich seemed to be almost thankful for such an occasion to remove himself). Ironically, though, as Roncaglia thought that Jauss and Köhler had never really given in to a modification in the general structure of their handbook, he pathetically announced his resignation in a letter of April 2, 1960: "Nell'interesse scientifico e editoriale del *Grundriß*, non saprei ormai suggerire se non d'affidare ad altri il compito di rinnovare un tentativo per il quale temo proprio d'aver esaurito le mie possibilità d'azione utile."

This was almost an event in the small world of the *Grundriß*, and, echoed by some rumors about politically motivated tensions among Italian philologists, it led Jauss and Köhler to curious conclusions. On April 12, 1960, they sent a letter to an Italian colleague, who had not had the honor of being invited to participate in the *Grundriß*, asking him for names of scholars *not* belonging to the Roncaglia group, and the following day they informed Jean Frappier about their new strategy:

> So können wir uns in aller Ruhe überlegen, wo wir andere Mit- arbeiter finden, die von der ansteckenden Krankheit des Crocismo und vom Dünkel der nationalen Literaturbetrachtung nicht in diesem Masse befallen sind. . . . Wir wenden uns an die Gegenpartei der italienischen Romanisten. Sie erinnern sich sicher noch daran, daß uns in Poitiers erzählt wurde, wie sehr die italienischen Romanisten in zwei feindselige Gruppen zerfallen sind. Roncaglia habe nur aus seiner Faktion ausgewählt. . . . Leider erinnere ich mich nicht mehr an die Namen, aus denen sich die andere Faktion zusammensetzt; Herr Köhler hat gleich an einen italienischen Freund geschrieben, um diese Namen zu erfahren. . . . Hoffen wir, daß die andere Faktion die Gegner Croces und zugleich tüchtige Romanisten in sich vereinigt.

No doubt, ideologically motivated divergences in their ways of reading medieval texts did exist among Italian scholars, but they had of course never reached such a degree of military order as the GRLMA editors imagined. Therefore the long lists of names that they estab- lished, assigning each of them to either the Croce/Roncaglia group or to the opposite side, could never generate the clearness they had hoped for.[15]

As the situation became more and more opaque—and desperate— for the editors, Jauss traveled to Venice in October 1960 for a consul- tation with Vittore Branca (who had been described as anti-Crocista) and was then easily won over to accept the very modifications in the general structure of the GRLMA that he and Köhler had refused to concede to Roncaglia. With the first eight volumes dedicated to the history of different genres up to A.D. 1300, parts 9, 10, and 11 should now comprehend "La transformation des traditions romanes médiévales au déclin du Moyen âge et au début de la Renaissance," opening up the possibility of describing national differences:

IX: La transformation des traditions médiévales communes par Dante, Boccace et Pétrarque

X: Les traditions littéraires (anciennes et nouvelles) au 14e siècle
   a) Italie
   b) France
   c) Espagne/Portugal

XI: Les traditions littéraires (anciennes et nouvelles) au 15e siècle
   a) Italie
   b) France
   c) Espagne/Portugal

This solution, which anticipated the definitive structure of the *Grundriß*'s second part (where volume 8 is now dealing with French; volume 9 with Spanish/Portuguese, and volume 10 with Italian fourteenth- and fifteenth-century literature), may have looked like an admirable diplomatic compromise (in a letter to Frappier, Jauss hailed it as "das glückliche Ergebnis meiner Verhandlungen in Italien"), but, introducing an interference between different perspectives, it cost the coherence of the whole handbook without finally having any impact on the Italian philologists' attitude. Roncaglia, who hastily declared his readiness to join again the ranks of the GRLMA in autumn 1960, took a very subtle revenge by dramatizing after that every epistemological or technical problem that his Italian countrymen happened to notice. As late as February 11, 1964, when Jauss and Köhler realized that Branca was no more help to them than any other Italian or Spanish collaborator, Roncaglia reminded them of what had happened in the fall of 1960:

Branca—perdonatemi se mi permetto di ricordarlo—fu officiato per la sua collaborazione proprio nel periodo in cui io avevo rinunciato alla mia. . . , perchè mi era stato detto che il piano dell'opera era ormai definito. Egli suggeri e ottenne un riesame del problema. Perchè non dovrebbe considerare possibile, oggi, un riesame anche d'altri problemi, che da parte mia sarebbe sbrigativo dichiarare insussistenti, ma chè sfuggono ovviamente ai miei poteri di

decisione? Per il resto, non è uomo da lasciarsi "hinauskomplimen-
tieren" senza farne pesare le conseguenze. E io non posso ora
prevedere quali sarebbero le conseguenze d'una sua estromissione
sugli altri collaboratori.

Neither Roncaglia nor Branca has ever written a single line for any
of the GRLMA volumes, but the obstinacy with which they stuck to
their specifically Italian way(s) of viewing medieval literature has
nevertheless left its traces. For it generated a new structure for the
handbook in which the genre aspect entered into conflict with the
principle of national differentiation and with a—at least for us—problematic periodization into "high" and "late" Middle Ages. It was only
through this new focus upon the fourteenth and fifteenth centuries
that the editors first realized in a memo from January 11, 1966, how
impossible it would be to fulfill the task of dedicating a documentation to every single "literary" text between 1100 and 1500: "Der
zweite Teil des GRLMA kann sowie nicht an dem Grundsatz der
Vollständigkeit festhalten. Es ist aber zu hoffen, daß er im Laufe der
Zeit ergänzt wird. Fazit: Mag die partie historique des GRLMA *monu-
mentum aere perennius* sein, die partie documentaire wird schon im
Augenblick ihrer Erscheinung in einem rapiden, unaufhaltsamen und
geradezu begrüssenswerten Prozeß des Überholtwerdens begriffen
sein."

In this context, the proposal was discussed (but never approved)
to publish the documentations in the form of loose files rather than as
a book. Astonishingly enough, Jauss and Köhler consulted their
Konredaktoren about the issue and, on February 22, 1966, they
received a long, thoroughly affirmative telegram from Roncaglia:
"Approvo proposta più calorosamente quanto più gravi risultano
difficoltè per documentazione lirica italiana mancando lavori pre-
paratori et essendo schedatura sinora fornita praticamente priva di
qualsiasi valore e fonte solo di disorientamento punto [sic] . . .
cordialissimi saluti Roncaglia." It was as if Jauss's and Köhler's epistemological goodwill had never made Roncaglia angry. For a short
while, academic diplomacy had triumphed over epistemology.

ORGANIZATION, CONSENSUS-ORIENTED AND COMPLEXITY-GENERATING

The basic working procedure that the editors invented for the
Grundriß seemed inspired by the industrial principle of the assembly

line—this would at least explain why it turned out to be grotesquely complex in relation to most medievalists' utterly individualistic working habits. Under the guidance of Köhler in Heidelberg (later in Freiburg) and Jauss in Münster (later in Giessen and finally in Constance), two teams of research assistants were supposed to establish files for each text pertaining to the field of the GRLMA and group them according to each volume's specific topic. In a second stage, those *fichiers* were to travel between Paris, Rome, and Barcelona, where the three *Konredaktoren* were expected to check and complete the information concerning "their" national literatures and to send them back to Germany. From there the *fichiers* were to be passed, in a third round, to the editors of each volume, whose task it was finally to distribute the files to the authors of the respective GRLMA chapters. It is easy to imagine that most of the files never finished their long journey (in fact, I have in my garage a couple hundred files regarding *Formes narratives brèves,* which apparently never made it from Giessen/Constance to Frappier's, Roncaglia's, or Riquer's desk).

But there were also a number of less "technical" obstacles. On the one hand, the intricate and complex philological questions of textual tradition had never been of specific interest to Jauss or Köhler, so that the German research teams' task often simply went beyond their competence. On the other hand, the more positivistically minded collaborators in France, Italy, and Spain seem to have anticipated right from the start that the goal of exhaustive documentation was impossible to achieve—and they were therefore lacking motivation to begin their work. In those rare cases where a *fichier* had indeed been established in Germany and was then completed in Paris, Rome, or Barcelona, it often turned out to be unclear who was the editor of the respective GRLMA volume to whose address the files had to be sent. The confusion increased because a constant flow of resignations and new appointments among the volume editors began almost as soon as the publisher and the *Hauptherausgeber* had signed the first respective contracts.

If, in rare cases, a file collection made it to its final destinations, long discussions would break out over the question of whether or not single texts were "adequately" located under the genres or historical periods that constituted the topic of the respective volume. As a result, the *Hauptherausgeber* gave up, in the mid-1960s, the principle of unequivocality according to which each medieval text was presented from a historical and a documentary perspective in only one volume of the GRLMA—and with this rigid approach they seemed to lose their belief that the structure of the handbook was capable of perfectly mirroring the structure of its object. From then on what they called *Doppelbehandlung* of single texts became legitimate.

This certainly was a wise move, but it deteriorated the GRLMA's practical function as a manual, and it was unfortunately followed by a new hierarchical distinction among *Doppelbehandlungen* into *Hauptbehandlung* und *Nebenbehandlung*. The criteria for the application of this distinction, however, turned out to be so complex that they forced Franz Koppe, a young philosopher who was earning some extra money as a research assistant for the *Grundriß* around 1970, to write an unironic seven-page treatise on this question for the instruction of the editors of future volumes. Koppe's text shared the fate of most written legislation: instead of clarity, it generated an infinite halo of interpretations.

But not only the process of text documentation was troubled by organizational problems. Jauss's and Köhler's correspondence with Martin de Riquer demonstrates that the existence of nationally differentiated approaches to literary history turned out to be the main problem for the *partie historique*. As early as November 9, 1959, Riquer had expressed his concern about how to handle such potential variety: "La mayor dificultad con que topo con todas las personas con que hablo es la falta de un 'modelo.' Convendría que Vds. redactaran un capítulo cualquiera del 'Grundriß,' de cualquier literatura, para que sirviera de orientación y guía para los futuros colaboradores. Todos me preguntan por la extensión, el tono, el estilo, la forma de citar, la bibliografía etc." This became Riquer's leitmotiv in the *GRLMA* concert, appearing in letters dated October 10 and 17, 1960, May 18 and December 18, 1961, and January 7, 1964. Undoubtedly, his awareness of historiographical style as a problematic dimension in the *Grundriß* had to do with the traditional Spanish ideal of "literary history" being a continuation of "the life of literature," but Riquer also frequently used it as an excuse for his own lack of activity as a *Konredaktor*.

The strategy took a picaresque tone when Riquer wrote to Köhler on May 18, 1961: "Me pide usted que le de nombres de colaboradores españoles. Hemos hecho hasta ahora bastantes gestiones, algunas fructuosas, otras no tanto, y no me sería difícil enviarle la lista que usted me pide. Pero prefiero no hacerlo por el momento. El prof. Noy les transmitió a ustedes en Heidelberg mi punto de vista: no adquirir compromisos definitivos hasta saber exactamente que hay que exigirle al colaborador." Finally, after receiving the so urgently requested *chapitre échantillon* in late 1963 (it was a first version of Jauss's now classic chapter on allegory, published in GRLMA 6.1), Riquer's tone switched from deferring to a rhetoric of liberty:

> Para cualquier colaborador es pesado, confuso y atemorizador el tener que estar pendiente de las normas generales del *Grundriß*, sobre todo abreviaturas y sigla. Creo que lo mejor sería que los colaboradores redactaran sus partes con cierta libertad en cuanto a la estructura y disposición material de los datos, pues muchos, aunque quieran ser fieles a las normas, en mas de una ocasión se apartaran de ellas o bien escribirán cohibidos. . . . Piense Vd. bien en ello: cuando llega el momento de redactar, todos nosotros obramos con cierta personalidad—o anarquía, si Vd. quiere—, y estoy seguro que la mayor dificultad con que topará la redacción del *Grundriß* será el temor de buenos especialistas, que no sabrán amoldarse a sus normas.

After five years of correspondence, after having financed month-long stays for at least three German research assistants in Barcelona to support Riquer's team (what they mostly experienced there was the art of "freundlich lächelnden Widerstand"), after a "diplomatische Mission" of Hans Jörg Neuschäfer, a young specialist in the field of Spanish literature during September 1962 (which Jauss, in a memo to the Deutsche Forschungsgemeinschaft, pretended to have undertaken himself), and after having covered the expenses for Riquer's collaborator Dr. Noy to come to Heidelberg (shortly after that visit Noy defected from academic life, becoming a journalist for *La Gaceta Ilustrada*), nobody could have blamed Jauss and Köhler for getting angry over Riquer's letter. But, different from their more active interventions on the Italian stage (and perhaps as an unconscious compensation for their deeply felt convictions about Spanish laziness), they continued treating him with exquisite epistolary courtesy. When Köhler finally proposed that Riquer step down from his role as *Konredaktor* on November 14, 1967, he explicitly mentioned that there was no need to pay back the honorarium received in 1959, and he even had somebody translate his letter into Riquer's native Catalan. According to the documents in my binders, Riquer responded to such inexplicable friendliness more than seven years later, on December 17, 1974, with some lines in German: "zu dem bevorstehenden Weihnachtsfest und neue [*sic*] Jahr möchte ich Ihnen meine besten Wünsche übermitteln. Gleichzeitig nütze ich die Gelegenheit aus, um Ihnen meine neue Adresse mitzuteilen . . . und hoffe, daß Sie mir einmal die Freude bereiten werden, mich in meinem neuen Heim zu besuchen."

At the same time, it is quite impressive to observe that the kind of consensus that Jauss and Köhler always anticipated but never really achieved in the collaboration with their (not only foreign) fellow scholars did indeed survive as a ground for their shared activities as GRLMA editors until Köhler's death in 1983. This seems all the more astonishing because, after the enthusiastic discovery of their complementary and parallel interests at Heidelberg in 1958–59, their thinking and their academic careers became more and more divergent. Whereas Köhler's international reputation was rapidly increasing in the 1960s (at one point in 1967 he mentions simultaneous offers from three American universities), the recognition of Jauss's work was first restricted to a much more modest range until his inaugural lecture at the newly founded University of Constance in spring 1967 was received as the founding document of a new school of literary theory. It was around this time, in Heidelberg, that the student movement cast a hypercritical light on Köhler's purely academic Marxism—a provocation to which Köhler, in a situation of constantly precarious health, never intellectually reacted. In general, there was hardly ever a moment in which Jauss's and Köhler's consensus came as a "natural" condition of their collaboration: it had to be constantly and actively achieved. When, for example, in late 1963 Köhler became aware that one of Jauss's collaborators had ironically criticized his rhetorical style in a letter to one of his own students, he bitterly complained about such an unheard-of incident. It was then Jauss who proposed an interpretation of this incident through which a principle of mutual tolerance was turned into the expression of a new "political" style in the academic world:

> Als zornige junge Männer, die den Übergang vom absolutistischen zum demokratischen Ordinariat vollzogen haben, erwarten wir beide gewiß nicht mehr, daß unsere Schüler nur in Tönen der Ehrfurcht über uns reden. . . . Kurzum, was ich zu dieser Sache jetzt noch zu sagen habe, ist nur, daß . . . wir uns auf "unserer Ebene" auch künftig rasch, unverhohlen und kräftesparend verständigen und die Briefe des anderen nach wie vor öffnen können, ohne befürchten zu müssen, sie könnten einfache Dinge kompliziert machen und die Summe der Unannehmlichkeiten vermehren.

This goodwill for consensus, which so often helped Köhler and Jauss to preserve mutual understanding, showed its almost devastating flip side whenever they projected it onto the organizational level of the *Grundriß*. Under the profound conviction that long deliberations would necessarily produce the best possible solutions (which had been intellectually dignified through the writings of Jauss's philosophical teacher Hans Georg Gadamer), they tried to discuss almost every single detail of the everyday GRLMA work with their assistants. A long exchange took place between Heidelberg and Giessen about typographical questions, abbreviations, footnotes, and so on, out of which emerged in 1965 a *Cahier de travail* with some seventy pages of "technical" instructions to be printed and distributed to all GRLMA authors. Quite naturally, the *Cahier de travail* seems to have had an almost lethal effect on their readiness to collaborate. For the key organizational (and financial) problem for the *Grundriß* was more and more shifting from the epistemological side to the question of how the authors could be brought to *start* the work to which they had committed themselves under such shockingly complex conditions.

There had been a strange economic optimism in the early years of the project, when Jauss and Köhler were guaranteed 2 percent of the sales price per copy of each single GRLMA volume, and each received a DM 2,000 advance in cash from Carl Winter Verlag (the volume editors' share was even fixed at 10 percent). This optimism was maintained over most of the first GRLMA decade. In June 1966, two years before the first *Grundriß* volume finally appeared, one of the *Hauptherausgeber,* finding himself in the process of financing the construction of a house for his family, proposed to the publisher to start "jährliche Abschlagszahlungen auf DM 1600 bis 2000 je Herausgeber," threatening that, in the case of a negative answer, he would have to postpone infinitely—if not to end—his work for the GRLMA. Only a few months later, with the work for the first volume far along, Jauss and Köhler, for quite unclear reasons, believed themselves to be in a situation where they could afford to give back part of a grant for research assistants to the Deutsche Forschungsgemeinschaft: "Für die in den nächsten Jahren bis zum Abschluß der Publikation (frühestens 1972) noch zu leistenden Arbeitsprogramme sollten nach Ansicht der Unterzeichneten nunmehr die Forschungsinstitute der anderen Länder eintreten." Paradoxically, the editors applied for a new grant only a few months after this generous gesture toward the finances of the German State.

What I could never find out, however, is whether Carl Winter Verlag ever started paying the *Hauptherausgeber* the advance they had requested in 1966. Should Winter have done so, it would have been a striking financial mistake. For, although the sales price of the first volumes published was comparatively modest (as a second-year student, I could afford the DM 48 for the more than three hundred pages of GRLMA 6.1), Winter never sold more than a few hundred of the two thousand copies that were initially printed. This was the beginning of a downward spiral, familiar to everybody who knows the academic publishing market in West Germany. In order to compensate for the deficit incurred, Winter started printing fewer copies which were sold at a higher price (the hard cover edition of GRLMA 4.1, which came out in 1978, cost more than DM 500). Then, instead of trying to turn the situation around by taking a greater financial risk, the publishers ended up applying for financial support with the Forschungsgemeinschaft, which required them to keep the number of copies low and the purchase price high. Although I was one of the three editors for GRLMA 11.1 (on medieval historiography), I never dared to confront this terrible reality by asking for its exact sales price (but I know that it was beyond DM 1,000 per copy). By that time, even in a country as wealthy as France, there was hardly any university library left that could afford to maintain its subscription to the ongoing GRLMA publications.

Meanwhile, a similar development had taken place regarding the cost of employing research assistants. As it became evident that the only realistic possibility of advancing the GRLMA lay in the establishment of small research groups formed by young scholars for each single volume, the amount invested in the *Grundriß* by the Forschungsgemeinschaft, the Conseil National de Recherche Scientifique, and several universities in France and West Germany came to a total of well over $1 million. And this, to be sure, is still far less than enough to ever finish the manual. There are certain articles and documentation series remaining to be written (among which are those on *cancioneros* and *romanceros*), each of which, in order to meet both the standards of what is now called the "New Philology" and the more traditional GRLMA principles, would require a specialist's working full time over a number of years.

Such tasks are normally not very appealing for scholars whose reputations would be established enough to obtain the research grants necessary for this kind of work. For naturally—if unfortunately—the institutions that provide such grants are reluctant to give them to young medievalists, even though they would have the necessary motivation to do the work. In addition, with the *Grundriß* having lost (or never achieved?) its international visibility on the publication market, it has become less of an honor and more of an unbearable risk to immerse the result of several years' research and writing into any of its volumes, instead of publishing a monograph on a topic of one's own choice. Thus, a few months ago, a former *Grundriß* collaborator, who has lost all perspective on what it takes to achieve a successful academic career (partly, I fear, by doing work for the GRLMA over too long a time), confronted me with an estimate of how much it would cost to have him finish one of the documentation volumes on an hourly wage equivalent to the salary of an administrative employee. He had no reason left to consider his continuous situation of underpayment as an investment toward a future in the university. Unfortunately, my only possible—and melancholic—reaction was to integrate his letter into my collection of GRLMA binders. The academic world has hardly any intrinsic means to take care of its victims.

Rhetoric, Bombastic and Innocent

Although there used to be much—sometimes self-ironic and sometimes self-indulgent—reference to the shrewdness of "GRLMA diplomacy" among the editors and their collaborators, the high-flying tone of so many letters and prefaces must have ultimately functioned as an efficient self-persuasion. This is why a number of young scholars believed that work for the *Grundriß* was a good investment toward an academic future, and this is also the only possible way to explain why it took even the editors so astonishingly long to become aware of the project's precarious status in a changing epistemological, organizational, and financial environment. What I find most striking about that rhetoric is the desire both to draw pretentious parallels between political events and the ongoing work for the *Grundriß* and implicitly to claim a moral superiority for the medievalists' *République des Lettres*. Restraining the self-reference to bare academic professionalism would probably have seemed just too narrow-minded to Jauss when he wrote the following words concerning the eternal problems with collaborators from Spain and Italy to Jean Frappier on March 18, 1963: "En ce temps de haute conjoncture pour la très officielle amitié franco-allemande, permettez-moi d'aborder aujourd'hui un problème quelque peu irritant. Vous aussi vous regardez, bien sur, l'axe Paris-Bonne-Madrid avec plus de méfiance que d'enthousiasme; nous sommes donc d'accord pour considérer que l'amitié des hommes de science ne saurait être sérieusement entamée par les embrassements ostentatoires de certain général et de certain vieillard."[16]

Such strange projections (together with a series of resignations that was particularly long in this case) may have been the unavowed reason why Maurice Delbouille, of whose work none of the *Grundriß* authorities seemed to be particularly fond in the beginning, emerged as the editor for the first volume in the late 1960s. For he was not only a professor of Romance philology at the University of Liège but also played a certain role in Belgian politics. On the occasion of his sixtieth birthday, he received a truly bombastic *Manifestation d'hommage,* which, toward its end, reflects the double perspective under which his colleagues perceived Delbouille: "À l'occasion du soixantième anniversaire et des trente-cinq années d'enseignement de Monsieur Maurice Delbouille, les Séminaires de philologie romane des Universités de Heidelberg et de Giessen et la rédaction centrale du *Grundriß der romanischen Literaturen des Mittelalters* s'unissent pour offrir leurs hommages et leurs voeux au savant, au maître, à l'irremplaçable collaborateur, à l'Européen, à l'ami." Similar congratulations were sent every year in March to Ramon Menendez Pidal, *éditeur honoris causa* of the first GRLMA volume, until he died in 1968 shortly before his hundredth birthday. If, however, the background for the Delbouille *hommage* had been the so-called process of European integration, of which the *Grundriß* always pretended to be an intellectual part, it was substituted in Menendez Pidal's case by the discourse of a strange theology of history, which was not too far from the official rhetoric of the Franco era:[17] "Que Diós le guarde, querido maestro, por muchos años y continue inspirándole en su trabajo—como lo ha hecho hasta ahora—para el bien y progreso de la Cultura y felicidad y alegría de todos."

The GRLMA rhetoric of more or less indirect self-celebration included, as a constitutive element, long passages on manifold diseases by which medievalists—and sometimes even their families[18]—were plagued. Although such complaints regularly served as an excuse for epistolary delays or for unfinished work, they also carried the connotation of a sacrifice that the scholars brought to the progress of wisdom: "Abgesehen von den Gehbehinderungen . . . , die sich zur Not bei der Schreibtischarbeit ertragen lassen, sind es neuerdings Schwindelanfälle und Gleichgewichtsstörungen, die sich zusätzlich eingestellt haben. Damit sind Sehstörungen verbunden, die bewirken, daß ich kaum länger als eine Viertelstunde auf beschriebenes oder bedrucktes Papier sehen kann. Ich bin in diesem Zustand arbeitsunfähig. Die Arbeit . . . am GRLMA ruht."

Such nosographic descriptions were normally answered by equally lengthy admonitions to reduce the respective workloads in the interest of the scholarly community (if not for the sake of Humanity): a heart attack that struck Jean Frappier during a GRLMA meeting at Rome on May 20, 1964, soon became an almost proverbial reference for similar recommendations extended to colleagues. Only Erich Köhler, who by that time already suffered from a terminal disease, was capable of writing about it with a slight tone of irony, which in the following lines might even allude to the Fisher-King from *Perceval*:

> Seit drei Tagen bin ich wieder in Freiheit, dieweil meine Ärzte die Tatsache, daß ich weiterhin ganz schön blute aus der noch nicht geschloßenen Operationswunde, offenbar für einen relativ normalen Vorgang halten. Da ich täglich noch eines zweimaligen Verbands- wechsels bedarf, bin ich geneigt, den heute abend in einem Fernsehinterview mit meinem ehemaligen Philosophielehrer Bloch gehörten tiefgründigen Satz vom "Überschuß des Möglichen im Vorhandenen" auf meinen ganz privaten Lebenssaft zu beziehen, der mir hartnäckig aus von rechts des Busens tropft.

In this context, it is interesting to see that Köhler, who was very seriously attacked by the student movement in 1968, made only occasional and superficial reference to these events, whereas most of his colleagues tended to profit from them as an additional potential to explain their flagrant lack of activity for the *Grundriß*—even though for many medievalists the continuous academic strikes would have been an ideal occasion to finally write their long-promised articles.

Among all the editors and authors of the GRLMA, *only Hans Robert Jauss, who by that time had just finished his work for volume 6 and was in the process of launching the publication of* GRLMA 1, did not need to make any apologies. Consequently, he proudly stated on December 12, 1968, that the academic revolution had not taken place at his new place of work: "In Konstanz allein ist alles anders: hier wurden die Reformen gemeinsam von Professoren, Assistenten und Studenten unternommen, wodurch sich eine Linie der Vernunft herausbildete, die nun bereits das Ärgernis der linksradikalen Gruppen an anderen Universitäten bildet." Once again, however, such belief in consensus implied a specific blindness. If the "Revolution" never took place at Constance, it was due, not to enlightened Reason, but to the fact that this university had started with an extremely small number of advanced students most of whom were attracted to south- ern Germany by excellent financial conditions (and an outstanding group of newly appointed professors who served as advisers for their doctoral dissertations).

A similar incapacity—or unwillingness?—to look behind the explicit or official meanings of events and texts constantly surfaces in the correspondence between the editors of the *Grundriß* and their German assistants. It is hard to imagine a young Italian or Spanish woman reporting to her professor on the pastime activities shared with one of his collaborators during a research stay in Paris with similarly candid words: "Inzwischen habe ich mich hier schon recht gut eingelebt und freue mich sehr, daß ich diese Zeit hier verbringen darf. Herr Warning ist auch eingetroffen, und wir unternehmen manches zusammen, in sehr übermütiger Laune, wenn wir auf Touristen in Paris spielen, sogar eine Eiffelturm-Besteigung."

It is equally touching to see how much she enjoyed browsing through the GRLMA *fichier* at the venerable Jean Frappier's home in March 1962: "Im übrigen sind die *séances de travail* immer durch Professor Frappiers *formule sacrée,* wie er sich ausdrückt, unterbrochen, nämlich *prenons des forces*—d.h. dann, daß Madame Frappier Tee serviert, oder man stärkt sich, ist sie ausgegangen, mit griechischem Wein." What looks mostly innocent in these letters can sometimes cause their readers embarrassment.

Shortly before the end of her pregnancy, another *Grundriß* collaborator writes to one of the editors: "Längst ist der Dank für Ihre letzten Bemühungen um das Schicksal meiner Familie fällig. Aber wie immer wollte ich ungern ohne ein kleines Zeichen eigener Produktivität antworten." A strange temporal inversion seems to have taken place, as she comes back to similar connotations three and a half years later: "Der Same, den Sie anläßlich meines . . . Besuchs im August 1971(?) legten, ist aufgegangen, nachdem er wie ein frisch gepflanzter Apfelbaum zunächst steril schien, um nach Skepsis erweckender Ruhezeit die ersten kümmerlichen Früchte zu zeitigen." Fortunately, life had provided the hermeneutic tools for the addressee's immediate understanding: "zumal mir das Gleichnis des frisch gepflanzten Apfelbaums, das ich als kümmerlicher Auch-Gärtner aus eigener, bitterer Erfahrung zu würdigen vermag, Ihre Situation so eindringlich vor Augen brachte."

On a less personal level, at least during the first decade following its establishment, the GRLMA's rapport with its immediate academic environment was oriented by a discourse that produced the flair of an academic *Doppelmonarchie*. Closely united through genealogical ties and represented by two crowns, a royal kinship believed its spiritual working and, sometimes, its physical suffering to be a sacrifice for the sake of humanity (or was it only a contribution toward the strength-

ening of the European Economic Market?). What made this construction so astonishingly immune, at least for some time, to intrinsic
skepticism and external disinterest was both its trust in explicit meanings and a certain number of exclusions. Early on, the name of the
celtomane Jean Marx had fulfilled this second function. Again and
again, Marx was referred to and his work was discussed—only to
confirm the eternal conclusion that he would not meet the intellectual
standards set for the *Grundriß*. But as time went on and the shining
self-image that the GRLMA rhetoric had built up began to crumble,
the selection criteria became much less academic—and, at least among
the German editors, more openly gender-oriented.

In autumn 1963 Frappier had mentioned the name of a then little
known female colleague from Belgium for a possible collaboration, to
which Jauss reacted with the heartfelt rejection, "denn diese schnat-
ternde und langweilige alte Tante sollte nicht in das 'Pantheon' des
Grundrißes aufgenommen werden." Köhler immediately agreed: "Sie
ist uns beiden ob ihrer Revolverschnauze nicht gerade bekömmlich."
What makes these remarks all the more scandalous—and all the more
confusing—is the fact that, in November 1967, through a letter con-
firming Köhler's participation in the Festschrift for Rita Lejeune that
she had organized, the same Belgian scholar felt compelled to extend
her warms thanks for a one-week invitation to Heidelberg: "Je voulais
vous exprimer mes vifs remerciements pour le charmant accueil que
vous-même et vos collaborateurs nous avez réservé au sein d'une
organisation si agréablement parfaite. J'ai été tres touchée des deux
photos souvenir de la charmante soirée passée dans votre si jolie
demeure, reflet de l'amabilité de sa charmante maitresse de maison."
Different from so many male medievalists whom Jauss and Köhler
had held in high esteem over many years, this woman has since
become co-editor of one of those *GRLMA* volumes that actually
appeared.

If this last incident perhaps indicates a slight change in *Grundriß*
diplomacy, one might say that the "Préface du GRLMA," *published as
an introduction to volume 1* in 1972, was a parallel step on the
epistemological level because it showed some self-critical cracks in the
editors' rhetoric. They admitted, for example, that their manual was
lacking a sociohistorical and an anthropological[19] dimension, which
they felt had become necessary through the most recent developments
in literary theory and literary history, and that they regretted having

given in—yielding to Branca's and Roncaglia's resistance, as we know—to the projection of national differences onto the structure of the *Grundriß*. At the same time, however, Jauss and Köhler declared that their main totalizing concepts—the unity of Romance languages and literatures, and the unity of medieval culture—were confirmed by the ongoing work for the GRLMA, and that—clearly under the impression of an ongoing discussion about the notion of the "literary system"20—more theoretical thought and historical research should have been dedicated to describe complementary relations between different medieval genres as a kind of meta-totality:

> Auch in dieser Hinsicht kann man dem GRLMA eher ein Zuwenig als ein Zuviel vorwerfen, nämlich daß die Bestandsaufnahme nicht über die Diachronie der Gattungsgeschichten hinaus zu einer Beschreibung der latenten Synchronie gattungshafter Aussageformen geführt und schließlich in der umfassenden Ordnung der symbolischen Ausdrucksformen verankert wurde, die gerade die Lebenswelt des Mittelalters vor anderen Epochen kennzeichnet.

Altogether, characterizing the *Grundriß* as "eher ein Zuwenig als ein Zuviel," the main perspective from which the editors tried to present their enterprise was that of a modest (but significant) anticipation of a "paradigm change" that, according to them, had taken place since 1960 under the influence of what, surprisingly enough, they now invoked as the salutary influence of the student movement.

If, after the foregoing account of the *Grundriß* history, it requires any further evidence to prove wrong this assessment of its character as "anticipation of a paradigm change," it lies in the loss of all the motivation and energy with which Jauss and Köhler had gotten the project under way around 1960. As so many times before, Jauss began to speak about the consequences of this change in a letter of June 1975. He proposed that he and Köhler share the responsibility of *Hauptherausgeber* with Ulrich Mölk and myself. The rhetoric of Jauss's confidential letter to his friend came close to the "Préface du GRLMA." Shining words of self-reference prevailed over some rather gentle self-critical undertones: "Die Gründung, Konzeption und Aufbauphase des GRLMA war eine andere Sache, die ohne unseren persönlichen Einsatz und unser persönliches Ansehen gewiss nicht zustandegekommen wären. Nachdem das Unternehmen sein Profil erhalten hat, das zweifellos immer mit unser beider Namen verbunden bleiben wird, geht das Unternehmen wie der Verlag nicht mehr ein echtes Risiko ein, wenn wir nun die Geschäftsführung in jüngere

Hände legen." Köhler had no objections, Mölk reluctantly accepted, and, for my part, I was about as enthusiastic about such a promotion as Jauss described: "Ich brauchte ihn nicht lange zu überreden: er war Feuer und Flamme."

In December 1975 the four of us signed a circular letter that was sent to more than a hundred medievalists who had agreed to become authors for the GRLMA. *We announced the restructuring of the Grundriß* organization and asked them to let us know whether they were still interested in that collaboration. Most of our colleagues did not even bother to answer. One exception was Vittore Branca, who sent a furious letter to the publisher offering his resignation (as he had done several times before): "Francamente questi continui cambiamenti e dispersioni e silenzi da parte vostra mi hanno piuttosto scoraggiato e disamorato dell'impresa; perciò, se voi credete, io non ho difficoltà a scogliervi da ogni impegno con me." But when Carl Winter accepted his proposal, Branca threatened that he was determined to take his revenge: "Resta da definire la somma che Voi mi dovrete versare come indennizzo, sia del lavoro che io avevo gia compiuto per il volume VII, lavoro che e a Vostra disposizione, sia per il danno morale e materiale che mi consegue dalla Vostra decisione." The publisher's only reaction was to ask Branca for those materials he pretended to have written for the GRLMA. They were never sent to Heidelberg (nor, I suppose, anywhere else). Thus his letters are indeed the only remaining trace of Branca's scarcely productive contribution to the *Grundriß.*

While this quite hilarious exchange was taking place, Mölk and I invited the GRLMA founders, as well as a number of old or potentially new authors from France and Germany and some representatives of neighboring academic disciplines, to a conference at the Zentrum für interdisziplinäre Forschung der Universität Bielefeld in May 1977[21] to discuss new guidelines for work on the twenty (out of twenty-three) volumes—ten belonging to the partie historique and ten to the partie documentaire—that by then remained to be published. What we decided coincided very much with the spirit of the 1972 "Préface du GRLMA": more attention was to be given to the texts' sociohistorical contexts, and the interrelations between vernacular and Latin culture should become an obligatory topic as well as the period transition between the Middle Ages and early modern times. A number of meetings were subsequently held with the authors of volumes 8, 10, and 11 to develop a consensus on the perspective and structure of their work. Daniel Poirion and August Buck, as volume editors for GRLMA

8 and 10, indeed provided the kind of initiative and support that had been so much lacking in earlier stages of the manual.

But, although I certainly hope that nobody will blame Mölk and me for having definitively ruined the *Grundriß,* it would probably be even less adequate to say that we "saved" the enterprise. Our—modest—positive record lies in the fact that by now there are just six volumes left that have not been at least partly published (though we probably spent much more research money than our predecessors and were unable to stop the publisher's almost lethal price decisions). The negative side is that, by altering its basic conception and by giving more independence to the editors and authors of each volume, we abandoned the principles of coherence and transparence that can be legitimately expected from a handbook. Volumes 8, 10, and 11, for example, are quite interesting collective works on the French four-teenth and fifteenth centuries, on the age of Dante, and on medieval historiography; their connection with the previously published vol-umes 4 and 6, however, is reduced to some regularly applied abbrevi-ations (which, by the way, caused an enormous amount of work for the manuscript editors), to the binding, and to the dark-red color of these books (even the typography changed). This must be the reason why even more libraries have meanwhile canceled their subscriptions to GRLMA.

Although smaller (and therefore less expensive) handbook pro-jects are thriving these days, especially in France,[22] the history of the *Grundriß* points to a number of changes inside and outside the academic institution that have perhaps not yet be sufficiently the-matized among all the well-deserved optimism caused by the success of "The New Medievalism." On an epistemological level, what counts, perhaps more than the "discovery" of the impossibility of conceiving of medieval culture or medieval literature as a "unity" (such "discoveries" are regularly followed by the more pragmatic "insight" into the pedagogic advantages of totalizations), is our pres-ent unwillingness to totalize. For reasons that are difficult but not impossible to explain, we prefer to look to whatever we identify as "margins," we are curious to see what is or was going on "behind the scenes," and we want to problematize rather than establish "canons." The new philological movement's insistence on the multiplicity of varying manuscripts that underly whatever we often still see as an "individual text" is only the most programmatically visible concreti-zation of this mood. In such an intellectual climate, the distance among different approaches to identical objects of research (if we at all continue to claim such object identity) is not only generally ac-knowledged, but has become one of our main fascinations. It partly motivates our interest in the multiple histories of academic disciplines that have become an almost dominating institutional concern during the past decade, and it explains why we prefer to organize colloquia and collective volumes in such a way that they generate controversies, rather than around models of complementarity.

Perhaps even more important, cultural historians have made their peace with the fact that they cannot count on a "natural" interest for their research outside the academic world. Instead of further cultivat-ing an attitude of disdain vis-à-vis this situation (which was never a very successful approach for compensating frustrations), we begin fondly to admit the remoteness of our objects and the lack of a practical motivation in our passion for them. This of course is the ground for the hermeneutic sublimation of "alterity and/as moder-nity," and we are happily surprised to see that, as a marketing strat-egy, alterity turns out to be far more successful than all the earnest claims and values of traditional humanism. Altogether, cultural his-tory and academic medievalism have become a lively market for projects of individualism, and, from this angle, the often ritualistic invocations of "resistance" and "subversiveness" as ultimate values are probably less "political" than we like to pretend. What we resist and what becomes subverted, at least for some more years down the road, is the disciplinary character of our intellectual and professional activities. Who would be ready, under these circumstances, to spend a thousand hours editing manuscripts with text documentations, and who could be tempted to pay a thousand dollars for a book that promises to eliminate any surprise and any individual perspective in its presentation of a medieval genre?[23]

NOTES

1. I worked for the GRLMA as a *Redaktionsassistent* from January 1971 until July 1972 at the University of Constance, have been one of its *Hauptherausgeber* (together with Hans Robert Jauss, Erich Köhler, und Ulrich Mölk) since 1976, and was among the volume editors for GRLMA 11 (with Ursula Link-Heer, Peter-Michael Spangenberg, and Dagmar Tillmann-Bartylla).

2. See Hans Robert Jauss, *Untersuchungen zur mittelalterlichen Tier-dichtung* (Tübingen: Max Niemeyer, 1959), 14ff.

3. Perhaps they were also encouraged by Leo Spitzer, to whose authority and approval many of the early letters in the GRLMA correspondence refer.

As one of the first academics who had left Germany during the Nazi period, Spitzer had been a visiting professor at Heidelberg in 1958. His *Vorlesung* "Interpretationen zur Geschichte der französischen Lyrik," was published in 1961 at Heidelberg by Helga Jauss-Meyer and Peter Schunck.

4. Krauss, who had been a *Wissenschaftlicher Assistent* of Erich Auerbach at the University of Marburg before 1933, was one of the very few German academics to participate actively in the resistance against Hitler. Sentenced to death, he survived the war in prison, where he wrote the remarkable satirical novel *PLN* (published in Frankfurt, 1949). For Krauss's biography, see Manfred Naumann, "Nachwort," in Werner Krauss, *Literaturtheorie, Philosophie und Politik. Das wissenschaftliche Werk I* (Berlin-Weimar: Verlag Akademie, 1984), 521–32. In my article "'Pathos of the Earthly Progress: Erich Auerbach's Everydays" (forthcoming in Seth Lerer, ed., *The Legacy of Erich Auerbach* [Stanford: 1995]), I present some new archival material on Krauss's biography.

5. Erich Köhler, *Ideal und Wirklichkeit in der höfischen Epik: Studien zur Form der frühen Artus- und Graldichtung* (Tübingen: M. Niemeyer, 1956), 1. On the theoretical orientations of Köhler's work, see Henning Krauss, "Historisch-dialektische Literaturwissenschaft: Zum Werk Erich Köhlers," in Henning Krauss and Dietmar Rieger, eds., *Mittelalterstudien: Erich Köhler zum Gedenken* (Heidelberg: C. Winter, 1984), 9–13.

6. See Bodo Harenberg, ed., *Chronik 1958*: Tag für Tag in Wort und Bild (Dortmund: Forschungstetle Ostmittel europa, 1987).

7. That the insistent presentation of the GRLMA project as a sort of "revised version" of Gustav Gröber's *Grundriß der romanischen Philologie*, which had appeared in its second edition at Strasbourg 1904–6, was used by Jauss and Köhler as a strategy of legitimation becomes evident from the fact that Gröber's manual contained chapters on both Romance languages and literatures and was not restricted to the Middle Ages.

8. *Parler du moyen âge* (Paris: Minuit, 1980), 57.

9. I have tried to describe the emergence of the discipline "Romanische Philologie" from this premise in "'Un souffle d'Allemagne ayant passé': Friedrich Diez, Gaston Paris and the Emergence of National Philologies," *Romance Philology* 40 (1986): 1–37.

10. Astonishingly, the GRLMA editors still highlighted this aspect twelve years later in their "Préface du GRLMA," *in Maurice Delbouille, ed., "Généralités," Grundriß der romanischen Literaturen des Mittelalters*, vol. 1 (Heidelberg: C. Winter, 1972), vi.

11. See my article "Zeitlosigkeit, die durchscheint in der Zeit: Ernst Robert Curtius' unhistorisches Verhältnis zur Geschichte," in Walter Berschin

and Arnold Rothe, eds., *Ernst Robert Curtius: Werk, Wirking, Zukunft-perpektiven: Heidelberger Symposium zum hundersten Geburtstag 1986* (Heidelberg: C. Winter, 1989), 227–41.

12. It finally materialized in an important (and very influential) article published by Jauss in the first issue of the journal *Poétique*. An extended German version appeared in GRLMA 1:107–38: "Theorie der Gattungen und Literatur des Mittelalters." *Gattungstheorie*, indeed, seems to have been the main concern of some of the most advanced medievalists in West Germany around 1960. See the philosophically sophisticated essays by the Germanist Hugo Kuhn, *Dichtung und Welt im Mittelalter* (Stuttgart: J. B. Metzler, 1959).

13. See the importance of the notion of "geschichtsnahe Perspektive" in "Préface du GRLMA."

14. See my article "Lebende Vergangenheit: Zur Typologie der 'Arbeit am Text' in der spanischen Kultur," in Ilse Nolting-Hauff and Joachim Schulze, eds., *Das fremde Wort: Studien zur Interdependenz von Texten. Festschrift für Karl Maurer zum 60. Geburtstag* (Amsterdam: Rudophi, 1988), 148–76.

15. Jeffrey Schnapp helped me understand that this investigation failed because it was based on an almost "paranoid" presupposition.

16. The references in this passage are not totally clear: "général" may refer to both de Gaulle and Franco, and "vieillard" to both Franco and Adenauer.

17. See my book *Eine Geschichte der spanischen Literatur* (Frankfurt: Suhrkamp, 1990), 975ff.

18. See the self-description of a scholar who, in a letter of March 26, 1968, proudly declares that he keeps working even in dramatic conditions: "Tutta la mia attività e da tempo scombinata . . . per gravi preoccupazioni famigliari, connesse alla cattiva salute dei miei genitori . . . e dei parenti di mia moglie . . . : une tensione psicologica e un cumulo di problemi pratici da non averne idea."

19. Different from the American use of the word "anthropology," *Anthropologie*, among cultural historians in Germany, refers to the search for metahistorically and transculturally "constant" features of human behavior or the inductive construction of a "transcendental subject."

20. See the table "Übersicht über die kleinen literarischen Gattungen der literarischen Rede im Mittelalter" in Jauss's *Alterität und Modernität der mittelalterlichen Literatur: Gesammelte Aufsätze 1956–1976* (Munich: W. Fink, 1977), 46f, and Köhler's article "Gattungssystem und Gesellschafts-system," in *Romanistische Zeitschrift für Literaturgeschichte* 1 (1977): 7–22.

21. The proceedings are published in "Literatur in der Gesellschaft des Spätmittelalters," *Begleitreihe zum* GRLMA, vol. 1 (Heidelberg: C. Winter, 1980).

22. Michel Zink, who wrote contributions to the volumes 4 and 8 of the GRLMA, has emerged as the unparalleled master of this—new?—academic and astonishingly popular genre. See his *Le moyen âge: Littérature française* (Nancy: Presses universitaires de Nancy, 1990), *Littérature française du moyen âge* (Paris: 1992), and the revised edition of *Dictionnaire des lettres françaises: Le moyen âage* (Paris: A. Fayard, 1993), ed. Michel Zink and Geneviève Hasenohr.

23. A few weeks before completing the manuscript for this chapter, in March 1993, I received a form letter from the *Amtsgericht Heidelberg* informing me that Carl Winter Verlag had filed for bankruptcy. The question of whether I wanted to report any financial requests in this context made me feel guilty. Had I not, for many years, been hammering a nail into the coffin of that venerable publishing house? On the other hand, this event makes the GRLMA history more conclusive than I had originally expected.

PART FIVE

DOCUMENT

SEVENTEEN

Preface to *Kinder- und Hausmärchen gesammelt durch die Brüder Grimm* (1819)

Translated and edited by
Hans Ulrich Gumbrecht and Jeffrey T. Schnapp

JACOB AND WILHELM GRIMM'S *Vorrede* to the 1819 edition of their *Kinder- und Hausmärchen* is one of the outstanding foundational documents for the academic discipline of literary studies. Nevertheless, owing to the broad international reception of this book as a reader for children, its preface has not been available in a modern English translation that gives attention to its singular historical importance.[1] For those who are familiar with its broader cultural context and who are, at the same time, interested in the genealogy of our profession, we think that the *Vorrede* by itself, without lengthy commentaries, will make obvious its relevance. We have therefore restricted ourselves to a relatively small number of translators' notes in order to provide some contextual references and linguistic commentaries that would otherwise only be available to Germanists. In this short introduction we want to explain briefly the specific perspective

Our English translation of the *Vorrede* to Jacob and Wilhelm Grimm's 1819 edition of the *Kinder- und Hausmärchen* is based on the recent edition by Heinz Roelleke: *Kinder- und Hausmärchen gesammelt durch die Bruder Grimm. Voillständige Ausgabe auf der Grundlage der dritten Auflage (1837)* (Frankfurt: Deutsch Klassiker Verlag, Bibliothek Deutscher Klassiker, vol. 5, 1985), 12–21.

from which the *Vorrede* must be understood as a milestone in the history of academic literary studies.

The publication history of Jacob and Wilhelm Grimm's *Kinder- und Hausmärchen* condenses, reveals, and represents a double movement of differentiation as the origin of our profession: a differentiation between a general fascination with cultural otherness, on the one side, that had increasingly occupied European intellectuals during the Enlightenment, and, on the other side, a more specific interest in the otherness of the national past, as it was rapidly gaining shape after 1800. It overlapped with a second differentiation between a situation where such longing for whatever appeared as culturally or historically remote was part of a general disposition within the reading public and the institutional articulation of this disposition as a new discipline and profession that began to emerge at some Prussian universities during the first decade of the nineteenth century.[2]

This then relatively young tendency of turning away from more exotic horizons of alterity was the context for Jacob and Wilhelm Grimm's decision to collect and edit texts that had been orally transmitted and were still being orally performed in their immediate geographical social environment. They probably even wanted to underline such a new orientation with the prefix *Haus-* in the title of their book. At the same time, we find, as a recurrent motif in the *Vorrede,* an insistence on three possible functions they hoped the *Kinder- und Hausmärchen* would fulfill. This complex concern of the authors and editors can be seen as a symptom for the beginning adaptation of a general interest in cultural materials from the national past to the narrower institutional framework of academic research and teaching.

The first of these functions discussed by the Grimms reflects the aesthetic taste of early Romanticism. They experience the tales they collect as a breath of "freshness and spontaneity," which will establish a gratifying contrast against a background of what they used to refer to as the "stiffness" of contemporary manners.[3] It is the same association that, in the *Vorrede,* constantly evokes metaphors of nature and childhood as discursive decorum characterizing the textual materials presented. If the second function they mention is, in their own words, more narrowly "educational," the famous—and exuberantly complex—notion of *Bildung* that they use in this context is neither identical with the then old-fashioned codes of socially defined "good manners" nor, of course, with the specific curriculum of professional formation. The concept of *Bildung* celebrates the emotionally and intellectually fully developed and mature individual—and it is in the name of this ideal that the Grimms unfold their polemic against the expectation that their texts should omit "all references to certain everyday conditions and circumstances that cannot (and will not) remain hidden." Finally, we repeatedly encounter the remark that "the mere existence" of the tales "is reason enough to protect them." This phrase, which could appear, at first glance, as pointing to a functional void, does indeed cover the most innovative perspective of the *Vorrede,* a perspective that did not exist prior to the incipient professionalization of the Romantic interest in the national past. It highlights the value of the *Kinder- und Hausmärchen* as a historical and ethnological document.[4]

It is their enthusiasm concerning the documentary value of the tales they collect that causes the Grimms to condemn in harsh words any form of "rewriting" such texts (which indeed was a favorite form of practice among contemporary Romantic poets), although we know today that their edition very strongly reflects Wilhelm Grimm's literary taste.[5] It is a corresponding interpretation of their task as editors that motivates the Grimm brothers to broadly describe, in their *Vorrede,* recording methods resembling early forms of anthropological field research, although their actual collecting activities were probably much closer to those forms of cultural exchange that prevailed in the eighteenth-century salons.[6] And it is, finally, an association between the texts' documentary value and a new scholarly self-image that makes the Grimms determined not only to resist early criticisms of the heaviness of their philological apparatus in the first edition of the *Märchen* from 1812,[7] but to extend their commentaries progressively and to end up publishing them in a separate volume from 1822 on. If Jacob and Wilhelm Grimm's *Vorrede* marks a decisive moment in the history of literary studies, it does so by revealing a desire for authenticity, which, along with innovative techniques of "philological craftsmanship," generated subtle strategies of textual fakes and manipulation—"for the sake of authenticity," so to speak.

But where did this longing for an "authenticity," of which certain texts were regarded as "documents," come from? Why was it cast into the form of an academic profession in Germany earlier than in other European countries? We have already alluded to a general alienation from the highly sophisticated life forms that had emerged during the seventeenth and eighteenth centuries as a general disposition implying a longing for cultural otherness. What intensified this disposition, what, at different chronological moments during the nineteenth century, within different European contexts, transformed it into an official interest of the state, and what directed the state's attention to the depths of national histories were situations of national defeat and humiliation.[8] Not by coincidence was the first fully remunerated professorship for German language and literature created at the University of Berlin in 1810, two years before the first edition of the *Kinder- und Hausmärchen* and three years before Prussia joined the war of liberation against Napoleon. On these premises, it was considered to be a task of public interest to preserve, edit, and present as "documents" to a new reading audience those texts that were supposed to contain and uncover the "essence" (*Wesen*) of the nation, for such "essence" was appreciated as the most important orientation for any political, social, cultural—and even legal—reforms. The Grimms' new understanding of text editing as a scholarly task, however, was feeding back to their nonscholarly activities as they were discussed in the *Vorrede*. The "freshness" of the texts began to become associated with the much-longed-for "youth of the nation," and the aesthetic pleasure they were said to produce could now, at least in part, be experienced as a pleasure stemming from a new closeness to the nation's historical and cultural roots. Likewise, the concept of *Bildung* acquired an additional semantic component that made "national character" appear as a central part of individuality.

It is true that, within this larger context, Jacob and Wilhelm Grimm were neither the first editors of a collection of orally transmitted folk tales nor the first intellectuals or scholars to become appointed professors of *Germanistik*. The specific importance of both the *Kinder- und Hausmärchen*'s publication history and the Grimms' professional biographies lies in the fact that they embrace, accompany, and reflect the longer process of that double (intellectual and institutional) differentiation in which we see the origin of literary studies. Similar editions of popular tales and poems had been published in Germany from as early as 1784 on,[9] most notably *Des Knaben Wunderhorn,* edited by three leading figures of the Romantic movement, Achim von Arnim, Clemens Brentano, and Joseph Görres, between 1805 and 1808. There is a direct, and probably more than barely anecdotal, link between this book and the initiation of Jacob and Wilhelm Grimm into what was to become "German studies." As students of law at the University of Marburg from 1802 on, they were attending Karl Friedrich von Savigny's lectures on the history of German law, which belonged to the very first academic articulations of the then innovative interest in national history.[10] When Savigny, in

1806, was approached by his brother-in-law Clemens Brentano with the request to recruit collaborators who would collect textual materials for further editions of *Des Knaben Wunderhorn,* this became the beginning of Jacob and Wilhelm Grimm's career as philologists. For the next four years, they worked closely with Clemens Brentano, who had just moved to Kassel, not too far from Marburg.

The Grimms, who had attended the *Gymnasium* in Kassel, quickly identified a number of informants for their philological enterprise in this provincial town, where they would finally become librarians of the Royal Library from 1808 on.[11] In 1810 they submitted the results of their research to Brentano. To the Grimms' disappointment, however, their mentor seemed to have lost his active interest in publishing the texts they had collected. In this situation, the poet Achim von Arnim encouraged them to prepare an edition independent of *Des Knaben Wunderhorn,* which finally appeared in 1812 and was dedicated to Arnim's wife, Bettine. In a market that was still dominated by the more literary aspects of the Romantic taste, the success of their book came late.[12] Despite mostly negative reactions and reviews (including Brentano's) following their edition of 1812, Jacob and Wilhelm Grimm brought forth a second volume of new tales in 1815.

The 1819 edition, whose *Vorwort* we present in English translation, was an enlarged version of the two previous collections. Its commentaries appeared, for the first time, as a separate book in 1822. At the same time, the 1819 edition marks the stage at which Wilhelm Grimm, probably the less academically ambitious of the two brothers, took over the work for all further publications of the *Kinder- und Hausmärchen.* He made the decision to present to the reading public, from 1825 on, a *Kleine Ausgabe* containing only 50 tales (as compared to the 150 texts of the 1812 and 1815 editions). This revised marketing strategy transformed the public image of the collection into that of a book for children, and the *Kleine Ausgabe* saw indeed ten further editions before Wilhelm Grimm's death in 1859. At the same time, however, with *Germanistik* becoming a well-respected and even popular academic discipline, the *Grosse Ausgabe* was enjoying the increasing success of five more editions. Interestingly enough, during Wilhelm Grimm's lifetime, both collections shared with the material they represented the key feature of textual flexibility (the very quality for which Paul Zumthor has coined the concept of *mouvance*): none of the altogether seventeen editions is identical in its text selection to any other edition.

Although the project that ultimately yielded the *Kinder- und Hausmärchen* had certainly had a decisive impact on Jacob and Wilhelm Grimm's involvement with the history of German culture, its end result was neither the first book that either of them would publish nor, for them, part of an exclusive concentration on German texts and the German language. Already in 1811, Jacob Grimm's book on late medieval German poetry (*Über den altdeutschen Meistergesang*) had appeared in Göttingen, and after three editions of early medieval German texts and the inauguration of a short-lived scholarly journal (*Altdeutscher Wälder*), he published, four years later in Vienna, a collection of Spanish *romances* (*Silva des romances viejos*). As works on non-German topics, his translation of a Serbian grammar and, again in brotherly collaboration, the translation of a collection of Irish *Fairy Legends* followed in 1824 and 1826 respectively.[13] The breadth of this agenda illustrates that the process of differentiation into "national-philological" fields and disciplines spanned several decades. The two works, however, that, together with the *Kinder- und Hausmärchen,* established the outstanding role of the Grimms within the German intellectual and institutional history of the nineteenth century were Jacob Grimm's *Deutsche Grammatik* (of which the first volume appeared in 1819, the very year his active collaboration in the collection of tales had come to an end) and their joint project of a *Deutsches Wörterbuch,* inaugurated in 1838.

Parallel to the rather slow development of their intellectual specialization, Jacob and Wilhelm Grimm became members of the academic institution at a relatively late moment in their lives. As early as 1816, Jacob Grimm had received, and rejected, the offer of a professorship at the University of Bonn.[14] It was possible for him and his brother—and indeed typical of the intellectual and institutional climate of their younger years—to pursue their research interests and build a singular international reputation while remaining in their position as librarians at Kassel. Not before 1830 did they accept professorships (which implied the continuation of their work as librarians) at the University of Göttingen. Seven years later, both Grimms, as members of a group of faculty protesting the cancelling of all constitutional rights by the king of Lower Saxony, were ousted from their academic positions. Although this incident has been frequently referred to in order to claim a necessary relationship between *Germanistik* and a politically critical attitude, what it actually reveals is their unconditional commitment to a specific interpretation of their profession in relation to nationhood as it had emerged in the years around the War of Independence of 1813–15. Retrospectively, it is therefore not at all surprising that an offer from the University of Berlin reached them in 1840. It was in the capital of the Prussian state that the convergence between intellectual specialization and a new ideology of national education, as it had been somehow vaguely outlined for the first time in Jacob and Wilhelm Grimm's *Vorrede* to the *Kinder- und Hausmärchen,* was then finding its most powerful institutional articulation.

PREFACE

When a tempest or some other heaven-sent calamity has felled a year's harvest, one sometimes happens upon a little place, hemmed in by a path's modest hedges or shrubs, that has weathered the storm and where some ears remain standing. If the sun then sheds its healing light anew, the ears will thrive alone and unobserved. No overhasty sickle will reap them for the silos; rather, poor hands will seek them out in late summer when ripe and full. These hands will place ear against ear, bind them carefully, and carry them home with greater ceremony than elsewhere honors entire sheaves: all in order that they may provide winterlong nourishment and perhaps also future seed.

Such was our predicament when we observed that little remained of so many things that had flourished in times of yore and that even their memory was soon to fade away, if it were not for folk songs, some books and legends,[15] and the innocent household tales.[16] Stoveside and ovenside seats, attic stairways, a few holidays still celebrated, fields and forests in their primeval stillness, but most of all, limpid Imagination:[17] these are the protective hedges that have ensured their survival through the ages.

Perhaps the time had come for these household tales to be preserved in writing, given the ever dwindling number of persons able to pass them on. To be sure, those who do know them often know a good many, for it is not tales but, rather, men who die off. Yet traditional customs continue to decline, just as the private nooks in homes and gardens that once endured from grandfather to grandson yield to an empty pomp not unlike the smile with which every mention of the tales is greeted: on the surface the smile seems noble enough, but little effort is expended. Wherever they are still to be found, the tales live on indifferently. One disregards whether they are good or bad, poetically evocative, or (for clever souls) silly. One simply knows them and loves them in the same manner in which one first encountered them, taking delight without a deeper reason or motivation. So magnificent is their living usage—poetry shares this with all things eternal—that one cannot but be swayed, whether willingly or unwillingly. (It is clear, incidentally, that the usage survived in places still receptive to poetry, places where the imagination remained unsullied by life's disturbances.) But our purpose here is not to praise these tales, and even less to defend them against contrary opinions. Their mere existence is reason enough to protect them. Anything that can bring us pleasure, move and teach us in such manifold ways, contains its own principle of necessity, as it must surely come from the same eternal source that bedews all of life, like a single drop cupped in a tiny leaf shimmering in the first dawn.

So the purity that runs through these poems is also that which makes children seem so wonderful and blessed to us. Both are graced, as it were, with the same glowing and immaculate white-blue eyes:[a] eyes that cannot grow any larger while the body's limbs remain tender, frail, and ill-adapted to the world's business. This is why, beyond its usefulness for the history of poetry and mythology, our collection's aim is that the poetry that breathes within it affect and gratify those susceptible to its pleasures. But the book's intent is also educational.[18]

Nevertheless, we do not aspire to the sort of "purity" that might have been achieved by dutifully omitting all references to certain everyday conditions and circumstances that cannot (and will not) remain hidden: a "purity" that is caught up in the illusion that what can be done in a printed book can also be accomplished in real life. We aspire instead to a purity grounded in the truthfulness of a narration that does not conceal anything wrong. In doing so we have carefully edited out of this new edition any expression that might be deemed inappropriate for children.[19] If one were to object that some parents will find some tales sufficiently embarrassing that they will not want the book to get into their children's hands, such concerns could be warranted in a case or two. Parents may thus choose to make their own selection; but, generally speaking, given a healthy state of mind, even this should prove unnecessary. Nothing can protect us better than Nature herself,[20] who has permitted these flowers and leaves to

[a]Which children themselves so much like to grasp (Fischarts Gargantua 129b 131b).

develop their distinctive shapes and colors. Whoever deems the latter unwholesome as a result of particular strictures ought not ask that they be recolored or recut. Similarly, rain and dew are sprinkled upon all of the earth's creatures as a blessing. If someone fears exposing his delicate plant to them due to the harm it might suffer, choosing instead to keep it indoors and shower it with chilled water, there is no reason that rain and dew should therefore cease. All natural things have the capacity to flourish, however, and that is what we ought to strive for. Besides, we know of no sound and substantial book that has edified the people—the Bible foremost of all—without causing a much higher degree of concern. Used in the proper manner, nothing evil will be found, but only, as a nice saying goes, a testimony of our hearts. Children fearlessly point to the stars, whereas others, under the impact of superstition, believe that, in doing so, they offend the angels.

It took us about thirteen years to connect these tales.[21] The first volume was published in 1812 and was made up largely of what we observed in the oral traditions of Hessia, and in the River Main and Kinzig area of the county of Hanau (where we ourselves come from).[22] The second volume was completed in the year 1814. It was produced in less time, in part because the book had earned itself friends, who, now that they clearly saw what and how it was intended, actively supported it; in part also because luck favored us—a sheer stroke of fate but one that often assumes the dogged and diligent collector. Once one has developed the habit of being attentive to similar things, they are found more frequently than one might first expect, and such is generally the case with people's customs, idiosyncratic quirks, proverbs, and jokes. To the special kindness and affection of friends we owe the beautiful tales in *Plattdeutsch*[23] from Münster and Paderborn, a region whose dialect is still particularly straightforward and internally complete. There, within those famed lands of German Liberty, the legends and tales have survived as a near-regular feature of holiday pastimes in some locales, and the people still abound with inherited customs and songs. Wherever writing has not yet disrupted things by importing what is foreign or by the deadening effect of sheer overabundance; wherever writing has not yet prompted memory to become negligent; as a general rule, wherever one encounters peoples whose literature[24] is insignificant, a stronger and more pristine tradition occupies its places. Thus in Lower Saxony more seems to have been preserved than in other regions. How much more complete and inwardly rich a collection it would have been possible to compile in the Germany of Hans Sachs[25] and Fischart,[26] in the fifteenth or even sixteenth century![b]

One such lucky coincidence befell us in the village of Niederzwehrn, near Kassel, where we made the acquaintance of a peasant woman who told us the greatest number and the most beautiful tales contained in the second volume. Still well preserved and not much over fifty years old, this woman's name was Viehmännin.[27] Her features had something firm, intelligent, and agreeable about them, and her wide-open eyes disclosed a clear and sharp gaze.[c] She was keeping the old legends firmly in her memory, a gift that not everybody shared, as she well noted, some people being unable to retain anything coherent at all. Her storytelling was deliberate, steady, and of an amazing liveliness (which she herself reveled in). It first issued forth spontaneously, but, if so requested, she would repeat her narrative once again slowly so that, with practice, it was possible to follow her in writing. Many of the tales were thus preserved word-for-word, and this fidelity is unmistakable. Those who are convinced that, as a rule, tradition is slightly distorted, negligently preserved, and therefore impossible to maintain over an extended time span, should have heard how carefully she stuck to her narrations and how zealously she was devoted to their correctness. Never did she alter anything important while repeating, and all oversights were corrected (as soon as noticed) in the very flow of her speech. Such attachment to tradition remains so strong

[b]It is noteworthy that, while writing was used for all other matters by the Gauls, the written transcription of handed-down songs was banned. Caesar, noting this is *De bello Gallico* 6.4, thinks that the ban's purpose was to prevent carelessness in the learning and memorization of traditional songs, due to excess confidence in writing. Also in Plato's *Phaedrus,* Thomas reminds Toth about the deleterious impact that writing would have on the development of memory.

[c]Our brother Ludwig Grimm has produced a very lifelike and natural etching of her, which will eventually appear in a collection of his works (a first portfolio has already been published). A fine scaled-down copy is supplied on this title page of our second volume. The war brought this good woman misfortune and misery which charitable persons could ease but not entirely alleviate. The father of her numerous grandchildren died of nerve fever, leaving her with his orphans who, in turn, brought illness and extreme poverty to her already impoverished cabin. She fell ill and died on November 17, 1816.

among persons who have continuously carried on the same way of life that, given our own proclivity to change, we are unable to understand it. Moreover, such an oft-tried and proven tradition possesses an urgent intimacy and inner aptitude of its own, which other things, though they may outwardly glisten far more brightly, will never acquire. The epic ground of popular poetry is similar to the manifold shades of the green spread out over the whole of Nature: they satisfy and soothe, but never bring fatigue.

Besides the tales of the second volume, we also received numerous supplements to the first volume, including improved versions of the narrations there presented, whether from the same source or from other similar ones. As a mountainous land, removed from busy highways[28] and mostly dedicated to farming, Hessia is better able to insure the preservation of old customs and traditions. A certain weightiness has thus endured, as has a healthy, industrious, and courageous frame of mind[29] (which history will not overlook); even the tall and beautiful stature of the men of these regions, the original home of the Chatten tribe,[30] has been preserved—all of which suggests that the lack of comforts and delicate manners, which inhabitants of regions like Saxony will surely remark, ought to be viewed as an advantage. One is also sensitive to the fact that to this world there corresponds a less hospitable (though often truly magnificent) countryside, as well as ways of life shaped by a certain severity and penury. Generally speaking, the Hessians[31] must be counted among the tribes of our Fatherland who, over the changing course of time, have held the fastest not only to their old dwelling places but also to the distinctiveness of their essential character as people.[32]

The book's second edition incorporates everything we have acquired for our collection up to the present date.[33] As a result, the first volume has been almost totally transformed: what was incomplete has been supplemented, some pieces have been narrated in a simpler and purer manner, and few will seem unimproved. We reviewed what appeared suspicious—that is, of having a foreign origin or of having been adulterated via later additions—and eliminated all such materials. In their place, we have inserted new pieces that were received in the meantime (and among them contributions from Austria and German Bohemia), so the reader may encounter many tales hitherto unfamiliar. While in the first edition we had reserved only meager space for annotations, given the wider scope of the present book, we are now able to dedicate a third volume to them. By this means it has become possible not only to provide what we reluctantly omitted in the earlier version, but also to append new, relevant passages, which we hope will all the more clearly underscore the scholarly[34] value of these traditions.

As regards the method of our collecting, its main concerns were fidelity and truth. For we have not added anything of our own nor embellished any legend's details or features, but have only reproduced its content exactly as received.[35] That the idiom[36] is for the most part our own is self-evident, but we have sought to capture any distinctive trait of which we became aware in order that the variety of Nature make itself felt also in this aspect of our collection. Besides, as anyone who has ever undertaken a similar labor understands, an inattentive and careless mode of reception[37] is impossible; on the contrary, attentiveness and discernment[38]—qualities acquired over the course of many years—are required in order to distinguish what is simpler, purer, and more perfect in itself from the adulterate. Various narratives completed one another to such a degree that, when merged, no contradictions resulted from their union:[39] these we have presented as one; others diverged, each one having its own distinctive features, in which case we have given preference to the best among them while preserving the other versions for the notes. Divergences of this sort seem to us far more noteworthy than to other scholars, who view them as little more than the alteration and disfigurement of a once-existing original;[40] whereas, on the contrary, they may simply represent manifold ways of approaching something inexhaustible that exists only in the Spirit.[41] Repetitions of single phrases, episodes, and prologues must be considered as epic formulae, which always recur in the context of a particular poetic tone—and cannot really be understood in another way.

We have gladly retained any dialect that was distinctive. Had this been the case with most of the tales, it would no doubt have benefited the narrative. The present context is one in which the achievement of a high degree of verbal polish, delicacy, and art would have been pernicious, and one cannot help but feel that a refined literary language,[42] however adaptable it might prove in other settings, gains in clarity and transparency but loses in flavor and is more distant from the pith. It is regrettable that the Lower Hessian dialect spoken in the vicinity of Kassel, this being the borderline region between the Saxon and Franconian province of Hessia, is an indistinct and not readily identifiable mixture of Lower Saxon and High German.

As far as we are aware, there exists in Germany no other similarly conceived collection of tales.[43] Hitherto, the tales were either preserved among the few that were accidentally transmitted, or they were regarded as little more than raw materials to be transformed into narratives of larger scope. We declare ourselves to be firmly opposed to this form of rewriting.[44] It is undeniable that any active feeling[45] that a poem is able to summon up rests upon a poetical casting and recasting,[46] without which any tradition would be sterile and dead. This is precisely the reason why the tales are narrated differently in every single province (according to its distinctive features) and by every single mouth. Yet there is a substantial discrepancy between such an almost unconscious unfolding from the immediate life source, which resembles the silent growth of plants, and an intentional, arbitrary knotting and pasting together of different versions. The latter transformations we cannot sanction. The only yardstick governing their composition is the poet's prevailing whim,[47] which is wholly dependent upon his training, whereas the singular character of natural recastings is shaped by the people's spirit, no individual bias being permitted to intrude. If one is willing to say that one finds preserved in them the conceptions and forms[48] of earlier times, it is self-evident that these rewritings must be detrimental to this value. But neither do they add to the value of the poems, for where can poetry be found, except in those places where it strikes the soul, where it deeply cools and refreshes, or warms and strengthens? Yet every rewriting of these legends that detracts from their simplicity, innocence, and unadorned purity tears them away from the circle in which they are heard and in which there exists an insatiable craving for them. It may well be—and this is the best possible scenario—that one obtains in exchange subtlety, genius, and especially the wit of our contemporary moment, as well as the tender hues of sentiment: all of which a civilization nourished by the poetry of so many peoples may achieve without much difficulty. But these gifts have rather more glimmer than value. Because they assume single hearings or readings, the customary mode of reception in our time, they condense and intensify the tales' charms. The wit, however, becomes tiresome when repeated, and only that endures which is quiet, tranquil, and pure. The writer's practiced hand resembles that cursed hand that had the unfortunate gift of transforming into gold all the objects it touched, including food: in the midst of all its riches, it is unable to satisfy and nourish us. How barren, how inwardly empty and shapeless appears a mythology created only from the imagination, furnished only with its fixed quota of images, despite all the best and most powerful words! This is said, naturally, only against any rewriting that would strive to render the tales more beautiful and more poetic, and of against their free appropriation in different poetic contexts; for who would wish to impose limits upon poetry?

So we pass this book along into benevolent hands,[49] thinking of the blessed force that they possess, and hoping that it will remain entirely hidden from those who would deny such crumbs of poetry to the poor and humble.

Kassel, July 3, 1819

NOTES

1. We became aware of its unavailability while establishing the reading materials for an undergraduate course. "The History of the Institution of Literature and Literary Studies," taught in the Department of Comparative Literature at Stanford University in the winter quarter of 1990–91. The only translation we could identify is not available at most university libraries: Edgar Taylor, *German Popular Stories, translated from the "Kinder- und Haus Märchen," collected by M. M. Grimm, from oral tradition* (London: C. Baldwyn, 1823).

2. This hypothesis of a double differentiation at the historical origin of literary studies is broadly discussed and documented in Hans Ulrich Gumbrecht, "'Un souffle d'Allemagne ayant passé'; Friedrich Diez, Gaston Paris and the Genesis of National Philologies," *Romance Philology* 40 (1986): 1–37.

3. See in this regard Jacob Grimm's descriptions of the professional milieu at the Kassel library in his autobiographical sketch published in *Selbstbiographie: Ausgewählte Schriften, Redenund Abhundlugen,* ed. Ulrich Wyss. (Munich: Deutscher Taschbuch Verlag, 1984), 25–39.

4. For the central importance of the concepts "document" and "monument" within nineteenth-century philology, see Bernard Cerquiglini, *Éloge de la variante: Histoire critique de la philologie* (Paris: Seuil, 1989).

5. See the excellent commentary by Rölleke to his edition of the *Kinder- und Hausmärchen,* 1158ff.

6. Roelleke, 1157, assumes that their informants were mostly eager to present the materials in a style adapted to Perrault's popular and highly artistic fairy tales.

7. See, in this regard, the document in Rölleke, 1162.

8. The relationship between national humiliation and the emergence of philology that we are postulating here for Germany (especially Prussia)

applies equally to the Italian *Risorgimento*, to the feeling of a national "bankruptcy" that prevailed in France after the Franco-Prussian War of 1870–71, and, for Spain, to the "Cuban disaster" of 1898. The by far most outstanding book on the intellectual and institutional history of *Germanistik* is Rainer Rosenberg's *Zehn Kapitel zur Geschichte der Germanistik. Literaturgeschichtsschreibung* (Berlin: Akademie Verlag, 1981).

9. Anselm Elwert's *Ungedruckte Reste alten Gesangs*. For this chapter of cultural history within German Romanticism, see Rölleke, 1151ff.

10. For Savigny's role in the intellectual context of German Romanticism, see Jutta Strippel, "Zum Verhältnis von deutscher Rechtsgeschichte und deutscher Philologie," in Joerg Jochen Müller, ed., *Germanistik und deutsche National 1806–1848: Zur Konstitution bürgerlichen Buwußtseins* (Stuttgart: 1975), 113–66.

11. Their title as "*Royal* Librarians" went back to the fact that, between 1806 and 1812, Kassel was the residence of Napoleon's brother Jerome, the king of Westphalia.

12. For details of the publication history, see Rölleke, 1178ff.

13. *Wuk Stephanowitch kleine Serbische Grammatik verdeutscht mit einer Vorrede* (Leipzig: G. Reimer, 1824; *Irische Elfenmärchen, Aus dem Englischen* (Leipzig: 1826) (a translation of Croston Croker's *Fairy Legends and Traditions of the South of Ireland*).

14. See *Selbstbiographie*, 35f. Under the influence of August-Wilhelm Schlegel, Friedrich Diez, whose role in the discipline of *Romanistik* is parallel to the Grimms' in *Germanistik,* was to become "lecturer for southern literatures and languages" at Bonn in 1821. Not dissimilar from Jacob and Wilhelm Grimm's intellectual career, Diez would only give up his research interest in German texts after this appointment. See Gumbrecht, 16ff.

15. *Sagen:* literally "sagas." We have translated the term as "legend" throughout, in order to avoid any confusion with the Icelandic and Norwegian sagas: lengthy prose narratives concerning the history of an ancient hero or his family. Nonetheless, it is worth noting that the Grimms often treat the *Hausmärchen* as a whole as a kind of saga of the German fatherland: the collective record of the German spirit.

16. *Hausmärchen:* this compound word, the label the Grimms assign to their entire collection, is nearly untranslatable. A *Märchen* is most often a work like a fairy tale in which the fabulous and magical prevail. A *Hausmärchen* is, by extension, a variety of "fairy tale" identified with the home, that intimate domestic/rural domain made up of "stoveside and ovenside seats, attic stairways," shaped by time-bound holiday rituals, and associated with the pursuit of traditional ways of life. With the addition of the prefix *Haus,* therefore, the semantic field of the word *Märchen* comes to embrace

not only notions of fantastic literature, but also, and most especially, the idea of the common literature belonging to a people as a whole.

17. *ungetrübte Phantasie:* "unclouded" or "untroubled" Fancy. Whereas terms such as *Einbildungskraft* or *Vorstellungskraft* are employed, in contemporary German philosophy, to describe the actual workings of the faculty of imagination, *Phantasie* describes the imagination's powers as a whole, particularly its "generative," "creative" powers.

18. *daß es als ein Erziehungsbuch diene:* the book is to "shape" and give proper form to the upbringing of children.

19. *Ihnen anstößig vorkomme:* probably refers to the scandal that some readers and the author of a review of the 1812 edition had taken in the wording of the tale *Rapunzel* which indirectly(!) referred to the title-protagonist's pregnancy. The incriminated sentence was substituted in the 1819 edition. See the commentary of Heinz Roelleke's edition, 1171f.

20. *als die Natur selber:* our translation ("Nature") underscores the aspect of conveying an animate character to the spontaneous physical power that informs the natural world.

21. *Seit etwa dreizehn Jahren:* appearing in a text of 1819, this reference dates back to the beginning of Jacob and Wilhelm Grimm's activity as collectors of folktales, the year 1806. It converges with what we know about Brentano's letter to Savigny of March 22, 1806, as the first—indirect—motivation for their interest.

22. *Wo wir her sind:* we know that the Grimms were not involved in any kind of recording that would resemble twentieth-century anthropological field research. It is unclear, however, whether this passage of their *Vorrede* is just unclear (as Roelleke, 1192, assumes), or whether it is part of the Grimms' effort to underscore the "scientific" character of their work—and their closeness to "authenticity."

23. *Plattdeutsch:* popular name for different forms of mainly orally preserved varieties of German, some of which are close to Dutch or English, often referred to as *Niederdeutsch.*

24. *Literatur:* used here in its pre-Romantic meaning of "written/printed texts (as opposed to oral communication)," which did not necessarily imply a connotation of "aesthetic quality."

25. *Hans Sachs:* (1492–1576), poet and playwright whose work is typical of the late-medieval city milieu, one of the heroes in Richard Wagner's *Meistersinger.*

26. *Fischart:* Johann Fischart (1546–90), humanist and author of numerous pamphlets against Franciscans, Jesuits, and the Catholic Counter-Reformation. His most important literary work is a German paraphrase of Rabelais's *Gargantua.*

27. *Viehmännin:* despite her fierce-looking family name (best translated as "Cattlewoman": it was normal in early-nineteenth-century German, although not grammatically obligatory, to refer to a married woman by the feminine version of her husband's father name) and despite the highly emotional footnote the Grimms dedicate to her, Dorothea Viehmann was not remotely as much of a living allegory for "authentic nature" nor as purely "German" as they obviously wanted her to be. According to Roelleke (1157, 1193), she was the daughter of an innkeeper and the wife of a tailor in the village of Niederzwehrn near Kassel. Through the fact that her family was descended from *Huguenot* immigrants, she was able, as were most of the persons on whose storytelling Jacob and Willhelm Grimm relied, to understand and speak French. It is therefore possible to trace a strong French influence in some of the tales which go back to her.

28. *Heerstraben:* the team alludes specifically to military routes.

29. *Gesinnung:* a body of principles revealing of the essential character of a subject or people. Built up from the word *Sinn* (consciousness, mind, wit, opinion).

30. *Chatten:* a Germanic tribe.

31. *Hessen:* the Hessian peoples inhabited three separate states within the German federation: Hesse-Kassel, Hesse-Homburg, and Hesse-Darmstadt—all three located in a region of densely forested plains between the Rhineland and northern Germany. Born in Hessen, Jacob and Wilhelm Grimm were Hessians.

32. *die Eigentümlichkeit ihres Wesens:* the phrase implies that there is a distinctive and essential "inner nature" (*Wesen*) that characterizes each people. Its conservation is insured by a particularly firm traditionalism among the Hessians.

33. *Wollen wir bei dieser zewiten Auflage dem Buch einverleiben:* refers to the edition of 1819 which, in addition to some newly discovered texts, contained the totality of the tales published in the two volumes of the Grimms' collection of 1812 and 1815.

34. *den wissenschaftlichen Wert:* this insistence on the "scientific worth" of the tales, their worthiness as objects of learned inquiry, stemming partly from the inclusion of a corpus of annotations, marks the main difference between the Grimms and their romantic predecessors. In the 1812 and 1815 editions, these annotations had been published together with the texts of the tales. From 1822 on, they appeared as a separate book.

35. *Ist es uns zuerst auf Treue und Wahrheit angekommen:* according to Roelleke, 1158ff, it is clear that Jacob and Wilhelm Grimm "rewrote" the texts that they had recorded about as much as their more poetically ambitious predecessors. In contrast to them, however, what they probably had mostly in

mind was a "toning down" of the highly stylized versions with which they were provided by many of their informants.

36. *Ausdruck:* literally, "expression." The word potentially encompasses here the verbal medium of the tales themselves, their form, and the stylistic decorum they observe.

37. *Auffassen:* a "taking in," "conceiving," and/or "understanding" of the material in question.

38. Literally, "tact," "taste."

39. *"sobald . . . keine Widerspruche wegzuschneiden waren":* literally, "as long . . . as no contradictions had to be cut off."

40. *Urbild:* an archetype or prototype.

41. *Einem im Geist bloss vorhandenen, unerschöpflichen:* this is an interesting rephrasing of what the Grimms call "ungetrübte Phantasie" earlier on in their text (see n. 17 above).

42. *Schriftsprache:* literally, "written speech" or, more generally, any educated or trained language use.

43. *Keine Sammlung von Märchen in Deutschland:* this of course only holds true as long as one is willing to trust the Grimms' claim that their own editing practice was radically different from the Romantic "rewriting" they criticized (see n. 35 above).

44. *Bearbeitung:* a "working on" or "reworking." The term has a stronger connotation of scholarship then the English "rewriting."

45. *in allem lebendigen Gefühl:* a feeling that is "living" in the sense of being animated by an inner vitality. *Gefühl* implies a strong subjective (i.e., nonanalytical) emotion.

46. *Bilden und Fortbilden:* literally, a "shaping and further shaping away" (with ideas of continuation prevailing). The phrase describes the process, characteristic of oral traditions as the Grimms understood them, by means of which every telling of a tale is always a retelling (with modifications, abridgments, and expansions implied).

47. *Ansicht:* figuratively, "opinion" or "judgment"; literally, "perspective" or the partial angle of vision from which an object is viewed.

48. *Anschauungen und Bildungen:* the first term may be translated as "view" but with the implication that the view in question grants the viewer an intuitive, but nonetheless analytical, access to the inner life of an object. The second term refers to "form" or "shape" but with the specific connotation of an educational value implied.

49. *Wohlwollenden Händen:* refers to "the hands of" Elisabeth von Arnim, the wife of the poet Achim von Arnim, who had first encouraged Jacob and Wilhelm Grimm to publish their collection of tales independently from Brentano's, Görres' and his own anthology *Des Knaben Wunderhorn.*

Contributors

R. HOWARD BLOCH is chair of the Department of French and Romance Philology at Columbia University. He is the author of *Medieval French Literature and Law* (1977), *Etymologies and Genealogies: A Literary Anthropology of the Middle Ages* (1983), *The Scandal of the Fabliaux* (1986), *Medieval Misogyny and the Invention of Western Romantic Love* (1991), *God's Plagiarist: Being an Account of the Fabulous Industry and Irregular Commerce of the Abbé Migne* (1994).

ALAIN BOUREAU is Directeur d'Études at the École des Hautes Études en Sciences Sociales, Paris, and chairs History of the Medieval Systems of Belief. He is the author of *La légende dorée: Le système narratif de Jacques de Voragine* (1984), *L'aigle: Chronique politique d'un emblème* (1985), *La papesse Jeanne* (1988), *Kantorowicz: Histoire d'un historien* (1990), *Le simple corps du roi* (1988), and *Le droit de cuissage* (1994).

E. JANE BURNS is Professor and Chair of Women's Studies at the University of North Carolina, Chapel Hill. She is the author of *Arthurian Fictions: Rereading the Vulgate Cycle* (1985), and *Bodytalk: When Women Speak in Old French Literature* (1993).

MICHAEL CAMILLE is Professor of Art History at the University of Chicago and the author of *The Gothic Idol: Ideology and Image-Making in*

493

Medieval Art (1989) and *Image on the Edge: The Margins of Medieval Art* (1992). He is currently working on a book project, *Illuminating Philosophy: Medieval Art and Science at the University of Paris,* as well as a short study of fourteenth-century images of the macabre.

ALAIN CORBELLARI, of l'Université de Paris IV, has written a study of the career and work of Joseph Bédier.

SUZANNE FLEISCHMAN is Professor of French and Romance Philology at the University of California, Berkeley. She is the author of *Modality in Grammar and Discourse* (1995), *Thought and Language* (1982),and *Tense and Narrativity* (1990), as well as numerous articles on aspects of Romance and historical linguistics and philology, medieval literature, the linguistics-literature interface, and narratology. She has coedited two collections of papers on topics in functional linguistics, *Discourse Pragmatics* and *The Verb, Mood and Modality* (1991).

JOHN M. GANIM is Professor of English at the University of California, Riverside, and the author of *Style and Consciousness in Middle English Narrative* (1983) and *Chaucerian Theatricality* (1990). He has written essays on *Annales* historiography and medieval literary studies in *The Idea of the Middle Ages* (1992) and on the legacy of E. K. Chambers's *Medieval Stage* in *Envoi.*

JOHN M. GRAHAM is Assistant Professor at the University of Michigan, Ann Arbor. His research and teaching centers on issues of social, textual, and literary authority in medieval France. He is currently completing a book on the medieval evolution and interpretation of troubadour lyric.

HANS ULRICH GUMBRECHT is Professor of Romance Languages and Comparative Literature (and from 1990–1994) Chair of the Department of Comparative Literature) at Stanford University. Gumbrecht's main working areas are the histories of French, Spanish, and Italian literatures. His more than 250 publications (translated into seventeen languages) include a complete history of Spanish literature and monographs on Zola, the history of aesthetic experience, and medieval narrative. His recent books in English include *Making Sense in Life and Literature* (1992); *Materialities of Communication* (1993), coedited with K. Ludwig Pfeiffer; a translation of his *History of Spanish Literature* (1994).

DAVID F. HULT is Professor of French at the University of Virginia. He is the author of *Self-fulfilling Prophecies: Readership and Authority in the First*

"Roman de la Rose" (1986), and editor of *Chrétien de Troyes, Le Chevalier sur Lion* (1994).

SARAH KAY is Reader of French at Cambridge University and Fellow of Girton College, Cambridge. Her main research interests are medieval Occitan poetry, the *Roman de la Rose,* and the Old French and Occitan chansons de geste. She has published a book on *Subjectivity in Troubadour Poetry* (1990) and an edition of *Raoul de Cambrai* (1992). Her most recent book is *The Chansons de Geste in the Age of Romance: Political Fictions* (1995).

LAURA KENDRICK, Professor in the English Department at Rutgers University and the Department of Humanities at the Université de Versailles at Saint-Quentin-en-Yvelines, has written *The Game of Love: Troubadour Wordplay* (1988), and *Comedy and Control in the Canterbury Tales* (1988).

ROBERTA L. KRUEGER is Professor of French at Hamilton College and the author of *Women Readers and the Ideology of Gender in Old French Verse Romance* (1993).

CARL LANDAUER, who has taught history at Yale, Stanford, and McGill universities, writes on the history of humanities and the history of legal theory.

SETH LERER is Professor of English at Stanford University. His publications include *Boethius and Dialogue: Literary Method in the Consolation of Philosophy* (1985), *Literary and Power in Anglo-Saxon Literature* (1991), and *Chaucer and His Readers: Imagining the Author in Late Medieval England* (1993), as well as numerous articles on medieval Latin, literary theory, and the history of scholarship.

STEPHEN G. NICHOLS is the James M. Beall Professor of French and Chair of the French Department at the Johns Hopkins University. Author of *Romanesque Signs: Early Medieval Narrative and Iconography* (1983, 1985), his recent projects include *The Whole Book: The Medieval Miscellany in Cultural Perspective* (1996), *The New Medievalism* (1991), *The New Philology* (1990), and *Commentary as Cultural Artefact* (1992). He is presently completing *La théâtralisation du rire au moyen âge* and *Marie de France's Common Places.*

PER NYKROG is Smith Professor of French and Spanish at Harvard University. He was Chairman of the Department of Romance Languages from 1986 to 1991. Born and educated in Denmark, he was Professor at the University of Aarhus from 1957 to 1979. His recent publications include *L'Amour et la Rose: Le Grand dessein de Jean de Meung* (1986) and *La recherche du don perdu: Points de repère dans le roman de Marcel Proust* (1987). His latest articles deal with George Sand and Balzac. He is currently working on a book-length project, *Chrétien de Troyes: Au fil du texte.*

JEFFREY M. PECK is Associate Professor of German, Center for German and European Studies, Georgetown University. His research focuses on cultural studies, especially the relationship between anthropology and literary studies, and the construction of national and ethic identities in the German context. He is currently completing a collaborative book of interviews and a video documentary on German Jews who returned to live in East and West Berlin.

JEFFREY T. SCHNAPP is Professor of Italian and Comparative Literature and Chair of Comparative Literature at Stanford University. He is the author of *The Transfiguration of History at the Center of Dante's "Paradise"* (1986), editor of *The Poetry of Allusion: Dante and Ovid in Dante's "Comedy"* (1991), and *Il Commento di Bernardino Daniello,* and *Staging Fascism* (1996).

HELEN SOLTERER is Associate Professor French at Duke University. She has recently completed *The Master and Minerva: Disputing Women in French Medieval Culture* (1995). She has published essays on pictorial narrative, allegory, and questions of feminine figuration. Her current research involves medieval theatricality and revivalism.